CATO HANDBOOK ON POLICY

6th EDITION

CATO INSTITUTE

Washington, D.C.

Library of Congress Cataloging-in-Publication Data

Cato Institute.
    Cato handbook on policy.— 6th ed.
       p. cm.
    Edited by David Boaz.
    Rev. ed. of: Cato handbook for Congress. ©2003.
    Includes bibliographical references.
    ISBN 1-930865-68-6
    1. Political planning—United States.   2. United States—Politics and government—2001-
    3. United States—Economic policy—2001-   4. United States—Social policy—1993-
    5. United States—Foreign relations—2001-   I. Boaz, David, 1953-   II. Cato Institute.
    Cato handbook for Congress.   III. Title.

    JK468.P64B38 2005
    320.6′0973′090511—dc22

                                             2004062887

Printed in the United States of America.

CATO INSTITUTE
1000 Massachusetts Ave., N.W.
Washington, D.C. 20001
www.cato.org

Contents

DOMESTIC POLICY

REGULATION

ENERGY AND ENVIRONMENT

Foreign and Defense Policy

International Economic Policy

1. Introduction

Today our federal government faces a monumental task: responding to the serious threat of terrorism. That challenge requires that we reconsider the priorities of our vast federal bureaucracy, to redefine and refocus our government on responsibilities that are truly governmental and truly national. This *Handbook* offers much advice on how and how not to confront the terrorist threat. It also offers advice on the proper constitutional boundaries of the federal government and the policies that would reflect those boundaries and enhance the liberty and prosperity of the American people.

In particular, we urge Congress and the president to move firmly toward the "ownership society" that President Bush called for in his campaign. An ownership society empowers individuals by giving them ownership of and control over important aspects of their own lives, such as retirement, health care, and education. We would note that in three national elections now, the old claim that Social Security is the "third rail of American politics" has been disproved. Most recently, in 2004 President Bush consistently talked about Social Security reform in his campaign for reelection; so did several senatorial candidates, who were attacked by their opponents and won. And that's no surprise, as numerous public opinion polls have shown support for private retirement accounts at anywhere from 56 to 70 percent. In Chapter 4 we offer a comprehensive plan for Social Security choice.

Social Security is not the only area where reform is needed. Congress and the president must reduce the burden of government on taxpayers and economic growth. They must deal with the unimaginably large fiscal imbalance in Medicare and allow more Americans to control their own health care dollars. They must learn to deal with homeland security within constitutional constraints, as the Supreme Court has recently reminded us in the *Padilla* and *Hamdi* cases. And they must find a way to extricate the United States from Iraq and confront the threat from Al Qaeda.

Defending the life, liberty, and property of Americans is the fundamental responsibility of the federal government. Clearly, that task requires a fairly

1

narrow focus on the part of the president, the federal agencies, and the Congress. A government that tries to do everything will do nothing well. It's remarkable that the president of the United States was in a Florida classroom reading to schoolchildren in a photo-op to promote more federal involvement in local education when Al Qaeda attacked America. Could there be a clearer example of essential vs. nonessential tasks for the federal government? Parents and teachers can read to schoolchildren. Only Congress and the president can guide the defense of the United States. Congress should read Article I, section 8, of the Constitution, which lays out the powers granted to the federal government, and resolve to begin shedding tasks that are inappropriate for the federal government. A good place to begin is by shedding responsibilities that more properly belong to the several states.

The Role of Federalism

Both the Bush and Clinton administrations have moved us away from our heritage as a federal constitutional republic with a government of limited powers and toward a centralized, national plebiscitary democracy with an essentially unconstrained national government.

Some people on both the left and the right, particularly when they view themselves as dominant in national politics, seem to want the national government to run everything from our health care system to our local schools. But many Americans still appreciate that the Constitution establishes a government of delegated, enumerated, and thus limited powers; that most political decisions should be made in the states and communities; that liberty and federalism are still the best foundation for freedom, prosperity, and social harmony.

The philosophy of centralized nationalism, so alien to the American Founding and heritage, underlies much of contemporary politics. Who, it is asked, can best comprehend the general will? Why, the national government, of course, and especially the one official elected by all the people— the president of the United States. Unlike Congress, it is said, he represents the national interest. The voters have chosen the president, we are told, and Congress should carry out his "mandate." If Congress refuses to do the general will, then presidents increasingly claim the power to rule by decree, through executive orders. Such a theory would replace the constitutional safeguards against majoritarianism with a president virtually unconstrained in his ability to do good, as he sees it, for the people.

It is odd that those who claim the mantle of liberalism would be so quick to toss aside federalism and constitutionalism, since divided powers protect minorities against the whims of the majority. We constrain our government because we know that any of us might be the minority in some dispute and also because we know that—when we're in the majority—we might be tempted to abuse our power. We seek to keep governance close to the people, partly because local government is more responsive and, even more important, because that gives individuals the chance to leave, to vote with their feet, and to find communities that better reflect their individual needs and preferences. About 50 years ago, the need to confront the problem of racist laws in some states led to an increase in the exercise of power by the federal government. The lingering effects of that struggle discredited "states' rights" and federalism, and federal power grew beyond what was necessary to guarantee individual rights in the states. Continuing to centralize the government of 290 million people in a distant capital is a tragic reversal of our liberal Founding. We should remember that the states are "laboratories of democracy" and let them make their own decisions about a wide range of policies.

Conservatives rightly charge liberals with overriding federalism to achieve their policy goals. They ask why New York, Mississippi, and Wyoming have to have the same abortion laws, the same environmental regulations, the same special education rules. But in recent years conservatives, heady with the thrill of national power, have also used that power to impose their own policy preferences. In the name of accountability and choice, the No Child Left Behind Act further centralizes education. The Bush administration, like the Clinton administration, has used its administrative powers and the federal courts to block state initiatives on medical marijuana and assisted suicide. President Bush and congressional Republicans have proposed a constitutional amendment to override state marriage laws. Suddenly liberals are beginning to see the wisdom of federalism and diversity among the states.

Federalism is not a good idea just for the side that is currently in the minority in Washington. It's the basis of the Constitution. The Founders feared concentrations of power. They believed that the best way to protect individual freedom and civil society was to limit and divide power. Thus it was much better to have decisions made independently by 13, or 50, states—each able to innovate or to copy successful innovations in other states—than to have one decision made for the entire country. As the country gets more complex, and especially as government amasses more power, the advantages of decentralization and divided power become even greater.

The Costs of Big Government

A popular desire for less government is always difficult to translate into substantive reform. It seems to be the nature of democracy that those who seek power and privilege from government are more energetic in the political arena than those who seek only to be left alone. Thomas Jefferson wrote, "The natural progress of things is for liberty to yield and government to gain ground." Economists have explained how every government program provides benefits to a few people while diffusing the costs over all taxpayers or consumers. Congress is more likely to hear from those who receive the concentrated benefits than from those who pay the diffused costs.

But we must recognize the real costs of excessive government. One obvious cost of our gargantuan government is reduced economic growth. In a world of global markets and rapid technological progress, we struggle along with annual growth rates far below what we achieved from World War II until the mid-1970s. With less taxation and less regulation, we could be far wealthier.

Another cost is the loss of our freedom. We still live in one of the freest countries in the world, but each new government program takes away just a little more of that freedom—the freedom to spend our money as we choose, to go into the businesses we choose, to negotiate with our employers over compensation and benefits.

A related cost of big government, but one not often recognized, is the harm it does to morality and responsibility. Expansive government undermines the moral character necessary to civil society. The "bourgeois virtues" of work, thrift, sobriety, prudence, fidelity, self-reliance, and a concern for one's reputation developed and endured because they are the virtues necessary in a world where wealth must be produced and people are responsible for their own flourishing. Government can't do much to instill those virtues in people, but it can do much to undermine them. People should be free to make their own decisions and to bear the consequences of those choices. When we take away freedom and responsibility, we get a society characterized not by thrift, sobriety, diligence, self-reliance, and prudence but by profligacy, intemperance, indolence, dependence, and indifference to consequences.

4

By taking away money, liberty, and responsibility, the growth of government necessarily shrinks civil society, that whole network of relationships among people, from families to businesses to charities and nonprofit associations, that are formed on the basis of consent. Communitarians who deplore the decline of community and cooperation should look to big government for an explanation.

The Beltway Cocoon

There exists in Congress a systemic bias toward seeing the expansion of government as a solution to almost every problem. That bias is not a fluke but a direct consequence of the current structure of American electoral politics. Whereas the Founders of the American Republic envisioned a government of citizen legislators for whom public service would be a solemn but *temporary* charge, we now see a regime composed almost exclusively of professional politicians. It was not always this way: average congressional tenure has risen steeply over the past century. Chief among the culprits responsible for this change is the huge and growing advantage enjoyed by House incumbents, who in recent years have seen reelection rates rise above 98 percent. Outside Texas, only three members of the House were defeated in November 2004. As David Broder noted in the *Washington Post,* the body that was "given the shortest terms . . . to ensure that they would be sensitive to any shifts in public opinion" has instead become "more like an American House of Lords."

In addition to all the traditional privileges afforded incumbents, sitting legislators are now protected by increasingly stringent campaign finance laws, which limit the ability of challengers to overcome those advantages through vigorous political speech. Even redistricting, which historically led to more competitive congressional races, has deteriorated into a bipartisan, computer-driven process of incumbent protection. In the 2001 redistricting, 30 of 32 incumbent Democratic representatives in California paid the legislatively appointed redistricting chief $20,000 each to protect their seats. But, as California Democratic chairman Art Torres noted: "This really is a bipartisan effort. You maintain the 20 Republican seats." Which tells us something about Golden State Republicans. They'd rather hold on to their own fiefdoms than advance Republican interests in Congress. Sadly, that is the norm in American politics today.

Incumbent advantage leads to a vicious cycle, wherein the most competent potential challengers are deterred from entering contests, except those for open seats, further tightening the incumbent's hold on power. As incumbent protection drives up average tenure, the amount of time one must be willing to commit to politics in order to achieve power in Congress also increases. Decades of this process have transformed politics into a game worth playing only for those determined to make a career of it. Whatever their motives, those who find the prospect of spending their lives in government attractive are also likely to have an inflated view of the role and importance of the state in American life. An old story about the chess genius Bobby Fischer has him interrupting a conversation about politics between some fellow players with the demand, ''What's that got to do with chess?'' Entrenched political classes are afflicted with a parallel sort of myopia. For them, discussion of any public benefit bubbling up from civil society or the private sector provokes the response, ''What's that got to do with a new federal program?'' To promote real political leadership, it may be necessary to change the institutional constraints that give rise to that kind of tunnel vision. In the meantime, however, legislators who sincerely desire to serve the public trust must force themselves to notice this pervasive bias and to overcome it.

The Role of Congress

In our system of government, Congress has an important role to play, as many of the chapters of this *Handbook* point out. Too often we assume that only the Supreme Court has the duty to uphold the law and the Constitution. In fact, every person elected or appointed to office takes an oath to ''support and defend the Constitution of the United States.'' The first duty of every official is to act within the authority of the Constitution and to ensure that other officials do so as well. Recent presidents have blithely exceeded the powers granted to them under the Constitution, and thanks to its negligence, Congress bears a significant part of the blame for presidential excesses. To live up to their oath of office, members of Congress should turn their attention to four tasks:

Rein in the President's War Powers

In affairs of state, no more momentous decision can be made than the decision to go to war. For that reason, in a democratic republic it is essential that that decision be made by the most broadly representative body: the legislature. That is where our Constitution lodges the power to declare war. The Clinton administration espoused a view of executive war-making authority that was as unconditional and unconstrained as that claimed by any president in American history. In fact, presidents from

Johnson and Nixon through Bush and Clinton asserted their authority to put American troops in harm's way without the consent of Congress, and the congressional resolution after September 11 delegated sweeping powers to President Bush. To ensure that we remain a constitutional republic, not a presidential empire, Congress must reclaim its power under the Constitution to make such momentous decisions and its obligation to debate and vote on war measures.

Stop the Abuse of Executive Orders

Lawmaking by the president, through executive orders, is a clear usurpation of both the legislative powers granted to Congress and the powers reserved to the states. The president's principal duty under the Constitution is to "take care that the laws be faithfully executed"—not to make law, as presidents increasingly have done. Like so many other threats to the rule of law, the problem did not begin with but was exacerbated by the Clinton administration. More so than previous presidents, Clinton employed executive orders to make law without any citation of specific constitutional or statutory authority—yet another example of using executive power to implement "the will of the people" outside the rule of law. A Clinton aide, Paul Begala, explained the attraction of executive orders colorfully: "Stroke of the pen, law of the land. Kind of cool." President Bush has used executive orders to grant himself extraordinary powers to deal with terrorism. No matter what agenda the president seeks to impose by executive order, Congress should stop him. The body to which the Constitution delegates "all legislative powers herein granted" must assert its authority.

Stop Delegating Lawmaking Authority to the Federal Bureaucracy

The Constitution clearly grants to Congress the power to make laws and to the executive branch the power to execute the laws. That separation of powers is a key element of the constitutional design. The Founders feared nothing more than the concentration of power in one set of hands. But since the 1930s Congress has gotten into the habit of passing broad laws and leaving the details up to administrative agencies. Congress likes to proclaim noble goals, promise good results, and leave it to unelected bureaucrats to deal with the inevitable tradeoffs and costs of such goals. Congress cannot constitutionally delegate its lawmaking authority to any other body, nor should it want to do so. Congress should accept its responsibility for making law and cease delegating legislation to the bureaucracy.

Consider the Constitutionality of Every Proposed Law

Ours is a government of delegated, enumerated, and thus limited powers. If a power is not granted to Congress in the Constitution, then Congress lacks the authority to legislate in that area. For too long we have drifted toward the idea that everything from our retirement insurance to our local schools to our marriage law is a proper subject for federal legislation. Members of Congress must not leave it to the Supreme Court to decide whether laws are constitutional. Every member must live up to his or her oath of office by considering the constitutionality of every proposed law. Before voting on any bill, each member should ask, "Where in the Constitution is the authority to pass this law?" If the authority cannot be found, members should not vote for the bill. If Congress accepts its responsibility in these matters, it will begin the renaissance of constitutional government in the United States.

Conclusion

For those who go into government to improve the lives of their fellow citizens, the hardest lesson to accept may be that Congress should often do nothing about a problem—such as education, crime, or the cost of prescription drugs. Critics will object, "Do you want the government to just stand there and do nothing while this problem continues?" Sometimes that is exactly what Congress should do. Remember the ancient wisdom imparted to physicians: First, do no harm. And have confidence that free people, left to their own devices, will address issues of concern to them more effectively outside a political environment.

Suggested Readings

Bastiat, Frederic. *The Law.* 1850. Irvington, NY: Foundation for Economic Education, 1998.

Boaz, David. *Libertarianism: A Primer.* New York: Free Press, 1997.

Constitution of the United States of America.

Crane, Edward H. *Defending Civil Society.* Cato's Letter no. 8. Washington: Cato Institute, 1994.

Epstein, Richard. *Simple Rules for a Complex World.* Cambridge, MA: Harvard University Press, 1995.

Friedman, Milton. *Capitalism and Freedom.* Chicago: University of Chicago Press, 1962.

Murray, Charles. *In Pursuit: Of Happiness and Good Government.* New York: Simon & Schuster, 1988.

—Prepared by Edward H. Crane and David Boaz

2. Limited Government and the Rule of Law

Congress should

- live up to its constitutional obligations and cease the practice of delegating legislative powers to administrative agencies; legislation should be passed by Congress, not by unelected administration officials;
- before voting on any proposed act, ask whether that exercise of power is authorized by the Constitution, which enumerates the powers of Congress;
- exercise its constitutional authority to approve only those appointees to federal judgeships who will take seriously the constitutional limitations on the powers of both the states and the federal government; and
- pass and send to the states for their approval a constitutional amendment limiting senators to two terms in office and representatives to three terms, in order to return the legislature to citizen legislators.

Limited government is one of the greatest accomplishments of humanity. It is imperfectly enjoyed by only a portion of the human race, and, where it is enjoyed, its tenure is ever precarious. The experience of the last century is surely witness to the insecurity of constitutional government and to the need for courage in achieving it and vigilance in maintaining it.

Advocates of limited government are not anti-government per se, as some people would charge. Rather, they are hostile to concentrations of coercive power and to the arbitrary use of power against right. With a deep appreciation for the lessons of history and the dangers of unconstrained government, they are for constitutionally limited government, with the delegated authority and means to protect our rights, but not so powerful as to destroy or negate them.

The American system was established to provide limited government. The independent existence of the United States was based on certain truths:

> that all Men are created equal, that they are endowed by their Creator with certain unalienable Rights, that among these are Life, Liberty, and the Pursuit of Happiness—That to secure these Rights, Governments are instituted among Men, deriving their just Powers from the Consent of the Governed, that whenever any Form of Government becomes destructive of these Ends, it is the Right of the People to alter or to abolish it, and to institute new Government, laying its Foundation on such Principles, and organizing its Powers in such Form, as to them shall seem most likely to effect their Safety and Happiness.

On that foundation the American Founders established a system of government based on delegated, enumerated, and thus limited powers.

The American Founders did not pluck those truths out of thin air, nor did they simply invent the principles of American government. They drew from their knowledge of thousands of years of human history, during which many peoples struggled for liberty and limited government. There were both defeats and victories along the way. The results were distilled in the founding documents of the American experiment in limited government: the Declaration of Independence, the Articles of Confederation, the state constitutions, and the Constitution of the United States.

The American Founders were careful students of history. It was Thomas Jefferson, in his influential *A Summary View of the Rights of British America*, prepared in 1774, who noted that "history has informed us that bodies of men as well as individuals are susceptible of the spirit of tyranny." Another Founder, Patrick Henry, devoted great attention to the study of history. He summed up the importance of history thus: "I have but one lamp by which my feet are guided, and that is the lamp of experience. I know of no way of judging the future but by the past." History—the lamp of experience—is indispensable to understanding and defending the liberty of the individual under constitutionally limited, representative government.

Through the study of history the Americans learned about the division of power among judicial, legislative, and executive branches; about federalism; about checks and balances among divided powers; about redress and representation; and about the right of resistance, made effective by the legal right to bear arms, an ancient right of free persons. Liberty and limited government were not invented in 1776; they were reaffirmed and strengthened. The American Revolution set the stage for the benefits of liberty and limited government to be extended to all. As John Figgis, professor of modern history at Cambridge University, noted at the beginning of the 20th century:

> The sonorous phrases of the Declaration of Independence . . . are not an original discovery, they are the heirs of all the ages, the depository of the emotions and the thoughts of seventy generations of culture.

The roots of the history of limited government stretch far back, to the establishment of the principle of the higher law by the ancient Hebrews and by the Greek philosophers. The story of the Golden Calf in the Book of Exodus and the investigations of nature by Aristotle both established— in very different ways—the principle of the higher law. Law is not merely an expression of will or power; it is based on transcendent principles. The legislator is as bound by law as is the subject or citizen; no one is above the law.

Many strands have been entwined to form the fabric of liberty:

- The struggle between church and state, which was put into high gear in the Latin West by Pope Gregory VII in the 11th century under the motto, "freedom of the church." That movement, which created an institutional distinction between the church and the secular authorities, could be seen as the first major "privatization" of a state-owned industry (the church) and provided the foundation for such important institutions as the rule of law and legal accountability, federalism, and the independent and self-governing associations that make up civil society.
- The growth of civil society in the self-governing chartered towns of Europe, in which the guiding principle was "city air makes one free." The independent cities of Europe were the seedbeds of modern civil society—of the market economy, of personal liberty, and of the security of person and property.
- The fixing of limits on the powers of monarchs and executives through written constitutions. The Magna Carta of 1215 is the most memorable of those documents to inheritors of the Anglo-Saxon political tradition. It included the requirement that taxes could not be imposed without the consent of the "general council of the realm," which provided the origin of the English parliament, as well as other very specific limitations on the king's power, including the stipulations that no

11

one be imprisoned or outlawed or exiled or his estate seized "except by the lawful judgment of his peers or the law of the land" and that "merchants shall have safe conduct in and out of England." That was the precursor of the Petition of Right of 1628, the Bill of Rights of 1689, the American Declaration of Independence, and the American Constitution and Bill of Rights.

Those various movements reinforced each other in a multitude of ways. The assertion of the freedom of the church and even of its supremacy over the secular powers was bound up with the idea of the higher law, by which all are judged—emperor, pope, and peasant alike. As legal scholar Henry Bracton, a judge during the reign of Henry III, noted of the royal authority, "The law makes him king. Let the king therefore give to the law what the law gives to him, dominion and power; for there is no king where will, and not law, bears rule." Were the king to consider himself above the law, it was the job of the king's council—the precursor of parliament—to rein him in: "if the king were without a bridle, that is, the law, they ought to put a bridle upon him." Not only was the nascent parliament above the king; the law was above the parliament, as Sir Edward Coke noted in the 17th century:

> when an act of Parliament is against common right and reason, or repugnant, or impossible to be performed, the common law will controul it, and adjudge such Act to be void.

The supremacy of the law over the exercise of power is a hallmark of the Western legal tradition. The rule of law is not satisfied by merely formal or ceremonial exercises, such as the publication of edicts in barely understandable form, whether in the archaic "Law French" of the king's courts or the pages of the *Federal Register*; the laws must be understandable and actually capable of being followed.

There was also widespread recognition of the principle of reciprocity between the holders of power and the general populace. Rights were spelled out in contractual form in constitutions and charters. Those rights were not gifts from the powerful, which could be taken away on a whim, but something on which one could take a stand. Tied up in the notion of a chartered right was the ancillary right to defend that right, even to the point of resistance with force of arms. The higher law, reciprocity and mutuality of obligations, written charters of rights, the right to be consulted on policy and to grant or refuse one's consent, and the right of resistance in defense of those rights are the foundations of constitutionally limited government. They were won over many centuries at great sacrifice.

Just how precious that heritage is can be gleaned from comparing it with the history of Russia, where, until very recently, there was no reciprocity between rulers and ruled and no independent power able to challenge the rulers. The principality of Muscovy and its successors were despotic to a high degree, with no charters of liberty, no power higher than the tsar (or his successor, the Communist Party), no limits on power—in effect, no law. As Harvard University historian Richard Pipes noted in his book *Russia under the Old Regime*, ''There is no evidence in medieval Russia of mutual obligations binding prince and his servitor, and, therefore, also nothing resembling legal and moral 'rights' of subjects, and little need for law and courts.'' The immense difficulties in establishing the rule of law, a system of well-defined and legally secure property, and a market economy are testimony to the great and vital importance of building on a tradition of stable, constitutionally limited government. They also remind us how important it is for us to maintain our heritage of limited government and the rule of law.

The struggle for limited government was a struggle of liberty against power. The demands for religious liberty and the protection of property were fused in the heroic resistance of the Netherlands to the Empire of Spain in their great revolt. The Dutch inspired the English to rise up against the Stuart kings, who sought to fasten upon the English the absolutism that had made such headway on the Continent. The American Revolution was one link in a long chain of revolutions for liberty. The historian John Lothrop Motley opened his magisterial history *The Rise of the Dutch Republic* by connecting the Dutch Republic with the United States of America:

> The rise of the Dutch Republic must ever be regarded as one of the leading events of modern times. . . . The maintenance of the right by the little provinces of Holland and Zealand in the sixteenth, by Holland and England united in the seventeenth, and by the United States of America in the eighteenth centuries, forms but a single chapter in the great volume of human fate; for the so-called revolutions of Holland, England, and America, are all links of one chain.

Motley continued,

> For America the spectacle is one of still deeper import. The Dutch Republic originated in the opposition of the rational elements of human nature to

13

sacerdotal dogmatism and persecution—in the courageous resistance of historical and chartered liberty to foreign despotism.

The Dutch, like the British and the Americans after them, became a shining example of what was possible when people were free: prosperity was possible without the guiding hand of the king and his bureaucrats; social harmony was possible without enforced religious conformity; law and government were possible without an unlimited and absolute sovereign.

The story of the attempts to institute absolutism in the Netherlands and in England was well known by the American Founders, who were, after all, British colonists. One cannot understand the American attempt to institute limited, representative government without understanding the history of England. What they were struggling against was the principle that the powers of the state are "plenary," that they fill up the whole space of power. King James I of England (then King James VI of Scotland) had written in 1598 that "the King is above the law, as both the author and giver of strength thereto." In 1610 James made *A Speech to the Lords and Commons of the Parliament at White-Hall* in which he railed against the notions of popular consent and the rule of law and stated that "as to dispute what God may do is blasphemy . . . so it is sedition in subjects to dispute what a king may do in the height of his power."

In other words, there are no limits to power. Distinct echoes of that view are still heard today. For example, the solicitor general of the United States, Drew Days, arguing in the 1995 case of *United States v. Lopez* before the Supreme Court, was unable to identify a single act of Congress, other than those expressly prohibited by the Constitution, that would be impermissible under the Clinton administration's expansive view of the Commerce Clause. Solicitor Days contended that the powers of Congress are plenary, that is, unlimited, unless, perhaps, specifically prohibited. That all-too-common view turns the notion of limited government on its head. Limited government means that government is limited both in the exercise of its delegated powers and in the means it can employ, which must be both "necessary and proper." The English Revolution of 1640, the Glorious Revolution of 1688, and the American Revolution of 1776 were fought precisely to combat unlimited government. What Americans need is not unlimited government, as Days proposed, but limited government under law, exercising delegated and enumerated powers. That is how the equal liberties of citizens are protected. As the philosopher John Locke, himself an active participant in the struggles for limited government in Britain and the primary inspiration of the American revolutionaries, argued in his *Second Treatise on Government*:

> *the end of Law* is not to abolish or restrain, but *to preserve and enlarge Freedom*: For in all the states of created beings capable of Laws, where *there is no Law, there is no Freedom*. For *Liberty* is to be free from restraint and violence from others, which cannot be, where there is no Law: But Freedom is not, as we are told, *A Liberty for every Man to do what he lists*: (For who could be free, when every other Man's Humour might domineer over him?) But a *Liberty* to dispose, and order, as he lists, his Person, Actions, Possessions, and his whole Property, within the Allowance of those Laws under which he is; and therein not to be subject to the arbitrary Will of another, but freely follow his own.

The American experiment in limited government generated a degree of liberty and prosperity that was virtually unimaginable only a few centuries before. That experiment revealed flaws, of course, none of which was more striking and repugnant than the toleration of slavery, or "man-stealing," as it was called by its libertarian opponents, for it deprived an individual of his property in his own person. That particular evil was eliminated by the Thirteenth Amendment to the Constitution, showing the self-correcting nature and basic resilience of the American constitutional system, which could survive such a cataclysm as the Civil War.

Other flaws, however, have been revealed or have surfaced since. Among them are the following:

- An erosion of the basic principles of federalism, as the federal government has consistently encroached on the authority of the states. Federal criminalization of acts that are already criminalized by the states, for example, usurps state authority (as well as circumventing—opinions of the Supreme Court notwithstanding—the prohibition of double jeopardy in the Fifth Amendment to the Constitution: "nor shall any person be subject for the same offense to be twice put in jeopardy of life or limb"). An even more striking contemporary example of the overreach of federal law is the continued exercise of federal controls over marijuana use in states, such as California and Arizona, that have legalized the medical use of that drug. The Tenth Amendment is quite explicit on this point: "The powers not delegated to the United States by the Constitution, nor prohibited by it to the States, are reserved to the States respectively, or to the people."
- Violation of the separation of powers between the various branches of government. In Article I, section 8, for example, the Constitution

15

explicitly reserves the power to declare war to the Congress, a power that the Congress has allowed to be usurped by the executive branch and which it should retake to itself.

- Failure of the legislative branch to fulfill its responsibilities when it delegates its legislative powers to administrative agencies of the executive branch, such as the Food and Drug Administration and the Federal Trade Commission. In addition to violating the Constitution, that has led to the erosion of the rule of law, as such administrative agencies have burdened the population with an unimaginably complex welter of edicts; the *Federal Register* ran 71,269 pages in 2003, reflecting a degree of minute regulation that is unreasonable and burdensome and that virtually guarantees that any citizen involved in a commercial transaction, for example, will run afoul of some part of it, no matter how well intentioned or scrupulous he or she may be. Such a situation is an invitation to the arbitrary exercise of power, rather than the application of law. That illegal delegation of powers is an abdication of the representative function described in the *Federalist Papers* and elsewhere by the Founders. Members of Congress are thereby converted from representatives of their constituents into ''fixers,'' who offer to intercede on behalf of constituents with the agencies that are illegally exercising the authority of the legislative branch. Thus, members of Congress can avoid responsibility for onerous laws but can take credit for gaining special treatment for their constituents. That system may be thoroughly congenial to the interests of the existing officeholders of both the executive and the legislative branch, but it is directly contrary to the doctrine of the separation of powers and to the very concept of representative government.

- Inattention to the important role of the federal judiciary as a check on arbitrary and unauthorized exercises of power. Especially since the Court-packing ''constitutional revolution of 1937,'' there has been too little attention by the federal judiciary—and by the Congress in ratifying judicial nominees—to fulfilling the role of the courts in enforcing constitutional restraints on both the federal and the state governments, as set out in Article III, section 2, of the Constitution. Sections of the Constitution that have suffered from relative neglect include Article I, section 1 (''All legislative Powers herein granted shall be vested in a Congress of the United States''); Article I, section 8 (enumerating and thus limiting the powers of Congress); Article I, section 10 (''No state shall . . . pass any . . . Law impairing the

Obligation of Contracts''); the Fifth Amendment (''No person shall be ... deprived of life, liberty, or property, without due process of law; nor shall private property be taken for public use without just compensation''); the Ninth Amendment (''The enumeration in the Constitution of certain rights shall not be construed to deny or disparage others retained by the people''); the Tenth Amendment (''The powers not delegated to the United States by the Constitution, nor prohibited by it to the States, are reserved to the States respectively, or to the people''); and the Fourteenth Amendment (''No state shall make or enforce any law which shall abridge the privileges or immunities of citizens of the United States''). Although the First and Fourteenth Amendments have indeed been the source of significant judicial activity, the Court has not consistently applied the prohibitions of the First Amendment to either commercial speech or political speech (the latter in the context of campaign finance), nor has the Court rectified the novel (and specious) distinction between personal liberties and economic liberties drawn by Justice Harlan F. Stone in *United States v. Carolene Products Co.* (1938).

- The failure to pass a constitutional amendment limiting members of the Senate to two terms and members of the House of Representatives to three terms. Just as the president is limited in the number of terms he or she can serve, so should be the other elected branch of government, to guarantee the rotation in office that the Founders believed essential to popular government.

Those flaws can, however, be corrected. What is needed is the courage to place the health of the constitutional order and the future of the American system above short-term political gain. The original American Founders were willing ''to mutually pledge to each other our Lives, our Fortunes, and our sacred Honor.'' Nothing even remotely approaching that would be necessary for today's members of Congress to renew and restore the American system of constitutionally limited government.

In defending the separation of powers established by the Constitution, James Madison clearly tied the arrangement to the goal of limiting government power:

> It may be a reflection on human nature that such devices should be necessary to control the abuses of government. But what is government itself but the greatest of all reflections on human nature? If men were angels, no government would be necessary. If angels were to govern men, neither external nor internal controls would be necessary. In framing a government which

is to be administered by men over men, the great difficulty lies in this: you must first enable the government to control the governed; and in the next instance oblige it to control itself. A dependence on the people is, no doubt, the primary control on the government; but experience has taught mankind the necessity of auxiliary precautions.

What is needed for the survival of limited government is a renewal of both of the forces described by Madison as controls on government: dependence on the people, in the form of an informed citizenry jealous of its rights and ever vigilant against unconstitutional or otherwise unwarranted exercises of power, and officeholders who take seriously their oaths of office and accept the responsibilities they entail.

Suggested Readings

Barnett, Randy. *Restoring the Lost Constitution.* Princeton, NJ: Princeton University Press, 2004.

Berman, Harold. *Law and Revolution: The Formation of the Western Legal Tradition.* Cambridge, MA: Harvard University Press, 1983.

Boaz, David. *Libertarianism: A Primer.* New York: Free Press, 1997.

Boaz, David, ed. *The Libertarian Reader: Classic and Contemporary Readings from Lao-tzu to Milton Friedman.* New York: Free Press, 1997.

Bramsted, E. K., and K. J. Melhuish, eds. *Western Liberalism: A History in Documents from Locke to Croce.* New York: Longman, 1978.

Brooks, David L., ed. *From Magna Carta to the Constitution: Documents in the Struggle for Liberty.* San Francisco: Fox & Wilkes, 1993.

Ely, James W., Jr. *The Guardian of Every Other Right: A Constitutional History of Property Rights.* New York: Oxford University Press, 1998.

Epstein, Richard A. *Simple Rules for a Complex World.* Cambridge, MA: Harvard University Press, 1997.

Hamilton, Alexander, James Madison, and John Jay, *The Federalist Papers.* New York: Mentor, 1961.

Hayek, F. A. *The Constitution of Liberty.* Chicago: University of Chicago Press, 1960.

Higgs, Robert. *Crisis and Leviathan: Critical Episodes in the Growth of American Government.* New York: Oxford University Press, 1987.

Jefferson, Thomas. "A Summary View of the Rights of British North America." In *The Portable Jefferson.* New York: Penguin Books, 1977.

Locke, John. *Two Treatises of Government.* 1690. Cambridge: Cambridge University Press, 1988.

—Prepared by Tom G. Palmer

3. Congress, the Courts, and the Constitution

Congress should

- encourage constitutional debate in the nation by engaging in constitutional debate in Congress, as was urged by the House Constitutional Caucus during the 104th Congress;
- enact nothing without first consulting the Constitution for proper authority and then debating that question on the floors of the House and the Senate;
- move toward restoring constitutional government by carefully returning power wrongly taken over the years from the states and the people; and
- reject the nomination of judicial candidates who do not appreciate that the Constitution is a document of delegated, enumerated, and thus limited powers.

Introduction

In a chapter devoted to advising members of Congress about their responsibilities under the Constitution, one hardly knows where to begin—so far has Congress taken us, over the 20th century, from constitutional government. James Madison, the principal author of the Constitution, assured us in *Federalist* no. 45 that the powers of the federal government under that document were "few and defined." No one believes that describes Washington's powers today. That raises fundamental questions about the constitutional legitimacy of modern American government.

For a while at century's end, after the realigning election of 1994, it looked like Congress was at last going to rethink its seemingly inexorable push toward ever-larger government. In fact, the 104th Congress saw the creation in the House of a 100-strong Constitutional Caucus dedicated to promoting the restoration of limited constitutional government. And shortly thereafter, President Clinton announced that the era of big government was over. But the spirit of that Congress has waned over time. By the 107th Congress, respect for constitutional limits on congressional power was all but gone. It was nowhere to be found in the 108th Congress.

The principles of the matter have not gone away, however; nor of course has the Constitution itself. It is still the law of the land, however little Congress heeds it. And the moral, political, and economic implications of limited constitutional government have not changed either. That kind of government is the foundation for liberty, prosperity, and the vision of equality that most people cherish. Indeed, that insight has been gaining ground around the world as the Leviathans of the 20th century have aged or crumbled. Yet all too many members of Congress seem still to believe that the good life is brought about primarily by government programs, not by individuals acting in their private capacities. And they believe equally that the Constitution authorizes them to enact such programs.

In growing numbers, however, Americans know better. Below the level that polling usually reaches, they have come to see that government rarely solves the problems it purports to solve; in fact, it usually makes those problems worse. More deeply, they have come to understand that a life dependent on government is too often not only impoverishing but impoverished. It is no accident, therefore, that the electoral trends for more than a quarter of a century have been in the direction of less government, even if Washington has been slow to appreciate that message.

In moving from a world in which government is expected to solve our problems to a world in which individuals, families, and communities assume that responsibility—indeed, take up that challenge—the basic questions are how much and how fast to reduce government. Those are not questions about how to make government run better—government will always be plagued by waste, fraud, and abuse—but about the fundamental role of government in this nation.

How Much to Reduce Government

The first of those questions—how much to reduce government—would seem on first impression to be a matter of policy; yet in America, if we take the Constitution seriously, it is not for the most part a policy question, a question about what we may or may not want to do. For the Founding Fathers thought long and hard about the proper role of government in our lives, and they set forth their thoughts in a document that explicitly enumerates the powers of the federal government.

Thus, setting aside for the moment all practical concerns, the Constitution tells us as a matter of first principle how much to reduce government by telling us, first, what powers the federal government in fact has and, second, how governments at all levels must exercise their powers—by respecting the rights of the people.

That means that if a federal power or federal program is not authorized by the Constitution, it is illegitimate. Given the present size of government, that is a stark conclusion, to be sure. But it flows quite naturally from the Tenth Amendment, the final statement in the Bill of Rights, which says, "The powers not delegated to the United States by the Constitution, nor prohibited by it to the States, are reserved to the States respectively, or to the people." In a nutshell, the Constitution establishes a government of delegated, enumerated, and thus limited powers. As the *Federalist Papers* make clear, the Constitution was written not simply to empower the federal government but to limit it as well.

Since the Progressive Era, however, the politics of government as problem solver has dominated our public discourse. And since the collapse of the Supreme Court during the New Deal, following President Roosevelt's notorious Court-packing scheme, the Court has abetted that view by standing the Constitution on its head, turning it into a document of effectively unenumerated and hence unlimited powers. (For a fuller discussion of the Constitution and the history of its interpretation, see Chapter 3 of the *Cato Handbook for Congress: 104th Congress*.)

Indeed, limits on government today, when we've had them, have come largely from political and budgetary rather than from constitutional considerations. Thus, it has not been because of any perceived lack of constitutional authority that government in recent years has failed to undertake a program but because of practical limits on the power of government to tax and borrow—and even those limits have failed in times of economic prosperity. That is not the mark of a limited, constitutional republic. It is the mark of a parliamentary system, limited only by periodic elections.

The Founding Fathers could have established such a system, of course. They did not. But we have allowed those marks of a parliamentary system to supplant the system they gave us. To restore truly limited government, therefore, we have to do more than define the issues as political or budgetary. We have to go to the heart of the matter and raise the underlying constitutional questions. In a word, we have to ask the most fundamental

21

question of all: does the government have the authority, the constitutional authority, to do what it is doing?

How Fast to Reduce Government

As a practical matter, however, before Congress or the courts can relimit government as it was meant to be limited by the Constitution, they need to take seriously the problems posed by the present state of public debate on the subject. It surely counts for something that a substantial number of Americans—to say nothing of the organs of public opinion—have little apprehension of or appreciation for the constitutional limits on activist government. Thus, in addressing the question of how fast to reduce government, we have to recognize that the Supreme Court, after nearly 65 years of arguing otherwise, is hardly in a position, by itself, to relimit government in the far-reaching way a properly applied Constitution requires. But neither does Congress at this point have sufficient moral authority, even if it wanted to, to end tomorrow the vast array of programs it has enacted over the years with insufficient constitutional authority.

For either Congress or the Court to be able to do fully what should be done, therefore, a proper foundation must first be laid. In essence, the climate of opinion must be such that a sufficiently large portion of the American public stands behind the changes that are undertaken. When enough people come forward to ask—indeed, to demand—that government limit itself to the powers it is given in the Constitution, thereby freeing individuals, families, and communities to solve their own problems, we will know we are on the right track.

Fortunately, a change in the climate of opinion on such basic questions has been under way for some time now. The debate today is very different than it was in the 1960s and 1970s. But there is a good deal more to be done before Congress and the courts are able to move in the right direction in any far-reaching way, much less say that they have restored constitutional government in America. To continue the process, then, Congress should take the lead in the following ways.

Encourage Constitutional Debate in the Nation by Engaging in Constitutional Debate in Congress, As Was Urged by the House Constitutional Caucus during the 104th Congress

Under the leadership of House freshmen like J. D. Hayworth and John Shadegg of Arizona, Sam Brownback of Kansas, and Bob Barr of Georgia, together with a few senior congressmen like Richard Pombo of California, an informal Constitutional Caucus was established in the "radical" 104th Congress. Its purpose was to encourage constitutional debate in Congress and the nation and, in time, to restore constitutional government. Unfortunately, the caucus has been moribund since then. It needs to be revived—along with the spirit of the 104th Congress—and its work needs to be expanded.

The caucus was created in response to the belief that the nation had strayed very far from its constitutional roots and that Congress, absent leadership from elsewhere in government, should begin addressing the problem. By itself, of course, neither the caucus nor the entire Congress can solve the problem. To be sure, in a reversal of all human experience, Congress in a day could agree to limit itself to its enumerated powers and then roll back the countless programs it has enacted by exceeding that authority. But it would take authoritative opinions from the Supreme Court, reversing a substantial body of largely post–New Deal decisions, to embed those restraints in "constitutional law"—even if they have been embedded in the Constitution from the outset, the Court's modern readings of the document notwithstanding.

The Goals of the Constitutional Caucus

The ultimate goal of the caucus and Congress, then, should be to encourage the Court to reach such decisions. But history teaches, as noted above, that the Court does not operate entirely in a vacuum, that to some degree public opinion is the precursor and seedbed of its decisions. Thus, the more immediate goal of the caucus should be to influence the debate in the nation by influencing the debate in Congress. To do that, it is not necessary or even desirable, in the present climate, that every member of Congress be a member of the caucus—however worthy that end might ultimately be—but it is necessary that those who join the caucus be committed to its basic ends. And it is necessary that members establish a clear agenda for reaching those ends.

To reduce the problem to its essence, every day members of Congress are besieged by requests to enact countless measures to solve endless problems. Indeed, listening to much of the recent campaign debate, one might conclude that no problem is too personal or too trivial to warrant the attention of the federal government. Yet most of the "problems" Congress spends most of its time addressing—from health care to day care to retirement security to economic competition—are simply the personal and economic problems of life that individuals, families, and firms,

23

not governments, should be addressing. What is more, as a basic point of constitutional doctrine, under a constitution like ours, interpreted as ours was meant to be interpreted, there is little authority for government at any level to address such problems.

Properly understood and used, then, the Constitution can be a valuable ally in the efforts of the caucus and Congress to reduce the size and scope of government. For in the minds and hearts of most Americans, it remains a revered document, however little it may be understood by a substantial number of them.

The Constitutional Vision

If the Constitution is to be thus used, however, the principal misunderstanding that surrounds it must be recognized and addressed. In particular, the modern idea that the Constitution, without further amendment, is an infinitely elastic document that allows government to grow to meet public demands of whatever kind must be challenged. More Americans than presently do must come to appreciate that the Founding Fathers, who were keenly aware of the expansive tendencies of government, wrote the Constitution precisely to check that kind of thinking and that possibility. To be sure, the Founders meant for government to be our servant, not our master, but they meant it to serve us in a very limited way—by securing our rights, as the Declaration of Independence says, and by doing those few other things that government does best, as spelled out in the Constitution.

In all else, we were meant to be free—to plan and live our own lives, to solve our own problems, which is what freedom is all about. Some may characterize that vision as tantamount to saying, "You're on your own," but that kind of response simply misses the point. In America individuals, families, and organizations have never been "on their own" in the most important sense. They have always been members of communities, of civil society, where they could live their lives and solve their problems by following a few simple rules about individual initiative and responsibility, respect for property and promise, and charity toward the few who need help from others. Massive government planning and programs have upset that natural order of things—less so in America than elsewhere, but very deeply all the same.

Those are the issues that need to be discussed, both in human and in constitutional terms. We need, as a people, to rethink our relationship to government. We need to ask not what government can do for us but what we can do for ourselves and, where necessary, for others—not through government but apart from government, as private citizens and organizations. That is what the Constitution was written to enable. It empowers government in a very limited way. It empowers people—by leaving them free—in every other way.

To proclaim and eventually secure that vision of a free people, the Constitutional Caucus should reconstitute itself and rededicate itself to that end at the beginning of the 109th Congress and the beginning of every Congress thereafter. Standing apart from Congress, the caucus should nonetheless be both of and above Congress—as the constitutional conscience of Congress. Every member of Congress, before taking office, swears to support the Constitution—hardly a constraining oath, given the modern Court's open-ended reading of the document. Members of the caucus should dedicate themselves to the deeper meaning of that oath. They should support the Constitution the Framers gave us, as amended by subsequent generations, not as "amended" by the Court's expansive interpretations.

Encouraging Debate

Acting together, the members of the caucus could have a major impact on the course of public debate in this nation—not least, by virtue of their numbers. What is more, there is political safety in those numbers. As Benjamin Franklin might have said, no single member of Congress is likely to be able to undertake the task of restoring constitutional government on his own, for in the present climate he would surely be hanged, politically, for doing so. But if the caucus hangs together, the task will be made more bearable and enjoyable—and a propitious outcome made more likely.

On the agenda of the caucus, then, should be those specific undertakings that will best stir debate and thereby move the climate of opinion. Drawn together by shared understandings, and unrestrained by the need for serious compromise, the members of the caucus are free to chart a principled course and employ principled means, which they should do.

They might begin, for example, by surveying opportunities for constitutional debate in Congress, then making plans to seize those opportunities. Clearly, when new bills are introduced, or old ones are up for reauthorization, an opportunity is presented to debate constitutional questions. But even before that, when plans are discussed in party sessions, members should raise constitutional issues. Again, the caucus might study the costs and benefits of eliminating clearly unconstitutional programs, the better to determine which can be eliminated most easily and quickly.

25

Above all, the caucus should look for strategic opportunities to employ constitutional arguments. Too often, members of Congress fail to appreciate that if they take a principled stand against a seemingly popular program—and state their case well—they can seize the moral high ground and prevail ultimately over those who are seen in the end to be more politically craven.

All of that will stir constitutional debate—which is just the point. For too long in Congress that debate has been dead, replaced by the often dreary budget debate. This nation was not established by men with green eyeshades. It was established by men who understood the basic character of government and the basic right to be free. That debate needs to be revived. It needs to be heard not simply in the courts—where it is twisted through modern "constitutional law"—but in Congress as well.

Enact Nothing without First Consulting the Constitution for Proper Authority and Then Debating That Question on the Floors of the House and the Senate

It would hardly seem necessary to ask Congress, before it enacts any measure, to cite its constitutional authority for doing so. After all, is that not simply part of what it means, as a member of Congress, to swear to support the Constitution? And if Congress's powers are limited by virtue of being enumerated, presumably there are many things Congress has no authority to do, however worthy those things might otherwise be. Yet so far have we strayed from constitutional thinking that such a requirement is today treated perfunctorily—when it is not ignored altogether.

The most common perfunctory citations—captured ordinarily in constitutional boilerplate—are to the General Welfare and Commerce Clauses of the Constitution. It is no small irony that both those clauses were written as shields against overweening government; yet today they are swords of federal power.

The General Welfare Clause

The General Welfare Clause of Article I, section 8, of the Constitution was meant to serve as a brake on the power of Congress to tax and spend in furtherance of its enumerated powers or ends: the spending that attended the exercise of an enumerated power had to be for the *general* welfare, not for the welfare of particular parties or sections of the nation.

That view, held by Madison, Jefferson, and most others, stands in marked contrast to the view of Hamilton—that the Constitution established an *independent* power to tax and spend for the general welfare. But as South Carolina's William Drayton observed on the floor of the House in 1828, Hamilton's view would make a mockery of the doctrine of enumerated powers, the centerpiece of the Constitution, rendering the enumeration of Congress's other powers superfluous: whenever Congress wanted to do something it was barred from doing by the absence of a power to do it, it could simply declare the act to be serving the "general welfare" and get out from under the limits imposed by enumeration.

That, unfortunately, is what happens today. In 1936 the Court came down, almost in passing, on Hamilton's side, declaring that there is an independent power to tax and spend for the general welfare. Then in 1937, in upholding the constitutionality of the new Social Security program, the Court completed the job when it stated the Hamiltonian view not as dicta but as doctrine, then reminded Congress of the constraints imposed by the word "general," but added that the Court would not police that restraint; rather, Congress would be left to police itself, the very Congress that was distributing money from the Treasury with ever greater particularity. Since that time the relatively modest redistributive schemes that preceded the New Deal have grown exponentially until today they are everywhere.

The Commerce Clause

The Commerce Clause of the Constitution, which grants Congress the power to regulate "commerce among the states," was also written primarily as a shield—against overweening *state* power. Under the Articles of Confederation, states had erected tariffs and other protectionist measures that impeded the free flow of commerce among the states. Indeed, the need to break the logjam that resulted was one of the principal reasons for the call for a convention in Philadelphia in 1787. To address the problem, the Framers gave *Congress* the power to regulate—or "make regular"—commerce among the states. It was thus meant to be a power primarily to facilitate free trade.

That functional account of the commerce power is consistent with the original understanding of the power, the 18th-century meaning of "regulate," and the structural limits entailed by the doctrine of enumerated powers. Yet today the functional account is all but unknown. Following decisions by the Court in 1937 and 1942, Congress has been able to regulate anything that even "affects" interstate commerce, which in principle is everything. Far from regulating to ensure the free flow of commerce among the states, much of that regulation, for all manner of social and economic purposes, actually frustrates the free flow of commerce.

As the explosive growth of the modern redistributive state has taken place almost entirely under the General Welfare Clause, so, too, the growth of the modern regulatory state has occurred almost entirely under the Commerce Clause. That raises a fundamental question, of course: if the Framers had meant for Congress to be able to do virtually anything it wanted under those two simple clauses alone, why did they bother to enumerate Congress's other powers, or bother to defend the doctrine of enumerated powers throughout the *Federalist Papers*? Had they meant that, those efforts would have been pointless.

Lopez *and Its Aftermath*

Today, as noted above, congressional citations to the General Welfare and Commerce Clauses usually take the form of perfunctory boilerplate. When it wants to regulate some activity, Congress makes a bow to the doctrine of enumerated powers by claiming that it has made findings that the activity at issue "affects" interstate commerce—say, by preventing interstate travel. Given those findings, Congress then claims it has authority to regulate the activity under its power to regulate commerce among the states.

Thus, when the 104th Congress was pressed in the summer of 1996 to do something about what looked at the time like a wave of church arsons in the South, it sought to broaden the already doubtful authority of the federal government to prosecute such acts by determining that church arsons "hinder interstate commerce" and "impede individuals in moving interstate." Never mind that the prosecution of arson has traditionally been a state responsibility, there being no general federal police power in the Constitution. Never mind that church arsons have virtually nothing to do with interstate commerce, much less with the free flow of goods and services among the states. The Commerce Clause rationale, set forth in boilerplate language, was thought by Congress to be sufficient to enable it to move forward and enact the Church Arson Prevention Act of 1996— unanimously, no less.

Yet only a year earlier, in the celebrated *Lopez* case, the Supreme Court had declared, for the first time in nearly 60 years, that Congress's power under the Commerce Clause has limits. To be sure, the Court raised the bar against federal regulation only slightly: Congress would have to show that the activity it wanted to regulate "substantially" affected interstate commerce, leading Justice Thomas to note in his concurrence that the Court was still a good distance from a proper reading of the clause. Nevertheless, the decision was widely heralded as a shot across the bow of Congress. And many in Congress saw it as confirming at last their own view that the body in which they served was simply out of control, constitutionally. Indeed, when it passed the act at issue in *Lopez*, the Gun-Free School Zones Act of 1990, Congress had not even bothered to cite any authority under the Constitution. In what must surely be a stroke of consummate hubris—and disregard for the Constitution—Congress simply assumed that authority.

But to make matters worse, despite the *Lopez* ruling—which the Court reinforced in May 2000 when it found parts of the Violence Against Women Act unconstitutional on similar grounds—Congress in September 1996 passed the Gun-Free School Zones Act again. This time, of course, the boilerplate was included—even as Sen. Fred Thompson of Tennessee was reminding his colleagues from the floor of the Senate that the Supreme Court had recently told them that they "cannot just have some theoretical basis, some attenuated basis" under the Commerce Clause for such an act. The prosecution of gun possession near schools—like the prosecution of church arsons, crimes against women, and much else—is very popular, as state prosecutors well know. But governments can address problems only if they have authority to do so, not from good intentions alone. Indeed, the road to constitutional destruction is paved with good intentions.

Congressional debate on these matters is thus imperative: it is not enough for Congress simply to say the magic words—"General Welfare Clause" or "Commerce Clause"—to be home free, constitutionally. Not every debate will yield satisfying results, as the examples above illustrate. But if the Constitution is to be kept alive, there must at least be debate. Over time, good ideas tend to prevail over bad ideas, but only if they are given voice. The constitutional debate must again be heard in the Congress of the United States as it was over much of our nation's history, and it must be heard before bills are enacted. The American people can hardly be expected to take the Constitution and its limits on government seriously if their elected representatives do not.

Move toward Restoring Constitutional Government by Carefully Returning Power Wrongly Taken over the Years from the States and the People

If Congress should enact no new legislation without grounding its authority to do so securely in the Constitution, so too should it begin repealing legislation not so grounded, legislation that arose by assuming power that rightly rests with the states or the people. To appreciate how daunting a task that will be, simply reflect again on Madison's observation that the powers of the federal government under the Constitution are "few and defined."

But the magnitude of the task is only one dimension of its difficulty. Let us be candid: there are many in Congress who will oppose any efforts to restore constitutional government for any number of reasons, ranging from the practical to the theoretical. Some see their job as one primarily of representing the interests of their constituents, especially the short-term interests reflected in the phrase "bringing home the bacon." Others simply like big government, whether because of an "enlightened" Progressive Era view of the world or because of a narrower, more cynical interest in the perquisites of enhanced power. Still others believe sincerely in a "living constitution," one extreme form of which—the "democratic" form—imposes no limit whatsoever on government save for periodic elections. Finally, there are those who understand the unconstitutional and hence illegitimate character of much of what government does today but believe it is too late in the day to do anything about it. All of those people and others will find reasons to resist the discrete measures that are necessary to begin restoring constitutional government. Yet, where necessary, their views will have to be accommodated as the process unfolds.

Maintaining Support for Limited Government

Given the magnitude of the problem, then, and the practical implications of repealing federal programs, a fair measure of caution is in order. As the nations of Eastern Europe and the former Soviet Union have learned, it is relatively easy to get into socialism—just seize all property and labor and place it under state control—but much harder to get out of it. It is not simply a matter of returning what was taken, for much has changed as a result of the taking. People have died and new people have come along. Public law has replaced private law. And new expectations and dependencies have arisen and become settled over time. The transition to freedom that many of those nations are experiencing is what we and many other nations around the world today are facing, to a lesser extent, as we too try to reduce the size and scope of our governments.

As programs are reduced or eliminated, then, care must be taken to do as little harm as possible—for two reasons at least. First, there is some sense in which the federal government today, vastly overextended though it is, stands in a contractual relationship with the American people. That is a very difficult idea to pin down, however, for once the genuine contract—the Constitution—has broken down, the "legislative contracts" that arise to take its place invariably reduce, when parsed, to programs under which some people have become dependent upon others, although neither side had a great deal to say directly about the matter at the outset. Whatever its merits, that contractual view is held by a good part of the public, especially in the case of so-called middle-class entitlements.

That leads to the second reason why care must be taken in restoring power to the states and the people, namely, that the task must be undertaken, as noted earlier, with the support of a substantial portion of the people—ideally, at the urging of those people. Given the difficulty of convincing people—including legislators—to act against their relatively short-term interests, it will take sound congressional judgment about where and when to move. More important, it will take keen leadership, leadership that is able to frame the issues in a way that will communicate both the rightness and the soundness of the decisions that are required.

In exercising that leadership, there is no substitute for keeping "on message" and for keeping the message simple, direct, and clear. The aim, again, is both freedom and the good society. We need to appreciate how the vast government programs we have created over the years have actually reduced the freedom and well-being of all of us—and have undermined the Constitution besides. Not that the ends served by those programs are unworthy—few government programs are undertaken for worthless ends. But individuals, families, private firms, and communities could bring about most of those ends, voluntarily and at far less cost, if only they were free to do so—especially if they were free to keep the wherewithal that is necessary to do so. If individual freedom and individual responsibility are values we cherish—indeed, are the foundations of the good society—we must come to appreciate how our massive government programs have undermined those values and, with that, the good society itself.

Redistributive Programs

Examples of the kinds of programs that should be returned to the states and the people are detailed elsewhere in this *Handbook*, but a few are in order here. Without question, the most important example of devolution to come from the "radical" 104th Congress was in the area of welfare. However flawed the final legislation may have been from both a constitutional and a policy perspective, it was still a step in the right direction.

31

Ultimately, as will be noted below in a more general way, welfare should not be even a state program. Rather, it should be a matter of private responsibility, as it was for years in this nation. But the process of getting the federal government out of the business of charity, for which there is no authority in the Constitution, has at least begun.

Eventually, that process should be repeated in every other "entitlement" area, from individual to institutional to corporate, from Social Security and Medicare to the National Endowment for the Arts to the Department of Agriculture's Market Access Program and on and on. Each of those programs was started for a good reason, to be sure, yet each involves taking from some to give to others—means that are both wrong and unconstitutional, to say nothing of monumentally inefficient. Taken together, they put us all on welfare in one way or another, and we are all the poorer for it.

Some of those programs will be harder to reduce, phase out, or eliminate than others, of course. Entitlement programs with large numbers of beneficiaries, for example, will require transition phases to ensure that harm is minimized and public support is maintained. Other programs, however, could be eliminated with relatively little harm. Does anyone seriously doubt that there would be art in America without the National Endowment for the Arts? Indeed, without the heavy hand of government grant making, the arts would likely flourish as they did long before the advent of the NEA—and no one would be made to pay, through his taxes, for art he abhorred.

It is the transfer programs in the "symbolic" area, in fact, that may be the most important to eliminate first, for they have multiplier effects reaching well beyond their raw numbers, and those effects are hardly neutral on the question of reducing the size and scope of government. The National Endowment for the Arts, the National Endowment for the Humanities, the Corporation for Public Broadcasting, the Legal Services Corporation, and the Department of Education have all proceeded without constitutional authority—but with serious implications for free speech and for the cause of limiting government. Not a few critics have pointed to the heavy hand of government in those symbolic areas. Of equal importance, however, is the problem of compelled speech: as Jefferson wrote, "To compel a man to furnish contributions of money for the propagation of opinions which he disbelieves is sinful and tyrannical." But on a more practical note, if Congress is serious about addressing the climate of opinion in the nation, it will end such programs not simply because they are without constitutional authority but because they have demonstrated a relentless tendency over the years in only one direction—toward even more government. Indeed, one should hardly expect those institutions to be underwriting programs that advocate less government when they themselves exist through government.

Regulatory Redistribution

If the redistributive programs that constitute the modern welfare state are candidates for elimination, so too are many of the regulatory programs that have arisen under the Commerce Clause. Here, however, care must be taken not simply from a practical perspective but from a constitutional perspective as well, for some of those programs may be constitutionally justified. When read functionally, recall, the Commerce Clause was meant to enable Congress to ensure that commerce among the states is regular, and especially to counter state actions that might upset that regularity. Think of the Commerce Clause as an early North American Free Trade Agreement, without the heavy hand of "managed trade" that often accompanies the modern counterpart.

Thus conceived, the Commerce Clause clearly empowers Congress, through regulation, to override state measures that may frustrate the free flow of commerce among the states. But it also enables Congress to take such affirmative measures as may be necessary and proper for facilitating free trade, such as clarifying rights of trade in uncertain contexts or regulating the interstate transport of dangerous goods. What the clause does not authorize, however, is regulation for reasons other than to ensure the free flow of commerce—the kind of "managed trade" that is little but a thinly disguised transfer program designed to benefit one party at the expense of another.

Unfortunately, most modern federal regulation falls into that final category, whether it concerns employment or health care or insurance or whatever. In fact, given budgetary constraints on the ability of government to tax and spend—to take money from some, run it through the Treasury, then give it to others—the preferred form of transfer today is through regulation. That puts it "off budget." Thus, when an employer, an insurer, a lender, or a landlord is required by regulation to do something he would otherwise have a right not to do, or not do something he would otherwise have a right to do, he serves the party benefited by that regulation every bit as much as if he were taxed to do so, but no tax increase is ever registered on any public record.

33

The temptation for Congress to resort to such "cost-free" regulatory redistribution is of course substantial, and the effects are both far-reaching and perverse. Natural markets are upset as incentives are changed; economies of scale are skewed as large businesses, better able to absorb the regulatory burdens, are advantaged over small ones; defensive measures, inefficient from the larger perspective, are encouraged; and general uncertainty, anathema to efficient markets, is the order of the day. Far from facilitating free trade, redistributive regulation frustrates it. Far from being justified by the Commerce Clause, it undermines the very purpose of the clause.

Federal Crimes

In addition to misusing the commerce power for the purpose of regulatory redistribution, Congress has misused that power to create federal crimes. Thus, a great deal of "regulation" has arisen in recent years under the commerce power that is nothing but a disguised exercise of a police power that Congress otherwise lacks. As noted earlier, the Gun-Free School Zones Act, the Church Arson Prevention Act, and the Violence Against Women Act are examples of legislation passed nominally under the power of Congress to regulate commerce among the states; but the actions subject to federal prosecution under those statutes—gun possession, church arson, and gender-motivated violence, respectively—are ordinarily regulated under *state* police power, the power of states, in essence, to "police" or secure our rights. The ruse of regulating them under Congress's commerce power is made necessary because there is no federal police power enumerated in the Constitution—except as an implication of federal sovereignty over federal territory or an incidence of some enumerated power.

That ruse should be candidly recognized. Indeed, it is a mark of the decline of respect for the Constitution that when we sought to fight a war on liquor earlier in the century we felt it necessary to do so by first amending the Constitution—there being no power otherwise for such a federal undertaking. Today, however, when we engage in a war on drugs— with as much success as we enjoyed in the earlier war—we do so without as much as a nod to the Constitution.

The Constitution lists three federal crimes: treason, piracy, and counterfeiting. Yet today there are more than 3,000 federal crimes and perhaps 300,000 regulations that carry criminal sanctions. Over the years, no faction in Congress has been immune, especially in an election year, from the propensity to criminalize all manner of activities, utterly oblivious to the lack of any constitutional authority for doing so. We should hardly imagine that the Founders fought a war to free us from a distant tyranny only to establish a tyranny in Washington, in some ways even more distant from the citizens it was meant to serve.

Policing the States

If the federal government has often intruded upon the police power of the states, so too has it often failed in its responsibility under the Fourteenth Amendment to police the states. Here is an area where federal regulation has been, if anything, too restrained—yet also unprincipled, oftentimes, when undertaken.

The Civil War Amendments to the Constitution changed fundamentally the relationship between the federal government and the states, giving citizens an additional level of protection, not against federal but against state oppression—the oppression of slavery, obviously, but much else besides. Thus, the Fourteenth Amendment prohibits states from abridging the privileges or immunities of citizens of the United States; from depriving any person of life, liberty, or property without due process of law; and from denying any person the equal protection of the laws. By implication, section 1 of the amendment gives the courts the power to secure those guarantees. Section 5 gives Congress the "power to enforce, by appropriate legislation, the provisions of this article."

As the debate that surrounded the adoption of those amendments makes clear, the Privileges or Immunities Clause was meant to be the principal source of substantive rights in the Fourteenth Amendment, and those rights were meant to include the rights of property, contract, and personal security—in short, our "natural liberties," as Blackstone had earlier understood that phrase. Unfortunately, in 1873, in the notorious *Slaughterhouse Cases,* a bitterly divided Supreme Court essentially eviscerated the Privileges or Immunities Clause. There followed, for nearly a century, the era of Jim Crow in the South and, for a period stretching to the present, a Fourteenth Amendment jurisprudence that is as contentious as it is confused.

Modern liberals have urged that the amendment be used as it was meant to be used—against state oppression; but they have also urged that it be used to recognize all manner of "rights" that are no part of the theory of rights that stands behind the amendment as understood at the time of ratification. Modern conservatives, partly in reaction, have urged that the amendment be used far more narrowly than it was meant to be used—for fear that it might be misused, as it has been.

35

The role of the judiciary under section 1 of the Fourteenth Amendment will be discussed below. As for Congress, its authority under section 5—"to enforce, by appropriate legislation, the provisions of this article"—is clear, provided Congress is clear about those provisions. And on that, we may look, again, to the debates that surrounded not only the adoption of the Fourteenth Amendment but the enactment of the Civil Rights Act of 1866, which Congress reenacted in 1868, just after the amendment was ratified.

Those debates give us a fairly clear idea of what it was that the American people thought they were ratifying. In particular, all citizens, the Civil Rights Act declared, "have the right to make and enforce contracts, to sue, be parties and give evidence; to inherit, purchase, lease, sell, hold, and convey real personal property, and to full and equal benefit of all laws and proceedings for the security of persons and property." Such were the privileges and immunities the Fourteenth Amendment was meant to secure.

Clearly, those basic common law rights, drawn from the reason-based classical theory of rights, are the stuff of ordinary state law. Just as clearly, however, states have been known to violate them, either directly or by failure to secure them against private violations. When that happens, appeal can be made to the courts, under section 1, or to Congress, under section 5. The Fourteenth Amendment gives no power, of course, to secure the modern "entitlements" that are no part of the common law tradition of life, liberty, and property: the power it grants, that is, is limited by the rights it is meant to secure. But it does give a power to reach even intrastate matters when states are violating the provisions of the amendment. The claim of "states' rights," in short, is no defense for state violations of individual rights.

Thus, if the facts had warranted it, something like the Church Arson Prevention Act of 1996, depending on its particulars, might have been authorized not on Commerce Clause grounds but on Fourteenth Amendment grounds. If, for example, the facts had shown that arsons of white churches were being prosecuted by state officials whereas arsons of black churches were not, then we would have had a classic case of the denial of the equal protection of the laws. With those findings, Congress would have had ample authority under section 5 of the Fourteenth Amendment "to enforce, by appropriate legislation, the provisions of this article."

Unfortunately, in the final version of the act, Congress removed citations to the Fourteenth Amendment, choosing instead to rest its authority entirely on the Commerce Clause. Not only is that a misuse of the Commerce Clause, inviting further misuse; but, assuming the facts had warranted it, it is a failure to use the Fourteenth Amendment as it was meant to be used, inviting further failures. To be sure, the Fourteenth Amendment has itself been misused, both by Congress and by the courts. But that is no reason to ignore it. Rather, it is a reason to correct the misuses.

In its efforts to return power to the states and the people, then, Congress must be careful not to misunderstand its role in our federal system. Over the 20th century, Congress assumed vast powers that were never its to assume, powers that belong properly to the states and the people. Those need to be returned. But at the same time, Congress and the courts do have authority under the Fourteenth Amendment to ensure that citizens are free from state oppression. However much that authority may have been underused or overused, it is there to be used; and if it is properly used, objections by states about federal interference in their "internal affairs" are without merit.

Reject the Nomination of Judicial Candidates Who Do Not Appreciate That the Constitution Is a Document of Delegated, Enumerated, and Thus Limited Powers

As noted earlier, Congress can relimit government on its own initiative simply by restricting its future actions to those that are authorized by the Constitution and repealing those past actions that were taken without such authority; but for those limits to become "constitutional law," they would have to be recognized as such by the Supreme Court, which essentially abandoned that view of limited government during the New Deal. Thus, for the Court to play its part in the job of relimiting government constitutionally, it must recognize the mistakes it has made over the years, especially following Roosevelt's Court-packing threat in 1937, and rediscover the Constitution—a process it began in *Lopez*, however tentatively, when it returned explicitly to "first principles."

But Congress is not powerless to influence the Court in that direction: as vacancies arise on the Court and on lower courts, it has a substantial say about who sits there through its power to advise and consent. To exercise that power well, however, Congress must have a better grasp of the basic issues than it has shown in recent years during Senate confirmation hearings for nominees for the Court. In particular, the Senate's obsession with questions about "judicial activism" and "judicial restraint," terms that in themselves are largely vacuous, only distracts it from the real issue—the nominee's philosophy of the Constitution. To appreciate those points more fully, however, a bit of background is in order.

From Powers to Rights

The most important matter to grasp is the fundamental change that took place in our constitutional jurisprudence during the New Deal and the implications of that change for the modern debate. The debate today is focused almost entirely on rights, not powers. Indeed, until the 107th Congress and its focus on ideology, the principal concern during Senate confirmation hearings had been with a nominee's views about what rights are "in" the Constitution. That is an important question, to be sure, but it must be addressed within a much larger constitutional framework, a framework too often missing from recent hearings.

Clearly, the American debate began with rights—with the protests that led eventually to the Declaration of Independence. And in that seminal document, Jefferson made rights the centerpiece of the American vision: rights to life, liberty, and the pursuit of happiness, derived from a premise of moral equality, itself grounded in a higher law discoverable by reason—all to be secured by a government of powers made legitimate through consent.

But when they set out to draft a constitution, the Framers focused on powers, not rights, for two main reasons. First, their initial task was to create and empower a government, which the Constitution did once it was ratified. But their second task, of equal importance, was to limit that government. Here, there were two main options. The Framers could have listed a set of rights that the new government would be forbidden to violate. Or they could have limited the government's powers by enumerating them, then pitting one against the other through a system of checks and balances—the idea being that where there is no power there is, by implication, a right, belonging to the states or the people. They chose the second option, for they could hardly have enumerated all of our rights, but they *could* enumerate the new government's powers, which were meant from the outset to be, again, "few and defined." Thus, the doctrine of enumerated powers became our principal defense against overweening government.

Only later, during the course of ratification, did it become necessary to add a Bill of Rights—as a secondary defense. But in so doing, the Framers were still faced with a pair of objections that had been posed from the start. First, it was impossible to enumerate all of our rights, which in principle are infinite in number. Second, given that problem, the enumeration of only certain rights would be construed, by ordinary methods of legal construction, as denying the existence of others. To overcome those objections, therefore, the Framers wrote the Ninth Amendment: ''The enumeration in the Constitution of certain rights shall not be construed to deny or disparage others retained by the people.''

Constitutional Visions

Thus, with the Ninth Amendment making it clear that we have both enumerated and unenumerated rights, the Tenth Amendment making it clear that the federal government has only enumerated powers, and the Fourteenth Amendment later making it clear that our rights are good against the states as well, what emerges is an altogether libertarian picture. Individuals, families, firms, and the infinite variety of institutions that constitute civil society are free to pursue happiness however they wish, in accord with whatever values they wish, provided only that in the process they respect the equal rights of others to do the same; and governments are instituted to secure that liberty and do the few other things their constitutions make clear they are empowered to do.

That picture is a far cry from the modern liberal's vision, rooted in the Progressive Era, which would have government empowered to manage all manner of economic affairs. But it is a far cry as well from the modern conservative's vision, which would have government empowered to manage all manner of social affairs. Neither vision reflects the true constitutional scheme. Both camps want to use the Constitution to promote their own substantive agendas. Repeatedly, liberals invoke democratic power for ends that are nowhere in the Constitution; at other times they invoke ''rights'' that are no part of the plan, requiring government programs that are nowhere authorized. For their agenda, conservatives rely largely on expansive readings of democratic power that were never envisioned, thereby running roughshod over rights that were meant to be protected.

From Liberty to Democracy

The great change in constitutional vision took place during the New Deal, when the idea that galvanized the Progressive Era—that the basic purpose of government is to solve social and economic problems—was finally instituted in law through the Court's radical reinterpretation of the Constitution. As noted earlier, following the 1937 Court-packing threat, the Court eviscerated our first line of defense, the doctrine of enumerated powers, when it converted the General Welfare and Commerce Clauses from shields against power into swords of power. Then in 1938 a cowed Court undermined the second line of defense, our enumerated and unenumerated rights, when it declared that henceforth it would defer to the political branches and the states when their actions implicated "nonfundamental" rights like property and contract—the rights associated with "ordinary commercial affairs." Legislation implicating such rights, the Court said, would be given "minimal scrutiny" by the Court, which is tantamount to no scrutiny at all. By contrast, when legislation implicated "fundamental" rights like voting, speech, and, later, certain "personal" liberties, the Court would apply "strict scrutiny" to that legislation, probably finding it unconstitutional.

With that, the Constitution was converted, without benefit of amendment, from a libertarian to a largely democratic document. The floodgates were now open to majoritarian tyranny, which very quickly became special-interest tyranny, as public-choice economic theory amply demonstrates should be expected. Once those floodgates were opened, the programs that poured through led inevitably to claims from many quarters that rights were being violated. Thus, the Court in time would have to try to determine whether those rights were "in" the Constitution—a question the Constitution had spoken to indirectly, for the most part, through the now-discredited doctrine of enumerated powers; and if it found the rights in question, the Court would then have to try to make sense of its distinction between "fundamental" and "nonfundamental" rights.

Judicial "Activism" and "Restraint"

It is no accident, therefore, that until very recently the modern debate has been focused on rights, not powers. With the doctrine of enumerated powers effectively dead, with government's power essentially plenary, the only issues left for the Court to decide, for the most part, are whether there might be any rights that would limit that power and whether those rights are or are not "fundamental."

Both liberals and conservatives today have largely bought into this jurisprudence. As noted above, both camps believe the Constitution gives a wide berth to democratic decisionmaking. Neither side any longer asks the first question, the fundamental question: do we have authority, constitutional authority, to pursue this end? Instead, they simply assume that authority, take a policy vote on some end before them, then battle in court over whether there are any rights that might restrict their power.

Modern liberals, fond of government programs, call upon the Court to be "restrained" in finding rights that might limit their redistributive and regulatory schemes, especially "nonfundamental" rights like property and contract. At the same time, even as they ignore those rights, liberals ask the Court to be "active" in finding other "rights" that were never meant to be among even our unenumerated rights.

But modern conservatives are often little better. Reacting to the abuses of liberal "activism," many conservatives call for judicial "restraint" across the board. Thus, if liberal programs have run roughshod over the rights of individuals to use their property or freely contract, the remedy, conservatives say, is not for the Court to invoke the doctrine of enumerated powers—that battle was lost during the New Deal—nor even to invoke the rights of property and contract that are plainly in the Constitution— that might encourage judicial activism—but to turn to the democratic process to overturn those programs. Oblivious to the fact that restraint in finding rights is tantamount to activism in finding powers, and ignoring the fact that it was the democratic process that gave us the problem in the first place, too many conservatives offer us a counsel of despair amounting to a denial of constitutional protection.

No one doubts that in recent decades the Court has discovered "rights" in the Constitution that are no part of either the enumerated or unenumerated rights that were meant to be protected by that document. But it is no answer to that problem to ask the Court to defer wholesale to the political branches, thereby encouraging it, by implication, to sanction unenumerated *powers* that are no part of the document either. Indeed, if the Tenth Amendment means anything, it means that there are no such powers. Again, if the Framers had wanted to establish a simple democracy, they could have. Instead, they established a limited, constitutional republic, a republic with islands of democratic power in a sea of liberty, not a sea of democratic power surrounding islands of liberty.

Thus, it is not the proper role of the Court to find rights that are no part of the enumerated or unenumerated rights meant to be protected by the Constitution, thereby frustrating authorized democratic decisions. But neither is it the proper role of the Court to refrain from asking whether those decisions are in fact authorized and, if authorized, whether their implementation is in violation of the rights guaranteed by the Constitution, enumerated and unenumerated alike.

The role of the judge in our constitutional republic is thus profoundly important and oftentimes profoundly complex. "Activism" is no proper posture for a judge, but neither is "restraint." Judges must apply the Constitution to cases or controversies before them, neither making it up nor ignoring it. They must appreciate especially that the Constitution is a document of delegated, enumerated, and thus limited powers. That will get the judge started on the question of what rights are protected by the document; for where there is no power there is, again, a right, belonging either to the states or to the people: indeed, we should hardly imagine that, before the addition of the Bill of Rights, the Constitution failed to protect most rights simply because most were not "in" it. But reviving the doctrine of enumerated powers is only part of the task before the Court; it must also revive the classical theory of rights if the restoration of constitutional government is to be completed correctly.

Those are the two sides—powers and rights—that need to be examined in the course of Senate confirmation hearings for nominees for the courts of the United States. More important than knowing a nominee's "judicial philosophy" is knowing his philosophy of the Constitution. For the Constitution, in the end, is what defines us as a nation.

If a nominee does not have a deep and thorough appreciation for the basic principles of the Constitution—for the doctrine of enumerated powers and for the classical theory of rights that stands behind the Constitution—then his candidacy should be rejected. In recent years, Senate confirmation hearings have become extraordinary opportunities for constitutional debate throughout the nation. Those debates need to move from the ethereal realm of "constitutional law" to the real realm of the Constitution. They are extraordinary opportunities not simply for constitutional debate but for constitutional renewal.

Alarmingly, however, in the 107th and 108th Congresses we saw the debate move not from "constitutional law" to the Constitution but in the very opposite direction—to raw politics. The demand that judicial nominees pass an "ideological litmus test"—that they reflect and apply the "mainstream values" of the American people, whatever those may be—is tantamount to expecting and asking judges not to *apply* the law, which is what judging is all about, but to *make* the law according to those values, whatever the actual law may require. The duty of judges under the Constitution is to decide cases according to the law, not according to whatever values or ideology may be in fashion. For that, the only ideology that matters is the ideology of the Constitution.

Conclusion

America is a democracy in the most fundamental sense of that idea: authority, or legitimate power, rests ultimately with the people. But the people have no more right to tyrannize each other through democratic government than government itself has to tyrannize the people. When they constituted us as a nation by ratifying the Constitution and the amendments that have followed, our ancestors gave up only certain of their powers, enumerating them in a written constitution. We have allowed those powers to expand beyond all moral and legal bounds—at the price of our liberty and our well-being. The time has come to return those powers to their proper bounds, to reclaim our liberty, and to enjoy the fruits that follow.

Suggested Readings

Bailyn, Bernard. *The Ideological Origins of the American Revolution.* Cambridge, MA: Belknap, 1967.

Barnett, Randy E. *Restoring the Lost Constitution: The Presumption of Liberty.* Princeton, NJ: Princeton University Press, 2004.

_____. *The Structure of Liberty: Justice and the Rule of Law.* New York: Oxford University Press, 1998.

Barnett, Randy E., ed. *The Rights Retained by the People: The History and Meaning of the Ninth Amendment.* Fairfax, VA: George Mason University Press, 1989.

Corwin, Edward S. *The "Higher Law" Background of American Constitutional Law.* Ithaca, NY: Cornell University Press, 1955.

Dorn, James A., and Henry G. Manne, eds. *Economic Liberties and the Judiciary.* Fairfax, VA: George Mason University Press, 1987.

Epstein, Richard A. *Principles for a Free Society: Reconciling Individual Liberty with the Common Good.* Reading, MA: Perseus Books, 1998.

_____. "The Proper Scope of the Commerce Power." *Virginia Law Review* 73 (1987).

_____. *Simple Rules for a Complex World.* Cambridge, MA: Harvard University Press, 1995.

_____. *Takings: Private Property and the Power of Eminent Domain.* Cambridge, MA: Harvard University Press, 1985.

Ginsburg, Douglas H. "On Constitutionalism." *Cato Supreme Court Review,* 2002–2003.

Hamilton, Alexander, James Madison, and John Jay. *The Federalist Papers.* New York: Mentor, 1961.

Lawson, Gary. "The Rise and Rise of the Administrative State." *Harvard Law Review* 107 (1994).

Lawson, Gary, and Patricia B. Granger. "The 'Proper' Scope of Federal Power: A Jurisdictional Interpretation of the Sweeping Clause." *Duke Law Journal* 43 (1993).

Locke, John. "Second Treatise of Government." In *Two Treatises of Government.* Edited by Peter Laslett. New York: Mentor, 1965.

Miller, Geoffrey P. "The True Story of Carolene Products." *Supreme Court Review* (1987).

Pilon, Roger. "Freedom, Responsibility, and the Constitution: On Recovering Our Founding Principles." *Notre Dame Law Review* 68 (1993).

_____. "How Constitutional Corruption Has Led to Ideological Litmus Tests for Judicial Nominees." Cato Institute Policy Analysis no. 446, August 8, 2002.

_____. "The Purpose and Limits of Government." *Cato's Letter,* no. 13 (1999).

_____. "Restoring Constitutional Government." *Cato's Letter,* no. 9 (1995).

Reinstein, Robert J. "Completing the Constitution: The Declaration of Independence, Bill of Rights and Fourteenth Amendment." *Temple Law Review* 66 (1993).

Shankman, Kimberly C., and Roger Pilon. "Reviving the Privileges or Immunities Clause to Redress the Balance among States, Individuals, and the Federal Government." Cato Institute Policy Analysis no. 326, November 23, 1998.

Siegan, Bernard H. *Economic Liberties and the Constitution.* Chicago: University of Chicago Press, 1980.

Sorenson, Leonard R. *Madison on the "General Welfare" of America.* Lanham, MD: Rowman & Littlefield, 1995.

Warren, Charles. *Congress as Santa Claus: Or National Donations and the General Welfare Clause of the Constitution.* 1932. Reprint, New York: Arno, 1978.

Yoo, John Choon. "Our Declaratory Ninth Amendment." *Emory Law Journal* 42 (1993).

—Prepared by Roger Pilon

ENTITLEMENT REFORM

4. Social Security

Congress should allow workers to privately invest at least half of their Social Security payroll taxes through individual accounts.

Social Security is not only the largest U.S. government program, accounting for roughly 23 percent of the federal budget; it is also the largest government program in the world. Few countries have budgets as large as the U.S. Social Security system. It is a program that touches almost every American. The Social Security payroll tax is the biggest tax paid by the average American family. In fact, nearly 80 percent of American workers pay more in Social Security payroll taxes than they do in federal income taxes. At the same time, millions of seniors rely on Social Security for their retirement income. More than half of seniors receive the majority of their retirement income through the program.

Yet Social Security is deeply flawed and facing a growing crisis. In less than 15 years, the national retirement program will begin to run a deficit, spending more on benefits than it takes in through taxes. The IOUs in the Social Security Trust Fund are merely a claim against future taxes, not real assets that can be used to pay benefits. Overall, the system is more than $26 trillion in debt.

Former president Bill Clinton laid out the very limited options for fixing the problem: raise taxes, cut benefits, or invest privately. Certainly it is possible to raise taxes or cut benefits enough to prop up the existing system for a little while longer. But the Social Security payroll tax is already the biggest tax that the average American family pays. Do we really want our legacy to our children and grandchildren to be the largest tax increase in American history? Cutting benefits is no better option. Already younger workers can expect a low, below-market return on their taxes. Benefit cuts would only make a bad deal worse.

That leaves private investment as the only viable option. By allowing younger workers to privately invest their Social Security taxes through individual accounts, we can

- help restore Social Security to long-term solvency, without massive tax increases;
- provide workers with higher benefits than Social Security would otherwise be able to pay;
- create a system that treats women, minorities, and young people more fairly;
- allow low-income workers to accumulate real, inheritable wealth for the first time in their lives; and
- give workers ownership of and control over their retirement funds.

Some people say that current budget deficits make Social Security reform, particularly individual accounts, impossible. They point to the "transition cost" of moving to individual accounts. Since current taxes are used to pay current beneficiaries, allowing younger workers to invest their taxes will require a replacement for current revenue to protect current retirees. But given Social Security's unfunded liabilities, the transition does not really represent a new cost. It is just making explicit an already implicit debt.

Of course, shifting to private investment would mean paying that debt now rather than later, so reforming Social Security will increase short-term budget deficits. But it will save trillions of dollars in the long term. In many ways, it is like refinancing your mortgage: you have to pay the points up front, but you save money in the long run.

Budget deficits are not a good thing. But to let current deficits stand in the way of Social Security reform is to saddle our children and grandchildren with a much bigger bill.

Quite simply, Social Security reform cannot be put off.

The Financial Crisis

Social Security as we know it is facing irresistible demographic and fiscal pressures that threaten the future retirement benefits of today's young workers. Although Social Security is currently running a surplus, according to the system's own trustees, that surplus will turn into a deficit within the next 15 years. That is, by 2018, Social Security will be paying out more in benefits than it takes in through taxes (Figure 4.1).

Figure 4.1
Current Social Security System

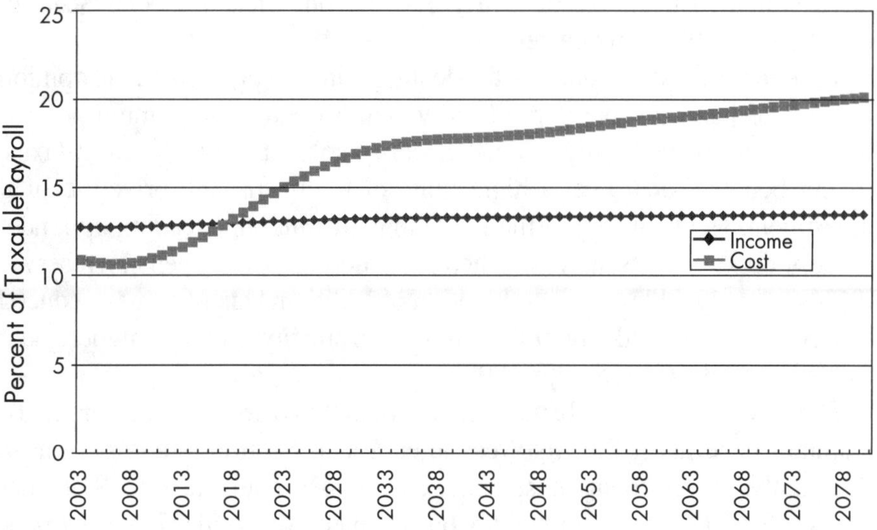

SOURCE: 2003 Trustees Report, Table IV.B1.

In theory, Social Security is supposed to continue paying benefits after 2018 by drawing on the Social Security Trust Fund. The trust fund is supposed to provide sufficient funds to continue paying full benefits until 2042, after which it will be exhausted. At that point, *by law,* Social Security benefits will have to be cut by approximately 27 percent.

However, in reality, the Social Security Trust Fund is not an asset that can be used to pay benefits. Any Social Security surpluses accumulated to date have been spent, leaving a trust fund that consists only of government bonds (IOUs) that will eventually have to be repaid by taxpayers. As the Clinton administration's fiscal year 2000 budget explained it:

> These [Trust Fund] balances are available to finance future benefit payments and other Trust Fund expenditures—but only in a bookkeeping sense. . . . *They do not consist of real economic assets that can be drawn down in the future to fund benefits.* Instead, they are claims on the Treasury that, when redeemed, will have to be financed by raising taxes, borrowing from the public, or reducing benefits or other expenditures. The existence of large Trust Fund balances, therefore, does not, by itself, have any impact on the Government's ability to pay benefits.

Even if Congress can find a way to redeem the bonds, the trust fund surplus will be completely exhausted by 2042. At that point, Social Security will have to rely solely on revenue from the payroll tax—but that revenue will not be sufficient to pay all promised benefits. Overall, Social Security faces unfunded liabilities of nearly $26 trillion. Clearly, Social Security is not sustainable in its current form.

There are really few options for dealing with the problem. This opinion is not held just by supporters of individual accounts. As Clinton pointed out, the only ways to keep Social Security solvent are to (a) raise taxes, (b) cut benefits, or (c) get a higher rate of return through private capital investment. Henry Aaron of the Brookings Institution, a leading opponent of individual accounts, agrees. "Increased funding to raise pension reserves is possible only with some combination of additional tax revenues, reduced benefits, or increased investment returns from investing in higher yield assets," he told Congress in 1999.

The tax increases or benefit cuts would have to be quite large. To maintain benefits in the first year after Social Security starts running a deficit, the government must acquire revenues equivalent to $197 per worker. By 2042 the additional tax burden increases to $1,976 per worker, and by 2078 it reaches an astounding $4,193 per worker (in constant 2003 dollars). And it continues to rise thereafter. Functionally, that would translate into either a huge increase in the payroll tax, from the current 12.4 percent to as much as 18.9 percent by 2077, or an equivalent increase in income or other taxes.

A Declining Rate of Return

Social Security taxes are already so high, relative to benefits, that Social Security has clearly become a bad deal for younger workers, providing a low, below-market rate of return. As Figure 4.2 shows, that return has been steadily declining and is expected to be less than 2 percent for most of today's workers.

That poor rate of return means that many young workers' retirement benefits will be far lower than if they had been able to invest those funds privately. A system of individual accounts, based on private capital investment, would provide most workers with significantly higher returns. Those higher returns would translate into higher retirement benefits, leading to a more secure retirement for millions of seniors.

Savings and Economic Growth

Social Security operates on a pay-as-you-go (PAYGO) basis, with almost all of the funds coming in being immediately paid out to current

Figure 4.2
Inflation-Adjusted Internal Real Rate of Return from OASI

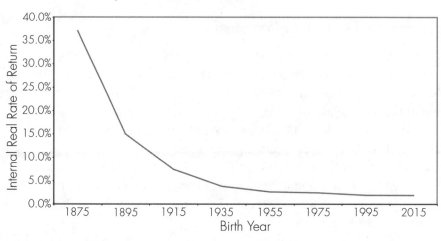

SOURCE: Dean R. Leimer, "Cohort-Specific Measures of Lifetime Net Social Security Transfers," Social Security Administration, Office of Research and Statistics, Working Paper no. 59, February 1994.

beneficiaries. This system displaces private, fully funded alternatives under which the funds coming in would be saved and invested for the future benefits of today's workers. The result is a large net loss of national savings, which reduces capital investment, wages, national income, and economic growth. Moreover, by increasing the cost of hiring workers, the payroll tax substantially reduces wages, employment, and economic growth as well.

Shifting to a private system, with hundreds of billions of dollars invested in individual accounts each year, would likely produce a large net increase in national savings, depending on how the government financed the transition. This would increase national investment, productivity, wages, jobs, and economic growth. Replacing the payroll tax with private retirement contributions would also improve economic growth because the required contributions would be lower and would be seen as part of a worker's direct compensation, stimulating more employment and output.

In 1997 Harvard economist Martin Feldstein estimated that if all Social Security payroll taxes were privately invested, it would produce $10 trillion to $20 trillion in present value net benefits to America. Most of that net benefit would probably come in the form of the higher returns and benefits

51

earned for retirees through the private investment accounts. But some would also come in the form of higher wages and greater employment.

Helping the Poor and Minorities

Low-income workers would be among the biggest winners under a system of privately invested individual accounts. Private investment would pay low-income workers significantly higher benefits than can be paid by Social Security. And that does not take into account the fact that blacks, Hispanics, and the poor have below-average life expectancies. As a result, they tend to live fewer years in retirement and collect less in Social Security benefits than do whites. In a system of individual accounts, by contrast, they would retain control over the funds paid in and could pay themselves higher benefits over their fewer retirement years, or leave more to their children or other heirs.

The higher returns and benefits of a privately invested system would be most important to low-income families, as they most need the extra funds. The funds saved in the individual retirement accounts, which could be left to children, would also greatly help families break out of the cycle of poverty. Similarly, the improved economic growth, higher wages, and increased jobs that would result from an investment-based Social Security system would be most important to the poor. Moreover, without reform, low-income workers will be hurt the most by the higher taxes or reduced benefits that will be necessary if we continue on our current course. Averting a financial crisis and its inevitable results would consequently be most important to low-income workers.

In addition, with average- and low-wage workers accumulating huge sums in their own investment accounts, the distribution of wealth throughout society would become far broader than it is today. That would occur, not through the redistribution of existing wealth, but through the creation of new wealth, far more equally held. Because a system of individual accounts would turn every worker into a stockowner, the old division between labor and capital would be eroded. Every laborer would become a capitalist.

Ownership and Control

After all the economic analysis, however, perhaps the single most important reason for transforming Social Security into a system of individual accounts is that it would give American workers true ownership of and control over their retirement benefits.

Many Americans believe that Social Security is an "earned right." That is, they think that, because they have paid Social Security taxes, they are entitled to receive Social Security benefits. The government encourages that belief by referring to Social Security taxes as "contributions," as in the Federal Insurance Contributions Act (FICA). However, the U.S. Supreme Court has ruled, in the case of *Flemming v. Nestor,* that workers have no legally binding contractual or property right to their Social Security benefits, and those benefits can be changed, cut, or even taken away at any time.

As the Court stated, "To engraft upon Social Security a concept of 'accrued property rights' would deprive it of the flexibility and boldness in adjustment to ever changing conditions which it demands." That decision built on a previous case, *Helvering v. Davis,* in which the Court had ruled that Social Security is not a contributory insurance program, stating that "the proceeds of both the employer and employee taxes are to be paid into the Treasury like any other internal revenue generally, and are not earmarked in any way."

In effect, Social Security turns older Americans into supplicants, dependent on the political process for their retirement benefits. If they work hard, play by the rules, and pay Social Security taxes their entire lives, they earn the privilege of going hat in hand to the government and hoping that politicians decide to give them some money for retirement.

In contrast, under a system of individual accounts, workers would have full property rights in their private accounts. They would own their accounts and the money in them the same way they own their individual retirement accounts (IRAs) or 401(k) plans. Their retirement benefits would not depend on future political choices.

Simple Rules for Reform

Social Security's problems have led to a growing movement for reform, including proposals to allow younger workers to privately invest some or all of their Social Security taxes through individual accounts.

Unfortunately, however, many of those proposals fell short of what was truly needed to truly fix Social Security. Many proposals contained only tiny accounts, leaving the majority of workers' retirement income subject to government control. Other plans overpromised, pretending that every retiree could become a millionaire with no cost to the taxpayers and no tough decisions.

In developing a plan to reform Social Security, Congress should bear in mind these simple rules:

Solvency Is Not Enough

The goal of Social Security reform should be to provide workers with the best possible retirement option, not simply to find ways to preserve the current Social Security system. After all, if solvency were the only goal, that could be accomplished with tax increases or benefit cuts, no matter how bad a deal that provided younger workers. Successful Social Security reform will result in a solvent system, not just in the short run, but sustainable over time as well. It will also improve Social Security's rate of return; provide better retirement benefits; treat women, minorities, and low-income workers more fairly; and give workers real ownership and control of their retirement funds.

Half Measures Avail Us Naught

You don't cut out half a cancer. Many proposals for Social Security reform would allow workers to privately invest only a small portion of their payroll taxes and continue to rely on the existing PAYGO Social Security system for the majority of Social Security benefits. But proposals for small accounts will not allow low- and middle-income workers to accumulate real wealth or achieve other objectives of reform. Individual accounts should be as large as feasible, ideally at least half of payroll taxes.

There Is No Free Lunch

Individual accounts will create a better, fairer, and more secure retirement system. But they cannot work miracles. They will provide higher retirement benefits than Social Security can pay. But they will not make everyone a millionaire. They will help solve Social Security's financial crisis and save taxpayers trillions of dollars over the long run. But there is no free lunch. There are short-term costs that will require tough choices by the president and Congress.

Although we should not minimize the difficulties of transition financing, it is also important to remember that the financing of the transition is a one-time event that will actually reduce the government's future liabilities. The transition moves the government's need for additional revenue forward in time, but—depending on the transition's ultimate design—it will not increase the amount of spending necessary. In effect, it is a case of "pay a little now or pay a lot later."

Cato's Social Security Plan

- Individuals would be able to privately invest **6.2 percentage points** of their payroll tax through individual accounts. People who choose to do so will forfeit all future accrual of Social Security benefits.
- Individuals who choose individual accounts will receive **a recognition bond** based on past contributions to Social Security. These zero-coupon bonds will be offered to all workers who have contributed to Social Security, regardless of how long they have been in the system but will be offered on a discounted basis.
- Allowable investment options for individual accounts will be based on a three-tiered system: a centralized, pooled collection and holding point; a limited series of investment options with a lifecycle fund as a default mechanism; and a wider range of investment options for individuals who accumulate a minimum level in their accounts.
- At retirement, individuals will be given an **option of purchasing a family annuity or taking a programmed withdrawal.** Those two options will be mandated only to a level required to provide an income above a minimum level. Funds in excess of the amount required to achieve this level of retirement income can be withdrawn in a lump sum.
- If individuals accumulate sufficient funds in their accounts to allow them to purchase an annuity that will keep them above a minimum income level in retirement, they will be **able to opt out** of the Social Security system entirely.
- The remaining 6.2 percentage points of payroll taxes will be used to pay transition costs and to fund disability and survivors' benefits. Once, far in the future, transition costs are fully paid for, this portion of the payroll tax will be reduced to the level necessary to pay survivors' and disability benefits.
- The Cato plan is offered in the context of payable Social Security benefits. That is, the Social Security system will be **restored to a solvent pay-as-you-go basis** prior to the development of individual accounts. Workers who choose to remain in the traditional Social Security system will receive whatever level of benefits Social Security can pay with existing levels of revenue. The best method for accomplishing this is to change the initial benefit formula from wage indexing to price indexing.

Conclusion

Social Security reform is not an option—it is a necessity. Every two-year election cycle that Congress waits to address Social Security drives up the ultimate price of reform by roughly $320 billion. Polls show that the American people are ahead of their political leaders in being willing to address the need for fundamental change. It is time for Congress to act.

Suggested Readings

Biggs, Andrew. "Perspectives on the President's Commission to Strengthen Social Security." Cato Institute Social Security Paper no. 27, August 22, 2002.

Ferrara, Peter, and Michael Tanner. *A New Deal for Social Security.* Washington: Cato Institute, 1998.

Piñera, José. "Empowering Workers: The Privatization of Social Security in Chile." *Cato's Letters* no. 10, May 1996.

Tanner, Michael, "The 6.2 Percent Solution: A Plan for Reforming Social Security." Cato Institute Social Security Paper no. 32, February 17, 2004.

Tanner, Michael, ed. *Social Security and Its Discontents: Perspectives on Choice.* Washington: Cato Institute, 2004.

—Prepared by Michael Tanner

5. Federal Welfare Reform

Congress should

- reauthorize the Personal Responsibility and Work Opportunity Reconciliation Act;
- strengthen welfare reform's work requirements;
- avoid federal funding of private charities;
- avoid federal marriage programs; and
- ultimately, replace welfare with private charity.

In 1996 Congress passed the Personal Responsibility and Work Opportunity Reconciliation Act (PRWORA), the most significant revision of the American welfare system since the Great Society. PRWORA replaced Aid for Families with Dependent Children (AFDC), the primary cash assistance program, with the Temporary Assistance for Needy Families (TANF) block grant. That effectively abolished most federal eligibility and payment rules, giving states much greater flexibility to design their own programs. The TANF block grant was a fixed amount for each state, largely based on the prereform federal contribution to that state's AFDC program. In addition, the block grants eliminated welfare's "entitlement" status, meaning that no one would have an automatic right to benefits.

Welfare reform brought about mixed, but generally positive, results. The number of welfare recipients declined by more than half. Approximately 4.7 million Americans have left the welfare rolls since 1996. And, in general, those people were modestly better off after leaving welfare. However, dependence on government programs remains widespread, and spending on government welfare programs, at both the federal and state levels, has actually increased. While out-of-wedlock birthrates have leveled off, they remain at unacceptably high levels. The work of welfare reform is far from complete.

However, since 2002, Congress has been deadlocked over proposals to reauthorize PRWORA (the original bill sunset after five years). The result has been a series of short-term continuing resolutions that preserve the basic structure of the 1996 reforms but prevent actions to either strengthen the reforms or move on to next steps.

Work Requirements

Among the most contentious areas of debate has been welfare reform's work requirements. Under PRWORA, most welfare recipients were required to "work" as a condition of receiving benefits. States were initially to have at least 40 percent of their welfare recipients either working or participating in work preparation activities; that percentage was to increase to 50 percent by 2002, although states were given wide discretion in designing work programs. In reality, however, states were given various credits and exemptions that significantly reduced the number of recipients actually required to work. For example, states are given a credit based on their caseload reductions, meaning that states with large numbers of people leaving welfare do not have to meet the stated levels of work participation for those remaining on the rolls. Without those credits, only 19 states would be meeting their participation requirements for single parents and only two states would be meeting the requirement for two-parent families. In fact, for 31 states, the credit reduced the actual work requirement to *zero*. In addition, roughly 14 states have continuing waivers, from the old AFDC program, that may override work requirements under TANF. Vermont, in fact, claims that existing waivers exempt it from *all* work requirements. Those exemptions make it possible for states to meet federal work participation mandates and make it seem like far more welfare recipients are working than actually are.

Moreover, the term "work" was interpreted so broadly that current work requirements have fallen far short of their goals. For example, in all 50 states, "job search," or simply looking for work, constitutes a work activity. Some states limit the amount of time that can be spent in job search, generally to six or eight weeks out of any 12-month period, but 29 states have no limit to the amount of job search a recipient can substitute for actual work. Nearly all states (47) count vocational education or training as a "work activity," and in six states there is no time limit on the training. In 12 other states, between 24 and 36 months of training can be substituted for work. In addition, 47 states consider adult education or the study of English as a second language to meet work activity requirements, and in at least 35 states there is no time limit on those activities. Training in "job readiness skills," such as completing a job application, writing résumés, interviewing skills, "life skills," career goal setting, and workplace expectations, count as work in 48 states. Finally, four states include alcohol and drug abuse treatment as work activities.

A great many welfare recipients are taking part in nonwork "work activities." In fact, only about 31 percent of the people that states consider "working" are in jobs, either subsidized community service jobs or private-sector employment.

Advocates of welfare reform have sought to rectify those problems by increasing the work requirement for recipients to 40 hours per week, at least 24 of which must be actual work, and by eliminating the "case load reduction" credit that has enabled many states to give the appearance of meeting work requirements without actually doing so. In contrast, some opponents of welfare reform have not only resisted those changes but have sought to further water down the definition of "work," to include more education and training, including college attendance.

Yet, study after study has shown that work is the surest route off welfare and out of poverty. The states with the strongest work requirements, and the most severe sanctions for failing to comply with those requirements, have been the most successful.

Moreover, the evidence strongly indicates that the most successful form of "work activity" is work itself. There have been several studies that compared "work-first" programs that attempt to push recipients into jobs as fast as possible with programs that emphasize education and training. The work-first programs increased earnings and decreased welfare dependence far more quickly than the education- and training-based alternatives. In particular, the National Evaluation of Welfare to Work Strategies, a comprehensive review of 11 welfare-to-work programs, conducted by HHS, followed former welfare recipients over a five-year period and found that employment-based programs were more successful at moving recipients into jobs and did so at far less cost than education and training programs. An even more telling study by Bruce Meyer of Northwestern University and Dan Rosenbaum of the University of North Carolina–Greensboro actually found a negative correlation between education and training programs and employment. Welfare recipients who participated in training programs were *less* likely to find work.

It is essential, therefore, for Congress to strengthen—not weaken—PRWORA's work requirements.

Federal Marriage Programs

One change that Congress should not adopt is proposals for the federal government to fund programs designed to encourage poor people to get married. Current legislation calls for spending roughly $2 billion over the next five years for this purpose. But such proposals not only represent a massive expansion of government into the most personal and private areas of our lives; they are also likely to fail as a matter of policy.

Of course marriage is a good thing. A substantial body of social science shows that marriage can benefit both individuals and society. But, before embarking on a massive new federally funded marriage program, we should consider several key problems with that approach.

First, and most obvious, there is the question of just whom poor women, especially poor pregnant women or single mothers, are supposed to marry. William Julius Wilson and others have shown that in high-poverty areas, with their attendant crime and unemployment, there are relatively few marriageable men. Several studies have looked at the fathers of children born out of wedlock and found them quite unprepared to support a family. More than a third lacked a high school diploma; 28 percent were unemployed; and another 20 percent had incomes of less than $6,000 per year. In addition, roughly 38 percent had criminal records.

An examination of attempts to collect child support payments from low-income unwed fathers found that a substantial number of them faced serious employment barriers, including criminal records and poor health. Many single mothers may remain single precisely because they find their unemployed and undereducated potential partners unattractive marriage material. Encouraging marriage to unsuitable partners may do more harm than good.

Second, marriage may do less to increase family income than supposed. Despite the evidence cited above that marriage leads to increased family income, the impact on low-income single mothers may be less than on others. About half of unwed mothers are in fact already living with their child's father. Another third are romantically involved with the father but living separately. The father can be presumed to be providing at least some resources under the circumstances, so any increase would be marginal. Moreover, given the economic conditions of the fathers described above, they may have few additional resources to bring to a marriage.

Forcing poor women into early marriage may also have unintended negative consequences. For example, if they marry, teen mothers are more likely to have a rapid second birth, which brings with it a variety of economic and other concerns. They are also more likely to leave school after they become pregnant and less likely to return to school later on. In addition, marriages of younger men and women are far less stable than those of people who delay marriage until they are older. The young divorce more frequently and after a shorter period of marriage. There are greater incidences of domestic violence.

In short, getting the federal government involved with marriage may do far more harm than good.

Prevent New Entrants to the Welfare System

Perhaps the most important step that Congress could take to end welfare dependence would be to prohibit new entrants to the system. Despite increased efforts at diversion under welfare reform, states continue to allow new and returning entrants into the cash assistance system. Consequently, caseloads have recently begun to level off or even grow in some states. That trend testifies to the fact that women will continue to drop out of school and have children out of wedlock so long as going on welfare remains an option.

Welfare reformers need to turn their efforts to encouraging young women to (1) finish high school; (2) not get pregnant outside marriage; and (3) get a job, any job, and stick with it. The most effective way Congress can communicate this message is to remove welfare as an alternative for young women who fail to make smart choices. While continuing to support and encourage work among those already receiving welfare, Congress should enact a prohibition against new, single mothers' signing onto the rolls.

This cutoff will have the effect of encouraging young women to think twice before entering into an unsustainable situation. Those who continue to have children they are unable to support will have to turn to their families and the community for assistance. Already, a rich variety of private-sector, voluntary, and faith-based initiatives is available to families attempting to surmount obstacles on the path from welfare to work. Such efforts would likely proliferate in the absence of the public cash assistance alternative.

Corrupting Charity

However, it is important to realize that shifting from government-run welfare to private charity does not mean that government should fund those charities.

President Bush has proposed that faith-based charities be eligible to receive billions of dollars in federal grants to provide social services. But, in doing so, he risks mixing government and charity in a way that could undermine the very things that have made private charity so effective.

Government dollars come with strings attached and raise serious questions regarding the separation of church and state. Charities that accept government funds could find themselves overwhelmed with paperwork and subject to a host of federal regulations. The potential for government meddling is tremendous, and even if the regulation is not abused, it will require a redirection of scarce resources away from charitable activities and toward administrative functions. Officials of charities may end up spending more time reading the *Federal Register* than the Bible.

As they became increasingly dependent on government money, those charities could find their missions shifting, their religious character lost, the very things that made them so successful destroyed. In the end, Bush's proposal may transform private charities from institutions that change people's lives into mere providers of services, little more than a government program in a clerical collar.

Most important, the whole idea of charity could become subtly corrupted, blurring the difference between the welfare state and true charity. After all, the essence of private charity is voluntariness, individuals helping one another through love of neighbor. In fact, in the Bible, the Greek word translated as charity is *agapeo*, which means love. But the essence of government is coercion, the use of force to make people do things they would not do voluntarily. As historian Gertrude Himmelfarb puts it, "Compassion is a moral sentiment, not a political principle." The difference is as simple as the difference between my reaching into my pocket for money to help another and my reaching into yours.

Conclusion

Six years after passage of the new welfare law, the country's cash assistance system shows modest improvement. More individuals are having to work for their benefits, fewer remain on the rolls, a greater number are finding employment after they exit the system, and fewer are losing out in the transition from welfare to work.

On an overwhelming number of measures, however, welfare as we once knew it remains firmly intact. The people who leave welfare for work continue to be short-term, transitional cases; individuals who remain on the rolls are still supported by a generous array of cash and in-kind benefits; life after welfare continues to be characterized by low-wage employment, heavy reliance on supplemental benefits, and frequent returns to the rolls; and the system continues to encourage dependence by allowing new entrants and providing generously for young women who give birth out of wedlock.

Congress needs to recognize that the solution to the country's dependence problem involves more than efforts to simply wean families off the welfare rolls. A more preventive approach is required, which involves making welfare no longer an attractive or viable alternative for single young women considering getting pregnant. Congress should encourage states to scale back bloated and ineffective welfare programs by eliminating the maintenance-of-effort spending requirement attached to receipt of federal TANF grants. Rather than require states to meet historic spending levels associated with much larger, prereform caseload numbers, Congress should permit states to divert saved welfare dollars to alternative efforts or, ideally, back to taxpayers. Ultimately, to dramatically reduce out-of-wedlock childbearing and life-long dependence, Congress should enact a prohibition against new entrants into the cash assistance system. Until welfare is no longer available to young women making crucial choices for themselves and their families, the country will continue to spend endless amounts of energy and taxpayer money trying to solve its dependence problem.

Suggested Readings

Blank, Rebecca, and Ron Haskins, eds. *The New World of Welfare.* Washington: Brookings Institution, 2001.

Murray, Charles. *Loosing Ground: American Social Policy: 1950–1980.* New York: Basic Books, 1984.

_____. *The Underclass Revisited.* Washington: American Enterprise Institute, 1999.

Tanner, Michael. *The Poverty of Welfare: Helping Others in Civil Society.* Washington: Cato Institute, 2003.

Zeigler, Jenifer. "Implementing Welfare Reform: A State Report Card." Cato Institute Policy Analysis no 529, October 19, 2004.

—Prepared by Michael Tanner

6. State Welfare Implementation

> **States should**
>
> - implement family caps,
> - enforce living requirements for minor parents,
> - make work mean work (tighten the definition of "work activities"),
> - promote diversion programs as an alternative to welfare,
> - impose time limits,
> - strengthen sanctions for failure to obey welfare rules, and
> - consider eliminating welfare altogether for new entrants.

States are the backbone of welfare reform. They are responsible for the innovative pilot programs after which federal legislation was modeled and for the successful administration of welfare reform. In 1996 states were granted tremendous flexibility to spend money and implement programs that would help recipients escape welfare's "cycle of dependence."

Some states have used that flexibility in a positive way. Following the spirit of welfare reform, they provide recipients with job experience for a better transition into the job market, rather than give them cash handouts for doing nothing. With job skills and an incentive to hurry off the rolls (time limits), families have been leaving welfare in record numbers.

Other states, however, have not used their flexibility in such a positive manner. They've undermined mandatory provisions, such as work requirements and the obligation of teen parents to live at home and finish school, through broad definitions and liberal exceptions. Some states have also failed to implement optional policies, such as family caps and diversion programs, which encourage self-sufficiency.

A recent Cato study graded the states on their policy decisions and results. Below are the states with the ten best and ten worst grades.

Best Grades			Worst Grades	
State	**Grade**		**State**	**Grade**
Idaho	A		Alaska	D
Ohio	A		Nebraska	F
Wyoming	A		Rhode Island	F
Wisconsin	A		Utah	F
Florida	B		New Hampshire	F
Connecticut	B		D.C.	F
Virginia	B		Maine	F
Illinois	B		North Dakota	F
New Jersey	B		Missouri	F
Indiana	B		Vermont	F

Grades are based on whether a state implemented policies to encourage personal responsibility and self-sufficiency. Such policies are necessary to truly reform welfare and help recipients to escape a life of dependence. States should adopt the following policies.

Family Caps

The Personal Responsibility and Work Opportunity Reconciliation Act (PRWORA) authorized states to impose a family cap, which would deny increased Temporary Assistance for Needy Families benefits to women on welfare who have additional children. Twenty-three states have established such caps. Family caps show recipients that welfare is a temporary safety net, not a subsidy for a life of dependence. If a family is not making it on its own, creating another mouth to feed is not the path to self-sufficiency.

Since a family cap is an elective policy, states can decide whether or how best to implement it. Family cap policies vary: some states do not give any cash increase for an additional child; other states do not halt cash increments but reduce the level; still other states technically have a family cap policy but rather than reduce the incremented benefit issue payment in the form of a voucher or to a third-party payee.

Teens at Home

PRWORA requires unmarried mothers under the age of 18 to remain in school and live with an adult. That was a priority in welfare reform since, by the early 1990s, half of unwed teen mothers went on welfare within one year of the birth of their first child, and an additional 25 percent were on welfare within five years. Nearly 55 percent of welfare expenditures are attributable to families that began with a birth to a teenager.

High school dropouts are roughly three times more likely to end up in poverty than are those who complete at least a high school education. If dropouts do find jobs, their wages are likely to be low. Wages for high school dropouts have declined (in inflation-adjusted terms) by 23 percent over the past 30 years. And the economic impact is intergenerational. Children whose parents have not completed high school are far more likely to live in poverty than children whose parents are more educated. Simply put, more education equals less poverty.

TANF allows high school attendance to fulfill the work requirement for minor teen mothers, who are supposed to remain in a parent's home while finishing school. All states are required to implement this policy, but the specific guidelines are at the discretion of each state. Unfortunately, many states have created broad definitions and extensive exceptions that make the federal law ineffective. Examples include exempting a teen who has lived away from her family for a year or is ''successfully living on her own.'' Just how ''successful'' is a teenager living on her own if she has an out-of-wedlock pregnancy and needs welfare assistance?

Work Policy

PRWORA's addition of work requirements to TANF benefits was one of the most substantial changes to the welfare system. By 2002 half of each state's eligible caseload had to be engaged in ''work-related'' activities at least 30 hours per week. Ninety percent of two-parent families on TANF had to be working 35 hours per week.

The U.S. Department of Health and Human Services divides jobs that qualify for work participation credit into categories for reporting purposes. Of the allowable work activity categories under TANF, the categories in which the recipient is actually working are subsidized and unsubsidized employment (public and private), community service, on-the-job training, and work experience. Unfortunately, states credit too much participation under the remaining categories: job search, job skills training, adult basic education/English as a second language classes, education directly related to employment, and vocational training. Those should not be considered actual work activities because they are education based and do not provide actual work experience.

In addition, caseload reduction credits essentially released states from their work participation rate obligations. Without credits, only five states would have met their single-parent participation requirements and only two states would have met the two-parent standard. Through credits, 17 states were able to reduce their work requirement to zero, and 16 states have carried over AFDC waivers that reduce or override TANF work requirements. Absent waivers, exemptions, and credits, the national participation rate for recipients in actual work activities is less than 30 percent.

States have made it very hard on themselves by not striving to meet the work requirement guidelines, regardless of credits. With weakened economies and tighter budgets, states must scramble to figure out how to create jobs for welfare recipients to meet work requirements and how to fund the administrative oversight such regulations require.

Diversion

Since PRWORA eliminated the welfare entitlement, states have been free to put conditions on the receipt of benefits. Thirty-four states and the District of Columbia have used this authority to establish diversion programs that prevent potential welfare recipients, particularly those considered job-ready or who have another potential source of income, from ever entering the system.

Generally, diversion programs fall into one of three categories. Most common are diversion programs that provide lump-sum payments in lieu of welfare benefits. Those programs assist families facing an immediate financial crisis or short-term need. The family is given a single cash payment in the hope that the immediate problem can be taken care of without going on welfare. In fact, a family is usually precluded from going on welfare for a period of time after accepting a diversion payment.

Most states do not restrict how lump-sum payments may be used; they have been used to pay off back debts, as well as for childcare, car repairs, medical bills, rent, clothing, and utility bills. Recipients may also use lump-sum payments for work-related expenses, such as purchasing tools, uniforms, and business licenses. A few states restrict the use of lump-sum payments to job-related needs, although that term can be defined broadly. For example, even moving expenses for a new job may qualify.

Another common diversion approach is a ''mandatory applicant job search,'' used by 27 states. Under this approach, welfare applicants are required to seek employment before they become eligible for benefits. In most cases the state will assist with the job search by providing job contacts and leads, access to a "resource room" where applicants can prepare résumés and conduct job searches, or classes in job search skills. They may also provide childcare and transportation assistance.

Finally, eight states have programs designed to encourage welfare applicants to use "alternative resources" before receiving TANF benefits. Those programs generally do not have specific guidelines but amount to caseworkers encouraging would-be applicants to seek help from family, private charity, or other government programs. Even in states with alternative resource referral programs, this approach is the least used, possibly because it is poorly understood by potential recipients and requires extensive caseworker involvement.

In Utah and Virginia, the states that have the most extensive diversion tracking information, between 81 and 85 percent of those initially diverted do not subsequently reapply for TANF.

Time Limits

Before welfare reform, pride and self-determination were the main forces driving recipients off welfare. Unfortunately, many recipients were comfortable with the lifestyle welfare benefits provided and saw no need to work their way out of the system. They had been told welfare benefits were an entitlement, and some dependents made welfare a way of life.

In an effort to deter such "career recipients," PRWORA set limits to how long someone can receive welfare. The federal TANF program imposes a lifetime limit of 60 months (5 years). States can reduce that period or continue to support recipients after that time with their maintenance-of-effort money or other state funds. States can also exempt up to 20 percent of their cases from the limit, and "child-only" cases—in which only the children in the family qualify for benefits—are not subject to federal time limits.

Since caseloads include on-again, off-again recipients, many are just now reaching the overall five-year moratorium on aid. As recipients begin to hit the federal time limit, states must decide whether to kick families off the rolls or continue benefits out of scarce state funds. Eighteen states have been spared the dilemma because they were granted waivers before PRWORA that allow for the exclusion of all or part of their caseloads from time limits. Many states have implemented categorical exemptions for various recipients, choosing to continue funding with their own money. State policies need to change as more and more recipients begin to reach their time limits, especially if state budgets continue to be stretched.

Sanctions

Obviously, it is not enough for states to just promulgate new welfare policies—those policies must be enforced. If welfare recipients fail to meet work requirements or violate other parts of a state's welfare policy, penalties must be imposed. Modest sanctions tend to deduct only the adult portion of the TANF benefit, not punishing any children in the household and thereby only minimally reducing the benefit. States with the most stringent sanctions withhold the entire TANF benefit upon the first violation. Then there are sanction policies that fall along the spectrum, allowing multiple violations as benefits are gradually reduced or withheld.

Michael New, postdoctoral fellow at the Harvard-MIT data center, evaluated the effectiveness of sanctions in a Cato Institute Policy Analysis titled "Welfare Reform That Works." New found that a state's sanction policy could affect caseload decline by as much as 20 percent, through both the indirect effect of encouraging recipients to get off the rolls and the direct effect of ending their eligibility. Not only is there a relationship between state sanction policy and caseload decline, New found, but that relationship is constant over several years.

Sanctions are not successful because they throw recipients off welfare; rather, they serve as a threat of actual consequences for failing to meet requirements or reaching time limits. Only about 6 percent of those leaving welfare have done so because of sanction enforcement. However, the percentage of the caseload affected by sanctions varies widely among the states. For example, in an average month in 1998, almost 30 percent of case closures in North Carolina were due to sanctions, while less than 1 percent of closures in California, Oklahoma, and Nebraska were sanction related.

The Future

The next step for states is to work on their own dependence problem and wean themselves from federal funding. Without the strings that come with federal dollars, states would have even greater flexibility to be innovative and efficient. By partnering with local nonprofits and community organizations, states could encourage a shift of the safety net back to civil society, where it belongs.

Charles Murray has called for at least one state, possibly one with a small caseload and a history of effective nongovernmental welfare, to cut off all benefits to women under the age of 21. But in the long run, we should aim even higher. Our ultimate goal should be to eliminate the entire welfare system for individuals able to work. That means eliminating not just TANF but also food stamps, subsidized housing, and all the rest. Individuals unwilling to support themselves through the job market should have to fall back on the resources of family, church, community, or private charity. As both a practical matter and a question of fairness, no child currently on welfare should be thrown off. However, a date should be set, after which no one new would be allowed into the welfare system.

What would happen to the poor if welfare were eliminated? First, without the incentives of the welfare state, fewer people would be poor. There would probably be far fewer children born into poverty. We have seen that the availability of welfare leads to an increase in out-of-wedlock births and that giving birth out of wedlock leads to poverty. If welfare were eliminated, the number of out-of-wedlock births would almost certainly decline. Studies suggest that women do make rational decisions about whether to have children and that a reduction in income (such as a loss of welfare benefits) would reduce the likelihood of their becoming pregnant or having children out of wedlock.

States have been rightly called the laboratories of democracy. We have seen positive results from their experiments with welfare reform. We urge them to take those experiments to the next level.

Suggested Readings

Murray, Charles. *The Underclass Revisited.* Washington: American Enterprise Institute, 1999.

New, Michael. "Welfare Reform That Works: Explaining the Welfare Caseload Decline, 1996–2000." Cato Institute Policy Analysis no. 435, May 7, 2002.

Tanner, Michael. *The Poverty of Welfare: Helping Others in Civil Society.* Washington: Cato Institute, 2003.

Zeigler, Jenifer. "Implementing Welfare Reform: A State Report Card." Cato Institute Policy Analysis no. 529, October 19, 2004.

—Prepared by Jenifer Zeigler

7. Health Care

State governments should

- preserve and strengthen health savings accounts, beginning with repealing laws that obstruct them;
- enact tax reforms to treat health expenditures no differently than nonhealth expenditures;
- allow consumers to purchase health insurance regulated by the state of their choice;
- allow patients and providers to avoid the costly medical tort system through voluntary contracts; and
- liberalize Medicaid.

The federal government should

- preserve and strengthen health savings accounts,
- enact tax reforms to treat health expenditures no differently than nonhealth expenditures,
- deregulate health insurance by allowing consumers to purchase health insurance regulated by the state of their choice,
- liberalize Medicare and Medicaid, and
- liberalize the regulation of pharmaceuticals and medical devices.

Too Important Not to Leave to the Market

A widely accepted premise in health policy discussions is that health care is a special case of market failure and that government intervention is, therefore, necessary. In America's health care system—the world's freest—that would seem to be the case. Medical inflation consistently outpaces general inflation. Consumers have few health insurance choices.

Health insurance premiums continue to climb by double digits year after year. Millions of Americans are unable to afford health insurance. Even those with insurance have their choices restricted by reimbursement rules, networks, and gatekeepers. Losing a job often means losing coverage. Doctors have little time to spend with patients. Prescriptions are too expensive for many people. Cost shifting is rampant. Competition is scant. Litigation threatens to drive doctors out of practice and deny patients access to care. And repeated efforts at reform seem to make no difference.

Careful observation, however, reveals that such supposed examples of market failure are actually manifestations of government failure; that is, the problems in America's health care sector are the result of government attempting to influence behavior or otherwise restrict individual liberty. Unsurprisingly, health care markets respond to such intervention as economic theory suggests markets would. The extent of America's health care difficulties can be explained by the fact that, according to University of Rochester health economist Charles Phelps, "the U.S. health care system, while among the most 'market oriented' in the industrialized world, remains the most intensively regulated sector of the U.S. economy."

Government involvement in the health care sector is harmful to patients and is a large and growing encroachment on individual liberty. The solution is to restore individual liberty by expanding the number of health care decisions made by individuals and reducing the number of decisions made by government.

The Third-Party Payer System

The primary way government interferes in health care markets is through policies that make the purchaser of health care someone other than the consumer. The result is America's "third-party payer" system: patients (the first party) consume medical care, and suppliers (the second party) are most often paid by some third party to the transaction. The two policies that created this system are the federal tax code (more precisely, the tax treatment of employment-based health insurance) and government health programs (principally Medicare and Medicaid).

Since World War II the federal government has exempted employer-provided health benefits from taxation. The immediate results were twofold. First, the price of employer-provided health insurance (including any medical care financed through such "insurance") dropped relative to that of other goods and services. If a worker's wages are taxed at 35 percent, the same pretax dollar can buy either $1 of health benefits or $0.65 of something else. Not taxing employer-provided health benefits the same as other forms of consumption makes the price of health insurance and medical care appear much lower relative to that of other forms of consumption. Thus, workers purchase more coverage and consume more care than they otherwise would. (This tax benefit initially applied only to third-party insurance, not to savings that individuals put aside for their health care expenses, also known as self-insurance.)

The second result has been that most Americans (roughly 60 percent in 2003) get their health insurance through their employers, and most of their medical bills are paid by employers or insurers. Such third-party payment magnifies the effects of the tax code and creates instability in the health care sector. Already encouraged to overconsume health care by distorted prices, workers are further insulated from the cost of their choices because someone else is writing the check. Since workers have few incentives to be cost-conscious, prudent consumers, demand for health care rises dramatically, and prices rise along with it.

In fact, third-party payment guarantees that prices will continue to rise. If government lowered the price of apples relative to that of other goods, consumers would buy more apples. However, as demand rose, so would prices. Consumers would eventually respond to higher prices by putting the brakes on their consumption, and prices would stabilize. But if a third party paid their apple bills, consumers would keep consuming and the price of apples would continue to climb. Double-digit percentage increases in health insurance premiums have become commonplace, even while overall inflation remains at or below 4 percent. From 1958 to 2002, there were only two periods (the high-inflation eras of 1973–74 and 1979–80) during which prices for nonmedical items rose faster than prices for medical care.

Since third-party payers end up paying those higher costs, they have attempted to constrain unnecessary spending with administrative controls that interfere with patients' medical decisions and how providers practice medicine. In other words, they create bureaucracies to constrain the consumption of patients who would constrain themselves if spending their own money. Managed care is a predictable outgrowth of third-party payment. Moreover, third-party payment diminishes national savings because people have less incentive to save for their future health needs. The distortions created by the tax code alone impose a deadweight loss on the economy of $106 billion per year.

Government health programs (chiefly Medicare and Medicaid), which provide medical care to roughly 27 percent of the population at reduced or no cost, have similar effects on consumer behavior. (Medicare and Medicaid are examined more closely in Chapter 8.) All told, 84 cents of every dollar spent on personal health care in the United States comes from someone other than the patient (see Figure 7.1). Despite enjoying the world's freest health care system, the United States pays for a greater share of its health care through third parties than do 17 other developed countries, including Canada and other socialist systems.

Tax Reform Is Health Care Reform

The primary goal of health care reform must be to eliminate government-imposed incentives for third-party payment. Ideally, the tax code would treat health expenditures like any other expenditure. If government imposes a tax, its purpose should be to raise revenue, not to favor some behaviors over others. However, merely repealing the current tax exclusion is politi-

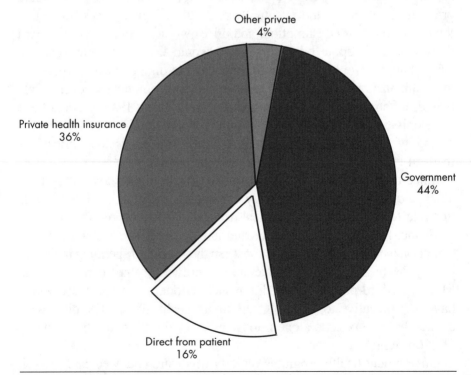

Figure 7.1
Sources of Payment for Personal Health Care Expenditures, 2002

Other private
4%

Private health insurance
36%

Government
44%

Direct from patient
16%

SOURCE: Centers for Medicare & Medicaid Services.

cally unfeasible and would amount to an enormous tax increase, as previously untaxed activity would become subject to taxation. (The exclusion provides a tax break estimated at $189 billion in 2004.)

Fundamental tax reform will be necessary to eliminate the differential tax treatment of health-related and other expenditures. (For more on this topic, see Chapter 11.) The current federal income tax should be replaced with a flat, low-rate tax system that treats health and nonhealth expenditures identically. Individuals would then make health care decisions according to what provided them the greatest value, not the greatest tax benefit. Moreover, health insurers would have to compete aggressively for customers, and the control that insurers and employers currently have over patients would disappear. Fundamental tax reform may take many years. Nonetheless, America will not have a free health care market until the differential tax treatment of health expenditures is eliminated.

Health Savings Accounts

In 2003 Congress took a giant leap toward health care reform with the creation of health savings accounts. Cato Institute scholars first proposed health savings accounts in the 1980s and were leaders in popularizing them among the public and policymakers. Although health savings accounts do not eliminate the price distortions that follow from the differential tax treatment of employer-provided health benefits, they greatly reduce the incentives for third-party payment.

Health savings accounts extend preferred tax treatment to self-insurance via a personal savings account dedicated to routine medical expenditures. The savings account is coupled with a low-cost, high-deductible health insurance policy for catastrophic expenses. Individuals and their employers deposit funds in the health savings account tax-free. Whatever the account owner does not spend grows tax-free.

Health savings accounts will rein in health care costs by encouraging patients to curb their consumption. People are much more careful consumers when spending their own money than when spending someone else's. With built-in incentives for consumers to make wise choices, many of the restrictions that insurers have placed on patients will begin to disappear. Because workers own their health savings accounts, they will have coverage when they switch jobs and be better able to afford insurance on their own. Health savings accounts will also make health insurance more affordable for the uninsured. Seventy-three percent of enrollees in a pilot health savings account program that began in 1997 previously had no health insurance.

As enacted, health savings accounts work as follows: Any American under the age of 65 who is covered by a qualified high-deductible health plan and who cannot be claimed as another's dependent for tax purposes is eligible to open a health savings account. A qualified individual health plan must have a deductible of at least $1,000 and a limit on out-of-pocket expenses (including deductibles and copayments) of $5,000. For families, the deductible is at least $2,000 and the out-of-pocket limit is $10,000. Only preventive care coverage is allowed below the deductible, though coverage for accidents, disability, dental, vision, and long-term care is also permitted.

The health savings account owner, her employer, a family member, or any combination thereof may contribute to the account. Annual contributions are limited by the health insurance deductible, with an upper limit of $2,600 for individuals and $5,150 for families. Contributions are permitted until the owner turns 65. Those aged 55–64 may make additional "catch-up" contributions of up to $500 in 2004, with the limit rising $100 annually until it reaches $1,000 in 2009. Health savings account funds may be invested in a variety of vehicles, including checking accounts, money market accounts, mutual funds, and certificates of deposit. Whatever funds the holder does not spend remain in the health savings account and grow tax-free.

Money withdrawn from a health savings account for medical expenses of the account holder, her spouse, or dependents is never taxed. However, health savings account funds spent on nonmedical items are subject to income taxes and an additional 10 percent tax. Upon the account holder's death, health savings account funds are transferred tax-free to the spouse or taxed as income if someone other than a spouse is the beneficiary.

Health savings accounts will be a disruptive influence. Consumers spending their own money will reveal different preferences (among insurance companies, medical professionals, pharmaceutical companies, and even public policies) than consumers who are spending someone else's money. Interest groups disfavored by consumers will try to save third-party payment by thwarting health savings accounts. Health savings accounts had barely been enacted before bills were introduced in Congress to repeal them. It is incumbent upon the federal and state governments to protect health savings accounts from defenders of the status quo and to strengthen those accounts so they may reform America's health care system from within.

How to Improve Health Savings Accounts

Many states have enacted health insurance regulations—requiring first-dollar coverage for certain treatments—that effectively prohibit many residents from opening a health savings account. Those regulations should be repealed, or at least rendered null with regard to health savings accounts. Further, states should allow residents to deduct their health savings account health insurance premiums from their state taxable income.

The federal government can do much more to make health savings accounts more flexible and widely available. First, it should allow individuals to deduct their health insurance premiums from their federal taxable income. Like state deductibility, this reform would bolster health savings accounts in the individual health insurance market. Second, health savings accounts should be open to all Americans, regardless of age or health insurance status. Health savings accounts are currently allowed only with high-deductible insurance and with specified limits on consumers' out-of-pocket exposure. Those who do not want or cannot obtain health insurance deserve the same access to health savings accounts as others. Likewise, an employer who cannot provide health insurance but can contribute to her workers' health savings accounts should have that option. Consumers, such as those who have built up large balances, also should be able to choose a larger out-of-pocket limit. There is no reason to limit consumers' choices in those areas. An individual should be permitted to open a health savings account on its own or in combination with any health insurance plan.

One reason to allow greater flexibility is to encourage more Americans to save for their health needs as opposed to handing their health care dollars over to a third party. Those reluctant to switch to a high-deductible health plan should be allowed to begin saving in a health savings account that would cover their deductibles and copayments. As they accumulate savings, many would gravitate away from third-party insurance toward higher-deductible plans. In South Africa health savings accounts may be coupled with any type of health insurance, and South Africans have responded by giving health savings accounts over half of the private health insurance market.

Third, contribution limits should be increased. In the absence of a health insurance requirement, health savings account contributions would have to be subject to some other limit. In general, annual limits should be set high enough for consumers to couple a health savings account with a true high-deductible health insurance policy and have no gaps in coverage.

For example, individuals could be allowed to contribute $3,000 per year and purchase a health insurance policy with a $3,000 deductible, while families could contribute $6,000 per year and have a $6,000 deductible. "Catch-up" contributions for those nearing retirement should also be increased by raising the maximum amount and lowering the age at which such contributions may start. Given employers' continuing curtailment of retiree health benefits and the fiscal crisis that faces Medicare in the coming decades, the federal government should encourage all Americans to save as much as possible for their health needs.

Fourth, the penalty on nonmedical withdrawals is an additional price distortion that further encourages owners to purchase medical care instead of other items. Disbursements for nonmedical expenses should be subject to income taxes with no additional penalty. Finally, the federal government should retool health reimbursement arrangements and flexible spending accounts to make them more closely resemble health savings accounts. Principally, this means balances in those "accounts" should be the property of the worker that she can carry over from year to year and take with her upon terminating employment.

Those enhancements to health savings accounts will go a long way— but not all the way—toward focusing America's health care system on the needs of consumers. Moreover, health savings accounts will ease the transition to fundamental tax reform. By habituating Americans to controlling their own health care, health savings accounts will mitigate the fear and dislocation that would result from going directly from the current system to one in which third-party payment receives no government encouragement.

Deregulating Health Care

Third-party payment is not the only way government distorts prices and robs patients and providers of their freedom to act. State and federal governments have enacted countless health care regulations that restrict the freedom of consumers and producers—often in response to the effects of previous government failures. Those include regulations governing health care facilities (hospitals, nursing homes, etc.), health professionals (doctors, nurses, and other providers), health insurance, pharmaceuticals, medical devices, and other products (through the Food and Drug Administration), and the medical liability system. Professor Chris Conover of Duke University estimates that the costs of such health care regulations exceed their benefits by two to one and impose a net annual cost on Americans of $169 billion. That is the equivalent of a tax of $1,500 per household, or of eliminating the gross state product of seven states. By increasing the cost of health care, such regulations make health insurance unaffordable for more than seven million Americans.

The federal and state governments should deregulate the health care sector wherever possible. Chapter 8 offers reforms that would decrease the amount of regulation attributable to Medicare and Medicaid. Chapter 40 discusses deregulating the Food and Drug Administration. (See below for reforms that would decrease the cost of the medical liability system.)

With regard to health insurance, the federal and state governments should allow purchasers to buy health insurance regulated by the state of their choice. Currently, purchasers are largely bound to the regulatory regime of the state where they reside (large employers can opt for federal regulation). If free to choose health insurance policies without regard to state borders, consumers will avoid regulations that impose unwanted costs and favor states whose regulations better meet their needs. For example, it has been estimated that states have enacted 1,823 separate requirements that insurance cover particular items. If a consumer lives in Minnesota but does not want to purchase all 60 types of coverage mandated there, she could choose to purchase health insurance regulated by Idaho, which has the fewest mandated benefits (13) or by a state whose laws are aligned more closely with her needs. Consumers could also avoid other costly regulations, such as price controls that increase the cost of coverage for many individuals. The *Wall Street Journal* has noted that regulations in New York make health insurance about 10 times more expensive there than in neighboring Connecticut. Millions of Americans shopping online for health insurance and health insurance regulation would put enormous pressure on states to deregulate. The federal government should give Americans this right immediately, but states can do so for their own residents without waiting for Congress to act. Such regulatory choice could serve as a model for deregulating other areas of the economy.

Medical Liability Reform

Torts are an important protection against those who do or would injure us, yet many people complain—with some reason—that the medical liability "system" in the United States is out of control. Frivolous lawsuits are brought too often, damages are exorbitant, and the aggrieved patients receive only a fraction of the monetary awards. Many specialists (neurosurgeons and obstetricians, to name two) report that they cannot afford the rising cost of medical liability insurance. Conover estimates that the U.S. medical liability "system" costs Americans $81 billion per year net of benefits.

Many observers have called on the federal government to correct the situation through federal medical liability reforms. As discussed in Chapter 18, Congress is not constitutionally authorized to impose substantive rules of tort law on the states. Although the federal government may enact technical procedural changes, state legislatures are the proper venue for correcting excesses in their civil justice systems. The fact that medical professionals can avoid states with inhospitable civil justice systems gives them significant leverage when advocating state-level medical liability reforms, and gives states incentives to enact such reforms. That some states have done so demonstrates that they have the ability.

What reforms should states consider? Arbitrary caps on damages may reduce the costs of frivolous lawsuits, but they foreclose adequate relief in extreme cases and prevent patients from bargaining for greater protection. So-called loser pays reforms would often reallocate the costs of frivolous lawsuits to the correct party; however, this rule deters less affluent patients from seeking legal redress for legitimate grievances.

A more patient-friendly and liberty-enhancing reform would be to allow patients and providers to avoid the costly medical tort system through voluntary contracts. Providers could offer to lower their prices if the patient agreed to certain limits on compensation in the event of an injury. If not, the patient could pay the higher price or seek a better deal from another provider. As John Goodman and Gerald Musgrave argue in *Patient Power*, this could lead to any number of innovations. For example:

> [O]ne sensible way to cut down on the litigation costs for simple negligence would be to have the hospital take out a life insurance policy on a patient prior to surgery. The hospital and the patient (or the patient's family) could agree that if the patient dies for any reason, the beneficiaries will accept the policy's payment as full compensation, even if there was negligence. The same principle could apply to other injuries, such as disability leading to a loss of income. Litigation costs would be avoided, and life insurance companies would have incentives to monitor the quality of hospital care.

In cases of ordinary negligence, patients could choose the level of protection they desired, rather than have that level (and the resulting higher prices) imposed on them by the tort system. Only in cases of intentional wrongdoing or reckless behavior would tort rules apply. As Goodman and Musgrave note: "The current legal system ignores contractual waivers of tort liability. What is needed is a legal change requiring the courts to honor certain types of contracts under which tort claims are waived in return for compensation.''

Suggested Readings

Cannon, Michael F. ''Health Savings Accounts: Making the Healthcare System Work for Women.'' Independent Women's Forum Position Paper no. 401, March 18, 2004.

Epstein, Richard. *Mortal Peril: Our Inalienable Right to Health Care?* Reading, MA: Addison-Wesley, 1997.

Federal Trade Commission and U.S. Department of Justice. ''Improving Health Care: A Dose of Competition.'' July 2004. http://www.ftc.gov/reports/healthcare/040723 healthcarerpt.pdf.

Friedman, Milton. ''How to Cure Health Care.'' *Public Interest*, Winter 2001.

Goodman, John C., and Gerald Musgrave. *Patient Power*. Washington: Cato Institute, 1992.

Miller, Tom. ''A Regulatory Bypass Operation.'' *Cato Journal* 22, no. 1 (Spring–Summer 2002).

—Prepared by Michael F. Cannon

8. Medicare and Medicaid

The federal government should

- maintain the Medicare Rx drug discount card program as an alternative to implementing the Medicare Rx benefit in 2006,
- allow seniors to opt out of Medicare entirely without loss of Social Security benefits,
- allow Medicare beneficiaries and their doctors to contract privately for Medicare-covered services,
- give current Medicare beneficiaries a risk-adjusted voucher to purchase health insurance and/or deposit in a health savings account,
- let workers save their Medicare payroll taxes in a retirement health savings account to purchase medical care and coverage in their golden years,
- freeze Medicaid spending at current levels and distribute Medicaid funds to states as unrestricted block grants, and
- eliminate Medicaid spending and cut taxes concomitantly.

State governments should

- demand full flexibility in administering Medicaid,
- experiment with Medicaid benefits structures that mirror health savings accounts, and
- deregulate health insurance markets to make health insurance more affordable for low-income individuals and families.

Introduction

Government directly finances health care for more than one-quarter of the U.S. population—some 77 million people in 2003. As shown in Chapter 7, that translates into nearly half (44 percent) of all medical care consumed in the United States. Two government programs account for most of the spending. Medicare is a federal program that creates a legal entitlement to health benefits for the elderly and disabled. Medicaid is a joint federal-state program that creates an entitlement to health benefits for the poor. Each was enacted by President Lyndon Johnson as part of the Great Society, and each will mark its 40th anniversary in July 2005. Their creation was a milestone for supporters of national health insurance, who had lobbied for greater federal involvement in the health care sector since before the New Deal.

In the 40 years since their enactment, Medicare and Medicaid have imposed a large and growing burden on taxpayers and the economy, a burden that soon will become unsustainable. According to the federal Office of Management and Budget, together they will account for one-fifth of all federal outlays in 2005 and one-fourth of outlays by 2009.

- In 2005 the federal government will spend $481 billion on Medicare and Medicaid (including the State Children's Health Insurance Program, a Medicaid offshoot), more than on national defense and homeland security combined ($478 billion).
- When state Medicaid spending is included, the two programs ($624 billion) dwarf even Social Security ($513 billion).

According to the Congressional Budget Office, Medicare spending will double from 2005 levels in eight years and federal Medicaid spending will nearly double in nine years (Figure 8.1). To keep funding those programs as they exist would require massive tax increases.

Those projections probably understate how much the programs will spend in the coming years. It is an iron-clad rule that government handouts grow beyond expectations. In 1965 the federal government projected that Medicare hospital insurance would cost $9 billion in 1990. Its actual cost in 1990 was $66 billion. Costs grow rapidly because people eligible for the handout both change their behavior to maximize their gain and pressure government to enlarge the handout. Recent examples of the latter include the addition of Medicare coverage for outpatient prescription drugs and obesity treatments.

Third-party payment insulates Medicare and Medicaid beneficiaries from the cost of care, leading to increased demand, overconsumption, higher prices, and enormous waste. Nobel laureate Milton Friedman estimates that third-party payment caused real per capita health spending to reach $3,625 in 1997, or more than twice what it otherwise would have

Figure 8.1
Projected Medicare and Medicaid Spending, 2003–14

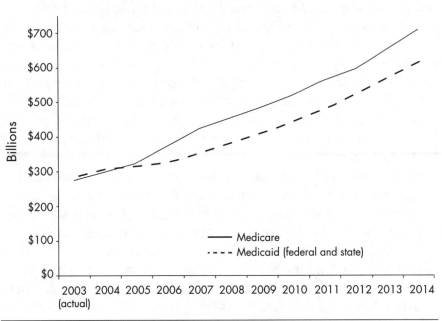

SOURCE: Congressional Budget Office and author's calculations.

been. Medicare and Medicaid accounted for 43 percent of the increase. A study by Dartmouth's Jonathan Skinner, Elliot Fisher, and John Wennberg found that nearly 20 percent of Medicare spending is wasted (i.e., "appears to provide no benefit in terms or survival, nor is it likely that this extra spending improves the quality of life"). That translates to more than $58 billion in 2005, a figure that does not include waste from medical care that provides some value but less than it costs.

Part of the waste is created by the efforts of government bureaucrats to determine what medical suppliers should be paid for providing services to beneficiaries. In a free health care market, the natural interplay between supply and demand would determine prices. Prices send signals that encourage suppliers to devote resources where they best satisfy consumers' needs. However, because prices for Medicare and Medicaid transactions are set by bureaucrats who cannot possibly have all the information captured by markets, pricing errors are inevitable. Prices no longer convey the information that consumers and producers need to coordinate their activities, and resources are diverted from where they are needed most.

Further waste is created as producers and patient groups expend vast resources to influence the price-setting process and other policies to their benefit. Medicare and Medicaid are leading reasons why health care interests spent more than $600 million on political contributions and lobbying activities in the 2001–02 election cycle, health professionals made the second-highest contributions to congressional campaigns, and health care groups ranked second in terms of dollars spent on lobbying activities in 2000. Moreover, Medicare and Medicaid crowd out private efforts to provide for their target populations, discourage saving and work, and infringe on the rights of individual Americans to control their income and medical decisions.

Neither program is sustainable in its current form. Unreformed, those programs will impose an ever-increasing burden on taxpayers, deliver fewer benefits to beneficiaries, and exacerbate the spiraling costs and loss of patient control that fuel calls for government-run health care.

The U.S. Constitution does not give Congress the power to create government health insurance schemes. The federal and state governments should hew to the Constitution and drastically liberalize these programs as a first step toward privately funding health care for the elderly and indigent. First and foremost, lawmakers should transform Medicare and Medicaid into programs that encourage responsible stewardship by giving beneficiaries ownership of their health care dollars. The federal and state governments should act before the 45th anniversary of Medicare and Medicaid.

Medicare

Though popular among seniors and those who might otherwise have to care for them, Medicare infringes on the right of workers to control their retirement savings and the freedom of seniors to control their own health care.

Medicare was founded on a number of premises that are either impractical or morally suspect, or both. One is that young workers should be taxed to pay for the health care needs of their elders, many of whom do not need it and many of whom never contributed to the program. The first generation of Medicare beneficiaries essentially got something for nothing, receiving subsidies without having contributed to the program. As if to immortalize this premise, the honorary first Medicare beneficiary was a man who neither contributed to Medicare nor needed it: former president Harry S Truman. Since Medicare's enactment, each generation of seniors has demanded that the debt it is owed by its elders be paid by its children and grandchildren. Moreover, successive generations of seniors have added to that debt burden by voting themselves greater subsidies to be financed by future generations. The most recent example is the prescription drug benefit added to Medicare by Congress and President Bush in 2003. (Often, benefit increases are not even subject to a vote. In 2004 the Bush administration unilaterally announced that Medicare would cover obesity treatments.)

Medicare's obligations and financing structure are unsustainable. A number of factors will fuel growth in Medicare spending in the coming years. First, demographic trends will reduce the number of workers available to finance Medicare relative to the number of beneficiaries. According to Medicare's trustees, the ratio will fall from about four workers per beneficiary in 2003 to about 2.4 workers per beneficiary in 2030 and continue to fall until there are only 2 workers per beneficiary in 2078. Second and related to that, those seniors will live longer. Social Security's trustees estimate that from 2003 to 2030 life expectancy at age 65 will grow from 16.0 years to 17.7 years for males and from 19.0 years to 20.3 years for females. Third, health care costs will continue to climb. In 2003 the Congressional Budget Office estimated that a mere 30 percent of Medicare's future growth would be due to society's aging, while 70 percent would be due to the rising cost of health care. Those factors exert a multiplying effect on each other; together they make Medicare as we know it unsustainable. Medicare's short-term cost growth is depicted in Figure 8.1.

Over the longer term, the situation becomes more severe. According to Medicare trustee Prof. Tom Saving, Medicare consumed 8 percent of federal income tax revenue in 2003—in addition to the Medicare payroll tax, beneficiary premiums, and other funding sources. As Medicare's implied promises come due, the share of federal income tax revenue that will have to be devoted to Medicare will grow, reaching half of all federal income tax revenue by 2042. Maintaining the Medicare program in its current form would require enormous tax increases. As a measure of how much Medicare has promised versus what its current funding mechanisms can deliver, Medicare's trustees calculate that we would need to deposit $61.6 *trillion* in an interest-bearing account in 2004 to cover all of Medicare's future deficits.

Another suspect premise is that government can or should devise a one-size-fits-all set of medical coverage benefits for tens of millions of senior citizens. The character of government subsidies is determined through the political process, which guarantees perverse results. Whereas insurance leaves individuals responsible for routine expenses and protects against catastrophic losses, Medicare does the opposite. Subsidies begin at very low levels of consumption and disappear when beneficiaries' needs become greatest. The reason is politics: popularly elected lawmakers win more votes by spreading the "insurance" around to many people than by concentrating it on the few who need it most. When Medicare was enacted, it effectively destroyed a large and growing private market for health insurance for seniors. By 1962 an estimated 60 percent of seniors had voluntary health insurance coverage, up from 31 percent in 1952. Today, seniors essentially have only one place to go for health insurance, though they may augment the coverage Medicare offers by signing up for a Medicare health maintenance organization or by purchasing Medicare supplemental or "Medigap" coverage. Often, those additional benefits make seniors even less price sensitive and more likely to overconsume medical care.

A third premise is that participation in Medicare is voluntary. In fact, Medicare greatly restricts the freedom of workers, seniors, and the medical community. Even if Medicare neither crowded out other health insurance options for seniors nor forced seniors who decline Medicare benefits to forfeit all past and future Social Security benefits, funding Medicare would still be compulsory for all Americans forced to pay the 2.9 percent Medicare payroll tax or other federal taxes that finance the program through general revenues. Augmented by participants' Medicare premiums, those funds are distributed to medical professionals who provide care to Medicare beneficiaries and to the Medicare bureaucracy that sets and enforces the terms of the exchange. Providers often find dealing with Medicare nightmarish. Improperly billing Medicare can lead to criminal prosecution for fraud. Yet the Government Accountability Office found that in 2004 Medicare call centers answered providers' billing questions accurately and completely only 4 percent of the time. It is no wonder, then, that the Department of Health and Human Services reports improper Medicare payments were $12.1 billion in 2001. Moreover, Medicare prohibits participating providers from delivering Medicare-covered services to beneficiaries on a private basis, an affront to the right of patients and doctors to make mutually beneficial exchanges that affect no one else.

Reforming Medicare will require a multipronged approach. First, Congress should immediately repeal or delay implementation of the prescription drug benefit enacted in 2003 before it takes effect in 2006. The Medicare trustees report that this program accounts for one-quarter of Medicare's projected deficits. This obligation would substantially increase the burden Medicare places on taxpayers and hinder further efforts at Medicare reform; it is already fueling calls for price controls on pharmaceuticals even before it has taken effect. A far less harmful alternative would be to retain the "transitional" drug subsidy that took effect in 2004. In that program, the federal government provides aid to low-income seniors primarily through a $600 subsidy in a quasi–health savings account for prescription drug expenses. In addition, Congress should immediately restore to seniors the freedom to contract privately with their physicians without penalty to either party and allow seniors to opt out of Medicare without forfeiting their Social Security benefits.

More fundamentally, Medicare must be transformed into a program in which seniors have an ownership interest in the money they are spending and medical care for the elderly is privately financed. The federal government should give all beneficiaries a voucher—which could be supplemented with private funds—to purchase health insurance from a variety of competing private insurers and/or to deposit in a health savings account. Any unused health savings account funds could be spent on nonmedical items. Seniors could then purchase coverage that suited their individual needs and would have incentives to be more prudent consumers. Seniors would conduct much more effective oversight of quality and fraud than the Medicare bureaucracy does because their own money would be on the line. Vouchers should be risk adjusted (less healthy seniors would receive larger amounts) to prevent insurers from accepting only healthy applicants. As Profs. Saving and Andrew Rettenmaier propose, the federal government should allow for long-term health insurance policies, which give insurers further incentive to pursue less-healthy seniors.

The federal government should allow workers to deposit some or all of their Medicare payroll taxes in a personal account for their health care needs in retirement. (This proposal would work much like Social Security personal accounts. See Chapter 4.) These funds would add to the capital stock, boost economic growth, and finance workers' health coverage in their golden years. It would move Medicare from a system of intergenerational transfers, with the inevitable political friction that results, to a prefunded system in which each generation pays its own way. In 1999 Harvard University Prof. Martin Feldstein estimated that diverting 1.4 percentage points of the current 2.9 percent Medicare payroll tax "would eventually be enough to pay for the full increase in the cost of Medicare, obviating a nine percentage point payroll tax increase.''

Medicaid

The federal government and state and territorial governments jointly administer Medicaid—or more precisely, the 56 separate Medicaid programs throughout the United States. Medicaid participation is ostensibly voluntary for states, if not for taxpayers. States that wish to participate (all states do) must provide a federally mandated set of health benefits to a federally mandated population of eligible individuals. In return, each state receives federal funds in proportion to what it spends. The ratio of federal to state contributions, or "match," is determined according to a state's relative wealth: poorer states receive a higher match, and wealthier states receive a lower match. On average, 57 percent of Medicaid funding comes from the federal government and 43 percent comes from the states. The more a state spends on its Medicaid program, the more it receives from the federal government. States can make their Medicaid benefits more generous than the federal government requires and can also extend eligibility to more people than the federal government requires. For beneficiaries, Medicaid is an entitlement. So long as they meet the eligibility criteria, they can receive benefits. Medicaid primarily serves four low-income groups: mothers and their children, the disabled, the elderly, and those needing long-term care.

Because the federal government provides an open-ended commitment to match state Medicaid spending, states have an incentive to underfund other priorities. Spending $1 on police buys $1 of police protection, but spending $1 on Medicaid buys $2 or more of health care. That financing structure also encourages states to pretend to increase Medicaid spending in order to draw down federal matching funds. States have used illegitimate schemes to lay hold of billions of federal dollars. The more a state expands its Medicaid program, the more harm it does to its health care sector. Medicaid eligibility induces many individuals (and their employers) to drop private coverage and take advantage of the "free" medical care, forcing taxpayers to purchase medical care for those who were able to obtain it anyway. Studies have shown that up to half of those who enrolled under Medicaid expansions already had private coverage. As Medicaid expands, more patients enter the medical marketplace with no regard for the cost of the items they consume.

It makes little sense for taxpayers to send money to Washington, DC, so those funds can be sent back to their state capitol with strings (and perverse incentives) attached. Control over Medicaid should be devolved to the states. The states can then decide whether and how to maintain their own programs and learn from the successes and failures of each other's experiments.

In 1996 Congress eliminated the federal entitlement to a welfare check, placed a five-year limit on cash assistance, and froze federal spending on such assistance, which was then distributed to the states in the form of block grants with fewer federal restrictions. The results were unquestionably positive. Welfare rolls were cut in half, and poverty reached the lowest point in a generation (see Chapter 5). The federal government should emulate this success by eliminating the entitlement to Medicaid benefits, freezing federal Medicaid spending at current levels, and distributing Medicaid funds to the states as unrestricted block grants. That would eliminate the perverse incentives that favor Medicaid spending over other state priorities and lead to gaming of Medicaid's funding rules. According to Congressional Budget Office projections, freezing Medicaid spending at 2005 levels would produce $749 billion in savings by 2014, or enough to reduce the cumulative 10-year federal deficit of $2.3 trillion by one-third. In time, the federal government should give the states full responsibility for Medicaid by eliminating federal Medicaid spending while concomitantly cutting federal taxes.

States should pressure the federal government for maximum flexibility in administering their Medicaid programs. With unrestricted Medicaid block grants, states that wanted to spend more on their Medicaid programs would be free to raise taxes to do so, and vice versa. States should redesign their Medicaid benefits to emulate health savings accounts. (For more on health savings accounts, see Chapter 7.) In essence, states should give beneficiaries vouchers (perhaps risk adjusted) to purchase private health insurance and/or deposit in a health savings account for their medical expenses. By giving beneficiaries ownership of their Medicaid benefits rather than an open-ended entitlement, states would encourage beneficiaries to avoid wasteful consumption. That would eliminate administrative costs and rein in medical inflation.

Granted, more beneficiaries may show up to claim Medicaid vouchers than currently show up for free medical care, which raises cost implications. Though states can experiment with ways to counteract this problem, all subsidies increase the incidence of that which is subsidized and become more attractive the more control they grant the recipient. Rather than an argument against Medicaid vouchers, however, this is an argument against subsidies. The only way to eliminate the problem is to eliminate the subsidy. Ultimately, states should phase out their Medicaid programs, cut taxes, and reduce regulations (see Chapter 7) to enable the market and private charities to meet the needs of the medically indigent.

Conclusion

Medicare and Medicaid reform must be waged on many fronts. In addition to giving individuals an ownership interest in their benefits under those programs, policymakers must simultaneously reform other areas of the health care system to curb rising health care costs and with them the burden of health care entitlements.

Suggested Readings

Blevins, Sue A. *Medicare's Midlife Crisis.* Washington: Cato Institute, 2001.

Edwards, Chris, and Tad DeHaven. "War between the Generations: Federal Spending on the Elderly Set to Explode." Cato Institute Policy Analysis no. 488, September 16, 2003.

Epstein, Richard. *Mortal Peril: Our Inalienable Right to Health Care?* Reading, MA: Addison-Wesley, 1997.

Feldstein, Martin. "Prefunding Medicare." National Bureau of Economic Research, Working Paper no. 6917, January 1999.

Friedman, Milton. "How to Cure Health Care." *Public Interest,* Winter 2001.

Goodman, John C., and Gerald Musgrave. *Patient Power.* Washington: Cato Institute, 1992.

Goodman, John C., Gerald Musgrave, and Devon Herrick. *Lives at Risk: Single-Payer National Health Insurance around the World.* Lanham, MD: Rowman & Littlefield, 2004.

Hoff, John S. *Medicare Private Contracting: Paternalism or Autonomy?* Washington: AEI Press, 1998.

Pipes, Sally. *Miracle Cure: How to Solve America's Health-Care Crisis and Why Canada Isn't the Answer.* San Francisco: Pacific Research Institute, 2004.

Rettenmaier, Andrew J., and Thomas R. Saving. *The Economics of Medicare Reform.* Kalamazoo, MI: W. E. Upjohn Institute for Employment Research, 2000.

Teske, Richard. "Abolishing the Medicaid Ghetto: Putting 'Patients First.'" American Legislative Exchange Council, The State Factor no. 0206, April 2002.

—Prepared by Michael F. Cannon

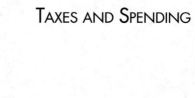

TAXES AND SPENDING

9. The Federal Budget

Congress should

- balance the budget without raising taxes;
- reduce domestic discretionary spending by more than $350 billion, thereby cutting the discretionary budget from 7.9 percent of GDP to 5 percent;
- reform Social Security by moving toward a system of individual savings accounts;
- reform Medicare to cut costs, and freeze Medicaid spending at current levels and distribute the funds to states as unrestricted block grants;
- establish a "sunset" commission to automatically review all federal programs on a rotating basis and propose major reforms and terminations;
- change the rules of the budget process to make it easier to keep spending under control; and
- institute a strong spending cap that does not allow government spending to grow faster than population plus inflation.

The federal government is estimated to have spent roughly $2.3 trillion in fiscal 2004. If the spending categories that account for the core functions of the federal government as outlined in the Constitution were subtracted from this amount, the government would still spend around $1.6 trillion. That means the federal government is currently at least three times bigger than it needs to be to carry out its enumerated powers. This spending bloat is a result of a multidecade accumulation of programs that expanded the reach, power, and cost of the federal government. Congress and the president need to arrest this growth as quickly as possible and return the federal government to its proper limits.

The Mess We're In

The estimated budget deficit for fiscal 2004 is $413 billion, and the deficit for fiscal 2005 is expected to be $348 billion. That puts the deficit in the range of 4 percent of GDP for 2004 and 3 percent for 2005. In fact, deficits exist for as far as the eyes of estimators can see: the estimated cumulative deficit for 2005–09 is $1.6 trillion.

Those deficits pale in comparison with the train wreck that awaits entitlement programs when the baby boomers start to retire. In just 13 years—by 2018—the Social Security Trust Fund will begin to run a deficit. And the amounts of unfunded liabilities that await everyone are staggering. Social Security's unfunded liability is estimated by its Board of Trustees to equal $10.4 trillion.

Economists Jagadeesh Gokhale and Kent Smetters estimate that in 2003 the federal government would have had to come up with $36 trillion to cover all of Medicare's future deficits. Now that the Medicare prescription drug benefit has been added and the population has aged a couple of years, the Board of Trustees of the Medicare system has estimated that the unfunded liabilities have grown to $61.6 trillion. That's close to 30 times the size of the federal budget today. It's obvious that any plan to balance the budget in the short term must also include reforms to entitlement programs for the long term.

How We Got into the Mess

The economic boom of the 1990s was good to everyone, including elected officials. Revenue flowed into state and federal coffers faster than they could spend it. That led, in 1998, to the first balanced budget since 1969. But by 2002—just four years later—the federal budget was in deficit again. What happened?

There was, very simply, too much spending. The surplus opened the floodgates of government expenditures. Consider this: In the four years before 1998, the average annual increase of total government spending was 3.1 percent. In the four years between 1998 and the return of the deficit in 2002, total government spending increased at an average annual rate of 5 percent.

In the years leading up to 1998, entitlement spending drove most of the spending growth. After 1998, however, out-of-control discretionary spending on defense and nondefense programs alike drove the spending binge. The average annual rate of growth in discretionary spending was

.5 percent between 1994 and 1998, but it exploded to 7.3 percent between 1998 and 2002 (Figure 9.1).

When the revenue began to dry up, one would have expected spending to slow, too. But spending grew even faster after the deficit appeared: the average annual increase in defense and nondefense discretionary spending from 2002 to 2004 was 11.2 percent.

Some observers argue that the terrorist attacks on September 11, 2001, and the subsequent invasions of Afghanistan and Iraq, not to mention the increased resources devoted to homeland security, drove much of the spending growth. Defense spending accounted for about 56 percent of discretionary spending growth between 2001 and 2004. The rest went for increases in pork projects, corporate welfare, and various government programs that are far outside the realm of a properly limited government. Those programs were not vital to the defense of the United States, and it is very hard to argue that overall spending had to go up as much as it has across the board to fight the war on terrorism.

Figure 9.1
Real Discretionary Outlays: Defense and Nondefense

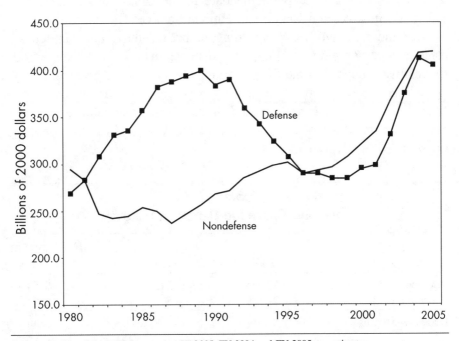

SOURCE: *Budget of the U.S. Government FY 2005.* FY 2004 and FY 2005 are estimates.

Some budget hawks argue that President Bush's tax cuts were a primary cause of the deficit. As it turns out, that's not true. A look at the numbers since 2000—the last year revenues posted a rise—shows that the revenue drop accounts for about 23 percent of the decline in federal finances. Indeed, revenue actually began to decline before most of the provisions of the Bush tax cut kicked in. There is no question that spending is driving the deficit: it accounts for 77 percent of the change (Table 9.1).

The main culprit is a culture of spending in Washington that has beaten the Republicans in Congress and the White House into submission. The class of Republican members of Congress who planned to aggressively cut government has lately presided over budget increases not seen since the days when "Tip" O'Neill and the Democrats controlled the House.

Indeed, Republicans in Congress over the past 10 years have completely lost their moorings on spending control. They originally promised to slash the federal budget to its bare essentials, but Leviathan is now substantially bigger than it was when they took control of the reins. In fact, by 2000—just six years after the 1994 electoral victory that came to be known as the Republican Revolution—95 of the largest programs they promised to eliminate had actually grown by 13 percent.

Four of the top five fastest growing agencies since fiscal 1995 are agencies that have no explicit mandate in the Constitution: Education, Labor, Commerce, and Health and Human Services (Figure 9.2).

Over the past two years, spending in both defense and nondefense categories grew rapidly. As Figure 9.1 depicts, this is quite a change from the relative prudence of the Reagan years when nondefense spending was cut to make room in the budget for the defense buildup of the 1980s. Indeed, it's even a change from the Clinton years, when defense spending was cut in the wake of the end of the Cold War and overall spending rates stayed relatively tame.

Table 9.1
Spending Drove the Deficit (in billions)

	2000	2004	Change in Dollars
Revenue	$2,025	$1,880	$154
Expenditures	$1,789	$2,293	$504
Deficit or Surplus	$236	−$413	$658

SOURCE: Author's calculations based on data from the Congressional Budget Office.

Figure 9.2
Growth in Outlays by Federal Department under the Republicans, FY1995–FY2004

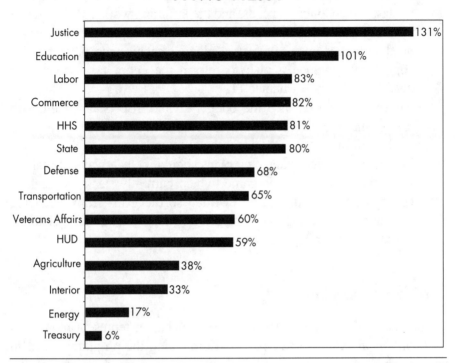

SOURCE: Veronique de Rugy, "The Republican Spending Explosion," Cato Institute Briefing Paper no. 87, March 3, 2004, p. 9.

To make matters worse, the Republican Congress and the Bush administration were able to do what no big-spending Democratic administration since Lyndon Johnson's has been able to do: pass the single biggest expansion to the Medicare program since its inception. The prescription drug benefit—debated on the floor of Congress under the false impression that it was going to cost $400 billion over 10 years, when the actual cost was closer to $534 billion—will only further damage the fiscal stability of the budget in the future.

Getting Out of the Mess

It is vital that Congress and the president get control of spending and reform increasingly expensive entitlement programs. Some ground rules need to be kept in mind:

1. Taxes should not be raised to balance the budget. As explained above, the problem is not that government is receiving too little money but that it is spending too much. More money to spend is the last thing Congress needs, and the last thing workers beleaguered by a complex tax code and an increasingly expensive tax burden need is higher taxes. In fact, a plan to balance the budget could conceivably include a plan to reform the entire tax system. For details on this, see Chapter 11.
2. Any attempt to balance the budget should also be an attempt to realign the priorities of the federal government and make it smaller while returning it to its constitutional boundaries.
3. Finally, any budget-balancing plans should include ways of making sure that the rules of the game, which currently stack the deck in favor of new spending, are rewritten so the gains from balancing the budget by cutting spending are not merely temporary victories but lasting contributions to fiscal restraint.

Cut Discretionary Spending

The cuts outlined in the Appendix to this chapter represent more than $350 billion in savings to taxpayers. Eliminating the programs listed in the Appendix from the federal budget—and keeping them out of the budget in the future—would balance the budget in five years. Not only would doing that allow the government to balance its books without raising taxes (indeed, it would balance the budget while simultaneously keeping intact all of President Bush's tax cuts), it would also show that Congress is serious about scaling back the role of the federal government.

Not all of the program terminations require the activities of the programs to disappear. Some of those government functions could be devolved to the state level. For instance, many of the Department of Transportation's (DOT's) activities are properly state and private-sector responsibilities. It makes no sense to collect gasoline taxes from citizens, send the money to Washington, then dole it back out to the states—minus the costs of the DOT bureaucracy (which has more than 100,000 full-time-equivalent employees) and its meddlesome rules. Moreover, Congress uses the DOT budget to deliver pork-barrel projects of dubious value. The federal government should end the federal gasoline tax and cease its highway, road, and mass transit spending functions. (For more on this subject, see Chapter 36.)

Even more savings can be found by privatizing federal assets and government-operated businesses. For instance, the federal government owns about one-third of the land in the United States and continues to accumulate more holdings. Yet only a fraction of federal land is of environmental significance, and the government has proven itself to be a poor land custodian. The process of federalizing the nation's land should be reversed by identifying low-priority holdings to sell back to citizens. In addition, numerous government-run enterprises, such as the U.S. Postal Service and Amtrak, could be run more efficiently by the private sector and should be privatized. For further information, see Chapter 33.

Reform Entitlement Programs

Social Security should be reformed to allow workers to invest a portion of their payroll taxes in accounts they own and control. See Chapter 4 for a plan to do just that. Medicare can be reformed through the widespread use of health savings accounts, and Medicaid spending can be frozen and the program block-granted to the states. (Reforms for Medicare and Medicaid are addressed in Chapter 8.)

Reject New Spending Programs if Unconstitutional

The U.S. Constitution confines federal spending authority to a few limited areas. Article I, section 8, allows for spending mainly on basic functions, such as establishing courts, punishing crime, and maintaining an army and navy. The General Welfare Clause in section 8 has been interpreted extremely broadly to provide a justification for much of today's federal spending. But much federal spending is not for the "general welfare" at all. It is for the benefit of particular groups and individuals. For example, corporate welfare spending is aimed at narrow interests, not the general interest. Members of Congress take an oath to uphold the Constitution. They should start taking that oath seriously. When a dubious program comes before them, they should ask whether there is proper constitutional authority for it.

Create a Federal "Sunset" Commission

To structure the process of terminating federal programs, Congress should establish a federal "sunset" commission. Sunsetting is the process of automatically terminating government agencies and programs after a period of time unless they are specifically reauthorized. One of the main problems today is that there are sunsets to tax cuts but not to spending programs. A sunset commission could review federal programs on a rotating basis and recommend major overhauls, privatization, or elimination.

Since the 1970s numerous state governments have adopted the sunset process, and it is currently used in about 16 states. In the late 1970s there was strong bipartisan support to pass a federal sunset law introduced by Sen. Edmund Muskie (D-ME) that would have sunset most federal programs every 10 years. Supporters at the time ranged from Sen. Jesse Helms (R-NC) to Sen. Edward Kennedy (D-MA). Although it gained strong support in the Senate, the legislative effort failed in the House.

Today, sunsetting is needed more than ever. There is no structured method to reform or terminate agencies when they no longer serve a public need or when better private alternatives become available. As a result, government agencies rarely disappear. For example, the Rural Utilities Service (formerly the Rural Electrification Administration) was created in the 1930s to bring electricity to rural homes. Virtually all American homes have had electricity for 20 years or more, yet the agency still survives. A sunset commission would make it much harder for such unjustifiable agencies to survive.

Changing the Budget Rules

Congress has done little to reform the budget rules that skew political decisionmaking in favor of ever-larger outlays. Now that the federal budget again has huge deficits, it is even clearer that lasting reforms to the budget process are needed. There has been much debate about which particular reforms would best restrain spending. But there is little to lose from experimenting with different budget control mechanisms, and any or all of the following reforms should be pursued.

Supermajority Tax Limitation Amendment

With a supermajority tax limitation, any tax increase would require a two-thirds vote in the House and Senate for passage. When the economy grows, federal tax revenues tend to grow faster than incomes, even without legislated increases. Given that automatic upward tax bias, taxpayers should be provided with the extra protection of such a limitation against legislative tax increases.

Zero-Based Budgeting

Zero-based budgeting would end the current practice of baseline budgeting. With baseline budgeting, most programs can exist on autopilot, since budgets are written to assume an expected growth rate in all government programs. The current system reinforces the ridiculous notion, for instance, that a 2 percent increase in spending can be called a "cut" if the expected baseline budget increase was supposed to be 3 percent. Zero-based budgeting would assume that every government program started the year with zero taxpayer money, and every program would have to justify its budget request from the bottom up.

Give the Budget Resolution the Force of Law

Currently, the budget resolution that outlines the budget "blueprint"—including the spending levels that both houses of Congress agree to at the beginning of each budget cycle—is mostly a symbolic document. That's because the Rules Committee in the House routinely exempts particular bills from the spending caps in the resolution. Thus, converting the present concurrent budget resolution into a joint budget resolution that requires a signature by the president would give the budget blueprint the force of law. The provisions in the budget blueprint, such as spending caps, would be harder to circumvent as a result.

Put Limits on "Emergency" Spending

So-called emergency spending is one of the biggest reasons for the budget bloat. Originally designed to modify the spending caps for genuine emergencies such as natural disasters or times of war, it has been abused dramatically over the last few years. For instance, in the 2000 budget the constitutionally mandated decennial Census was treated as an unexpected "emergency" expense. Between 1999 and 2002 the Congressional Budget Office estimates that Congress spent $154 billion on "emergencies," only a fraction of which can honestly be worthy of the distinction. Safeguards need to be put in place to keep the emergency clause from being abused. Creating a law that defines explicitly what can qualify as an emergency expense would go a long way toward remedying the problem.

Freeze "Advance" Appropriations

One of the games that Congress plays with the budget is shifting funding into a future budget to get around the spending caps. The abuse of this practice should end. Congress should be required to pay for all spending it intends to do in the year in which it intends to do it.

Require a Two-Thirds Majority to Waive Spending Caps

Currently, spending caps can be waived by a three-fifths majority. Although a two-thirds majority will not always keep a tight lid on spending, it would certainly make it harder for big spenders to ignore the fiscal restraint required by the rules of the budget process.

Enact a Tax and Expenditure Limitation

Although many of the budget process reforms listed above would make it harder for Congress to expand government without a few hurdles, they may not necessarily effectively limit government growth. An innovative way of doing that would be to enact a cap that restrains the growth of government spending each and every year. The cap would hold government spending to a growth pattern no faster than that of population plus inflation.

The experience of the states that have some sort of strong spending cap has been very positive. Colorado's innovative Taxpayer's Bill of Rights (TABOR) has been the most successful budget cap of them all. (For more information on the success of these limits, see Chapter 35.)

An upper limit on spending would create an incentive to reprioritize the federal government. If there is a spending ceiling that Congress can't overturn by a simple majority or ignore, cuts in nonessential programs become more feasible. Adding this limit to the constitution would ensure the strongest possible fiscal restraint, but it is not necessary. Some of the budget process rules discussed above could be successful in controlling spending if coupled with a TABOR-like proposal.

Conclusion

Bold reform is needed if Congress and the White House are serious about getting the federal government's fiscal house in order. Business as usual is not going to reduce the deficit or cut spending. Policymakers need to realize that the federal government does far more than it should. Cutting spending is only the first step. Reforming entitlements and changing the rules of the game are also vital.

Appendix: Proposed Program Terminations (FY2004 outlays in $millions)

Department of Agriculture
Economic Research Service	$71
National Agricultural Statistics Service	$124
Agricultural Research Service	$1,154
Cooperative State Research, Educ., and Extension Serv.	$1,082
Agricultural Marketing Service	$1,021
Risk Management Agency	$4,034
Farm Services Agency	$15,780
Rural Development	$1,043
Rural Housing Service	$1,549
Rural Business Cooperative Service	$107
Rural Utilities Service	$108
Foreign Agricultural Service	$1,917
Forest Service: Land Acquisition Programs	$154
Forest Service: State and Private Forestry	$455
Total Cuts to Department of Agriculture	$28,599

Department of Commerce
Economic Development Administration	$417
International Trade Administration	$364
Minority Business Development Agency	$22
Fisheries Loans and Marketing	$32
National Marine Fisheries Service	$754
Office of Oceanic and Atmospheric Research	$557
Advanced Technology Program	$195
Manufacturing Extension Program	$40
Other Nat. Inst. of Standards & Tech. Programs	$421
National Telecommunications & Info. Admin.	$104
Total Cuts to Department of Commerce	$2,906

Department of Defense (see Chapter 51)

Department of Education
Eliminate entire agency	$62,815

(continued next page)

(Appendix continued)

Department of Energy

General Science, Research, and Development	$3,405
Energy Supply	$714
Fossil Energy, Research and Development	$590
FreedomCAR	$246
Other Energy Conservation Programs	$636
Strategic Petroleum Reserve	$171
Energy Information Administration	$78
Clean Coal Technology	$19
Power Marketing Administration Subsidies	$155
Total Cuts to Department of Energy	$6,014

Department of Health and Human Services

Health Professions Education Subsidies	$409
National Health Service Corps	$170
Family Planning	$278
Healthy Start	$98
Community-based Abstinence Grants and Education	$95
Indian Health Service	$2,584
Substance Abuse and Mental Health Serv. Admin.	$3,133
Agency for Health Care Research and Quality	$327
Temporary Assistance for Needy Families	$18,866
Payments to States for Family Support Programs	$4,098
Low-Income Home Energy Assistance	$1,892
Promoting Safe and Stable Families	$414
National Institutes of Health: Applied R&D	$12,500
Child Care Entitlements to States	$2,866
Block Grants to States for Child Care and Dev.	$2,237
Social Services Block Grant	$1,767
Grants to States for Foster Care and Adoption	$6,442
Head Start	$6,775
Children and Families Services Faith-Based Centers	$1
Administration on Aging	$1,313
Total Cuts to Department of Health and Human Services	$66,265

Department of Housing and Urban Development
Eliminate entire agency $46,177

Department of Homeland Security
    State and Local Programs $3,768
    Firefighter Assistance Grants $399
    Transportation Security Administration $2,810
    Coast Guard—Boat Safety Grants $65
Total Cuts to Department of Homeland Security $7,042

Department of the Interior
    Bureau of Indian Affairs $2,180
    Bureau of Reclamation $1,234
    U.S. Geological Survey $840
    State and Tribal Wildlife Grants $65
    Sport Fish Restoration Fund $336
    Land Acquisition and State Assistance Programs $249
Total Cuts to Department of the Interior $4,904

Department of Justice
    Antitrust Investigations $133
    Juvenile Justice Programs $208
    Community Oriented Policing Services (COPS) $1,271
    State and Local Law Enforcement Assistance $1,516
    Weed and Seed Program $31
    Drug Enforcement Administration $1,642
Total Cuts to Department of Justice $4,801

Department of Labor
    Training & Employment Services $5,600
    Welfare to Work $181
    Community Service for Seniors $445
    Occupational Safety and Health Administration $456
    Trade Adjustment Assistance $770
    International Labor Affairs $110
Total Cuts to Department of Labor $7,562

(continued next page)

(Appendix continued)

Department of State/International Assistance Programs	
Education and Cultural Exchange Programs	$325
United Nations	$317
United Nations Peacekeeping Operations	$893
Inter-American Organizations	$129
Org. for Economic Cooperation & Dev. (OECD)	$82
Migration and Refugee Assistance	$782
Int. Narcotics Control & Law Enforcement	$520
Andean Counterdrug Initiative	$966
East-West Center	$20
Economic Support Fund	$3,760
Multilateral International Assistance	$2,632
Foreign Military Financing Program	$5,432
Foreign Military Sales	$3
Total Cuts to Department of State/International Assistance Programs	$15,861
Department of Transportation	
Eliminate entire agency	$58,010
Department of the Treasury	
Community Development Financial Institutions	$43
Total Cuts to Department of the Treasury	$43
Executive Office of the President	
Office of National Drug Control Policy	$27
Office of Science and Technology Policy	$7
Total Cuts to Executive Office of the President	$34
Other Agencies and Activities	
Accounting Oversight Board	$97
Agency for International Development	$4,613
Appalachian, Delta, Denali Commissions	$94
Cargo Preference Program	$443
Commission on Civil Rights	$9
Corporation for National and Community Service	$609

Corporation for Public Broadcasting	$437
Davis-Bacon Act	$1,100
Drug Control Programs	$500
Army Corps of Engineers	$4,308
Equal Employment Opportunity Commission	$325
Environmental Protection Agency	$8,129
FTC—Antitrust Enforcement	$82
International Military Training	$89
International Trade Commission	$60
Legal Services Corporation	$341
Millennium Challenge Corporation	$298
Military Bases (excess facilities)	$5,000
NASA	$14,604
National Endowment for the Arts (NEA)	$118
National Endowment for the Humanities (NEH)	$132
National Labor Relations Board	$242
National Mediation Board	$11
Neighborhood Reinvestment Corp.	$114
Peace Corps	$302
Selective Service System	$26
Service Contract Act	$610
Small Business Administration	$3,978
Trade and Development Agency	$62
U.S. Postal Service Subsidies	$60
Total Cuts to Other Agencies and Activities	$46,793
Total Proposed Budget Savings	$357,826

Suggested Readings

Coburn, Tom, with John Hart. *Breach of Trust: How Washington Turns Outsiders into Insiders*. Nashville, TN: WND Books, 2003.

Congressional Budget Office. "A 125-Year Picture of the Federal Government's Share of the Economy, 1950 to 2075." July 3, 2002. www.cbo.gov.

de Rugy, Veronique. "The Republican Spending Explosion." Cato Institute Briefing Paper no. 87, March 3, 2004.

Edwards, Chris. "Downsizing the Federal Government." Cato Institute Policy Analysis no. 515, June 2, 2004.

———. "Sunsetting to Reform and Abolish Federal Agencies." Cato Institute Tax & Budget Bulletin no. 6, May 2002.

Gokhale, Jagadeesh, and Kent Smetters. *Fiscal and Generational Imbalances: New Budget Measures for New Budget Priorities*. Washington: American Enterprise Institute, 2003.

Moore, Stephen, and Stephen Slivinski. "The Return of the Living Dead: Federal Programs That Survived the Republican Revolution." Cato Institute Policy Analysis no. 375, July 24, 2000.

—Prepared by Stephen Slivinski

10. "Starving the Beast" Will Not Work

Congress should

- *not* expect a reduction of federal revenues to reduce federal spending and
- continue to reduce the most distortive federal tax rates but accept the responsibility to reduce federal spending as a necessary complement to the reduction in tax revenues.

For nearly three decades, many conservatives and libertarians have argued that reducing federal tax rates, in addition to increasing long-term economic growth, would reduce the growth of federal spending by "starving the beast." That position has been endorsed by, among others, Nobel laureates Milton Friedman and Gary Becker in *Wall Street Journal* columns in 2003.

Friedman summarized this perspective as follows:

> . . . how can we ever cut government down to size? I believe there is one and only one way: the way parents control spendthrift children, cutting their allowance. For governments, that means cutting taxes. Resulting deficits will be an effective—I would go as far as to say, the only effective—restraint on the spending propensities of the executive branch and the legislature. The public reaction will make that restraint effective.

Becker and his colleagues describe this effect as "The Double Benefit of Tax Cuts."

There are two problems with this perspective. The first is that this perspective has *not* been consistent with the evidence, at least since the late 1970s.

In a brief note in a professional book that was published in 2002, I presented evidence that the relative level of federal spending from 1981 through 2000 was coincident with the relative level of the federal tax

113

burden in the *opposite* direction; in other words, there was a strong *negative* relation between the concurrent relative levels of federal spending and tax revenues during this period, as illustrated by Figure 10.1. Controlling for the unemployment rate, the federal spending share of GDP *declined* by about 0.5 times the increase in the federal revenue share of GDP.

What is going on? The most direct interpretation of this relation is that it represents a demand curve—that the demand for federal spending by current voters declines with the amount of that spending financed by current taxes. Future voters will bear the burden of any resulting deficit but are apparently not effectively represented by those making the current fiscal choices.

Figure 10.1
Federal Spending and Revenue as a Percent of GDP
1981 through 2000

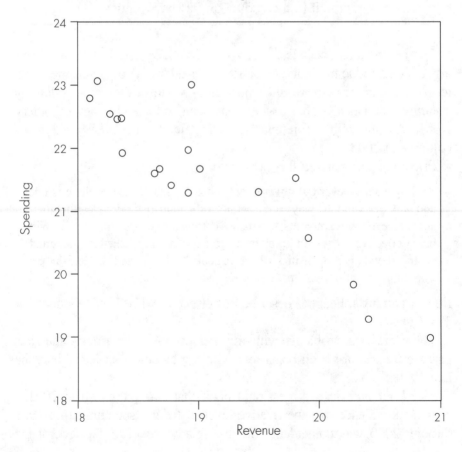

An update of this test confirms that there was a significant negative relation between the relative levels of federal spending and tax revenues (lagged one year) for the 25 years from 1979 through 2003, again controlling for the unemployment rate. An estimate of this equation for the prior 25 years from 1954 through 1978 also indicated a negative relation between the relative level of federal spending and tax revenues (again, lagged one year) but one that was not statistically significant. For no extended period did these estimates reveal a significant positive relation between the relative level of federal spending and tax revenues, the necessary condition for the "starve the beast" hypothesis to be confirmed.

At the limit, of course, the "starve the beast" hypothesis must be correct; there must be some maximum tolerable deficit that would force Congress to reduce spending by an amount equal to any reduction in tax revenues. The evidence of the above tests, however, is that there has been no such effective limit in the past 50 years.

The second problem is that the "starve the beast" perspective has led too many conservatives and libertarians to be casual about the sustained political discipline necessary to control federal spending directly, succumbing to the fantasy that tax cuts would solve this problem. President George W. Bush, for example, has proposed and won the approval of most congressional Republicans for large increases in federal spending for agriculture, defense, education, energy, homeland security, Medicare, and transportation, and he has yet to veto a single spending bill. As a consequence, real per capita federal spending during the Bush administration increased at the highest rate since the Johnson administration.

The political discipline necessary to control federal spending must involve a sustained commitment to principle. Members of the administration and Congress must increasingly ask *why* federal taxpayers should finance some program, rather than only how or how much. The necessary discipline requires that members of Congress address the following questions in both the authorizing and appropriation processes: Does the Constitution include explicit authority for the program or activity? Is the federal government better qualified to perform the activity than state and local governments or the private sector? Is the proposed federal activity the best of alternative ways to accomplish the shared goal? Is the marginal benefit of the federal activity higher than the marginal cost to the economy of the taxes necessary to finance the activity? A negative answer to any of those questions should be sufficient to reduce or eliminate the activity, whether it is among those already funded or those proposed. Other chapters of this *Cato Handbook* identify numerous current federal programs or activities that should be reduced or eliminated on the basis of one or more of these criteria. A focus on domestic discretionary spending other than for homeland security will not be enough; such spending is now only 18 percent of total outlays and includes much of the spending that benefits specific districts and is especially protected by members of Congress.

Conclusion

Above all, keep in mind that the size of government is best measured by the level of spending and regulation, not by the level of taxes. Reducing tax revenues without a commensurate reduction of federal spending only shifts part of the burden of current government spending to future generations—including *your* children and grandchildren.

Suggested Readings

Becker, Gary S., Edward O. Lazear, and Kevin M. Murphy. "The Double Benefit of Tax Cuts." *Wall Street Journal*, October 7, 2003.
Edwards, Christopher. "Downsizing the Federal Government." Cato Institute Policy Analysis no. 515, June 2, 2004.
Friedman, Milton. "What Every American Wants." *Wall Street Journal*, January 2003.
Niskanen, William A. "Comment." In *American Economic Policy in the 1990s*. Edited by Jeffrey A. Frankel and Peter R. Orszag. Cambridge, MA: MIT Press, 2002.

—Prepared by William A. Niskanen

11. Federal Tax Reform

Congress should

- make permanent the tax cuts enacted in 2001 and 2003, including the income tax rate reductions and dividend and capital gains tax cuts;
- reenact the 50 percent expensing provision for business investment that was established in 2003;
- repeal the estate tax permanently;
- repeal the individual and corporate alternative minimum taxes (AMTs);
- turn Roth individual retirement accounts (IRAs) into large, all-purpose savings accounts available to every family by repealing withdrawal restrictions and liberalizing contribution and income limits;
- simplify the tax code by combining further rate cuts with the elimination of social engineering provisions, such as education and homeowner tax breaks; and
- replace the income tax with a low-rate consumption-based tax—either a Hall-Rabushka flat tax, a consumed-income tax, a national retail sales tax, or another tax that is flat, neutral, and simple.

The Burden of Taxes

At the beginning of the 20th century, federal taxes accounted for 3 percent of the nation's gross domestic product, and the tax code and related regulations filled just a few hundred pages. Today, federal taxes account for 17 percent of GDP, rising to 20 percent of GDP by 2014 if recent tax cuts expire as scheduled. According to CCH Inc., federal tax rules and regulations spanned 60,044 pages in 2004—48 percent more pages than when the Republicans took over Congress in 1995.

The extraction of $2 trillion in federal taxes from families and businesses each year comes at an enormous cost. The most obvious cost is that Americans are left with less money to meet their needs for food, clothing, housing, and other items, and businesses are left with fewer funds to invest and build the economy.

In addition, the tax system imposes large compliance burdens and "deadweight losses" on the economy. *Compliance burdens* are the time and administrative costs of dealing with the tax system's rules and paperwork. *Deadweight losses* are created by taxes distorting the market economy by changing relative prices and altering the behavior of workers, investors, businesses, and entrepreneurs.

Consider a working woman who is considering launching a small business on the side to earn more income. If the government raises marginal tax rates and dissuades her from those entrepreneurial plans, the nation loses the production and innovative ideas that she could have added to the economy.

Such economic damage increases more than proportionally as marginal tax rates rise. In particular, deadweight losses rise by the square of the tax wedge between pre- and posttax income. For example, a doubling of the tax wedge causes deadweight losses to quadruple. That is why a flatter tax structure with lower marginal rates would be much more efficient than the highly graduated rate structure that we have today.

In sum, every new $1 million government program costs taxpayers much more than $1 million. In addition to direct tax costs of $1 million, taxpayers are burdened by higher compliance costs and deadweight losses. Estimates of the size of deadweight losses vary, but generally each added dollar of income tax revenue creates a loss to the economy of 25 cents or more. Harvard professors Martin Feldstein and Daniel Feenberg estimated that the Bush tax cut in 2001 reduced deadweight losses by 38 cents for each dollar of the tax cut. Another Harvard professor, Dale Jorgenson, figures that deadweight losses of the income tax system are 35 cents on each added tax dollar and estimates that switching to a consumption-based tax system would reduce that burden substantially.

Congress should cut the overall size of the federal government to reduce these tax burdens. But even given the current level of federal taxes, the tax system can be redesigned to increase economic growth by reducing deadweight losses and compliance costs. The following sections look at key problems of the income tax and reforms that would create a simpler, fairer, and more efficient system.

Income Tax Complexity

In 1976 president-to-be Jimmy Carter called for "a complete overhaul of our income tax system. I feel it's a disgrace to the human race." Since Carter's attack, the number of pages of federal tax rules has roughly tripled. More recently, President Bush's first treasury secretary, Paul O'Neill, called the tax code an "abomination." Unfortunately, policymakers have done little to fix the problem, and Table 11.1 shows that complexity has risen in recent years.

The following are five types of costs created by the income tax's excessive complexity.

1. Compliance and Enforcement Burdens

Americans spend 6.5 billion hours annually filling out tax forms, keeping records, and learning tax rules, according to the Office of Management and Budget. A huge public and private "tax industry" is needed to administer, plan, and enforce the complex system, requiring the efforts of some of the smartest people in the country. The costs of complying with federal income taxes are roughly $200 billion per year. In addition to the costs of filing tax returns, taxpayers face the burden from audits, notices, liens, levies, seizures, and the 30 million penalties assessed each year by the IRS. Those burdens fall on individuals both directly and indirectly through the costs imposed on businesses. For example, the paperwork for a large corporation's tax return can run more than 10,000 pages. All Americans would gain if businesses spent less time on such paperwork and more time creating good products.

2. Errors

Tax complexity causes taxpayers and the IRS to make frequent and costly errors. The IRS routinely gets up to half the answers to taxpayer phone inquiries wrong. The problem is that Congress has filled the tax code with complex features such as the Earned Income Tax Credit. Almost one-third of EITC payments—about $9 billion annually—are erroneous. These EITC errors occur despite a big effort by the IRS to fix the problem with a special $200 million annual budget allocation.

Table 11.1
Rising Tax Complexity

Item	Initial Year	Recent Year
a) Total pages of federal tax rules	1995 40,500	2004 60,044
b) Number of IRS tax forms	2000 475	2004 529
c) Number of income tax loopholes for education and training	1994 16	2004 28
d) Percent of taxpayers using paid tax preparers	1995 50%	2003 62%
e) H&R Block U.S. tax preparation revenues	1996 $740 million	2003 $1.9 billion
f) Hours Americans spend filling out tax forms	1995 5.3 billion	2004 6.5 billion
g) Pages in Form 1040 instruction book	1995 84	2003 131
h) Average time to complete Form 1040 and Schs. A, B, D.	1995 21.2 hours	2003 28.5 hours

SOURCE: Author, based on
  a) CCH Inc. Includes tax code, regulations, and IRS rulings.
  b) IRS, Tax Forms and Publications Division.
  c) Author's count of official "tax expenditures."
  d) National Taxpayers Union.
  e) H&R Block. Annual reports for various years.
  f) Office of Management and Budget, "Information Collection Budget."
  g) National Taxpayers Union.
  h) National Taxpayers Union.

3. Decisionmaking Complications

Tax complexity impedes efficient decisionmaking by families and businesses. For example, the growing number of saving vehicles under the income tax greatly confuses family financial planning. If a family makes the wrong savings choice, it could result in lower returns, less liquidity, and payment of withdrawal penalties. Saving would be vastly simplified under a consumption-based tax.

For businesses, the complex and always changing income tax rules inject uncertainty into decisions such as those about capital investment.

Major tax laws can alter hundreds of tax provisions causing a flood of changes to tax forms, tax regulations, and IRS guidance notices. More complexity means more errors for everyone in the tax industry and more disputes between taxpayers and the IRS. Audits, appeals, and litigation over disputed business tax items can drag on for years.

4. Inequity and Unfairness

Although equality under the law is a bedrock American principle, individuals pay greatly different tax rates under the income tax. For example, IRS data for 2002 show that income taxes averaged 26.2 percent of adjusted gross income for those earning more than $200,000, but 10.5 percent for those earning between $50,000 and $100,000. Joint Tax Committee data for 2003 show that 60 million of 152 million U.S. households paid no income tax at all.

Even people with similar incomes are treated unequally by the tax code as a result of special exemptions, deductions, and credits. As Congress has added more special preferences for favored groups, inequities have increased. Tax incentives for education, home ownership, alternative fuels, and other items unfairly favor some Americans over others. Special tax breaks should be repealed and overall tax rates reduced.

5. Avoidance and Evasion

Tax complexity leads to greater noncompliance with the tax system. That stems partly from greater taxpayer confusion. But complexity also fosters multiple interpretations of the law, thereby stimulating more aggressive tax planning. Taxpayers take risks on their tax returns in the hope that complexity will hide their strategies from the IRS. The economy would be better off if tax rules were simple and transparent so that taxpayers focused on productive endeavors, rather than on playing cat-and-mouse games with the IRS.

Income Tax Bias against Saving

Saving is a key source of economic growth because it provides businesses with the investment funds they need to expand and modernize the nation's capital stock. The income tax system taxes saving and investment but not current consumption, which creates a damaging bias that reduces economic growth. Also, the income tax system applies different tax burdens to different forms of savings and investment, thus complicating and distorting economic decisionmaking.

To solve those problems, all recent tax reform proposals would switch from an income tax base to a consumption tax base. That would remove the bias against saving, and it would create neutrality between different forms of savings and investment. The nation's saving would increase and investment would flow to the highest-valued uses in the economy. For individuals, a consumption-based tax would make saving simpler and more lucrative. With greater savings, families would be more financially secure and could rely less on government safety nets.

Different consumption tax reform plans would treat saving similar to either regular IRAs or Roth IRAs. In the first case, initial saving is deducted but withdrawals from saving are taxed. Reform proposals for a "consumed-income" or "saving-deferred" tax would treat all saving this way. In the second case, no deduction is given for initial saving but withdrawals are tax-free. The Hall-Rabushka "flat tax" adopts this treatment by taxing wages but exempting individuals from taxes on dividends, interest, and capital gains. To move toward tax reform, current Roth IRAs could be expanded into large, all-purpose savings accounts, similar to the Hall-Rabushka approach.

Short-Term Reforms

Make the Income Tax Rate Cuts Permanent

In 2001 Congress enacted the Economic Growth and Tax Relief Reconciliation Act based on President Bush's tax reduction plan. That act took a number of positive steps, including reducing individual statutory tax rates, liberalizing the tax rules on savings vehicles, and taking steps toward estate tax repeal. However, those provisions are set to expire at the end of 2010, thus creating the possibility of a massive tax hike in 2011. To avert such a tax shock, Congress should extend the 2001 tax cuts permanently.

Make the Capital Expensing Reforms Permanent

To spur economic growth, Congress enacted a business tax cut in 2002 that allowed companies to "expense" (or immediately deduct) 30 percent of the cost of qualified capital purchases. In the Jobs and Growth Tax Relief Reconciliation Act of 2003, Congress increased the expensing provision to 50 percent and extended it to the end of 2004. The 2003 act also increased the limit for small business capital expensing. Small businesses may now immediately deduct up to $100,000 of qualified investments. Those provisions should be made permanent to create sustained growth in business investment. Consumption-based tax plans, such as the Hall-Rabushka flat tax and the Simplified USA tax of Rep. Phil English (R-PA), incorporate 100 percent expensing for all capital investment.

Make the Dividend and Capital Gains Tax Cuts Permanent

The 2003 tax law cut the maximum capital gains tax rate from 20 to 15 percent and the maximum tax rate on dividends from 35 to 15 percent. Those tax cuts, which are set to expire at the end of 2008, should be made permanent as part of a general policy of reducing taxes on capital income. Most major nations have cut capital income taxes in recent years, but the United States has lagged behind (see Chapter 13). Before the 2003 tax cut, the United States had the second-highest tax burden on dividends among the 30 OECD countries, taking into account both corporate and individual taxes. The United States also lags behind the reform leaders on capital gains taxation. Austria, Belgium, the Czech Republic, Germany, Greece, Hong Kong, Mexico, the Netherlands, New Zealand, Poland, and Switzerland all have a tax rate of zero on individual capital gains, although holding periods and other conditions apply in some countries.

Expand Roth IRAs into Universal Savings Accounts

One approach to reducing taxes on savings would be to liberalize the rules on Roth IRAs. Contributions to Roth IRAs are from after-tax earnings, but qualified withdrawals are tax-free. Contribution limits on Roth IRAs were recently liberalized, but further reforms could revolutionize saving in America. The key is to repeal the Roth IRA restrictions on withdrawals. Currently, individuals face a 10 percent penalty on most withdrawals prior to retirement. The result is that the liquidity of IRAs is reduced and families are dissuaded from using the accounts for fear that they may need their money before retirement. This restriction especially affects moderate-income families, who may decide not to use IRAs at all so as to keep their savings in more liquid form.

Roth IRAs should be turned into all-purpose savings accounts that allow withdrawals for any reason, not just for purposes specified by the government. That was the idea behind the Bush administration's Lifetime Savings Accounts proposal. Such accounts would encourage families to build up larger pools of savings that could be used for any contingency, such as medical expenses, home buying, unemployment, college, or unexpected crises. All personal savings—not just retirement savings—creates greater individual financial stability and thus should be encouraged. Universal savings accounts would also simplify the tax code because the plethora of current special purpose accounts could be phased out.

Repeal the Estate Tax

The 2001 tax law repealed the federal estate tax, but only for the single year of 2010. After 2010 the "death tax" returns in full force with a top tax rate of 55 percent. The estate tax raises only about 1 percent of federal revenues, but it is very costly to the economy. The chairman of the Council on Economic Advisers, Greg Mankiw, noted at a November 2003 Treasury conference that as a tax on savings, the estate tax suppresses growth and reduces average workers' wages. He concluded that "the repeal of the estate tax would stimulate growth and raise incomes for everyone."

The estate tax is probably the most inefficient tax in America. It has created a huge and wasteful estate-planning industry to help wealthy Americans avoid the tax if they hire enough lawyers and accountants. Studies indicate that for every dollar raised by the tax, roughly one dollar is lost to avoidance, compliance, and enforcement costs.

In addition, the estate tax may not actually raise any money for the government, as noted at the Treasury conference by Mankiw. The tax has the effect of suppressing income tax collections, thus offsetting estate tax receipts. Mankiw concluded that "estate tax repeal . . . could actually increase total federal revenue." Congress should complete the job it started and permanently repeal the estate tax.

Enact Simplification Measures

Nearly every member of Congress expresses concern about income tax complexity but puts little effort into actually simplifying the code. One place to start would be the Joint Committee on Taxation's 1,300-page report from 2001 that proposed more than 100 simplification reforms, including repeal of the corporate and individual AMTs. Congress should take seriously the proposals of its own experts at the JCT and enact those reforms.

Further progress could be made by assembling groups of narrow tax breaks to eliminate in a reform package that included substantial tax rate cuts. For example, education incentives, energy tax breaks, and the mortgage interest deduction could be repealed in combination with a large cut to middle-income tax rates.

124

Certainly, Congress should not pass laws that make the tax code more complex. Yet that seems to be the fate of the Foreign Sales Corporation/ Extraterritorial Income Exclusion tax legislation. The original FSC/ETI bill from Ways and Means chairman Bill Thomas (R-CA) would have simplified the complex tax rules on corporate foreign investments. But by the end of the 108th Congress, House and Senate versions of the bill were massive pieces of legislation that would add new complexities to the code. Congress should start from scratch and simply repeal the FSC/ ETI tax break and enact a substantial corporate tax rate cut.

Repeal the Alternative Minimum Tax

The corporate and individual AMTs are complex income tax systems that operate parallel to the ordinary income tax. There is broad agreement that the AMTs should be repealed since they serve no economic purpose. Indeed, the corporate AMT adds distortions and uncertainty to business decisionmaking. AMT repeal has been recommended by the JCT and the American Bar Association. Former IRS national taxpayer advocate Val Oveson called the AMT ''absolutely, asininely stupid.'' Under JCT projections, 30 million taxpayers will be subject to the ''asinine'' individual AMT by 2010 unless Congress acts to repeal it.

Continue Reforming the Tax Policy Process

When Congress considers raising or cutting taxes, changes in federal revenues are estimated by the JCT. Those estimates are very important in policy debates, yet they are often erroneous and incomplete. A key problem is that JCT revenue estimates have traditionally been ''static,'' meaning that they do not take into account the effects that tax changes have on the macroeconomy. If marginal tax rates are cut, for example, the economy will grow and generate a partially offsetting increase in federal revenues. Such macroeconomic feedbacks are captured in ''dynamic'' estimates of tax changes.

In recent years, the JCT (and the Congressional Budget Office) has begun to modernize its tax-estimating apparatus, and some recent analyses have included macroeconomic modeling results. Economic modeling should be made a routine part of the tax policy process. One benefit would be to help members of Congress understand that tax changes are not just about gaining and losing money for the budget; they can create substantial impacts on the economy.

Other aspects of the tax policy process also need reform. The estimating techniques used by government economists should be opened to peer review. In addition, the traditional presentation of tax estimation results in the form of "distributional" tables should be reexamined to ensure fairness and accuracy.

Cut Spending

Although President Bush and Congress have enacted some important tax cuts in recent years, they have let federal spending and the deficit soar. Federal outlays rose 31 percent under President Bush between FY01 and FY05. That has become a hurdle to future tax reforms because some policymakers will use the resulting deficit as an excuse to oppose tax cuts and to support tax increases. Chapter 9 describes how to restrain and reduce federal spending.

Fundamental Tax Reform

Raising the bulk of federal revenue from a broad-based income tax was a historic mistake. It has led to excessive complexity, multiple economic distortions, and a reduction in U.S. economic growth. To correct those problems, fundamental tax reform proposals would replace the income tax with a low-rate consumption-based system.

The difference between an income and a consumption-based tax is the treatment of saving and investment. The federal income tax is loosely based on a broad measure of income economists call Haig-Simons income. Taxing Haig-Simons income means imposing a heavy tax burden on saving and investment. For example, a full Haig-Simons-based tax would tax all capital gains accrued on paper every year, whether or not those gains were actually received by taxpayers. It would also tax items that individuals would not normally think of as income, such as the implicit rent received from owning one's home and the buildup of wealth in life insurance policies.

A few decades ago, many tax policy experts supported taxing such an expansive Haig-Simons income base. Yet there is no good economic argument for such a tax base. For example, the accrual taxation of capital gains would result in inefficient double taxation. (A rise in an asset's projected future return creates an immediate capital gains tax, which comes on top of taxes that will be paid when the asset generates income in the future.) The attraction of a Haig-Simons income tax base stemmed mainly from the egalitarian impulse to impose a heavy load of taxation on those with high incomes.

Today, there is much greater understanding that income-based taxes are both economically damaging and cannot be made simple. The current income tax relies on a huge array of ad hoc rules. Current tax law has no consistent standard for what constitutes income or when it should be taxed. Capital gains are treated on a realization basis, which creates planning difficulties for investors who must optimally time asset sales and try to offset gains with losses. Also, inflation wreaks havoc with income taxes by making capital gains, depreciation, and other items difficult to measure properly.

A consumption-based tax would be much simpler than the current income-based system, as summarized in Table 11.2. For example, capital gains taxation would be eliminated, as would depreciation deductions. Also, inflation is not a problem for consumption-based taxes. After 90 years of struggling with the complex and unstable income tax, it is time for America to try a different tax base. A consumption-based tax would be simpler, more transparent, and more favorable to economic growth.

Tax Reform Options

To replace the individual and corporate income taxes with a low-rate consumption-based tax, Congress can begin by enacting the short-term reforms listed above. At the same time, it should start considering consumption-based proposals, including the flat tax, a national retail sales tax, a consumed-income tax, and other ideas.

The flat tax was originally proposed by Robert Hall and Alvin Rabushka of the Hoover Institution and was most recently championed by former house majority leader Dick Armey. Leading retail sales tax proposals have included a plan by Rep. Billy Tauzin (R-LA) to replace individual and corporate income taxes with a 15 percent retail sales tax and Rep. John Linder's (R-GA) FairTax plan to replace those taxes plus federal payroll taxes with a 23 percent sales tax.

Other ideas include the Simplified USA tax of Rep. Phil English (R-PA) and the Inflow-Outflow tax plan of the Institute for Research on the Economics of Taxation. Rep. Jim DeMint (R-SC) introduced a plan that would replace the corporate income tax with a 9 percent consumption-based tax and the individual income tax with a 9 percent retail sales tax.

All those plans would reduce taxes on saving and investment. They would, however, differ in their mechanics and pose tradeoffs with regard to administration, simplicity, and civil liberties. Table 11.2 summarizes the advantages of a Hall-Rabushka flat tax, but similar gains could be achieved under other low-rate consumption-based systems.

Table 11.2.
Advantages of a Low-Rate Consumption-Based Tax
A Hall-Rabushka flat tax compared to the income tax

Advantages for Individuals

Low marginal tax rate: A consumption-based tax with a low rate would increase incentives for working, saving, and entrepreneurship. Many small businesses and the self-employed would face a lower marginal tax rate, spurring growth and investment.

Interest and dividends: Interest and dividends would not be taxed at the individual level. That would make saving simpler, enhance financial privacy, and increase incentives for families to save for retirement and other needs. Half a billion 1099s and other IRS forms would be eliminated. The tax code's complex and distortionary treatment of interest, such as the municipal bond preference, would be eliminated.

Capital gains: Capital gains taxation—perhaps the most complex part of the tax code—would be eliminated. Investor decisions would not be distorted by such capital gains issues as the timing of realizations, matching gains with losses, and calculating basis. Ending gains taxation would stimulate the birth and expansion of entrepreneurial growth companies, which rely on investors who earn returns through capital gains.

Savings vehicles: The current plethora of savings vehicles, including pensions, 401(k)s, and IRAs, would be phased out as tax hurdles to all types of savings were removed. Retirement would become individually based, ending the risks of being tied to company plans. Families could save for their own reasons, not just for reasons favored by Congress. Families could save as much as they wanted, would not have complex restrictions on their saving choices, and could withdraw their savings tax-free.

Social engineering: Social engineering through the tax code would end, and fairness would increase as tax provisions that favored narrow groups were eliminated. All taxpayers would face a simple, fair, and neutral tax system.

Advantages for Businesses

Low marginal tax rate: Lower corporate and small business tax rates would provide increased incentives for hiring and investment. A low corporate rate would make the United States a magnet for foreign investment inflows. A low tax rate would also reduce tax avoidance and evasion efforts and kill the wasteful corporate tax shelter industry. Compliance and enforcement costs of the tax system would fall.

Capital income: All types of capital income would receive the same neutral treatment and be taxed only once. Structural distortions, such as the tax bias in favor of corporate debt financing, would be eliminated. Tax rates across industries and asset types would be equalized.

Depreciation: All capital investment would be immediately expensed, thus ending the complex and distortionary depreciation rules. Business investment would increase, leading to higher productivity and rising wages across the economy. A consumption-based tax would also eliminate other rules for the capitalization of assets, such as the complicated business inventory rules.

Capital gains: Elimination of corporate capital gains taxation would simplify business reorganizations and reduce distortions such as the "lock-in" of investment holdings. Ending capital gains taxation would mean that a main building block of corporate tax shelters would disappear.

Inflation: Distortions caused by inflation under the income tax for such items as depreciation, inventory, and capital gains would be eliminated under a consumption-based tax.

International tax rules: Under a consumption-based tax, businesses would be taxed on a territorial basis, thus eliminating many complex tax rules, such as the foreign tax credit. A territorial business tax would make the United States a great place to locate the headquarters of multinational corporations, thus spurring high-end job creation.

Business types: All businesses would be taxed under the same rules, thus ending the different rules for C and S corporations, LLCs, sole proprietorships, and partnerships. Business reorganizations would be simpler and opportunities for tax sheltering reduced.

Conclusion

Consumption-based tax proposals have gained widespread support because they would simplify the tax code and spur greater economic growth. Given the nine-decade reign of the income tax, it is surprising what a weak case there is for it compared with a consumption-based tax. In congressional testimony a few years ago, the former chairman of the Council of Economic Advisers, Glenn Hubbard, called the income tax "fundamentally flawed" because of its inefficiency, complexity, and unfairness.

Major tax reform will move back onto the Washington agenda for a number of reasons. First, tax complexity continues to spiral upward and the AMT will soon be hitting 30 million American households, which will create demands for change. Second, the corporate income tax is headed for a train wreck as other countries continue to cut their tax rates and global investment capital becomes ever more mobile. A U.S. response to rising global tax competition is needed.

Third, the last decade of tax policy debate has shown that tax cuts and tax reform ideas are very popular with the public. The tax reform ingredient that is needed right now is a bipartisan group of congressional leaders to move ahead with reforms. In the 1980s tax reform was a bipartisan concern. For example, Democrats Dennis DeConcini of Arizona and Leon Panetta of California introduced versions of the then-new Hall-Rabushka flat tax in Congress in 1982. Forward-thinking Democrats and Republicans need to work together to cut the high and rising burden of taxes by scrapping the income tax and adopting a simple and low-rate consumption-based system.

Suggested Readings

Adams, Charles. *Those Dirty Rotten Taxes: The Tax Revolts That Built America.* New York: Free Press, 1998.

Bradford, David. *Untangling the Income Tax.* Cambridge, MA: Harvard University Press, 1999.

Burton, David. "Reforming the Federal Tax Policy Process." Cato Institute Policy Analysis no. 463, December 17, 2002.

Burton, David, and Dan R. Mastromarco. "Emancipating America from the Income Tax: How a National Sales Tax Would Work." Cato Institute Policy Analysis no. 272, April 15, 1997.

Edwards, Chris. "Dividend Tax Cuts: U.S. Has the Second Highest Rate." Cato Institute Tax & Budget Bulletin no. 12, January 2003.

———. "Replacing the Scandal-Plagued Corporate Income Tax with a Cash-Flow Tax." Cato Institute Policy Analysis no. 484, August 14, 2003.

———. "Simplifying Federal Taxes: The Advantages of Consumption-Based Taxation." Cato Institute Policy Analysis no. 416, October 17, 2001.

Hall, Robert, and Alvin Rabushka. *The Flat Tax.* 2d ed. Stanford, CA: Hoover Institution Press, 1995.

Kotlikoff, Laurence J. "The Economic Impact of Replacing Federal Income Taxes with a Sales Tax." Cato Institute Policy Analysis no. 193, April 15, 1993.

McCaffery, Edward. "Grave Robbers: The Case against the Death Tax." Cato Institute Policy Analysis no. 353, October 4, 1999.

Metcalf, Gilbert. "The National Sales Tax: Who Bears the Burden?" Cato Institute Policy Analysis no. 289, December 8, 1997.

Moore, Stephen, and John Silvia. "The ABCs of the Capital Gains Tax." Cato Institute Policy Analysis no. 242, October 4, 1995.

—Prepared by Chris Edwards

12. Fiscal Federalism

Congress should

- begin terminating the 716 federal grant programs that provide state and local governments with more than $400 billion annually for education, housing, community development, and other nonfederal responsibilities;
- turn Medicaid into a block grant as a first step to cutting the explosive spending growth in this federal-state program; and
- eliminate federal highway and transit funding and repeal the federal gasoline tax that funds these transportation programs.

Introduction

The federal government was designed to have specific limited powers, with most basic government functions left to the states. The Tenth Amendment to the Constitution states this clearly: "The powers not delegated to the United States by the Constitution, nor prohibited by it to the states, are reserved to the states respectively, or to the people." But during recent decades, the federal government has undertaken a large number of activities that were traditionally and constitutionally reserved to the states.

The primary mechanism that the federal government has used to extend its power into state affairs is grants to state and local governments ("grants-in-aid"). In FY04 federal grants totaling $418 billion were to be paid out to lower levels of government for a huge range of activities including health care, transportation, housing, and education. Grants to state and local governments increased from 7.6 percent of total federal outlays in FY60 to 18.0 percent in FY04.

The federal grant structure is massive and complex. One can get a sense of the complexity of the grant-making apparatus by examining the 1,800-

page "Catalog of Federal Domestic Assistance" at www.cfda.gov. The CFDA details 716 different federal grant programs aimed at state and local governments. Grant programs range from the giant $177 billion Medicaid to hundreds of more obscure programs that most taxpayers have never heard of. The CFDA lists a $10 million grant program for "Nursing Workforce Diversity" and a $59 million program for "Boating Safety Financial Assistance." One Environmental Protection Agency program hands out $25,000 grants to local governments for projects that "raise awareness" about environmental issues.

Since they were expanded greatly in the 1960s, federal grants to state and local governments have proven to be a terribly wasteful way of providing government services to Americans. Congress should begin large-scale cuts to federal grants.

Grants Are Good Politics but Bad Economics

The increase in federal grants in recent decades has occurred because of political logic, not economic logic. Federal grants have allowed the federal government to sidestep concerns about expansion of its powers over traditional state activities. By using grants, federal politicians can become activists in areas such as education, while overcoming state concerns about encroachment on their power by shoveling cash into state coffers.

Support for grants—and support for centralization of government power in Washington in general—comes from policymakers who favor funding government through the heavily graduated federal income tax system, rather than through the more proportional state tax systems.

Support also comes from those who think that the federal government should redistribute income from rich to poor regions of the country. But such geographic redistributions are neither constitutionally nor economically sound. Besides, politics usually undermines the goal of taking from rich regions and giving to poor regions. Although the initial goal of a grant program may be to aid poor areas, every member of Congress ultimately wants a piece of program spending for his or her district. Grant programs must sprinkle funds broadly to many districts to gain political support, rather than just the areas that really need help.

A good example is the $6 billion Community Development Block Grant program. The program was created in 1974 to channel federal money to low-income urban areas for key services such as firefighters and police. But today the program spreads taxpayer largesse widely to some of the wealthiest areas of the country, often for dubious projects. Today all urban areas with 50,000 or more people are eligible for the program, not just the needy ones, and it funds projects such as the installation of traffic lights in wealthy Newton, Massachusetts.

The Department of Education's $10 billion Title I program provides another example of the difficulty in targeting federal grants to the poor. A 2002 statistical analysis by Nora Gordon of the University of California, San Diego, found that while Title I is supposed to steer money to poor school districts, the actual effect is different. She found that within a few years of a grant being given, state and local governments used the federal funds to displace their own funding of poor schools. Thus, poor schools ended up being no further ahead than they had been without the federal program.

Six Reasons to Cut Grants

The following are six further reasons why grants are wasteful and inefficient—six reasons for Congress to begin cutting the $418 billion grant empire.

1. Grant Bureaucracy Is Wasteful

The source of federal grant money paid to the states is, of course, the taxpayers who live in the 50 states. Taxpayer money is sent to Washington where it is reallocated by Capitol Hill horse-trading and routed through layers of departmental bureaucracy. The depleted funds are then sent down to state and local agencies coupled with long lists of complex federal regulations with which they must comply.

Taxpayers and the economy lose out from the unproductive activities of the huge bureaucracies that are needed to administer $418 billion of intergovernmental flows of money. The federal-state grant superstructure is intensely bureaucratic. To take one example, the $59 million "Weed and Seed" anti-drug program for schools has a 74-page application kit that references 1,300 pages of regulations with which grant recipients must comply.

Many grant programs involve three levels of bureaucracy—federal, state, and local—before funds are disbursed for a project. That is "trickle-down economics" at its worst. For example, the $441 million Safe and Drug Free Schools program sends money to state education bureaucracies, which in turn use complex procedures to send funds down to local school boards. School boards need expert bureaucrats to apply for the funds and to follow state and federal rules. After all that, reviews of the program have concluded that schools have tended to spend the money wastefully.

Federal grants for local "first responder" activities were popular in the wake of 9/11, but they too got bogged down in bureaucracy. There are 16 overlapping grant programs that fund first responders, such as firefighters, according to an April 2003 General Accounting Office report. The House Select Committee on Homeland Security reported in April 2004 that $5.2 billion of $6.3 billion in first responder grants since 9/11 "remains stuck in the administrative pipeline at the state, county, and city levels." The committee reported that much of the first responder money went to dubious projects of little value. Indeed, much of the funding went to states on the basis of factors such as population, not terrorism risk.

2. Grants Spur Wasteful State Spending

Federal grants set off a gold-rush response by state and local governments and create irresponsible overspending decisions. States have little incentive to spend grant money efficiently because it comes to them "free." With federal matching grants, state politicians can spend an added dollar on their constituents while only charging them a fraction of a dollar in state taxes. That makes program expansion very attractive. With Medicaid, for example, state governments have expanded benefits and the number of eligible beneficiaries beyond reasonable levels because of the generous federal match.

Medicaid also illustrates how states can abuse the handouts they receive from Washington. In recent years, numerous states have literally bilked the federal government out of billions of dollars with complex schemes to maximize Medicaid payments. For example, some states imposed taxes on health care providers that were at the same time rebated back to the providers. The effect was to increase reported state Medicaid spending and boost federal matching funds. State gamesmanship to maximize federal grants goes back to at least the 1960s.

One partial solution short of terminating grants is to convert matching grants to block grants. Block grants provide a fixed sum to states and give them flexibility on program design. For example, the 1996 welfare reform law turned Aid to Families with Dependent Children, a traditional open-ended matching grant, into Temporary Assistance for Needy Families, a lump-sum block grant.

Today, a ripe reform target for Congress is to convert Medicaid into a block grant and freeze its overall federal funding. That would help the federal government to reduce its huge deficit, and it would force the states to cut back on this massively bloated program. For example, if federal Medicaid spending were frozen at its FY05 level, by FY09 it would be saving the federal government $51 billion annually, which could be used to reduce the deficit.

3. Redistributing Income between the States Is Unfair and Inefficient

The huge federal grant machine has centralized U.S. fiscal power in the hands of the federal government. While utopian grant planners may dream of rationally redistributing money between the states, raw political power ultimately determines spending outcomes, which creates much inefficiency. For example, states receive varying amounts of highway grants for each dollar of gasoline taxes sent to Washington. While some congested and fast-growing states that need new highways lose out, slow-growing states get unneeded "highways to nowhere" if they have champion pork-barrel politicians representing them, such as Sen. Robert Byrd (D-WV) and former representative Bud Shuster (R-PA). It makes far more sense for the states to raise money for their own highways from their own taxpayers since each state has different needs and priorities. For their part, states should move ahead with private highway projects that avoid taxpayer burdens altogether.

4. Grants Reduce State Policy Diversity

Federal grants reduce state government innovation and diversity because federal money comes with regulations that limit policy flexibility. Grants put the states in a costly straitjacket of federal rules. Medicaid has perhaps the most complicated top-down rules of any grant program. The FY05 federal budget notes, for example, that the "complex array of Medicaid laws, regulations, and administrative guidance is confusing, overly burdensome, and serves to stifle state innovation and flexibility."

The classic one-size-fits-all federal regulation imposed through the grant machinery was the 55 mph national speed limit. The speed limit was enforced between 1974 and 1995 by federal threats to withdraw state highway grant money. It never made any sense that the same speed limit should be imposed in the wide-open western states as the crowded eastern states. Congress finally listened to motorists and repealed the law.

But federal policymakers are increasing their intrusions in other areas, such as education. The cost of federal education grant spending exploded under President Bush. With higher spending have come complex new mandates under the No Child Left Behind law of 2002, which is a major source of frustration for state and local policymakers.

5. Grants Divert Attention from Crucial National Concerns

A serious problem caused by the huge scope of federal grant activity is that federal politicians end up spending their time dealing with local issues rather than crucial national issues. For example, members of Congress spend much of their time holding hearings and considering legislation on local issues such as K-12 schools. In addition, the 716 federal grant projects generate unending opportunities for members of Congress to steer pork projects to their home districts. The chase for hometown pork consumes much of a typical member's time.

As a consequence, Congress has had little time left over for serious oversight of agencies such as the FBI and CIA, to avert serious failings before they happen, or for considering crucial national issues such as terrorism. The *Washington Post* reported on April 27, 2004, two and a half years after 9/11, that most members on the intelligence committees in the House and Senate had been too busy on other activities to have read crucial terrorism reports or to have held oversight hearings to rectify intelligence agency problems. Congress finally did get around to considering the government failures that led to 9/11 later in 2004, but the federal government is still far too big to oversee adequately.

6. Grants Make Government Responsibilities Unclear

Federal grants create problems for the voting public because it is difficult for citizens to figure out which level of government is responsible for certain policy outcomes. Federal, state, and local governments all play big roles in such areas as transportation and education, thus making accountability very difficult. When the schools fail, which government should parents blame? For their part, politicians have become skilled at pointing fingers at the other levels of government when policies go badly. As Ronald Reagan pointed out in his 1983 budget message, "What had been a classic division of functions between the federal government and the state and localities has become a confused mess."

Cutting Federal Grants

Ronald Reagan tried to sort out the "confused mess" of federal grants. The Reagan administration's policy of "New Federalism" attempted to re-sort federal and state priorities so that each level of government would have full responsibility for financing its own programs. For example, Reagan proposed that the federal government fully run Medicaid but that welfare and food stamps be fully operated and financed by the states. Reagan sought to terminate spending in areas that were properly state activities: he tried to abolish the Department of Education, calling it "President Carter's new bureaucratic boondoggle" in the 1980 presidential campaign.

Figure 12.1, which shows federal grant spending in constant 2004 dollars, indicates that Reagan made modest progress in cutting federal grants. Between 1980 and 1985, Reagan cut overall grant spending by 15 percent in constant dollars and nonhealth grants by 21 percent. Unfortunately, the cuts were short-lived, and grant spending has since increased rapidly. Under a Republican Congress, total grant outlays in nominal dollars increased from $225 billion in FY95 to $418 billion in FY04. Outlays on the Department of Education soared from $36 billion in FY01 to $63 billion in FY04 under President Bush.

The same pattern is evident when one looks at the total number of federal grant programs, as shown in Figure 12.2. Reagan made some

Figure 12.1
Real Federal Grants to State and Local Governments

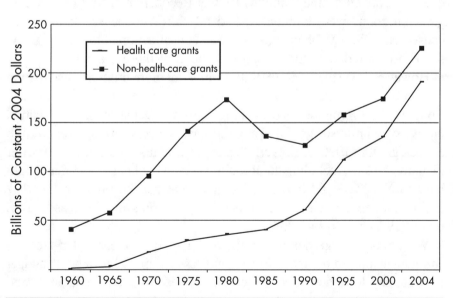

SOURCE: Author's calculations based on *Budget of the U.S. Government, FY2005, Analytical Perspectives,* p. 120. Fiscal years.

137

Figure 12.2
Number of Federal Grant Programs for State and Local Governments

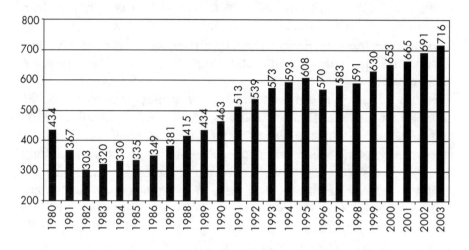

SOURCE: Office of Management and Budget, based on www.cfda.gov.

progress in cutting the number of programs, but the progress was subsequently reversed. In the Omnibus Budget Reconciliation Act of 1981, 59 grant programs were eliminated, and 80 narrowly focused grants were consolidated into 9 block grants. That consolidation into block grants succeeded in reducing the regulatory burden of those programs.

However, since the mid-1980s the number of grant programs has soared, with only a brief retrenchment in the mid-1990s under the new Republican Congress. The Republicans sought to abolish the Department of Education but were again unsuccessful. They did have success turning welfare into a block grant in 1996. However, President Clinton's veto pen was a barrier to many reforms, including the Republican budget plan in 1995 that would have turned Medicaid into a block grant and cut the program by $187 billion over seven years. The number of grant programs increased from 608 in 1995 to 716 by 2003.

With today's large deficit and the massive cost increases that face the entitlement programs, there is less and less room in the federal budget for state and local activities. Policymakers need to revive federalism and transfer programs back to the states. State and local governments are in a better position to determine whether residents need more roads, schools, and other items. By federalizing such spending we are asking Congress to do the impossible—to efficiently plan for the competing needs of a diverse country of almost 300 million people.

Suggested Readings

Budget of the U.S. Government, FY2005, Analytical Perspectives, "Aid to State and Local Governments."

Edwards, Chris. "Downsizing the Federal Government." Cato Institute Policy Analysis no. 515, June 2, 2004. This report has citations for facts and data used in this chapter.

General Accounting Office. "Federal Assistance: Grant System Continues to Be Highly Fragmented." GAO-03-718T, April 29, 2003.

Government Printing Office. *Catalog of Federal Domestic Assistance.* www.cfda.gov.

—Prepared by Chris Edwards

13. International Tax Competition

Congress should

- cut the federal corporate income tax rate from 35 percent to 20 percent;
- pursue fundamental tax reform by replacing the individual and corporate income taxes with a consumption-based tax system;
- oppose policies that would make U.S. companies more uncompetitive in foreign markets, such as raising taxes on foreign subsidiaries and restricting the reincorporation of companies abroad;
- retain U.S. fiscal sovereignty by opposing international tax harmonization initiatives; and
- oppose anti-competitive regulations such as the IRS effort to mandate greater reporting of foreign investor deposits in U.S. banks.

Globalization is knitting separate national economies into a single world economy. That process is occurring through rising trade and investment flows, greater labor mobility, and rapid transfers of technology. As economic integration increases, individuals and businesses gain the freedom to take advantage of foreign economic opportunities. Individuals have more choices about where to work and invest, and businesses have more choices about where to locate production, research, and headquarters facilities.

Taxation is having an increasing impact on investment and location decisions. As a result, there is rising pressure on countries to reduce tax rates to avoid losing their tax bases. International "tax competition" is increasing as capital and labor mobility rises.

Some governments are pursuing misguided defensive measures in an effort to shield their tax bases from competition. Those measures include restrictive tax rules on the foreign operations of companies and attempts to harmonize taxes across countries. Such measures do nothing to reform inefficient tax systems, and they can increase tax complexity.

Cutting Tax Rates

High tax rates are more difficult to sustain in the new competitive global economy. That is particularly true for taxes on capital income, including taxes on business profits, dividends, interest, and capital gains. Taxes on capital income create an increasing drag on growth as capital mobility increases. High taxes on capital income both reduce domestic savings and investment and drive out foreign capital, with a negative impact on productivity, wages, and incomes.

Recognizing that fact, nearly all industrial nations have cut their personal and corporate income tax rates in recent years. Table 13.1 shows that the average statutory corporate tax rate for the 30-nation Organization for Economic Cooperation and Development was cut from 37.6 percent in 1996 to 30.0 percent by 2004. By contrast, the U.S. corporate tax rate is 40 percent, including the 35 percent federal rate and the average state corporate tax rate. The U.S. rate is the second-highest among the 30 nations.

The average top individual income tax rate for 26 OECD countries fell from 67 percent in 1980 to 44 percent by 2002, as shown in Table 13.2. The average rate for four newer OECD countries not in the table (the Czech Republic, Hungary, Poland, and the Slovak Republic) was 38 percent in 2002. Note that the top U.S. rate fell from 40 percent in 2000, to 39 percent in 2001 and 2002, to 35 percent in 2003 but is scheduled to rise to 40 percent again in 2011.

For each country, Table 13.2 includes the national government rate plus the rate in the lowest-tax state or province. For the United States, the table includes zero for the state part of the tax because a few U.S. states do not have individual income taxes. But note that the most populous state, California, has a top individual income tax rate of 9.3 percent.

Countries have cut other types of taxes on capital. Capital gains taxes have been cut; special taxes on wealth have been eliminated; and there has been a trend to cut withholding taxes, which are taxes on cross-border payments of interest, dividends, and other investment returns.

Imposing Defensive Tax Rules on Corporations

Tax competition has caused governments to adopt defensive rules to prevent businesses and individuals from enjoying lower tax rates abroad.

Table 13.1
Top Corporate Income Tax Rates in the OECD
(Includes national and state/provincial taxes)

Country	1996	1997	1998	1999	2000	2001	2002	2003	2004
Australia	36.0	36.0	36.0	36.0	36.0	34.0	30.0	30.0	30.0
Austria	34.0	34.0	34.0	34.0	34.0	34.0	34.0	34.0	34.0
Belgium	40.2	40.2	40.2	40.2	40.2	40.2	40.2	34.0	34.0
Canada	44.6	44.6	44.6	44.6	44.6	42.1	38.6	36.6	36.1
Czech Rep.	39.0	39.0	35.0	35.0	31.0	31.0	31.0	31.0	28.0
Denmark	34.0	34.0	34.0	32.0	32.0	30.0	30.0	30.0	30.0
Finland	28.0	28.0	28.0	28.0	29.0	29.0	29.0	29.0	29.0
France	36.7	36.7	41.7	40.0	36.7	35.3	34.3	34.3	34.3
Germany	57.4	57.4	56.7	52.3	51.6	38.4	38.4	39.6	38.3
Greece	40.0	40.0	40.0	40.0	40.0	37.5	35.0	35.0	35.0
Hungary	33.3	18.0	18.0	18.0	18.0	18.0	18.0	18.0	16.0
Iceland	33.0	33.0	30.0	30.0	30.0	30.0	18.0	18.0	18.0
Ireland	38.0	36.0	32.0	28.0	24.0	20.0	16.0	12.5	12.5
Italy	53.2	53.2	41.3	41.3	41.3	40.3	40.3	38.3	37.3
Japan	51.6	51.6	51.6	48.0	42.0	42.0	42.0	42.0	42.0
Korea	33.0	30.8	30.8	30.8	30.8	30.8	29.7	29.7	29.7
Luxembourg	40.3	39.3	37.5	37.5	37.5	37.5	30.4	30.4	30.4
Mexico	34.0	34.0	34.0	35.0	35.0	35.0	35.0	34.0	33.0
Netherlands	35.0	35.0	35.0	35.0	35.0	35.0	34.5	34.5	34.5
New Zealand	33.0	33.0	33.0	33.0	33.0	33.0	33.0	33.0	33.0
Norway	28.0	28.0	28.0	28.0	28.0	28.0	28.0	28.0	28.0
Poland	40.0	38.0	36.0	34.0	30.0	28.0	28.0	27.0	19.0
Portugal	39.6	39.6	37.4	37.4	35.2	35.2	33.0	33.0	27.5
Slovak Rep.	n/a	n/a	n/a	n/a	n/a	29.0	25.0	25.0	19.0
Spain	35.0	35.0	35.0	35.0	35.0	35.0	35.0	35.0	35.0
Sweden	28.0	28.0	28.0	28.0	28.0	28.0	28.0	28.0	28.0
Switzerland	28.5	28.5	27.8	25.1	25.1	24.7	24.5	24.1	24.1
Turkey	44.0	44.0	44.0	33.0	33.0	33.0	33.0	33.0	33.0
United Kingdom	33.0	31.0	31.0	31.0	30.0	30.0	30.0	30.0	30.0
United States	40.0	40.0	40.0	40.0	40.0	40.0	40.0	40.0	40.0
Average—									
30 countries	37.6	36.8	35.9	34.8	34.0	32.8	31.4	30.9	30.0

SOURCE: Author based on KPMG data.
NOTE: Figures include the average state or provincial tax rate, as applicable.

For businesses, such defensive measures have generally increased the complexity of the tax code and reduced their ability to compete in foreign markets.

The tax rules that countries apply to the foreign operations of businesses are an important factor in tax competitiveness. According to a 2004 PricewaterhouseCoopers survey, most OECD countries have ''territorial'' tax systems that do not tax the regular business income of foreign subsidiaries. By contrast, the United States taxes corporations on their global income, although foreign business income is generally not taxed until repatriated to the United States. That is, taxation is ''deferred'' until profits are sent home.

Table 13.2
Top Personal Income Tax Rates in the OECD
(Includes national and state/provincial taxes)

Country	1980	1985	1990	1995	2000	2002
Australia	62	60	49	47	47	47
Austria	62	62	50	50	50	50
Belgium	76	76	55	58	58	50
Canada	60	50	44	44	44	39
Denmark	66	73	68	64	59	59
Finland	65	64	57	54	51	51
France	60	65	53	51	54	53
Germany	65	65	53	57	56	51
Greece	60	63	50	45	43	40
Iceland	63	56	40	47	45	46
Ireland	60	65	56	48	42	42
Italy	72	81	66	67	51	47
Japan	75	70	65	65	50	50
Korea	89	65	64	48	44	40
Luxembourg	57	57	56	50	49	40
Mexico	55	55	40	35	40	35
Netherlands	72	72	60	60	52	52
New Zealand	62	66	33	33	39	39
Norway	75	64	51	42	48	48
Portugal	84	69	40	40	40	40
Spain	66	66	56	56	48	35
Sweden	87	80	61	46	51	52
Switzerland	31	33	33	35	31	31
Turkey	75	63	50	55	45	40
United Kingdom	83	60	40	40	40	40
United States	70	50	33	40	40	39
Average—						
26 countries	67	63	51	49	47	44

SOURCE: James Gwartney and Robert Lawson, *Economic Freedom of the World: 2004 Annual Report.*
NOTE: Figures include the lowest state or provincial tax rate, as applicable.

However, the United States limits such tax deferral more aggressively than other countries. In 2003 the Treasury's assistant secretary for tax policy, Pam Olson, testified to Congress that ''no other country has rules for the immediate taxation of foreign-source income that are comparable to the U.S. rules in terms of breadth and complexity.'' Dow Chemical testified to Congress in 2003 that 78 percent of its 7,800-page U.S. tax return relates to the rules on foreign income. Those complex tax rules impose a high burden on foreign subsidiaries and cause U.S. companies to lose out in global markets.

That became an issue during the 2004 election because John Kerry proposed that the United States further increase taxes on U.S. foreign subsidiaries. If such a policy were enacted, U.S. companies would lose sales to foreign competitors that had lower tax costs. Over time, U.S. subsidiaries would be closed or sold off to foreign companies, and U.S. firms would have to downsize their U.S. operations. Domestic headquarters jobs in research, marketing, management, and other fields would be lost.

The mistake made by Senator Kerry and other corporate critics is to assume that foreign subsidiaries hurt the U.S. economy. In fact, foreign subsidiaries mainly complement U.S.-based production. For example, subsidiaries are a main conduit through which U.S. goods are exported abroad. By damaging the competitiveness of subsidiaries, the Kerry plan would have damaged the U.S.-based activities that depend on expanded foreign business opportunities.

Policymakers who support legislation to prevent U.S. companies from moving their place of incorporation to lower-tax countries make a similar mistake. The Treasury announced in 2002 that there had been a marked increase in the number of companies pursuing this option because of the unattractive U.S. tax system. Those companies are seeking to reduce taxes paid to the U.S. government on their foreign operations. They would, however, continue to pay U.S. taxes on their U.S. operations even if they are incorporated abroad.

Rather than try to ban such transactions, Congress should fix the underlying problem. The problem is that the United States is a bad place, from a tax perspective, to locate the headquarters of a multinational corporation. However, the corporate tax bill enacted in October 2004 takes a few positive steps to improve the competitiveness of the U.S. tax code.

Instead of trying to penalize U.S. companies that have succeeded in foreign markets, policymakers should pursue tax reforms to create a consumption-based territorial tax system that would not tax companies on their foreign operations at all. That way, U.S. companies could increase their global sales and profitability, which would boost U.S. job creation and economic growth.

International Tax Harmonization

Some governments have responded to rising tax competition by trying to coordinate tax systems across countries to limit competition in the manner of a cartel. The European Union has been a leader in that approach and has pushed its member countries to harmonize their tax systems. For example, in 1992 the EU imposed a minimum standard value-added tax rate of 15 percent for member countries.

The EU and some European leaders have tried to get EU countries to harmonize corporate income tax rates. In 2001 France's prime minister condemned tax competition as "fiscal dumping" and said that corporate taxes should be harmonized to prevent companies from moving to low-tax areas. Some European leaders have called for integrating European taxation to fully end tax competition.

Those developments are important for the United States because the arguments used to support European tax harmonization are being heard in global forums. For example, a United Nations panel in 2001 proposed creating an International Tax Organization that would develop norms for tax policy, engage in surveillance of tax systems, and try to get countries to desist from so-called harmful tax competition. The UN has also called for creating a "global source of funds" from a "high yielding tax source," that is, a world tax imposed by the UN.

The Paris-based OECD launched a drive to squelch "harmful tax competition" in an influential 1998 report, *Harmful Tax Competition: An Emerging Global Issue*. It has tried to get the United States and other countries to take action against low-tax countries. The focus has been on indirect methods of nullifying tax competition, such as greater sharing of tax information between governments. The idea is to give tax collectors access to data on the economic activities of citizens abroad to eliminate the attractiveness of low-tax countries.

The OECD has also pressed to create international tax standards and agreements. A 2000 report, *Towards Global Tax Co-operation: Progress in Identifying and Eliminating Harmful Tax Practices,* stated that "harmful tax competition is by its very nature a global phenomenon and therefore its solution requires a global endorsement and global participation." But the United States should not participate in tax agreements and information exchanges that reduce U.S. citizens' financial privacy, threaten U.S. sovereignty, or restrict the ability of countries to cut taxes.

The efforts to suppress tax competition are partly driven by the politics of redistribution. The primary tax used for redistribution, the income tax, has the most mobile of tax bases and is thus the most affected by tax competition. Because tax competition is a threat to highly graduated income taxes, some politicians are trying to squelch competition any way they can. But graduated, or "progressive," income taxes are very inefficient. Tax competition is beneficial if it can limit the use of those taxes and act as a constraint on government redistribution. The United States should make sure that international groups do not push for global standards that lock in inefficient income tax systems and prevent consumption-based tax reforms.

IRS Regulations on Foreign Investment in the United States

Efforts to stifle tax competition are not just occurring overseas; some efforts are being pushed domestically. Interest earned on U.S. bank deposits paid to foreign investors has been tax-free for decades, as affirmed by Congress on a number of occasions. That pro-competition policy has worked to the U.S. economy's advantage because it has drawn billions of dollars of foreign investment into the U.S. financial system.

However, in 2002 the IRS issued a proposed regulation (REG-133254-02) that would force U.S. banks to report on interest paid to account holders from certain other countries. The proposed regulation is designed to help foreign governments collect their taxes and would not affect U.S. taxes. There is roughly $2 trillion held in U.S. bank deposits by foreigners, with about $0.5 trillion vulnerable to flowing out of the country if the IRS imposes this regulation. Some of those funds would be shifted to low-tax countries that have greater protections for financial privacy. Congress should oppose this regulation and other policies that risk driving investment capital out of the U.S. economy.

Responding to Tax Competition with Tax Cuts and Tax Reform

The United States led the world in 1986 by cutting the federal corporate tax rate from 46 to 34 percent. Most major countries followed suit and continued cutting in the 1990s, with the result that the United States now has a higher corporate tax rate than all other major countries except Japan.

It is time for the United States to regain the lead in tax reform by cutting the federal corporate rate from 35 percent to 20 percent. That would greatly improve U.S. competitiveness and generate large flows of investment into the United States. Such a cut would all but end the problems of U.S. companies reincorporating abroad and companies engaging in Enron-style tax sheltering.

To not increase the deficit, a corporate rate cut could be paired with cuts to federal spending on business subsidies, which currently total about

$90 billion per year (see Chapter 34). Such a reform package would increase investment and employment incentives for all firms, while reducing government favoritism and economic distortions.

Beyond a rate cut, Congress should consider repealing the corporate income tax, or replacing it with a consumption-based cash-flow tax. The business portion of former house majority leader Dick Armey's flat tax is an example of a cash-flow tax. A cash-flow tax would allow full expensing of capital investment, which would make the United States a great place for global corporations to locate their production facilities.

A cash-flow tax would be a territorial tax and thus would not impose U.S. taxes on the foreign operations of U.S. companies. That would allow U.S. companies to compete in global markets on a level playing field with foreign companies. A territorial system would also be much simpler than the current worldwide tax system. With a low-rate territorial cash-flow tax, global corporations would be encouraged to move their headquarters, operations, and profits to the United States.

If the United States pursued such tax reforms, other countries would likely follow suit. As tax rates on capital income fell around the world, economic distortions caused by taxes would be cut and global growth would increase. If governments or international agencies do not block tax competition, and countries around the world compete to adopt more efficient tax systems, citizens in every nation will be winners.

Suggested Readings

Center for Freedom and Prosperity at www.freedomandprosperity.org. This site provides an extensive collection of articles on tax competition.

de Rugy, Veronique, and Richard W. Rahn. "Threats to Financial Privacy and Tax Competition." Cato Institute Policy Analysis no. 491, October 2, 2003.

Edwards, Chris. "Replacing the Scandal-Plagued Corporate Income Tax with a Cash-Flow Tax." Cato Institute Policy Analysis no. 484, August 14, 2003.

———. "The U.S. Corporate Tax and the Global Economy." Cato Institute Tax & Budget Bulletin no. 18, September 2003.

Edwards, Chris, and Veronique de Rugy. "International Tax Competition, A 21st-Century Restraint on the Government." Cato Institute Policy Analysis no. 431, April 12, 2002.

KPMG. "Corporate Tax Rates Survey." January 2004. www.kpmg.com/Rut2000_prod/Documents/9/2004ctrs.pdf.

Mitchell, Daniel. "Making American Companies More Competitive." Heritage Foundation Backgrounder no. 1691, September 25, 2003.

PricewaterhouseCoopers. Testimony of Peter R. Merrill before the House Budget Committee on "Competitiveness of the U.S. Tax Code." July 22, 2004.

U.S. Department of the Treasury. "Corporate Inversion Transactions: Tax Policy Implications." May 2002.

—Prepared by Chris Edwards

GOVERNMENT REFORM

14. The Delegation of Legislative Powers

> **Congress should**
>
> - require all "lawmaking" regulations to be affirmatively approved by Congress and signed into law by the president, as the Constitution requires for all laws; and
> - establish a mechanism to force the legislative consideration of existing regulations during the reauthorization process.

Separation of Powers: The Bulwark of Liberty

When the legislative and executive powers are united in the same person, or in the same body of magistrates, there can be no liberty.

—Montesquieu, *The Spirit of the Laws*

Article I, section 1, of the U.S. Constitution stipulates, "All legislative powers herein granted shall be vested in the Congress of the United States, which shall consist of a Senate and House of Representatives." Article II, section 3, stipulates that the president "shall take care that the laws be faithfully executed." Thus, as we all learned in high school civics, the Constitution clearly provides for the separation of powers between the various branches of government.

The alternative design—concentration of power within a single governmental body—was thought to be inimical to a free society. John Adams wrote in 1776 that "a single assembly, possessed of all the powers of government, would make arbitrary laws for their own interest, and adjudge all controversies in their own favor." James Madison in *Federalist* no. 47 justified the Constitution's separation of powers by noting that it was a necessary prerequisite for "a government of laws and not of men."

Further, he wrote, "The accumulation of all powers, legislative, executive, and judiciary, in the same hands, whether of one, a few, or many, and whether hereditary, self-appointed, or elective, may justly be pronounced the very definition of tyranny."

For the first 150 years of the American Republic, the Supreme Court largely upheld the original constitutional design, requiring that Congress rather than administrators make the law. The suggestion that Congress could broadly delegate its lawmaking powers to others—particularly the executive branch—was generally rejected by the courts. And for good reasons. First, the Constitution was understood to be a document of enumerated and thus limited powers, and nowhere was Congress either explicitly or even implicitly given the power to delegate. Second, the fear of power concentrated in any one branch still animated both the Supreme Court and the legislature. Third, Americans believed that those who make the law should be directly accountable at the ballot box.

The upshot was that the separation of powers effectively restrained federal power, just as the Founders had intended. As Alexis de Tocqueville observed, "The nation participates in the making of its laws by the choice of its legislators, and in the execution of them by the choice of agents of the executive government." He also observed that "it may also be said to govern itself, so feeble and so restricted is the share left to the administrators, so little do the authorities forget their popular origins and the power from which they emanate."

The New Deal: "Delegation Running Riot"

The sense of political crisis that permeated the 1930s effectively buried the nondelegation doctrine. In his first inaugural address, Franklin Roosevelt compared the impact of the ongoing economic depression to a foreign invasion and argued that Congress should grant him sweeping powers to fight it.

Shortly after taking office, Congress in 1933 granted Roosevelt virtually unlimited power to regulate commerce through passage of the Agricultural Adjustment Act (which authorized the president to increase agricultural prices via administrative production controls) and the National Industrial Recovery Act (known as the NIRA), which authorized the president to issue industrial codes to regulate all aspects of the industries they covered.

The Supreme Court, however, temporarily arrested the tide in 1935 in its unanimous opinion in *A.L.A. Schechter Poultry Corp. v. United States.* The Court overturned the industrial code provisions of the NIRA, and, in a separate opinion, Justice Benjamin Cardozo termed the NIRA—and thus the New Deal—"delegation running riot." That same year, the Court struck down additional NIRA delegations of power in *Panama Refining Co. v. Ryan.*

Largely because of the *Schechter* and *Panama Refining* decisions, President Roosevelt decried the Court's interference with his political agenda and proposed legislation enlarging the size of the Court so that he could appoint additional justices—the so-called Court-packing plan. He lost that battle but won the war. Although the Court never explicitly reversed its 1935 decisions and continues to articulate essentially the same verbal formulas defining the scope of permissible delegation—indeed, *Schechter* and *Panama Refining* theoretically are good law today—it would be nearly 40 years before the Court again struck down business regulation on delegation grounds.

As long as Congress articulates some intelligible standard (no matter how vague or arbitrary) to govern executive lawmaking, courts today are prepared to allow delegation, in the words of Justice Cardozo, to run riot. John Locke's admonition that the legislature "cannot transfer the power of making laws to any other hands, for it being but a delegated power from the people, they who have it cannot pass it over to others," is a forgotten vestige of an era when individual liberty mattered more than administrative convenience. As Federal District Judge Roger Vinson wrote in *United States v. Mills* in 1989:

> A delegation doctrine which essentially allows Congress to abdicate its power to define the elements of a criminal offense, in favor of an unelected administrative agency such as the [Army] Corps of Engineers, does violence to this time-honored principle. . . . Deferent and minimal judicial review of Congress' transfer of its criminal lawmaking function to other bodies, in other branches, calls into question the vitality of the tripartite system established by our Constitution. It also calls into question the nexus that must exist between the law so applied and simple logic and common sense. Yet that seems to be the state of the law.

Delegation: The Corrosive Agent of Democracy

The concern over congressional delegation of power is not simply theoretical and abstract, for delegation does violence, not only to the ideal construct of a free society, but also to the day-to-day practice of democracy itself. Ironically, delegation does not help to secure "good government"; it helps to destroy it.

Delegation Breeds Political Irresponsibility

Congress delegates power for much the same reason that Congress ran budget deficits for decades. With deficit spending, members of Congress can claim credit for the benefits of their expenditures yet escape blame for the costs. The public must pay ultimately, of course, but through taxes levied at some future time by some other officials. Likewise, delegation allows legislators to claim credit for the benefits that a regulatory statute airily promises yet escape the blame for the burdens it will impose, because they do not issue the laws needed to achieve those high-sounding benefits. The public inevitably must suffer regulatory costs to realize regulatory benefits, but the laws will come from an agency that legislators can then criticize for imposing excessive burdens on their constituents.

Just as deficit spending allows legislators to appear to deliver money to some people without taking it from others, delegation allows them to appear to deliver regulatory benefits without imposing regulatory costs. It provides, in the words of former Environmental Protection Agency deputy administrator John Quarles, "a handy set of mirrors—so useful in Washington—by which politicians can appear to kiss both sides of the apple."

Delegation Is a Political Steroid for Organized Special Interests

As University of Miami law professor John Hart Ely has noted, "One reason we have broadly based representative assemblies is to await something approaching a consensus before government intervenes." The Constitution was intentionally designed to curb the "facility and excess of law-making" (in the words of James Madison) by requiring that statutes go through a bicameral legislature and the president.

Differences in the size and nature of the constituencies of representatives, senators, and the president—and the different lengths of their terms in office—increase the probability that the actions of each will reflect a different balance of interests. That diversity of viewpoint, plus the greater difficulty of prevailing in three forums rather than one, makes it far more difficult for special-interest groups or bare majorities to impose their will on the totality of the American people. Hence, the original design effectively required a supermajority to make law as a means of discouraging the selfish exercise of power by well-organized but narrow interests.

Delegation shifts the power to make law from a Congress of all interests to subgovernments typically representative of only a small subset of all interests. The obstacles intentionally placed in the path of lawmaking disappear, and the power of organized interests is magnified.

That is largely because diffuse interests typically find it even more difficult to press their case before an agency than before a legislature. They often have no direct representation in the administrative process, and effective representation typically requires special legal counsel, expert witnesses, and the capacity to reward or to punish top officials through political organization, press coverage, and close working relationships with members of the appropriate congressional subcommittee. As a result, the general public rarely qualifies as a "stakeholder" in agency proceedings and is largely locked out of the decisionmaking process. Madison's desired check on the "facility and excess of law-making" is thus smashed.

Delegation Breeds the Leviathan State

Perhaps the ultimate check on the growth of government rests in the fact that there is only so much time in a day. No matter how many laws Congress would like to pass, there are only so many hours in a session to do so. Delegation, however, dramatically expands the realm of the possible by effectively "deputizing" tens of thousands of bureaucrats, often with broad and imprecise missions to "go forth and legislate." Thus, as Jacob Weisberg has noted in the *New Republic:* "As a labor-saving device, delegation did for legislators what the washing machine did for the 1950s housewife. Government could now penetrate every nook and cranny of American life in a way that was simply impossible before."

The Threadbare Case for Delegation

Although delegation has become so deeply embedded in the political landscape that few public officials even recognize the phenomenon or the issues raised by the practice, political observers are becoming increasingly aware of the failure of delegation to deliver its promised bounty of good government.

The Myth of Technical Expertise

It was once maintained that delegation produces more sensible laws by transferring lawmaking from elected officials, who are beholden to concentrated interests, to experts, who can base their decisions solely on a cool appraisal of the public interest. Yet most agency heads are not scientists, engineers, economists, or other kinds of technical experts; they are political operatives. Since the Environmental Protection Agency's inception in 1970, for example, the overwhelming majority of its administrators and assistant administrators have been lawyers. As MIT professor Michael Golay wrote in *Science:* "Environmental protection policy disagreements are not about what to conclude from the available scientific knowledge; they represent a struggle for political power among groups having vastly differing interests and visions for society. In this struggle, science is used as a means of legitimizing the various positions . . . science is a pawn, cynically abused as may suit the interests of a particular protagonist despite great ignorance concerning the problems being addressed." Perhaps that's why the EPA's own Science Advisory Board was forced to concede in a 1992 report that the agency's science "is perceived by many people both inside and outside the agency to be adjusted to fit policy."

We should not necessarily bemoan the lack of agency expertise, for it is not entirely clear that government by experts is superior to government by elected officials. There is no reason to believe that experts possess superior moral knowledge or a better sense of what constitutes the public good. Indeed, specialization often impairs the capacity for moral judgment and often breeds professional zealotry. Likewise, specialized expertise provides too narrow a base for the balanced judgments that intelligent policy requires.

Although both agency administrators and legislators often lack the expertise to evaluate technical arguments by themselves, they can get help from agency and committee staff, government institutes (such as the Centers for Disease Control and the Government Accountability Office), and private sources such as medical associations, think tanks, and university scientists. After all, that is what the hearings process is supposed to be about.

And only someone naive about modern government would seriously claim today that the winds of politics blow any less fiercely in administrative meeting rooms than they do in the halls of Congress. As Nobel laureate economist James Buchanan and others have observed, public officials have many incentives to pursue both private and political ends that often have little to do with their ostensible missions.

Is Congress Too Busy?

New Dealers once argued that "time spent on details [by Congress] must be at the sacrifice of time spent on matters of the broad public policy." But Congress today spends little time on "matters of broad public policy," largely because delegation forces Congress to spend a large chunk of its time constructing the legislative architecture—sometimes over a thousand pages of it—detailing exactly how various agencies are to decide important matters of policy. Once that architecture is in place, members of Congress find that a large part of their job entails navigating through those bureaucratic mazes for special interests jockeying to influence the final nature of the law. Writing such instructions and performing agency oversight to ensure that they are carried out would be unnecessary if Congress made the rules in the first place.

Moreover, delegation often works to prolong disputes and keep standards of conduct murky because pressures from legislators and the complicated procedures imposed upon agencies turn lawmaking into an excruciatingly slow process. Agencies typically report that they have issued only a small fraction of the laws that their long-standing statutory mandates require. Competing interests devote large sums of money and many of their best minds to this seemingly interminable process. For example, it took the EPA 16 years to ban lead in gasoline despite the fact that the 1970 Clean Air Act explicitly gave them the authority to do so. Simply making the rules the first time around in the legislative process would take less time than the multiyear regulatory sausage machine requires to issue standards.

Complex Rules for a Complex World

Perhaps the most widely accepted justification for some degree of delegation is the complex and technical nature of the world we live in today. As the Supreme Court opined in 1989, "Our jurisprudence has been driven by a practical understanding that in our increasingly complex society, replete with ever changing and more technical problems, Congress simply cannot do its job absent an ability to delegate power under broad general directives."

Yet the vast majority of decisions delegated to the executive branch are not particularly technical in nature. They are instead hotly political, for the reasons mentioned above. If Congress must regulate, it could (and probably should) jettison micromanagerial command-and-control regulations that make up the bulk of the *Federal Register* and instead adopt regulations that are less prescriptive and more performance based or market oriented. Most regulatory analysts on both the left and the right agree that this would also have the happy consequences of decreasing regulatory costs, increasing regulatory efficiency, and decreasing the burden on regu-

157

lators. In addition, a Congress not skewed toward regulation by delegation would rediscover practical reasons for allowing many matters to be left to state and local regulators.

Conclusion

Forcing Congress to vote on each and every administrative regulation that establishes a rule of private conduct would prove the most revolutionary change in government since the Civil War—not because the idea is particularly radical, but because we are today a nation governed, not by elected officials, but by unelected bureaucrats. The central political issues of the 109th Congress—the complex and heavy-handed array of regulations that entangle virtually all manner of private conduct, the perceived inability of elections to affect the direction of government, the disturbing political power of special interests, the lack of popular respect for the law, the sometimes tyrannical and self-aggrandizing exercise of power by government, and populist resentment of an increasingly unaccountable political elite—are but symptoms of a disease largely caused by delegation.

"No regulation without representation!" would be a fitting battle cry for the 109th Congress if it is truly interested in fundamental reform of government. It is a standard that both the left and the right could comfortably rally around, given that many prominent constitutional scholars, policy analysts, and journalists—from Nadine Strossen, president of the American Civil Liberties Union, to former judge Robert Bork—have expressed support for the end of delegation.

Some observers complain that voting on all regulations would overwhelm Congress. Certainly, federal agencies do issue thousands of regulations every year. However, the flow of new rules is no argument against congressional responsibility. Congress could bundle relatively minor regulations together and vote on the whole package. Both houses could then give major regulations—those that impose costs of more than $100 million annually—close scrutiny.

Of course, forcing Congress to take full and direct responsibility for the law would not prove a panacea. The legislature, after all, has shown itself to be fully capable of violating individual rights, subsidizing special interests, writing complex and virtually indecipherable law, and generally making a hash of things. But delegation has helped to make such phenomena, not the exception, but the rule of modern government. No more crucial—and potentially popular—reform awaits the attention of the 109th Congress.

Suggested Readings

Anthony, Robert. "Unlegislative Compulson: How Federal Agency Guidelines Threaten Your Liberty." Cato Institute Policy Analysis no. 312, August 11, 1998.

Breyer, Stephen. "The Legislative Veto after Chadha." Thomas F. Ryan lecture. *Georgetown Law Journal* 72 (1984).

DeLong, James. *Out of Bounds—Out of Control: Regulatory Enforcement at the EPA.* Washington: Cato Institute, 2002.

Lawson, Gary. "Delegation and the Constitution." *Regulation* 22, no. 2 (1999).

Lowi, Theodore. *The End of Liberalism: The Second Republic of the United States.* 2d ed. New York: W. W. Norton, 1979.

Schoenbrod, David. "Politics and the Principle That Elected Legislators Should Make the Laws." *Harvard Journal of Law and Public Policy* 26 (Winter 2003): 238–80.

―――. *Power without Responsibility: How Congress Abuses the People through Delegation.* New Haven, CT: Yale University Press, 1993.

Smith, Nick. "Restoration of Congressional Authority and Responsibility over the Regulatory Process." *Harvard Journal on Legislation* 33 (1996).

—Prepared by David Schoenbrod and Jerry Taylor

15. Term Limits

> **Each member of Congress should**
>
> - pledge to be a citizen legislator by limiting his or her time in office to no more than three additional terms in the House of Representatives and no more than two additional terms in the Senate and
> - keep that pledge.

Americans are dissatisfied with Washington. For more than a generation, polls have found a steady decline in the proportion of citizens who believe Washington can be trusted to do what is right. Most people believe that politics has nothing to do with their lives or that it is run for the benefit of a few. Not surprisingly, a poll by Princeton Survey Research Associates revealed that only 12 percent of the electorate have a great deal of confidence in Congress as an institution.

Americans can reclaim their democracy. They can have a government that is accountable to their will, a government for and by the people. They can have a citizen legislature in Washington and in every statehouse in America. Citizen legislators will make laws that make sense to ordinary people and revive our national faith in representative government.

How can we have citizen legislatures? The power of office has virtually put incumbents beyond the reach of the people. Restoring democracy requires term limits for incumbents. All members of Congress should pledge to limit their stay on Capitol Hill.

The People Support Term Limits

Members of Congress should listen to the good sense of the American people on this issue. For years, national polls have found that three of four voters support term limits. In a June 2000 poll by Diversified Research, Inc., 69 percent of Californians said they still approved of the original

(1990) term limits initiative. In March 2002, a ballot initiative designed to weaken California's term limits law was soundly defeated at the polls, despite a 10-to-1 spending advantage over term limit defenders. According to Paul Jacob, executive director of U.S. Term Limits, "If the people of this country got a chance tomorrow to vote on term limits for members of Congress, you would see them rush to the nearest polling place."

Indeed, the people have spoken loudly and clearly on term limits in virtually all of the states that provide an opportunity to do so. Twenty-two states representing nearly half of Congress had term limited their delegations by 1994. The great majority of those states had opted to limit their representatives to three terms, and all of those states had limited their senators to two terms. Only two of the 22 states chose six terms for the House.

From 1990 to 1995, state legislative term limits passed in 18 states. In November 2000, Nebraska became the 19th state to limit the terms of state legislators. The first 19 states passed term limits by an average of 67 percent of the vote. Moreover, almost every effort by incumbents to roll back term limits has been defeated by voters. Between 1996 and 2004, term limits affected 1,218 legislative seats. Term limits prevented 261 legislators in 12 states from running for reelection in the 2004 elections.

Despite the overwhelming support of the American people for term limits, the incumbent establishment has made it extremely difficult for the will of the people to be translated into law. When the Supreme Court declared that states could not limit the terms of their representatives in Washington, advocates of term limits petitioned the new Republican Congress—which had put term limits in its "Contract with America"—to pass a constitutional amendment to impose nationwide term limits. Incumbent members of Congress had an obvious conflict of interest on the issue, and they did not pass an amendment.

Take the Pledge

Americans believe term limits will make Congress a citizen legislature. But a Congress controlled by career politicians will never pass a term limits amendment. So the term limits movement, one of the most successful grassroots political efforts in U.S. history, has set out to change Congress from a bastion of careerism into a citizen legislature the best way it can—district by district.

George Washington set the standard. Perhaps the most popular and powerful American in history, Washington nevertheless stepped down after two terms as president. He handed back to the people the immense power and trust they had given to him—dramatically making the case that no one should monopolize a seat of power.

The tradition of a two-term limit for the president lasted uninterrupted for almost a century and a half. When Franklin D. Roosevelt broke the tradition, Congress moved to codify the term limit by proposing the Twenty-Second Amendment to the Constitution, which the states ratified in just 12 short months. The presidential term limit remains tremendously popular.

We can establish such a tradition in Congress. Since 1994 several dozen new faces have entered the halls of Congress, serious about changing the culture of Washington and after pledging to limit themselves to three terms in the House or two terms in the Senate. Those pledges have resonated with the voters who understand that a lawmaker's career interests do not always coincide with the interests of the people back home. A poll by Fabrizio-McLaughlin and Associates asked, "Would you be more likely to vote for a candidate who pledges to serve no more than three terms in the House, or a candidates who refuses to self limit?" Seventy-two percent of respondents said they would be more likely to vote for the self-limiter.

Self-limiters serve their constituents well. Rep. Matt Salmon of Arizona, in reaffirming the pledge he made in 1994 to serve only three terms in the House, said:

> The independence that comes from limiting my terms has enabled me to vote against the bloated budget deal of 1997, and to challenge my own party's leadership when I feel it would be best for the people of Arizona. Instead of looking ahead to my own career in the House, I am able to put my Arizona constituents first.

Self-limiters also resist Washington's culture of spending. They are able to vote for spending limits because of the freedom of conscience afforded by their term limit pledge. The self-limiters' collective experience suggests that self-limitation helps to discipline a politician's legislative behavior. Self-limiters exercise greater independence than their non-term-limited peers and appear less fearful of incurring the wrath of either party power brokers or special interest groups. During the past several years, many self-limiters stood out as the most fiscally conservative members of Congress.

Not surprisingly, self-limiters have spearheaded opposition to pork-barrel spending and committee budget increases. They have demanded honest accounting and pioneered the political push for real reform of flawed government programs such as Social Security and Medicare—so often used by professional politicians as political footballs.

Term Limits on Committee Chairs

Most laws begin life in congressional committees led by powerful chairs who act as gatekeepers for floor votes on legislation. For decades the average tenure of a committee chair was about 20 years. The seniority system allowed entrenched politicians from the least competitive districts to wield power over other members, not on the basis of merit, but because of their longevity. In the past the only way to lose a chair was by death, resignation, retirement, or electoral defeat.

The seniority system increased the level of pork-barrel spending and blocked much needed change. For example, in a Cato Institute Policy Analysis, "Term Limits and the Republican Congress," Aaron Steelman examined 31 key tax and spending proposals in the 104th and 105th Congresses. He found that junior Republicans in Congress were "more than twice as likely to vote for spending or tax cuts as were senior Republicans." Steelman pointed out that "veteran Republican legislators have proven they are comfortable with big government. It is unlikely that fundamental change in Washington will occur while they continue to control legislative debate and action."

For those reasons, in 1995 the Speaker of the House decided to limit the terms of House committee chairs to three terms, totaling six years. Those limits are an important dent in a corrupt system. Term limits on those powerful positions make the House more responsible and open the way for newer members to influence policy. In 1996 the Republican caucus imposed six-year limits on GOP committee chairs. As a consequence, some changes have occurred on the traditional Senate leadership career path. But the pace of change should be quickened, not slowed down. The 109th Congress should retain term limits on committee chairs in the House and extend them to Senate committee chairs.

Why We Need a Citizen Legislature

Why are term limits so popular? Americans believe that career legislators and professional politicians have created a gaping chasm between themselves and their government. For democracy to work, it must be representative—a government of, by, and for the people. Democracy in America requires a citizen legislature.

To be a citizen legislator, a member of Congress should not be far removed from the private sector. The members of the House of Representatives, in particular, should be close to the people they represent. As Rhode Island's Roger Sherman wrote at the time of our nation's founding: "Representatives ought to return home and mix with the people. By remaining at the seat of government, they would acquire the habits of the place, which might differ from those of their constituents." In the era of year-round legislative sessions, the only way to achieve that objective is through term limits.

What should be the limit on terms? Some observers have proposed as many as six terms (or 12 years) for the House. Three terms for the House is better for several reasons. America is best served by a Congress whose members are there out of a sense of civic duty but who would rather live their lives in the private sector, holding productive jobs in civil society, far removed from government and politics. Such individuals might be willing to spend two, four, or even six years in Washington, but not if the legislative agenda is being set by others who have gained their authority through seniority. Twelve-year "limits," which amount to a mini-career, do little to remove this major obstacle to a more diverse and representative group of Americans seeking office.

We have solid evidence that short, three-term limits enhance the democratic process: Proposition 140 in California, which was passed by the voters there in 1990 and limited the state assembly to three two-year terms. The 1992 assembly elections witnessed a sharp increase in the number of citizens seeking office, with a remarkable 27 freshmen elected to the 80-member lower house of the California legislature. In an article on that freshman class, the *Los Angeles Times* said:

> Among the things making the group unusual is that most of them are true outsiders. For the first time in years, the freshman class does not include an abundance of former legislative aides who moved up the ladder to become members. . . . Among the 27 are a former U.S. Air Force fighter pilot, a former sheriff-coroner, a paralegal, a retired teacher, a video store owner, a businesswoman-homemaker, a children's advocate, an interior designer, a retired sheriff's lieutenant, and a number of businessmen, lawyers, and former city council members.

A scholarly study of the California legislature by Mark Petracca of the University of California at Irvine found that the strict term limits Californians passed in 1990 had the following consequences:

- Turnover in both legislative chambers increased markedly.
- The number of incumbents seeking reelection dropped sharply.
- The percentage of elections in which incumbents won reelection dropped significantly.
- The number of women in both houses increased.
- The number of uncontested races declined.
- The number of candidates seeking office in both chambers increased.
- The winning margin of incumbents declined.

While perhaps not attractive to people seeking to be career politicians, all those developments please the great majority of Americans who favor a return to citizen legislatures.

Similarly, a three-term limit for the U.S. House of Representatives would return control of the House—not just through voting but also through participation—to the people. We must make the possibility of serving in Congress a more attractive option for millions more Americans.

A second reason for shorter term limits is that the longer one is in Congress, the more one is exposed to and influenced by the "culture of ruling" that permeates life inside the Beltway. Groups such as the National Taxpayers Union have shown that the longer people serve in Congress, the bigger spenders, taxers, and regulators they become. That is just as true of conservatives as it is of liberals. It is also understandable. Members of Congress are surrounded at work and socially by people who spend other people's money and regulate their lives. It is the unusual individual— although such people do exist—who is not subtly but surely affected by that culture.

Three terms rather than six would better serve as an antidote to the growing "professionalization" of the legislative process. As Mark Petracca has written:

> Whereas representative government aspires to maintain a proximity of sympathy and interests between representative and represented, profession- alism creates authority, autonomy, and hierarchy, distancing the expert from the client. Though this distance may be necessary and functional for lawyers, nurses, physicians, accountants, and social scientists, the qualities and characteristics associated with being a "professional" legislator run counter to the supposed goals of a representative democracy. Professional- ism encourages an independence of ambition, judgment, and behavior that is squarely at odds with the inherently dependent nature of representative government.

Finally, shorter limits for the House would enhance the competitiveness of elections and, as previously noted, increased the number and diversity of Americans choosing to run for Congress. The most competitive races (and the ones that bring out the largest number of primary candidates) are for open seats.

At least a third of all House seats would be open each election under three-term limits, and it is probable that as many as half will not feature an incumbent seeking reelection. We also know from past experience that women and minorities have greater electoral success in races for open seats.

The members of a true citizen legislature literally view their time in office as a leave of absence from their real careers. Their larger ambitions lie in the private sector, not in expanding the ambit of government. Citizen legislators are true public servants, not the new masters of the political class.

State Legislative Term Limits Are Working

Term limits are taking effect all over the country in state legislatures—and they are working. Term limits were intended to end careerism among legislators. Scholarly research on the effects of term limits suggests that they have substantially attained that goal. Congress should take note:

- Term limits remain popular with state electorates long after their introduction.
- Term limits stimulate electoral competition in state legislative elections.
- Term limits enable nontraditional candidates to run for seats in state legislatures. Female, Hispanic, and Asian candidates find it easier to enter term-limited legislatures than non-term-limited bodies.
- Term limits weaken seniority systems in state legislatures.
- Term limits have not strengthened interest groups, state bureaucracies, or legislative staffs as predicted by critics of term limits.
- Term limits foster public policies that serve to halt, or at least reduce, the growth in the size and scope of government. Term-limited politicians demonstrate greater respect than their non-term-limited colleagues for taxpayers' money.

Clearly, term limits are working. Congress can't hold out forever.

Conclusion

The term limits movement is not motivated by disdain for the institution of Congress. It is motivated by a sincere desire on the part of the American

167

people to regain control of the most representative part of the federal government. Resistance to this movement on the part of elected federal legislators only underscores the image of an Imperial Congress.

Those who sign the Term Limits Declaration are on the record as citizen legislators. Increasingly, that pledge will make the difference in winning competitive seats in Congress. The seniority system, rotten at its core, cannot survive a Congress where more and more members are under term limits. Nor can wrong-headed policies and wasteful spending projects survive a Congress with so many citizen legislators.

On May 22, 1995, a five-to-four Supreme Court ruling in *U.S. Term Limits, Inc. v. Thornton* overturned the congressional term limits imposed by 23 states. Eight of the Supreme Court justices are now at least 65 years old, and as many as four justices may retire during the next Congress. The replacement of even one justice could significantly affect future rulings. The potential for turnover on the Court over the next few years may offer an opportunity to revisit the congressional term limits issue in the near future.

Term limits remain an issue to be reckoned with. Public support is even stronger and deeper for candidates making personal term limits commitments than for a term limits amendment. Voters seek to replace career politicians with dedicated citizen legislators as the best solution to what ails us in Washington. Political leaders who understand the problems created by a permanent ruling elite in Washington—or who simply want to abide by the overwhelming will of their constituents—will pledge to serve no more than three additional terms in the House or two in the Senate.

Suggested Readings

Bandow, Doug. "The Political Revolution That Wasn't: Why Term Limits Are Needed Now More Than Ever." Cato Institute Policy Analysis no. 259, September 5, 1996.

Basham, Patrick. "Assessing the Term Limits Experiment: California and Beyond." Cato Institute Policy Analysis no. 413, August 31, 2001.

———. "Defining Democracy Down: Explaining the Campaign to Repeal Term Limits." Cato Institute Policy Analysis no. 490, September 24, 2003.

Carey, John M., Richard G. Niemi, and Lynda W. Powell. *Term Limits in the State Legislatures*. Ann Arbor: University of Michigan Press, 2000.

Crane, Edward H., and Roger Pilon, eds. *The Politics and Law of Term Limits*. Washington: Cato Institute, 1994.

Elhauge, Einer. "What Term Limits Do That Ordinary Voting Cannot." Cato Institute Policy Analysis no. 328, December 16, 1998.

O'Keefe, Eric. *Who Rules America? The People vs. the Political Class*. Spring Green, WI: Citizen Government Foundation, 1999.

O'Keefe, Eric, and Aaron Steelman. "The End of Representation: How Congress Stifles Electoral Competition." Cato Institute Policy Analysis no. 279, August 20, 1997.

Owings, Stephanie, and Rainald Borck. "Legislative Professionalism and Government Spending: Do Citizen Legislators Really Spend Less?" *Public Finance Review* 23 (2000): 210–25.

Steelman, Aaron. "Term Limits and the Republican Congress." Cato Institute Briefing Paper no. 41, October 27, 1998.

—Prepared by Edward H. Crane and Patrick Basham

16. Campaign Finance

Congress should

- repeal the prohibition on soft money fundraising in the Bipartisan Campaign Reform Act of 2002 (BCRA),
- repeal the provisions of BCRA related to electioneering communications,
- eliminate taxpayer funding of presidential campaigns,
- reject proposals to mandate electoral advertising paid for by the owners of the television networks,
- reform the Federal Election Commission to bring it under the rule of law, and
- deregulate the current campaign finance system.

The 107th Congress passed the most sweeping new restrictions on campaign finance in a generation, the Bipartisan Campaign Reform Act of 2002 (BCRA). During the 108th Congress, the Supreme Court endorsed almost all of BCRA. Proponents of more restrictions will urge the 109th Congress to criminalize the fundraising of 527 groups, force taxpayers to spend more on presidential campaigns, mandate "free" political advertising for candidates, and replace the current Federal Election Commission with a new agency modeled on the Federal Bureau of Investigation. BCRA and the proposed changes in current law reflect the mistaken assumptions of the so-called reformers.

Freedom and Corruption

The Constitution prohibits the government from abridging freedom of speech. In the seminal case of *Buckley v. Valeo* (1976), the Supreme Court recognized that restrictions on political spending abridge political speech:

> A restriction on the amount of money a person or group can spend on political communication during a campaign necessarily reduces the quantity

of expression by restricting the number of issues discussed, the depth of their exploration, and the size of the audience reached. This is because virtually every means of communicating ideas in today's mass society requires the expenditure of money.

Note that the Court did not say, "Money equals speech." It said that political speech requires spending money. Restrictions on money thus translate into restrictions on speech.

We should encourage, not restrict, campaign spending. John J. Coleman of the University of Wisconsin found that campaign spending increases public knowledge of the candidates across all groups in the population. Less spending on campaigns is not likely to increase public trust, involvement, or attention. Implicit or explicit spending limits reduce public knowledge during campaigns. Getting more money into campaigns benefits American democracy.

Unfortunately, contributions to campaigns do not enjoy the same constitutional protections as spending. In 1974 Congress limited campaign contributions to prevent "corruption or the appearance of corruption." Until recently those ceilings have governed American elections without being adjusted for inflation. BCRA raised the limits on "hard money" contributions, but their real value remains well below the ceilings enacted in 1974.

The lower protection afforded contributions makes little sense. Political candidates spend money to obtain the means (often television time) to communicate with voters; such spending, as noted earlier, is protected speech. But contributors give to candidates for the same reason—to enable candidates to present their views to the electorate. Moreover, ceilings on contributions complicate raising money and thus inevitably reduce "the quantity of expression by restricting the number of issues discussed, the depth of their exploration, and the size of the audience reached" by the candidate.

What about corruption? We have more than 200 pages of federal laws regulating campaign finance. All of those laws purport to prevent corruption or the appearance of corruption in national politics.

What is corruption? Bribery is a clear case of corruption. Bribery involves secretly giving public officials something of value (usually money) in exchange for political favors. Officials then spend bribes on private consumption. Campaign contributions also involve giving money to public officials or their agents. However, by law the recipients may spend contributions only for political purposes. Anyone who spends campaign contributions on fancy cars and lavish houses commits a felony. Unlike bribes, contributions are publicly disclosed.

Critics argue that contributors influence the judgment of legislators and receive favors for their donations. The evidence says otherwise. Three leading scholars examined 41 studies of the influence of money on legislative voting. They conclude: "The evidence that campaign contributions lead to a substantial influence on votes is rather thin. Legislators' votes depend almost entirely on their own beliefs and the preferences of their voters and their party. Contributions explain a minuscule fraction of the variation in voting behavior in the U.S. Congress. Members of Congress care foremost about winning reelection. They must attend to the constituency that elects them, voters in a district or state, and the constituency that nominates them, the party." The assumption that money corrupts and more money corrupts even more comes up short on the evidence.

What about preventing the appearance of corruption? We might first wonder why the mere appearance of illegality should be sufficient reason to restrict First Amendment rights. Proponents argue that campaign contributions appear to corrupt the political process, thereby undermining public confidence in government. Once again the evidence runs against proponents of campaign finance restrictions. John Coleman found that campaign spending had no effect on public confidence in government. Nathaniel Persily and Kelli Lammie discovered that Americans' "confidence in the system of representative government" is associated with individuals' positions in society, their general tendency to trust others, their beliefs about what government should do, and their ideological or philosophical disagreement with the policies of incumbent officeholders. On the other hand, they found our system of campaign finance had no effect on public confidence.

Congressional Conflicts of Interest

The intense interest in campaign finance regulation shown by members of Congress—substantially greater than the interest shown by most Americans—should hardly surprise. Campaign finance law affects their prospects for reelection. Campaign finance regulation brings every member face to face with the problem of self-dealing—not only the self-dealing the regulations are supposed to prevent but, more immediately, the self-dealing that is inherent in writing regulations not simply for oneself but for those who would challenge one's power to write such regulations in the first place.

Only one congressional election since 1974 has seen an incumbent reelection rate lower than 90 percent. Even in the "revolution" of 1994, which changed control of the House of Representatives, 90 percent of incumbents were reelected. The last three elections have seen reelection rates of more than 98 percent.

Campaign finance restrictions may not fully explain the lack of competition for incumbents in American politics. But those restrictions encumber entry into the political market and thus discourage credible challenges to incumbents. A challenger needs large sums to campaign for public office, especially at the federal level. He needs big money to overcome the manifest advantages of incumbency—name recognition, the power of office, the franking privilege, a knowledgeable staff, campaign experience, and, perhaps most important, easy access to the media. Yet current law limits the supply of campaign dollars: an individual can give no more than $2,000 to a candidate, and a political party or a political action committee (PAC) can give no more than $5,000.

In a free and open political system, challengers would find a few "deep pockets" to get them started, then build support from there, unrestrained by any restrictions save for the traditional prohibitions on vote selling and vote buying. That is how liberal Eugene McCarthy challenged an incumbent president in 1968. It is how conservative James Buckley challenged an incumbent senator and a major party challenger in 1970. Candidates following their examples today would be criminals. Challengers living within the law incur massive compliance costs, including the risk of future litigation and prosecution. Many are discouraged, in all likelihood, from mounting a challenge. That is not healthy for democracy.

The Soft Money Ban

BCRA makes things worse. By banning "soft money"—unregulated contributions given to the political parties—Congress has complicated the lives of challengers. Parties have traditionally directed soft money contributions to races in which challengers might have a chance. A Cato Institute study found, not surprisingly, that state restrictions on giving to parties (regulations similar to BCRA's soft money ban) reduce the overall competitiveness of elections. At the same time, BCRA does not affect donations by PACs, most of which go to incumbents. BCRA does loosen federal contribution limits for candidates running against self-funding individuals. Apparently, contributions over $2,000 corrupt politics—unless an incumbent faces a self-funding millionaire. That strains credulity. BCRA seems little more than an incumbent protection law, a monument to the dangers of self-dealing.

Activists have circumvented the soft money ban by raising unlimited contributions on behalf of groups organized under Section 527 of the Internal Revenue Code. BCRA's sponsors will urge Congress to restrict the activities of those groups. Indeed, the FEC has already passed regulations to that end to take effect after the 2004 election. Instead of adding more restrictions, Congress should repeal the soft money prohibition, thereby removing the rationale for the existence of the 527 groups.

Political Advertising

Congress's conflict of interest does not end with the ban on soft money. For several years, interest groups and the political parties funded aggressive advertising criticizing members of Congress during their reelection campaigns. To be sure, some of those ads were unfair or inaccurate, but the Constitution protects the right to be both. BCRA prohibits such advertising funded by corporations and unions if it mentions a candidate for federal office. If such ads are coordinated with a campaign, their funding is subject to federal election law including contribution limits.

Those restrictions mean future elections will have fewer ads, less debate of public matters, and less criticism of elected officials. Congress has decided either to prohibit or to complicate the fundraising and political activities of its critics. The Supreme Court went along with that harassment of free speech. To restore the First Amendment, the 109th Congress should repeal all provisions of BCRA relating to electioneering communications.

Taxpayer Financing of Campaigns

Some people believe the United States can preclude corruption or its appearance only by prohibiting all private contributions, whether designated as campaign contributions or not, and moving to a system of taxpayer-financed campaigns.

Taxpayers now finance primary and general election campaigns for president. Compared with the system it replaced, presidential public financing has not increased competition in the party primaries or the general election. The system borders on insolvency because ever-fewer taxpayers check off the contribution box on their income tax return. The declining support for the program makes sense. Polls show Americans reject public financing as "welfare for politicians." Congress should eliminate this unpopular multi-billion-dollar boondoggle.

Proponents of campaign finance reform want the 109th Congress to force the television networks to pay for political advertising. The networks would be required to "donate" airtime, which would be given to the political parties as vouchers. The shareholders of the companies that own the networks would be taxed to fund this advertising. Proponents claim such taxes are a fair price for the use of public property, the airwaves. In fact, economist Thomas Hazlett has shown that government's claim to "ownership" of the airwaves amounts to nothing more than imposing political control over the media of radio and television. Even if we grant for purposes of argument that the airwaves belong to the public, we might ask why the broadcasters have to pay for political advertising. After all, trucking companies pay taxes for the upkeep of roads, but they are not required to haul freight for members of Congress.

The Federal Election Commission

Proponents of "reform" argue that the Federal Election Commission has failed to enforce election law and has undermined BCRA. They urge Congress to replace the FEC with a stronger agency—one with a law enforcement mission, a kind of Federal Bureau of Investigation for elections and political campaigns.

The juxtaposition of the FBI and political campaigns should trouble Americans. Do we want a federal law enforcement agency investigating the campaigns of members of Congress and those who challenge them for office? That is an invitation for political or partisan abuse. The late, unlamented Independent Counsel statute comes immediately to mind. Do members of Congress want every detail of their last campaigns subject to investigation by an agency controlled either by their political enemies or by the reformers themselves?

Congress should get rid of the FEC as part of a broader deregulation of political speech and electoral campaigns. Absent that, Congress should move to reform the FEC to make its procedures comport with the rule of law.

Defendants before the FEC have few due process safeguards. When a complaint comes before the commission, its general counsel makes the case against the alleged lawbreaker, who has no right to appear before the commission. The general counsel provides the commission with a report that summarizes and criticizes the legal arguments of the accused and is present to answer questions from the commissioners. Those reports are not given to the accused even though they may contain new arguments or information.

The FEC also sends out discovery subpoenas on the recommendation of its general counsel. To contest a subpoena, a citizen must appeal to the FEC itself, which turns the matter over to its Office of General Counsel. The commission rarely grants motions to quash its own subpoenas. It often will not provide the accused with documents that might aid the defendant. How could all of this accord with the rule of law?

The FEC has hardly been a pussycat in enforcing federal restrictions on campaign finance. Like most burgeoning bureaucratic empires, it has continually tried to extend its regulatory authority. Prior to BCRA, the FEC continually sought to regulate issue advertising, a protected form of speech.

The FEC has attacked political speech in other ways as well. Thus, the government can constitutionally regulate "political committees." Some people on the FEC argue that spending on issue advocacy, a protected freedom, makes a group a political committee and thus subjects it to regulation. In the Orwellian world of the FEC, exercising constitutional freedom justifies government coercion. Federal law also regulates electoral activities if they are coordinated with a candidate. The FEC has always pushed a broad concept of coordination, the better to bring more political activity under its control.

Not surprisingly, those aggressive FEC attacks have chilled political activities at the grassroots. Individuals and small groups lack the resources to take on a bevy of specialized, zealous lawyers supported by taxpayers. The FEC is yet another expansive federal bureaucracy that should be reined in by Congress in the near term and eliminated over the long term.

The Real Problem

The campaign finance laws have made our politics less competitive by favoring incumbents over challengers, thereby striking at the very heart of democratic government. As James Madison said in *Federalist* no. 51, a dependence on the people is the primary control on government. That dependence can only have meaning in elections with vigorous competition. By undermining competitive elections, campaign finance laws undermine democracy. Moreover, to the extent that incumbency is correlated with ever-larger government, as studies repeatedly show, our present law exacerbates the very problem it was meant to reduce—corruption.

We come, then, to the heart of the matter. Campaign finance "reform" distracts us from the real issue, the ultimate source of potential corruption—ubiquitous government. Government today fosters corruption of every form because it exercises vast powers over virtually every aspect of life. Given that reality, is it any wonder that special interests—indeed that every interest but the general—should be trying either to take advantage of that or to protect themselves from it?

The Founders understood the problem of what they called "factions." They understood that interests would be tempted to capture government for their own ends. To reduce that temptation, they wrote a constitution that granted government only limited powers.

Far from forcing everyone to contribute to campaigns, the Founders left individuals free to decide the matter for themselves—and free also to decide how much to contribute. The Founders were mindful of the potential for real corruption, which they left to traditional legal means to ferret out.

The Founders had a pair of better ideas about how to handle the various forms of corruption. The first was to rely on competition, to construct a system that enabled interest to be pitted against interest. There is no shortage, after all, of special interests. But if you fetter them all, through some grand regulatory scheme, you stifle the natural forces that are necessary for the health of the system. No individual, no committee of Congress, no blue-ribbon committee of elders can fine-tune the system of political competition. It has to be free to seek its own equilibrium.

The second idea was equally simple, yet equally profound: limit power in the first place, the better to limit the opportunities for corruption. If a member of Congress has only limited power to sell, there will be limited opportunities to buy.

Once we recognize corruption as a breach of the trust that is grounded in the oath of office to uphold the Constitution, we see that the problem is much broader than is ordinarily thought. In fact, people who try to reduce the issue to one of money—big money buying access—miss the larger picture entirely. Money may induce a member to vote for an interest narrower than the general good—the evidence notwithstanding—but when we ratified the Constitution we gave members the opportunity to do so only to a very limited degree. In fact, it was because we understood, as Lord Acton would later put it, that power tends to corrupt and absolute power corrupts absolutely, that we so limited our officials. And we realized that they would be tempted to breach their oaths of office not only for money but for power as well—indeed, for the office itself. Thus, it was not "special interests" alone that the Founders feared but the people too: The Founders wanted to protect against the capture of government by that ever-changing special interest known as "the majority." For that reason too—no, especially—they limited government's powers.

The federal government now has an all but unlimited power to redistribute and regulate at will, an ambit that virtually ensures that members of Congress will act not for the general good, the good of all, but for some narrower interest. Indeed, the modern state and politics are corrupt by nature. When government takes from some to give to others, it does not serve the *general* good—and cannot, *by definition.* When candidates promise "free" goods and services from government in exchange for votes, they are selling their office, plain and simple: "Vote for me and I'll vote to give you these goods." That is where corruption begins. It begins with the corruption—or death (the root of "corruption")—of the oath of office. For not remotely does our Constitution authorize the kind of redistributive state we have in this nation today (see Chapter 3 for a detailed discussion).

To root out the generalized corruption endemic to modern government, one should begin with the Constitution and the oath of office. The Constitution establishes a government of delegated, enumerated, and thus limited powers. It sets forth powers that are, as Madison put it in *Federalist* no. 45, "few and defined." Thus, it addresses the problem of self-dealing by limiting the opportunities for self-dealing. If Congress has only limited power to control citizens' lives—if citizens are otherwise free to plan and live their own lives—Congress has little influence to sell, whether for cash, for perquisites, or for votes.

Before they take the solemn oath of office, therefore, members of Congress should reflect on whether they are swearing to support the Constitution as written and understood by those who wrote and ratified it or the Constitution the New Deal Court discovered in 1937. The contrast between the two could not be greater. One was written for limited government; the other was crafted for potentially unlimited government. As that potential has materialized, the opportunities for corruption have become ever more manifest, as members know only too well. Indeed, to appreciate the point, we need only notice the corruption that is endemic to totalitarian systems—the ultimate redistributive states—despite draconian sanctions against it. It goes with ubiquitous government.

Conclusion

The answer to the corruption that is thought to attend our system of private campaign financing is not more campaign finance regulations but fewer such regulations. The limits on campaign contributions, in particular, should be removed, for they are the source of many of our present problems. More generally, however, the opportunities for corruption that were so expanded when we abandoned constitutionally limited government need to be radically reduced. Members of Congress can do that by taking the Constitution and their oaths of office more seriously.

Suggested Readings

Ansolabehere, Stephen, John M. de Figueiredo, and James M. Snyder Jr., "Why Is There So Little Money in U.S. Politics?" *Journal of Economic Perspectives* 17 (Winter 2003): 105–30.

Basham, Patrick. "It's the Spending, Stupid! Understanding Campaign Finance in the Big Government Era." Cato Institute Briefing Paper no. 64, July 18, 2001.

Coleman, John J. "The Benefits of Campaign Spending." Cato Institute Briefing Paper no. 84, September 4, 2003.

Hazlett, Thomas W. "The Rationality of U.S. Regulation of the Broadcast Spectrum." *Journal of Law and Economics* 33 (April 1990): 133–75.

Persily, Nathan, and Kelli Lammie. "Perceptions of Corruption and Campaign Finance: When Public Opinion Constitutes Constitutional Law." *University of Pennsylvania Law Review* 153 (December 2004).

Pilon, Roger. "Freedom, Responsibility, and the Constitution: On Recovering Our Founding Principles." *Notre Dame Law Review* 68 (1993).

Samples, John. "The Failures of Taxpayer Financing of Presidential Campaigns." Cato Institute Policy Analysis no. 500, November 25, 2003.

Samples, John, ed. *Welfare for Politicians: Taxpayer Financing of Campaigns and American Democracy.* Washington: Cato Institute, 2005.

Samples, John, and Adam D. Thierer. "Why Subsidize the Soapbox? The McCain Free Airtime Proposal and the Future of Broadcasting." Cato Institute Policy Analysis no. 480, August 6, 2003.

Smith, Bradley A. "Campaign Finance Regulation: Faulty Assumptions and Undemocratic Consequences." Cato Institute Policy Analysis no. 238, September 13, 1995.

———. *Unfree Speech: The Folly of Campaign Finance Reform.* Princeton, NJ: Princeton University Press, 2001.

Smith, Bradley A., and Stephen M. Hoersting. "A Toothless Anaconda: Innovation, Impotence and Overenforcement at the Federal Election Commission." *Election Law Journal* 1 (2002): 145–71.

—Prepared by Roger Pilon and John Samples

17. Reclaiming the War Power

> **Congress should**
> - cease trying to shirk its constitutional responsibilities in matters of war and peace,
> - insist that hostilities not be initiated by the executive branch unless and until Congress has authorized such action, and
> - oppose any effort to reshape national security doctrine in a manner that denies congressional supremacy over the war power.

The horror of September 11, 2001, changed many things: it ended a certain American innocence and sense of invincibility; it taught Americans that our enemies could strike at us on our own soil; and it provided ample justification for defending ourselves by waging war on Al Qaeda and its nation-state allies. It did not, however, amend the Constitution. Indeed, President Bush has repeatedly made it clear that the fight against terrorists is a fight to maintain our free institutions and the way of life they sustain. Six days after the destruction of the World Trade Center and the attack on the Pentagon, President Bush issued a proclamation in honor of our Constitution. In it, he declared that "today, in the face of the terrorist attacks of September 11, 2001, we must call upon, more than ever, the Constitutional principles that make our country great."

No constitutional principle is more important than congressional control over the decision to go to war. In affairs of state, no more momentous decision can be made. For that reason, in a democratic republic, it is essential that that decision be made by the most broadly representative body: the legislature. As James Madison put it, "In no part of the constitution is more wisdom to be found, than in the clause which confides the question of war or peace to the legislature, and not to the executive department."

The Constitutional Framework

In the Constitution as Madison and the other Framers designed it, the president lacks the authority to initiate hostilities. In the Framers' view, absent prior authorization by Congress, the president's war powers were purely defensive; if the territory of the United States or U.S. forces were attacked, the president could respond. But he could not undertake aggressive actions without prior congressional authorization.

On August 17, 1787, the Constitutional Convention considered the recommendation of the Committee of Detail that the legislature should have sole power "to make war." Only one delegate, South Carolina's Pierce Butler, spoke in favor of granting that authority to the executive. As Madison's notes from the Convention tell us, that idea was not warmly received. "Mr. [Elbridge] Gerry [of Massachusetts said he] never expected to hear in a republic a motion to empower the Executive alone to declare war." For his part, George Mason of Virginia "was agst. giving the power of war to the Executive, because not to be trusted with it. . . . He was for clogging rather than facilitating war."

However, the delegates did take seriously the objection, raised by Charles Pinckney of South Carolina, that the House of Representatives was too large and unwieldy, and met too infrequently, to supervise all the details attendant to the conduct of a war. For that reason, "Mr. M[adison] and Mr. Gerry moved to insert '*declare*,' striking out '*make*' war; leaving to the Executive the power to repel sudden attacks." Roger Sherman of Connecticut "thought [the proposal] stood very well. The Executive shd. be able to repel and not to commence war." The motion passed.

The document that emerged from the convention vests the bulk of the powers associated with military action in Congress, among them the powers "to declare War, [and] grant Letters of Marque and Reprisal." Other important war-making powers include the power "to raise and support Armies, but no Appropriation of Money to that Use shall be for a longer Term than two years," and "to provide for calling forth the Militia to execute the Laws of the Union, suppress Insurrections and repel invasions."

Significantly, several of the enumerated powers allocated to Congress involve the decision to initiate military action. Viewed in this light, Congress's power to issue "letters of Marque and Reprisal" and its power to call out the militia inform our understanding of Congress's authority to declare war. A letter of marque and reprisal is a legal device (long fallen into disuse) empowering private citizens to take offensive action against citizens of foreign countries, usually privateers attacking ships. Since military attacks carried out by American citizens might well be considered acts of war by foreign powers, and accordingly embroil the United States in hostilities, the Constitution vests the important decision to grant this power in the most deliberative body: the legislature. Similarly, Article I, sec. 8 gives Congress power over the militia, allowing Congress to decide when domestic unrest has reached the point where military action is required.

In contrast, the grant of authority to the executive as "Commander-in-Chief" of U.S. Armed Forces is entirely supervisory and reactive. The president commands the Army and Navy and leads them into battle, should Congress choose to declare war. He commands the militia to suppress rebellions, should the militia be "called into the actual Service of the United States." In this, as Hamilton noted in *Federalist* no. 69, the president acts as no more than the "first General" of the United States. And generals, it should go without saying, are not empowered to decide with whom we go to war. The Constitution leaves that decision to Congress. As Constitutional Convention delegate James Wilson explained to the Pennsylvania ratifying convention: "This system will not hurry us into war; it is calculated to guard against it. It will not be in the power of a single man, or a single body of men, to involve us in such distress; for the important power in declaring war is vested in the legislature at large."

Congressional Abdication

Given that constitutional framework, 2002's debate about war with Iraq left a lot to be desired. At first, Bush administration officials proceeded as if no authorization were necessary. Then, in August 2002 the White House Counsel's Office brazenly insisted that the administration already had congressional authorization for Gulf War II, in the form of the 1991 joint resolution that authorized Gulf War I. How could a resolution passed in 1991 to give a previous president authority to expel Saddam Hussein from Kuwait authorize another president to take Baghdad 11 years later? A good question, the answer to which was not at all apparent from reading the 1991 resolution. Such tendentious stretching of legal authority might have been appropriate for a trial lawyer zealously pressing his client's interest. But for a president sworn to uphold the Constitution, and seeking legal justification to lead troops into battle, something more than clever lawyering was required: new and independent authorization for a new war.

Of course, the administration eventually sought, and secured, congressional authorization for use of force against Iraq. It did so despite the fact that some prominent members of Congress did not want to be burdened with the vast responsibility the Constitution places on their shoulders. Then–senate minority leader Trent Lott (R-MS), for instance, treated the Democrats' push for congressional authorization as a partisan annoyance rather than a solemn constitutional duty, calling it "a blatant political move that's not helpful."

In some ways, that was nothing new. Throughout the 20th century, congressional control of the war power eroded, not simply as a result of executive branch aggrandizement, but also because of congressional complicity. The imperial presidency continues to grow, largely because many legislators want to duck their responsibility to decide the question of war and peace, delegate that responsibility to the president, and reserve their right to criticize him, should military action go badly.

Indeed, even in authorizing the president to use force, Congress attempted to shirk its responsibility to decide on war. After voting for the resolution, which gave the president all the authority he needed to attack Iraq, prominent members of Congress insisted they hadn't really voted to use force. That was for the president to decide. As Senate Majority Leader Tom Daschle (D-SD) put it: "Regardless of how one may have voted on the resolution last night, I think there is an overwhelming consensus . . . that while [war] may be necessary, we're not there yet." But it is not for the president to decide whether we are "there yet." The Constitution leaves that question to Congress.

In the rush to war, most members couldn't even be bothered to use due diligence on the Iraq issue—to examine the available intelligence and decide for themselves whether they thought a serious threat existed. Throughout the fall of 2002, copies of the 92-page National Intelligence Estimate on the Iraq threat were kept in two guarded vaults on Capitol Hill—available to any member of the House or Senate who wanted to review it. In March 2004 the *Washington Post* revealed that only six senators and a handful of House members found it worth the effort to go and read the whole document. Sen. Jay Rockefeller explained that general reluctance to read intelligence briefings by saying that, when you're a senator, "everyone in the world wants to come see you" in your office and getting away to the secure room—across the Capitol grounds at the Hart Senate Office Building—is "not easy to do." He added that intelligence briefings tend to be "extremely dense reading."

This will not do. When our representatives vote to wage war, it's not too much to ask that they've absorbed the available information and made an informed decision. Too often, however, it seems they'd prefer to punt the decision to the president and hold him accountable for a decision that's theirs to make.

Congressional scholar Louis Fisher compares the Iraq vote to the Gulf of Tonkin Resolution that empowered Lyndon Johnson to expand the Vietnam War. As was the Iraq war resolution, the Gulf of Tonkin Resolution was broadly worded to allow the president to make the final decision about war all by himself. Lyndon Johnson compared the resolution to "grandma's nightshirt" because it "covered everything." And, as with Iraq, the president did not immediately use the authority granted him. It would be six months later, after Johnson defeated Goldwater in the November election, before the war escalated with a sustained bombing campaign in North Vietnam. In Iraq, President Bush waited five months before launching Operation Iraqi Freedom. As Fisher put it, "In each case [Vietnam and Iraq], instead of acting as the people's representatives and preserving the republican form of government, [Congress] gave the president unchecked power." In each case, it was easier to dodge the issue than to take responsibility.

That's how Sen. John F. Kerry and Sen. John Edwards both saw it at the time. In the run-up to the vote, Edwards said, "In a short time Congress will have dealt with Iraq and then we'll be on to other issues." Kerry echoed: "We will have done our vote. . . . You're not going to see anything happen in Iraq until December, January, February, sometime later. . . . And we will go back to the real issues."

But the question of war *is* a "real issue," if anything is. It's the gravest issue the Constitution requires Congress to decide. That prominent senators—and presidential candidates—squirm to avoid responsibility for it does not bode well for the future health of either Congress or the executive branch.

Thus far in the war on terror, though, Congress has dodged that responsibility, delegating it to the president. The use-of-force resolution Congress passed immediately after September 11 contains an even broader delegation of authority to the president, authorizing him to make war on "those nations, organizations, or persons *he determines* planned, authorized, committed, or aided the terrorist attacks that occurred on Sept. 11, 2001, or harbored such organizations or persons" (emphasis added). By its plain terms, the resolution leaves it to the president to decide when the evidence that a target nation has cooperated with Al Qaeda reaches a level that justifies war. President Bush has exercised that authority in good faith so far; he might have used the flimsy evidence for a Hussein–Al Qaeda connection to invoke the September 2001 resolution, instead of securing separate authorization for the Iraq War. But the text of the September 2001 resolution allows the president to decide whom and when to attack. If Congress wants input on whether we should go to war with Iran or Syria or any number of other nations the president may target in the future, it may have a difficult case to make.

Such broad delegations of legislative authority are constitutionally suspect in the domestic arena; surely they are no less so when it comes to questions of war and peace. As Madison put it:

> Those who are to *conduct a war* cannot in the nature of things, be proper or safe judges, whether *a war ought* to be *commenced,* [or] *continued. . . .* They are barred from the latter functions by a great principle in free government, analogous to that which separates the sword from the purse, or the power of executing from the power of enacting laws" (emphasis in original).

Preemptive Wars

The administration's national security doctrine, which emphasizes preemptive military strikes, may have equally troubling consequences for congressional control over the war power. Under the doctrine, rogue nations in the process of developing nuclear, chemical, or biological weapons will be vulnerable at any time to preemptive attacks by the United States. In a graduation speech given at West Point on June 1, 2002, President Bush discussed the new strategy: "The war on terror will not be won on the defensive," he said, "we must take the battle to the enemy . . . [and] be ready for preemptive action when necessary." The administration formalized the policy in the National Security Strategy of the United States of America, released in September 2002. That document does not discuss whether preemptive wars will be conducted pursuant to congressional authorization or launched unilaterally, in the form of surprise attacks by the president. In the case of Iraq, the president did not use the doctrine as an excuse to bypass the constitutional requirement of congressional authorization. But the development of the doctrine must be carefully monitored by this Congress and future ones, lest it become a pretext for unilateral presidential war making.

Granted, the Constitution does not categorically rule out unilateral military action by the president. No sane person would argue that when missiles are in the air or enemy troops are landing on our shores the president is obliged to call Congress into session before he can respond. As Madison's notes from the Constitutional Convention make clear, the consensus of the Framers was that though Congress had the power to "commence war," the president would have "the power to repel sudden attacks." Within that power, there's some latitude for preemptive strikes. If a rogue state plans a nerve gas attack on the New York subway system, the president need not and should not wait until enemy agents are ashore before he orders military action.

But if the preemptive strike doctrine morphs in the future into a free-standing justification for presidential wars, that will have grave consequences for the constitutional balance of power. The doctrine applies whether or not any specific attack on the United States is planned and whether or not U.S. intelligence has credible evidence that the target has weapons of mass destruction (WMD). It could be used by this administration or future ones to avoid the inconvenient task of securing authority from Congress. That would change the constitutional power to repel sudden attacks into a dangerous and unconstitutional power to *launch* sudden attacks.

Moreover, such a power would be ripe for abuse. Firm evidence of WMD capability is very hard to come by—as we've learned to our regret in the case of Iraq. Justifications for preemptive wars will necessarily be speculative and susceptible to manipulation. The potential for politically driven attacks would be enormous.

President Bush will not be the last president to wield the broad new powers his administration is forging in the domestic and foreign affairs arenas. The war on Al Qaeda terror will take years, and if and when victory is achieved, we may not know with any certainty that we've won.

Our entire constitutional system repudiates the notion that electing good men is a sufficient check on abuse of power. As President Bush himself noted in his September 17 proclamation, "In creating our Nation's Constitutional framework, the Convention's delegates recognized the dangers inherent in concentrating too much power in one person, branch, or institution." It's imperative that Congress resist this tendency toward concentration of power and the further growth of the imperial presidency.

Suggested Readings

Fisher, Louis. *Congressional Abdication on War and Spending.* College Station: Texas A&M University Press, 2000.

———. *Presidential War Power.* Lawrence: University Press of Kansas, 1995.

Healy, Gene. "Arrogance of Power Reborn: The Imperial Presidency and Foreign Policy in the Clinton Years." Cato Institute Policy Analysis no. 389, December 13, 2000.

Levy, Leonard W. *Original Intent and the Framers' Constitution.* New York: Macmillan, 1988.

Schlesinger, Arthur. *The Imperial Presidency.* Boston: Houghton-Mifflin, 1973.

Wormuth, Francis D., and Edwin B. Firmage. *To Chain the Dog of War.* Dallas: Southern Methodist University Press, 1986.

—Prepared by Gene Healy

18. Tort and Class Action Reform

State legislatures should

- enact punitive damages reforms,
- eliminate joint and several liability,
- require that government pay all legal costs if it loses a civil case, and
- outlaw contingency fees paid by government to private attorneys.

Congress should

- constrain courts' long-arm jurisdiction over out-of-state defendants and
- implement class action reforms.

Four years ago, a Florida jury conjured up punitive damages of $145 billion for a class of tobacco plaintiffs. Two years later, a California jury recommended a $28 billion treasure trove for a single claimant. So it goes. Not just tobacco; but guns, asbestos, and a cross section of American industry that has grown into the Mass Tort Monster.

Since 1930 litigation costs have increased four times faster than the overall economy. Federal class actions tripled over the last 10 years. Class actions in state courts ballooned by more than 1,000 percent. The Chamber of Commerce estimates that the annual cost of the tort system translates into $809 per person—the equivalent of a 5 percent tax on wages. The trial lawyers' share—roughly $40 billion in 2002—exceeds the annual revenues of Microsoft.

When costs explode, proposals for reform are never far behind. As a result, we've been deluged by congressional schemes to ban lawsuits against gun makers and fast food distributors, cap medical malpractice awards, and otherwise enlist the federal government in the tort reform battle. But no matter how worthwhile a goal may be, if there is no constitutional authority to pursue it, then the federal government must step aside and leave the matter to the states or to private citizens.

Can Tort Reform and Federalism Coexist?

In its quest for constitutional authority, Congress often cites the Commerce Clause. Consider medical malpractice. No doubt we have a nationwide mess. But not every national problem is a federal problem. More than three dozen states have passed damage caps, and all 50 states are considering various other reforms. Mississippi is a case in point. Because of "jackpot justice," doctors fled, 71 insurance companies pulled out, and the state lost an $800 million bid for a Toyota plant. The result: a new law, effective September 2004, that caps pain-and-suffering, medical malpractice, and punitive damages.

That's an example of tort reform that is compatible with federalism. Nowhere in the Constitution is there a federal power to set rules that control lawsuits by in-state plaintiffs against in-state doctors for in-state malpractice. The substantive rules of tort law are not commerce and they're not the business of Congress. On those occasions when a state attempts to expand its sovereignty beyond its borders, federal procedural reforms can curb any abuses (see below).

State-Based Tort Reform

With that in mind, here are six remedies that can be implemented by the states without federal involvement. The first three are directed at punitive damage awards; the final three apply to tort reform more broadly.

First, take the dollar decision away from the jury. For example, the jury might be instructed to vote yes or no on an award of punitive damages. Then the amount would be set by a judge in accordance with preset guidelines.

Second, limit punitive damages to cases involving actual malice or intentional wrongdoing or gross negligence. Whatever the heightened standard, the idea is that accidental injuries arising from ordinary, garden-variety negligence are unlikely to require the deterrence for which punitive damages are designed.

Third, states could implement procedural guarantees like those available under criminal law. Punitive awards serve the same purposes as criminal penalties, but defendants are not accorded the protections applicable in a criminal case. Among those protections is a higher burden of proof than the usual civil standard, which is preponderance of the evidence. Also, no double jeopardy. Current rules allow punitive damage awards for the same conduct in multiple lawsuits. Last, no coerced self-incrimination, which criminal defendants can avoid by pleading the Fifth Amendment. In civil cases, compulsory discovery can be self-incriminating.

Fourth, states ought to dispense with joint and several liability. That's the "deep pockets" rule that permits plaintiffs to collect all of a damage award from any one of multiple defendants, even if the paying defendant was responsible for only a small fraction of the harm. A better rule is to apportion damages in accordance with the defendants' degree of culpability.

Fifth, government should pay attorneys' fees when a governmental unit is the losing party in a civil lawsuit. In the criminal sphere, defendants are already entitled to court-appointed counsel if necessary; they're also protected by the requirement for proof beyond reasonable doubt and by the Fifth and Sixth Amendments to the Constitution. No corresponding safeguards against abusive public-sector litigation exist in civil cases. Limiting the rule to cases involving government plaintiffs preserves access to the courts for less-affluent private plaintiffs seeking remedies for legitimate grievances. And defendants in government suits will be able to resist baseless cases that are brought by the state solely to ratchet up the pressure for a large financial settlement.

Sixth, contingency fee contracts between private lawyers and government entities should be prohibited. When a private lawyer subcontracts his services to the government, he bears the same responsibility as a government lawyer. He's a public servant beholden to all citizens, including the defendant, and his overriding objective is to seek justice. Imagine a state attorney paid a contingency fee for each indictment, or state troopers paid a bonus for each speeding ticket. The potential for corruption is enormous.

Federal Procedural Tort Reform

Aside from state-imposed reforms, there are at least three areas where the federal government can intervene without offending long-established state prerogatives. The guiding principle is that federal legislatures and courts are authorized to act when there is a high risk that states will appropriate wealth from the citizens of other states. One federal reform consistent with that principle is to amend the rules that control state exercise of so-called long-arm jurisdiction over out-of-state businesses.

Congress could, for example, preclude a local court from hearing a case unless the defendant engages directly in business activities within the state. A company's mere awareness that the stream of commerce could sweep its product into a particular state should not be sufficient to confer jurisdiction. Instead, jurisdiction should be triggered only if the company purposely directs its product to the state—i.e., the company itself exerts control over the decision to sell in the state. A sensible rule like that would give firms an exit option—they could withdraw from a state and thereby avoid the risk of a runaway jury, even if a product somehow ends up in-state. Today, federal limits on long-arm statutes remain lax or ambiguous. For that reason, oppressive state tort laws remain a threat to out-of-state defendants.

There's a second federal reform that's compatible with federalist principles—a federal choice-of-law rule for product liability cases. Here's how that might work:

Basically, choice of law is the doctrine that determines which state's laws control the litigation. Generally, plaintiffs can and will select the most favorable forum state, in part, on the basis of its tort laws. But suppose a federal choice-of-law rule were enacted for cases in which the plaintiff and defendant are from different states. Suppose further that the applicable law were based on the state where the manufacturer was located. A manufacturer could decide where to locate, and its decision would dictate the applicable legal rules. Consumers, in turn, would evaluate those rules when deciding whether to buy a particular manufacturer's product. If a manufacturer were located in a state that didn't provide adequate legal remedies for defective products, consumers would buy from rival companies.

Would there be a race to the bottom by manufacturers searching for the most defendant-friendly tort law? Maybe. But more likely, states would balance their interest in attracting manufacturers against the interest of in-state consumers, who want tougher product liability laws. In effect, healthy competition among the states would enlist federalism as part of the solution rather than raise federalism as an excuse for failing to arrive at a solution.

Class Action Reform

The third procedural reform that Congress can and should enact is aimed at class actions. In the past 20 years, class actions have morphed from a rarely used procedural device, designed to litigate a large number of unusually similar claims, into a commonly used device for coercing a settlement from companies that haven't done anything wrong.

The 108th Congress attempted to address that problem in the Class Action Fairness Act—by giving defendants and class members the power to pull some class suits into federal courts. But the root problem is not with courts that administer class actions. It's with the class device itself. Congress can, and should, do more to directly address key problems associated with modern class actions at the state and federal levels. Here are four suggestions:

First, put the burden on trial lawyers to convince persons to join their class actions. Currently, the modern class action rule creates a presumption that persons out of court, who have no connection to the class proceeding, favor being "represented" by a trial lawyer who files a class action on their putative behalf. That presumption is based on nothing more than the trial lawyer's say-so. Considering that modern class action lawyers often claim to "represent" the interests of thousands—or even millions—of persons, the presumption is a legal fiction. Many litigants have no idea that their interests are being represented in court, and so serve as mute pawns of plaintiffs' lawyers seeking to coerce settlements and line their pockets. The rule should be changed by putting the burden on trial lawyers to convince people to affirmatively "opt in" to a class action (for example, by mailing a consent form to the court) before they can be counted as part of the "class."

Second, prohibit class actions that deprive defendants of their due process right to fairly litigate individualized defenses. Currently, vague rules dictate what kind of claims get certified. For example, classes are certified even when a governing statute or common law rule requires that key elements of proof—such as reliance, causation, or damages—be proved on an individual basis. That means trial lawyers can use the class device to combine tens of thousands of factually dissimilar claims into one proceeding, making it impossible for defendants to adequately smoke out and identify weak or meritless individual claims. In a series of cases, the U.S. Courts of Appeals for the Fourth, Fifth, and Seventh Circuits have rejected that use of the class device. So should Congress—by enacting a rule stating that, in the absence of a clear legislative statement to the contrary, class actions cannot be used to litigate legal claims when the governing law requires case-by-case proof of each plaintiff's claim.

Third, ensure that only class actions that have some merit get certified. Under current law, class certification decisions are made very early—

before a judge has even considered the merits of the claims and before plaintiffs have demonstrated that they have some evidence to back up their allegations. That allows trial lawyers to game the system by including large numbers of meritless claims in one lawsuit in the hopes that corporate defendants will settle before the suit goes to trial. That's not a bad strategy, given the stakes involved: Even when companies are faced with clearly weak claims, the enormity of large classes—which can encompass millions of individual suits—means that few corporations want to bet the company that a jury will get the case right. Congress should nip meritless class actions in the bud by providing that classes may be certified only after the class "representative"—the main plaintiff—is able to make a preliminary factual showing that he has a reasonable likelihood of success on the merits.

Finally, Congress must address state class actions—which are often just as troublesome as the federal kind. The 108th Congress proposed to tackle the problem by expanding federal diversity jurisdiction over "interstate" class claims. That's not enough: For one, it does nothing to curb rich trial lawyers from bankrolling a number of duplicative intrastate class actions in state court, in order to "put the squeeze" on a beleaguered company involved in simultaneous proceedings in federal court. That's a major abuse of our federal system—one that is a hallmark of the most troublesome multidistrict class actions, like the recent "managed care litigation" against health maintenance organizations. Expanding diversity jurisdiction over "interstate" state class actions does nothing to solve that problem.

Moreover, a key component of the plan to expand diversity jurisdiction could be struck down by federal courts. A provision of the Class Action Fairness Act treats hypothetical members of a proposed class as "parties" for purposes of establishing federal jurisdiction, even though a class hasn't been certified and class members therefore aren't yet an official part of the judicial proceedings. That goes against the grain of Chief Justice John Marshall's ruling 180 years ago, in *Osborn v. Bank of the United States*, that a federal court cannot look to the citizenship of unnamed persons who are not in court when assessing whether the court has diversity jurisdiction. In the 2002 case of *Devlin v. Scardelletti*, the modern Court similarly cast doubt on the proposition that "nonnamed class members" are parties for purposes of establishing diversity.

194

We propose a different solution—one that will not be struck down by courts, will address the worst components of state class actions, and will give states an incentive to take control of local court procedure. It's a two-step reform. First, Congress has the power to expand federal question jurisdiction over class claims that raise defenses under federal law—including claims that a proposed class action is so large and unwieldy that it might violate due process. Federal courts have broad power over such lawsuits—even if the due process problems haven't yet materialized. Nonetheless, under current law, many such claims can't be litigated in federal court. That should be changed by giving federal courts power to assert jurisdiction over class actions—intrastate and interstate—that might raise defenses under federal law, including due process and other constitutional provisions, and by empowering state court defendants to remove such actions to federal court.

But expanding federal question jurisdiction, and federal removal jurisdiction, is not enough: To combat intrastate class actions effectively, states must take responsibility for class action reform. Congress can give them an incentive to do so by creating a "safe harbor"—one that provides that states can keep control over large class actions filed in state court, even those class actions that raise federal defenses, if they adopt federal class action reforms, including "opt in," a ban on the use of the class device to deny defendants the power to litigate individualized defenses, and a rule that classes will be certified only when the main plaintiff has a reasonable likelihood of success on the merits. That provides an incentive for states to enact far-reaching reforms at the state level, and so harnesses a key component of federalism—competition between state and federal judicial systems—to cure what ails the modern class action regime.

Conclusion

When a state exercises jurisdiction beyond its borders or discriminates against out-of-state businesses, federal intervention may occasionally be appropriate. For the most part, however, the states have reformed and are continuing to reform their civil justice systems. Under those circumstances, time-honored principles of federalism dictate that each state exercise dominion over its substantive tort law. Congress can then focus on procedural matters. In that regard, we suggest three reforms: First, tighten long-arm jurisdiction over out-of-state defendants. Second, implement a federal choice-of-law regime. Third, restructure the rules for class actions.

Suggested Readings

Barnett, Randy E. *Restoring the Lost Constitution*. Princeton, NJ: Princeton University Press, 2004.

Connor, Martin F. "Taming the Mass Tort Monster." National Legal Center for the Public Interest, October 2000.

Epstein, Richard A. "Class Actions: Aggregation, Amplification, and Distortion." *University of Chicago Legal Forum* (2003): 475–518.

Krauss, Michael I. "Product Liability and Game Theory: One More Trip to the Choice-of-Law Well." *Brigham Young University Law Review* (2002): 759–826.

Krauss, Michael I., and Robert A. Levy. "Can Tort Reform and Federalism Coexist?" Cato Institute Policy Analysis no. 514, April 14, 2004.

Levy, Robert A., ed. *Shakedown: How Corporations, Government, and Trial Lawyers Abuse the Judicial Process*. Washington: Cato Institute, 2004.

Moller, Mark K. "Class Actions and the Constitution: A Primer for Meaningful Class Action Reform." Cato Institute Policy Analysis, forthcoming.

Olson, Walter K. *The Rule of Lawyers: How the New Litigation Elite Threatens America's Rule of Law*. New York: St. Martin's, 2003.

Osborn v. Bank of the United States, 22 U.S. (9 Wheat.) 738, 856–57 (1824) (opinion of Chief Justice John Marshall) (discussing constitutional limits on the scope of federal diversity jurisdiction).

Tager, Evan M. "The Constitutional Limitations on Class Actions." Mealey's Litigation Report: Class Actions, 2001. http://www.appellate.net/articles/Tagercom.pdf.

—Prepared by Robert A. Levy and Mark K. Moller

THREATS TO CIVIL LIBERTIES

19. The Patriot Act

Congress should

- let all of the Patriot Act provisions that were originally designated to "sunset" expire on schedule in December 2005,
- repeal the "Delayed Notification" or "Sneak and Peek" provision of the Patriot Act, and
- repeal the money laundering provisions of the Patriot Act and the Bank Secrecy Act of 1970.

The Patriot Act: An Inglorious Birth

Congress normally holds hearings on legislative proposals in order to study their merits and demerits before bringing any measure to the floor for a vote. That deliberative process was scorned in the aftermath of the September 11, 2001, terrorist attacks. Within days of those attacks, President Bush and Attorney General John Ashcroft proposed an omnibus package of "anti-terrorism" measures for congressional approval. Attorney General Ashcroft demanded quick action by the legislative branch. The richest and most powerful government in world history was portrayed as a weakling vis-à-vis Al Qaeda terrorists. Until that legislative package was enacted, America was supposedly at a grave disadvantage.

When House Majority Leader Dick Armey (R-TX) called for separate votes on the various measures within the Ashcroft "package," he was overruled by congressional leaders who did not want to be criticized by the attorney general in the newspapers. The Bush administration wanted a single vote on the entire package because it perceived a political advantage in framing the matter in terms of whether legislators were going to "support" President Bush's attempt to "strengthen" America's laws—or not. Congressional leaders labeled the package of proposals the USA

Patriot Act (Uniting and Strengthening America by Providing Appropriate Tools Required to Intercept and Obstruct Terrorism) to intimidate members who were skeptical about the law and how it would impact liberty and privacy in America. They went so far as to schedule a vote even before members of Congress could actually obtain copies of the proposal. Since few politicians wanted to be seen as opposing the "Patriot" act, the measure passed overwhelmingly. The entire episode was a parody of deliberative policymaking.

Since more terrorist attacks on the American homeland seem inevitable, it is vitally important that policymakers not repeat the unfortunate experience that led to the hasty enactment of the Patriot Act. Periodic policy adjustments make sense, but omnibus legislation vastly increases the chances of a bad proposal finding its way onto the federal law books. Thus, gigantic anti-terrorism legislative "packages" should be rejected outright in the future. If a proposal cannot find legislative and executive support on its own merits, it should not become the law of the land.

Patriot Act Misfires

Although the Patriot Act contains several controversial measures, it is also true that the law has been on the receiving end of misplaced criticism. That is because the Patriot Act has become something of a catchall phrase for a range of controversial, but distinct, policies of the Bush administration. Since reasoned debate over the proper parameters of the government's police powers cannot proceed when there is widespread confusion with respect to what certain laws and policies actually do, it will be useful to briefly clarify what is—and what is not—covered by the Patriot Act. The following matters have garnered a fair amount of media attention over the past three years, but these measures are *not* related to the Patriot Act.

- The arrest, imprisonment, and treatment, of hundreds of individuals, mostly immigrants, in the months following the September 11 attacks.
- The policy of eavesdropping on attorney-client conversations.
- The Pentagon's Total Information Awareness database.
- The creation of the Department of Homeland Security.
- The creation of the Transportation Security Administration and airport search procedures.
- The creation of a prison camp at Guantanamo Bay, Cuba.
- The policy of trials before military commissions.
- The imprisonment of American citizens ("enemy combatants") in military brigs.

The merits of those policies are certainly debatable, but they should not be confused with the provisions of the Patriot Act.

The Patriot Act covers a range of subjects—from surveillance procedures to border procedures to money laundering to victim compensation funds. It is not a "free-standing" law but rather a jumble of provisions that amend and expand a host of preexisting federal laws. It is thus difficult to appreciate the impact of the Patriot Act by simply reading it. One must first understand how all of the preexisting federal laws are enforced, which can be very complicated.

The Coming Battle over the "Sunset" Provisions

Although it was impossible to stop, or even slow, the congressional passage of the Patriot Act in the weeks following the Al Qaeda attacks on the Pentagon and the World Trade Center, conscientious lawmakers were successful in attaching "sunset" provisions to most of the surveillance-related measures within the act. A sunset provision is basically a procedural mechanism that establishes an "expiration date" for certain laws. The sunset concept was perfectly suited for the Patriot Act. Members of Congress were hard-pressed to resist a plea from Attorney General Ashcroft for "necessary tools" that could avert imminent mass murder. But it was equally difficult for Ashcroft to resist the idea of a sunset date for his rushed proposals. After all, if those proposals really had merit, Congress could simply reenact them at a later date. During the temporary, "probationary" period Congress could study the new law carefully to determine whether the initial plea of "necessity" was genuine or exaggerated. The sunset provisions of the Patriot Act will take effect in December 2005. It is safe to say that a legislative battle over the reenactment of the Patriot Act will take place in the next Congress.

Congress should resist the lobbying efforts of the intelligence and law enforcement agencies. Particular proposals may have merit, but the best way to encourage deliberation and debate would be to let all the pertinent provisions expire on schedule. That would put the burden of persuasion on the executive branch, where it belongs. If discrete proposals really have merit, it is very likely that Congress will approve them in short order. As noted above, sweeping renewal "packages" ought to be rejected outright.

As the debate heats up, one should note that supporters of the Patriot Act tend to emphasize portions of the law that are not controversial. Over and over again, the public is told that the Patriot Act merely "updates" the law so that new technologies are "covered." Such claims are true, but they direct attention away from the measures that present real threats to civil liberties. In July 2004, for example, the Justice Department released a report that purported to show how the Patriot Act had furthered specific terrorism investigations. The report does not discuss the Patriot Act's hotly contested provisions, and that is a telling indication that the Justice Department is anxious to avoid close scrutiny of the entire law.

What are the most controversial provisions of the Patriot Act? One of the most serious threats to liberty comes from Section 215. According to the Department of Justice, that section allows investigators to obtain "business records" for terrorism investigations pursuant to a federal "court order." In fact, the provision is not limited to business records. Federal agents can use that section of the Patriot Act to seize any tangible item (correspondence, film, personal belongings) directly from a person's home. The "court order" is nothing but a façade because the Patriot Act says the judge "shall" issue such orders whenever the executive branch claims it is conducting a terrorism investigation.

Most shocking of all, Section 215 makes it a crime for anyone to speak out about its use. Any person who speaks to a relative, a neighbor, or a reporter about the government's demand can be jailed. Defenders of the Patriot Act demand specific examples of "abuses" of the law, but they fail to mention that the Section 215 gag provision keeps anyone affected from coming forward. That will obviously make it very difficult for Congress to assess how the orders are actually being used.

The second threat to civil liberties comes from Section 505 of the Patriot Act. Under that provision, federal agents can use so-called national security letters to seize transactional records, such as bank and rental car receipts. That Patriot Act provision bypasses the Constitution's search warrant procedure by vesting a secret subpoena power directly within the executive branch. Instead of having to apply for judicially approved warrants, federal agents can unilaterally threaten businesspeople with jail if they do not surrender employee and customer records. This represents an enormous change in American law. Congress has steadfastly denied subpoena powers to the FBI and the CIA because it was deemed to be too much power for the executive branch. Now that both agencies have acquired the power, they will not surrender it easily. These subpoenas also contain "gag" provisions for Americans who receive them.

The third threat to liberty comes from the Patriot Act's expansion of the Foreign Intelligence Surveillance Act (FISA)—a law that created a special federal court to approve electronic surveillance of citizens and resident aliens alleged to be acting on behalf of a foreign power. Previously, the FISA court granted surveillance authority if foreign intelligence was the primary purpose of an investigation. But Section 218 of the Patriot Act allows the government to conduct surveillance if foreign intelligence is only a "significant" purpose of an investigation. That may seem like a trivial change, but it is not. Because the standard for FISA approval is lower than "probable cause," and because FISA now applies to ordinary criminal matters if they are characterized as "national security" inquiries, the new rules offer federal agents another avenue to bypass the Constitution's search warrant requirements. The result: rubber-stamp judicial consent to phone and Internet surveillance, even in regular criminal cases.

Limit Power, Restore Privacy

The sunset provisions do not apply to all of the Patriot Act's problematic sections. This means that Congress must affirmatively act to repeal police power sections that threaten liberty in America. Three sections stand out above all the others.

The first section is the so-called sneak and peek power. Section 213 of the Patriot Act empowers agents to conduct covert entries into homes and businesses. Agents still apply for a judicial search warrant, but the homeowner does not know about the entry until days or weeks later. This section of the Patriot Act is defended as an important "tool to fight terrorism," but it can be used for any federal criminal investigation. Such a power crept into the law with electronic surveillance devices. When a judge approves a bugging operation, it makes sense to allow agents to enter without notifying the subject. But the Patriot Act's expansion of those secret searches to ordinary physical searches is a departure from constitutional norms that cannot be justified.

The second section concerns the sharing of grand jury information. Federal officials often exaggerate when they say that they were "unable to speak to one another" and that the Patriot Act "fixes" that. In fact, federal agents could share information discovered in a grand jury investigation with the CIA. But before they did so, they had to receive the permission of a federal judge. The Patriot Act removes the judge from that "gatekeeper" role and now permits information sharing without advanced judicial approval. The Patriot Act threatens to turn federal grand jurors into employees of the intelligence community. The next Congress should restore federal judges to their gatekeeper role.

The third section of the Patriot Act concerns the expansion of federal money laundering laws. The Bank Secrecy Act of 1970 required banks to spy on their customers and report suspicious transactions to federal law enforcement officials. The Patriot Act expands the surveillance network by requiring mortgage companies, pawnbrokers, used car dealerships, and many other businesses to keep tabs on customers and report activity to the federal government. Any business that shirks its law enforcement responsibilities will be bludgeoned with fines. In 2004, for example, Riggs Bank was fined $25 million for insufficient assistance with money laundering probes. In a free society, the government would rely upon the voluntary cooperation of business institutions for investigative assistance. The Patriot Act, however, conscripts scores of new businesses into a regime of coercive mandates.

Conclusion

American institutions tend to look for "quick-fix" solutions to problems. American policymakers must recognize, however, that the danger posed by Al Qaeda is not a short-term crisis but a long-term security dilemma for the United States. If Congress rushes to enact anti-terrorism legislation in the aftermath of every attack, no one can deny that Americans will lose their liberty over the long term. Now that more than three years have passed since the shock and horror of September 11, Congress will have an opportunity to seriously deliberate the constitutional issues that were initially skirted. No one doubts that a legislative battle is looming with respect to whether the Patriot Act's provisions will expire or be made permanent. Policymakers should not make the mistake of underestimating the American people. Of course, the electorate wants safety, but it wants the federal government to secure that safety by fighting the terrorists themselves, not by turning America into a surveillance state.

Suggested Readings

Bovard, James. *Terrorism and Tyranny*. New York: Palgrave/Macmillan, 2003.

Dash, Samuel. *The Intruders*. Piscataway, NJ: Rutgers University Press, 2004.

Dillard, Thomas W., Stephen R. Johnson, and Timothy Lynch. "A Grand Façade: How the Grand Jury Was Captured by Government." Cato Institute Policy Analysis no. 476, May 13, 2003.

Hentoff, Nat. *The War on the Bill of Rights—And the Gathering Resistance*. New York: Seven Stories, 2003.

Lynch, Timothy. "Breaking the Vicious Cycle: Preserving Our Liberties While Fighting Terrorism." Cato Institute Policy Analysis no. 443, June 26, 2002.

Schulhofer, Stephen. *The Enemy Within*. New York: Century Foundation Press, 2002.

—Prepared by Timothy Lynch

20. Militarization of the Home Front

Congress should

- refuse to enact further exceptions to, or otherwise weaken, the Posse Comitatus Act;
- closely monitor the executive branch to ensure that the military remains a last resort, not a first responder, for addressing the problem of terrorist attacks on the home front; and
- repeal the "drug war exceptions" to the Posse Comitatus Act.

Americans hold the U.S. military in high regard for very good reasons. Despite the current difficulties in Iraq, America's armed forces have overthrown two tyrannical regimes in the space of two years—and they have done so quickly and overwhelmingly. In fact, the military has been so impressive abroad that some federal officials have come to see it as a panacea for domestic security problems posed by the terrorist threat. But on the home front there are many tasks for which the military is ill suited and for which its deployment would be dangerous.

Americans have long been wary of the use of standing armies to keep the peace at home. Despite that reluctance, top figures in Congress and the Bush administration have proposed weakening the Posse Comitatus Act, the 126-year-old statute that restricts the government's ability to use the U.S. military as a police force. Calls abound for bringing military resources to bear in areas ranging from border control to domestic surveillance. Sen. John Warner (R-VA), head of the Armed Services Committee, has said that the doctrine of Posse Comitatus may have had its day. And Gen. Ralph E. Eberhardt, the head of the new Northern Command, which directs all military forces within North America, said, "We should always be reviewing things like Posse Comitatus . . . if we think it ties our hands in protecting the American people."

The Posse Comitatus Act

What is the Posse Comitatus Act (PCA), and does it "tie the hands" of the government in protecting the American people? Passed in 1878, the PCA forbids law enforcement officials from employing the U.S. military to "execute the laws." The rationale behind the act, as one federal court has explained, is that "military personnel must be trained to operate under circumstances where the protection of constitutional freedoms cannot receive the consideration needed in order to assure their preservation. The Posse Comitatus statute is intended to meet that danger."

But the PCA is not a total prohibition on domestic use of the military, and it hardly ties the government's hands with regard to any *legitimate* use of the military on the home front. First, the act applies only to troops that are acting under federal command. It does not forbid state governors from using the National Guard to perform policing duties. The troops stationed in the nation's airports after September 11, 2001, were operating under the command of the state governors, and therefore the Posse Comitatus Act didn't apply.

Second, the courts have generally held that only hands-on policing violates the act. That means that arresting people, searching them, interrogating them, restricting their movement, and other coercive activities are proscribed. But if the Army provides training or equipment to domestic authorities, it's not violating the act.

Third, Congress can pass exceptions to the law, and it has done so repeatedly. For example, there are statutes on the books that allow the military to act in an emergency situation involving weapons of mass destruction.

Finally, the courts recognize a "military purpose exception" to the PCA even when there is no specific statute in place allowing the use of the military. So if a latter-day Pancho Villa invades California, we don't have to send in state and local police; instead, the Army can respond. The same analysis applies to the fighter jets patrolling American skies for hijacked jetliners after 9/11. They were there to defend our cities against a military-style attack, and no one has suggested that was a violation of the Posse Comitatus Act.

Clearly then, the Posse Comitatus Act doesn't tie the government's hands. What the law does is reaffirm the principle that a free country relies on civilian peace officers to keep the peace. We call the troops in only as a last resort in extraordinary circumstances. And that is entirely appropriate.

Past Abuses

Unfortunately, we've deviated from that principle in the past. And those mistakes show how important it is to resist militarization of the home front. For example:

- In the late 19th and early 20th century, the military was used repeatedly to suppress labor unrest and crush unions, putting whole areas of the country under martial law. Particularly egregious was the Army's suppression of the 1899 miners' strike in Coeur d'Alene, Idaho. Army regulars engaged in house-to-house searches and assisted in more than a thousand arrests. Troops arrested every adult male in the area and jailed the men without charging them for weeks.
- During World War I, Army intelligence agents had arrest powers and free rein throughout the country. They used that power to harass labor leaders, opponents of the war, and politically active minorities. They carried out some six million investigations during the war and caught a grand total of one German spy.
- In the 1960s, the military got back into the spy business. Senate hearings in 1971 revealed that military intelligence agents kept thousands of files on suspected radicals, including such dangerous characters as Adlai Stevenson, the ACLU, and Americans for Democratic Action.

More recently, the Army played a key role in the Waco disaster in 1993. It provided the equipment and advice that helped lead to the deaths of more than 80 people, including 27 children. The drug war exceptions to the Posse Comitatus Act allowed federal agents to get M1 Abrams tanks. And it was U.S. Army Delta Force operatives on the scene who advised federal agents to launch a tank and CS gas assault on buildings full of women and children.

A few years later, in 1997, a Marine Corps anti-drug patrol shot and killed an 18-year-old American high school student named Esequiel Hernandez. Hernandez was herding goats and carrying a .22 caliber rifle near his family's farm in Redford, Texas, when he ran into the Marines, who were heavily camouflaged and hidden in the brush. Shots were exchanged. Instead of identifying themselves, or trying to defuse the situation, the Marines hunted Hernandez for 20 minutes. When Hernandez raised his rifle again, a Marine shot him, and Hernandez bled to death without receiving first aid. An internal Pentagon investigation of the incident said that the soldiers were ill prepared for contact with civilians, as the Marines' military training had instilled "an aggressive spirit while teaching basic combat skills."

That's the kind of training soldiers should have. But that training can lead to tragic collateral damage when we try to turn soldiers into peace officers.

A Blunt Instrument

Policymakers who would give the military a greater role in internal security should keep those abuses in mind. And they should also consider how ineffective and wasteful domestic use of the military is likely to be.

We simply cannot surround every high-value target in America with troops, even if we want to. The first responders to any terror attack are almost always going to be civilians and local law enforcement. Moreover, in most cases, a military response is ill suited to the domestic fight against Al Qaeda. The army is a blunt instrument—fantastic for destroying columns of enemy tanks or toppling rogue regimes. But at home we're fighting an asymmetric war against a clandestine enemy. That is the kind of fight that calls for investigative skills and smart policing—not overwhelming firepower.

Public officials have forgotten that and called for domestic uses of the military that are ill-conceived and wasteful. For example, over Thanksgiving weekend in 2001, Florida authorities stationed a tank outside Miami International Airport. However impressive and ominous that looked, it was rather unlikely that Al Qaeda was about to roll up in an armored column. And a tank would be utterly useless against knives or explosives smuggled aboard an airplane—a far more likely form of attack.

Worse still, after September 11, Transportation Secretary Norman Mineta called for putting Delta Force operatives on domestic flights to guard against hijackers. It's hard to think of a more unproductive use of military resources than having highly trained commandos warming seats on flights to Los Angeles. Delta Force soldiers ought to be hunting Al Qaeda operatives overseas, not collecting frequent flier miles.

Moreover, having troops sitting around airports and border stations undermines military preparedness. That's what the General Accounting Office concluded when it studied DoD home-front operations in the wake of September 11. In a July 2003 report, the GAO noted:

> While on domestic military missions, combat units are unable to maintain proficiency because these missions provide less opportunity to practice the varied skills required for combat and consequently offer little training value. In addition, . . . the present force structure may not be sufficient to address

the increase in domestic and overseas military missions. As a result, U.S. forces could experience an unsustainable pace that could significantly erode their readiness to perform combat missions and impact future personnel retention.

Mission Creep

Nonetheless, pressure is building to give the Army a greater domestic role. Despite the lessons we should have learned with the tragic death of Esequiel Hernandez, there are growing calls to militarize our borders with Canada and Mexico and turn armed soldiers into border patrol agents. In fact, in 2002 the Pentagon undertook a limited militarization of our borders with Canada and Mexico—deploying some 1,600 federalized National Guardsmen to the borders for six months. Though the deployment was temporary, it was carried out in violation of the Posse Comitatus Act—a disturbing indication of the government's willingness to violate the law.

There are also troubling signs that the military is getting back into the domestic surveillance business. First, there was Total Information Awareness, the Pentagon's research on data-mining technology that could be used to generate a dossier on every American citizen. In the fall of 2003 Congress cut off funding for TIA. But military analyst and former Army intelligence officer William M. Arkin reports that research continues on domestic data mining, and military intelligence agents have been assigned to FBI field offices.

Then there's the Pentagon's response to the sniper incident in the D.C. area in 2002, which suggests that the restraints on domestic use of the military are eroding. In the hunt for the sniper, the Pentagon provided surveillance planes, despite the fact that there was no evidence that the incident involved international terrorism. In the future, we may see pressure to get the military involved in every high-profile crime that might conceivably be linked to terrorism. If we weaken the Posse Comitatus Act, as Senator Warner and others have suggested, that involvement will not be limited to a support role—it could involve hands-on policing, with all the threats to life and civil liberty that entails.

True, Defense Secretary Donald Rumsfeld has said that he sees no need to amend the Posse Comitatus Act. But that's hardly reassuring, given that other administration officials appear ready to interpret the act out of existence. Peter Verga, the Pentagon's number-two man on homeland security, told the September 11 commission in January 2004 that when Congress voted to authorize war with Al Qaeda and Afghanistan seven days after the September 11 attacks, that authorization "was not limited to overseas use of the military forces." If so, then there are no legal restraints on what the military can do domestically to fight the war on terror. If the president so chooses, armed soldiers on the home front can search, interrogate, arrest, and possibly shoot to kill. But the debate over the September 2001 use-of-force resolution does not contain any reference to the Posse Comitatus Act, and there's no indication that anyone who voted for it thought he was authorizing militarization of the home front.

Verga's boss, Paul McHale, assistant secretary of defense for homeland security, gave a similarly narrow account of the restrictions Posse Comitatus imposes on military involvement in the domestic war on terror. In a March 2004 hearing before the Senate Armed Services Committee, McHale told Senator Warner that the PCA does not restrict the use of U.S. armed forces when they're employed for anti-terror purposes. Such deployments, he argued are not "for law-enforcement purposes. They're deploying to defeat Al Qaeda. That activity is not covered by posse comitatus."

It's true that the so-called military purpose exception allows some uses of U.S. armed forces domestically; as mentioned above, it allows the Air Force to guard American skies against a repeat of 9/11. However, McHale appears to want to make the military purpose doctrine the exception that swallows the rule. It is not a fair interpretation of the doctrine to say that because a particular domestic use of the military is ultimately aimed at catching a terrorist, anything goes. Terrorists forge IDs and they sometimes engage in the drug trade or smuggle cigarettes. Are those military matters now? To slide down that slope is essentially to say that the act does not apply during wartime so long as there may be clandestine foreign enemies on American soil. That is not a proviso that Congress ever chose to write into the law, and it is quite a dangerous view. Given the Bush administration's broad view of its powers to use the military on the home front, Congress should closely monitor the Pentagon's homeland security activities to guard against abuses.

Demilitarize the War on Drugs

Congress should also move to end military involvement in the drug war. In a series of statutory revisions passed in the 1980s, Congress made the war on drugs a bona fide war, with the Pentagon a central player in the struggle. Though those statutory provisions are commonly referred to as the "drug war exceptions" to the Posse Comitatus Act, they do not grant soldiers arrest authority. However, the provisions do encourage the Pentagon's involvement in surveillance and drug interdiction near the national borders. In some cases, the loopholes also promote direct involvement by soldiers in law enforcement.

In 1990 Congress authorized the secretary of defense to fund National Guard involvement in state-level drug war operations. That funding has encouraged the use of uniformed National Guardsmen in state drug interdiction operations, which range from leveling crack houses to lecturing high school students about the dangers of drug abuse. One state-level anti-drug program, California's Campaign against Marijuana Planting, has long been a source of friction between rural residents and law enforcement. Under CAMP, National Guard helicopters buzz California farms and Guardsmen and police officers invade private property looking for marijuana plants during growing season. As one irate Californian said of CAMP: "It's like a Boy Scout outing for law enforcement. It is a kick. . . . They get up here, and everyone in the countryside is a criminal."

Rumsfeld has referred to military efforts to stop drug trafficking as "nonsense." In his confirmation hearing in January 2001, he noted that "the drug problem in the United States is overwhelmingly a demand problem and to the extent that demand is there and it is powerful, it is going to find ways to get drugs in this country." Former defense secretary Caspar Weinberger has been equally blunt, arguing that military involvement in the war on drugs has been "detrimental to military readiness and an inappropriate use of the democratic system."

Weinberger is right. The militarization of the drug war has led to abuses of power at home and abroad. Abroad, U.S. Army involvement in the fight against drugs has destabilized Latin American governments and cost scores of innocent lives, including those of Americans. In April 2001 in Peru, for example, a U.S. surveillance plane identified a small Cessna airplane as a possible drug-trafficking vehicle. The Peruvian air force sent up an A-37B Dragonfly attack plane, which fired on the Cessna, killing an innocent American missionary, Roni Bowers, and her infant daughter.

The loopholes for military participation in the drug war have done damage enough. By putting heavily armed and inappropriately trained Marines on the U.S.-Mexican border, the "drug war" exceptions to the Posse Comitatus Act led inexorably to the death of Esequiel Hernandez. And by encouraging the transfer of military ordnance to civilian peace officers, the drug war exceptions have encouraged a dangerous culture of paramilitarism in police departments. It is time to demilitarize the war on drugs.

Eternal Vigilance

In the past, when America has departed from its tradition of civilian law enforcement, the results have been tragic. We should be loath to make those mistakes again. Proud as we are of our armed forces, we Americans have fought to keep our Republic free from domestic militarization. As James Madison put it in *Federalist* no. 41: "The liberties of Rome proved the final victim to her military triumphs. . . . A standing force, therefore, is a dangerous, at the same time that it may be a necessary, provision. On the smallest scale it has its inconveniences. On an extensive scale its consequences may be fatal. On any scale it is an object of laudable circumspection and precaution." In other words, remain vigilant. Take care that the institution that helps defend our liberties can never become a threat to our liberties. That warning has never been more important.

Suggested Readings

Cooper, Jerry M. "Federal Military Intervention in Domestic Disorders." In *The United States Military under the Constitution of the United States, 1789–1989*, ed. Richard H. Kohn. New York: New York University Press, 1991.

Healy, Gene. "Deployed in the USA: The Creeping Militarization of the Home Front." Cato Institute Policy Analysis no. 503, December 17, 2003.

Jensen, Joan M. *Army Surveillance in America, 1775–1980*. New Haven, CT: Yale University Press, 1991.

Kopel, David B. "Militarized Law Enforcement: The Drug War's Deadly Fruit." In *After Prohibition: An Adult Approach to Drug Policies in the 21st Century*, ed. Timothy Lynch. Washington: Cato Institute, 2000.

Smith, Lamar. *Oversight Investigation of the Death of Esequiel Hernandez, Jr.* Report to the Subcommittee on Immigration and Claims of the House Committee on the Judiciary, 105th Cong. Washington: Government Printing Office, November 1998.

—Prepared by Gene Healy

21. Regulation of Electronic Speech and Commerce

Congress should

- resist the urge to regulate offensive content on the Web;
- allow the market to address privacy, security, and marketing concerns;
- let technical solutions have the primary role in suppressing Internet pathologies such as spam, spyware, and unwanted pop-ups;
- make certain that "Internet governance" remains minimal administration of technical standards and not broad social or economic regulation;
- reject preemptive regulation of new technologies such as RFID;
- reject legislation or regulation that protects incumbent businesses or business models from competition; and
- avoid burdensome and unconstitutional Internet tax collection schemes.

One of the most important things to understand about the Internet is that it is more like a language than a tangible thing. The Internet is a set of protocols that computers use to allow people, businesses, and other entities to communicate among themselves faster than ever before. Many attempts at Internet regulation are analogous to regulating the English language because people sometimes use it to do harmful or anti-social things. The Internet is also worldwide, meaning that no country can control the content of the Internet or the behavior of the online world.

Although it is true that the Internet helps bad people to do bad things, much more important, it allows good people to do good things. Never before have consumers and citizens had so much access to information about their governments, so much diversity in the viewpoints they can hear, and so much ability to comparison shop among service providers and sellers.

The burst of creativity, communication, and commerce that the Internet has brought in the past decade or so is only the beginning of a wave of innovation and progress that the Internet medium will foster. It should be kept an unfettered, entrepreneurial realm so that we can get the maximum benefits from creative, industrious Internet communicators and business-people the world over.

But the technology and telecommunications sectors are increasingly under assault at the local, state, federal, and international levels. Some common refrains are coming from U.S. lawmakers and international bureaucrats alike: They blame the Internet for the social ills it reveals. They promise their constituents "protection" from practices that are better cured by new technology, education, choice, and responsible use of the Internet. Likewise, they attempt to shape the Internet and its use with subsidy programs and proposals for Internet governance that are actually just social and economic regulation.

Policymakers must resist intervention in the Internet and the Internet economy. Whether governments act as regulators or promoters of high-tech, they will impose needless costs and create unintended, unwanted consequences. Solutions to problems with the Internet can be found on the Internet itself. The collective intelligence and creativity of Internet users vastly outstrip those of any governmental, quasi-governmental, or bureaucratic organization.

Offensive Content

The Internet allows people to communicate about the things that interest them, and there is no doubt that sex is a fascinating subject for many people. That means that the Internet contains a lot of frank content relating to sex and eroticism, including content that caters to some quite peculiar interests. Because of the potential exposure of children to material that many people find immoral or offensive, Congress has made repeated attempts to regulate Internet speech.

The Communications Decency Act (CDA), passed to ban pornography on the Internet, was struck down by the Supreme Court in 1997. In 2002 the Supreme Court upheld a portion of the Child Online Protection Act (COPA), passed by Congress in 1998 to shield children from online pornography by requiring that website operators verify the age of visitors. The Court held that free speech is not necessarily violated by the imposition of community standards on a national scale. But, after additional review in lower courts, the Supreme Court revisited COPA in 2004 and found that the government had not proven that COPA was the least restrictive means of accomplishing its stated purpose.

Although the Supreme Court does not reject the notion of "contemporary community standards," lower courts got it right when arguing that the community standards notion lets the most squeamish dictate what all others can see on the Web. In the name of protecting children, the law interferes with content that adults should have the right to see under the First Amendment. On an Internet that is increasingly capable of direct peer-to-peer communication and broadcast, individual choices and behavior replace "community standards."

The best and least restrictive defense against unwanted display of sexual content is parental supervision. Helpful tools, including filtering software and filtered online services, are available in the private sector. Filtered online services can also limit the receipt of unwanted salacious e-mail, for which COPA is no use. Another tool at parents' disposal is tracking software that lets them monitor everything a child does or has done on the Internet.

In countries that do not have as strong a tradition of free speech as the United States, governments have attempted to censor controversial speakers such as racists or businesses that sell artifacts of Nazism. The cure for harmful speech is not censorship but more speech to counter obnoxious ideas. The Internet helps to make sure that even the most despicable ideas, such as racism and Holocaust denial, can be fully aired, debunked, and laid to rest.

Privacy, Security, and Marketing

In the early days of the Internet, users did not understand how information moves in this medium. They were naturally concerned to know what information they revealed when they went online, how that information was protected, and how it would be used. Government regulators have clamored to answer those questions and impose their visions of online commerce. But the best answers are emerging from competition among firms to serve consumers. It is very easy to jump among competing firms online, so consumers are highly empowered to reward and punish online businesses on the basis of their privacy, security, and marketing practices.

Without regulation, online firms have instituted the practice of posting privacy policies for interested consumers to review. One hundred percent of legitimate retailers engage in this practice—again, without regulation requiring it. This allows individuals and activists to review and critique privacy policies. Occasionally, criticism of a company's practices hits a nerve among consumers, and their rebuke is swift. The entire universe of online retailers learns the lesson.

The best example of this is the episode several years ago when Double-Click proposed to combine click-stream information with real-world consumer profiles. The plan was cancelled long before it was implemented because of public concern. Though often used to illustrate the privacy threat, this demonstrates how responsive Internet companies are to consumers' interests and concerns.

While many consumers are concerned about privacy, many others are relatively indifferent, and those differences are rational. The availability of consumer information to manufacturers, retailers, and marketers means that products can be better designed, more economically delivered, and appealingly offered to the public. Individuals save time and money when businesses have information they can use to customize offerings, provide good customer service, and make well-targeted offers. They rarely suffer any harm from having information about their commercial behavior available to these companies.

Market forces, similarly, dictate appropriate security practices. Companies that have lost or exposed customers' personal information as a result of security breaches have suffered devastating hits in terms of public relations and lost business. They also give up competitive advantage if customer information or business strategy is revealed to competitors.

There is no need to require companies to use security procedures that are appropriate for them. It is already in their interest to do so. If a regulation requires appropriate security measures from a company that would not otherwise have them, that just preserves a company that should go out of business.

The state of California has passed a law to require notice to consumers when a security breach has revealed customer information that is particularly susceptible to identity fraud. A rigid rule like that may have perverse results: Consumers may be needlessly agitated if a security breach ultimately has no negative consequences. Because notice may interfere with a law enforcement investigation, notice can be delayed, but then the consumer will learn of a breach long after it might have mattered.

A more sensible rule would be to make holders of personal information responsible for reasonably foreseeable harms caused by security breaches.

A common law rule like this would emphasize the importance of security by placing the data holder's assets at risk. It would put the burden on the data holder to decide how best to respond to any breach on the basis of the particular facts of each case. And it would protect consumers because they could be made whole if a breach caused them harm.

The marketing practices of legitimate e-commerce companies are usually covered in their privacy policies and enforced through active consumerism. The market is converging around "opt-in" e-mail policies because consumers distrust and reject companies that e-mail them without permission, though some may continue to do so. Studies have shown that companies only rarely violate marketing policies. If they do so, they risk offending potential customers, drawing adverse publicity, and being sued for breach of contract or under other theories of liability.

Spam, Spyware, and Other Pathologies

Today, huge quantities of unwanted e-mail travel the Internet, forcing Internet service providers (ISPs) to overbuild their systems and expend enormous effort on filtering and blocking software. In consumers' inboxes, spam is often a waste of time, sometimes a vehicle for fraud, and, once in a while, a way to find an Internet bargain.

Spammers use a variety of techniques to avoid detection as spam and to avoid tracing of their e-mails' sources. They do this both to avoid retribution and to avoid legal liability. They have been enormously successful at both.

In particular, spammers have been able to avoid nearly every law aimed at them. By late 2003 more than half of the states had passed anti-spam laws that attempted a welter of different approaches to get at spam. Those laws had little effect other than to confuse legitimate e-mailers and in some cases expose them to draconian liability and extortive lawsuits.

To clean up the mess made by the states, particularly an awfully written California law, Congress passed the CAN-SPAM Act. CAN-SPAM placed a number of regulations on commercial e-mail and preempted state regulation of e-mail, except for anti-fraud and -deception laws. While the CAN-SPAM regulations have been tolerated so far, they and other regulations drive up legal and compliance costs, particularly for small business.

Most important, though, the CAN-SPAM Act has had no effect so far on the amount of unwanted e-mail traversing the Internet, which appears only to have grown since the act was passed. This illustrates the difficulty of regulating a medium that is international, complex, and useable by anonymous parties.

A variety of technical approaches hold out the greatest chance of truly suppressing the spam problem. Typically used at the ISP level are services that filter out spam using a variety of techniques, including key-word scanning and IP banning. Anti-virus vendors have begun incorporating anti-spam capabilities into their software. Many Internet users have adopted white lists and challenge-response systems. A white list is a list of e-mail addresses from which the recipient is willing to receive e-mails. E-mails from addresses not on the list may be deleted or sent to a "Junk" file. Challenge-response systems ask the sender of a first-time e-mail to verify that he or she is a real person. Once a sender verifies him- or herself, future e-mails from that source are accepted automatically.

An anti-spam approach that has a great deal of potential is a sender verification protocol. In sender verification, e-mailers would publish a list of authorized e-mail servers from which they send. When e-mail is received by an ISP or individual, their system would check to see that it came from an authorized server. E-mails not from an authorized server are probably spam and could be sent to a "Junk" file or immediately deleted. Technical solutions like these are the most likely to suppress spam. Legal solutions have been no solution at all.

The same is probably true of spyware. "Spyware" is the colloquial name given to software that is surreptitiously downloaded or attached to other downloads and that reports user behavior or information without the user's knowledge or acceptance. To date, the spyware problem has been poorly defined, nearly guaranteeing that it will not be handled well. A few states have begun to legislate about spyware in much the same way they did spam.

As with spam, the most likely solutions to spyware problems are technical ones. There are already a number of software producers whose programs search users' computers for spyware. When these programs detect spyware, they remove or quarantine it and reverse unwanted changes to computer settings.

Though it pales in comparison with spyware and spam, the pop-up problem is another Internet pathology that is best addressed by technical solutions. Though some spyware legislation has thrown a net over pop-ups, this discrete problem is best solved by pop-up-blocking software. Internet browsers can give consumers choice about which sites to allow pop-ups from, just as consumers can decide which sites to accept cookies from. Legislative solutions in this area will be too late for advancing technology and likely do more harm than good.

Internet Governance

"Internet governance" is an emerging issue that goes to the core of what the Internet of the future will look like. When the Internet was a small project used by researchers to communicate with one another, there was no need for a formal governance structure. With the growth of the Internet to its present vast proportions and importance to the economy, a couple of organizations have asserted a need for central control of the Internet's functioning.

The leader has been the U.S. government, which, because it funded much of the research that brought about the Internet, has asserted the power to govern it. Though the source of this power is dubious and it has never been formalized by congressional act or otherwise, the Clinton administration handled the problem rather deftly by distancing control of the Internet from any U.S. government agency. Instead, the nominal governor of the Internet is a nonprofit organization called the Internet Corporation for Assigned Names and Numbers (ICANN) that answers to the U.S. Department of Commerce.

ICANN's most important responsibility is ensuring that the Internet's protocols are functioning and the Domain Name System is properly administered. Unfortunately, it has rapidly adopted a broader vision of its role and dabbled in economic and social regulation of both what products Internet registries and registrars may provide and what people may do on the Internet. ICANN has quickly become a bloated and confusing bureaucracy. It has sought large expansions in its budget to facilitate further regulatory behavior.

Despite those defects, ICANN is preferable to the other leading contender for control of "Internet governance." The International Telecommunications Union, acting in conjunction with the United Nations, is seeking to bring the Internet under the control of those international bureaucracies. The recent World Summit on the Information Society signaled the UN's likely desire to seek control of the Internet's core architecture. That would subject the Internet to regulation by a confusing and remote bureaucracy that would surely think its mandate covered matters well beyond technical functioning. Already, UN actors have talked about worldwide rules for Internet communication and commerce, as well as taxation schemes to provide subsidies to special pleaders at the UN.

219

The widespread assumption that Internet governance is a problem for public law should be challenged. Ultimately, the Internet is a language, or an agreement on how computers talk to one another. It should be treated more as a contract than as an entity that is appropriate for external, formal regulation. Private agreements or arrangements like the Internet are more appropriately dealt with by contract law, which determines the scope of the agreement, implied terms, and expectations of the parties. Other than to interpret the agreement, there probably should not be a role for government bodies in saying what the terms of the Internet are.

New Internet Technologies

The Internet we know today is mostly used to connect computers to one another so that individuals, businesses, and governments can communicate with each other—that is, share information from organization to organization. The most prominent next generation of Internet communications will bring communication among machines, devices, and products. Radio Frequency Identification technology (RFID) is poised to create Internet connections (of a sort) for the billions of durable goods, machines, consumer goods, and spare parts that constantly flow through our economy.

By rationalizing and streamlining the movement of objects on factory floors, in stores, on trucks and trains, and in warehouses, RFID may bring substantial new efficiencies to the economy. Logistics managers know how much time and effort are wasted just finding things and moving them from Point A to Point B so that they can be put into service. RFID will use connections across the Internet to give managers information they need to manufacture and deliver the goods that consumers want and need at lower cost.

Unfortunately, the excitement and hype about the substantial benefits of RFID have caused some activists to believe that substantial privacy invasions will come from the technology. While that is certainly possible, it is less likely than is often assumed. Nonetheless, some activists, proregulatory groups, and legislators have called for prospective regulation of this entire suite of technologies, before anything more than experimental implementations have been put in place.

To win the substantial consumer benefits that RFID promises, it should be deployed and tested while all effects on consumer interests, such as privacy, low cost, and convenience, are considered. Should there be privacy consequences to certain implementations of RFID, economic incentives probably hold the solution, as consumers will refuse to buy products with unwanted RFID tags, or refuse to shop at stores that use RFID in unwanted ways.

Without experience, it is impossible to know how technologies like RFID may be used and what consequences they may have for good or bad. They should move forward and their adverse and beneficial consequences should be considered in real-world contexts. They should not be the subject of regulation based on speculation or projections about worst-case scenarios.

State and Local Restraints of Electronic Trade

New York Times reporter John Markoff noted in a December 2000 column, "In a remarkably short period, the World Wide Web has touched or has promised to alter—some would say threaten—virtually every aspect of modern life." Of course, not everyone has enthusiastically embraced the changes the Internet has brought, *especially* those who feel threatened by it. That is particularly true in the business marketplace where many well-established industries and older institutions fear that the Net is displacing their businesses or perhaps entire industry sectors by bringing consumers and producers closer together.

That older industries fear newer ones is nothing new, of course. Any new and disruptive technology will attract its fair share of skeptics and opponents. Steamboat operators feared the railroads; railroaders feared truckers; truckers feared air shippers; and undoubtedly horse and buggy drivers feared the first automobiles that crossed their paths.

Fear of technological change is to be expected; the problem is that older industries often have clout in the political marketplace and can convince policymakers to act on their behalf. State licensing or franchising laws are often the favored club for entrenched industries that are looking for a way to beat back their new competitors. Demanding that producers comply with a crazy-quilt of state and local regulations will often be enough to foreclose new market entry altogether.

That is simply old-fashioned industrial protectionism. But requiring national or even global commercial vendors—as is clearly the case with e-commerce and Internet sellers—to comply with parochial laws and regulations is antithetical to the interests of consumers and the economy in general. Consumers clearly benefit from the development of online commercial websites and value the flexibility such sites give them to do business directly with producers and distributors. More important, the development of a vibrant online commercial sector provides important benefits for the economy as a whole in terms of increased productivity. The Progressive Policy Institute has estimated that protectionist laws and regulations could cost consumers more than $15 billion annually in the aggregate.

Lawmakers must be flexible in crafting public policies so as to not upset the vibrant, dynamic nature of this marketplace and be willing to change existing structures, laws, or political norms to accommodate or foster the expansion of new technologies and industry sectors. The fact that some "old economy, manufacturing-age" interests may not like the emergence of the new economy, information-age sectors and technologies does not mean policymakers should seek to accommodate older interests by stifling the development of the cybersector. Such a Luddite solution will hurt consumers and further set back the development of the online marketplace. Congress must exercise its powers under the Commerce Clause of the Constitution to protect interstate electronic commerce when it is seriously threatened by state and local meddling.

Internet Taxation

A remarkably contentious battle has taken place in recent years over the Internet Tax Freedom Act of 1998 and the federally imposed moratorium on state and local taxation of the Internet. The ITFA moratorium does not prohibit states or localities from attempting to collect sales or use taxes on goods purchased over the Internet; it merely prohibits state and local government from imposing "multiple or discriminatory" taxation of the Internet or special taxes on Internet access. What pro-tax state and local officials are really at war with is not the ITFA but 30 years of Supreme Court jurisprudence that has not come down in favor of state or local government. The Court has ruled that states can require only firms with a physical presence, or "nexus," in those states to collect taxes on their behalf.

The effort to tax the Internet is a classic case of misplaced blame. In their zeal to find a way to collect taxes on electronic transactions to supposedly "level the (sales tax) playing field," most state and local officials conveniently ignore the fact that the current sales tax system is perhaps the most unlevel playing field anyone could possibly have designed. Several politically favored industries and sensitive products receive generous exemptions from sales tax collection obligations or even from the taxes themselves. And the vast majority of "service-sector" industries and professions receive a blanket exemption from sales tax obligations.

Citizens should be cognizant of the deficiencies of the current system and not allow state and local policymakers to trick them into thinking that the Internet is to blame for the holes in their sales tax bases. Electronic commerce sales have never represented more than 2 percent of aggregate retail sales according to U.S. Department of Commerce data. In light of this, it's hard to see how the Internet is to blame for the declining sales tax base.

Congress must also take an affirmative stand against efforts by state and local governments to create a collusionary multistate tax compact to tax interstate sales. Other options exist that state and local government can pursue before looking to impose unconstitutional tax burdens on interstate commerce. Of course, getting runaway state spending under control would go a long way toward solving many of their supposed problems. But if lawmakers really want to find a way to "level the playing field" and tax Internet transactions, an origin-based sales tax system would allow them to do so in an economically efficient and constitutionally sensible way. In the meantime, however, Congress would be wise to permanently extend the existing ITFA moratorium on multiple and discriminatory taxes, as well as Internet access taxes, and let Supreme Court precedents continue to govern the interstate marketplace for electronic commerce transactions.

Suggested Readings

Bell, Tom W. "Internet Privacy and Self-Regulation: Lessons from the Porn Wars." Cato Institute Briefing Paper no. 65, August 9, 2001. www.cato.org/pubs/briefs/bp-065es.html.

Corn-Revere, Robert. "Caught in the Seamless Web: Does the Internet's Global Reach Justify Less Freedom of Speech?" Cato Institute Briefing Paper no. 71, July 24, 2002. www.cato.org/pubs/briefs/bp-071es.html.

Crews, Clyde Wayne Jr. "Human Bar Code: Monitoring Biometric Technologies in a Free Society." Cato Institute Policy Analysis no. 452, September 17, 2002. http://www.cato.org/pubs/pas/pa-452es.html.

———. "Why Canning 'Spam' Is a Bad Idea." Cato Institute Policy Analysis no. 408, July 26, 2001. www.cato.org/pubs/pas/pa-408es.html.

Harper, Jim. "Understanding Privacy—And the Real Threats to It." Cato Institute Policy Analysis no. 520, August 4, 2004. http://www.cato.org/pubs/pas/pa-520es.html.

Singleton, Solveig. "Privacy as Censorship: A Skeptical View of Proposals to Regulate Privacy in the Private Sector." Cato Institute Policy Analysis no. 295, January 22, 1998. www.cato.org/pubs/pas/pa-295.html.

———. "Will the Net Turn Car Dealers into Dinosaurs? State Limits on Auto Sales Online." Cato Institute Briefing Paper no. 58, July 25, 2000. www.cato.org/pubs/briefs/bp-058es.html.

Thierer, Adam, and Clyde Wayne Crews Jr. *Who Rules the Net? Internet Governance and Jurisdiction.* Washington: Cato Institute, 2003.

Thierer, Adam, and Veronique de Rugy. ''The Internet Tax Solution: Tax Competition, Not Tax Collusion.'' Cato Institute Policy Analysis no. 494, October 23, 2003. http://www.cato.org/pubs/pas/pa-494es.html.

—Prepared by Jim Harper and Adam Thierer

22. Property Rights and Regulatory Takings

Congress should

- enact legislation that specifies the constitutional rights of property owners under the Fifth Amendment's Just Compensation Clause;
- follow the traditional common law in defining "private property," "public use," and "just compensation";
- treat property taken through regulation the same as property taken through physical seizure; and
- provide a single forum in which property owners may seek injunctive relief and just compensation promptly.

America's Founders understood clearly that private property is the foundation not only of prosperity but of freedom itself. Thus, through the common law and the Constitution, they protected property rights—the rights of people to freely acquire and use property. With the growth of the modern regulatory state, however, governments at all levels today are eliminating those rights through so-called regulatory takings—regulatory restraints that take property rights, reducing the value of the property, but leave title with the owner. And courts are doing little to protect such owners because the Supreme Court has yet to develop a principled, much less comprehensive, theory of property rights. That failure has led to the birth of the property rights movement in state after state. It is time now for Congress to step in—to correct its own violations and to give guidance to the courts as they adjudicate complaints about state violations.

When government condemns property outright, taking title from the owner, courts require it to compensate the owner for his losses under the Fifth Amendment's Takings or Just Compensation Clause: "nor shall private property be taken for public use without just compensation." The modern problem is not there—provided the compensation is just—but with regulatory takings that provide goods for the public at the expense of owners, who are often left with worthless titles. Courts have been reluctant to award compensation in such cases because they have failed to grasp the principles of the matter—due in part to an unwarranted deference to the regulatory state. As a result, owners sometimes lose their entire investment in their property, and they can do nothing about it. Meanwhile, governments are only encouraged to further regulation since the goods that are thus provided are cost free to the public.

Over the past decade, however, the Supreme Court has chipped away at the problem and begun to require compensation in some cases—even if its decisions are largely ad hoc, leaving most owners to bear the losses themselves. Thus, owners today can get compensation when title is actually taken, as just noted; when their property is physically invaded by government order, either permanently or temporarily; when regulation for other than health or safety reasons takes all or nearly all of the value of the property; and when government attaches conditions that are unreasonable or disproportionate when it grants a permit to use property. Even if that final category of takings were clear, however, those categories would not constitute anything like a comprehensive theory of the matter, much less a comprehensive solution to the problem. For that, Congress (or the Court) is going to have to turn to first principles, much as the old common law judges did. The place to begin, then, is not with the public law of the Constitution but with the private law of property.

Property: The Foundation of All Rights

It is no accident that a nation conceived in liberty and dedicated to justice for all protects property rights. Property is the foundation of every right we have, including the right to be free. Every legal claim, after all, is a claim to something—either a defensive claim to keep what one is holding or an offensive claim to something someone else is holding. John Locke, the philosophical father of the American Revolution and the inspiration for Thomas Jefferson when he drafted the Declaration of Independence, stated the issue simply: "Lives, Liberties, and Estates, which I call by the general Name, *Property*." And James Madison, the principal author of the Constitution, echoed those thoughts when he wrote that "as a man is said to have a right to his property, he may be equally said to have a property in his rights."

Much moral confusion would be avoided if we understood that all of our rights—all of the things to which we are "entitled"—can be reduced to property. That would enable us to separate genuine rights—things to which we hold title—from specious "rights"—things to which other people hold title, which we may want. It was the genius of the old common law, grounded in reason, that it grasped that point. And the common law judges understood a pair of corollaries as well: that property, broadly conceived, separates one individual from another and that individuals are independent or free to the extent that they have sole or exclusive dominion over what they hold. Indeed, Americans go to work every day to acquire property just so they can be independent.

Legal Protection for Property Rights

It would be to no avail, however, if property, once acquired, could not be used and enjoyed—if rights of acquisition, enjoyment, and disposal were not legally protected. Recognizing that, common law judges, charged over the years with settling disputes between neighbors, have drawn upon principles of reason and efficiency, and upon custom as well, to craft a law of property that respects, by and large, the equal rights of all.

In a nutshell, the basic rights they have recognized, after the rights of acquisition and disposal, are the right of sole dominion—or the right to exclude others, the right against trespass; the right of quiet enjoyment—a right everyone can exercise equally, at the same time and in the same respect; and the right of active use—at least to the point where such use violates the rights of others to quiet enjoyment. Just where that point is, of course, is often fact dependent—and is the business of courts to decide. But the point to notice, in the modern context, is that the presumption of the common law is on the side of free use. At common law, that is, people are not required to obtain a permit before they can use their property—no more than people today are required to obtain a permit before they can speak freely. Rather, the burden is upon those who object to a given use to show how it violates their right of quiet enjoyment. That amounts to having to show that their neighbor's use takes something they own free and clear. If they fail, the use may continue.

Thus, the common law limits the right of free use only when a use encroaches on the property rights of others, as in the classic law of nuisance. The implications of that limit, however, should not go unnoticed, especially in the context of such modern concerns as environmental protection. Indeed, it is so far from the case that property rights are opposed to environmental protection—a common belief today—as to be just the opposite: the right against environmental degradation is a *property* right. Under common law, properly applied, people cannot use their property in ways that damage their neighbors' property—defined, again, as taking things those neighbors hold free and clear. Properly conceived and applied, then, property rights are self-limiting: they constitute a judicially crafted and enforced regulatory scheme in which rights of active use end when they encroach on the property rights of others.

The Police Power and the Power of Eminent Domain

But if the common law of property defines and protects private rights—the rights of owners with respect to each other—it also serves as a guide for the proper scope and limits of public law—defining the rights of owners and the public with respect to each other. For public law, at least at the federal level, flows from the Constitution; and the Constitution flows from the principles articulated in the Declaration—which reflect, largely, the common law. The justification of public law begins, then, with our rights, as the Declaration makes clear. Government then follows, not to give us rights through positive law, but to recognize and secure the rights we already have. Thus, to be legitimate, government's powers must be derived from and consistent with those rights.

The two public powers that are at issue in the property rights debate are the police power—the power of government to secure rights—and the power of eminent domain—the power to take property for public use upon payment of just compensation, as set forth, by implication, in the Fifth Amendment.

The police power—the first great power of government—is derived from what Locke called the Executive Power, the power each of us has in the state of nature to secure his rights. Thus, as such, it is legitimate, since it is nothing more than a power we already have, by right, which we gave to government, when we constituted ourselves as a nation, to exercise on our behalf. Its exercise is legitimate, however, only insofar as it is used to secure rights, and only insofar as its use respects the rights of others. Thus, while our rights give rise to the police power, they also limit it. We cannot use the police power for non-police-power purposes. It is a power to secure rights, through restraints or sanctions, not some general power to provide public goods.

A complication arises with respect to the federal government, however, for it is not a government of general powers. Thus, there is no general federal police power, despite modern developments to the contrary (which essentially ignore the principle). Rather, the Constitution establishes a government of delegated, enumerated, and thus limited powers, leaving most powers, including the police power, with the states or the people, as the Tenth Amendment makes clear. (See Chapter 3 for greater detail on this point.) If we are to abide by constitutional principle, then, we have to recognize that whatever power the federal government has to secure rights is limited to federal territory, by implication, or is incidental to the exercise of one of the federal government's enumerated powers.

But if the police power is thus limited to securing rights, and the federal government's police power is far more restricted, then any effort to provide public goods must be accomplished under some other power—under some enumerated power, in the case of the federal government. Yet any such effort will be constrained by the Just Compensation Clause, which requires that any provision of public goods that entails taking private property—whether in whole or in part is irrelevant—must be accompanied by just compensation for the owner of the property. Otherwise the costs of the benefit to the public would fall entirely on the owner. Not to put too fine a point on it, that would amount to plain theft. Indeed, it was to prohibit that kind of thing that the Founders wrote the Just Compensation Clause in the first place.

Thus, the power of eminent domain—which is not enumerated in the Constitution but is implicit in the Just Compensation Clause—is an instrumental power: it is a means through which government, acting under some other power, pursues other ends—building roads, for example, or saving wildlife. Moreover, unlike the police power, the eminent domain power is not inherently legitimate: indeed, in a state of nature, none of us would have a right to condemn a neighbor's property, however worthy our purpose, however much we compensated him. Thus, it is not for nothing that eminent domain was known in the 17th and 18th centuries as "the despotic power." It exists from practical considerations alone—to enable public projects to go forward without being held hostage to holdouts seeking to exploit the situation by extracting far more than just compensation. As for its justification, the best that can be said for eminent domain is this: the power was ratified by those who were in the original position; and it is "Pareto superior," as economists say, meaning that at least one party (the public) is made better off by its use while no one is made worse off—provided the owner does indeed receive just compensation.

When Is Compensation Required?

We come then to the basic question: When does government have to compensate owners for the losses they suffer when regulations reduce the value of their property? The answers are as follows.

First, when government acts to secure rights—when it stops someone from polluting on his neighbor or on the public, for example—it is acting under its police power and no compensation is due the owner, whatever his financial losses, because the use prohibited or "taken" was wrong to begin with. Since there is no right to pollute, we do not have to pay polluters not to pollute. Thus, the question is not whether value was taken by a regulation but whether a *right* was taken. Proper uses of the police power take no rights. To the contrary, they protect rights.

Second, when government acts not to secure rights but to provide the public with some good—wildlife habitat, for example, or a viewshed or historic preservation—and in doing so prohibits or "takes" some otherwise *legitimate* use, then it is acting, in part, under the eminent domain power and it does have to compensate the owner for any financial losses he may suffer. The principle here is quite simple: the public has to pay for the goods it wants, just like any private person would have to. Bad enough that the public can take what it wants by condemnation; at least it should pay rather than ask the owner to bear the full cost of its appetite. It is here, of course, that modern regulatory takings abuses are most common as governments at all levels try to provide the public with all manner of amenities, especially environmental amenities, "off budget." As noted above, there is an old-fashioned word for that practice: it is "theft," and no amount of rationalization about "good reasons" will change that. Even thieves, after all, have "good reasons" for what they do.

Finally, when government acts to provide the public with some good and that act results in financial loss to an owner but takes no right of the owner, no compensation is due because nothing the owner holds free and clear is taken. If the government closes a military base, for example, and neighboring property values decline as a result, no compensation is due those owners because the government's action took nothing they owned. They own their property and all the uses that go with it that are consistent with their neighbors' equal rights. They do not own the value in their property.

Some Implications of a Principled Approach

Starting from first principles, then, we can derive principled answers to the regulatory takings question. And we can see, in the process, that there is no difference in principle between an "ordinary" taking and a regulatory taking, between taking full title and taking partial title—a distinction that critics of property rights repeatedly urge, claiming that the Just Compensation Clause requires compensation only for "full" takings. If we take the text seriously, as we should, the clause speaks simply of "private property." As the quote above from Madison suggests, "property" denotes not just some "underlying estate" but all the estates—all the uses—that can rightly be made of a holding. In fact, in every area of property law except takings we recognize that property is a "bundle of sticks," any one of which can be bought, sold, rented, bequeathed, what have you. Yet takings law has clung to the idea that only if the entire bundle is taken does government have to pay compensation.

That view enables government to extinguish nearly all uses through regulation—and hence to regulate nearly all value out of property—yet escape the compensation requirement because the all but empty title remains with the owner. And it would allow a government to take 90 percent of the value in year one, then come back a year later and take title for a dime on the dollar. Not only is that wrong, it is unconstitutional. It cannot be what the Just Compensation Clause stands for. The principle, rather, is that property is indeed a bundle of sticks: take one of those sticks and you take something that belongs to the owner. The only question then is how much his loss is worth.

Thus, when the Court a few years ago crafted what is in effect a 100 percent rule, whereby owners are entitled to compensation only if regulations restrict uses to a point where all value is lost, it went about the matter backwards. It measured the loss to determine whether there was a taking. As a matter of first principle, the Court should first have determined whether there was a taking, then measured the loss. It should first have asked whether otherwise legitimate uses were prohibited by the regulation. That addresses the principle of the matter. It then remains simply to measure the loss in value and hence the compensation that is due. The place to start, in short, is with the first stick, not the last dollar.

The principled approach requires, of course, that the Court have a basic understanding of the theory of the matter and a basic grasp of how to resolve conflicting claims about use in a way that respects the equal rights of all. That is hardly a daunting task, as the old common law judges demonstrated. In general, the presumption is on the side of active use, as noted earlier, until some plaintiff demonstrates that such use takes the quiet enjoyment that is his by right—and the defendant's right as well. At that point the burden shifts to the defendant to justify his use: absent some defense like the prior consent of the plaintiff, the defendant may have to cease his use—or, if his activity is worth it, offer to buy an easement or buy out the plaintiff. Thus, a principled approach respects equal rights of quiet enjoyment—and hence environmental integrity. But it also enables active uses to go forward—though not at the expense of private or public rights. Users can be as active as they wish, provided they handle the "externalities" they create in a way that respects the rights of others.

What Congress Should Do

The application of such principles is often fact dependent, as noted earlier, and so is best done by courts. But until the courts develop a more principled and systematic approach to takings, it should fall to Congress to draw at least the broad outlines of the matter, both as a guide for the courts and as a start toward getting its own house in order.

In this last connection, however, the first thing Congress should do is recognize candidly that the problem of regulatory takings begins with regulation. Doubtless the Founders did not think to specify that regulatory takings are takings too, and thus are subject to the Just Compensation Clause, because they did not imagine the modern regulatory state: they did not envision our obsession with regulating every conceivable human activity and our insistence that such activity—residential, business, what have you—take place only after a grant of official permission. In some areas of business today we have almost reached the point at which it can truly be said that everything that is not permitted is prohibited. That is the opposite, of course, of our founding principle: everything that is not prohibited is permitted—where "permitted," means "freely allowed," not allowed "by permit."

Homeowners, developers, farmers and ranchers, mining and timber companies, businesses large and small, profit making and not for profit, all have horror stories about regulatory hurdles they confront when they want to do something, particularly with real property. Many of those regulations are legitimate, of course, especially if they are aimed, preemptively, at securing genuine rights. But many more are aimed at providing some citizens with benefits at the expense of other citizens. They take rights from some to benefit others. At the federal level, such transfers are not likely to find authorization under any enumerated power. But even if constitutionally authorized, they need to be undertaken in conformity with the Just Compensation Clause. Some endangered species, to take a prominent modern example, may indeed be worth saving, even if the authority for doing so belongs to states, and even if the impetus comes from a relatively small group of people. We should not expect a few property owners to bear all the costs of that undertaking, however. If the public truly wants the habitat for such species left undisturbed, let it buy that habitat or, failing that, pay the costs to the relevant owners of their leaving their property unused.

In general, then, Congress should review the government's many regulations to determine which are and are not authorized by the Constitution. If not authorized, they should be rescinded, which would end quickly a large body of regulatory takings now in place. But if authorized under some enumerated power of Congress, the costs now imposed on owners, for benefits conferred on the public generally, should be placed "on budget." Critics of doing that are often heard to say that if we did go on budget, we couldn't afford all the regulations we want. What they are really saying, of course, is that taxpayers would be unwilling to pay for all the regulations the critics want. Indeed, the great fear of those who oppose taking a principled approach to regulatory takings is that once the public has to pay for the benefits it now receives "free," it will demand fewer of them. It should hardly surprise that when people have to pay for something they demand less of it.

It is sheer pretense, of course, to suppose that such benefits are now free, that they are not already being paid for. Isolated owners are paying for them, not the public. As a matter of simple justice, then, Congress needs to shift the burden to the public that is demanding and enjoying the benefits. Among the virtues of doing so is this: once we have an honest, public accounting, we will be in a better position to determine whether the benefits thus produced are worth the costs. Today, we have no idea about that because all the costs are hidden. When regulatory benefits are thus "free," the demand for them, as we see, is all but unbounded.

But in addition to eliminating, reducing, or correcting its own regulatory takings—in addition to getting its own house in order—Congress needs to enact general legislation on the subject of takings that might help to restore respect for property rights and reorient the nation toward its own first principles. To that end, Congress should

Enact Legislation That Specifies the Constitutional Rights of Property Owners under the Fifth Amendment's Just Compensation Clause

As already noted, legislation of the kind here recommended would be unnecessary if the courts were doing their job correctly and reading the Just Compensation Clause properly. Because they are not, it falls to Congress to step in. Still, there is a certain anomaly in asking Congress to do the job. Under our system, after all, the political branches and the states represent and pursue the interests of the people within the constraints established by the Constitution; and it falls to the courts, and the Supreme Court in particular, to ensure that those constraints are respected. To do that, the Court interprets and applies the Constitution as it decides cases brought before it—cases often brought against the political branches or a state, as here, where an owner seeks either to enjoin a government action on the ground that it violates his rights or to obtain compensation under the Just Compensation Clause, or both. Thus, it is somewhat anomalous to ask or expect Congress to right wrongs that Congress itself may be perpetrating. After all, is not Congress, in its effort to carry out the public's will, simply doing its job?

The answer, of course, is yes, Congress is doing its job, and thus this call for reform—against the "natural" inclination of Congress, if you will—is somewhat anomalous. But that is not the whole answer. For members of Congress take an oath to uphold the Constitution, which requires them to exercise independent judgment about the meaning of its terms. In doing that, they need to recognize that we do not live in anything like a pure democracy. The Constitution sets powerful and far-reaching restraints on the powers of all three branches of the federal government and, since ratification of the Civil War Amendments, on the states as well. Thus, the simple-minded majoritarian view of our system—whereby Congress simply enacts whatever some transient majority of the population wants enacted, leaving it to the Court to determine the constitutionality of the act—must be resisted as a matter of the oath of office. The oath is taken on behalf of the people, to be sure, but through and in conformity with the Constitution. When the Court fails to secure the liberties of the people, there is nothing in the Constitution to prevent Congress from exercising the responsibility entailed by the oath of office. In fact, that oath requires Congress to step into the breach.

There is no guarantee, of course, that Congress will do a better job of interpreting the Constitution than the Court. In fact, given that Congress is an "interested" party, it could very well do a worse job, which is why the Founders placed "the judicial Power"—entailing, presumably, the power ultimately to say what the law is—with the Court. But that is no reason for Congress to ignore its responsibility to make its judgment known, especially when the Court is clearly wrong, as it is here. Although nonpolitical in principle, the Court does not operate in a political vacuum— as it demonstrated in 1937, unfortunately, after Franklin Roosevelt's notorious Court-packing threat. If the Court can be persuaded to undo the centerpiece of the Constitution, the doctrine of enumerated powers, one imagines it can be persuaded to restore property rights to their proper constitutional status.

Thus, in addition to rescinding or correcting legislation that now results in uncompensated regulatory takings, and enacting no such legislation in the future, Congress should also enact a more general statute that specifies the constitutional rights of property owners under the Fifth Amendment's Just Compensation Clause, drawing upon common law principles to do so. That means that Congress should

Follow the Traditional Common Law in Defining "Private Property," "Public Use," and "Just Compensation"

As we saw above, property rights in America are not simply a matter of the Fifth Amendment—of positive law. Indeed, during the more than two years between the time the Constitution was ratified and took effect and the time the Bill of Rights was ratified, property rights were protected not only against private but against public invasion as well. That protection stemmed, therefore, not from any explicit constitutional guarantee but from the common law. Thus, the Just Compensation Clause was meant simply to make explicit, against the new federal government, the guarantees that were already recognized under the common law. (Those guarantees were implicit in the new Constitution, of course, through the doctrine of enumerated powers; for no uncompensated takings were therein authorized.) With the ratification of the Civil War Amendments—and the Fourteenth Amendment's Privileges or Immunities Clause in particular—the common law guarantees against the states were constitutionalized as well. Thus, because the Just Compensation Clause takes its inspiration and meaning from the common law of property, it is there that we must look to understand its terms.

Those terms begin with "private property": "nor shall private property be taken for public use without just compensation." As every first-year law student learns, "private property" means far more than a piece of

235

real estate. Were that not the case, property law would be an impoverished subject indeed. Instead, the common law reveals the many significations of the concept "property" and the rich variety of arrangements that human imagination and enterprise have made of the basic idea of private ownership. As outlined above, however, those arrangements all come down to three basic ideas—acquisition, exclusive use, and disposal—the three basic property rights, from which more specifically described rights may be derived.

With regard to regulatory takings, however, the crucial thing to notice is that, absent contractual arrangements to the contrary, the right to acquire and hold property entails the right to use and dispose of it as well. As Madison said, people have "a property" in their rights. If the right to property did not entail the right of use, it would be an empty promise. People acquire property, after all, only because doing so enables them to use it, which is what gives it its value. Indeed, the fundamental complaint about uncompensated regulatory takings is that, by thus eliminating the uses from property, government makes the title itself meaningless, which is why it is worthless. Who would buy "property" that cannot be used?

The very concept of "property," therefore, entails all the legitimate uses that go with it, giving it value. And the uses that are legitimate are those that can be exercised consistent with the rights of others, private and public alike, as defined by the traditional common law. As outlined above, however, the rights of others that limit the rights of an owner are often fact dependent. Thus, legislation can state only the principle of the matter, not its application in particular contexts. Still, the broad outlines should be made clear in any congressional enactment: the term "private property" includes all the uses that can be made of property consistent with the common law rights of others, and those uses can be restricted without compensating the owner only to secure such rights, not to secure public goods or benefits.

The "public use" requirement also needs to be tightened, not least because it is a source of private-public collusion against private rights. As noted above, eminent domain was known in the 17th and 18th centuries as "the despotic power" because no private person would have the power to condemn, even if he had a worthy reason and did pay just compensation. Yet we know that public agencies often do condemn private property for such private uses as auto plant construction, casino parking lots, and tax-enhancing commercial development. Those are rank abuses of the public use principle: they amount to implicit grants of private eminent domain—

and invitations to public graft and corruption. Every private use has spillover benefits for the public, of course. But if that were the standard for defining "public use," then every time someone wanted to expand his business over his neighbor's property, he could go to the relevant public agency and ask that the neighbor's property be condemned since the expansion would benefit the public through increased jobs, business, taxes, what have you. He would no longer need to bargain with his neighbor but could simply ask—or "pay"—the agency to condemn the property "for the public good."

Because it is a despotic power, even when just compensation is paid, eminent domain should be used sparingly and only for a truly *public* use. That means for a use that is broadly enjoyed by the public, rather than by some narrow part of the public; and in the case of the federal government it means for a constitutionally authorized use. More precisely, it means for a use that is owned or controlled by the public. Condemnation, after all, transfers title—either in part, for a regulatory taking, or in whole, for a full taking. If the condemnation transfers title from one private party to another, with minimal public control thereafter, it is simply illegitimate.

Thus, condemnation for building a sports stadium may be authorized under some state's constitution, but if the stadium is then owned and managed by and for the benefit of private parties, the "public use" standard has been abused, whatever the spillover "public" benefits may be. Here title settles the matter. Yet even if the public keeps the title, but the effect of the transfer is to benefit a small portion of the public rather than the public generally, the condemnation is also likely to be illegitimate because it is not truly for a "public" use. If some small group wants the benefits provided by the condemnation, private markets provide ample opportunities for obtaining them—the right way. To avoid abuse and the potential for corruption, then, Congress needs to define "public use" rigorously, with reference to titles, use, and control.

Finally, Congress should define "just compensation" with reference to its function: it is a remedy for the wrong of taking someone's property. That the Constitution implicitly authorizes that wrong does not change the character of the act, of course. As noted above, eminent domain is "justified" for practical reasons—and because "we" authorized it originally, although none of us today, of course, was there to do so. Given the character of the act, then, the least the public can do is make the victim whole. That too will be a fact-dependent determination. But Congress should at least make it clear that "just" compensation means compensation for all losses that arise from the taking, plus an added measure to acknowledge the fact that the losses arise not by mere accident, as with a tort, but from a deliberate decision by the public to force the owner to give up his property.

It should be noted, however, that not every regulatory taking will require compensation for an owner. Minimal losses, for example, may be difficult to prove and not worth the effort. Moreover, some regulatory restrictions may actually enhance the value of property or of particular pieces of property—say, if an entire neighborhood is declared "historic." Finally, that portion of "just compensation" that concerns market value should reflect value before, and with no anticipation of, regulatory restrictions. In determining compensation, government should not benefit from reductions in value its regulations bring about. Given the modern penchant for regulation, that may not always be easy. But in general, given the nature of condemnation as a forced taking, any doubt should be resolved to the benefit of the owner forced to give up his property.

If Congress enacts general legislation that specifies the constitutional rights of property owners by following the common law in defining the terms of the Just Compensation Clause, it will abolish, in effect, any real distinction between full and partial takings. Nevertheless, Congress should be explicit about what it is doing. Any legislation it enacts should

Treat Property Taken through Regulation the Same As Property Taken through Physical Seizure

The importance of enacting a unified and uniform takings law cannot be overstated. Today, we have one law for "full takings," "physical seizures," "condemnations"—call them what you will—and another for "partial takings," "regulatory seizures," or "condemnations of uses." Yet there is overlap, too: thus, as noted above, the Court recently said that if regulations take all uses, compensation is due—perhaps because eliminating all uses comes to the same thing, in effect, as a "physical seizure," whereas eliminating most uses seems not to come to the same thing.

That appearance is deceptive, of course. In fact, the truth is much simpler—but only if we go about discovering it from first principles. If we start with an owner and his property, then define "property," as above, as including all legitimate uses, it follows that any action by government that takes any property is, by definition, a taking—requiring compensation for any financial losses the owner may suffer as a result. The issue is really no more complicated than that. There is no need to distinguish "full" from "partial" takings: *every* condemnation, whether "full" or "partial," is a taking. Indeed, the use taken is taken "in full." Imagine that the property were converted to dollars—100 dollars, say. Would we say that if the government took all 100 dollars there was a taking, but if it took only 50 of the 100 dollars there was not a taking? Of course not. Yet that is what we say under the Court's modern takings doctrine because, as one justice recently put it, "takings law is full of these 'all-or-nothing' situations."

That confusion must end. Through legislation specifying the rights of property owners, Congress needs to make it clear that compensation is required whenever government eliminates common law property rights and an owner suffers a financial loss as a result—whether the elimination results from regulation or from outright condemnation.

The promise of the common law and the Constitution will be realized, however, only through procedures that enable aggrieved parties to press their complaints. Some of the greatest abuses today are taking place because owners are frustrated at every turn in their efforts to reach the merits of their claims. Accordingly, Congress should

Provide a Single Forum in Which Property Owners May Seek Injunctive Relief and Just Compensation Promptly

In its 1998 term the Supreme Court decided a takings case that began 17 years earlier, in 1981, when owners applied to a local planning commission for permission to develop their land. After having submitted numerous proposals, all rejected, yet each satisfying the commission's recommendations following a previously rejected proposal, the owners finally sued, at which point they faced the hurdles the courts put before them. Most owners, of course, cannot afford to go through such a long and expensive process, at the end of which the odds are still against them. But that process today confronts property owners across the nation as they seek to enjoy and then to vindicate their rights. If it were speech or voting or any number of other rights, the path to vindication would be smooth by comparison. But property rights today have been relegated to a kind of second-class status.

The first problem, as noted above, is the modern permitting regime. We would not stand for speech or religion or most other rights to be enjoyed only by permit. Yet that is what we do today with property rights, which places enormous, often arbitrary power in the hands of federal, state, and local "planners." Driven by political goals and considerations—

notwithstanding their pretense to "smart growth"—planning commissions open the application forum not only to those whose *rights* might be at stake but to those with *interests* in the matter. Thus is the common law distinction between rights and interests blurred and eventually lost. Thus is the matter transformed from one of protecting rights to one of deciding whose "interests" should prevail. Thus are property rights effectively politicized. And that is the end of the matter for most owners because that is as far as they can afford to take it.

When an owner does take it further, however, he finds the courts are often no more inclined to hear his complaint than was the planning commission. Federal courts routinely abstain from hearing federal claims brought against state and local governments, requiring owners to litigate their claims in state courts before they can even set foot in a federal court on their federal claims. Moreover, the Supreme Court has held that an owner's claim is not ripe for adjudication unless (1) he obtains a final, definitive agency decision regarding the application of the regulation in question, and (2) he exhausts all available state compensation remedies. Needless to say, planners, disinclined to approve applications to begin with, treat those standards as invitations to stall until the "problem" goes away. Finally, when an owner does get into federal court with a claim against the federal government, he faces the so-called Tucker Act Shuffle: he cannot get injunctive relief and compensation from the same court but must instead go to a federal district court for an injunction and to the Federal Court of Claims for compensation.

The 105th and 106th Congresses tried to address those procedural hurdles through several measures, none of which passed both houses. They must be revived and enacted if the unconscionable way we treat owners, trying simply to vindicate their constitutional rights, is to be brought to an end. This is not a matter of "intruding" on state and local governments. Under the Fourteenth Amendment, properly understood and applied, those governments have no more right to violate the constitutional rights of citizens than the federal government has to intrude on the legitimate powers of state and local governments. Federalism is not a shield for local tyranny. It is a brake on tyranny, whatever its source.

Conclusion

The Founders would be appalled to see what we did to property rights over the course of the 20th century. One would never know that their status, in the Bill of Rights, was equal to that of any other right. The time has come to restore respect for these most basic of rights, the foundation of all of our rights. Indeed, despotic governments have long understood that if you control property, you control the media, the churches, the political process itself. We are not at that point yet. But if regulations that provide the public with benefits continue to grow, unchecked by the need to compensate those from whom they take, we will gradually slide to that point—and in the process will pay an increasingly heavy price for the uncertainty and inefficiency we create. The most important price, however, will be to our system of law and justice. Owners are asking simply that their government obey the law—the common law and the law of the Constitution. Reduced to its essence, they are saying simply this: Stop stealing our property; if you must take it, do it the right way—pay for it. That hardly seems too much to ask.

Suggested Readings

Bethell, Tom. *The Noblest Triumph: Property and Prosperity through the Ages*. New York: St. Martin's, 1998.

Coyle, Dennis J. *Property Rights and the Constitution: Shaping Society through Land Use Regulation*. Albany: State University of New York Press, 1993.

DeLong, James V. *Property Matters: How Property Rights Are under Assault—And Why You Should Care*. New York: Free Press, 1997.

Eagle, Steven J. *Regulatory Takings*. Charlottesville, VA: Michie Law Publishers, 1996.

Ely, James W. Jr. *The Guardian of Every Other Right: A Constitutional History of Property Rights*. 2d ed. New York: Oxford University Press, 1998.

Epstein, Richard A. *Takings: Private Property and the Power of Eminent Domain*. Cambridge, MA: Harvard University Press, 1985.

Farah, Joseph, and Richard Pombo. *This Land Is Our Land: How to End the War on Private Property*. New York: St. Martin's, 1996.

Locke, John. "Second Treatise of Government." In *Two Treatises of Government*. Edited by Peter Laslett. New York: Mentor, 1965.

Madison, James. "Property." In *National Gazette*, March 29, 1792. Reprinted in *The Papers of James Madison*, vol. 14, *6 April 1791–16 March 1793*. Edited by Robert A. Rutland et al. Charlottesville: University Press of Virginia, 1983.

Pilon, Roger. "Are Property Rights Opposed to Environmental Protection?" In *The Moral High Ground: An Anthology of Speeches from the First Annual New York State Conference on Private Property Rights*. Edited by Carol W. LaGrasse. Stony Creek, NY: Property Rights Foundation of America, 1995.

————. "Property Rights, Takings, and a Free Society." *Harvard Journal of Law and Public Policy* 6 (1983).

Pipes, Richard. *Property and Freedom: How through the Centuries Private Ownership Has Promoted Liberty and the Rule of Law*. New York: Alfred A. Knopf, 1999.

Siegan, Bernard H. *Property and Freedom: The Constitution, the Courts, and Land-Use Regulation*. New Brunswick, NJ: Transaction Press, 1997.

Siegan, Bernard H., ed. *Planning without Prices: The Takings Clause As It Relates to Land Use Regulation without Just Compensation*. Lexington, MA: Lexington Books, 1977.

—Prepared by Roger Pilon

23. Tobacco and the Rule of Law

Congress should

- deny funding for the Justice Department's racketeering suit against cigarette makers,
- enact legislation to abrogate the multistate tobacco settlement, and
- reject proposed legislation to regulate cigarette manufacturing and advertising.

Introduction

Ten months after tobacco companies and 46 state attorneys general settled their differences for a quarter of a trillion dollars, the U.S. Department of Justice decided that it wanted a share of the plunder. DOJ's complaint alleged that cigarette companies had been conspiring since the 1950s to defraud the American public and conceal information about the effects of smoking. Specifically, the government contended that industry executives knowingly made false and misleading statements about whether smoking causes disease and whether nicotine is addictive.

On the one hand, DOJ promoted its novel lawsuit against cigarette makers. On the other hand, the same watchdog agency stood idly by while tobacco companies and state attorneys general teamed up to violate the antitrust laws. The multistate tobacco settlement, a cunning and deceitful bargain between the industry and the states, allows the tobacco giants to monopolize cigarette sales and foist the cost onto smokers.

Congress can take affirmative steps to counteract those abuses of executive power: first, by denying funds for DOJ's ongoing lawsuit and, second, by enacting legislation that abrogates the multistate tobacco settlement.

At the same time, Congress should reject any attempt to regulate cigarette advertising or the content of tobacco products.

Deny Funding for DOJ's Racketeering Suit against Cigarette Makers

In its litigation against the tobacco industry, the federal government demanded billions of dollars to pay for health care expenditures—mostly Medicare outlays—related to smoking. DOJ's legal theory was modeled after the states' lawsuits, which were designed to replenish depleted Medicaid coffers. Like the states, the federal government argued that it could sue tobacco companies without stepping into the shoes of each smoker. That way, so the theory goes, DOJ would not be subject to the "assumption-of-risk" defense that had been a consistent winner for the industry over four decades of litigation.

As you would expect, government officials understood the assumption-of-risk principle perfectly well. Indeed, former veterans affairs secretary Jesse Brown invoked it when the government itself was threatened with liability for having provided soldiers with cigarettes over many years. It would be "borderline absurdity" to pay for "veterans' personal choice to engage in conduct damaging to their health," he said. "If you choose to smoke, you are responsible for the consequences."

Evidently, that principle applied only if the defendant was a government agency. When private companies were sued, DOJ asserted that it could recover from the tobacco industry merely because smoking injured someone covered by Medicare—even if that person, having voluntarily assumed the risk of smoking, could not recover on his own. The same tobacco company selling the same cigarettes to the same smoker, resulting in the same injury, would be liable only if the smoker was a Medicare recipient and the government was the plaintiff. Otherwise, the assumption-of-risk defense would apply. Liability hinged on the injured party's Medicare status, a happenstance unrelated to any misconduct by the industry.

The federal government also wanted the court to ignore the traditional tort law requirement that causation be demonstrated on a smoker-by-smoker basis. Instead, DOJ wanted to adduce only aggregate statistics, indicating a higher incidence of certain diseases among smokers than among nonsmokers. For example, statistics showed that smokers are more likely than nonsmokers to suffer burn injuries. So tobacco companies would have to pay for many careless persons who fell asleep with a lit cigarette. Similarly, the industry would have to shell out for persons who had heart attacks and other "smoking-related" diseases but who never smoked. Without individualized corroborating evidence, aggregate statistics might suggest liability. Only common sense would dictate otherwise.

To reinforce and supplement its bizarre tort theories, DOJ relied on three statutes: the Medical Care Recovery Act, the Medicare Secondary Payer Act, and the civil provisions of the Racketeer Influenced and Corrupt Organizations Act. Federal judge Gladys Kessler dismissed both the MCRA and MSPA claims out of hand. She allowed the RICO claim to go forward, although she expressed some reservations about the government's ability to prove damages.

Nowadays, RICO is used as a standard bullying tactic by plaintiffs' attorneys, even though the act was supposed to be invoked against organized crime. This time, however, DOJ had to deal with an embarrassing admission, tucked away in the final sentence of the press release that announced its lawsuit: "There are no pending Criminal Division investigations of the tobacco industry."

Two dozen prosecutors and FBI agents had conducted a five-year, multi-million-dollar inquiry during which they dissected allegations and plowed through documents for evidence that tobacco executives perjured themselves and manipulated nicotine levels. Whistleblowers and company scientists testified before grand juries. The outcome: not a single indictment of a tobacco company or industry executive.

Nonetheless, then–attorney general Janet Reno somehow conjured up a RICO claim that accused the industry of the very same infractions for which grand juries could not find probable cause. Here's just one example, count number three: In November 1959, the industry "did knowingly cause a press release to be sent and delivered by the U.S. mails to newspapers and news outlets. This press release contained statements attacking an article written by then–U.S. surgeon general Leroy Burney about the hazards of smoking." There you have it—racketeering, in all its sordid detail.

Clinton administration insiders knew that the charges were trumped up. Former Clinton aide Rahm Emanuel put it this way: "If the White House hadn't asked, [Reno] would never have looked at it again." So it's politics, not law, that's driving this litigation. The American public needs to know that our tort system is rapidly becoming a tool for extortion. Sometimes opportunistic politicians seek money; sometimes they pursue policy goals; often they abuse their power. When Clinton was unable to persuade Congress to enact another tax on smokers, he simply bypassed the legislature and asked a federal court to impose damages in lieu of taxes. Evidently, anything goes—and the rule of law goes out the window.

Inexplicably, the Bush administration has taken up the case and is pursuing the RICO charges. But Congress can do better. Call off the government's anti-tobacco crusade. Put an immediate stop to DOJ's power grab by denying funds to continue its lawsuit.

Enact Legislation to Abrogate the Multistate Tobacco Settlement

While DOJ presses its campaign to extort money from giant tobacco companies, the Antitrust Division looks the other way as those same companies, in collaboration with state attorneys general, commit what is arguably the most egregious antitrust violation of our generation—a collusive tobacco settlement that is bilking millions of smokers out of a quarter of a trillion dollars.

The Master Settlement Agreement, signed in November 1998 by the major tobacco companies and 46 state attorneys general, transforms a competitive industry into a cartel, then guards against destabilization of the cartel by erecting barriers to entry that preserve the dominant market share of the tobacco giants. Far from being victims, the big four tobacco companies are at the very center of the plot. They managed to carve out a protected market for themselves—at the expense of smokers and tobacco companies that did not sign the agreement.

To be sure, the industry would have preferred that the settlement had not been necessary. But given the perverse legal rules under which the state Medicaid recovery suits were unfolding, the major tobacco companies were effectively bludgeoned into negotiating with the states and the trial lawyers. Finding itself in that perilous position, the industry shrewdly bargained for something pretty close to a sweetheart deal.

The MSA forces all tobacco companies—even new companies and companies that were not part of the settlement—to pay "damages," thus foreclosing meaningful price competition. Essentially, the tobacco giants have purchased (at virtually no cost to themselves) the ability to exclude competitors. The deal works like this: Philip Morris, Reynolds, Lorillard, and Brown & Williamson knew they would have to raise prices substantially to cover their MSA obligations. Accordingly, they were concerned that smaller domestic manufacturers, importers, and new tobacco companies that didn't sign the agreement would gain market share by underpricing cigarettes. To guard against that likelihood, the big four and their state collaborators added three provisions to the MSA:

First, if the aggregate market share of the four majors were to decline by more than two percentage points, then their "damages" payments would decline by three times the excess over the two-percentage-point threshold. Any reduction would be charged against only those states that did not adopt a "Qualifying Statute," attached as an exhibit to the MSA. Naturally, because of the risk of losing enormous sums of money, all of the states have enacted the statute.

Second, the Qualifying Statute requires all tobacco companies that did not sign the MSA to post pro rata damages—based on cigarette sales—in escrow for 25 years to offset any liability that might hereafter be assessed! That's right—no evidence, no trial, no verdict, no injury, just damages. That was the stick. Then came the carrot.

Third, if a nonsettling tobacco company agreed to participate in the MSA, the new participant would be allowed to increase its market share by 25 percent of its 1997 level without paying damages. Bear in mind that no nonsettling company in 1997 had more than 1 percent of the market, which, under the MSA, could grow to a whopping 1.25 percent. Essentially, the dominant companies guaranteed themselves a commanding market share in perpetuity.

Perhaps as troubling, the settlement has led to massive and continuing shifts of wealth from millions of smokers to concentrated pockets of the bar. Predictably, part of that multi-billion-dollar booty has started its roundtrip back into the political process. With all that money in hand, trial lawyers have seen their political influence grow exponentially. Every day that passes more firmly entrenches the MSA as a fait accompli, and more tightly cements the insidious relationship between trial attorneys and their allies in the public sector. The billion-dollar spigot must be turned off before its corrupting effect on the rule of law is irreversible.

An obvious way to turn off the spigot is to abrogate the MSA. If it is allowed to stand, the MSA will create and finance a rich and powerful industry of lawyers who know how to manipulate the system and are not averse to violating the antitrust laws. Congress should dismantle the MSA to restore competition. That's a tall order, but the stakes are immense.

Reject Proposed Legislation to Regulate Cigarette Manufacturing and Advertising

Under legislation periodically reintroduced in Congress, the Food and Drug Administration would be authorized to regulate cigarette ads and ingredients, including nicotine. Lamentably, Philip Morris—the industry leader with the most to gain from restrictions on would-be competitors—quickly chimed in to support many of the proposals. Yet, if tobacco is to be regulated as a drug, Congress will simply be guaranteeing a pervasive black market in tobacco products. FDA regulation that makes cigarettes taste like tree bark, coupled with higher prices, will inevitably foment illegal dealings dominated by criminals and terrorists hooking underage smokers on an adulterated product freed of all the constraints on quality that competitive markets usually afford.

The war on cigarettes, like other crusades, may have been well-intentioned at the beginning; but as zealotry takes hold, the regulations become foolish and ultimately destructive. Consider the current attempt to control tobacco advertising. Not only are the public policy implications harmful; there are obvious First Amendment violations that should concern every American who values free expression.

Industry critics point to the impact of tobacco ads on uninformed and innocent teenagers. But the debate is not about whether teens smoke; they do. It's not about whether smoking is bad for them; it is. The real question is whether tobacco advertising can be linked to increases in aggregate consumption. There's no evidence for that link. The primary purpose of cigarette ads, like automobile ads, is to persuade consumers to switch from one manufacturer to another.

In 1983, the Supreme Court held that government may not "reduce the adult population . . . to reading only what is fit for children." Thirteen years later, the Court affirmed that even vice products like alcoholic beverages are entitled to commercial speech protection. More recently, the Court threw out Massachusetts regulations banning selected cigar and smokeless tobacco ads. Those ads are not the problem. Kids smoke because of peer pressure, because their parents smoke, and because they are rebelling against authority.

If advertising were deregulated, newer and smaller tobacco companies would vigorously seek to carve out a bigger market share by emphasizing health claims that might bolster brand preference. In 1950, however, the Federal Trade Commission foreclosed health claims—such as "less smoker's cough"—as well as tar and nicotine comparisons for *existing* brands. To get around that prohibition, aggressive companies created *new* brands, which they supported with an avalanche of health claims. Filter cigarettes grew from roughly 1 percent to 10 percent of domestic sales within four years.

Then in 1954, the FTC tightened its restrictions by requiring scientific proof of health claims, even for new brands. The industry returned to promoting taste and pleasure; aggregate sales expanded. By 1957, scientists had confirmed the benefit of low-tar cigarettes. A new campaign of "Tar Derby" ads quickly emerged, and tar and nicotine levels collapsed 40 percent in two years. To shut down the flow of health claims, the FTC next demanded that they be accompanied by epidemiological evidence, of which none existed. The commission then negotiated a "voluntary" ban on tar and nicotine comparisons.

Not surprisingly, the steep decline in tar and nicotine ended in 1959. Seven years later, apparently alerted to the bad news, the FTC reauthorized tar and nicotine data but continued to proscribe associated health claims. Finally, in 1970 Congress banned all radio and television ads.

Today, the potential gains from health-related ads are undoubtedly greater than ever—for both aggressive companies and health-conscious consumers. If, however, government regulation expands, those gains will not be realized. Instead of "healthy" competition for market share, we will be treated to more imagery and personal endorsements—the very ads that anti-tobacco partisans decry.

If the imperative is to reduce smoking among children, the remedy lies with state governments, not the U.S. Congress. The sale of tobacco products to youngsters is illegal in every state. Those laws need to be vigorously enforced. Retailers who violate the law must be prosecuted. Proof of age requirements are appropriate if administered objectively and reasonably. Vending machine sales should be prohibited in areas such as arcades and schools where children are the main clientele. And if a minor is caught smoking or attempting to acquire cigarettes, his parents should be notified. Parenting is, after all, primarily the responsibility of fathers and mothers, not the government.

Instead, government has expanded its war on tobacco far beyond any legitimate concern with children's health. Mired in regulations, laws, taxes, and litigation, we look to Congress to extricate us from the mess it helped create. Yet if Congress authorizes the FDA to regulate cigarette ads and control the content of tobacco products, it will exacerbate the problem. Equally important, Congress will have delegated excessive and ill-advised legislative authority to an unelected administrative agency.

Of course, the machinery of regulation, once set in motion, will not stop with ameliorative changes. Listen to former commissioner David A. Kessler, outlining his concept of FDA oversight: "Only those tobacco products from which the nicotine had been removed or, possibly, tobacco products approved by FDA for nicotine-replacement therapy would then remain on the market.'' In other words, cigarettes as we know them would cease to exist.

In 1919 Americans understood that Congress could not prohibit the sale of alcoholic beverages, so Prohibition was effectuated by constitutional amendment. Today, when it comes to tobacco, our lifestyle police argue that we require neither a constitutional amendment nor even an intelligible statute—just an amorphous delegation to an unelected administrative agency, which can ban ingredients it doesn't think ''uninformed'' citizens should consume. So much for limited government. We are left with the executive state—return of the king.

Just as bad, assigning quasi-legislative authority to the FDA will drive another nail into the coffin of personal responsibility. A federal agency will be empowered to dictate the form and composition of a legal product about which consumers have exhaustive knowledge. Throughout the 20th century, incessant warnings about the risks of tobacco came from doctors, public health sources, and thousands of scientific and medical publications. By the 1920s, 14 states had prohibited the sale of cigarettes. A warning has appeared on every pack of cigarettes lawfully sold in the United States for almost four decades. Nicotine content by brand has been printed in every cigarette ad since 1970.

That isn't enough for the anti-tobacco crowd, for whom cigarettes are only the first in a long list of products that the nanny state will monitor. If we know anything at all about government, it is that bureaucrats are likely to have an expansive view of their mission. So what comes next—coffee, soft drinks, red meat, dairy products, sugar, fast foods, automobiles, sporting goods? The list is endless—all in pursuit of so-called public health.

But smoking is a private, not a public, health question. The term ''public,'' if it is to have any substantive content, cannot be used to describe all health problems that affect lots of people. Instead, ''public'' should refer only to those cases requiring collective action, when individual harms cannot be redressed without a general societal solution. Smoking, for example, would be a public health problem if it were contagious. But it isn't. Similarly, cigarettes do not infect us as they cross state borders. Nor has nicotine shown up in biological or chemical weapons.

An adult's decision to smoke is a voluntary, private matter. It's time to rein in the administrative state and restore a modicum of individual liberty.

Suggested Readings

Bulow, Jeremy, and Paul Klemperer. ''The Tobacco Deal.'' In *Brookings Papers on Economic Activity: Microeconomics 1998.* Washington: Brookings Institution, 1998.

Calfee, John E. "The Ghost of Cigarette Advertising Past." *Regulation*, November–December 1986.

Levy, Robert A. "Tobacco-Free FDA." *Administrative Law & Regulation News* 2, no. 3 (Winter 1998).

——. *Shakedown: How Corporations, Government, and Trial Lawyers Abuse the Judicial Process*. Washington: Cato Institute, 2004.

O'Brien, Thomas C. "Constitutional and Antitrust Violations of the Multistate Tobacco Settlement." Cato Institute Policy Analysis no. 371, May 18, 2000.

—Prepared by Robert A. Levy

24. The War on Drugs

Congress should

- repeal the Controlled Substances Act of 1970,
- repeal the federal mandatory minimum sentences and the mandatory sentencing guidelines,
- direct the administration not to interfere with the implementation of state initiatives that allow for the medical use of marijuana, and
- shut down the Drug Enforcement Administration.

Ours is a federal republic. The federal government has only the powers granted to it in the Constitution. And the United States has a tradition of individual liberty, vigorous civil society, and limited government. Identification of a problem does not mean that the government ought to undertake to solve it, and the fact that a problem occurs in more than one state does not mean that it is a proper subject for federal policy.

Perhaps no area more clearly demonstrates the bad consequences of not following such rules than does drug prohibition. The long federal experiment in prohibition of marijuana, cocaine, heroin, and other drugs has given us crime and corruption combined with a manifest failure to stop the use of drugs or reduce their availability to children.

In the 1920s Congress experimented with the prohibition of alcohol. On February 20, 1933, a new Congress acknowledged the failure of alcohol prohibition and sent the Twenty-First Amendment to the states. Congress recognized that Prohibition had failed to stop drinking and had increased prison populations and violent crime. By the end of 1933, national Prohibition was history, though many states continued to outlaw or severely restrict the sale of liquor.

Today Congress confronts a similarly failed prohibition policy. Futile efforts to enforce prohibition have been pursued even more vigorously since the 1980s than they were in the 1920s. Total federal expenditures for the first 10 years of Prohibition amounted to $88 million—about $982 million in 2004 dollars. Drug enforcement costs about $19 billion a year now in federal spending alone.

Those billions have had some effect. Total drug arrests are now more than 1.5 million a year. Since 1989 more people have been incarcerated for drug offenses than for all violent crimes combined. There are now about 400,000 drug offenders in jails and prisons, and more than 60 percent of the federal prison population consists of drug offenders.

Yet, as was the case during Prohibition, all the arrests and incarcerations haven't stopped the use and abuse of drugs, or the drug trade, or the crime associated with black-market transactions. Cocaine and heroin supplies are up; the more our Customs agents interdict, the more smugglers import. And most tragic, the crime rate has soared. Despite the good news about crime in the past few years, crime rates remain at high levels.

As for discouraging young people from using drugs, the massive federal effort has largely been a dud. Despite the soaring expenditures on anti-drug efforts, about half the students in the United States in 1995 tried an illegal drug before they graduated from high school. Every year from 1975 to 2003, at least 82 percent of high school seniors said they found marijuana "fairly easy" or "very easy" to obtain. During that same period, according to federal statistics of dubious reliability, teenage marijuana use fell dramatically and then rose significantly, suggesting that cultural factors have more effect than the "war on drugs."

The manifest failure of drug prohibition explains why more and more people—from Nobel laureate Milton Friedman to conservative columnist William F. Buckley Jr., former secretary of state George Shultz, and former governors Jesse Ventura and Gary Johnson—have argued that drug prohibition actually causes more crime and other harms than it prevents.

Repeal the Controlled Substances Act

The United States is a federal republic, and Congress should deal with drug prohibition the way it dealt with alcohol prohibition. The Twenty-First Amendment did not actually legalize the sale of alcohol; it simply repealed the federal prohibition and returned to the several states the authority to set alcohol policy. States took the opportunity to design diverse liquor policies that were in tune with the preferences of their citizens. After 1933 three states and hundreds of counties continued to practice prohibition. Other states chose various forms of alcohol legalization.

The single most important law that Congress must repeal is the Controlled Substances Act of 1970. That law is probably the most far-reaching federal statute in American history, since it asserts federal jurisdiction over every drug offense in the United States, no matter how small or local in scope. Once that law is removed from the statute books, Congress should move to abolish the Drug Enforcement Administration and repeal all of the other federal drug laws.

There are a number of reasons why Congress should end the federal government's war on drugs. First and foremost, the federal drug laws are constitutionally dubious. As previously noted, the federal government can exercise only the powers that have been delegated to it. The Tenth Amendment reserves all other powers to the states or to the people. However misguided the alcohol prohibitionists turned out to have been, they deserve credit for honoring our constitutional system by seeking a constitutional amendment that would explicitly authorize a national policy on the sale of alcohol. Congress never asked the American people for additional constitutional powers to declare a war on drug consumers. That usurpation of power is something that few politicians or their court intellectuals wish to discuss.

Second, drug prohibition creates high levels of crime. Addicts commit crimes to pay for a habit that would be easily affordable if it were legal. Police sources have estimated that as much as half the property crime in some major cities is committed by drug users. More dramatic, because drugs are illegal, participants in the drug trade cannot go to court to settle disputes, whether between buyer and seller or between rival sellers. When black-market contracts are breached, the result is often some form of violent sanction, which usually leads to retaliation and then open warfare in the streets.

Our capital city, Washington, D.C., has become known as the "murder capital" even though it is the most heavily policed city in the United States. Make no mistake about it, the annual carnage that accounts for America's still high murder rates has little to do with the mind-altering effects of a marijuana cigarette or a crack pipe. It is instead one of the grim and bitter consequences of an ideological crusade whose proponents will not yet admit defeat.

Third, since the calamity of September 11, 2001, U.S. intelligence officials have repeatedly warned us of further terrorist attacks. Given that danger, it is a gross misallocation of law enforcement resources to have federal police agents surveilling marijuana clubs in California when they could be helping to discover sleeper cells of terrorists on U.S. territory. The Drug Enforcement Administration has 9,000 agents, intelligence analysts, and support staff. Their skills would be much better used if those people were redeployed to full-time counterterrorism investigations.

Fourth, drug prohibition is a classic example of throwing money at a problem. The federal government spends some $19 billion to enforce the drug laws every year—all to no avail. For years drug war bureaucrats have been tailoring their budget requests to the latest news reports. When drug use goes up, taxpayers are told the government needs more money so that it can redouble its efforts against a rising drug scourge. When drug use goes down, taxpayers are told that it would be a big mistake to curtail spending just when progress is being made. Good news or bad, spending levels must be maintained or increased.

Fifth, drug prohibition channels more than $40 billion a year into the criminal underworld that is occupied by an assortment of criminals, corrupt politicians, and, yes, terrorists. Alcohol prohibition drove reputable companies into other industries or out of business altogether, which paved the way for mobsters to make millions in the black market. If drugs were legal, organized crime would stand to lose billions of dollars, and drugs would be sold by legitimate businesses in an open marketplace.

Drug prohibition has created a criminal subculture in our inner cities. The immense profits to be had from a black-market business make drug dealing the most lucrative endeavor for many people, especially those who care least about getting on the wrong side of the law.

Drug dealers become the most visibly successful people in inner-city communities, the ones with money and clothes and cars. Social order is turned upside down when the most successful people in a community are criminals. The drug war makes peace and prosperity virtually impossible in inner cities.

Students of American history will someday ponder the question of how today's elected officials could readily admit to the mistaken policy of alcohol prohibition in the 1920s but recklessly pursue a policy of drug prohibition. Indeed, the only historical lesson that recent presidents and Congresses seem to have drawn from Prohibition is that government should not try to outlaw the sale of booze. One of the broader lessons that they should have learned is this: prohibition laws should be judged according to their real-world effects, not their promised benefits. If the 109th Congress will subject the federal drug laws to that standard, it will recognize that the drug war is not the answer to problems associated with drug use.

Respect State Initiatives

The failures of drug prohibition are becoming obvious to more and more Americans. A particularly tragic consequence of the stepped-up war on drugs is the refusal to allow sick people to use marijuana as medicine. Prohibitionists insist that marijuana is not good medicine, or at least that there are legal alternatives to marijuana that are equally good. Those who believe that individuals should make their own decisions, not have their decisions made for them by Washington bureaucracies, would simply say that that's a decision for patients and their doctors to make. But in fact there is good medical evidence of the therapeutic value of marijuana— despite the difficulty of doing adequate research on an illegal drug. A National Institutes of Health panel concluded that smoking marijuana may help treat a number of conditions, including nausea and pain. It can be particularly effective in improving the appetite of AIDS and cancer patients. The drug could also assist people who fail to respond to traditional remedies.

More than 70 percent of U.S. cancer specialists in one survey said they would prescribe marijuana if it were legal; nearly half said they had urged their patients to break the law to acquire the drug. The British Medical Association reports that nearly 70 percent of its members believe marijuana should be available for therapeutic use. Even President George Bush's Office of National Drug Control Policy criticized the Department of Health and Human Services for closing its special medical marijuana program.

Whatever the actual value of medical marijuana, the relevant fact for federal policymakers is that in 1996 the voters of California and Arizona authorized physicians licensed in those states to recommend the use of medical marijuana to seriously ill and terminally ill patients residing in the states, without being subject to civil and criminal penalties.

It came as no surprise when the Clinton administration responded to the California and Arizona initiatives by threatening to bring federal criminal charges against any doctor who recommended medicinal marijuana or any patient who used such marijuana. After all, President Clinton and his lawyers repeatedly maintained that no subject was beyond the purview of federal officialdom.

President Bush, on the other hand, has spoken of the importance of the constitutional principle of federalism. Shortly after his inauguration, Bush said, "I'm going to make respect for federalism a priority in this administration." Unfortunately, the president's actions have not matched his words. When the Ninth Circuit Court of Appeals ruled that the Controlled Substances Act could not extend so far as to reach two Californians who grew their own marijuana for medical use and who did not engage in commercial activity or interstate commerce, the Bush administration appealed the case, *Ashcroft v. Raich,* to the Supreme Court. Instead of supporting the Supreme Court's recent landmark rulings that have revived the constitutional principle of federalism, Bush administration lawyers are embracing the arguments of liberal academics. That is, the federal government can pass a law about anything "affecting" interstate commerce, which turns out to be virtually everything.

The Bush administration is also undermining the landmark federalism precedents in Congress and at the state and local levels. Federal police agents and prosecutors continue to raid medical marijuana clubs in California and Arizona. And both of the president's drug policy officials, drug czar John Walters and DEA chief Karen Tandy, have been using their offices to meddle in state and local politics. If it is inappropriate for governors and mayors to entangle themselves in foreign policy—and it is—it is also inappropriate for federal officials to entangle themselves in state and local politics. In the 108th Congress, Reps. Barney Frank (D-MA), Dana Rohrabacher (R-CA), and Ron Paul (R-TX) jointly proposed the States' Rights to Medical Marijuana Act, which would have prohibited federal interference with any state that chose to enact a medical marijuana policy. The 109th Congress should enact a similar bill without delay.

One of the benefits of a federal republic is that different policies may be tried in different states. One of the benefits of our Constitution is that it limits the power of the federal government to impose one policy on the several states.

Repeal Mandatory Minimums

The common law in England and America has always relied on judges and juries to decide cases and set punishments. Under our modern system, of course, many crimes are defined by the legislature, and appropriate penalties are defined by statute. However, mandatory minimum sentences and rigid sentencing guidelines shift too much power to legislators and regulators who are not involved in particular cases. They turn judges into clerks and prevent judges from weighing all the facts and circumstances in setting appropriate sentences. In addition, mandatory minimums for nonviolent first-time drug offenders result in sentences grotesquely disproportionate to the gravity of the offenses.

Rather than extend mandatory minimum sentences to further crimes, Congress should repeal mandatory minimums and let judges perform their traditional function of weighing the facts and setting appropriate sentences.

Conclusion

Drug abuse is a problem for those involved in it and for their families and friends. But it is better dealt with as a moral and medical than as a criminal problem—"a problem for the surgeon general, not the attorney general," as former Baltimore mayor Kurt Schmoke puts it.

The United States is a federal republic, and Congress should deal with drug prohibition the way it dealt with alcohol prohibition. The Twenty-First Amendment did not actually legalize the sale of alcohol; it simply repealed the federal prohibition and returned to the several states the authority to set alcohol policy. States took the opportunity to design diverse liquor policies that were in tune with the preferences of their citizens. After 1933 three states and hundreds of counties continued to practice prohibition. Other states chose various forms of alcohol legalization.

Congress should repeal the Controlled Substances Act of 1970, shut down the Drug Enforcement Administration, and let the states set their own policies with regard to currently illegal drugs. They would do well to treat marijuana, cocaine, and heroin the way most states now treat alcohol: It should be legal for stores to sell such drugs to adults. Drug sales to children, like alcohol sales to children, should remain illegal. Driving under the influence of drugs should be illegal.

With such a policy, Congress would acknowledge that our current drug policies have failed. It would restore authority to the states, as the Founders envisioned. It would save taxpayers' money. And it would give the states the power to experiment with drug policies and perhaps devise more successful rules.

Repeal of prohibition would take the astronomical profits out of the drug business and destroy the drug kingpins who terrorize parts of our cities. It would reduce crime even more dramatically than did the repeal of alcohol prohibition. Not only would there be less crime; reform would also free federal agents to concentrate on terrorism and espionage and free local police agents to concentrate on robbery, burglary, and violent crime.

The war on drugs has lasted longer than Prohibition, longer than the Vietnam War. But there is no light at the end of this tunnel. Prohibition has failed, again, and should be repealed, again.

Suggested Readings

Benjamin, Daniel K., and Roger Leroy Miller. *Undoing Drugs: Beyond Legalization.* New York: Basic Books, 1991.

Boaz, David. "A Drug-Free America—Or a Free America?" *U.C. Davis Law Review* 24 (1991).

Boaz, David, ed. *The Crisis in Drug Prohibition.* Washington: Cato Institute, 1991.

Buckley, William F. Jr., et al. "The War on Drugs Is Lost." *National Review,* February 12, 1996.

Luna, Erik. "The Misguided Guidelines: A Critique of Federal Sentencing." Cato Institute Policy Analysis no. 458, November 1, 2002.

Lynch, Timothy, ed. *After Prohibition: An Adult Approach to Drug Policies in the 21st Century.* Washington: Cato Institute, 2000.

Masters, Bill. *Drug War Addiction.* St. Louis: Accurate Press, 2002.

McNamara, Joseph. "The Defensive Front Line." *Regulation* (Winter 2001): 19–21.

Nadelmann, Ethan A. "An End to Marijuana Prohibition." *National Review,* July 12, 2004.

Ostrowski, James. "The Moral and Practical Case for Drug Legalization." *Hofstra Law Review* 18 (1990).

Pilon, Roger. "The Medical Marihuana Referendum Movement in America: Federalism Implications." Testimony before the House Crime Subcommittee, October 1, 1997.

—Prepared by David Boaz and Timothy Lynch

25. Restoring the Right to Bear Arms

Congress should

- reeducate itself about the original meaning and current constitutional implications of the Second Amendment,
- use its constitutional authority over the District of Columbia to overturn D.C.'s handgun ban and enact a "shall-issue" concealed carry licensing statute, and
- repeal the Gun Control Act of 1968.

For decades, the Second Amendment was consigned to constitutional exile, all but erased from constitutional law textbooks and effectively banished from the nation's courts. But no more. Recent developments in the law and in political culture have begun the process of returning the amendment to its proper place in our constitutional pantheon. Congress now has a historic opportunity, not simply to stave off new gun-control proposals, but to begin restoring Americans' right to keep and bear arms.

Understanding the Second Amendment

Ideas have consequences, and so does constitutional text. Though elite opinion reduced the Second Amendment to a constitutional inkblot for a good part of the 20th century, gun enthusiasts and grassroots activists continued to insist that the amendment meant what it said. And slowly, often reluctantly, legal scholars began to realize that the activists were right. Liberal law professor Sanford Levinson conceded as much in a 1989 *Yale Law Journal* article titled "The Embarrassing Second Amendment." UCLA Law School's Eugene Volokh took a similar intellectual journey. After a 1990 argument with a nonlawyer acquaintance who loudly maintained that the Second Amendment protected an individual right, Volokh concluded that his opponent was a "blowhard and even a bit of a kook." But several years later, as he researched the subject, he discovered to his "surprise and mild chagrin, that this supposed kook was entirely right": the amendment secures the individual's right to keep and bear arms.

That's also what the Fifth Circuit Court of Appeals concluded in October 2001 when it decided *United States v. Emerson*. It held that the Constitution "protects the right of individuals, including those not then actually a member of any militia . . . to privately possess and bear their own firearms . . . that are suitable as personal individual weapons."

U.S. Attorney General John Ashcroft has endorsed the *Emerson* court's reading of the amendment. First, in a letter to the National Rifle Association, Ashcroft stated his belief that "the text and the original intent of the Second Amendment clearly protect the right of individuals to keep and bear firearms." That letter was followed by Justice Department briefs before the Supreme Court in the *Emerson* case and in *United States v. Haney*. For the first time, the federal government argued in formal court papers that the "Second Amendment . . . protects the rights of individuals, including persons who are not members of any militia . . . to possess and bear their own firearms, subject to reasonable restrictions designed to prevent possession by unfit persons or . . . firearms that are particularly suited to criminal misuse."

The Right of the People

What's driving the new consensus? Let's look at the amendment's text: "A well regulated Militia, being necessary to the security of a free State, the right of the people to keep and bear Arms, shall not be infringed."

The operative clause ("the right of the people to keep and bear Arms, shall not be infringed") secures the right. The explanatory clause ("A well regulated Militia, being necessary to the security of a free State") justifies the right. That syntax was not unusual for the times. For example, the free press clause of the 1842 Rhode Island Constitution states: "The liberty of the press being essential to the security of freedom in a state, any person may publish his sentiments of any subject." That provision surely does not mean that the right to publish protects only the press. It protects "any person"; and one reason among others that it protects any person is that a free press is essential to a free society. Analogously, the Second Amendment protects "the people"; and one reason among others that it protects the people is that it ensures a well-regulated militia.

As George Mason University law professor Nelson Lund puts it, imagine if the Second Amendment said, "A well-educated Electorate, being necessary to self-governance in a free state, the right of the people to keep and read Books shall not be infringed." Surely, no rational person would suggest that only registered voters have a right to read. Yet that is precisely the effect if the text is interpreted to apply only to a well-educated electorate. Analogously, the Second Amendment cannot be read to apply only to members of the militia.

The Second Amendment, like the First and the Fourth, refers explicitly to "the right of the people." Consider the placement of the amendment within the Bill of Rights, the part of the Constitution that deals exclusively with rights of individuals, not powers of the state. No one can doubt that First Amendment rights (speech, religion, assembly) belong to us as individuals. Similarly, Fourth Amendment protections against unreasonable searches and seizures are individual rights. In the context of the Second Amendment, we secure "the right of the people" by guaranteeing the right of each person. Second Amendment protections are not for the state but for each individual against the state—a deterrent to government tyranny.

And not just against government tyranny. The Second Amendment also secures our right to protect ourselves from criminal predators. After all, in 1791 there were no organized, professional police forces to speak of in America. Self-defense was the responsibility of the individual and the community and not, in the first instance, of the state. Armed citizens, responsibly exercising their right of self-defense, are an effective deterrent to crime.

Today, states' incompetence at defending citizens against criminals is a more palpable threat to our liberties than is tyranny by the state. But that incompetence coupled with a disarmed citizenry could well create the conditions that lead to tyranny. The demand for police to defend us increases in proportion to our inability to defend ourselves. That's why disarmed societies tend to become police states. Witness law-abiding inner-city residents, many of whom have been disarmed by gun control, begging for police protection against drug gangs—despite the terrible violations of civil liberties, such as curfews and anti-loitering laws, that such protection entails. The right to bear arms is thus preventive—it reduces the demand for a police state. George Washington University law professor Robert Cottrol put it this way: "A people incapable of protecting themselves will lose their rights as a free people, becoming either servile dependents of the state or of the criminal predators."

Over the years, our elected representatives have adopted a dangerously court-centric view of the Constitution: a view that decisions about constitutionality are properly left to the judiciary. But members of Congress also swear an oath to uphold the Constitution. Congress can make good on that oath by taking legislative action to restore our right to keep and bear arms. To that end, Congress should take the following steps.

Repeal D.C.'s Handgun Ban and Enact Concealed Carry

No jurisdiction in the United States works as doggedly to disarm citizens as does the District of Columbia, our nation's capital and on-again, off-again murder capital. Yes, the city council grudgingly legalized pepper spray in 1993 (provided, of course, that it's properly registered), but that brief concession to self-defense hasn't led to any revision of the District's gun laws, which are still among the most restrictive in America.

With very few exceptions, no handgun can be registered in D.C. Even those pistols grandfathered prior to the District's 1976 ban cannot be carried from room to room in the home without a license, which is never granted. Moreover, all firearms in the home, including rifles and shotguns, must be unloaded and either disassembled or bound by a trigger lock. In effect, no one in the District can possess a functional firearm in his or her own residence. And the law applies not just to "unfit" persons like felons, minors, or the mentally incompetent but across the board to ordinary, honest, responsible citizens. If "reasonable" regulations are those that prohibit bad persons from possessing massively destructive firearms, then the District's blanket prohibitions on handguns are patently unreasonable.

Some violations of the D.C. gun ban are prosecuted by the U.S. attorney for the District of Columbia, an employee of the Justice Department— the same Justice Department that is now on record as favoring an individual rights theory of the Second Amendment. To be sure, Attorney General Ashcroft had declared in an internal memorandum that the Justice Department "will continue to defend the constitutionality of all existing federal firearms laws." But D.C. law, although enacted pursuant to congressional delegation, is not federal law.

It's one thing for Ashcroft to endorse the individual right to bear arms in a letter to a friendly interest group, or to affirm it in a footnote in a legal brief. It's quite another to follow up words with action. As an official with the District's Public Defender Service puts it, Ashcroft's Justice Department "is currently prosecuting individuals solely for 'bearing' a pistol, even though many of those individuals have no prior convictions and are adult citizens of full mental capacity. Thus the United States persists in prosecuting District of Columbia residents for conduct that the Attorney General has expressly deemed protected by the United States Constitution.''

Whatever the reasons for Attorney General Ashcroft's perplexing decision to continue prosecuting gun-ban violations, Congress has the constitutional authority to protect District residents' right to bear arms. Article I, section 8, clause 17, of the Constitution gives Congress the power "to exercise exclusive legislation in all cases whatsoever" over the District of Columbia. Congress can and should use that authority to repeal the District's gun ban and enact a "shall-issue" concealed carry licensing statute. Such statutes mandate that handgun permits be issued to citizens who satisfy certain objective criteria such as mental competence, lack of a criminal record, and completion of a firearms training course.

More than 30 states have shall-issue laws, and, as exhaustive research by American Enterprise Institute scholar John R. Lott Jr. has shown, they deter crime. Lott found that "the reductions in violent crime are greatest in the most crime prone, most urban areas. Women, the elderly and blacks gained by far the most from this ability to protect themselves."

In contrast, since 1976 D.C. residents have served as guinea pigs in a public policy experiment in near-total gun prohibition. That experiment has failed catastrophically. Congress can and should end that illegitimate experiment and restore District residents' right to keep and bear arms. Unlike armed criminals in D.C., the city's disarmed residents pay their taxes and obey the laws. But the District of Columbia government says that if someone breaks into their houses, their only choice is to call 911 and pray that the police arrive in time. That's not good enough. The right to bear arms includes the right to defend your property, your family, and your life. No government should be permitted to take that right away.

Repeal the Gun Control Act of 1968

The Gun Control Act of 1968, with subsequent amendments, is bad law and bad public policy. It ought to be repealed. Full repeal is not a radical step; Ronald Reagan endorsed it in 1980. But until that can be accomplished, Congress should, at a minimum, repeal the most oppressive sections:

The 1994 Ban on So-Called Assault Weapons

Automatic firearms have been heavily regulated since 1934. Semiautomatic weapons, which fire only one round each time the trigger is pulled, have been available for more than 100 years. They are used by tens of millions of Americans for hunting, self-defense, target shooting, and in formal competitions, including the Olympics. Police statistics from around the nation show that such guns are rarely used in crime. Felons, drug addicts, illegal aliens, minors, and incompetents cannot legally buy firearms—semiautomatic or otherwise. Moreover, semiautomatic weapons are not more powerful than other guns. Indeed, they fire smaller bullets at lower velocities than do most well-known rifles used for hunting big game.

The ban on assault weapons expired in September 2004. The statute was purely cosmetic—banning guns because of politically incorrect features such as bayonet lugs (as if drive-by bayoneting were a problem) or a rifle grip that protrudes ''conspicuously'' from the gun's stock. The ban did little to curb criminal violence, but it did a great deal to inhibit the full exercise of Second Amendment rights. Congress should resist any attempt to re-enact the ban.

The 1994 Ban on Possession of Handguns by Persons under 18

Assuming that a ban on underage possession of a handgun by a 17-year-old could survive Second Amendment scrutiny, it is a topic that should be addressed by state, not federal, law. The statute does include some exceptions—for example, a parent may take a child target shooting—but, even if the child is under direct and continuous parental supervision, the parent commits a federal crime unless she writes a note giving the child permission to target shoot and the child carries the note at all times. The 1994 prohibition usurps traditional state powers, is overbroad, and encroaches on parental rights, despite a paucity of empirical evidence that the ban will reduce gun accidents or gun-related violence.

The Ban on Gun Possession by Specified Adults

When adult behavior is regulated, the Second Amendment weighs more heavily than when restrictions are imposed on minors. Even if Second Amendment constraints are somehow satisfied, the federal government has no constitutional authority in this area. Particularly unfair, whether imposed by federal or state law, is the ban on gun possession by anyone who is subject to a domestic restraining order, routinely issued by divorce courts without any finding that the subject of the order is a danger to another person. Such provisions ought not to be allowed to stand.

Conclusion

The broader principle is this: Governments frequently fail to perform their single most important function—protecting American citizens against aggression. Armed civilians can deter aggression. That means safer homes, shopping malls, schools, and other public places. Law enforcement officers can't be everywhere, but an armed, trained citizenry can be.

For too long, elite opinion in America has been implacably opposed to armed self-defense. The underlying philosophy, expressed by Pete Shields, former president of Handgun Control, is that "the best defense is . . . no defense—give them what they want." After 9/11, that philosophy is no longer valid, if it ever was. It's time for Congress to repudiate it.

Suggested Readings

Halbrook, Steven P. "Second Class Citizenship and the Second Amendment in the District of Columbia." *George Mason University Civil Rights Law Journal* 5 (1995).

Kopel, David B. *The Samurai, the Mountie, and the Cowboy: Should America Adopt the Gun Controls of Other Democracies?* Amherst, NY: Prometheus Books, 1992.

Lott, John R. Jr. *More Guns, Less Crime: Understanding Crime and Gun-Control Laws.* 2d ed. Chicago: University of Chicago Press, 2000.

Lund, Nelson. "A Primer on the Constitutional Right to Keep and Bear Arms." Virginia Institute for Public Policy Report no. 7, June 2002.

Snyder, Jeffrey R. "Fighting Back: Crime, Self-Defense, and the Right to Carry a Handgun." Cato Institute Policy Analysis no 284, October 22, 1997.

United States v. Emerson, 270 F.3d 203 (5th Cir. 2001).

—Prepared by Gene Healy and Robert A. Levy

26. The Nanny State

Policymakers should

- respect the concept of personal responsibility when making public policy,
- respect Americans' right to make their own decisions about risk and vice and their consequences, and
- avoid the temptation to use government to "protect us from ourselves."

One of the more disturbing trends in government expansion over the last 30 years has been the collection of laws, regulations, and binding court decisions that make up the "nanny state." Those laws and regulations represent government at its most arrogant. Their message is clear: politicians and bureaucrats know more about how to live your life, manage your health, and raise your kids than you do. Former president Ronald Reagan once said: "Government exists to protect us from each other. Where government has gone beyond its limits is in deciding to protect us from ourselves." Today's policymakers would do well to heed Reagan's words.

Unfortunately, they haven't. Lawmakers at all levels of government have shown increasing contempt for personal responsibility and an increasing tendency to employ the power of the state to influence behavior. Government today pressures us to avoid risks, even risks that many of us knowingly and willingly take. There seems to be a consensus among nanny-statists that, with enough public service announcements, awareness campaigns, and social engineering efforts, Americans will start behaving as the nanny-statists want them to.

The largest, most expensive, and most obvious example of government-as-nanny is America's failed drug war. Though drug use directly harms no one but drug users, we continue to prohibit certain drugs, either because policymakers believe government should protect users from themselves or because they believe drug use has detrimental effects on society at large, or on the "public health."

Of course, the detrimental effects of drug use largely arise precisely *because* of government interference. It isn't drug use itself that has turned inner cities into war zones; it is the *prohibition* of drug use, which makes selling banned drugs quite lucrative and thus an attractive investment for the criminal element and an attractive lifestyle for people with few prospects. The same could be said about drug abuse's affect on the health care system. If each of us were solely responsible for our own health care, only drug users would bear the consequences of their habits. It is only because we have a quasi-public health care system that the costs of drug abuse are passed on to the rest of the population.

The same philosophy that entrenched the government in the drug war has allowed ensuing nanny-state endeavors to blossom. Once we're comfortable with government control over what pharmaceuticals we're permitted to put into our bodies, the case for restrictions, regulations, and controls on tobacco and alcohol isn't difficult to make. And from there, government can cite, and has cited, the "public health" effects of obesity as reason to extend its tentacles into our refrigerators and onto our dinner plates. In fact, once policymakers have bought the notion of a "public health" in need of protection and nurturing by government, they can be comfortable giving the state pervasive control over nearly every facet of our lives— from mandating that we wear our seatbelts, to telling us what risks we should allow our children to take, to telling us what foods we should eat and how much and how often we should eat them.

Just a few examples of the growing nanny state:

- Every state but one now requires motorists to wear seatbelts.
- All but three states now require some or all motorcycle riders to wear helmets.
- After hundreds of years of use by humans, the federal government banned the stimulant ephedra in 2004. Despite widespread use, ephedra has been loosely connected to only about a hundred deaths (a recent RAND study has implicated it in only two).
- The Reason Public Policy Institute has compiled a list of products and activities that have recently been banned by local, state, or federal government. It includes sex toys, nude dancing, strip clubs, beer advertisements, snowmobiles, all-terrain vehicles, "pocket bikes," motor scooters, exotic pets, and smoking in public places.

- In 2000 the Consumer Product Safety Commission proposed banning a type of bath seat for infants, not because the product wasn't safe, but because it was *too* safe, which CPSC argued could lull parents into a false sense of security.
- The National Transportation Safety Board has suggested that parents be required to buy extra airplane tickets for infants and that infants be secured in child safety seats, despite the fact that NTSB could identify only three cases in the last 20 years in which obeying such a rule might have saved an infant's life. The cost of an extra ticket might also persuade a parent to drive, which is more dangerous than flying.

The list goes on. There seems to be no sphere of life in regard to which government doesn't have an opinion about how we should live and doesn't feel obligated to help us live correctly—through excise taxes, tax breaks, regulation, restrictions on advertising, zoning laws, or outright prohibition.

Today we have well-funded, well-staffed federal agencies whose sole mission is to discourage Americans from using alcohol and tobacco. Implementing or raising existing excise taxes on both alcohol and cigarettes is again gaining favor in state legislatures, particularly in states facing a budget crunch. In 2004 the U.S. Department of Justice pressed charges against two California pornography producers and has publicly said it plans to press charges against others. Since 2000 DOJ has also aggressively pursued online gambling companies, going so far as to threaten credit card companies, online payment services such as Paypal, and advertisers with prosecution if they do business with gaming websites. Federal prosecutors have also recently stepped up efforts to enforce laws against prostitution, medical marijuana, prescription pain medication, and physician-assisted suicide—all crimes that take no victims.

The nanny state's latest crusade makes Americans even more intimate with their government, bringing the state to our mouths, frying pans, and waistlines. Responding to a rash of media reports announcing that Americans, and American children in particular, are getting heavy, nanny-statists have called for a host of new government programs, regulations, and measures intended to persuade, encourage, or outright coerce Americans to eat properly and exercise regularly. Some of those measures are relatively innocuous, such as government-sponsored "public awareness" campaigns. Others are more troubling, including "fat taxes" on calorie-dense foods, class action litigation against food producers, and restrictions on portion sizes in restaurants. And the most costly obesity-related proposal was never voted on by lawmakers at all. Medicare's recent decision to consider covering obesity treatments could mean that U.S. taxpayers will be asked to pay for the diet plans, nutritional counseling, and even "stomach-stapling" surgery of as many as 20–25 million people, a number that could double if Medicaid follows Medicare's lead.

The nanny state mindset extends across partisan lines. Vice President Al Gore once said that government shouldn't oversee our lives but should be "more like grandparents in the sense that grandparents perform a nurturing role." Though President Bush has at least intimated a desire to give Americans more control over their own lives, he has offered little in the way of actual policy. Andrew Card, his chief of staff, has said that President Bush "sees America as we think about a 10-year-old child." Despite his advocacy of an "ownership society," the president devoted more time in his 2004 State of the Union address to fighting steroids than he did, for example, to giving Americans ownership of their Social Security contributions.

Lawmakers should respect Americans' control over their own lives. We need to rethink the idea of "public health," so that it encompasses only serious threats to public safety, threats such as deadly diseases or chemical or biological terrorism—threats to which no one would willingly expose himself.

Individual Americans will make better decisions about risk and lifestyle when they and they alone bear the consequences of those decisions. Of course, what makes a good or bad decision is subjective, which is precisely why personal decisions should be beyond the purview of government. More fundamentally, what we eat, drink, or otherwise put into our bodies; what we do with our bodies; the people we choose to sleep with and how we choose to sleep with them; and what health, financial, or safety risks we elect to take simply are not legitimate concerns of the state. Once government simply leaves Americans alone on these matters, responsibility for decisions about risk and vice and their consequences becomes limited to individual Americans. It's only when government gets involved that the costs of risk are dispersed across the rest of the public.

It's time to roll back the nanny state. Policymakers should let Americans live their lives as they please, so long as they do not harm anyone else. They should heed former president Reagan's words and concentrate on protecting Americans from terrorists and criminals instead of wasting time, money, and resources on protecting Americans from themselves.

Suggested Readings

Balko, Radley. "It's the Parents, Stupid." Tech Central Station, July 13, 2004.
———. "Post-Reductio America." Tech Central Station, November 19, 2003.
Boaz, David. "Obesity and 'Public Health?' " Cato Institute Daily Commentary, July 20, 2004.
Niskanen, William. "The Nanny State Strikes Again." *FoxNews.com,* December 26, 2003.
———. "Obesity and Medicare." Cato Institute Daily Commentary, July 17, 2004.
Sullivan, Andrew. "The Nanny in Chief." *Time,* February 2, 2004.
Volokh, Eugene. "Obscenity Crackdown: What Will the Next Step Be?" Cato Institute TechKnowledge, April 12, 2004.

—Prepared by Radley Balko

27. National ID Cards

> **Congress should** resist the establishment of a national identification card and encourage the development and acceptance of private identification systems.

In the wake of a calamitous terrorist attack, such as the one that America experienced on September 11, 2001, it is appropriate for policymakers to review our laws, policies, and customs with an eye to changes that would enhance our safety and security. Identification systems, and the question of whether there should be a uniform national ID, have been significant features of public debate since it came to light that several of the terrorists acquired false identification papers.

Every policy proposal should be carefully examined for effectiveness and consistency with our values and freedoms. A national or uniform ID system offers less protection at greater cost to freedom than it appears to. Verifying identity is just one, fallible, way of attempting to secure transportation systems and infrastructure. A national or uniform ID system would be a small but significant step toward future impingements on freedom, including mandates that all Americans carry identity cards at all times, the creation of an internal passport system, and government tracking of individuals' travels and financial transactions.

Congress should not hastily enact any proposal simply because it is packaged as an ''anti-terrorism'' measure. Rather, it should encourage market solutions that allow people and institutions to choose how identity is to be established and how people's suitability for access to transportation systems, buildings, military bases, and other infrastructure is to be determined. The happenstance that nearly everyone carries a driver's license is not a sound basis for federally mandated or unified identity cards.

Security Benefits Are Illusory

It was only a matter of days after the attack of September 11 before some members of Congress proposed a national ID card system as a way of thwarting additional terrorist attacks. In the past, a national ID card has been pushed as a way of finding illegal immigrants. Since September 11, the proposal has been repackaged as a "security" measure.

A national or uniform ID card would be a very bad deal for America because it would require some 250 million people to surrender some of their freedom and some of their privacy but not offer substantial protection from terrorist attack. An ID card with biometric identifiers may seem impenetrable, but there are several ways that terrorists will be able to get around such a system. They can bribe the employees who issue the cards or the employees who check the cards, for example. Terrorists could recruit people who possess valid cards—U.S. citizens or lawful permanent residents—to support and carry out attacks.

Indeed, past incidents of terrorism have been carried out by people born and raised in the United States, people who had been issued proper, fully valid identification. Knowing who a person is reveals little about his or her plans or motivations, and a national ID system would do nothing to distinguish first-time terrorists before they attack. Terrorist recruits or people who newly adopt terrorist methods will not be revealed by a national ID system until after our security has failed and disaster has struck. Identity-based security is valid in some contexts, but it is not a substitute for security programs that harden critical infrastructure against likely tools and methods of attack and that develop intelligence on the people and groups who wish to do our country harm.

Proponents of national ID systems point to countries in Europe, such as France, that already have national ID card systems. But the experience of those countries is nothing to brag about. The people in those countries have surrendered their privacy and their liberty, yet they continue to experience terrorist attacks. National ID cards simply do not deliver the security that is promised.

The Loss of Liberty Will Be Real

The establishment of a national ID card system would dilute civil liberties and pave the way for further intrusions on anonymity and freedom. The Fourth Amendment to the Constitution protects Americans against unreasonable arrests and the Fifth Amendment prohibits the government from forcing people to incriminate themselves. The Supreme Court recently upheld the arrest of a man who invoked his right to remain silent when a police officer asked him for identification. As strange as it may sound, standing quietly and peacefully on a public sidewalk can now be a crime in America. Although the Supreme Court declined to say that the police can demand identification whenever they want, the police have essentially acquired that power as a practical matter. That is because it is almost impossible for a layperson to know precisely when he can lawfully refuse such a request. The law on the matter is just too nuanced for nonlawyers to comprehend.

If a national ID system were enacted, pressure would inevitably build to enhance the government's power even further by making it crystal clear that citizens must produce identification in any and all circumstances. The proof of this is at hand: In the countries that already have national ID card systems, the police have acquired the power to demand identification at will. Implemented widely, such power would become an "internal passport" system. "Your papers, please" could again become a familiar request, harking back to the worst totalitarian states of the last century. Americans are rightly suspicious of national IDs for this reason. A uniform requirement to carry and produce identification could quickly devolve into a comprehensive tracking mechanism, used by government at first to investigate ordinary crime but over time to systematically track and control ordinary, law-abiding citizens.

It is important to note that many of the proponents of the national ID card—such as Alan Dershowitz of Harvard Law School and Larry Ellison from Oracle—present the idea in its most innocuous form. The proponents say the card will be "voluntary" and that people will have to present it only at airports. And the card will reveal only a few basic pieces of information, such as name and address. But, over time, the amount of information on the card will surely expand. (The Pentagon has already moved to create a Total Information Awareness database that would contain medical and financial information on citizens.) The number of places where one will have to present an ID card will also expand, and it will eventually become compulsory. And, sooner or later, a legal duty to produce identification whenever a government official demands it could be created.

Government officials warn us to expect more terrorist attacks. It is a safe bet that there will be more anti-terrorism proposals in the wake of such attacks. Perhaps there will be an attack a year from now, and a limited national ID card will be proposed and enacted. Maybe three years later, America will be attacked again; people will die, and law enforcement will go to Congress and say, "We have a national ID card, but the problem is that it is voluntary, not compulsory." Thus, by increments, America will get the full-blown national ID card system that is now in place in other countries. Congress should avoid this slippery slope by focusing its attention on more effective security measures. A national ID card expands the power of government over law-abiding citizens, but it will not really enhance security.

Rather than focus on government-issued ID cards, federal policy should encourage and foster the variety of identification systems that exist in the private marketplace today. People carry many types of privately issued identification, and these systems could be expanded and modified for security purposes. Many people, for example, carry credit cards that allow them to pay for goods or services. A variety of privately issued access cards allow people entry into buildings or access to automobiles. Many of these systems already provide better assurance of identity and trustworthiness than many government-issued ID cards. The government should accept privately issued identification that sufficiently authenticates the holders and the suitability of the holder for access to transportation systems and critical infrastructure. In a marketplace for identification services, consumers would be able to choose what methods they use to identify themselves, how much information they share for this purpose, and whether records are kept of their activities. A national ID system would deprive Americans of choices like these, which they should have.

Conclusion

It is very important that policymakers not lose sight of what we are fighting for in the war on terrorism. The goal should be to fight the terrorists within the framework of a free society. The federal government should be taking the battle to the terrorists, to their base camps, and killing the terrorist leadership; it should not be transforming our free society into a surveillance state. Proposals for uniform national identification would take America in the direction of a "Show us your papers" surveillance state.

Suggested Readings

Crews, Clyde Wayne Jr. "Human Bar Code: Monitoring Biometric Technologies in a Free Society." Cato Institute Policy Analysis no. 452, September 17, 2002.

Kopel, David. "You've Got Identity: Why a National ID Is a Bad Idea." *National Review Online*, February 5, 2002.

Lynch, Timothy. "Breaking the Vicious Cycle: Preserving Our Liberties While Fighting Terrorism." Cato Institute Policy Analysis no. 443, June 26, 2002.

———. "Cooperate, Or Else!" *Reason Online*, June 25, 2004. www.reason.com/hod/tl062504.shtml.

Twight, Charlotte. "Watching You: Systematic Federal Surveillance of Ordinary Americans." Cato Institute Briefing Paper no. 69, October 17, 2001.

Watner, Carl, and Wendy McElroy, eds. *National Identification Systems.* Jefferson, NC: McFarland, 2004.

—Prepared by Timothy Lynch and Jim Harper

DOMESTIC POLICY

28. U.S. Department of Education

> **Congress should**
>
> - abolish the Department of Education and
> - return education to the state, local, or family level, as provided by the Constitution.

The powers not delegated to the United States by the Constitution, nor prohibited by it to the States, are reserved to the States respectively, or to the people.

—Tenth Amendment to the U.S. Constitution

The U.S. Department of Education, formed in 1979 during the Carter administration, represents an intrusion by the federal government into an aspect of American society over which it has no constitutional authority. The U.S. Constitution gives Congress no authority whatsoever to collect taxes for, fund, or operate schools. Therefore, under the Tenth Amendment, education should be entirely a state and local matter.

For more than 200 years, the federal government had left education to those who were in the best position to oversee it—state and local governments and families. Richard L. Lyman, president of Stanford University, who testified at the congressional hearings on forming the new department, pointed out that "the two-hundred-year-old absence of a Department of Education is not the result of simple failure during all that time. On the contrary, it derives from the conviction that we do not want the kind of educational system that such arrangements produce."

Without question, the Framers intended that most aspects of American life would be outside the purview of the federal government. They never envisioned that Congress or the president would become involved in funding schools or mandating policy for classrooms. As constitutional scholar Roger Pilon has said: "From beginning to end the [Constitution] never mentioned the word 'education.' The people, in 1787 or since, have never given the federal government any power over the subject—despite a concern for education that surely predates the Constitution.''

Why then was the Department of Education created? President Jimmy Carter, during whose watch the new department came into being, had promised the department to the National Education Association. Contemporary editorials in both the *New York Times* and the *Washington Post* acknowledged that the creation of the department was mainly in response to pressure from the NEA. According to Rep. Benjamin Rosenthal (D-NY), Congress went along with the plan out of ''not wanting to embarrass the president.'' Also, many members of Congress had made promises to educators in their home districts to support the new department. The *Wall Street Journal* reported the admission of one House Democrat: ''The idea of an Education Department is really a bad one. But it's NEA's top priority. There are school teachers in every congressional district and most of us simply don't need the aggravation of taking them on.'' Former house minority leader Bob Michel termed the Department of Education the ''Special Interest Memorial Prize'' of the year.

The new department started with a $14 billion budget and more than 4,000 employees, all transferred from other departments. Proponents claimed that cost savings would be realized, but opponents pointed out that a new department would require not only a new secretary but also the corresponding assistant secretaries, under secretaries, support staff, office space, regional offices, cars, and other amenities. All of those would be necessary for the new department to look and act like a bona fide cabinet department. Critics of the department also pointed to the Department of Energy, formed two years earlier, which had been the subject of a tangle of regulations and confusing policies. Rep. John Rousselot (R-CA) said: ''If you like the Department of Energy, you'll love the Department of Education. You'll have every bureaucrat in Washington looking at your school district.''

Has the Department of Education produced budget savings or a streamlining of federal education programs? No. The department's budget has continually increased, from $14.5 billion in 1979 to a proposed $57.3 billion for 2005. According to analyses of federal education spending before and after the creation of the Department of Education, after its creation, federal spending on education increased at twice the rate it had before.

Chester Finn, who served as assistant secretary of education from 1985 until 1988, made the following observation about why education spending increased faster once we had a Department of Education:

When budget time rolls around, a department is able to exert more clout in pressing for larger funding from Congress than can smaller agencies. It carries a bureaucratic momentum and muscle all its own. Since it no longer has to compete with health and welfare, as it did under HEW, the new department will be able to exert the full brunt of the education lobby in its behalf upon the Congress. Make no mistake about it, the principal reason the NEA and the administration wanted to elevate the Office of Education to a full-fledged department was to give it the political power and prestige to seek bigger budget increases for federal education programs.

Along with the budget, the maze of federal education programs continues to expand under the Department of Education. Wayne Riddle, representing the Congressional Research Service, testified before a 1995 congressional hearing that the potential overlap of Department of Education programs with those of other federal agencies has probably increased since 1979 in such areas as vocational education and job training, science education, and early childhood education. Currently, there are more than 760 education-related programs spread across 39 federal agencies costing taxpayers $108 billion per year. President Bush's 2005 budget calls for federal spending on myriad education programs that are clearly local in nature— from special reading and after-school programs to tutoring preschoolers to job training for their parents.

Also, the Department of Education and its nearly 5,000 employees have had virtually no positive effect on the performance of schools or the academic gains of school children. The department's own national history report card issued in May 2002 found that only 43 percent of the nation's 12th graders had at least a basic understanding of U.S. history, unchanged from 1994, the last time the test was given. On one question, the majority of high school seniors chose Germany, Japan, or Italy as a U.S. ally in World War II. Diane Ravitch, education adviser to the Bush I administration and professor of education at New York University, called the results "truly abysmal." "Since the seniors are very close to voting age or have already reached it," she observed, "one can only feel alarm that they know so little about their nation's history and express so little capacity to reflect on its meaning." Comparisons of U.S. students with students in other countries show that U.S. students still lag behind students in countries such as Finland, Australia, and New Zealand.

It's fair to say that the Department of Education has had no apparent positive effect on the academic performance of U.S. school children. Instead, its major effect has been to move the focus on improving education from parents and local districts to Washington, D.C. Federal guidelines now cover such topics as how schools discipline students, the content of sex education courses, and the gender of textbook authors. Former secretaries of education Lamar Alexander and William Bennett have stated that the department has "an irresistible and uncontrollable impulse to stick its nose into areas where it has no proper business. Most of what it does today is no legitimate affair of the federal government. The Education Department operates from the deeply erroneous belief that American parents, teachers, communities and states are too stupid to raise their own children, run their own schools and make their own decisions."

American taxpayers have spent hundreds of billions of dollars on the Department of Education since its founding in 1979, yet test scores and other measures indicate no improvement in American education (Figure 28.1). The benefits promised by the proponents of the department plainly

Figure 28.1
Federal Education Spending and Average Student Performance

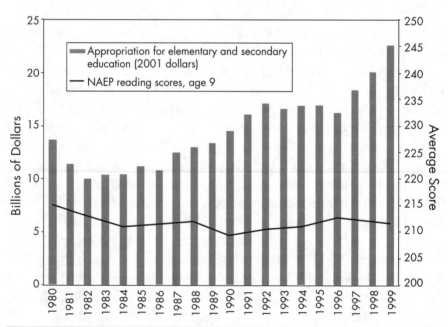

NOTE: The time period chosen corresponds to the data available from the NAEP 1999 "Trends in Academic Progress: Three Decades of Student Performance," Table B.1, Appendix B, p. 100, U.S. Department of Education, National Center for Education Statistics, http://www.nces.ed.gov/pubsearch/pubsinfo.asp? pubid = 2000469. Expenditures are from "Education Department Budget History Table: FY 1980–present," http://www.ed.gov/about/overview/budget/history/edhistory.pdf.

have not materialized. There is simply no legitimate reason to continue this failed experiment.

No Child Left Behind Act

The foremost policy initiative of the Bush administration to date has been the No Child Left Behind Act. In its original form, the act included a number of reforms that would have allowed flexibility for districts and increased choice for parents—including choice of private schools—but most of these provisions were removed in committee.

The bill passed in June 2002 provided the Department of Education with $27.9 billion for spending on NCLB programs. At the same time, it perpetuated most of the older federal education programs, many of which are ineffective and wasteful. The total cost for NCLB climbed to more than $37 billion this year.

Instead of decreasing the role of the federal government in education, NCLB places a plethora of mandates on local schools. Although some of the mandates prescribe what appear to be reasonable practices (like requiring that schools test students annually in reading and math and show annual progress), imposing them from Washington represents a departure from the American tradition that education is a state and local matter.

During his presidential campaign, Bush emphasized that he did not want to become the "federal superintendent of schools." But NCLB gives the president and the federal government far too much power over local schools and classrooms. Instead of proposing more top-down fixes for education, the president should use his position to push for the return of control of education to states and localities and urge state-level reforms that return the control of education to parents.

New Directions

There is a growing awareness that parents, not distant government bureaucrats, should have more power over their children's education. After years of legal battles over school choice in places like Cleveland, Ohio, and Milwaukee, Wisconsin, the U.S. Supreme Court ruled in June 2002 that school vouchers were constitutional and that parents could use them at either secular or religious private schools. School choice programs now exist in Ohio, Wisconsin, Florida, Pennsylvania, Arizona, Maine, Iowa, Minnesota, Vermont, Illinois, and Washington, D.C. Many more states will consider school choice legislation during the coming two years.

The way for Congress to improve American education is to step aside and let the states experiment with choice in a variety of ways. Some will expand charter schools or experiment with private management. Others will institute scholarship tax credits, parental tax credits, or vouchers either on a limited basis or open to all students. The most successful policies and programs will be emulated by other states.

Since Congress has no authority under the Constitution to collect taxes for, fund, or regulate schools, it should not tax Americans to fund a huge federal education bureaucracy that exercises dictatorial control over curriculum, standards, and policy. The only actions that should be taken at the federal level are those that deregulate education. For example, Congress should repeal the many regulations and mandates governing special education and allow states to set up their own programs for educating special needs children. Instead of mandating tests or other accountability measures and subsidizing the public school monopoly, it should return tax funds to the states, eliminate the myriad unnecessary and unconstitutional federal programs, and allow the states to take the lead in reforming education.

Except in Washington, D.C., where Congress has constitutional authority over legislative matters, it should not set up demonstration projects or fund voucher programs. Federal tax credits for parents who use private schools may seem attractive, but, since Congress has no constitutional authority to collect taxes for education, it would be better to simply institute a tax cut for all Americans, eliminate the wasteful and meddlesome Department of Education, and allow individual Americans to decide how best to spend that money. We must remember that parents, not politicians, are in the best position to make decisions about the education of their children.

James Madison, who proclaimed that the powers of the federal government should be few and enumerated, would be shocked at what the president and Congress are doing today in relation to an aspect of family life that was never intended to come under the control of Congress, the White House, or any federal agency. Congress should take the enlightened view, consistent with that of the nation's Founders, and draw a line in the sand that won't be crossed. Education is a matter reserved to the states.

Eliminating the federal intrusion into education is not anti-education or anti-child and it's not just about saving money. It's about returning money and power to those who are better able than federal bureaucrats to determine what is best for their children. Keeping federal politicians out of American education is a time-honored and constitutionally sound policy and is the most likely to produce the best quality educational options for children.

Nine Reasons to Abolish the Department of Education

1. The Constitution provides no authority whatsoever for the federal government to be involved in education. Eliminating the department on those grounds would help to reestablish the original understanding of the enumerated powers of the federal government.

2. No matter how brilliantly designed a federal government program may be, it creates a uniformity among states that is harmful to creativity and improvement. Getting the federal government out of the picture would allow states and local governments to create better ways of addressing education issues and problems.

3. If education were left at the local level, parents would become more involved in reform efforts. Differences in school effectiveness among states and communities would be noted, and other regions would copy the more effective programs and policies.

4. The contest between Congress and state legislatures to demonstrate who cares more about education would be over, allowing members of Congress to focus on areas and problems for which they have legitimate responsibility.

5. Since most information about the problems and challenges of education is present at the local level, Congress simply does not have the ability to improve learning in school classrooms thousands of miles away. These problems are best understood and addressed by local authorities and parents.

6. The inevitable pattern of bureaucracy is to grow bigger and bigger. The Department of Education should be eliminated now, before it evolves into an even larger entity consuming more and more resources that could be better spent by parents themselves.

7. The $57.3 billion spent each year by the Department of Education could be much better spent if it were simply returned to the American people in the form of a tax cut. Parents themselves could then decide how best to spend that money.

8. The Department of Education has a record of waste and abuse. For example, the department reported losing track of $450 million during three consecutive General Accounting Office audits.

9. The Department of Education is an expensive failure that has added paperwork and bureaucracy but little value to the nation's classrooms.

Suggested Readings

Boaz, David, ed. *Liberating Schools: Education in the Inner City.* Washington: Cato Institute, 1991.

Coulson, Andrew. *Market Education: The Unknown History.* New Brunswick, NJ: Transaction, 1999.

Finn, Chester E. Jr., and Michael J. Petrilli. "Washington versus School Reform." *Public Interest* 133 (Fall 1998).

Harmer, David. *School Choice: Why You Need It, How You Get It.* Washington: Cato Institute, 1994.

McClusky, Neal. "A Lesson in Waste: Where Does All the Federal Education Money Go?" Cato Institute Policy Analysis no. 518, July 7, 2004.

Richman, Sheldon. "Parent Power: Why National Standards Won't Improve Education." Cato Institute Policy Analysis no. 396, April 26, 2001.

Salisbury, David F. "What Does a Voucher Buy? A Closer Look at the Cost of Private Schools." Cato Institute Policy Analysis no. 486, August 28, 2003.

Salisbury, David, and Casey Lartigue. *Educational Freedom in Urban America:* Brown v. Board *after 50 Years.* Washington: Cato Institute, 2004.

Subcommittee on Oversight and Investigations of the House Committee on Education and the Workforce. "Education at the Crossroads: What Works and What's Wasted in Education Today." 105th Cong., 2d sess., July 17, 1998.

—Prepared by David Salisbury

29. Higher Education

Congress should

- phase out federal student aid *except* aid directly related to national security (such as ROTC scholarships),
- phase out federal aid to institutions,
- eliminate all grant programs and research not related to national security, and
- end pork by requiring all federal grants to universities to be competitively bid.

In his book *Universities in the Marketplace*, former Harvard University president Derek Bok writes something federal policymakers should never forget: "Universities share one characteristic with compulsive gamblers and exiled royalty: there is never enough money to satisfy their desires." When combined with another central guide for policymakers, the Constitution's Tenth Amendment, which states that "the powers not delegated to the United States by the Constitution, nor prohibited by it to the states, are reserved to the states respectively, or to the people," the message is clear: the federal government must get out of higher education.

The 109th Congress has an excellent opportunity to begin doing just that. The Higher Education Act, the primary federal law governing colleges and universities, is due to be reauthorized this year, a carryover from the 108th Congress. Legislators can make changes to the act that will initiate the federal withdrawal, ultimately deflating higher education's perpetually ballooning price and freeing taxpayers—almost half of whom have never taken a single college class, and nearly three-quarters of whom do not have a bachelor's degree—from subsidizing higher education.

Where Are We Now?

Over the last nearly 40 years, the federal government has provided an increasingly massive amount of higher education funding. According to the National Center for Education Statistics (NCES), between 1965 and 2002 federal spending on postsecondary education rose from $5.6 billion, adjusted for inflation, to an estimated $22.8 billion. In addition, federal expenditures on university-based research exploded, from $8.4 billion to an estimated $25.7 billion. And the federal presence is likely to keep growing: the Department of Education's *Fiscal Year 2005 Budget Summary* shows that the president has requested more than $22.2 billion for student aid in 2005, as well as more than $2.3 billion for efforts like aid to minority-serving institutions, programs to encourage disadvantaged students to pursue higher education, and efforts to improve teacher preparation. If enacted, that would bring the department's 2005 higher education spending to more than $24.5 billion.

The Adverse Effects of Federal Student Aid

According to *The College Cost Crisis*, a report from the U.S. House Subcommittee on 21st-Century Competitiveness, "America's higher education system is in crisis. Decades of uncontrolled cost increases are pushing the dream of a college degree further out of reach for needy students." Surprisingly, the evidence suggests that student aid itself is actually a major force behind the explosion.

In part, it is simple supply and demand. Over the years, increasing numbers of people have desired to go to college, pushing its price higher. Ordinarily, the upward pressure on price would have been restrained by consumers' willingness and ability to pay; people have limited funds and will pay only so much before deeming a good either unaffordable or unworthy of its price. But in *Going Broke by Degree: Why College Costs Too Much*, Ohio University economist Richard Vedder explains that because third parties like the federal government absorb tuition increases, the budget constraints that come when individuals pay their own way have been eliminated: "The shift to the right of the demand curve for students—and the resulting higher tuition—has been aided and abetted by a large and proliferating number of government assistance programs—some grants, some guaranteed student loans, some work-study programs." Figure 29.1 bears this trend out, showing that between 1990 and 2000 (the most recent year for which data are available) as college prices rose, federal aid did too. Indeed, except between 1991 and 1992 and 1999 and 2000, federal student aid actually grew faster than tuition, fees, and room and board (TFRB). To put this in perspective, in 1990

Figure 29.1
Growth in Average Inflation-Adjusted Federal Aid per Full-Time-Equivalent Student and Growth in Inflation-Adjusted Average Tuition, Fees, Room and Board per Full-Time-Equivalent Student, 1990–2000

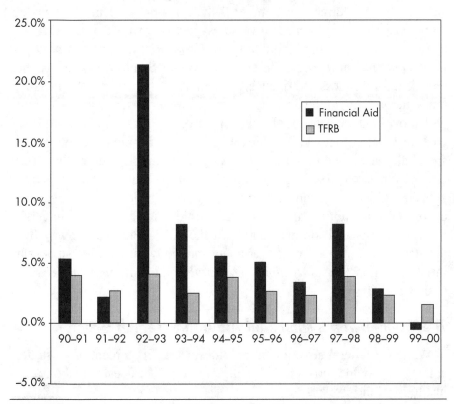

SOURCES: U.S. Department of Education, National Center for Education Statistics, *Digest of Education Statistics 2002*, Tables 200 and 312; and College Board, *Trends in Student Aid 2003*, Table 2 and Appendix B. "Financial Aid" is the average amount of federal aid per full-time-equivalent student, determined by dividing *Trends in Student Aid* "total federal aid" data by *Digest*, Table 200, enrollment figures. TFRB is from *Digest*, Table 312. Note that average aid per student includes graduate students, while average TFRB is only for undergraduates. Separate per student federal aid totals for undergraduates were not available.

federal student aid covered about 34 percent of the average student's TFRB, but it covered 46 percent in 2000.

Explaining the supply side is the so-called Bennett Hypothesis, put forth in 1987 by then–secretary of education William Bennett, who argued that "increases in financial aid in recent years have enabled colleges and universities blithely to raise tuitions, confident that Federal loan subsidies would help cushion the increase." In other words, colleges will charge

293

every penny they think the market will bear, and, as Figure 29.1 shows, student aid has ensured that it will bear a lot.

Of course, no schools have actually confessed to setting tuition at levels designed to capture student aid, so the Bennett Hypothesis is controversial. But several college presidents and administrators *have* admitted that universities grab every dime they can get their hands on, student aid included. As noted earlier, Bok likened universities' greed to that of deposed dictators and compulsive gamblers. Similarly, in *Honoring the Trust: Quality and Cost Containment in Higher Education*, former Stanford University vice president for business and finance William Massy writes that "universities press their pricing to the limits that markets, regulators, and public opinion will allow" and cites former Princeton University president Howard Bowen's declaration that "universities will raise all the money they can and spend all the money they raise." Finally, in testimony before the House Subcommittee on 21st-Century Competitiveness, Murray State University president F. King Alexander acknowledged that colleges and universities do indeed raise tuition to absorb student aid: "Murray State University has not ... opted to dramatically shift the educational costs away from the state and to the federal government indirectly through the student by inflating tuition *like many higher cost states and institutions have done*" (italics added).

The Trouble with Institutional Aid and Research Grants

While the federal government provides nearly 70 percent of all student aid, states provide most aid to institutions. But that doesn't make federal institutional aid irrelevant.

Generally, federal aid is sent to special classes of schools. For example, Education's *2005 Budget Summary* reports that in 2004 the department sent nearly $223 million to Historically Black Colleges and Universities (HBCUs), almost $11 million to Alaska Native and Native-Hawaiian-serving Institutions, and $94 million to Hispanic-serving Institutions. In addition, two schools received separate federal support: Howard University, a historically black school in Washington, D.C., got nearly $239 million in 2004, and Gallaudet University, a school for deaf students, also in Washington, received more than $100 million. All told, the federal government doled out more than $833 million in institutional aid in 2004.

That aid is limited but still presents problems, the most fundamental being that it takes money from taxpayers and gives it to schools favored by politicians. Moreover, it gives receiving schools unfair advantages over competing institutions. For instance, in 2004 Howard University received almost $239 million in federal support, while 104 other HBCUs had to share $223 million and most other schools got nothing.

A much larger problem is federal research funding, which NCES estimates totaled nearly $25.7 billion in 2002, and which the Association of American Universities said accounted for nearly 60 percent of all university research.

Why the big federal investment in research? The argument is that few private organizations will undertake basic research that promises little or no immediate profit, leaving the federal government to finance it. As Bok says, "The most important inquiries in science often involve questions no company will support because the answers take the form of general laws of nature that hold no special rewards for the enterprise that funds the research."

Vedder finds, however, that much university research is neither necessary nor likely to be undertaken only by the federal government. He points out that researchers often seek grants after their research is nearly complete, frequently use grants to refine already completed research, and undertake projects that industry is willing to do.

In addition, universities' growing emphasis on research has come at the expense of their central mission: teaching. "For many institutions, the balance between research and education has tilted too far toward research," declares Massy. "Faculty time represents the university's most important asset . . . [but] there are only so many hours in a day, and even the most highly motivated professors have finite amounts of energy. Therefore, increases in research activity will, sooner or later, come at the expense of time devoted to educational tasks."

Vedder seconds Massy, identifying a decades-long trend away from teaching and toward research. "Faculty members," he writes, "do what they like best and/or what is most likely to advance their careers . . . faculty have demanded and received lighter teaching loads to allow them to do more research."

Pork

One final source of federal money is described by the *Chronicle of Higher Education* as "directed, noncompetitive appropriations," that is, pork. As the *Chronicle* reported in its September 26, 2003, article, "Academic Pork Barrel Tops $2-Billion for the First Time," pork projects, typically pushed by members of Congress after they've been lobbied for by receiving institutions, are costing taxpayers more money every year: from $296 million in 1996, to more than $2 billion by 2003. And what has the barrel produced? According to *Lobbying for Higher Education* by Vanderbilt University professor Constance Ewing Cook, such gems as $8 million to build a planetarium for Delta College in Michigan, a two-year community college that offers no major in the sciences, and a $21 million grant to Wheeling Jesuit College, a bounty almost twice the size of the college's annual budget, earmarked by Sen. Robert Byrd (D-WV).

Remove the Federal Government from Higher Education

James Madison wrote in *Federalist* no. 45 that "the powers delegated by the proposed Constitution to the federal government are few and defined . . . [they] will be exercised principally on external objects, as war, peace, negotiation, and foreign commerce." Since the Constitution grants the federal government no role in higher education, it may be involved only in ways that support legitimate federal concerns such as national defense, allowing continued involvement in such things as the Senior Reserve Officer Training Corps (ROTC), the service academies, and national defense–related research. It must withdraw from all other higher education activities.

It cannot, however, withdraw immediately. Given how deeply entangled the federal government is in higher education, to do so would send disastrous shocks to students and schools. Abruptly ending student aid in just a year or two, for instance, would leave millions of students scrambling for funds to make up for lost Pell grants and loans and would overwhelm private lenders, schools, and charitable organizations that have conducted planning based on expected levels of federal involvement. A gradual withdrawal must occur to allow students, schools, and private lenders to adjust to a changing higher education landscape. What follows is an overview of a six-year withdrawal plan that does that and at the same time sets a clear path for dissociating the federal government from higher education.

Immediately: Pork-barrel spending must be prohibited; only federal grants that are competitively bid can be sent to colleges. No new research projects unrelated to national security may be awarded to universities, but projects currently under way may continue to completion. Finally, the consolidated loan program, which allows individuals who have already completed college to consolidate multiple loans into a single loan, often at a rate lower than they otherwise would have paid, must be eliminated.

Four Years: Federal aid to institutions ends. Institutions currently receiving aid will need to either economize or find new sources of revenue. The four-year timeframe offers an adequate transition period, because federal aid accounts for only a tiny part of most institutions' overall budgets.

Six Years: All federal student aid programs—grants, loans, and tax benefits—should be eliminated. Each year between enactment of the revised HEA and the end of the six-year period, the maximum Pell grant value, incorporating cost-of-living adjustments pegged to inflation, should be reduced in equal increments. Similarly, maximum loan sizes and government subsidy rates must be reduced for all federal loan programs in equal six-year increments. Information about all new rates and ceilings must be made readily available to the public.

Top Five Signs There's Too Much Money in Higher Education

1. According to the *New York Times*, Washington State University boasts that its Jacuzzi, which can seat 53 people at one time, is the largest on the west coast.

2. Also according to the *Times*, the University of Southern Mississippi is planning a water park with water slides, a meandering river, and something called a "wet deck" that helps keep sunbathers cool.

3. The ACT reports that at four-year public colleges only 41.2 percent of students graduate within *five* years of entering school.

4. According to the National Association of Student Financial Aid Administrators, married taxpayers making up to $130,000 per year—ten times the poverty level for a family of two—are eligible to take tax deductions for enrolling in one or more college courses.

5. A recent Harris Poll found that 90 percent of college students own a computer, 62 percent a stereo, 84 percent a television, 74 percent a DVD player, and 55 percent a video game system. Meanwhile, the College Board reports that nearly 60 percent receive some form of financial aid, and NCES reports that almost 80 percent go to heavily subsidized public colleges and universities.

Conclusion

The federal presence in higher education is both unconstitutional and harmful. Federal student aid drives up the cost of tuition, ultimately destroying most of the aid's real value while costing taxpayers ever more. Federal institutional aid, university-based federal research projects, and higher education pork also cost taxpayers billions of dollars every year. There is only one acceptable solution to these problems: the federal government must remove itself from higher education.

Suggested Readings

College Board. *Trends in Student Aid 2003* and *Trends in College Pricing 2003*. www. collegboard.com.

Congressional Budget Office. "Private and Public Contributions to Financing College Education." January 2004.

Massy, William F. *Honoring the Trust: Quality and Cost Containment in Higher Education.* Bolton, MA: Anker, 2003.

Palacios, Miguel. "Human Capital Contracts: 'Equity-like' Instruments for Financing Higher Education." Cato Institute Policy Analysis no. 462, December 16, 2002.

Vedder, Richard. *Going Broke by Degree: Why College Costs Too Much.* Washington: American Enterprise Institute, 2004.

Winter, Greg. "Jacuzzi U: A Battle of Perks to Lure Students." *New York Times*, October 5, 2003.

Wolfram, Gary. "The Threat to Independent Education: Public Subsidies and Private Colleges." Cato Institute Policy Analysis no. 278, August 15, 1997.

—Prepared by Neal McCluskey

30. Improving K-12 Education

> **States should**
> - stop spending money on ineffective public school reforms and
> - institute school choice on a wide scale.

By most measures, America's K–12 public schools continue on a path of mediocrity and stagnation. SAT scores have risen slightly since the 1980s but remain well below the levels attained in 1967. Scores on the National Assessment of Educational Progress have remained tellingly flat since the test's inception in 1969, and U.S. students continue to come in at the middle of the pack or worse in comparison with students in other developed countries. And according to the Educational Testing Service's most recent poll, parents give U.S. public schools lower grades than ever before.

During the last few decades, state governments (and to some degree the federal government) have attempted to implement reforms in hopes of remedying declines in public school performance. Most of those reforms sought to improve public education through more funding. In spite of the fact that per pupil spending has increased 60 percent in real dollars since 1982, there is little to indicate that the infusion of dollars has led to any improvement in student achievement.

The fact that such reforms have consistently failed to produce improvements has led analysts and reformers to take a serious look at what is wrong with the American education system. Increasingly, reformers have pointed to monopoly and centralization as the core malady with public schools.

In 1989 Albert Shanker, president of the American Federation of Teachers, noted that U.S. public education operates like a government-planned economy, "a bureaucratic system" with "few incentives for innovation and productivity." "It's no surprise," he observed, "that our school system doesn't improve: It more resembles the communist economy than our own market economy.'' The U.S. public schools remain a rare American monopoly and enjoy ever-increasing levels of funding. According to a 2004 report by the Nelson A. Rockefeller Institute of Government, state spending on U.S. public schools rose by 17 percent in real dollars over and above enrollment growth during the six-year period between 1997 and 2002. Citing the nearly $370 billion the states spend each year on K–12 public education, a recent *Wall Street Journal* editorial posed this question: Is there any other part of American life that would receive tens of billions more dollars if it kept showing no improvement in performance?

In response to that stagnation coupled with ever-increasing levels of funding, policymakers in a number of states have sought to implement changes that would instill consumer choice and market discipline into American education. As of this writing, 11 states and the District of Columbia have instituted school choice programs either through vouchers or by offering tax credits to parents who choose private schools rather than government-run schools. Figure 30.1 shows the states that have implemented school vouchers or tuition tax credits. In addition, 41 states now have charter schools and 15 states have instituted choice within public

Figure 30.1
The Growth of School Choice in the States

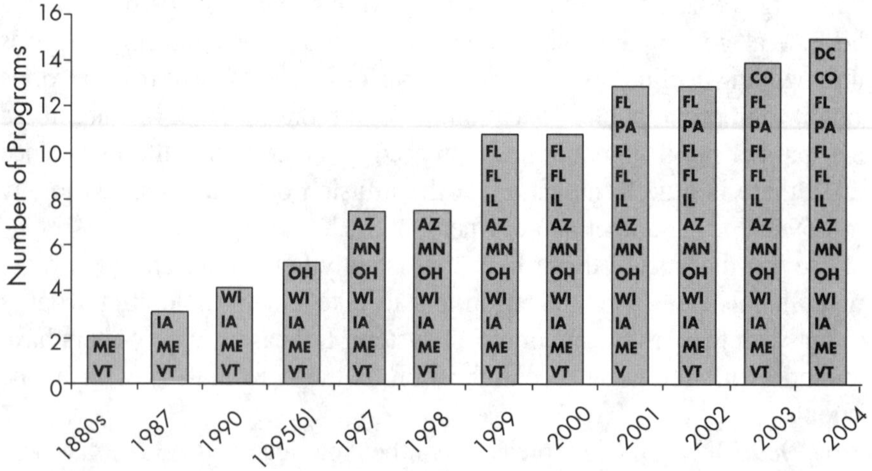

NOTE. Since the last 1880s, Maine and Vermont have used vouchers for students living in communities without public schools. Many of those communities continue using vouchers to send children to private schools rather than build public schools. Also note that Florida has three different school choice programs.

schools. All of those reforms have been intended to encourage choice and competition based on consumer preference. Overall, evaluations of those programs show that benefits from school choice programs exceed those that have been attained by other types of reforms.

Unfortunately, virtually all of those programs place limitations on the number of students who can participate or restrict participation to children from the poorest schools or poorest families. Such restrictions dilute the potential benefits that would result from allowing a universal competitive marketplace to arise.

The Next Step

What needs to happen next is for an entire state, or at least a major city, to give *every* child a voucher or tax credit that can be used at the public or private school of the parent's choice. Rather than a meagerly low voucher amount, the voucher or tax credit should be adequate to cover tuition at most local private schools.

Government figures show that in 1999–2000 the average private elementary school tuition in America was less than $3,500 (Table 30.1). The average tuition at private secondary schools was $6,052. Since the average per pupil spending for public schools is now $9,354, most states could propose a voucher or tax credit of these tuition amounts and still realize substantial savings. Education is the largest category of state spending in virtually every state. Therefore, school choice constitutes a golden opportunity to improve education while conserving our tax dollars. From a fiscal perspective, choice eases the enrollment burden on public schools without decreasing their per student level of funding. At the same time, it imposes the discipline of the market on public and private schools, motivating schools to improve.

Vouchers or Tax Credits?

A universal school choice plan could be achieved through vouchers or tax credits. The tax structure and school funding procedures in each state will influence which approach will be best. Voucher programs are simple in that a set amount of funds would be made available to every child in the state to be spent on tuition at the private or public school of the parent's choice. Because private secondary education is generally more expensive than tuition at the elementary grades, the voucher amount for secondary school could be more than for elementary school grades.

Table 30.1
Private School Tuition, by Type of School and Level, 1999–2000

Type of School	Average Tuition
All private schools	$4,689
Elementary	$3,267
Secondary	$6,052
Combined	$6,779
Catholic schools	$3,263
Elementary	$2,451
Secondary	$4,845
Combined	$6,780
Other religious schools	$4,063
Elementary	$3,503
Secondary	$6,536
Combined	$4,260
Nonsectarian schools	$10,992
Elementary	$7,884
Secondary	$14,638
Combined	$12,363

SOURCE: Based on National Center for Education Statistics, *Digest of Education Statistics, 2002,* Table 61 (1999–2000). These are the most recent figures available. Elementary schools have grades six or lower and no grade higher than eight. Secondary schools have no grade lower than seven. Combined schools have grades lower than seven and higher than eight. Excludes prekindergarten students.

A tax credit approach works somewhat differently for middle- or higher-income parents (who pay state income taxes) than for lower-income parents who pay little or no state income taxes. Higher-income parents who chose a private school for their children would be required to pay tuition out of their own pockets, then claim a dollar-for-dollar credit on their state income tax each year at tax time. Under a universal approach, grandparents or other individuals could pay tuition for a child and claim a tax credit on their state income taxes. Lower-income parents apply for scholarships from scholarship-granting organizations. Businesses or individuals in the state can donate to those scholarship organizations and claim a tax credit on their state income tax equal to their contribution. Scholarship tax credits make funds available to low-income children whose parents pay little or no state income tax and who therefore cannot claim the credit themselves.

One disadvantage of credits over vouchers is that credits make less money available for private school tuition, since most parents don't pay enough in state income tax to cover the cost of tuition, especially if they have several children in school. This disadvantage can be overcome by allowing taxpayers to, in addition, claim a credit against property taxes paid for public schools. Parents who pay private school tuition could receive a certificate or form that could be used as full or partial payment of property taxes. Likewise, parents who rent rather than own property could pass the form or certificate along to their landlord as partial rent payment. The landlord could then use the certificate toward payment of property taxes. As of this writing, lawmakers in South Carolina are considering a school choice tax credit plan that involves income as well as property tax credits.

One advantage of tax credits over vouchers is that credits do not involve direct state spending. Direct state spending causes all taxpayers to be involuntary contributors to private schools, creating pressure to regulate those schools. Universal tax credits can offer the same benefits as vouchers without forcing anyone to contribute to private schools. Tax credits also avoid some potential state constitutional impediments as pretax dollars contributed to scholarships are private funds, not state funds.

Guidelines for Good School Choice Legislation

For the maximum benefits of school choice to be realized, the program must ensure independence for private schools and greater flexibility for public schools. In particular, private schools must be allowed to remain free of regulations that would prohibit specialization, innovation, and creativity. Public schools, likewise, must be given the flexibility to respond to increased demand in creative ways. The goal of school choice is to create a true market environment where creative ideas and best practices can emerge and where customer demands and preferences are met. The following guidelines are critical to crafting school choice legislation that will lead to the greatest benefits.

1. Autonomy for Private Schools

To create a vibrant and creative marketplace, good school choice policy should allow private schools to be truly independent in terms of admissions policies, hiring, standards, and pricing.

Requiring private schools to accept all applicants severely jeopardizes the ability of private schools to focus on specific types of students. Experience has shown that private schools are interested in serving difficult-to-educate children as well as children who are academically gifted. So policymakers should not worry that private schools will focus only on the brightest students.

Likewise, private schools should be allowed to select staff on the basis of criteria specific to their various distinctive missions rather than hire only state-certified teachers. Many private schools find that people with subject matter expertise who feel strongly about the mission or objectives of the school are effective teachers, even without state certification.

Since each private school has its own standards and measures of quality, private schools should not be required to administer state tests or adopt state curriculum guidelines or "standards." Most private schools already administer standardized tests as a way to measure student academic progress, but there is wide variation among private schools in terms of test preference. Some private schools reject standardized tests altogether, favoring more holistic methods of measuring student progress. Requiring private schools that participate in school choice to adopt particular tests, state "standards," or state-constructed tests would be a drastic blow to the diversity that exists in the private school community.

There is reason to believe that many private schools will not participate in school choice programs if those programs require that they give up their curriculum, religious environment, or ability to admit students based on the school's unique specialization or mission. According to a 1998 U.S. Department of Education survey, at least half of all private schools would decline to participate in a school choice program if they were unable to exercise control over admissions policies or were required to change their religious environment or mission.

Finally, private schools should be able to set their own price. Attempts by government to limit tuition to the quantity covered by a voucher or tax credit amounts to "price control." Price controls are unhealthy because they limit the ability of some schools to develop, implement, or disseminate new approaches that may be, in their initial stages, somewhat more costly. As in all economic sectors, wealthier people provide the initial capital to finance experimentation and innovation. Later, experience and competition bring costs down, making the innovation available to everyone. Without the freedom to pay more than the average price for schooling innovations in the early stage, many new and important innovations and breakthroughs will never get onto the drawing board or be adopted by schools. For this reason, there should be no restrictions on parents who wish to "top up" the voucher or tax credit by paying additional fees. There will be plenty of schools available for students whose parents cannot or do not wish to pay additional fees, but those students and those who follow in the future will benefit from the innovations and practices developed in other schools.

2. Aid Must Go to Parents, Not Schools

To avoid constitutional challenges, a school choice program must offer only indirect aid to religious schools. Therefore, vouchers should be made out to parents who endorse the voucher over to the private school. Vouchers can be mailed to the private school the parents have selected but must be endorsed by the parent before they can be accepted as payment. The June 2002 U.S. Supreme Court decision that upheld the Ohio school voucher program stipulated that the indirect nature of aid to religious schools, routed first through parents, is a necessary ingredient in a constitutionally sound school choice program.

3. Available to All Students

For school choice to drive innovation and overall improvement in education generally, a program should make vouchers or tax credits available to *all* students rather than just certain subgroups. It is attractive politically to limit benefits to children from failing schools or from low-income families, but ultimately those children lose the benefits that would emerge from a larger market. The fewer students who have the ability to choose private schools, the fewer private schools will compete for those students. In addition, new private schools will not be attracted into a market where only a limited number of "customers" have choice.

In the interest of fairness, students already attending private schools should be included in the program. However, since those students are currently costing the state nothing, including them initially may make the program prohibitively expensive. For that reason, the program in its early stage may have to focus the funds on students switching from public schools to private schools or those entering kindergarten. As more students migrate to private schools, the increased savings can be used to pay for vouchers or tax credits for those students already in private schools.

4. Easy Access to Scholarships

Under a tax credit program, lower-income parents should have easy access to scholarships. A parent needing a scholarship should be able to visit any private school and obtain information about sources of scholarships. Also, information about scholarships should be available through various community sources (libraries, newspapers, radio, scholarship fairs, and the Internet). As scholarship-granting organizations are private entities, they should be allowed to develop their own criteria for granting scholarships and their own application procedures. Some scholarship-granting organizations may choose to focus on children from particular backgrounds or with particular interests. As long as new scholarship organizations are allowed to form and offer scholarships, the ability to specialize will be healthy and will promote easy access to scholarships for those who need them most.

5. High Dollar Amount (for adequate nonreligious options)

A sound school choice program should offer a dollar amount that is adequate to cover tuition at most local private schools. Admittedly, many private schools charge substantially less in tuition than is spent per student in public schools, but these are mostly schools that are religiously affiliated and that receive subsidies from their religious bodies. A low dollar amount, therefore, will skew choices toward religious schools and will appear to be biased toward religious private schools. A program organized around the cost of the lowest-priced private schools will do little more than fill unused seating capacity in these schools and will not attract new private schools into the market. Policymakers should look to low-cost nonreligious private schools and charter schools for a more realistic estimate of the minimum cost of education.

6. Limited Regulation

State lawmakers who are crafting the program should not assume that a regulation is acceptable just because few existing private schools oppose it. Private schools today exist in a unique environment and focus on a few niche markets where customers are willing to pay over and above their school taxes for such schools. But in a school choice environment, private school operators will need the freedom to be innovative and pioneer new methods and approaches. Regulations and entry barriers must not be too great. Therefore, regulations on private schools should be limited to those that already exist, and guarantees should be made that no new regulations will be added once a school choice program is in place. Teachers and others wishing to establish new private schools will be reluctant to do so if they fear that new regulations will be enacted down the road. Lawmakers must remember that it is the independence and uniqueness of private schools that make them attractive in the first place.

Therefore, they should not seek to impose new regulations on private schools in exchange for participation in school choice programs.

7. Reliance on Private Consumer Groups to Report Results to Parents

Some sponsors of school choice legislation may feel it necessary for a state agency (such as the state's office of education or local school districts) to collect and disseminate evaluative information about private school performance to parents or to evaluate the success of the school choice program. Although we may like to think they are, government agencies cannot be totally unbiased in their assessments and should not be expected to provide positive evaluations of private schools, which under a school choice program become direct competitors to government schools. Rather than ask a government agency to perform the role of evaluator, the program should rely on private consumer groups to report information and results to parents.

Experience has shown that the private sector can perform this role. Wherever school choice has been implemented, new organizations and information sources have emerged to provide parents and others with evaluative information about public and private schools. One example is GreatSchools.net, a nonprofit organization that provides in-depth profiles of schools on its website. In addition to a list of a state's public and private schools, the site contains various "tools" for parents, including links to compare schools or match their child's needs with available schools. Other examples of private consumer research groups are Florida Child, Utah Schools at a Glance, the school report cards published by the Denver-based Education Policy Center, and Standard & Poor's "School Evaluation Services," which includes customized data and reports for parents and school leaders. Private groups have an interest in providing unbiased, objective information to parents, and there is no need to have government agencies duplicate many of their efforts with potentially less objective evaluative consumer information.

8. Multiyear Permanent Program

One of the primary goals of school choice is to motivate educators and innovators to open new schools that will compete with existing schools. School choice will attract new school operators only if there is a high degree of certainty about the future and stability of the program. If school operators face uncertainties about government policies, financial support, or political support for a school choice program, they will be much less likely to risk time and money on starting new schools. Therefore, states should not pass school choice programs that are considered "experimental" or label a school choice program as strictly a "pilot" program. School operators will be hesitant to start up new schools in such an environment. Rather, programs should be implemented with a minimum of 10 years duration so that the market is potentially attractive to long-term effort and investment.

9. New Dynamics of Governance and Control

For school choice to work, it must institute a new means of governing; it cannot leave in control those who benefit from the status quo. If it does, then those people can use their positions of power to stifle competition and impose government control over private schools.

Rather than place regulatory power and accountability controls in the hands of school districts or state education agencies, states should allow private school accreditation groups, brand name reputations, private regulatory bodies such as exist in other industries, insurance companies, consumer watchdog groups, and parents themselves to become the regulatory structure over education. Increases in the quality of education will come about only if government steps aside and allows consumer pressure and competition to ensure a high standard of quality.

What Makes Good School Choice Legislation?

1. Autonomy for Private Schools
2. Aid Must Go to Parents, Not Schools
3. Available to All Students
4. Easy Access to Scholarships
5. High Dollar Amount (for adequate nonreligious options)
6. Limited Regulation
7. Reliance on Private Consumer Groups to Report Results to Parents
8. Multiyear Permanent Program
9. New Dynamics of Governance and Control

Conclusion

The reason public schools don't improve is not a lack of funds. State and local governments have increased spending for K–12 education by more than 17 percent in real dollars since 1997 and by more than 60 percent since 1982. In spite of this influx of dollars, student academic performance remains stagnant.

Rather than throw even more money at the problem, states should institute school choice on a broad scale, moving toward a competitive education market. The only way to transform the system is to break up the long-standing government monopoly and use the dynamics of the market to create innovations, better methods, and new schools.

To realize the positive effects of a competitive education market, school choice programs must ensure autonomy and independence for private schools and flexibility for public schools. Therefore, states should not impose regulations on existing private schools or create regulatory barriers that prevent new private school operators from entering the market. Only in this way will school choice produce the better education American children deserve.

Suggested Readings

Bolick, Clint. *Voucher Wars: Waging the Legal Battle over School Choice.* Washington: Cato Institute, 2003.

Boyd, Donald J. "K–12 Education: Still Growing Strongly." Nelson A. Rockefeller Institute of Government, Albany, NY, June 21, 2004.

Gryphon, Marie. "True Private Choice: A Practical Guide to School Choice after *Zelman v. Simmons-Harris.*" Cato Institute Policy Analysis no. 466, February 4, 2003.

Hoxby, Caroline M. "School Choice and School Productivity (or Could School Choice Be the Tide That Lifts all Boats?)" National Bureau of Economic Research, Working Paper no. 8873, April 2002.

Ormand, H. Lillian. "The Struggle for School Choice Policy after *Zelman:* Regulation vs. the Free Market." Cato Institute Policy Analysis no. 495, October 29, 2003.

Salisbury, David. "What Will a Voucher Buy? A Closer Look at the Cost of Private Schools." Cato Institute Policy Analysis no. 486, August 28, 2003.

—Prepared by David Salisbury

31. Agricultural Policy

Congress should

- phase down and terminate all crop subsidies, a process that was supposed to begin with passage of the 1996 Freedom to Farm law;
- move farmers toward use of market-based insurance and other financial instruments to protect against price and weather fluctuations;
- eliminate federal controls that create producer cartels in the dairy, tobacco, and sugar markets; and
- eliminate trade protections on agricultural goods while working through the World Trade Organization to pursue liberalization in global markets.

Enriching the Few at the Expense of the Many

Much of the U.S. agricultural sector operates in a fairly free market environment. Products that account for 64 percent of U.S. farm production, such as fruits and vegetables, generally do not receive federal subsidies. Products that account for the other 36 percent of farm production receive roughly $20 billion of direct subsidies each year. More than 90 percent of those subsidies go to farmers of just five crops—wheat, corn, soybeans, rice, and cotton.

The federal government also imposes restrictions and import controls on products such as sugar and milk. Those rules enrich a few producers at the expense of American consumers. For example, sugar prices are three times higher in the United States than elsewhere because of federal controls. Another problem is that farm subsidies and controls are an

311

impediment to world trade negotiations, which are designed to bring greater prosperity to every country.

In addition to subsidies and controls, the U.S. Department of Agriculture (USDA) runs a huge array of marketing, loan, statistical, and research programs for farmers. The USDA has 110,000 employees and 7,400 offices scattered throughout the country. No other industry in America is so coddled.

Reversal of the 1996 Reforms

With the backing of the Bush administration, Congress passed a new farm law in 2002 that moved away from the "Freedom to Farm" reforms of 1996. Direct farm subsidies and related support programs will cost taxpayers $104 billion during FY05 to FY09, according to the federal budget. The costs may end up being higher; subsidies under the 1996 farm law were projected to cost $47 billion over seven years but ended up costing more than $120 billion.

The 1996 farm law aimed to move agriculture away from the command-and-control regime in place since the 1930s. The law increased planting flexibility, eliminated some crop supports, and was supposed to phase down subsidies. But after enactment, Congress ignored agreed-upon subsidy limits and passed a number of large supplemental subsidy bills. As a result, farm subsidies have soared to about $20 billion annually in recent years from less than $10 billion annually in the mid-1990s.

The Structure of Crop Subsidies

Large-scale federal manipulations of agriculture began as "temporary" measures in the 1930s under the New Deal. Farm programs have flourished ever since, despite a dramatic drop in the importance of agriculture to the U.S. economy. Crop subsidies have usually been delivered in the form of price supports, which create chronic problems of overproduction.

Prior to 1996 the main farm subsidy program paid "deficiency" payments based on legislated price levels called target prices. Eligible commodities included crops such as wheat, corn, and rice. Farmers were paid for their base acreage in each crop, which they were stuck producing if they wanted to get the full subsidy. To stem overproduction, the government paid farmers not to farm on set-aside land.

The resulting absence of flexibility and land idling created large "deadweight" economic losses, or inefficiency costs. The most efficient selection of crops was not being planted, and good farmland was going unused. Those inefficiencies provided an important justification for the 1996 reforms. A combination of high commodity prices and the Republican takeover of Congress created support for cutting intervention in the farm sector under the 1996 farm law.

1996 Reforms

The centerpiece of the 1996 farm law was the replacement of price supports with production flexibility contracts (PFCs) that were fixed payments decoupled from market prices. The government set total PFC subsidy payments on a declining scale from $6 billion in 1996 to $4 billion in 2002.

The reforms affected farmers of corn, wheat, grain sorghum, barley, oats, cotton, and rice. Farmers were allowed to plant any crop they chose and their subsidy payment would be at a fixed level. The new rules led to significant reductions in deadweight economic losses and allowed farmers to respond to changing market conditions.

Nonetheless, farm subsidies continue to promote oversupply because they increase farmer wealth and thus encourage farm expansion, and they prop up marginal farms that should be allowed to fail. Also, the marketing loan program was not ended and it continues to promote oversupply.

Another continuing subsidy program is the conservation reserve program (CRP), which idles millions of acres of land by paying farmers not to farm. Almost one-third of land idled under the CRP is owned by retired farmers, so many recipients do not even have to work to get subsidies. Instead of the CRP, a simpler way to stop overproduction and conserve the environment would be to eliminate all farm subsidies.

Undoing Reforms with the 2002 Farm Bill

The 2002 farm bill reversed progress made in 1996. It added a new price support, or "countercyclical," program to provide bigger subsidies when prices are low. In addition, the marketing loan program, which acts as a price support, was expanded in the 2002 bill to cover chickpeas, lentils, dry peas, honey, wool, and mohair.

Congress ignored the experts, who generally agree that price supports are counterproductive. For example, the U.S. Department of Agriculture noted in a major report in September 2001 that "government attempts to hold prices above those determined by commercial markets have simply made matters worse time after time" by causing overproduction and inflating land prices.

The 2002 bill also retains the multi-billion-dollar PFC program. The intent of the PFC program introduced in 1996 was to wean farmers off subsidies. Instead, the 2002 farm bill simply turns the program into another long-term handout.

The 2002 bill continued other Soviet-style farm policies. Protectionist sugar measures that cost consumers billions of dollars were kept in place. Complex milk supports and regulations were retained. Peanut farmers are now eligible for direct subsidies.

When passed, the 2002 farm bill was expected to cost taxpayers $190 billion over 10 years. The ultimate cost will be higher if Congress continues its bad habit of passing expensive supplemental farm spending bills.

Welfare for the Well-to-Do

Politicians love to discuss the plight of the small farmer, but they actually give most farm subsidies to the largest farms. For example, the top 10 percent of recipients received 65 percent of all farm subsidies in 2002. Much of the subsidy payout goes to wealthy individuals and companies that clearly do not need taxpayer help, as data from the Environmental Working Group shows (see www.ewg.org). Farm subsidy recipients include Fortune 500 companies, well-off members of Congress, and millionaires such as David Rockefeller and Ted Turner.

USDA figures show that farmers have above-average incomes. The average farm household income was $65,757 in 2002, which is 14 percent higher than the average U.S. household income of $57,852. Even if one accepts the notion that the government should redistribute income from rich to poor, farm subsidies do the reverse.

Also, as there is in virtually all government giveaway programs, there is a great deal of fraud and abuse in farm subsidies. In April 2004 the General Accounting Office reported that millions of dollars of subsidies were going to people who should not receive them due to lax USDA oversight. Some money is going to people who have only a very marginal involvement in farming. In other cases, farm businesses have concocted schemes to get around legal subsidy limits through complex organizational structures. Those abuse problems are a further reason to end farm subsidies.

Repealing Farm Subsidies Is Economically and Politically Feasible

Despite the policy reversals of 2002, efforts to reform farm subsidies will come back on the agenda because of the continuing unfairness and distortions that they cause. In addition, global trade agreements may be successful in bringing down farm subsidies both here and abroad.

During the debate over the 2002 farm bill, Sen. Richard Lugar (R-IN) offered an interesting alternative to the current system. His plan would phase out current subsidies and replace them with a voucher system that would promote reliance on insurance and other financial instruments. Although Lugar's proposals did not go far enough, they suggest that with some political courage Congress might take some innovative steps forward.

The experience of New Zealand in eliminating its farm subsidies in the 1980s shows that full subsidy removal makes economic and political sense. In 1984 New Zealand's Labour government ended all farm subsidies in that country. That was a remarkably bold policy since New Zealand's economy is roughly five times more dependent on farming than is the U.S. economy.

Subsidy elimination in New Zealand was swift and sure. Although the plan was initially met with massive protests, the subsidies were quickly ended. New Zealand farming has never been healthier than it is today. The value of farm output has soared since subsidies were repealed, and farm productivity has grown strongly.

Forced to adjust to new economic realities, New Zealand farmers cut costs, diversified their land use, sought nonfarm income, and altered production as market signals advised. As a report by the Federated Farmers of New Zealand noted, the country's experience "thoroughly debunked the myth that the farming sector cannot prosper without government subsidies." Reformers in Congress should continue working to debunk that same myth in this country.

Suggested Readings

Edwards, Chris, and Tad DeHaven. "Farm Reform Reversal." Cato Institute Tax & Budget Bulletin no. 2, March 2002.
———. "Farm Subsidies at Record Levels As Congress Considers New Farm Bill." Cato Institute Briefing Paper no. 70, October 18, 2001.
Federated Farmers of New Zealand. "Life after Subsidies." www.fedfarm.org.nz.
General Accounting Office. "Farm Program Payments: USDA Needs to Strengthen Regulations and Oversight to Better Ensure Recipients Do Not Circumvent Payment Limitations." GAO-04-407, April 2004.
Lamb, Russell. "The New Farm Economy." *Regulation* 26, no. 4 (Winter 2003–04).
McNew, Kevin. "Milking the Sacred Cow: A Case for Eliminating the Federal Dairy Program." Cato Institute Policy Analysis no. 362, December 1, 1999.
Orden, David. "Reform's Stunted Crop." *Regulation* 25, no. 1 (Spring 2002).

—Prepared by Chris Edwards

32. Cultural Agencies

> **Congress should**
> - eliminate the National Endowment for the Arts,
> - eliminate the National Endowment for the Humanities, and
> - defund the Corporation for Public Broadcasting.

In a society that constitutionally limits the powers of government and maximizes individual liberty, there is no justification for the forcible transfer of money from taxpayers to artists, scholars, and broadcasters. If the proper role of government is to safeguard the security of the nation's residents, by what rationale are they made to support exhibits of paintings, symphony orchestras, documentaries, scholarly research, and radio and television programs they might never freely choose to support? The kinds of things financed by federal cultural agencies were produced long before those agencies were created, and they will continue to be produced long after those agencies are privatized or defunded. Moreover, the power to subsidize art, scholarship, and broadcasting cannot be found within the powers enumerated and delegated to the federal government under the Constitution.

The National Endowment for the Arts, an "independent" agency established in 1965, makes grants to museums, symphony orchestras, individual artists "of exceptional talent," and organizations (including state arts agencies) to "encourage individual and institutional development of the arts, preservation of the American artistic heritage, wider availability of the arts, leadership in the arts, and the stimulation of non-Federal sources of support for the Nation's artistic activities." Among its more famous and controversial grant recipients were artist Andres Serrano, whose exhibit featured a photograph of a plastic crucifix in a jar of his own urine, and the Institute of Contemporary Art in Philadelphia, which sponsored a traveling exhibition of the late Robert Mapplethorpe's homoerotic photographs. (Thanks to an NEA grantee, the American taxpayers once paid $1,500 for a poem, "lighght." That wasn't the title or a typo. That was the entire poem.) The NEA's fiscal 2004 budget was $122 million, back up after modest cuts by the 104th and 105th Congresses.

The National Endowment for the Humanities, with a fiscal year 2004 budget of $135 million, "funds activities that are intended to improve the quality of education and teaching in the humanities, to strengthen the scholarly foundation for humanities study and research, and to advance understanding of the humanities among general audiences." Among the things it has funded are controversial national standards for the teaching of history in schools, the traveling King Tut exhibit, and the documentary film *Rosie the Riveter*.

The 37-year-old Corporation for Public Broadcasting—FY04 budget, $437 million—provides money to "qualified public television and radio stations to be used at their discretion for purposes related primarily to program production and acquisition." It also supports the production and acquisition of radio and television programs for national distribution and assists in "the financing of several system-wide activities, including national satellite interconnection services and the payment of music royalty fees, and provides limited technical assistance, research, and planning services to improve system-wide capacity and performance." Some of the money provided local public radio and television stations is used to help support National Public Radio and the Public Broadcasting Service.

Note that the amount of arts funding in the federal budget is quite small. That might be taken as a defense of the funding, were it not for the important reasons to avoid *any* government funding of something as intimate yet powerful as artistic expression. But it should also be noted how small federal funding is as a percentage of the total arts budget in this country. The NEA's budget is about 1 percent of the $13.1 billion contributed to the arts by private corporations, foundations, and individuals in 1996. According to the American Arts Alliance, the nonprofit arts are a $53 billion industry. Surely they will survive without whatever portion of the NEA's budget gets out of the Washington bureaucracy and into the hands of actual artists or arts institutions. Indeed, when the NEA budget was cut in 1995, private giving to the arts rose dramatically.

In 1995 the first Republican Congress voted to phase out the NEA over three years. The new Congress should revive that commitment and also end federal involvement with the National Endowment for the Humanities and the Corporation for Public Broadcasting.

Poor Subsidize Rich

Since art museums, symphony orchestras, humanities scholarship, and public television and radio are enjoyed predominantly by people of greater-than-average income and education, the federal cultural agencies oversee a fundamentally unfair transfer of wealth from the lower classes up. It's no accident that you hear ads for Remy Martin and "private banking services" on NPR, not for Budweiser and free checking accounts. *Newsweek* columnist Robert J. Samuelson is correct when he calls federal cultural agencies "highbrow pork barrel." As Edward C. Banfield has written, "The art public is now, as it has always been, overwhelmingly middle and upper-middle class and above average in income—relatively prosperous people who would probably enjoy art about as much in the absence of subsidies." Supporters of the NEA often say that their purpose is to bring the finer arts to those who don't already patronize them. But Dick Netzer, an economist who favors arts subsidies, conceded that they have "failed to increase the representation of low-income people in audiences." In other words, lower-income people are not interested in the kind of entertainment they're forced to support; they prefer to put their money into forms of art often sneered at by the cultural elite. Why must they continue to finance the pleasures of the affluent?

Corruption of Artists and Scholars

Government subsidies to the arts and humanities have an insidious, corrupting effect on artists and scholars. It is assumed, for example, that the arts need government encouragement. But if an artist needs such encouragement, what kind of artist is he? Novelist E. L. Doctorow once told the House Appropriations Committee, "An enlightened endowment puts its money on largely unknown obsessive individuals who have sacrificed all the ordinary comforts and consolations of life in order to do their work." Few have noticed the contradiction in that statement. As author Bill Kauffman has commented, Doctorow "wants to abolish the risk and privation that dog almost all artists, particularly during their apprenticeships. 'Starving artists' are to be plumped up by taxpayers. . . . The likelihood that pampered artists will turn complacent, listless, and lazy seems not to bother Doctorow." Moreover, as Jonathan Yardley, the *Washington Post*'s book critic, asked, "Why should the struggling young artist be entitled to government subsidy when the struggling young mechanic or accountant is not?"

Politicizing Culture

James D. Wolfensohn, former chairman of the Kennedy Center for the Performing Arts, decried talk about abolishing the NEA. "We should not allow [the arts] to become political," he said. But it is the subsidies that have politicized the arts and scholarship, not the talk about ending them. Some artists and scholars are to be awarded taxpayers' money. Which artists and scholars? They can't all be subsidized. The decisions are ultimately made by bureaucrats (even if they are advised by artists and scholars). Whatever criteria the bureaucrats use, they politicize art and scholarship. As novelist George Garrett has said: "Once (and whenever) the government is involved in the arts, then it is bound to be a political and social business, a battle between competing factions. The NEA, by definition, supports the arts establishment." Adds painter Laura Main, "Relying on the government to sponsor art work . . . is to me no more than subjecting yourself to the fate of a bureaucratic lackey."

Mary Beth Norton, a writer of women's history and a former member of the National Council on the Humanities, argues that "one of the great traditions of the Endowment [for the Humanities] is that this is where people doing research in new and exciting areas—oral history, black history, women's history to name areas I am familiar with—can turn to for funding." When the NEH spent less money in the mid-1980s than previously, Norton complained, "Now, people on the cutting edge are not being funded anymore." But if bureaucrats are ultimately selecting the research to be funded, how cutting-edge can it really be? How can they be trusted to distinguish innovation from fad? And who wants scholars choosing the objects of their research on the basis of what will win favor with government grant referees?

Similar criticism can be leveled against the radio and television programs financed by the CPB. They tend (with a few exceptions) to be aimed at the wealthier and better educated, and the selection process is inherently political. Moreover, some of the money granted to local stations is passed on to National Public Radio and the Public Broadcasting Service for the production of news programs, including *All Things Considered* and the *Newshour with Jim Lehrer*. Why are the taxpayers in a free society compelled to support news coverage, particularly when it is inclined in a statist direction? Robert Coonrod, former president of CPB, defends the organization, saying that "about 90 percent of the federal appropriation goes back to the communities, to public radio and TV stations, which are essentially community institutions." Only 90 percent? Why not leave 100 percent in the communities and let the residents decide how to spend it? Since only 16 percent of public broadcasting revenues now come from the federal government, other sources presumably could take up the slack if the federal government ended the appropriation.

It must be pointed out that the fundamental objection to the federal cultural agencies is not that their products have been intellectually, morally, politically, or sexually offensive to conservatives or even most Americans. That has sometimes, but not always, been the case. Occasionally, such as during the bicentennial of the U.S. Constitution, the agencies have been used to subsidize projects favored by conservatives. The brief against those agencies would be the same had the money been used exclusively to subsidize works inoffensive or even inspiring to the majority of the American people.

The case also cannot be based on how much the agencies spend. In FY04 the two endowments and the CPB were appropriated about $694 million total, a mere morsel in a $2.3 trillion federal budget. (Total federal support for the arts—ranging from military bands to Education Department programs to the Kennedy Center for the Performing Arts—amounts to $2 billion, not a minuscule amount. Congress should critically review all of those expenditures in light of the lack of constitutional authority for such programs, the burden they place on taxpayers, and the principle of subsidiarity or federalism.) The NEA's budget is about 0.2 percent of the total amount spent on the nonprofit arts in the United States.

No, the issue is neither the content of the work subsidized nor the expense. Taxpayer subsidy of the arts, scholarship, and broadcasting is inappropriate because it is outside the range of the proper functions of government, and as such it needlessly politicizes, and therefore corrupts, an area of life that should be left untainted by politics.

Government funding of anything involves government control. That insight, of course, is part of our folk wisdom: "He who pays the piper calls the tune." "Who takes the king's shilling sings the king's song."

Defenders of arts funding seem blithely unaware of this danger when they praise the role of the national endowments as an imprimatur or seal of approval on artists and arts groups. Former NEA chair Jane Alexander said: "The Federal role is small but very vital. We are a stimulus for leveraging state, local and private money. We are a linchpin for the puzzle of arts funding, a remarkably efficient way of stimulating private money." Drama critic Robert Brustein asks, "How could the NEA be 'privatized' and still retain its purpose as a funding agency functioning as a stamp of approval for deserving art?"

The politicization of whatever the federal cultural agencies touch was driven home by Richard Goldstein, a supporter of the NEH. Goldstein pointed out:

> The NEH has a ripple effect on university hiring and tenure, and on the kinds of research undertaken by scholars seeking support. Its chairman shapes the bounds of that support. In a broad sense, he sets standards that affect the tenor of textbooks and the content of curricula. . . . Though no chairman of the NEH can single-handedly direct the course of American education, he can nurture the nascent trends and take advantage of informal opportunities to signal department heads and deans. He can "persuade" with the cudgel of federal funding out of sight but hardly out of mind.

The cudgel (an apt metaphor) of federal funding has the potential to be wielded to influence those who run the universities with regard to hiring, tenure, research programs, textbooks, curricula. That is an enormous amount of power to have vested in a government official. Surely, it is the kind of concentration of power that the Founding Fathers intended to thwart.

Separation of Conscience and State

We might reflect on why the separation of church and state seems such a wise idea to Americans. First, it is wrong for the coercive authority of the state to interfere in matters of individual conscience. If we have rights, if we are individual moral agents, we must be free to exercise our judgment and define our own relationship with God. That doesn't mean that a free, pluralistic society won't have lots of persuasion and proselytizing—no doubt it will—but it does mean that such proselytizing must remain entirely persuasive, entirely voluntary.

Second, social harmony is enhanced by removing religion from the sphere of politics. Europe suffered through the Wars of Religion, as churches made alliances with rulers and sought to impose their theology on everyone in a region. Religious inquisitions, Roger Williams said, put towns "in an uproar." If people take their faith seriously, and if government is going to make one faith universal and compulsory, then people must contend bitterly—even to the death—to make sure that the *true* faith is established. Enshrine religion in the realm of persuasion, and there may be vigorous debate in society, but there won't be political conflict—and people can deal with one another in secular life without endorsing the private opinions of their colleagues.

Third, competition produces better results than subsidy, protection, and conformity. "Free trade in religion" is the best tool humans have to find the nearest approximation to the truth. Businesses coddled behind subsidies and tariffs will be weak and uncompetitive, and so will churches, synagogues, mosques, and temples. Religions that are protected from political interference but are otherwise on their own are likely to be stronger and more vigorous than a church that draws its support from government.

If those statements are true, they have implications beyond religion. Religion is not the only thing that affects us personally and spiritually, and it is not the only thing that leads to cultural wars. Art also expresses, transmits, and challenges our deepest values. As the managing director of Baltimore's Center Stage put it: "Art has power. It has the power to sustain, to heal, to humanize ... to change something in you. It's a frightening power, and also a beautiful power. . . . And it's essential to a civilized society." Because art is so powerful, because it deals with such basic human truths, we dare not entangle it with coercive government power. That means no censorship or regulation of art. It also means no tax-funded subsidies for arts and artists, for when government gets into the arts funding business, we get political conflicts. Conservatives denounce the National Endowment for the Arts for funding erotic photography and the Public Broadcasting System for broadcasting *Tales of the City,* which has gay characters. (*More Tales of the City,* which appeared on Showtime after PBS ducked the political pressure, generated little political controversy.) Civil rights activists make the Library of Congress take down an exhibit on antebellum slave life, and veterans' groups pressure the Smithsonian to remove a display on the bombing of Hiroshima. To avoid political battles over how to spend the taxpayers' money, to keep art and its power in the realm of persuasion, we would be well advised to establish the separation of art and state.

Suggested Readings

Banfield, Edward C. *The Democratic Muse.* New York: Basic Books, 1984.

Boaz, David. "The Separation of Art and the State." *Vital Speeches,* June 15, 1995. www.cato.org/speeches/sp-as53.html.

Cowen, Tyler. *In Praise of Commercial Culture.* Cambridge, MA: Harvard University Press, 1998.

Gillespie, Nick. "All Culture, All the Time." *Reason,* April 1999.

Grampp, William. *Pricing the Priceless.* New York: Basic Books, 1984.

Kauffman, Bill. "Subsidies to the Arts: Cultivating Mediocrity." Cato Institute Policy Analysis no. 137, August 8, 1990.

Kostelanetz, Richard. "The New Benefactors." *Liberty,* January 1990.

Lynes, Russell. "The Case against Government Aid to the Arts." *New York Times Magazine,* March 25, 1962.

Samuelson, Robert J. "Highbrow Pork Barrel." *Newsweek,* August 21, 1989.

Subcommittee on Oversight and Investigations of the House Committee on Education and the Workforce. *The Healthy State of the Arts in America and the Continuing Failure of the National Endowment for the Arts.* 105th Cong., 1st sess., September 23, 1997. Serial no. 105-A.

—Prepared by Sheldon Richman and David Boaz

33. Privatization

Congress should

- end rail subsidies, privatize Amtrak, and allow the company to terminate unprofitable routes;
- privatize the air traffic control system, privatize airport screening and security, end subsidies to airports, and encourage state and local airport privatization;
- privatize federal electric utilities, including the Tennessee Valley Authority and the four Power Marketing Administrations;
- privatize the U.S. Postal Service and repeal the legal restrictions on competitive delivery of mail; and
- encourage federal agencies to increase competitive sourcing for needed government services.

Introduction

Many federal government activities are commercial in nature and could be carried out by private firms in competitive markets. In some cases, private companies are currently prevented from offering services to the public because of government restrictions. For example, the U.S. Postal Service has a legal monopoly on first-class mail. Such restrictions should be repealed.

In other cases, the government performs services that are readily available in the private sector. For example, USPS parcel delivery competes with private parcel services. Another example is the federal government's National Zoo in Washington, which has been rocked by scandals regarding its poor treatment of animals. There is no need for the government to be in the zoo business—some of the best zoos in the country are private, such as those in San Diego and the Bronx.

Privatization has many benefits, including opening new opportunities for entrepreneurs, creating higher-quality and lower-cost services, and reducing the government budget deficit and debt. For those reasons, dozens of countries have pursued privatization during the past two decades. Governments on every continent have sold electric utilities, airlines, oil companies, railroads, and other businesses to private investors. Even postal services are being privatized. Britain, Finland, Germany, the Netherlands, New Zealand, and Sweden have either opened postal services to private competition or privatized their national mail companies. Unfortunately, Americans continue to be saddled with the 774,000-employee USPS and other inefficient government businesses.

There has been an occasional attempt to bring privatization reforms to this country. Ronald Reagan established a President's Commission on Privatization that proposed modest reforms in 1988, but Congress generally did not act on them. Nonetheless, a few federal entities have been sold in recent decades. Conrail, a freight railroad in the Northeast, was privatized in 1987. The Alaska Power Administration was privatized in 1996. The U.S. Enrichment Corporation, which provides enriched uranium to the nuclear industry, was privatized in 1998.

Today, privatization makes more sense than ever for a number of reasons. First, sales of federal assets would cut the huge federal budget deficit. Second, by reducing the responsibilities of the government, members of Congress could better focus on their core responsibilities, such as national security. Third, there is now vast foreign privatization experience that could be drawn on in pursuing U.S. reforms. Fourth, privatization would spur economic growth by opening new markets to entrepreneurs. For example, privatization of USPS and the repeal of its monopoly would bring major innovation to the mail business, just as the 1980s' breakup of the AT&T monopoly brought innovation to the telecommunications business.

One roadblock to privatization is the view that certain activities, such as air traffic control (ATC), are too important to leave to the private sector. But the reality is just the opposite. The government has shown itself to be a failure at providing efficient and high-quality ATC, passenger rail, and other services. Those industries are too important to miss out on the innovations and likely greater safety that private entrepreneurs could bring to them. For example, privatized ATC would probably be safer because private firms could access capital markets in order to invest in the newest technologies. By contrast, the federal government's ATC has often lagged behind in technology because of budget constraints and mismanagement.

Privatization vs. Competitive Sourcing

In a government-wide analysis, the Bush administration determined that about half of all federal employees perform tasks that are also performed in the marketplace and thus are not "inherently governmental." The administration made a push to open some of those activities to allow private firms to bid for work that had previously been performed in-house. The administration estimates that the cost savings from such "competitive sourcing" averages about 20 percent.

Those are positive steps, but competitive sourcing is not the same as privatization. Competitively sourced services still consume taxpayer dollars and are government-directed activities. Policymakers go astray when they support competitive sourcing of programs that should, instead, be fully privatized or terminated. Privatization gets spending off the government's budget entirely and provides for much greater dynamism, efficiency, and innovation than is possible through government contracting.

In addition, privatization avoids a serious pitfall of contracting—opening the government to corruption. A Pentagon scandal reported by the *Washington Post* in December 2003 provides a good example. Two senior procurement officials were convicted of receiving sexual favors and $1 million in cash for awarding minority set-aside defense contracts to particular firms. One of the men headed the Pentagon's Office of Small and Disadvantaged Business Utilization, which helps minority firms win contracts. In this case, the best reform is not competitive sourcing but termination of this unneeded Pentagon office.

Privatizing Stand-Alone Businesses

The federal government operates numerous business enterprises that could be converted into publicly traded corporations, including the USPS, Amtrak, and a number of electric utilities. Other countries have in-depth experience in privatizing such services that Congress can use when it moves ahead with reforms.

- **Postal Services:** A 2003 report by the President's Commission on the U.S. Postal Service and other studies have concluded that the outlook for the USPS is bleak because of declining mail volume and rising costs. The way ahead is to privatize the USPS and repeal the first-class mail monopoly that it currently holds. New Zealand and Germany have implemented reforms that Congress should examine. Since 1998 New Zealand's postal market has been open to private competition, with the result that postage rates have fallen and labor productivity at New Zealand Post has risen markedly. Germany's Deutsche Post was privatized in 2000, with the result that the company has improved productivity and expanded into new lines of business.

- **Electric Utilities:** The U.S. electricity industry has always been dominated by publicly traded corporations. The exceptions are the federal government's Tennessee Valley Authority and four Power Marketing Administrations, which sell power in 33 states. Those government power companies have become an anachronism as utility privatization has proceeded around the world from Britain to Brazil and Argentina to Australia. TVA and PMA privatization would reduce the federal deficit, eliminate the utilities' artificially low power rates that encourage excess consumption, and increase efficiency in utility operations and capital investment. President Clinton proposed to sell off the four PMAs in his fiscal year 1996 budget. It is time to dust off those plans and move ahead with reforms.
- **Passenger Rail:** Subsidies to Amtrak were supposed to be temporary after the passenger rail agency was created in 1970. That has not occurred, and Amtrak has provided second-rate passenger rail service for 30 years while consuming more than $25 billion in federal subsidies. Reforms elsewhere show that private passenger rail can work. Full or partial rail privatization has occurred in Argentina, Australia, Britain, Germany, Japan, New Zealand, and other countries.

Privatizing Infrastructure

Before the 20th century, transportation infrastructure such as roads was often financed and built by the private sector. But during much of the 20th century, transportation infrastructure was thought of as a government function. By the 1980s that started to change, and governments around the world began selling off, or letting private firms build, billions of dollars worth of airports, highways, bridges, and other infrastructure.

Just about any service that can be supported by consumer fees can be privatized. A big advantage of privatized airports, ATC, highways, bridges, and other infrastructure is that private companies can freely tap debt and equity markets for capital expansion to meet rising demand and to reduce congestion. By contrast, government infrastructure today is often congested because upgrades are constrained by lack of government funding and poor long-term planning by governments.

- **Air Traffic Control:** Numerous countries have partly or fully privatized their ATC services. Canada's reforms provide a good model for the United States. In 1996 Canada set up a fully private, nonprofit ATC corporation, Nav Canada, which is self-supported from charges on aviation users (see www.navcanada.ca). The Canadian system has received rave reviews for investing in the latest technology and reducing air congestion. Meanwhile, the Federal Aviation Administration has been struggling to modernize U.S. air traffic control for two decades. The FAA's upgrade efforts have frequently fallen behind schedule and gone far over budget, according to the General Accounting Office. ATC is far too important for government mismanagement; privatization is long overdue.

- **Highways:** A number of states and foreign countries have started experimenting with privately financed and operated highways. The Dulles Greenway in Northern Virginia is a 14-mile private highway opened in 1995. It was financed through private bond and equity issues and uses an electronic toll system to maximize efficiency for drivers. In Richmond, the 895 Connector project is being financed by private capital and will be operated by a nonprofit firm. Fluor Daniel, a leading engineering company, has proposed building private highways in Virginia, including widening the Capital Beltway with four new electronic toll lanes. The company also has a $1 billion plan to build toll lanes running 56 miles south from Washington. Similar private road projects are being pursued in California, Texas, North Carolina, and South Carolina. There is clearly a strong private-sector interest in funding and building highways. Policymakers should pave the way for entrepreneurs to help reduce the nation's congestion and save taxpayer money.

- **Airports:** Most major airports in the United States are owned by municipal governments, with the federal government providing subsidies. The United States lags reforms that are taking place abroad—airports have been fully or partially privatized in Auckland, Copenhagen, Frankfurt, London, Melbourne, Naples, Rome, Sydney, Vienna, and other cities. The British led the way with the 1987 privatization of British Airports Authority, which owns London's Heathrow. In the United States, Congress needs to take the lead on airport privatization because there are numerous federal roadblocks that make U.S. cities hesitant to proceed. For example, government-owned airports can issue tax-exempt debt, which gives them a financial advantage over private airports.

Privatizing Loan Programs

The federal government runs a large array of loan and loan guarantee programs for farmers, students, small businesses, utilities, shipbuilders, weapons purchasers, exporters, fishermen, and other groups. The Federal Credit Supplement in the federal budget lists 59 different loan programs and 70 loan guarantee programs. Loan guarantees are promises to private creditors that the government will cover borrower defaults. At the end of 2003 there was $249 billion in outstanding federal loans and $1.2 trillion in loan guarantees.

In the 1970s federal loans and loan guarantees grew rapidly as politicians discovered that they could pay off special interests with loan programs, while not paying any political cost for supporting higher spending directly. Like other federal programs, loan programs that make no economic sense can survive by creating an ''iron triangle'' of interests that resist reform. Loan program supporters include loan beneficiaries, financial institutions, federal loan administrators, and congressional committees that authorize loan programs.

In the 1980s the Reagan administration tried to cut federal loan programs but did not have much success. Policymakers should revive Reagan's initiatives and begin terminating or privatizing federal loan programs. The provision of credit is a centuries-old market institution that does not need government help, especially given the sophistication and liquidity of financial markets today.

Some federal loan programs target borrowers who could have received private financing. In such cases, there is no need for government loans because they simply displace private loans. Other loan programs target borrowers who cannot secure private financing. In that case, federal loans support borrowers who are poor credit risks, and taxpayer money is likely to be wasted when loans are defaulted on. For example, Farm Service Agency loans are aimed at farmers who are unable to obtain private credit at market interest rates. But such farmers are probably bad credit risks with poor business prospects. Indeed, FSA loans have high default rates.

The FY05 federal budget says that government loan programs are needed because private markets suffer from ''imperfections,'' such as lack of perfect information about borrowers. For example, banks might be more hesitant to lend to start-up businesses because they do not have lengthy credit histories. But it is appropriate that start-up firms face more scrutiny and pay higher interest rates because of their higher risk of failure. Since failure creates economic waste, it is good that creditors are more hesitant to lend to riskier businesses. Government loan subsidies result in too many loans going to excessively risky and low-value projects.

Free-market allocation of credit is far from perfect, but markets have developed mechanisms for funding risky endeavors. For example, venture capital and angel investment pumps tens of billions of dollars of investment into new businesses every year. There is no need for the government to compete with such private financial mechanisms.

Government distortions are a bigger problem than market "imperfections." For example, federal loan guarantees make financial institutions overeager to lend to those with shaky credit because the government will cover losses in case of default. Also, federal loan programs are generally poorly managed. For example, federal student loans have been on GAO's high-risk list for waste, fraud, and abuse every year since 1990. Lax enforcement of student loan repayments has led to large losses from defaults, costing taxpayers billions of dollars.

Privatizing Federal Buildings and Real Estate

At the end of FY03 the federal government owned about $1 trillion in buildings and equipment, $200 billion in inventory, $550 billion in land, and $650 billion in mineral rights. Many federal assets are neglected or abused and would be better cared for in the private sector. It is common to observe government property that is in poor shape, with public housing being perhaps the most infamous federal eyesore. The GAO finds that "many assets are in an alarming state of deterioration" and has put federal property holdings on its high-risk waste list (GAO-03-122). The solution is to sell federal assets that are in excess of public needs and to better manage a smaller set of holdings.

The federal government owns about one-fourth of the land in the United States. But only a portion of that land is of environmental significance, and the government has proven itself to be a poor land custodian. There are widely reported maintenance backlogs on lands controlled by the Forest Service, Park Service, and Fish and Wildlife Service. The solution is not a larger maintenance budget but to trim down holdings to fit limited taxpayer resources.

The government owns billions of dollars worth of excess buildings. The GAO has found that the government has "many assets it does not need," including 30 vacant Veterans Affairs buildings and 1,200 excess Department of Energy facilities. The GAO figures that the Pentagon spends up to $4 billion each year maintaining its excess facilities. The Pentagon owns excess supply depots, training facilities, medical facilities, research labs, and other installations. Federal asset sales would help reduce the deficit, allow improved maintenance of remaining assets, and improve economic efficiency by putting assets into more productive private hands.

Suggested Readings

Edwards, Chris. "Downsizing the Federal Government." Cato Institute Policy Analysis no. 515, June 2, 2004. This report provides cites for facts and data used in this chapter.

General Accounting Office. "High-Risk Series: Federal Real Property." GAO-03-122. January 1, 2003.

Hudgins, Edward L., ed. *Mail @ the Millennium: Will the Postal Service Go Private?* Washington: Cato Institute, 2000.

Poole, Robert W. Jr., and Viggo Butler. "How to Commercialize Air Traffic Control." Reason Public Policy Institute Policy Study no. 278, February 2001.

Reason Public Policy Institute, www.rppi.org, for studies and news on privatization around the world.

Vranich, Joseph, and Edward L. Hudgins. "Help Passenger Rail by Privatizing Amtrak." Cato Institute Policy Analysis no. 419, November 1, 2001.

—Prepared by Chris Edwards

34. Corporate Welfare

Congress should

- end programs that provide direct grants to businesses,
- end programs that provide marketing and other commercial services to businesses,
- end programs that provide subsidized loans and insurance to businesses,
- eliminate trade barriers intended to protect U.S. industries from foreign competition at the expense of U.S. consumers,
- eliminate domestic regulatory barriers that favor particular companies with monopoly power,
- create financial transparency with a detailed listing in the federal budget of companies that receive direct business subsidies and the amounts thereof, and
- establish a corporate welfare elimination commission modeled after the Base Realignment and Closure Commission.

By the end of fiscal 2004, the federal government had spent at least $90 billion on more than 65 programs that subsidize businesses. There have been numerous efforts to cut those wasteful and unfair programs, but total corporate welfare spending keeps rising. A somewhat serious attempt was made after the Republicans took control of both houses of Congress in the 1990s, but those efforts failed.

The Bush administration had promised a renewed attack on corporate welfare in its first year in office. Indeed, then–budget director Mitch Daniels stated that it was "not the federal government's role to subsidize, sometimes deeply subsidize, private interests." By its second year in office, the Bush administration had basically abandoned any direct campaign against corporate welfare programs. While taxpayers wait for reforms, the government continues to subsidize private interests *directly* through such programs as aid to farmers and subsidized loans for exporters. And private interests continue to receive billions of dollars of *indirect* subsidies through programs such as federal energy research and trade barriers. With the federal budget in deficit in 2005 by an estimated $348 billion, corporate welfare is the perfect place to start cutting excess spending.

What Is Corporate Welfare?

Corporate welfare consists of government programs that provide unique benefits or advantages to specific companies or industries. Corporate welfare includes programs that provide direct grants to businesses, programs that provide indirect commercial support to businesses, and programs that provide subsidized loans and insurance.

Many corporate welfare programs provide private industry with useful services, such as insurance, statistics, research, loans, and marketing support. Those are all functions that the private sector does every day for itself without government help in many industries. If commercial activities are useful and efficient, then private markets should be able to support them free of subsidies.

In addition to spending programs, corporate welfare includes barriers to trade that attempt to protect U.S. industries from foreign competition at the expense of U.S. consumers and U.S. companies that use foreign products. Corporate welfare also includes domestic legal barriers that favor particular companies with monopoly power against free-market competitors.

Corporate welfare sometimes supports companies that are already highly profitable. Such companies clearly do not need any extra help from taxpayers. In other situations, corporate welfare programs prop up businesses that are failing in the marketplace. Such companies should be allowed to fail because they weigh down the economy and reduce overall U.S. income levels.

Which Agencies Dish It Out and Who Receives It?

The federal budget supports a broad array of corporate welfare programs in most cabinet-level agencies. The leading corporate welfare providers are the Departments of Agriculture, Commerce, Energy, Housing and Urban Development, and Transportation. Many smaller independent federal agencies, such as the Export-Import Bank, also dole out corporate welfare.

Many recipients of corporate welfare are among the biggest companies in America, including the Big Three automakers, Boeing, Archer Daniels Midland, and now-bankrupt Enron. Most of the massive handouts to agricultural producers go to large farming businesses. Once companies are successful in securing a stream of taxpayer goodies, they defend their stake year after year with the help of their state's congressional delegation.

The Dirty Dozen: 12 Most Odious Corporate Welfare Programs

1. Advanced Technology Program (Department of Commerce)
2. Economic Development Administration (Department of Commerce)
3. International Trade Administration (Department of Commerce)
4. Market Access Program (Department of Agriculture)
5. Foreign Military Financing (Department of Defense)
6. FreedomCAR (Department of Energy)
7. Maritime Administration's Guaranteed Loan Subsidies
8. Export-Import Bank
9. Agency for International Development
10. Small Business Administration
11. Energy Supply Research and Development
12. Agricultural Research Service

A Sampler of Corporate Welfare Programs to Cut

The following are some corporate welfare programs that are long overdue for elimination. Eliminating just these 12 programs would yield $94 billion in savings over five years. The spending total next to each program below is for FY2004—in the cases in which outlay figures were unobtainable, budget authority is listed.

Direct Subsidies

- Commerce Department—Advanced Technology Program ($195 million). This program gives research grants to high-tech companies. Handouts to successful firms make no sense because they could have relied on private venture capital instead. Handouts to unsuccessful firms make no sense because they force taxpayers to subsidize economic waste.

- Commerce Department—Economic Development Administration ($417 million). The programs within the EDA give grants to state and local government, nonprofit corporations, and private businesses to, among other things, fund the construction of private industrial office parks. The EDA also funds the Trade Adjustment Assistance program, which doles out grants to firms and industries that lose business as a result of free trade.
- Commerce Department—International Trade Administration ($364 million). The ITA's role is to "develop the export potential of U.S. firms" by conducting export promotion programs and protecting inefficient industries by enforcing antidumping regulations. A handful of other corporate welfare programs survive under the umbrella of ITA.
- Agriculture Department—Market Access Program ($103 million). This program gives taxpayer dollars to exporters of agricultural products to pay for their overseas advertising campaigns.
- Department of Defense—Foreign Military Financing ($5.4 billion). Through this program, U.S. taxpayers fund weapons purchases by foreign governments from U.S. weapons makers. This program is estimated to be the largest single subsidy program for U.S. weapons exporters.
- Department of Energy—FreedomCAR ($246 million). This program, the brainchild of President Bush, replaces the Partnership for a New Generation of Vehicles, a longtime target of opponents of corporate welfare. This program supports research on lightweight automotive technology, electronic power controls, and hybrid engines. It even includes money to research a hydrogen-fueled engine. This is research that the big automakers could easily finance on their own.

Subsidized Loans and Insurance

- Maritime Administration—Guaranteed Loan Subsidies ($55 million). Provides loan guarantees for purchases of ships from U.S. shipyards. The United States has vast and liquid financial markets making credit available to all businesses that have reasonable risks. It makes no sense to use taxpayer funds to duplicate functions of private financial markets.

- Export-Import Bank ($1.5 billion). This program uses taxpayer dollars to subsidize the financing of foreign purchases of U.S. goods. It makes loans to foreigners at below-market interest rates, guarantees the loans of private institutions, and provides export credit insurance. (See Chapter 68 for more details.)

Indirect Subsidies to Businesses

- Agency for International Development ($4.6 billion). AID is the main U.S. foreign aid agency. It establishes investment funds with taxpayer money, which indirectly subsidizes American businesses. As the agency itself proudly admits: "The principal beneficiary of America's foreign assistance programs has always been the United States. Close to 80 percent of the [U.S. AID] contracts and grants go directly to American firms."
- The Small Business Administration ($4 billion). The SBA provides subsidized loans and loan guarantees to small businesses. Because government can't properly pick winners and losers in a complex economy, the program's track record is abysmal. Around 15 percent of SBA loans become delinquent in any given year, and taxpayers are left holding the bag. Small businesses should compete for capital just like any other business.
- Energy Department—Energy Supply Research ($714 million). This program aims to develop new energy technologies and improve existing ones. The energy industry itself and private research institutes should fund such work.
- Agriculture Department—Agricultural Research Service ($1.1 billion). This program aims to improve product quality and find new uses for a variety of agricultural products. In most industries, such commercial activities are financed by the businesses selling the product, not taxpayers.

What Is Wrong with Corporate Welfare?

As some of the above examples illustrate, there are many problems with corporate welfare programs. Here are seven:

1. **Corporate welfare is a big drain on the taxpayer**. In FY03, around $90 billion of taxpayer money was spent on programs that subsidize businesses. By eliminating those programs, Congress could provide every household in the country with an $842 per year tax rebate.

2. **Corporate welfare creates an uneven playing field**. By giving selected businesses and industries special advantages, corporate subsidies put businesses that are less politically connected at an unfair disadvantage.

3. **Corporate welfare programs are anti-consumer**. By helping particular businesses, the government often damages consumers. For example, the protectionist federal sugar program costs consumers several billion dollars per year in higher product prices.

4. **The government does a poor job of picking winners**. It is the role of private entrepreneurs and investors to take technology risks in the venture capital and stock markets. Government by its nature cannot possibly collect, use effectively, or even fathom enough information to successfully direct the capital markets.

5. **Corporate welfare fosters an incestuous relationship between government and corporations.** Corporate welfare generates an unhealthy relationship between business and the government. In Washington today industry trade associations and lobbying firms continually pressure lawmakers to give out new business subsidies or to protect old ones. All of the corporate welfare money that Enron received over the years is a perfect example of that. If, on the other hand, the federal government got out of the business of handing out favors, that demand would diminish.

6. **Corporate welfare depletes private-sector strength**. While "market entrepreneurs" work hard to create new businesses, corporate welfare helps create "political entrepreneurs" who spend their energies seeking government handouts. Corporate welfare draws talented people and firms into wasteful subsidy-seeking activities and away from more productive pursuits. Besides, companies receiving subsidies usually become weaker and less efficient, not stronger.

7. **Corporate welfare is unconstitutional.** Corporate subsidy programs lie outside Congress's limited spending authority under the U.S. Constitution. Nowhere in the Constitution is the government granted the authority to spend taxpayer dollars on specific industries.

Eliminating Corporate Welfare

A two-pronged attack should be taken to overcome the political difficulty of ending corporate welfare. Because corporate welfare is doled out by dozens of federal agencies, it is difficult for taxpayers to find out which firms are receiving what amounts of money. A first reform step should be financial transparency. The administration should begin providing a detailed cross-agency listing of companies and cash received for all direct business subsidies in its annual budget documents.

Beyond full disclosure, a corporate welfare elimination commission, akin to the successful military base closing commissions of the 1990s, should be established,. Ending corporate welfare will require altering the incentives of legislators. No one senator or representative will vote for a bill that lowers the budget for his or her favored program without a corresponding decrease in someone else's favored program. In other words, no one wants to unilaterally defund a favorite program since the money will just be reallocated elsewhere.

Also, member of Congress A knows that voting for a decrease in member B's favored program might result in future reprisals. That is the reason that tackling these programs one by one, or in a small group, during the appropriations process is not likely to yield results. An institutional problem of this sort requires an institutional solution.

General guidelines for a bill creating a corporate welfare elimination commission could be as follows:

- The commission would not be composed of sitting members of Congress. It would be chosen by bipartisan agreement between the president and the leadership of both houses of Congress.
- The commission would convene for the purpose of proposing a list of corporate welfare programs that should be eliminated.
- No corporate welfare spending program should be considered "off the table."
- The commission's list of recommended program terminations would be voted on by both houses of Congress, with no amendments, within 60 days of the commission's final report.

A commission structured along those lines would solve two main problems:

- The Special Interests Dilemma: Because the members of the commission would not be incumbent lawmakers, there would be few, if any, incentives for the members to think about reelection prospects or other political factors. Admittedly, there would still be special interest pressure on the commission. Instead of lobbying members of Congress, supporters of corporate welfare programs would lobby the commission. However, the political dynamic would be different enough that lobbying would be likely to be less, if at all, effective.

- The Collective Choice Dilemma: Because every program would be terminated by an up-or-down vote on an unamendable bill, there would be no vote trading on the specifics of the bill as there is during the normal appropriations process. The commission would have the ability to cast a wider net and create a list of programs that would hit a larger number of special interest constituencies than any one member of, or group within, Congress would propose. To avoid other attendant political dynamics, the commission could present to Congress its list of program terminations in a nonelection year.

This idea has an ancestor in the Base Realignment and Closure Commission. The BRAC grew out of the understanding that even though the military base structure at the time made little sense on the whole, Congress could not bring itself to close specific bases. Although many members of Congress wanted to close military bases in the abstract, they were rarely willing to vote for a bill that would close a base in their district. As in the case of corporate welfare programs, Congress soon found itself unable, because of institutional and political biases, to downsize the defense budget at a time when doing so was widely and often cited by members of both parties as an important goal.

Another benefit for taxpayers of having a commission address the issue of corporate welfare is that these egregious programs could be discussed openly and publicly in a focused proceeding. The exposure of a substantial portion of the federal budget—indeed, an overall reappraisal of what the federal government does—is a long-needed corrective to the current state of affairs.

Suggested Readings

Congressional Budget Office. "Federal Financial Support of Business." July 1995.

Edwards, Chris, and Tad DeHaven. "Corporate Welfare Update." Cato Institute Tax & Budget Bulletin no. 7, May 2002.

Hartung, William. "Corporate Welfare for Weapons Makers: The Hidden Costs of Spending on Defense and Foreign Aid." Cato Institute Policy Analysis no. 350, August 12, 1999.

Lukas, Aaron, and Ian Vásquez. "Rethinking the Export-Import Bank." Cato Institute Trade Briefing Paper no. 15, March 12, 2002.

Rodgers, T. J. "Silicon Valley versus Corporate Welfare." Cato Institute Briefing Paper no. 37, April 27, 1998.

———. "Why Silicon Valley Should Not Normalize Relations with Washington, D.C." Cato Institute monograph, February 9, 2000.

Slivinski, Stephen. "The Corporate Welfare Budget: Bigger Than Ever." Cato Institute Policy Analysis no. 415, October 10, 2001.

—Prepared by Stephen Slivinski

35. State Fiscal Policy

> **State legislatures should**
> - return all future surpluses to taxpayers by cutting taxes or issuing tax refunds and
> - control spending by enacting a strong tax and expenditure limitation.

The State Spending Spree

The state fiscal crunch that most legislatures confronted recently resulted from excess spending during the last decade. For starters, the state governments grew faster than the federal government. Between 1990 and 2002, total federal government spending rose by 60 percent. State spending doubled during the same period. That is far faster than population growth plus inflation.

As the economy slowed and large budget gaps started appearing, state budgets did not shrink in size even if the rates of growth declined. Spending continued to rise: in 2002, for example, when revenue was expected to decline by an average of .7 percent, state appropriations still rose by 1.2 percent.

After adjusting for inflation and population growth, the budgets of seven states (Mississippi, Arkansas, West Virginia, Missouri, Pennsylvania, New Mexico, and Utah) more than doubled between 1991 and 2002 (Table 35.1). Real state spending grew faster in the 1990s (4 percent annually) than in the go-go 1980s (3.4 percent annually).

This is a case of history repeating itself. In the 1980s few states resisted the pressure to use surplus revenues from the economic boom to create costly new programs. As a result, when the economy slipped into recession in the early 1990s, many states found themselves in the worst fiscal crunch

Table 35.1
Real per Capita Spending Increases, 1991–2002

Rank	State	Increase	Rank	State	Increase
1	Mississippi	137%	26	Nebraska	76%
2	Arkansas	117%	27	South Dakota	76%
3	West Virginia	116%	28	New Hampshire	75%
4	Missouri	114%	29	Montana	74%
5	Pennsylvania	108%	30	Indiana	73%
6	New Mexico	103%	31	Illinois	73%
7	Utah	102%	32	Florida	72%
8	Oklahoma	99%	33	Washington	70%
9	Minnesota	97%	34	Maryland	70%
10	North Carolina	95%	35	Georgia	68%
11	Tennessee	95%	36	Connecticut	68%
12	South Carolina	95%	37	Rhode Island	67%
13	Kentucky	93%	38	Vermont	67%
14	Texas	93%	39	Virginia	67%
15	Oregon	89%	40	Michigan	63%
16	California	88%	41	Delaware	63%
17	Colorado	88%	42	New York	62%
18	Maine	86%	43	New Jersey	62%
19	Kansas	86%	44	Louisiana	59%
20	Alabama	83%	45	Massachusetts	50%
21	Wisconsin	83%	46	Nevada	49%
22	Iowa	81%	47	Hawaii	47%
23	Ohio	80%	48	Wyoming	46%
24	Idaho	79%	49	Arizona	36%
25	North Dakota	76%			

SOURCE: Authors' calculations based on Bureau of Census data.
NOTE: Alaska is excluded.

in decades. The recession caused revenue growth to slow, but demands to meet all the new spending commitments did not slow.

Deficits Caused by Spending, Not Tax Cuts

Some analysts try to blame recent tax cuts for the budget gaps. Although there was widespread tax cutting in the late 1990s, tax cuts tapered off substantially in FY02, and tax increases began anew in FY03. Besides, the tax cuts of the 1990s were very modest compared with the huge spending increases that took place. Indeed, roughly two of every three surplus dollars between 1996 and 2002 went to new spending, with just one dollar going to tax cuts. In other words, spending increases were twice as big as recent tax cuts.

Even with tax cuts in many states in the 1990s, state revenues still boomed. In fact, the states that had the 10 highest rates of growth in revenue per $1,000 in personal income between 1995 and 2002 had larger deficits as a percentage of state spending than the 10 states that had the lowest revenue growth rates. The same holds true for spending trends: the states with the 10 fastest rates of growth in real per capita spending had larger deficits on average than the states that maintained control over spending.

If states had not cut taxes in the 1990s, today's budget gaps would be even larger because extra revenue would have fueled even more spending. It is simply not true that states that cut taxes had higher deficits than those that did not. Indeed, the opposite is true. If the money is available, it will be spent. Tax cuts are valuable not just because they lower tax burdens but also because they remove the temptation to spend.

Tax Policy and Economic Growth in the 1990s

It is important to emphasize the value of tax cuts in general, and income tax cuts in particular, because the evidence shows that states that reduce taxes improve their prospects for economic growth. For example, a 1996 study by Zsolt Besci of the Federal Reserve Bank of Atlanta found that "relative marginal tax rates have a statistically significant negative relationship with relative state growth averaged for the period from 1961 to 1992." The message of the study for state governments is that "lowering aggregate state and local marginal tax rates is likely to have a positive effect on long-term growth rates." A study for the Joint Economic Committee of Congress by Richard Vedder of Ohio University came to a similar conclusion. A study by Thomas Dye of Florida State University found that states with no income tax had higher personal income growth (and smaller government growth) than states that had an income tax.

Tax changes enacted in the states in the 1990s offer a useful laboratory in which to explore the effects of tax policy. It is useful to compare the economic performance of the 10 states that increased taxes the most with the economic performance of the 10 states that cut taxes the most during 1990–2002 (see Table 35.2). The results suggest that when states reduce taxes they improve their relative economic performance.

Businesses and jobs migrated to low-tax states in the 1990s. Job growth averaged 25 percent in the top 10 tax-cutting states, higher than the national

Table 35.2
Taxes and State Economic Performance, 1990–2002

	Top 10 Tax-Cutting States	50-State Average	Top 10 Tax-Hiking States
1990–2002 revenue increases (per $1,000 of personal income)	($8.23)	$3.10	$15.35
Employment, 1990–2002	24.63%	22.34%	17.62%
Personal income, 1990–2002	91.7%	86.43%	78.6%
Population growth, 1990–2002	17.5%	16.01%	14.4%

SOURCE: Authors' calculations.

average of 22 percent, while the top 10 tax-hiking states experienced employment growth of just under 18 percent.

Wealth grew faster in the tax-cutting states than in the tax-hiking states. Indeed, tax-cutting states saw personal income grow over 5 percentage points faster than the national average, while the tax-hiking states saw below-average personal income growth.

Citizens voted with their feet and migrated to the tax-cutting states in greater numbers. Population growth averaged 17.5 percent in tax-cutting states but only 14.4 percent in the tax-hiking states. Again, growth in this variable outstripped the national average in the tax-cutting states.

If tax cuts caused fiscal deterioration as some observers allege—indeed, many of the tax hikes promoted over the past few years were predicated on "saving" a particular state's bond rating—then the bond ratings of the 10 tax-cutting states should be worse than the bond ratings of the 10 tax-raising states. But the opposite is true. For the tax-cutting states, the average Standard and Poor's bond rating in 2002 was between AAA and AA. For the tax-raising states, the average bond rating was between AA and A.

Restraining Government Growth in the States

The big problem for the people who tried to restrain the growth of government in the 1990s was not just fighting the spending appetites of members of both parties but also the tide of revenue that fueled those spending desires. With an economic recovery on the horizon, the time is ripe to put into place restrictions on government growth before the genie of the revenue boom is out of the bottle. Once states find themselves in surpluses again, the temptation to spend it all is likely to be irresistible to many. That acquiescence to more spending will only put the states back into the same, or worse, position they were in at the end of the 1990s once revenue flags again in the next economic downturn.

The best thing a state can do is to put into place a strong tax and expenditure limitation (TEL) that keeps government from growing without bound. Those limits, which are usually very popular with voters and taxpayers, would restrict the ability of state legislatures to spend beyond a particular growth rate.

During the tax revolt in the 1970s, a number of states adopted TELs as a mechanism to limit the growth of government. By 1982 TELs had been enacted in 17 states. TEL enactment slowed along with the fervor of the tax revolt in the prosperous 1980s; only 3 states enacted TELs between 1983 and 1990. However, during the early and mid-1990s, TELs enjoyed a resurgence of sorts; by 1996, 6 additional states had enacted TELs. Currently, 26 states operate under some kind of TEL.

Not all TELs are created equal. Some work better than others. Indeed, most of the TELs in the states currently are either toothless or don't hold spending to a strict enough baseline.

What Makes a Good TEL?

Property 1: Limiting the Growth of Expenditures and Revenues to the Inflation Rate Plus Population Growth

An overwhelming majority of the TELs that have been passed since 1976 limit growth in state expenditures and revenues to state personal income growth. However, two states, Colorado and Washington, have recently enacted TELs that limit growth in state expenditures to the inflation rate plus population growth.

That is a more stringent limit. Over the years the rate of growth in personal income has been significantly greater than the inflation rate. Between 1980 and 1990, growth in real personal income exceeded the inflation rate plus population growth by more than 38 percentage points. It should also be noted that holding increases in expenditures to increases in personal income, as most TELs do, sets a relatively low limit for a state to maintain. Between 1980 and 1990, the ratio of state and local direct general expenditures to personal income actually fell in 27 of the 49 states considered in our analysis.

Property 2: Refunding Surpluses to Taxpayers Immediately

Another feature that is worth examining is the provision that mandates immediate refunds of any surpluses to taxpayers. Thus far, four states (Colorado, Michigan, Missouri, and Oregon) have enacted TELs that mandate immediate refunds of revenues that exceed the limit established by the TEL. Such a provision would strengthen any TEL because it would make it difficult for state government to collect or spend excess revenues. In addition, it would give citizens and watchdog groups a greater incentive to see that the provisions of the TEL were enforced. An examination of the recent budgetary history of the four states that require immediate refunds indicates that such refund provisions enhance the effectiveness of TELs in another way. Namely, they create a strong incentive for state legislators to cut taxes when it appears that revenues are going to exceed the limit.

If a state enacts a TEL that mandates immediate refunds of surplus revenues, state legislators have the option of allowing revenues to exceed the limit and then subsequently refunding the revenue. However, there are logistical and political problems with doing that. First, it is nearly impossible to refund the sales tax. Also, although it is possible to enact refunds of income or property taxes, legislators dislike doing so. That is because high-income citizens would obtain a high percentage of the refunds, and legislators do not like to be charged with favoring the rich over everyone else. As a result, a powerful incentive is created for legislators to cut taxes before the end of the fiscal year so that revenues will no longer exceed the limit. Indeed, case studies indicate that Michigan, Missouri, and Colorado (three of the four states that mandate taxpayer refunds) have enacted tax cuts in response to the prospect of having revenues exceed the limit mandated by their TELs.

How Well Do These Sorts of TELs Work?

Regression analysis can examine this question. In our model, the dependent variable is the annual change in per capita state and local direct general expenditures in 1996 dollars. The analysis examines the effects of TELs with provisions for immediate refunds and TELs that limit growth in expenditures to the inflation rate. Demographic and economic variables are also included to take into account the uniqueness of each state.

The results, which are summarized in Figure 35.1, support the idea that certain features can greatly enhance the effectiveness of a TEL. From this

Figure 35.1
Effectiveness of TELs by Feature

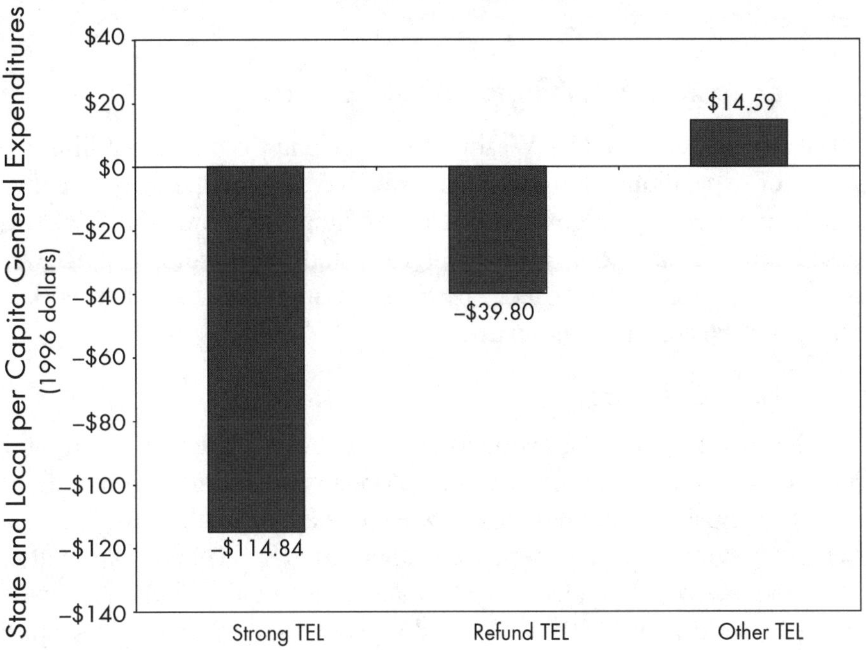

SOURCE: Authors' calculations.

regression it appears that TELs that limit increases in spending and revenue to the inflation rate plus population growth have the most promise for reducing spending. If a state passes a TEL that limits expenditures to the inflation rate plus population growth, the regression equation predicts that every year the TEL will reduce per capita state and local direct general expenditures by approximately $114.84. The results indicate that we can be more than 98 percent confident that these TELs have a negative effect on state and local direct general expenditures.

Likewise, if a state passes a TEL that does not limit state expenditures to the inflation rate plus population growth but includes a refund provision, the regression equation predicts that the TEL will reduce per capita direct general expenditures by $39.80 annually.

Finally, the regression analysis suggests that other TELs that neither limit expenditures to inflation nor have immediate refund provisions appear ineffective at reducing state expenditures. Indeed, the model predicts that if a state passes a TEL that has neither of these two provisions, that state's per capita direct annual general expenditures will actually increase by $14.59. Overall, this analysis provides strong evidence that TELs can be effective tools for limiting the growth of state expenditures, but only if they are designed properly.

A Closer Look at Washington and Colorado

The two TELs passed by Washington State and Colorado that limit the growth of expenditures to the inflation rate have been especially effective at reducing per capita government expenditures. Colorado's TEL was passed in 1992 and took effect in FY94, and Washington's TEL was passed in 1993 and took effect in FY96. Taking a look at what worked well—and what didn't—is instructive.

Case Study: Colorado

In the past 25 years Colorado has enacted three separate TELs. In 1977 Colorado was one of the first states to adopt a general fund appropriations limit. The legislation limited increases in state appropriations to 7 percent over the previous year's general fund appropriations. Due to expire after FY83, the law was amended in 1979 and extended indefinitely. However, during the mid to late 1980s Colorado's economy suffered a downturn due to the collapse of the energy and construction industries, and revenues were consistently below the limit mandated by the TEL.

In 1991 the General Assembly of Colorado adopted another statutory general fund appropriations limit. This one reduced the existing limit by one percentage point, mandating that general fund expenditures could increase by no more than 6 percent. However, this legislation included generous exemptions for spending on education and federal mandates. Colorado's citizens became increasingly frustrated by what they believed to be government inefficiency and the perceived inequities in the state tax system. Many people became involved with a grassroots movement to reform state and local taxes. In 1986, 1988, and 1990 they succeeded in placing on the ballot initiatives that would limit taxes and spending. Those initiatives lost by narrower margins each time.

Finally, in 1992 the Taxpayer Bill of Rights (TABOR), also known as Amendment One, passed and added Article X, sec. 20, to the state constitution. TABOR has three primary components. First, all tax increases have to be approved by taxpayers. Second, it mandates that the existing TELs, passed in 1977 and 1991, cannot be weakened without taxpayer approval. Third, it includes the most stringent TEL of any state. TABOR limits growth in state spending and tax increases to inflation plus population growth. It mandates that any revenue collected over the limit be refunded to the taxpayers. It requires that the limit be adjusted when responsibility for government programs is transferred. Finally, the limit is constitutional, not statutory, which makes it difficult to amend.

This particular ballot initiative generated a firestorm of controversy. Gov. Roy Romer, a Democrat, sharply criticized the measure on numerous occasions. He said that defeating the measure was the "moral equivalent of fighting the Nazis at the Battle of the Bulge." He warned of an economic Armageddon with passage of TABOR and said that the Colorado border would soon have to be posted with signs reading "Colorado is closed for business." Public employee unions and the education lobby quickly lined up in opposition to TABOR. Even the *New York Times* criticized TABOR, calling it potentially the most radical change in any state government that year.

Others argued that TABOR was bad policy because the demands for state services, such as schools, prisons, and highways, seemed likely to increase faster than the rate of inflation. They also contended that Colorado needed to spend more on those services because, in previous years, Colorado's spending increases for education and highways had been considerably below the national average. Despite those warnings, TABOR passed with more than 53 percent of the vote in 1992 and took effect in FY94.

Since 1994 the legislature has had to rebate substantial amounts of tax revenues to stay underneath the limit. Colorado enacted taxpayer refunds of $139 million in 1997, $563 million in 1998, $679 million in 1999, and $941 million in 2000. In addition to its rebate provisions, TABOR forces both state and local government to obtain voter approval to raise taxes. Although many municipalities have sought and won voter approval to increase taxes, statewide initiatives have fared poorly. In every year from 1993 to 1999 a proposal to either increase taxes or circumvent TABOR was on the Colorado ballot. Those included a 1993 initiative to increase the sales tax, a 1997 gas tax increase, and a 1999 effort to use part of the surplus for road and school construction. Each of those statewide initiatives was defeated. However, in 2000 Colorado residents did approve Amendment 23, which increased state aid to public education and reduced the TABOR surplus for both 2000 and 2001.

Case Study: Washington State

During the last 20 years Washington State has passed two TELs by citizen initiative. The first one, Initiative 62, was passed in 1979 and limited increases in state revenues to the rate of growth in personal income. However, the state suffered a recession shortly after passage of the initiative, and it never became a serious constraint since the limit was higher than what the state could spend. In fact, in 1993 the legislature was able to pass a $1 billion tax increase to balance the FY94–95 budget and remain within the limit. However, that tax increase provoked a backlash and provided the impetus for putting another TEL, Initiative 601, on the ballot in 1993.

Initiative 601 imposed a limit that was stricter than the limit set by Initiative 62. Initiative 601 limited increases in state expenditures to the inflation rate. In addition, it stopped the legislature from circumventing the limit by devolving functions of state government to the localities. It explicitly prohibited the legislature to impose on local governments any responsibility for new programs unless the legislature fully reimbursed the local governments for the cost of the programs. Initiative 601 passed by 1 percent of the vote.

In 1994 the Washington legislature passed a supplemental budget to ensure that it was in compliance with the TEL that was scheduled to take effect in FY96. The legislature instituted some targeted budget cuts, mostly in administration, social services, and prisons, to save more than $120 million in the new biennium. The legislature increased spending for some items, such as highways and school construction, on the grounds that those were one-time-only expenses and would be off the budget in FY96. As a result, the budget base was not swollen from previous spending levels and would be easier to sustain in the new biennium.

Finally, some agencies were directed to begin planning for cuts. For instance, public colleges were directed to trim expenses by $39 million to help pay for faculty and staff pay raises. Because of those spending reductions, the budget was under the TEL's limit in FY96 and FY97. In subsequent years the state legislature took steps to reduce taxes when it appeared that the government was collecting high levels of revenue. In FY98 and FY99 the legislature instituted modest targeted tax cuts of $38.5 million and $19.7 million, respectively.

Since spending was being restrained, voters in the state of Washington desired more substantial tax relief. In 1998 Washington voters passed Initiative 695, which reduced the motor vehicle excise tax by $30 and saved taxpayers $256 million. In 1999 Washington residents voted to repeal the motor vehicle excise tax. That reduced the tax burden on Washington residents by an additional $1.1 billion over two years.

However, Washington's Initiative 601 was weaker than Colorado's Taxpayer Bill of Rights in one important respect. Initiative 601 was a statutory measure whereas TABOR is a constitutional amendment. That makes Initiative 601 easier to amend, and possibly weaken. Indeed, that is precisely what happened in the spring of 2000 when the Washington legislature wanted to pass a budget that would have exceeded the limit mandated by the TEL. The legislature succeeded in obtaining the necessary supermajority to suspend the TEL, and the governor signed the budget into law. The long-term effects on the budgetary practices of the state of Washington remain to be seen.

Conclusion

It is vital that state legislatures control their spending habits. The surpluses that are bound to appear again when the economy picks up steam will be a temptation to those who like big government. Strong spending restraints are very popular with voters in the states in which they have been tried. Legislators would be well advised to keep that in mind next time they risk alienating taxpayers by creating an expensive new government program.

Suggested Readings

Becsi, Zsolt. "Do State and Local Taxes Affect Relative State Growth?" Federal Reserve Bank of Atlanta *Economic Review,* March–April 1996.

Edwards, Chris, Stephen Moore, and Phil Kerpen. "States Face Fiscal Crunch after 1990s Spending Surge." Cato Institute Briefing Paper no. 80, February 12, 2003.

New, Michael. "Limiting Government through Direct Democracy: The Case of State Tax and Expenditure Limitations." Cato Institute Policy Analysis no. 420, December 13, 2001.

_____. "Proposition 13 and State Budget Limitations: Past Successes and Future Options." Cato Institute Briefing Paper no. 83, June 19, 2003.

Vedder, Richard. "The Effects of Taxes on Economic Growth: What the Research Tells Us." Texas Public Policy Foundation, March 29, 2002.

—Prepared by Michael New and Stephen Slivinski

36. Federal Highway Programs

Congress should

- eliminate the federal fuel tax,
- eliminate the Federal Highway Trust Fund,
- eliminate subsidies to mass transit programs, and
- devolve to the states full responsibility for highway construction and financing.

The federal system of financing major state roads was enacted in June 1956. The most recent reauthorization expired in September 2003. Looking at the history of the current system and the adverse incentives it breeds, it becomes obvious that Congress should extract the federal government from the highway business to the fullest extent possible. Ways to devolve highway programs to the states should be the focus of any congressional action on highway funding.

A Brief History of the Federal Highway System

The Highway Revenue Act of 1956 created the Federal Highway Trust Fund (FHTF) as a source of funding for highway construction, without the federal government having to borrow the money required. President Eisenhower signed the Federal Aid Highway Act of 1956 into law on June 29 of that year. It stated that, among other things,

- the program would fund the construction of a national 41,250-mile Interstate and Defense Highways System;
- $25 billion would be authorized to finance the 90 percent federal share of the cost;
- the system would be completed by fiscal year 1969;
- the powers of the federal government in the highway realm would expire in 1972; and

- disbursement to the states would be based on a formula taking into account factors such as the geographical area, the length of the road network, and the number of motor vehicles.

Instead of expiring, the powers of the 1956 act were renewed and changed several times after 1972. The length of the designated Interstate Highway System (IHS) was increased to 46,726 miles. Its construction was phased out in 1996, but federal financing of state roads was retained for a newly defined 155,000-mile National Highway System.

Since the inception of the FHTF, the composition of the taxes dedicated to it has changed, but the main sources of funds, accounting for about 85 percent of receipts, are the taxes on motor fuels. The federal gasoline tax was 3 cents a gallon in 1956 and 4 cents in 1959. It has since been raised to 18.4 cents a gallon—24.4 cents for diesel fuel.

The 1991 Intermodal Surface Transportation Efficiency Act (ISTEA), spearheaded by Sen. Daniel Patrick Moynihan and supported by environmental and transit advocacy groups, expanded the reach of the federal government in transportation affairs. It substituted "flexibility" and "intermodalism" for the exclusive "dedication" of revenues raised from road users to highways. That opened the door for all sorts of pork-barrel projects. The change of focus from highways exclusively to transportation generally indicated that, from then on, any political group could lay claim to federal highway money for any purpose related, loosely or otherwise, to transportation.

Unfortunately, the ability of Congress to play games with the so-called trust fund had been long-standing. The FHTF is not, and never was, a trust fund in any meaningful sense, and its custodians are under no obligation to spend its revenues for the benefit of road users. Legally, the FHTF is a separate account (with the name Highway Trust Fund) maintained in the U.S. Treasury, from which the Federal Highway Administration (FHA) can draw amounts determined annually by Congress. The FHA disburses those revenues to state governments for the federal share of expenditures previously made by the states. Congress is free to attach any conditions it wishes to the appropriation of FHTF revenues (such as, until recently, 55-mile-per-hour speed limits) and is also free to decline to appropriate them, so that they can accumulate to reduce the overall budget deficit.

Advantages of the Federal Highway Financing System

The main accomplishment of the 1956 financing arrangements was the completion, at a comparatively small cost to road users, of the 46,726-

mile Interstate Highway System, probably the greatest public works achievement since the fall of the Roman Empire. Those familiar with the difficulty of getting any government project achieved will be particularly appreciative of the success of the men and women involved in getting this magnificent road network completed.

It is not easy to discern other advantages to the federal financing of state roads now that this goal has been met, however. Some federal highway activities—research on safety issues, for example—could well be beneficial, but they do not involve the financing of infrastructure. In other words, the days when a federally financed construction project was the most cost-effective way of achieving the desired results are over.

Problems with the Federal Highway Financing System

There are several disadvantages to the current financing system, and keeping it in place will only perpetuate the adverse incentives inherent in the system.

Federal Financing Encourages Low-Priority and Unnecessary Projects

The states retain formal responsibility for their highways but do not have to meet more than a small percentage of the bills—for which federal contributions range from 75 to 90 percent. That allows states to break ground on less-vital projects and boondoggles at the expense of road users in other states. The federal funding of state roads tends to result in excessive demands for expensive facilities, because to the states—which are only nominally responsible for the funding—federal funds are virtually costless. States will naturally line up to receive this relatively "free" money. Thus, the system allows the construction of expensive projects, such as Boston's Central Artery/Tunnel project (popularly known as the "Big Dig") for which local funding would probably never have been considered. Initially estimated at $3.3 billion, the cost has ballooned to more than $14.6 billion. Speaker of the House "Tip" O'Neill, who represented a Boston district, led the push for the use of federal funds.

Fuel Taxes Can't Act as User Fees since They Are Used to Fund All Sorts of Nonhighway Spending

The large-scale diversion of money from the Federal Highway Trust Fund started in 1982 with the opening in the FHTF of the Mass Transit Account and was accelerated by the 1991 Intermodal Surface Transportation Efficiency Act. The expenditures authorized for the latest enacted highway bill—the 1998 Transportation Equity Act for the 21st Century (TEA-21)—offer an example of this diversion. Some of the items, such as "Interstate Maintenance Program," are for expenditures on roads; others, such as "Miscellaneous Studies," might or might not be for roads; while others, such as "Recreational Trails Program," are clearly not for roads.

Some of the items authorized for nonroad purposes are listed in Table 36.1, which shows, for each nonroad item, the total for six fiscal years— 1998 through 2003—and the percentage that each item takes of the total $218 billion TEA-21 program for the six years. The main diversions are as follows:

- *Transit (18.83 percent).* This diversion results from 2.86 cents per gallon of motor fuel being taken for the Mass Transit account of the FHTF. The funds are used to subsidize transit services that have so little appeal to passengers that users are not willing to pay even the operating costs. Passenger-mile costs for light rail average $1.20 and

Table 36.1
Nonroad Programs Authorized in TEA-21

Program	Total Authorized for Program ($ millions)	Total Authorized for Program as a Percentage of the Total for TEA-21 (%)
One-tenth of Surface Transportation Program	3,333	1.53
Congestion Mitigation/Air Quality Improvement	8,123	3.73
Recreational Trails Program	270	0.12
National Scenic Byways Program	148	0.07
Puerto Rico Highway Program	660	0.30
MAGLEV Transportation Technology Deployment Program	60	0.03
MAGLEV Transportation Technology Deployment Program (subject to appropriation)	950	0.44
Federal Transit Administration Programs	41,000	18.83
Total	54,544	25.05

SOURCE: TEA-21 Authorization Table, http://www.fhwa.dot.gov/tea21/sumauth.htm.

for bus transit $0.75—both well in excess of the cost of travel by car, which averages $0.34 per vehicle-mile. Transit use is concentrated in a few places—74 percent of the ridership in 2000 took place in seven metropolitan areas: Boston, Chicago, Los Angeles, New York, Philadelphia, San Francisco, and Washington, D.C. It is by no means clear why farmers in Kansas should subsidize local travel in Los Angeles.

- *Congestion Mitigation and Air Quality (CMAQ) provisions (3.73 percent).* The CMAQ program is intended to assist states in improving the quality of their air. These funds are not used to finance road improvement, despite the fact that studies have shown that an increase in road capacity can actually reduce congestion and improve air quality.
- *Surface Transportation Program (1.53 percent).* Since 1991 one-tenth of the Surface Transportation Program has had to be spent on nonroad "enhancements," such as bicycle and pedestrian facilities, historic preservation, and scenic easements.

The other items marked as "nonroad" need no explanation, except perhaps the $660 million for the Puerto Rico Highway Program. These funds are definitely for roads, but not for roads traveled by those who pay into the FHTF, as Puerto Rico road users do not pay into the fund.

The total of all the "nonroad" items comes to at least 25 percent—in other words, at least a quarter of every fuel tax dollar goes to something other than highways.

Federal Financing Inflates Road Costs

Federal financing inflates road costs in three ways:

- States are required to adopt labor regulations, such as the Davis-Bacon rules and "Buy America" provisions, both of which can raise highway costs substantially. Davis-Bacon rules, by themselves, can increase project costs by 30 percent or more.
- Federal specifications for road construction can be higher, and therefore more expensive, than state standards.
- There are significant administrative costs in sending monies from the states to the federal government and back again. Published data indicate that, in FY02, administrative costs attributable to federal involvement, at both federal and state levels, were of the order of 5 percent of road costs.

Ralph Stanley, the entrepreneur who conceived and launched the Dulles Greenway—a 14-mile privately financed toll road from Dulles airport to Leesburg in Northern Virginia—estimated that federal involvement increased project costs by 20 percent. Robert Farris, who was commissioner of the Tennessee Department of Transportation (1981–85) and federal highway administrator (1987–89), has suggested similar estimates.

Federal Financing Misallocates Funds between States

A major inequity is that some states persistently get more from the FHTF than they pay into it. The distribution of benefits in these transportation programs probably has more to do with political clout of particular senators and representatives than it does with transportation needs.

Table 36.2 lists the share of money taken from the FHTF as a ratio of what money the state paid into the fund. Notice that there is a tendency for southern states to subsidize those in the northeast. Since 1982 this has been exacerbated by the diversion of payments by road users to mass-transit systems, many of which are in the northeast.

The numbers in Table 36.2 do not take into account the diversions from the FHTF, namely the 25 percent paid out to nonroad uses, the administrative costs, and the increased costs in each state due to federal standards and regulations. If these were taken into account, road users in almost all states would be paying more than they gain from the current system of federal highway financing.

Federal Financing Allows Politicians to Buy Votes with Pork and "Earmarks"

In 1982 the usual practice of not appropriating taxpayer money for specific roads was broken by the funding of 10 "demonstration projects" costing $362 million. "Demonstration projects" subsequently grew to 1,850 in the 1998 reauthorization bill, costing taxpayers a total of $9.3 billion. These pork projects are also known as "Congressionally mandated special projects," "High Priority Projects," and, more recently, simply "earmarks." Their growth can be seen in Table 36.3.

Traditionally, earmarks were used to help members of Congress get reelected, but during the 2003–04 deliberations on reauthorization, they were also used to get the bill passed. Members were offered $14 million worth of earmarks if they supported the bill. Members of the Transportation and Infrastructure Committee got, on average, $40 million each. The ranking minority member got $90 million, and the chairman more than

Table 36.2
Highway Trust Fund Return Ratio (per dollar contributed)

State	2003 Ratio	State	2003 Ratio
Alaska	5.17	Nebraska	1.00
D.C.	3.31	Washington	1.00
Rhode Island	2.38	Nevada	0.98
South Dakota	2.14	Massachusetts	0.96
Montana	2.11	Kentucky	0.95
North Dakota	2.11	Missouri	0.95
West Virginia	1.90	Maine	0.94
Vermont	1.81	Mississippi	0.94
Hawaii	1.74	Illinois	0.93
Delaware	1.57	Louisiana	0.93
Wyoming	1.47	New Jersey	0.92
Connecticut	1.39	Oklahoma	0.89
Idaho	1.38	Utah	0.89
New York	1.32	Colorado	0.88
Wisconsin	1.21	South Carolina	0.88
Virginia	1.20	Michigan	0.87
Maryland	1.16	North Carolina	0.87
Kansas	1.15	Ohio	0.87
Pennsylvania	1.15	Tennessee	0.87
Arkansas	1.11	California	0.86
New Mexico	1.10	Texas	0.86
Iowa	1.05	Florida	0.84
New Hampshire	1.05	Georgia	0.84
Alabama	1.03	Arizona	0.81
Minnesota	1.02	Indiana	0.81
Oregon	1.02		

SOURCE: Federal Highway Administration.

$440 million for his home state of Alaska. The house speaker ($160 million) and minority leader ($120 million) were not forgotten. Only South Dakota got nothing—possibly because its representative was in jail and not available to claim its share.

The list of House earmarks includes

- $125 million for a bridge to link Ketchikan, Alaska, to a sparsely inhabited island;
- $1.5 million for the Henry Ford Museum in Dearborn, Michigan;

Table 36.3
Growth of "Earmarks" Since Fiscal Year 1982

Year	Number of Earmarks	Total Appropriated ($ millions)
1982	10	362
1987	152	1,400
1991	538	6,230
1998	1,850	9,360
2004	3,248*	10,600*

SOURCE: Authors' calculations.
*Preliminary estimates

- $593,175 for a sidewalk revitalization project in Eastman, Georgia;
- $5 million for a parking garage in Bozeman, Montana;
- $500,000 to provide transportation infrastructure for visitors to James-town Island;
- $3.2 million for a pedestrian walkway at Coney Island;
- $4 million for transit improvements at Eastlake Stadium, a stadium for a minor-league baseball team;
- $10 million to construct a new interchange on I-85 between the Greenville Spartanburg Airport and the SC Highway 101 interchanges; and
- $5 million for Home Furnishing Market for terminals and parking in High Point, North Carolina.

Getting the Feds Out of Highway Finance

Congress needs to devolve to the states the responsibility for construction and maintenance of highways. There is no sense in making states send fuel tax money all the way to Washington just to have a few cents on each dollar shaved off in administrative expenses before it is sent back to the states. Devolution would also remedy the inequity of the current system under which politically influential representatives and senators are able to extract a larger amount for their constituents.

There have been various plans to end the federal role in the highway system. The idea—called a "turnback" proposal—was floated during the days of the Reagan administration and ended up being promoted in the 1990s by Rep. John Kasich of Ohio and Sen. Connie Mack of Florida.

The current version of this idea is in a bill sponsored by Rep. Jeff Flake of Arizona. A turnback proposal could include the following elements:

- elimination of the federal fuel tax,
- elimination of the Highway Trust Fund, and
- devolution to the states responsibility for funding the maintenance and construction of their highway systems.

If enacted, those proposals would enable each state to finance its roads in accordance with the wishes of its voters. Some might follow the example of Oregon and develop road-financing methods that do not rely on the taxation of fuel. Some might wish to retain political control of their roads, and others might prefer to commercialize them. New approaches to highway funding could be tested.

States fully responsible for their own roads would have stronger incentives to ensure that funds paid by road users were spent efficiently. For example, in the absence of federal grants for new construction, some states might prefer to better manage and maintain their existing roads, rather than build new ones. Others might find ways to encourage the private sector to assume more of the burden of road provision (e.g., by contracting with private firms to maintain their roads to designated standards or to provide new roads). Some states might stop discriminating against privately provided roads, most of which are currently ineligible to receive funding from the Federal Highway Trust Fund, although their users pay the required federal taxes. New arrangements would be noticed by other states, and those that brought improvements could be copied, while failed reforms would be avoided. In time, road users would get better value for their money, and some would even get the road services for which they were prepared to pay.

Congress should reassert its commitment to federalist principles by getting out of the highway business once and for all.

Suggested Readings

Roth, Gabriel. "A Road Policy for the Future." *Regulation*, Spring 2003.

———. ed. *Paving the Way: Competitive Markets for Roads*. San Francisco: Independent Institute, forthcoming.

Utt, Ronald D. "Reauthorization of TEA-21: A Primer on Reforming the Federal Highway and Transit Programs." Heritage Foundation Backgrounder no. 1643, April 2003.

VanDoren, Peter. "Let the Market Free Up Transportation in the U.S." *The Hill*, May 19, 2003.

—Prepared by Gabriel Roth and Stephen Slivinski

REGULATION

37. Health and Safety

> **Congress should**
> - eliminate goals of zero risk in statutes governing occupational and environmental health and
> - establish the purpose of safety and health agencies as the identification of opportunities to improve safety and health at costs that are much less than the market value of the benefits.

Before the 1970s, the health and safety regulations that we now take for granted were completely absent from the American economy, with the exception of selected regulations for food safety and prescription drugs. The rise of the consumer movement and environmental concerns led to the establishment of the National Highway Traffic Safety Administration in 1966, the Occupational Safety and Health Administration in 1970, the Environmental Protection Agency in 1970, the Consumer Product Safety Commission in 1972, and the Nuclear Regulatory Commission in 1974.

Scholarly assessment of the three decades of experience with regulation and government oversight concludes that health and safety regulations have largely failed to fulfill their initial promise, but many of the initial promises were infeasible goals. There continue to be major opportunities to improve regulatory performance by targeting existing inefficiencies and using market mechanisms (rather than strict command-and-control mechanisms) to achieve regulatory goals.

Why Should the Government Regulate Risk?

Government action in the health and safety arena can be justified when there are shortcomings in risk information. The goal of regulatory agencies that address health and safety risks should be to isolate instances in which misinformation about health risks prevents people from making optimal tradeoffs and to isolate instances in which health risks are not internalized in market decisions.

The existence of a health risk does not necessarily imply the need for regulatory action. For example, as long as workers understand the risks they face in various occupations, they will receive wage compensation through normal market forces sufficient to make them willing to bear the risk; the health risk is internalized into the market decision.

In situations in which the risks are not known to workers, as in the case of dimly understood health hazards or situations in which the labor market is not competitive, market forces might not operative effectively to internalize the risk. Those cases provide an opportunity for constructive, cost-effective government intervention, although, in practice, such intervention may be worse than nothing.

Zero vs. Optimal Risk

Unfortunately, the rationale of correcting market failures has never been a major motivation of regulatory intervention. The simple fact that risks exist has provided the impetus for the legislative mandates of the health and safety regulatory agencies. To this day, very few regulatory impact analyses explore in any meaningful way the role of potential market failure in the particular context and the constructive role that market forces may already play in that context.

The conventional regulatory approach to health and safety risks is to seek a technological solution either through capital investments in the workplace, changes in the safety devices in products, or similar kinds of requirements that do not entail any additional care on the part of the individual. Stated simply, the conventional view is that the existence of risks is undesirable and, with appropriate technological interventions, we can eliminate those risks. That perspective does not recognize the cost tradeoffs involved; the fact that a no-risk society would be so costly as to make it infeasible does not arise as a policy concern of consequence.

The economic approach to regulating risk is quite different. The potential role of the government is not to eliminate risk but rather to address market failures that lead to an inefficient balance between risk reduction and cost. A necessary but not sufficient argument for government regulation arises when regulation can generate benefits to society that are worth more than the costs that are incurred and can address the market failures using a cost-effective approach. To achieve those goals, the focus should not simply be on rigid technological standards but on flexible regulatory mechanisms that meet the performance goals. Even in cases in which intervention clears such hurdles, however, it still may fail because it is implemented by political institutions.

How Should Risks Be Evaluated?

Because government policies, at best, reduce risks of death rather than eliminate certain death for identified individuals, the correct benefit value is society's willingness to pay for the reduction in risk. For example, if a regulation would reduce risk by 1 in 1 million to everyone in a population of 1 million, then the regulation would save 1 statistical life. If the average willingness to pay for that risk reduction is $6 per person, then the value of a statistical life is $6 million.

Using detailed data on wages and prices, economists have estimated people's tradeoffs between money and fatality risk, thus establishing a value of statistical lives based on market decisions. For workers in jobs of average risk, the estimates imply that, in current dollars, workers receive premiums in the range of $600 to face an additional annual work-related fatality risk of 1 chance in 10,000. Put somewhat differently, if there were 10,000 such workers facing an annual fatality chance of 1 in 10,000, there would be 1 statistical death. In return for that risk, workers would receive total additional wage compensation of $6 million. The compensation establishes the value of a statistical life, based on workers' own attitude toward risks.

The estimates suggest that in situations in which there is an awareness of the risk, market forces are enormously powerful and create tremendous safety incentives. Thus, we are not operating in a world in which there are no constraints other than regulatory intervention to promote safety. Powerful market forces already create incentives for safety that should not be overridden by intrusive regulations.

Assessing Regulatory Performance

Although many agencies use reasonable measures of the value of a statistical life for the purposes of assessing benefits, the cost per life saved for the regulations actually promulgated often far exceeds the estimated benefits. The restrictive nature of agencies' legislative mandates often precludes consideration of costs in the regulatory decision.

Table 37.1 lists various health and safety regulations and their estimated cost per life saved. The table also lists the cost per normalized life saved

Table 37.1
A Sample of U.S. Health and Safety Regulations and Their Cost per Life Saved

Regulation	Year	Agency	Cost per Life Saved (millions of 1990 $)	Cost per Normalized Life Saved (millions of 1995 $)
Unvented space heater ban	1980	CPSC	0.1	0.1
Aircraft cabin fire protection standard	1985	FAA	0.1	0.1
Seatbelt/air bag	1984	NHTSA	0.1	0.1
Steering column protection standard	1967	NHTSA	0.1	0.1
Underground construction standards	1989	OSHA	0.1	0.1
Trihalomethane in drinking water	1979	EPA	0.2	0.6
Aircraft seat cushion flammability	1984	FAA	0.5	0.6
Alcohol and drug controls	1985	FRA	0.5	0.6
Auto fuel system integrity	1975	NHTSA	0.5	0.5
Auto wheel rim servicing	1984	OSHA	0.5	0.6
Aircraft floor emergency lighting	1984	FAA	0.7	0.9
Concrete and masonry construction	1988	OSHA	0.7	0.9
Crane suspended personnel platform	1988	OSHA	0.8	1.0
Passive restraints for trucks and buses	1989	NHTSA	0.8	0.8
Auto side-impact standards	1990	NHTSA	1.0	1.0
Children's sleepwear flammability ban	1973	CPSA	1.0	1.2
Auto side-door supports	1970	NHTSA	1.0	1.0
Low-altitude windshear equipment	1988	FAA	1.6	1.9
Metal mine electrical equipment standards	1970	MSHA	1.7	2.0
Trenching and excavation standards	1989	OSHA	1.8	2.2
Traffic alert/collision avoidance systems	1988	FAA	1.8	2.2
Hazard communication standard	1983	OSHA	1.9	4.8

Regulation	Year	Agency	Cost per Life Saved (millions of 1990 $)	Cost per Normalized Life Saved (millions of 1995 $)
Truck, bus, and MPV side-impact standard	1989	NHTSA	2.6	2.6
Grain dust explosion prevention standards	1987	OSHA	3.3	4.0
Rear lap/shoulder belts for cars	1989	NHTSA	3.8	3.8
Stds for radionuclides in uranium mines	1984	EPA	4.1	10.1
Benzene NESHAP (original)	1984	EPA	4.1	10.1
Ethylene dibromide in drinking water	1991	EPA	6.8	17.0
Benzene NESHAP (revised)	1988	EPA	7.3	18.1
Asbestos occupational exposure limit	1972	OSHA	9.9	24.7
Benzene occupational exposure limit	1987	OSHA	10.6	26.5
Electrical equipment in coal mines	1970	OSHA	11.0	13.3
Arsenic emissions from glass plants	1986	MSHA	16.1	40.2
Ethylene oxide occupational exposure limit	1984	EPA	24.4	61.0
Arsenic/copper NESHAP	1986	EPA	27.4	68.4
Petroleum sludge hazardous waste listing	1990	EPA	32.9	82.1
Cover/move uranium mill tailings (inactive)	1983	EPA	37.7	94.3
Benzene NESHAP (revised)	1990	EPA	39.2	97.9
Cover/move uranium mill tailings (active)	1983	EPA	53.6	133.8
Acrylonitrile occupational exposure limit	1978	OSHA	61.3	153.2
Coke ovens occupational exposure limit	1976	OSHA	75.6	188.9
Lockout/tagout	1989	OSHA	84.4	102.4
Arsenic occupational exposure limit	1978	OSHA	127.3	317.9
Asbestos ban	1989	EPA	131.8	329.2
Diethylstilbestrol cattle feed ban	1979	FDA	148.6	371.2

(continued)

Table 37.1
(continued)

Regulation	Year	Agency	Cost per Life Saved (millions of 1990 $)	Cost per Normalized Life Saved (millions of 1995 $)
Benzene NESHAP (revised)	1990	EPA	200.2	500.2
1,2-Dichloropropane in drinking water	1991	EPA	777.4	1,942.1
Hazardous waste land disposal ban	1988	EPA	4,988.7	12,462.7
Municipal solid waste landfills	1988	EPA	22,746.8	56,826.1
Formaldehyde occupational exposure limit	1987	OSHA	102,608.5	256,372.7
Atrazine/alachlor in drinking water	1991	EPA	109,608.5	273,824.4
Wood preservatives hazardous waste listing	1990	EPA	6,785,822.0	16,952,364.9

SOURCE: W. Kip Viscusi, Jahn K. Hakes, and Alan Carlin, "Measures of Mortality Risks," *Journal of Risk and Uncertainty* 14 (1997): 213–33.

(in 1995 dollars), which accounts for the duration of life lost and the existence of discounting of future lives. Because the legislative mandate varies across regulations, one sees great variance in the cost per life saved. Indeed, the cost varies even within certain regulatory agencies. For example, EPA's regulation of trihalomethane in drinking water has an estimated cost per normalized life saved of $600,000, whereas the regulation of Atrazine/alachlor in drinking water has an estimated cost per normalized life saved of $274 billion. A regulatory system based on sound economic principles would reallocate resources from the high- to the low-cost regulations. That would result in more lives saved at the same cost to society (or, equivalently, shifting resources could result in the same number of lives saved at lower cost to society).

The focus of policy debates should not be on whether regulations that cost $7 million per life saved or $12 million per life saved are desirable. Rather, policy debates should emphasize the enormous opportunity costs associated with regulations that cost hundreds of millions of dollars or even billions of dollars per statistical life saved.

Effect of Regulation on Accident Rates

What has been the overall effect of health and safety regulations since the early 1970s? One yardstick of performance is to see whether accident rates have declined. Figure 37.1 summarizes fatality rates of various kinds, including motor vehicle accidents, work accidents, home accidents, public non-motor-vehicle accidents, and an aggregative category of all accidents.

Since the 1970s, accidents of all kinds have declined. Improvements in safety over time typically lead to annual press releases on the part of the regulatory agencies in which they take credit for the improvements and attribute the gains to their regulatory efforts. There are exceptions, as there are some years in which accident rates increase—and regulatory officials typically blame cyclical factors for such trends.

Figure 37.1
Accidental Death Rates

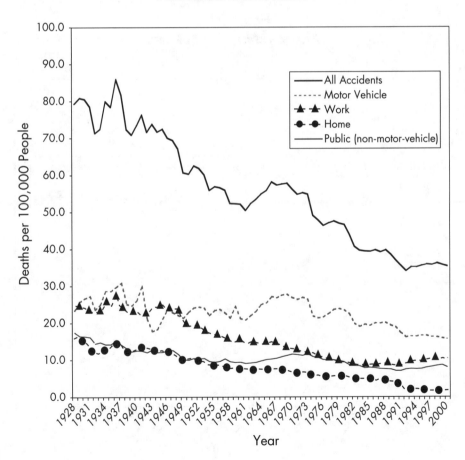

The basic message of Figure 37.1 is that accident rates have been declining throughout the past 100 years. The improvement in our safety is not a new phenomenon that began with the advent of regulatory agencies commissioned to protect the citizenry. There is, for example, no significant downward shift in Figure 37.1's trend for job fatality risk after the establishment of OSHA.

Perhaps the main exception has been motor vehicle accidents, but assessments of annual death rates associated with motor vehicles are complicated by the fact that many more people drive than did in previous years, and there have been considerable changes in the amount of driving, traffic congestion, and highway design.

Figure 37.2 provides an explanation of motor vehicle accident rates that attempts to adjust to some of the aspects of driving intensity rather than simply tally the motor vehicle fatality rate per person. As can be

Figure 37.2
Motor Vehicle Death Rates

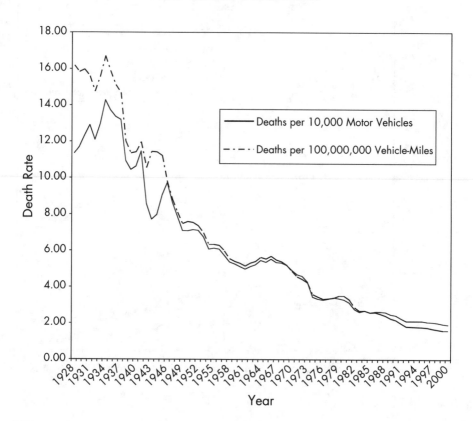

seen from the figure, deaths per 10,000 motor vehicles as well as deaths per 100 million vehicle-miles each have declined steadily throughout the last 100 years. As in the case of the other accident statistics, there is no evidence of a sharp, discontinuous break in the downward trend's occurring with the advent of regulatory policies.

Although regulation may play a beneficial safety-enhancing role, the steady decrease in risk throughout the century supports the hypothesis that improvements in societal wealth have greatly increased our demand for safety over time. Coupling that wealth with technological improvements— many of which have been stimulated by the greater demand for safety— has led to dramatic improvements in our individual well-being. Market forces rather than regulatory policy have likely been the most important contributor to safety improvements since early last century.

Reform Agenda

Almost from its inception, health and safety regulation has been the target of proposed reform. Some policy improvements have occurred, such as elimination of some of the nitpicking of safety standards, the increased use of informational approaches to regulation, and enhanced enforcement efforts. However, health and safety regulations have fallen short of any reasonable standard of performance.

The underlying difficulty can be traced to the legislative mandates of the regulatory agencies. Instead of focusing regulations on instances of market failure, the emphasis is on reductions of risk irrespective of cost. The regulatory approach has also been characterized by an overly narrow conceptualization of the potential modes of intervention. The emphasis has been on command-and-control regulations rather than performance-oriented standards. More generally, various forms of injury taxes that would parallel the financial incentives created by workers' compensation or various environmental tradable permits programs could establish incentives for safety while at the same time offering firms leeway to select the most cost-effective means of risk reduction. A glaring omission from the regulatory strategy has been adequate attention devoted to the role of consumer and worker behavior and the potential for exploiting the benefits that can derive from promoting safety-enhancing actions by individuals rather than relying simply on technological controls.

Defenders of the current regulatory approach have long seized the moral high ground by claiming that their uncompromising efforts protect individual health; less consequential concerns such as cost should not

373

interfere with that higher enterprise. The fallacy of such thinking is that high-cost, low-benefit safety regulations divert society's resources from a mix of expenditures that would be more health enhancing than the allocations dictated by the health and safety regulations. Agencies that make an unbounded financial commitment to safety frequently are sacrificing individual lives in their symbolic quest for a zero-risk society. It is unlikely that this situation will be remedied in the absence of fundamental legislative reform.

Suggested Readings

Adams, John. "Cars, Cholera, and Cows: The Management of Risk and Uncertainty." Cato Institute Policy Analysis no. 335, March 4, 1999.

Hahn, Robert W., and Jason K. Burnett. "A Costly Benefit." *Regulation* 24, no. 3 (2001).

Kniesner, Thomas J., and John D. Leeth. "Abolishing OSHA." *Regulation* 18, no. 4 (1995).

Miller, Henry I., and Peter VanDoren. "Food Risks and Labeling Controversies." *Regulation* 23, no. 1 (2000).

Niskanen, William A. "Arsenic and Old Facts." *Regulation* 24, no. 3 (2001).

Scalia, Eugene. "OSHA's Ergonomics Litigation Record: Three Strikes and It's Out." Cato Institute Policy Analysis no. 370, May15, 2000.

Viscusi, W. Kip, and Ted Gayer. "Safety at Any Price?" *Regulation* 25, no. 3 (2002).

Wilson, Richard. "Regulating Environmental Hazards." *Regulation* 23, no. 1 (2000).

———. "Underestimating Arsenic's Risk." *Regulation* 24, no. 3 (2001).

—Prepared by Peter Van Doren

38. Transportation

Policymakers should

- end all federal transportation subsidies,
- repeal the Railway Labor Act of 1926 and the Railroad Retirement Act of 1934,
- privatize Amtrak,
- privatize the air traffic control system,
- eliminate all federal regulations that prevent airports from being privately owned or operated,
- repeal laws that prevent foreign airlines from flying domestic routes in the United States, and
- repeal the Jones Act.

Historically, the federal government regulated the U.S. transportation system with a heavy hand. Beginning in the 1950s, a series of academic studies showed that regulation protected incumbent firms rather than the public. The result was higher prices and poorer service.

Deregulation of the Airlines

Congress passed the Airline Deregulation Act in October 1978. This legislation eliminated federal control over routes by December 1981 and over fares by January 1983. The Civil Aeronautics Board, which directed much of federal regulation of air transportation, was abolished at the end of 1984. The new law authorized airlines to abandon routes but established an Essential Service Air Program to provide subsidies for service to small communities.

The effect of this legislation on the market value of the various airlines has been remarkable. Southwest has gone from virtually "zero" to a market capitalization of around $12 billion. On the other hand, United went from a market value in real terms of $2 billion to bankruptcy at the end of 2001.

The percentage of passengers traveling on discount fares has increased dramatically. In 1976, on long flights, only 27 percent of those flying in coach between major metropolitan areas managed to get a discount ticket; by 1983, 73 percent were getting special fares. Virtually all passengers today, except for a handful of business travelers, are paying less than the full coach fare. From 1977 to 2003, after adjusting for inflation, airfares fell some 53 percent. Figure 38.1 shows how the average fare has declined since the early 1970s. The Federal Trade Commission estimated in 1988 that, after adjusting for fuel costs, the flying public was paying 25 percent less because of deregulation. Steven Morrison, professor of economics at Northeastern University, calculated that deregulation produced a net benefit, in 2001 dollars, of about $15 billion, most of which was in the form of lower prices for consumers.

Lower fares have boosted load factors—from 49 percent in 1976 to 75 percent in the first half of 2004—which means that travelers are finding planes and airports far more crowded. Higher load factors, however, make

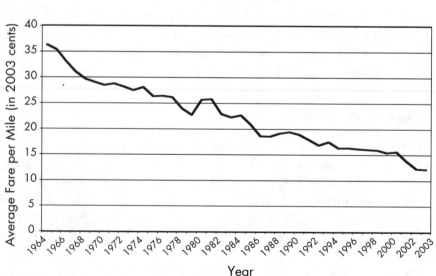

Figure 38.1
Airline Fares, 1964–2003

SOURCE: Air Transport Association, *Annual Passenger Prices (Yield)*, http://www.airlines.org/econ/print. aspx?nid = 1035.

it possible for the airlines to make money at lower prices. Over the quarter of a century since deregulation, the number of passengers flying has roughly doubled while passenger-miles have nearly tripled, proving the success of deregulation.

Deregulation of Air Freight

While passenger airlines were receiving greater authority to compete, Federal Express was lobbying to open up freight air traffic. The Civil Aeronautics Board had granted it only a commuter license that limited FedEx to small aircraft, restricting its ability to compete. It wanted authorization to fly large aircraft to and from any state or city in the country. In 1976 the CAB recommended that air freight transportation be largely deregulated. With support for less federal control from other freight carriers and no visible opposition, President Jimmy Carter, in November 1977, signed H.R. 6010, which deregulated air freight transportation.

Although little attention has been paid to the abolition of air freight regulation, it has been hugely successful. Prior to deregulation, air freight had been growing around 11 percent per year. In the first year of decontrol, 1978, revenue ton-miles jumped by 26 percent. That early success helped build support for exempting passenger transportation from control.

Deregulation of Rail Freight

In the fall of 1980 Congress passed the Staggers Act to provide additional pricing and route abandonment freedoms to the railroad industry. The Staggers Act gave railroads the ability to set prices within wide limits. Rail lines could enter into contracts with shippers to carry goods at agreed-upon rates. Tariffs could not be considered unreasonable, even for "captive" shippers, unless they exceeded 180 percent of variable costs. To qualify as "captive," shippers also had to prove that there was no effective competition, a provision designed to protect coal, chemical, and other bulk commodity shippers. Railroads were also given new authority to abandon routes.

The Interstate Commerce Commission was abolished and the Surface Transportation Board established on January 1, 1996, as an independent body housed within the U.S. Department of Transportation, with jurisdiction over certain surface transportation economic regulatory matters. Its authority is largely confined to railroad pricing and merger issues. This act also effectively deregulated intrastate controls on motor carriers, which had been blocking a fully competitive trucking industry.

The Staggers Act was highly beneficial for carriers as well as for shippers. The rail industry withstood well the sharp recession of 1981–82 and enjoyed record profit levels in 1983, notwithstanding a sharp drop in revenue per ton-mile. By 1988 railroad rates had fallen from 4.2 cents per ton-mile in the 1970s to 2.6 cents. After 1984 rail rates continued to fall, declining over the following 15 years by 45 percent. Competition and the Staggers Act have been a great success.

Deregulation of Trucking

Deregulation of the trucking industry, completed only in the 1990s, resulted in lower rates and better service to shippers. It also resulted in lower wages for truck drivers as the Teamsters Union lost power. The price of trucking licenses, which had been as much as millions of dollars, declined significantly to a few thousand dollars as the ICC made new licensing relatively simple and easy. Even though bankruptcies increased, the number of licensed trucking firms increased sharply in the first few years of deregulation.

Standard & Poor's found that the cost of shipping by truck had fallen by $40 billion from the era of regulation to 1988. Improved flexibility enabled business to operate on the basis of "just-in-time delivery," thus reducing inventory costs. The Department of Transportation calculated that the outlays necessary to maintain inventories had plummeted in today's dollars by more than $100 billion.

Further Reform

Although great progress has been made in reducing regulation of transportation, further steps would improve the U.S. system. Currently, the motor carrier industry is subject to no economic controls; consequently there need be no change in policy.

Railroads are still subject to some price controls, limits on abandonment, and control over mergers. Rail passenger service, particularly Amtrak, has been a problem ever since it was established in the 1970s.

Government limits on air passenger transportation continue through cabatoge restrictions, federal administration of air traffic controllers, and government ownership of airports. Finally, as a result of the September

11, 2001, attacks, security considerations have burgeoned, making air travel more time-consuming and perhaps safer.

Water transportation regulation and subsidies have not been a part of the regulatory reforms of the last 25 years and remain stubbornly resistant to change.

Rail Freight

Today, the rail industry remains the most closely supervised mode of transport with limits on abandonment; mergers; labor usage; ownership of other modes; and even, in certain situations, pricing. The Surface Transportation Board oversees the rail industry and administers the Staggers Act, under which the board must ensure that rates charged to "captive shippers" are fair.

Under federal law, the STB can exempt railroad traffic from rate regulation whenever it finds such control unnecessary to protect shippers from monopoly power or wherever the service is limited. Congress has legalized individual contracts between shippers and rail carriers, allowing competitive pricing. The Staggers Act authorizes railroads to price their services freely, unless a railroad possesses "market dominance." Congress continues a prohibition on intermodal ownership and requires the maintenance of labor protection.

All rail mergers, for example, require STB approval; once given the green light, however, those mergers are relieved from challenge under the antitrust laws or under state and local legal barriers. Railroads face a stringent review by the STB that, in addition to general antitrust considerations, includes the effect on other carriers, the fixed charges that would arise, and the effect on employees. In particular, the board must provide protection in any consolidation for employees who might be adversely affected. That provision is very popular with rail labor unions; the industry views it as employment protection, which makes achieving significant savings from mergers difficult.

Under current law, railroads must seek STB permission to abandon lines, build new track, or sell any service. Because users and other interested parties employ the law to slow or even block change, which adds to costs, those rules should be repealed.

Federal law also enjoins the STB to regulate rates charged "captive shippers"—those that can ship by only one line and enjoy no satisfactory alternative. Coal and grain companies have exploited this provision to gain lower rates. The markets for coal and grain are highly competitive,

379

so the producers cannot sell their output at more than the market price. Consequently, a railroad that drives shipping costs up to the point where the cost of producing the coal or grain and then moving it exceeds the competitive price will find that it has no traffic. In other words, although the railroad has no direct competition, it, too, is constrained by the market.

If a coal company enjoys significantly lower costs because of a favorable location or a rich and easily exploited mine, it could reap higher profits than less favorably sited enterprises. However, if the mine has only one option for shipping its product, that is, a single railroad, the rail carrier will be able to secure much of that above-normal profit. In that case, the stockholders of the railroad will gain at the expense of the stockholders of the mining corporation. There exists no rationale for the government to intervene by favoring one company over another. The captive shipper clause must go.

Congress should also repeal the ban on railroads' owning trucking companies or certain water carriers. Federal regulations proscribe railroad ownership of trucking firms, although the STB and the ICC, in earlier decades, have granted many exceptions. From the time of building the Panama Canal, the Interstate Commerce Act has prohibited railroad possession of water carriers that ply that waterway. Early in the 20th century, the public believed that those huge companies needed the competition of water carriers to keep down transcontinental rates. Like the prohibition on ownership of water carriers, the ban on owning trucking firms stems from the unwarranted fear of railroad power. With the plethora of options available to shippers today, such rules are totally unnecessary. The restrictions simply limit the ability of railroads, trucking firms, and water carriers to offer the most efficient multimodal services.

The Staggers Act authorized railroads to negotiate contracts with shippers but only with government approval. In addition, all rates must be filed with the STB, and tariffs that are either "too high" or "too low" can be disallowed. Congress should repeal these vestigial regulatory powers. At best, they add to paperwork and to the cost of operation; at worst, they slow innovation and reduce competition.

Amtrak

Over 33 years, Amtrak has spent some $34 billion in an effort to turn itself into a self-sustaining enterprise.

Congress should face the facts: passenger rail transportation cannot be made profitable, except in a few corridors, such as between Washington and New York and perhaps Boston. That portion of the system can probably cover its operating costs but most likely will be unable to cover its capital costs. With a few minor exceptions, passenger rail is not profitable anywhere in the world; there is no reason to believe it can be made profitable here. The appropriate policy would be to auction off the assets of the current system, favoring investors who would attempt to continue some passenger service. It seems likely that the East Coast corridor between Washington and points north would survive, albeit with a lower paid workforce. If all union contracts and employees are kept, the system can survive only with taxpayers' funds.

Air Travel

Although airline deregulation has been a great success, the industry has been plagued with crowding; delays; and, on some routes, dominance of a single carrier. The causes lie in the failure to deregulate other essential features of the industry. The air traffic control system, in particular, remains a ward of the FAA. Government entities own virtually all airports. The federalization of airport security has added more government bureaucracy with no clear effect on security.

Air Traffic Control. The FAA runs the current air traffic control (ATC) system. Because the FAA is a government agency, annual congressional appropriations control its finances. Its rules follow normal bureaucratic practices with congressional committees looking over its actions. Moreover, the FAA must regulate itself—a major conflict of interest.

As a government agency, the FAA has been unable to bring on line quickly new technologies that would improve safety and reduce delays. While computer technology changes every year or two, the FAA's procurement processes require five to seven years to complete. It still has 1960-era mainframe computers, equipment that depends on vacuum tubes, and obsolete radars. As a consequence, equipment breaks down frequently and planes must be spaced farther apart than would be necessary with state-of-the-art computers and radars.

Congress has held numerous hearings and put great pressure on the FAA to modernize, but it has been unable to improve matters significantly. To create and maintain a modern system, air traffic control must be separated from the FAA. The Clinton administration recommended a government corporation to run the ATC system; but another government corporation, such as the post office or Amtrak, although it would probably be an improvement over the current arrangement, is not the solution.

A number of other countries—Canada, the Czech Republic, Germany, Latvia, New Zealand, South Africa, Switzerland, Thailand, and the United Kingdom—have wrestled with this problem and have found that separating the ATC system from government oversight while maintaining government safety regulations works well.

Although no country has fully privatized its ATC system, Canada has created a private nonprofit corporation owned by the users. Its system has successfully reduced delays. The other freestanding ATC systems are at least partially government owned. Given the restrictions that the federal government puts on its government-owned corporations, such as Amtrak and the post office, it would be preferable to follow Canada's example by establishing a nonprofit corporation owned and controlled by airlines and other users of the ATC system.

Most ATC systems are funded through user fees. The problem that arises is what to charge general aviation. Because the FAA currently subsidizes general aviation, owners and pilots oppose any notion of a freestanding corporation dependent on user fees. Nevertheless, client pay is a good rule. Noncommercial general aviation pilots, who typically fly single-engine planes, should be charged only when they file a flight plan or land at an airport with a control tower. Commercial general aviation planes, such as corporate jets, should pay their share of the costs of the system.

Airline Cabotage. It is time for the United States to drop its restrictions on foreign ownership and operation of air carriers. Under current law, non-Americans can own no more than 25 percent of the voting stock of U.S. airlines. America has no similar restrictions on investment in steel, autos, or most other industries. There is no reason to make an exception for the airlines. Other private carriers should be free to invest in the United States. At the moment, several U.S. carriers are in financial difficulties. Purchase by a healthy foreign airline would make great sense, bringing new capital and new competition to the American market. Virgin Atlantic Airways, for example, is interested in building a low-cost U.S. carrier to feed its international service.

At the same time, the long-standing policy of negotiating ''open skies'' agreements with other governments should be based not on what U.S. carriers get out of the agreement but on the benefits to American travelers. Cathay Pacific, based in Hong Kong, could offer improved service and competition both in the domestic market and internationally. British Air might invest in US Air to provide nationwide connections to Europe. The introduction of such foreign carriers would strengthen competition in the American market, bringing additional benefits to travelers.

Airport Privatization. Because the Airport and Airways Trust Fund moneys have been available only to government-owned airports, private airports are ineligible for any of the funds that are raised from taxes on fuel and passengers. Because those airports eligible for grants are subject to federal appropriations, even state and local government-owned airports cannot plan and count on money from the trust fund. Repealing the federal taxes on aviation and allowing airports to impose their own fees, which could vary by time of day to reflect peak use, would give airports incentives to expand their capacity and introduce technologies that would reduce delays.

Maritime Policy

Unlike the regulations affecting other transportation sectors, maritime regulations and subsidies have been strikingly resistant to reform. A hodge-podge of conflicting and costly policies—subsidization, protectionism, regulation, and taxation—unnecessarily burdens the U.S.-flag fleet, forces U.S. customers to pay inflated prices, and curbs domestic and international trade. The list of rules and regulations governing shipping is too exhaustive to catalog here, but one thing is clear: shipping policies must be thoroughly reviewed and revamped. Congress should pay special attention to deregulation of ocean shipping and other trade- and consumer-oriented reforms.

In particular, Congress should repeal the Jones Act (sec. 27 of the Merchant Marine Act of 1920). The Jones Act prohibits shipping merchandise between U.S. ports "in any other vessel than a vessel built in and documented under the laws of the United States and owned by persons who are citizens of the United States." The act essentially bars foreign shipping companies from competing with American companies. A 1993 International Trade Commission study showed that the loss of economic welfare attributable to America's cabotage restriction was some $3.1 billion per year. Because the Jones Act inflates prices, many businesses are encouraged to import goods rather than buy products manufactured in other parts of the United States.

The primary argument made in support of the Jones Act is that we need an all-American fleet on which to call in time of war. But during the Persian Gulf War, only 6 vessels of the 460 that shipped military supplies came from America's subsidized merchant fleet. Repealing the Jones Act would allow the domestic maritime industry to be more competitive and would enable American producers to take advantage of lower prices resulting from competition among domestic and foreign suppliers. Ships used in domestic commerce could be built in one country, manned by citizens of another, and flagged by still another. That would result in decreased shipping costs, with savings passed on to American consumers and the U.S. shipping industry. The price of shipping services, now restricted by the act, would decline by an estimated 25 percent.

Conclusion

Transportation is inherently competitive. Since elimination of most of the economic controls on trucking, railroads, and airlines, those industries have flourished. Although the performance of those sectors has improved greatly since the 1970s when the federal government controlled entry, rates, and routes, problems remain. The difficulties stem in part from the success of deregulation, which, for example, has democratized air travel while the infrastructure has remained in government hands. Decontrol has demonstrated that the market works much better free from government controls than with government oversight. We need to apply that lesson to the remaining problems and remove federal ownership and control from administration of air traffic control, the airports, and the security system.

The government should free the freight railroads from the remaining constraints on that industry. The government should recognize that passenger rail transport is never going to be profitable, especially when run by the government. Only the private sector can possibly run a profitable passenger train system and then only if free from government controls on labor and pricing. Unlike other transportation policies, maritime policy has been resistant to reform and should receive the immediate attention of reform-minded members of Congress.

Suggested Readings

Button, Kenneth. "Toward Truly Open Skies." *Regulation* 25, no. 3 (2002).

Moore, Thomas Gale. "Moving Ahead." *Regulation* 25, no. 2 (2002).

Poole, Robert W. Jr., and Viggo Butler. "Airline Deregulation: The Unfinished Revolution." *Regulation* 22, no. 1 (1999).

Vranich, Joseph, Cornelius Chapman, and Edward L. Hudgins. "A Plan to Liquidate Amtrak." Cato Institute Policy Analysis no. 425, February 8, 2002.

—Prepared by Peter Van Doren

39. Antitrust

Congress should

- repeal the Sherman Act of 1890;
- repeal the Clayton Act of 1914;
- repeal the Federal Trade Commission Act of 1914;
- repeal the Robinson-Patman Act of 1936;
- repeal the Celler-Kefauver Act of 1950;
- repeal the Antitrust Procedures and Penalties Act of 1975;
- repeal the Hart-Scott-Rodino Act of 1976; and
- pending repeal, curb the states' authority to enforce federal antitrust laws.

Introduction

Antitrust is thought by some to be the bulwark of free enterprise. Without the continued vigilance of the Justice Department and the Federal Trade Commission, so the argument goes, large corporations would ruthlessly destroy their smaller rivals and soon raise prices and profits at consumers' expense. When megamergers grab headlines and a federal judge decides that the nation's leading software company should be dismembered, the importance of vigorous antitrust law enforcement seems to be obvious.

But antitrust has a dark side. The time for modest reform of antitrust policy has passed. Root-and-branch overhaul of what Federal Reserve chairman Alan Greenspan a generation ago referred to as a "jumble of economic irrationality and ignorance"—and what modern scholarship has shown over and over again to be a playground of special pleaders—is called for.

Here are seven reasons why the federal antitrust laws should be repealed.

No. 1: Antitrust Debases the Idea of Private Property

Frequently when government invokes the antitrust laws, it transforms a company's private property into something that effectively belongs to the public, to be designed by government officials and sold on terms congenial to rivals who are bent on the market leader's demise. Some advocates of the free market endorse that process, despite the destructive implications of stripping private property of its protection against confiscation. If new technology is to be declared public property, future technology will not materialize. If technology is to be proprietary, then it must not be expropriated. Once expropriation becomes the remedy of choice, the goose is unlikely to continue laying golden eggs.

The principles are these: No one other than the owner has a right to the technology he creates. Consumers can't demand that a product be provided at a specified price or with specified features. Competitors aren't entitled to share in the product's advantages. By demanding that one company's creation be exploited for the benefit of competitors, or even consumers, government is flouting core principles of free markets and individual liberty.

No. 2: Antitrust Laws Are Fluid, Nonobjective, and Often Retroactive

Because of murky statutes and conflicting case law, companies never can be quite sure what constitutes permissible behavior. If a company cannot demonstrate that its actions were motivated by efficiency, conduct that is otherwise legal somehow morphs into an antitrust violation. Normal business practices—price discounts, product improvements, exclusive contracting—become violations of law. When they're not accused of monopoly price gouging for charging too much, companies are accused of predatory pricing for charging too little or collusion for charging the same!

No. 3: Antitrust Is Based on a Static View of the Market

In real markets, sellers seek to carve out minimonopolies. Profits from market power are the engine that drives the economy. So what might happen in a utopian, perfectly competitive environment is irrelevant to the question whether government intervention is necessary or appropriate. The proper comparison is with the marketplace that will evolve if the antitrust laws, by punishing success, eliminate incentives for new and improved products. Markets move faster than antitrust laws could ever move. Consumers rule, not producers. And consumers can unseat any product and any company no matter how powerful and entrenched. Just ask WordPerfect or Lotus or IBM.

No. 4: Antitrust Remedies Are Designed by Bureaucrats Who Don't Understand How Markets Work

Economic losses from excessive regulation can do great damage to producers and consumers. But government moves forward in the name of correcting market failure, apparently without considering at all the possibility of government failure. Proponents of antitrust tell us that government planners know which products should be withdrawn from the market, no matter what consumers actually prefer. The problem with that argument is that it leads directly to paternalism, to the idea that an elite corps of experts knows our interests better than we do—and can regulate our affairs to satisfy those interests better than the market does.

The real issue is not whether one product is better than another but who gets to decide—consumers, declaring their preferences by purchases in the market, or specialists at the Justice Department or the Federal Trade Commission rating the merits of various goods and services. When we permit government to make such decisions for us and allow those decisions to trump the subjective choices of consumers, we abandon any pretense of a free market. In the process, we reduce consumer choice to a formalistic appraisal centering on technical features alone, notwithstanding that products are also desired for quality, price, service, convenience, and a host of other variables.

No. 5: Antitrust Law Is Wielded by Business Rivals and Their Allies in the Political Arena

Instead of focusing on new and better products, disgruntled rivals try to exploit the law—consorting with members of Congress, their staffers, antitrust officials, and the best lobbying and public relations firms that money can buy. Soon enough, the targeted company responds in kind. Microsoft, for example, once conspicuously avoided Washington, D.C., politicking—but no longer. And America's entrepreneurial enclave, Silicon Valley, has become the home of billionaire businesspeople who use political influence to bring down their competitors. That agenda will destroy what it sets out to protect. Politicians are mostly order takers. So we'll get the kind of government we ask for—including oppressive regulation. Citizens who are troubled by huge corporations dominating private markets should be even more concerned if those same corporations decide that political clout better serves their interest—politicizing competition to advance the private interests of favored competitors.

No. 6: Barriers to Entry Are Created by Government, Not Private Businesses

Under antitrust law, the proper test for government intervention is whether barriers to entry foreclose meaningful competition. But what is a "barrier"? When a company advertises, lowers prices, improves quality, adds features, or offers better service, it discourages rivals. But it cannot bar them. True barriers arise from government misbehavior, not private power—from special-interest legislation or a misconceived regulatory regime that protects existing producers from competition. When government grants exclusive licenses to cable, electric, and telephone companies, monopolies are born and nurtured at public expense. When Congress decrees targeted tax benefits, subsidies, insurance guarantees, and loans or enacts tariffs and quotas to protect domestic companies from foreign rivals, that creates the same anti-competitive environment that the antitrust laws were meant to foreclose. The obvious answer, which has little to do with antitrust, is for government to stop creating those barriers to begin with.

No. 7: Antitrust Will Inevitably Be Used by Unprincipled Politicians as a Political Bludgeon

Too often, the executive branch has exploited the antitrust laws to force conformity by "uncooperative" companies. Remember that when President Nixon wanted to browbeat the three major TV networks, he used the threat of an antitrust suit to extort more favorable media coverage. On a widely publicized tape, Nixon told his aide, Chuck Colson: "Our gain is more important than the economic gain. We don't give a goddamn about the economic gain. Our game here is solely political. . . . As far as screwing the networks, I'm very glad to do it." If Nixon were the only culprit, that would be bad enough. But former *New York Times* reporter David Burnham, in his 1996 book, *Abuse of Power*, shows that presidents from Kennedy through Clinton routinely demanded that the Justice Department bend the rules in pursuit of political ends.

The lesson is clear. The threat of abusive public power is far larger than the threat of private monopoly. It's time for Congress to get rid of the federal antitrust laws. Meanwhile, pending repeal of those laws, Congress must ensure that enforcement by state authorities does not duplicate federal enforcement. Government must not be given two bites at the antitrust apple, nor should defendants be exposed to double jeopardy.

Curb the States' Authority to Enforce Federal Antitrust Laws

It's time to rein in the power of state attorneys general. For most of American history they did vital, but routine and distinctly unglamorous, legal work for their states. But beginning in the 1980s, some attorneys general challenged the Reagan administration's policies in antitrust and environmental law, pursuing their own agendas through litigation. In the antitrust context, activist attorneys general have relied on their so-called *parens patriae* power to sue on behalf of state residents under federal statutes.

The Microsoft case is perhaps the most egregious example of duplicative federal and state antitrust enforcement. Nine states—relying on the same trial, the same facts, the same conclusions of law, and the same injuries to the same people—tried to override a settlement between Microsoft and the federal government, supported by 41 of the 50 states. In a legal brief to a federal judge, the Justice Department offered persuasive reasons why the states should not be allowed an end run around the federal settlement.

First, "The United States is the sole enforcer of the federal antitrust laws on behalf of the American public." Second, the states' remedies would affect competition and consumers outside their borders—raising "for the very first time the prospect that a small group of states, with no particularized interests to vindicate, might somehow obtain divergent relief with wide-ranging, national economic implications." Third, "The public interest is best served when federal and state antitrust activity is complementary, not duplicative or conflicting." Fourth, the nine holdout states had "neither the authority nor the responsibility to act in the broader national interest, and the plaintiff with that authority and responsibility [that is, the United States] has taken a different course."

Still worse, continued the Justice Department, the relief sought by the nonsettling states could "harm consumers, retard competition, chill innovation, or confound compliance" with the federal settlement. Echoing the Supreme Court, the Justice Department warned that antitrust redress requires a showing of "harm to competition not competitors." Remedies

389

must be crafted for the benefit of the public, not for the private gain of politically favored rivals.

Consider the remarks of respected Judge Richard Posner of the Seventh Circuit Court of Appeals, who mediated an abortive Microsoft settlement. Posner offered these recommendations in the *Antitrust Law Journal:* "I would like to see, first, the states stripped of their authority to bring antitrust suits, federal or state, except . . . where the state is suing firms that are fixing the prices of goods or services that they sell to the state. . . . [States] are too subject to influence by . . . competitors. This is a particular concern when the [competitor] is a major political force in that state. A situation in which the benefits of government action are concentrated in one state and the costs in other states is a recipe for irresponsible state action."

Congress is constitutionally authorized to intervene whenever actual or imminent state practices threaten the free flow of commerce. Congress should use that power and curb the *parens patriae* authority of the states to enforce federal antitrust laws. Otherwise, some states will continue to abuse their existing authority—exercising it to impose sovereignty beyond their borders and cater to the parochial interests of influential constituents.

Here are the rules that ought to govern when states propose to vindicate the private rights of their residents under federal antitrust law: First, states should not be allowed to litigate on behalf of private parties who, on their own, have unhindered access to the courts. Second, injury claims must be those related to residents collectively or to a state's overall economy, not particular parties. That reduces the likelihood that the litigation will be instigated by special interests. Third, relief should be in the form of money damages only, not conduct remedies. The problem with conduct remedies is that they invariably affect out-of-state residents. Finally, no state should be permitted to sue if a federal agency is also suing, unless there are state-specific injuries that are not addressed in the federal suit.

Would constraints on state antitrust enforcement powers violate time-honored principles of federalism? Not at all. Federalism isn't simply a matter of states' rights. Nor is it exclusively about devolution of power or promoting efficient government. First and foremost, federalism is about checks and balances based on dual sovereignty. Most often, the states are a counterweight to excessive power in the hands of the federal government. Yet antitrust is an obvious case in which the federal government must curb excessive power in the hands of the states.

Conclusion

More than two centuries ago, in the *Wealth of Nations*, Adam Smith observed that "people of the same trade seldom meet together ... but the conversation ends in a conspiracy against the public or in some contrivance to raise prices." Coming from the father of laissez faire, that warning has been cited ad nauseam by antitrust proponents to justify all manner of interventionist mischief. Those same proponents, whether carelessly or deviously, rarely mention Smith's next sentence: "It is impossible indeed to prevent such meetings, by any law which either could be executed, or would be consistent with liberty and justice."

Antitrust is bad law, bad economics, and bad public policy. It deserves an ignominious burial—sooner rather than later.

Suggested Readings

Armentano, Dominick T. *Antitrust and Monopoly: Anatomy of a Policy Failure.* New York: Wiley, 1982.

DeBow, Michael. "Restraining State Attorneys General, Curbing Government Lawsuit Abuse." Cato Institute Policy Analysis no. 437, May 10, 2002.

Greenspan, Alan. "Antitrust." In *Capitalism: The Unknown Ideal.* Edited by Ayn Rand. New York: Signet, 1966.

Levy, Robert A. *Shakedown: How Corporations, Government, and Trial Lawyers Abuse the Judicial Process.* Washington: Cato Institute, 2004.

Shughart, William F. II. "The Government's War on Mergers: The Fatal Conceit of Antitrust Policy." Cato Institute Policy Analysis no. 323, October 22, 1998.

—Prepared by Robert A. Levy

40. Food and Drug Administration

> **The federal government should**
>
> - allow market-based certification of the safety and efficacy of initial uses of new drugs and medical devices, just as markets certify the efficacy of subsequent uses; and
> - restore individuals' freedom to use any non-FDA-approved product.

Under current law, the Food and Drug Administration must approve all pharmaceuticals and medical devices before they can be marketed. Although the process is often termed "FDA testing," that agency does little if any actual testing. The developer of a new drug uses its own labs or hires another private company to conduct animal tests on the drug for safety before proceeding to clinical trials for safety and efficacy in people. A medical school or a consulting firm often conducts those tests. When each phase of the testing is completed, the pharmaceutical company submits the details of the testing process, evidence of adherence to FDA protocols, and the test results to the FDA.

FDA officials review the test results at each step, and if they are satisfied, they give the pharmaceutical company permission to proceed to the next step in the testing process. When all the tests and trials are complete, FDA officials review all the information—often measured in hundreds of pounds or linear feet of reports rather than number of pages—and decide whether the company can market the drug and advertise it to physicians for the treatment of specific diseases and conditions. The FDA exercises very strict authority over what manufacturers can say about their products. In particular, manufacturers can only promote uses of the product that have been approved by the FDA.

As an agency, the FDA has strong incentives to delay the time when new products reach patients. If the FDA approves a product, it runs the risk of patients being harmed, which would lead to criticism of the agency. If the FDA delays approval or requires more tests, the same number of patients (or more) may be harmed by not having access to a beneficial product, but the FDA does not come under criticism because its role is unseen. As Dr. Henry Miller explained:

> In the early 1980s, when I headed the team at the FDA that was reviewing the [new drug application] for recombinant human insulin, the first drug made with gene-splicing techniques, we were ready to recommend approval a mere four months after the application was submitted (at a time when the average time for NDA review was more than two and a half years). . . . [M]y supervisor refused to sign off on the approval—even though he agreed that the data provided compelling evidence of the drug's safety and effectiveness. "If anything goes wrong," he argued, "think how bad it will look that we approved the drug so quickly." . . . The supervisor was more concerned with not looking bad in case of an unforeseen mishap than with getting an important new product to patients who needed it.

The bias toward delay can be readily observed. From 1977 to 1995 the number of clinical trials required to bring a new drug to market doubled and the number of patients involved in those trials nearly tripled. It now takes up to 15 years to complete the FDA-regulated development, testing, and review processes. Joseph DiMasi, Ronald Hansen, and Henry Grabowski estimate that the cost of bringing a new drug to patients has doubled since 1987, to more than $800 million in 2003, while a new drug discovered in 2003 would cost $1.9 billion to bring to patients 12 years hence.

The Human Cost of FDA Delays

Certainly, it is desirable to make all products as safe as possible. But every day that the FDA delays approving a product, many patients who might be helped suffer or die needlessly. Dr. Louis Lasagna, former director of Tufts University's Center for the Study of Drug Development, estimated that the seven-year delay in the approval of beta-blockers as heart medication cost the lives of as many as 119,000 Americans. During the three and a half years it took the FDA to approve the drug Interleukin-2, 25,000 Americans died of kidney cancer even though the drug had already been approved for use in nine other countries. Eugene Schoenfeld, a cancer survivor and president of the National Kidney Cancer Association, maintains that "IL-2 is one of the worst examples of FDA regulation known to man." Patients also suffer needlessly when the FDA causes drugs never to be developed. Researchers have estimated that FDA regulation cut by 60 percent the number of new drugs introduced in the 1960s and 1970s. Prof. Christopher Conover of Duke University has estimated that the increased morbidity and mortality due to FDA regulation imposed a net economic cost of $42 billion in 2002 alone.

In the past few decades, patients' groups have become more vocal in demanding timely access to new medication. AIDS sufferers led the way. The Internet allows patients to organize, exchange information, and take more control of their treatment. Patients can track the progress of possible treatments as they are tested for safety and efficacy and are quite conscious of how the FDA can stand in the way of their health and even their survival. In 2003 the Abigail Alliance for Better Access to Developmental Drugs brought suit against the FDA to expand access to unapproved drugs for terminally ill patients with no other hope. After all, if an individual is expected to live for only six months, another year of testing does that person no good.

From FDA Certification to Market-Based Certification

It is past time for Congress to break the FDA monopoly on initial safety and efficacy certification and restore the right of individuals to control their own health care. A model for reform already exists in the private sector.

The United States already has an essentially free-market process for certifying drug efficacy. Even though the FDA approves a drug for one particular use, which goes on the drug's label, physicians may—and do— prescribe drugs for other uses. Examples include

- aspirin, designed for pain relief, which turns out to be effective in preventing heart attacks, and
- Viagra, intended as a treatment for angina, which turns out to be a remedy for erectile dysfunction and has been used to treat pulmonary hypertension, even in premature babies.

Lack of FDA certification does not mean such uses are dangerous or unproven: these so-called "off-label" uses are suggested or discovered by doctors and scientists, tested, discussed worldwide in medical journals and symposia, and (if validated) appear in medical textbooks, the *U.S. Pharmacopeia Drug Information*, the *American Hospital Formulary Service Drug Information*, and other authoritative sources. In fact, off-label uses often become the standard of care, particularly in fighting cancer and other diseases. Doctors so frequently rely on market-based certification (which arguably includes foreign governments' certifications) that more than half of known drug uses are off-label uses.

Market-based certification respects the freedom of doctors and patients to make treatment decisions according to individual circumstances. It is also more efficient than government certification; one researcher found that off-label uses that were later certified by the FDA were certified by the market (in the *U.S. Pharmacopeia Drug Information*) an average of 2.5 years sooner.

The federal government should build on that success and allow companies to seek initial certification of their products from such market organizations. Those organizations would certify *new* drugs for new uses, just as they now certify *existing* drugs for new uses. They would design and execute the laboratory tests and human studies appropriate for evaluating the safety and efficacy of personalized drugs. To survive, market organizations would have to be scrupulously honest: just as Underwriters Laboratories and *Consumer Reports* sell their reputations, the *U.S. Pharmacopeia* or other organizations would sell their reputations and lose customers if their reputations came into question. Market-based certification and restoring patients' freedom to use any non-FDA-approved product would help Americans capture the benefits of future pharmaceutical innovations, including individually tailored drugs, that the current FDA certification process is likely to suppress.

Some manufacturers will oppose liberalization. Larger companies especially are used to doing business with the FDA. They are comfortable with the confidence the public has in the FDA, and they may view regulations as costs that they can absorb but that their smaller competitors cannot. Such attitudes are even more reason to allow market-based certification.

In a free society, individuals should be free to care for their physical well-being as they see fit, which includes the freedom to choose the medical treatments they think best. Such liberty does not open the door for fraud or abuse any more than does a free market in other products. In fact, informed consent by patients will become more sophisticated as the market for information about medical treatments becomes more free and open.

Suggested Readings

Campbell, Noel D. "Replace FDA Regulation of Medical Devices with Third-Party Certification." Cato Institute Policy Analysis no. 288, November 12, 1997.

Conover, Christopher J. "Health Care Regulation: The $169 Billion Hidden Tax." Cato Institute Policy Analysis no. 527, October 4, 2004.

Goldberg, Robert M. "Breaking Up the FDA's Medical Information Monopoly." *Regulation* 18, no. 2 (1995).

Higgs, Robert. "Wrecking Ball: FDA Regulation of Medical Devices." Cato Institute Policy Analysis no. 235, August 7, 1995.

Hollis, Aidan. "Closing the FDA's Orange Book." *Regulation* 24, no. 4 (2001).

Klein, Daniel B., and Alexander Tabarrok. "Who Certifies Off-Label?" *Regulation* 27, no. 2 (2004).

———. www.FDAReview.org.

Miller, Henry I. *To America's Health: A Proposal to Reform the Food and Drug Administration*. Stanford, CA.: Hoover Institution Press, 2000.

Tabarrok, Alexander. "The Blessed Monopolies." *Regulation* 24, no. 4 (2001).

Walker, Steven, and Dan Popeo. "A Break for Those with Nothing Left to Lose." *Milken Institute Review*, First Quarter 2004, pp. 7–13. http://www.milkeninstitute.org/publications/review/2004_3/07_13mr21.pdf.

—Prepared by Michael F. Cannon

41. Telecommunications, Broadband, and Media Policy

Congress should

- level the telecom playing field by placing all carriers on an equal legal footing and comprehensively deregulate all carriers to accomplish this goal,
- sunset all forced-access regulatory mandates,
- reform and devolve universal service subsidies and the "E-Rate" program,
- quarantine broadband wireless Internet telephone services from remaining federal and state regulation,
- clean up the telecom industry tax mess,
- reject new cable and satellite regulations,
- enact comprehensive spectrum reform and privatization, and
- allow comprehensive media ownership reform to advance.

Revising Telecom Regulation

The telecommunications sector is just beginning to emerge from the meltdown that decimated stocks, destroyed billions in shareholder value, and left once-proud industry giants scrambling to avoid bankruptcy. The reverberations of this meltdown were also felt well beyond the boundaries of the telecom sector as upstream and downstream industries, especially the equipment market, took a hit as well.

Although there were many business causes for the market meltdown, public policy has had an equally important impact on this sector. While markets and technologies have evolved rapidly, the communications policy landscape remains encumbered with many outdated rules and regulations. That is largely because when Congress last attempted to address these matters seven years ago in the Telecommunications Act of 1996, legislators intentionally avoided providing clear deregulatory objectives to the Federal Communications Commission (FCC) and instead delegated broad and remarkably ambiguous authority to the agency and state regulators. That left the most important deregulatory decisions to regulators who, not surprisingly, did a very poor job of following through with a serious liberalization agenda.

As policymakers look to the future, they must acknowledge just how much the world has changed and modify telecom law accordingly. Traditionally, the industry was regulated because of the lack of competition and the need to ensure universal service, but those concerns are no longer an issue. America long ago achieved universal connectivity, and the market has grown increasingly competitive with each passing year. Millions of Americans are now "cutting the cord" entirely by switching to wireless cellular service, and countless more are switching from their traditional wireline provider to Internet telephone providers, or "VoIP" (voice over Internet protocol). Meanwhile, energy companies are on the cusp of breaking into the telecom market to provide yet another wire into the home for broadband over powerline systems. In a world where consumers have multiple wireline and wireless options, Congress must recognize that the old rationales for regulation have been either satisfied or rendered moot by the relentless march of technology. Consequently, the mistakes of the Telecom Act must not be repeated in upcoming legislation; indeed they must now be undone to protect future competitors and technologies from repressive regulatory burdens.

Regulatory Asymmetry

The Telecom Act's most serious flaw was its backward-looking focus on correcting the market problems of a bygone era. Instead of thoroughly cleaning out the regulatory deadwood of the past, legislators and regulators decided to instead rework archaic legal paradigms and policies that were outmoded decades ago. The act kept in place increasingly unnatural legal distinctions, such as the artificial separation of local and long-distance wireline telephone services even though those two services can be bundled and sold as one service as they are by wireless cellular providers.

In particular, the Telecom Act did not address the underlying regulatory asymmetry that governs formerly distinct industry sectors. That is, regulators have traditionally grouped providers into categories such as common carriers, cable services, wireless, and mass media and broadcasting. But technological convergence in this industry has meant that those formerly distinct industry sectors and companies are now integrating and rivals are searching for ways to offer consumers a bundled set of communications, broadband, and even media services under a single brand name. Increasingly, providers are referring to themselves as information services providers, broadband providers, or network services providers. Yet the Telecom Act endorsed the paradigms of the past and allowed increasingly interchangeable services to be regulated under different legal standards: telecom, cable, wireless, broadcasting, and so on.

Therefore, the first step Congress must take to begin seriously reforming communications policy is to end this asymmetry, not by "regulating up" to put everyone on an equal footing, but rather by "deregulating down." Placing everyone on the same *deregulated* level playing field should be at the heart of telecommunications policy. The easiest way for Congress to tear down the old regulatory paradigms and achieve regulatory parity would be to borrow a page from trade law and adopt the equivalent of a "most favored nation" principle for communications. In a nutshell, this policy would state that "any communications carrier seeking to offer a new service or entering a new line of business should be regulated no more stringently than its least regulated competitor." That would create regulatory simplicity and parity without any new regulation.

The Perils of Forced Access

Next, Congress must clean out the most burdensome regulatory deadwood in the telecom sector by closing the book on "open-access" regulation for good. This was the second serious problem with the Telecom Act: its fundamentally flawed premise that competition could be micromanaged into existence through open-access—or as they are more appropriately called, "forced-access"—mandates. The act included provisions that required local telephone companies to unbundle and share elements of their networks with rivals at a regulated rate. The theory behind those interconnection and unbundling rules was that smaller carriers needed a chance to get their feet wet in this market before they could invest in facilities of their own to serve consumers. To encourage entry by smaller carriers, Congress delegated broad and undefined authority to the FCC to create rules that would allow independent carriers to lease capacity from incumbent network owners at a regulated (and very low) price so that the new rivals could resell that capacity to customers and still earn a profit.

The danger inherent in that scheme should have been apparent from the start: If regulators went to the extreme and set the regulated rate for leased access too low, then new rivals would come to rely on infrastructure sharing as their core business model and avoid making the facilities-based investments necessary for true competition to develop. That is essentially what happened in the wake of the Telecom Act as the FCC overzealously implemented the act's network-sharing provisions. That encouraged new entrants to engage in a crude form of regulatory arbitrage as they pushed for regulators to constantly suppress the regulated price of access to existing telephone networks. Meanwhile, those resellers largely ignored investment in new networks of their own through which legitimate competition could have developed. In other words, the goal of federal telecom policy became infrastructure sharing instead of infrastructure building. But sharing is not competing, and infrastructure socialism was never a sensible prescription for bringing about true communications competition or innovation.

Luckily, despite the best efforts of the FCC and state regulators to retain the current forced-access regulatory system, the courts have repeatedly struck down elements of that scheme. The District Court of Appeals' March 2004 decision in *USTA v. FCC* might have been the final nail in the coffin of infrastructure socialism. In that case, the court blasted the FCC for overstepping its authority and converting the Telecom Act into a regulatory instead of a deregulatory measure. When the Bush administration refused to appeal the decision to the Supreme Court, it signaled to many observers that the forced-access crusade might have seen its final days. But Congress still needs to take action to formally close the door on that counterproductive chapter of telecom history, especially in light of the fact that the rules now threaten emerging technologies.

Protecting New Services and Preempting the States

A third flaw of the Telecom Act was its failure to shield emerging technologies from the new forced-access regulations or other "legacy" regulations. In particular, Congress failed to realize the potential threat state and local regulators might pose to new or existing communications technologies and thus failed to include language in the act preempting them.

The gravity of that threat was exposed in the late 1990s when several state and municipal regulatory officials began advocating the extension of forced-access mandates to cable providers and their broadband offerings in particular. Regulators argued that the same infrastructure-sharing logic that applied to old telephone networks needed to apply to the new high-speed services cable companies were rolling out. Ironically, federal regulators rejected such calls for forced-access regulation of cable largely because some at the FCC wanted to make sure cable companies were well positioned to compete against telephone companies. But the FCC lacked the clear authority to preempt the state and local governments altogether. Thus, the debate is still raging today, and litigation is pending.

Equally troubling is the threat state and local regulation poses to VoIP and wireless services. Recently, some state officials have openly advocated greater regulation and taxation of both those services under the guise of "consumer protection." But no amount of rhetoric can disguise what this effort really is: a turf battle. State and local officials are increasingly concerned that emerging technologies are eroding their very raison d'être.

These jurisdictional regulatory issues demand immediate attention by Congress. Federal lawmakers must take the same bold steps they have while deregulating previous network industries (railroads, trucking, airlines, banking) by preempting a great deal of the economic regulation state and local governments engage in today.

Ending Universal Service Entitlements

The fourth flaw of the Telecom Act was Congress's unwillingness to dismantle or even reform the universal service subsidies and regulations that continue to distort market pricing and competitive entry in this market. The system has been riddled with inefficient cross-subsidies, artificially inflated prices, geographic rate averaging, and hidden phone bill charges for average Americans. Although some reform efforts have been undertaken in recent years, they have been quite limited.

To make matters worse, section 254 of the Telecommunications Act mandated that the FCC take steps to expand the definition of universal service. It did not take the agency long to follow up on that request. In May 1997 the agency created the "E-Rate" program (known among its critics as the "Gore tax" since it was heavily promoted by then–vice president Al Gore), which unilaterally established a new government bureaucracy to help wire schools and libraries to the Internet. The FCC then dictated that the American people would pick up the $2.25 billion per year tab for the program by imposing a hidden tax on everyone's phone bills. Although the constitutionality of the E-Rate program was questioned initially, the program withstood court challenges and early legislative reform efforts. Consequently, the E-Rate threatens to become yet another entrenched Washington entitlement program and further set back needed reform efforts.

In addition, there is now growing a new crop of federal spending initiatives that cover broadband, the Internet, and the high-technology sector in general. Although not a formally unified effort, the combined effect of federal legislative activity on this front is tantamount to the creation of what might be called a "Digital New Deal." That is, just as policymakers proposed a litany of "New Deal'" programs and spending initiatives during the Depression, lawmakers are today devising myriad new federal programs aimed at solving the many supposed emergencies or disasters that will befall industry or consumers without government assistance. The recent troubles of the dot-com and telecommunications sectors have only added fuel to the fire of interventionism.

The new communications-, cyberspace-, and Internet-related spending initiatives that policymakers are considering, or have already implemented, can basically be grouped into four general categories: (1) broadband deployment; (2) digital education, civic participation, and cultural initiatives; (3) cybersecurity; and (4) research and development. Dozens of new federal programs were proposed in those areas during the past two sessions of Congress. And dozens of other promotional programs already exist.

The dangers of this cyberpork should be obvious. Washington subsidy and entitlement programs typically have a never-ending lifespan and often open the door to increased federal regulatory intervention. Political meddling of this variety could also displace private-sector investment efforts or result in technological favoritism by favoring or promoting one set of technologies or providers over another. Moreover, subsidy programs aren't really necessary in an environment characterized by proliferating consumer choices but also uncertain market demand for new services. Finally, and most profoundly, perhaps the leading argument against the creation of a Digital New Deal is that, by inviting the feds to act as a market facilitator, the industry runs the risk of becoming more politicized over time.

Congress should abolish the current system of federal entitlements and devolve to the states responsibility for any subsidy programs that are deemed necessary in the future. A federal telecommunications welfare state is not justified. If schools desire specific technologies or communications connections, for example, they can petition their state or local leaders for funding the same way they would for textbooks or chalkboards: through an accountable, on-budget state appropriation. There is nothing unique about communications or computing technologies that justifies a federal entitlement program paid for by hidden telephone taxes while other tools of learning are funded through state and local budgets.

Rejecting New Paradigms Based on Old Regulations

As Congress looks to reopen and revise the Telecom Act, it must be wary of proposals to adopt new regulatory paradigms that are really little more than a repackaging of the misguided schemes of the past. In particular, some policymakers have become enamored with so-called Net neutrality and network layers regulatory paradigms.

Network layers models divide our increasingly packet-based Internet world into at least four distinct layers: (1) content layer, (2) applications layer, (3) logical/code layer, and (4) physical/infrastructure layer. The layers model is an important analytical tool that could help lawmakers rethink and eventually eliminate the increasingly outmoded policy paradigms of the past, which pigeonhole technologies and providers into discrete industrial regulatory categories. That does not mean, however, that the layers model should be taken a step further and be formally enshrined as a new regulatory regime. In particular, a layer breaker should not be considered a lawbreaker. Vertical integration across layers can create efficiencies and ensure that firms achieve the scale necessary to become major competitors.

Net neutrality regulatory models are built on the layers model and are also at war with the notion of vertical integration. Net neutrality mandates would limit efforts by physical infrastructure owners to integrate into other layers, especially content, on the grounds that infrastructure providers will leverage market power in one segment of the industry into another and destroy innovation in the process. Net neutrality proposals illustrate how the layers model could be used to restrict vertical integration in this sector by transforming the layers concept into a set of regulatory firewalls between physical infrastructure; code, or applications; and content. You can offer service in one layer, but not another.

Quite obviously, Net neutrality mandates or a network layers paradigm would entail a great deal of ongoing regulation of the communications and Internet sectors. But such regulations are not needed in today's marketplace since it has grown increasingly competitive. Net neutrality or network layers regulation would discourage added facilities-based competition and innovation by instead opting for the short-term optimization of activities on current networks at the expense of longer-term investment and innovation. Finally, the regulatory regime envisioned by Net neutrality mandates would also open the door to a great deal of potential "gaming" of the regulatory system and allow firms to use the system to hobble competitors. Worse yet, it will encourage more FCC regulation of the Internet and broadband markets in general.

Agency Power

Finally, Congress must rectify what may have been the Telecom Act's most glaring omission: the almost complete failure to restrain or cut back the size and power of the FCC. During previous deregulatory experiments, Congress wisely realized that comprehensive and lasting reform was possible only if the agencies that oversaw the sectors involved were also reformed or even eliminated. In the telecom world, by contrast, the FCC grew bigger and more powerful in the wake of reform, and we witnessed spending go up by 37 percent, a tripling of the number of pages in the *FCC Record*, and 73 percent more telecom lawyers after the act than before. It is safe to say that you cannot deregulate an industry by granting regulators more power over that industry.

This situation must be reversed to achieve lasting reform. The next cut at a Telecom Act must do more than just hand the FCC vague forbearance language with the suggestion that the agency take steps to voluntarily regulate less. Regulators cannot be expected to voluntarily reduce their own powers. Congress needs to impose clear sunsets on existing FCC powers, especially the infrastructure sharing provisions of the last act. Sunsets must also be imposed on any new transitional powers granted to the FCC in the next revision of Telecom Act. And funding cuts should also be imposed. Without such agency reforms and cuts, Congress will be forced to continuously revisit telecom policy and correct the FCC's mistakes, which markets could handle on their own.

Cleaning Up the Telecom Industry Tax Mess

Regulation is not the only thing holding back America's communications and broadband sector. Burdensome and unique tax rules also remain a serious threat. That is largely due to the fact that policymakers at the state and local levels have long treated this sector as a cash cow from which they could draw substantial sums. They justified such heavy levies by arguing that the industry was a natural monopoly. But the telecommunications industry is no longer being treated as a regulated monopoly, so policymakers should stop taxing it as though it were. That is, as competition comes to communications in America, tax policies based on the regulated monopoly model of the past must be comprehensively reformed.

Some of the taxes are federal in nature and can be addressed by Congress or the FCC. A good example is the federal 3 percent excise tax on telecommunications put in place during the Spanish-American War of 1898. That anachronistic tax should be repealed immediately. And the hidden taxes associated with the E-Rate, or "Gore Tax," program should also be repealed or at least devolved to a lower level of government for administration.

The more problematic tax policy issues, however, arise from burdensome state and local mandates. For example, many states impose discriminatory ad valorem taxes on interstate communications services by taxing telecommunications business property at rates higher than other property, driving up costs for consumers. Federal protections against such taxes—already in effect for railroads, airlines, and trucking—should be extended to telecommunications. Many governments impose multiple and extremely high taxes on communications services. Such taxes should be slashed to a single tax per state and locality, and filing and auditing procedures should be radically streamlined. Finally, taxes and tolls on Internet access should be permanently banned since those charges represent a burdensome levy on the free flow of information and the construction of new interstate broadband networks. The recent congressional effort to extend the Internet Tax Freedom Act moratorium on Internet access taxes as well as other "multiple and discriminatory" Internet taxes, was a good start that should be broadened to incorporate tax protection of other services including nationwide VoIP and wireless offerings.

Rejecting New Cable Regulations

The American cable and satellite sectors are dramatic examples of what free markets can accomplish once regulators step out of the way. The direct broadcast satellite (DBS) industry didn't even exist 25 years ago but today offers hundreds of channels of service to every American home. And after Congress repealed the disastrous price controls mandated by the Cable Act of 1992 as part of the Telecom Act, the cable sector responded with $85 billion in new investment, hundreds of new digital channels, and high-speed Internet services. Cable firms are also rapidly deploying competitive phone service to square off against telephone giants.

Instead of celebrating this as a great capitalist success story, many members of Congress complain that consumers now have *too much* choice from cable and satellite television, but not the choice they are looking for. Some legislators are proposing that cable and DBS companies be forced to give customers the ability to pick and choose every channel on an à la carte basis, instead of picking from tiers of service with their dozens of bundled channels. In theory, an à la carte mandate would presumably give cable subscribers more choice and help lower overall rates since consumers could reject more expensive channels that inflate the cost of any given tier. In reality, however, mandatory à la carte regulation would have potentially devastating implications for the cable

407

industry and consumers alike and would result in less channel choice and higher prices in the long term.

Consider first the cost of time for both industry and consumers. Presumably, an à la carte mandate would require that cable operators provide each household a channel checklist (either on paper, online, or over the phone) that would need to be filled out. In a 500-channel universe, how many hours will consumers need to spend on their computers, or on the phone with cable representatives? Second, the technology upgrades that would be necessary to make à la carte a reality could be quite expensive. An "addressable converter box" would need to be installed in each home to ensure that channel selections could be properly scrambled if they were not selected by the consumer. Thus, "cable ready" TV sets would no longer be an option; everyone would need a set-top box under an à la carte system, and that means higher costs for many households since most currently do not have such boxes.

More important, à la carte regulation would undermine the economic model that has driven the success of the cable sector and helped create so much program diversity. Proponents of à la carte foolishly assume that program bundling and tiering hurt consumers when, in reality, the exact opposite is the case. Sometimes the whole is much greater than the sum of the parts. For example, newspapers bundle issue sections together instead of selling them individually because an à la carte approach would not attract as great a customer or advertiser base. The same is true of cable and DBS. Programming tiers that include a diversity of channels increase value for advertisers and consumers alike. And if advertising dollars dry up, cable bills will likely increase.

Thus, à la carte regulation would likely curtail the overall amount of niche or specialty programming on cable networks. The current tiering approach keeps many smaller channels afloat. In fact, as a business matter, many programmers refuse to sell their channels to cable operators unless they are included in a specific tier. An à la carte regulatory mandate would need to nullify existing contracts in order to immediately offer consumers unrestricted channel choice. But doing so would likely cut back the overall range of consumer choices in the long term. And how would consumers even find new niche channels in an à la carte environment? An October 2003 General Accounting Office report notes that "subscribers place value in having the opportunity to occasionally watch networks they typically do not watch." In other words, viewers place a high value on channel surfing since it allows them to sample new channels and programs. But à la carte regulations would discourage that process and suppress the development of new niche programming options. For those reasons, the GAO report argued that à la carte regulation would have dangerous unintended consequences, namely, diminished consumer choice, less program diversity, and a likely increase in overall rates.

Equally insidious are regulatory proposals to break up existing tiers and create new bundles that offer consumers different types of programming options (perhaps over "mini-" or "micro-tiers.") In particular, some people suggest that requiring cable and DBS operators to offer "themed" tiers, such as a "family-friendly" tier, might be one way of expanding consumer choices or helping "clean up" cable and satellite TV. This is dangerous thinking. A themed-tier programming requirement potentially puts Congress or the FCC in the content regulation business with a vengeance. If video programmers are required to offer the public a "family-friendly" tier of programming, it means someone must define what that term means. The "light touch" regulatory approach would simply mandate that firms offer such a tier but then allow the interaction of operators, program suppliers, and consumers to determine what fell into that mix. But how long would it be before some consumers cried foul about one channel or another, which they did not regard as being truly "family friendly," being thrown into that mix?

Enough consumer complaints would likely produce calls for government assistance in defining "family friendly." Hence, a censorship regime is born. A regime based not necessarily on direct regulation of certain channels, programs, or content (although that might be the end result) but instead an indirect censorship regime based on "regulation by raised eyebrow," in which policymakers provide informal feedback to cable and DBS operators regarding what they'd like to see included in any "family-friendly" tier. In the end, neither Congress nor the FCC has the legal authority to censor programming that appears on private video networks. Cable and satellite television are not licensed to operate "in the public interest" like broadcasters and, therefore, cannot be subjected to the same sort of indecency regulatory scheme that covers broadcasters. But à la carte regulation or "themed-tier" mandates might force this question in the courts and lead to protracted legal battles that would benefit neither industry nor consumers.

Spectrum Reform and Privatization

The Telecommunications Act largely ignored the wireless sector and spectrum reform in general. That was a highly unfortunate oversight by Congress, given the ongoing problems associated with centralized bureaucratic management of the electromagnetic spectrum. For more than seven decades, the FCC has treated the spectrum as a socialized public resource, and the results have been predictable: gross misallocation, delayed innovation, and the creation of artificial scarcity.

In recent years, however, the FCC has gradually come to accept the logic of a free market in spectrum allocation and management. The shift to the use of auctions in the early 1990s was a major step forward in this regard. Previously, all spectrum allocations had been made through comparative hearings or random lotteries. Although not all new spectrum allocations are made through auctions, many are, meaning that people who value the resource most highly are now obtaining the spectrum.

Moreover, the FCC has recently signaled its interest in allowing spectrum license holders greater flexibility in use to ensure that this valuable resource can be put to its most efficient use. Although the agency has not yet followed through on this reform, recent FCC Spectrum Policy Task Force meetings and initiatives suggest that the agency is at least moving in the right direction.

But auctions and flexible use, while important steps, are not enough. The task of spectrum reform will be complete only when policymakers grant property rights in spectrum. Just as America has a full-fledged private property rights regime for real estate, so too should wireless spectrum properties be accorded the full protection of the law. As long as federal regulators parcel out spectrum under a licensing system, the process will be a politicized mess. The alternative—a pure free market for the ownership, control, and trade of spectrum properties—should be a top priority.

To begin this task, Congress should grant incumbent spectrum holders a property right in their existing or future allocation. That means spectrum holders would no longer lease their allocation from the federal government but instead would own it outright and be able to use it (or sell it) as they saw fit. That also means that all arbitrary federal regulatory oversight of the spectrum would end, including content or speech controls on broadcasters. Federal regulators would be responsible only for dealing with technical trespass (interference) violations and disputes that arose between holders of adjoining spectrum.

Auctions should be used to allocate scarce spectrum to which there are competing claims. Auctions should not be one-time events; they can be ongoing as spectrum claims develop and multiply. Policymakers should not rig the auctions in any way, either to favor certain demographic groups or to artificially boost the amount of money raised for the federal Treasury by such auctions. The primary goal of spectrum auctions is to allocate spectrum to its most highly valued use by offering it up for competitive bidding, not to funnel money into the federal coffers.

Under this new system, spectrum owners—better thought of as "band managers" of the bands of spectrum they will own and manage—would henceforth have complete freedom to use, sublease, combine, or sell spectrum in any way they saw fit. Government agencies and public-sector users should purchase the spectrum they need at ongoing auctions. It should be noted that government agencies already control a significant portion of the spectrum, so under this scheme, they would be granted rights to their existing holdings. Congress or state governments should ensure that public-sector spectrum users have money in their budgets for ongoing spectrum acquisition.

Finally, as Table 41.1 shows, regarding spectrum "commons" areas—or portions of the electromagnetic spectrum that are less scarce and can be shared by many users without assigning specific rights—the government has three options: (1) It can directly allocate certain bands of spectrum for commons use, much as it purchases large portions of land for public parks, and then open those areas to common use. (2) At the opposite end of the spectrum, so to speak, government could simply rely on private band managers to contract with independent users to create commons areas within their allocation. Practically speaking, however, it might be very difficult for commons areas to develop under this model, given the need for coordination across many bands. The transaction costs would be enormous. (3) A compromise between those two extremes would be for public officials to designate certain ceilings and floors above and below which certain noninterfering uses of the spectrum would be tolerated. In spectrum parlance, those ceilings and floors are known as "overlay" and "underlay" rights or areas. That is a quite practical solution, as such "easements" already exist today in some bands of the spectrum.

Those three options represent practical and legitimate solutions to the need for ongoing spectrum commons areas. One option, however, should be taken off the table, the pure commons regime for the spectrum. Some spectrum engineers and academics—infatuated with the exciting technologies emerging today that enable reuse and efficient sharing of the spectrum—have called for adoption of a pure spectrum commons model to govern ongoing spectrum allocations. Those theorists believe that new technologies such as software-defined radios and smart antennas can allow

Table 41.1
Property Rights vs. a Spectrum Commons: What Are the Options?

	Requires Ongoing Regulatory Oversight	Requires Little Continuing Oversight
Emphasis on Importance of Property Rights	**Ceilings and Floors—Easements Model**: Use auctions and property rights for mutually exclusive uses but impose federal ceiling and floor requirements ("easements") above or below which band managers have no control. So long as they do not meaningfully interfere, allow unlimited overlay or underlay across all private bands. Possible historical models: airline traffic above private property or subsoil mineral or oil drilling rights.	**Pure Property Rights Model**: Grant incumbent spectrum holders property rights in their allocations. Use auctions and property rights for new mutually exclusive uses of spectrum. Grant spectrum owners the absolute right of excludability and flexible use. Rely on private band managers to subdivide and sublease portions of their band to common uses.
Emphasis on Importance of Commons	**Public Parks Model**: Most of spectrum fully privatized but feds (perhaps states and localities or even private associations) purchase large swaths of spectrum and open it up for free use to create a spectrum commons. Or the FCC could just generously expand "Part 15" rules for unlicensed spectrum.	**Pure Commons—Homesteading Model**: No exclusive property rights. Let overlay and underlay users tap into spectrum as they wish and fight about the interference later in the courts or have faith that new devices ("agile radio," or software-defined radios) will allow everyone to work things out voluntarily.

users to infinitely divide the spectrum and shatter the notion of spectrum scarcity in the process.

But that is a stretch. There will almost certainly be *some* scarcity at work within the spectrum, just as there is for all natural resources. If nothing else, the limits of the human imagination create scarcities within the spectrum. More practically, commons areas are likely to encourage overuse and congestion, which will force many parties to search out privately managed bands where they could pay a premium for uninterrupted use. And the commons crowd does not have a useful transitional solution to the issue of spectrum incumbency. Existing users, many of whom have controlled a specific swath of spectrum for several decades, would not take lightly the idea of sharing their allocation with newcomers. And a good case can be made that they should not be forced to share that spectrum, given their long-standing control and use of the resource. It would be better to grandfather them into a property rights model by granting them complete ownership and flexible use rights to that spectrum.

Under the property rights regime envisioned above, the FCC would get out of the spectrum management business altogether. Residual regulatory functions, such as the adjudication of interference disputes or international coordination, could be left to some sort of "spectrum court," which would be a set of administrative law judges with particular expertise in resolving technical spectrum disputes.

Congress and the FCC are currently engaged in an effort to balance private and commons spectrum by putting some spectrum up for auction and exclusive use while setting aside other chunks of spectrum for commons or unlicensed uses. That is an experiment worth continuing, but the balance should not tilt too far in favor of unlicensed set-asides since evidence shows that a commons is rarely the most efficient way of ensuring the optimal use of a resource. Private ownership ensures that owners understand or incur the opportunity costs associated with misallocation of resources. Consequently, markets—including spectrum markets—tend to work best when most property is owned by someone. Nonetheless, a good argument can be made that some spectrum should be set aside for unlicensed spectrum applications—from garage door openers and TV remote controls to regional "wi-fi" and "wi-max" broadband networks.

Ending Arbitrary Media Ownership Regulations

Following the June 2, 2003, release by the FCC of revised guidelines regarding media ownership structures, a remarkably contentious debate erupted in Congress and the general public over this arcane regulatory matter. Although the FCC's order only moderately revised existing standards, many special interest groups and members of Congress mounted a vociferous campaign to overturn the new FCC rules. The critics of media decontrol argued that the FCC's liberalization of ownership rules would result in greater levels of industry consolidation and, more generally, be "bad for democracy" because it would result in "fewer voices."

413

On the objective question of whether media are more concentrated today than in the past, the evidence suggests this claim is generally untrue, with some sectors showing slightly greater levels of concentration but others actually exhibiting less. Of course, such comparisons with the past are complicated by the fact that the media marketplace has evolved rapidly in recent decades and entirely new technologies and industry sectors have emerged and displaced older ones.

The critics of media decontrol have actually had greater success with their subjective and quite emotional sociopolitical rationales for media reregulation. But claims about a lack of "diversity" and scarcity of "high-quality news and entertainment" do not square with marketplace realities. Again, if objective facts are taken into account, such emotional rhetoric and hypothetical fears are found to be baseless. Indeed, by all impartial measures, it is difficult to see how citizens and consumers are not better off today than they were in the past. Regardless of what the underlying business structures or ownership patterns look like, the real question should be "Do citizens and consumers have more news, information, and entertainment choices at their disposal today than in the past?" The answer to that question is an unambiguous yes.

What, then, explains the unusual passion of the pro-regulation media critics? It generally boils down to the fact that a lot of people have an axe to grind with the media for one reason or another. Psychologists describe this as the "third-person effect": self-proclaimed media "experts" and cultural elitists will often overestimate the influence that mass media have on the attitudes and behavior of others, all the while arguing that the media have no impact on them. That phenomenon helps explain why critics on both the left and the right decry "bias" in media, when in reality they are just concerned that particular programs are not to their liking and don't want others in the public to hear those viewpoints.

To correct for such perceived "bias," many cultural elitists want to remake the media in their preferred image, arguing the quality of news or journalism can be improved through structural ownership controls among other regulatory methods. Others have a love affair going with the notion of "localism" in broadcasting and journalism; they are committed to doing whatever it takes to preserve it even though they don't always make it clear what that means or how it should be accomplished. Finally, others simply loathe the fact that the media business is a business at all and declare that commercialism has destroyed diversity and quality in American journalism and entertainment.

But while the media critics keep complaining, the media marketplace keeps evolving and now offers citizens more choices than ever before. Ours is now a world characterized by information abundance, not information scarcity. Information and entertainment cannot be monopolized. Today's media marketplace is a dynamic sector subject to intensely competitive pressures. It would be impossible for any single entity or individual to control the flow of information and entertainment in a free society, especially considering the nature of the new technological age in which we live.

Policymakers must decide if the debate over media ownership policy will be governed by facts or fanaticism, evidence or emotionalism. The hyperbolic rhetoric, shameless fear-mongering, and unsubstantiated claims, which have thus far driven the absurd backlash to media liberalization, have no foundation in reality and must be rejected.

Suggested Readings

Crandall, Robert W. "A Somewhat Better Connection." *Regulation* (Summer 2002): 22–28.

Hazlett, Thomas W. "Economic and Political Consequences of the 1996 Telecommunications Act." *Regulation* 23, no. 3 (2000): 36–45. www.cato.org/pubs/regulation/regv23n3/hazlett.pdf.

Leighton, Wayne A. "Broadband Deployment and the Digital Divide: A Primer." Cato Institute Policy Analysis no. 410, August 7, 2001. www.cato.org/pubs/pas/pa-410es.html.

Thierer, Adam. " 'Net Neutrality' Digital Discrimination or Regulatory Gamesmanship in Cyberspace?" Cato Institute Policy Analysis no. 507, January 9, 2004. http://www.cato.org/pubs/pas/pa-507es.html.

_____. "Number Portability Decision Adds to Wireline Telecom Sector's Perfect Storm." Cato Institute TechKnowledge no. 66, November 20, 2003. http://www.cato.org/tech/tk/031120-tk.html.

_____. "Telecom Newspeak: The Orwellian World of Broadband 'Deregulation.' " In *Telecrisis: How Regulation Stifles High-Speed Internet Access*, edited by Sonia Arrison, pp. 9–31. San Francisco: Pacific Research Institute, January 2003. http://www.pacificresearch.org/pub/sab/techno/telecrisis.pdf.

_____. "A 10-Point Agenda for Comprehensive Telecom Reform." Cato Institute Briefing Paper no. 63, May 8, 2001. www.cato.org/pubs/briefs/bp-063es.html.

_____. "Thinking about the Next Telecom Act." Testimony before the Senate Commerce Committee, April 28, 2004. http://www.cato.org/testimony/ct-at040428.html.

_____. "Three Cheers for the FCC Spectrum Task Force Report." Cato Institute TechKnowledge no. 44, November 21, 2002. http://www.cato.org/tech/tk/021121-tk.html.

Thierer, Adam, and Clyde Wayne Crews Jr. *What's Yours Is Mine: Open Access and the Rise of Infrastructure Socialism*. Washington: Cato Institute, 2003. http://www.catostore.org/index.asp?fa = ProductDetails&pid = 1441099.

—Prepared by Adam Thierer

42. The Limits of Monetary Policy

> **Congress should**
>
> - uphold their constitutional duty to maintain the purchasing power of the dollar by enacting legislation that makes long-run price stability the primary objective of Federal Reserve monetary policy;
> - recognize that the Fed cannot fine-tune the real economy but can achieve price stability by limiting the growth of base money to a noninflationary path;
> - hold the Fed accountable for achieving expected inflation of 0–2 percent a year;
> - abolish the Exchange Stabilization Fund, since the Fed's role is to stabilize the domestic price level, not to stabilize the foreign exchange value of the dollar by intervening in the foreign exchange market; and
> - offer no resistance to the emergence of digital currency (money stored in digital form on microchips embedded in computer hard drives or in "smart cards") and other substitutes for Federal Reserve notes, so that free-market forces can help shape the future of monetary institutions.

History has shown that monetary stability—money growth consistent with a stable and predictable value of money—is an important determinant of economic stability. Safeguarding the long-run purchasing power of money is also essential for the future of private property and a free society. In the United States, persistent inflation has eroded the value of money and distorted relative prices, making production and investment decisions more uncertain. In the early 1970s, wage-price controls were imposed that attenuated economic freedom and increased government discretion, thus undermining the rule of law. Although those controls have been removed and inflation appears to be under control, there is no guarantee of future price-level stability.

Current law specifies no single objective for monetary policy and lacks an enforcement mechanism to achieve monetary stability. The multiplicity of goals and the absence of an appropriate penalty-reward structure to maintain stable money are evident from section 2A of the amended Federal Reserve Act:

> The Board of Governors ... and the Federal Open Market Committee shall maintain long-run growth of the monetary and credit aggregates commensurate with the economy's long-run potential to increase production, so as to promote effectively the goals of maximum employment, stable prices, and moderate long-term interest rates. .... Nothing in this Act shall be interpreted to require that the objectives and plans with respect to the ranges of growth or diminution of the monetary and credit aggregates disclosed in the reports submitted under this section be achieved.

From 1975 to 1999, the Federal Reserve reported its monetary targets to Congress. *It no longer does.* Alan Greenspan has done a commendable job of keeping inflation relatively low since he took office in 1987, but his performance is no guarantee of future success in achieving money of stable value.

The U.S. monetary system continues to be based on discretionary government fiat money, with no legally enforceable commitment to long-run price stability as the sole objective of monetary policy. Clark Warburton's 1946 characterization of U.S. monetary law as "ambiguous and chaotic" still rings true.

The large amount of discretion exercised by the Fed and the uncertainty it entails reflect Congress's failure to provide an adequate legal framework for stable money, as intended in Article I, section 8, of the Constitution. If the Fed were subject to a monetary rule, stop-go monetary policy—an extremely important factor in generating business fluctuations—could be halted. There is a growing consensus among economists and Fed officials that long-run price stability should be the focus of monetary policy, but Congress has yet to enact legislation that would bind the Fed to that objective and hold the chairman accountable for erratic changes in the quantity of money and persistent rises in the price level.

In his July 2000 "Monetary Report to the Congress," Greenspan stated: "Irrespective of the complexities of economic change, our primary goal is to find those policies that best contribute to a noninflationary environment and hence to growth. The Federal Reserve, I trust, will always remain vigilant in pursuit of that goal.'' But will it? And should the public trust the discretionary power of an ''independent'' central bank not bound by any rule?

William Poole, president of the Federal Reserve Bank of St. Louis and a proponent of zero inflation, has pointed to the market disruption caused by the lack of a clear monetary rule to guide Fed policy:

> The fact that markets so often respond to comments and speeches by Fed officials indicates that the markets today are not evaluating monetary policy in the context of a well-articulated and well-understood monetary rule. The problem is a deep and difficult one.

Congress should face that problem and retain the power to regulate the value of money by mandating that maintaining price stability is the Fed's primary duty.

Mandate Price Stability as the Fed's Primary Duty

Congress should amend the Federal Reserve Act to make long-run price stability—i.e., expected inflation of 0–2 percent a year—the sole goal of monetary policy. (If price indexes correctly measured inflation, zero expected inflation would be the preferred target. But since price indexes typically understate the extent of quality improvement, zero expected inflation can be in fact deflation.)

The Fed's function is not to set interest rates or to target the rate of unemployment or real growth. The Fed cannot control relative prices, employment, or output; it can directly control only the monetary base (currency held by the public and bank reserves) and thereby affect money growth, nominal income, and the average level of money prices. In the short run, the Fed can affect output and employment, as well as real interest rates, but it cannot do so in the long run.

The tradeoff between unemployment and inflation that is the basis for the Phillips curve is not a viable monetary policy option for the Fed. Market participants learn quickly and will revise their plans to account for the inflationary impact of faster money growth designed to reduce unemployment below its so-called natural rate. The results of those revisions—such as demanding higher money wages to compensate for expected inflation—will frustrate politicians intent on using monetary policy to stimulate the real economy. Cato Institute chairman William Niskanen, in a recent empirical study, made the following points.

419

- "There is *no* tradeoff of unemployment and inflation except in the same year."
- "In the long term, the unemployment function is a *positive* function of the inflation rate."
- "The minimum sustainable unemployment rate is about 3.7 percent and can be achieved only by a *zero* steady-state inflation rate."

Evidence also shows that inflation and long-run growth are *inversely* related (Figure 42.1). Inflation—that is, a *persistent* rise in the average level of money prices—introduces distortions into the financial system and impedes the efficient allocation of resources. Those distortions and others have a negative impact on economic growth. Since inflation is primarily a monetary phenomenon (caused by excess growth of the money supply over and above long-run output growth), it cannot increase real

Figure 42.1
Real Growth and Inflation Move in Opposite Directions

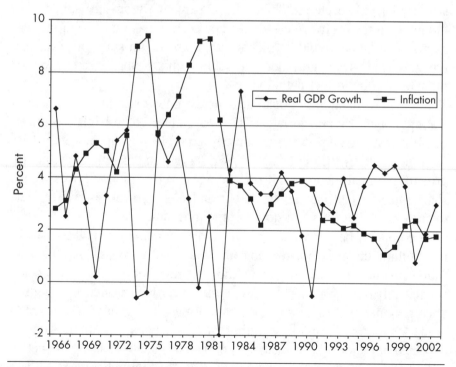

SOURCE: Alan Reynolds, "The Fed's Whimsical Monetary Tinkering," Figure 1, as updated.
NOTE: Inflation is calculated from the GDP chain-type index.

growth—but it can *decrease* it. That is why monetary stability and, hence, price-level stability are so important.

The Fed cannot attain more than one policy target with one policy instrument. The only instrument the Fed has direct control over is the monetary base; the surest target is long-run price stability. The Fed could use either an adaptive feedback rule, such as that proposed by Carnegie Mellon economist Bennett McCallum, or an inflation-targeting rule, such as New Zealand has successfully used. With the feedback rule, the Fed would adjust the growth of the monetary base to keep nominal GDP (or domestic final sales) on a smooth noninflationary growth path. With an inflation target, the Fed would adjust the monetary base so that the growth rate of the price level was approximately zero in the long run. There would be some rises and falls in the price level due to supply-side shocks, either positive or negative, but *expected* inflation would remain close to zero (in the 0–2 percent range) over time.

Congress need not dictate the exact rule for the Fed to follow in its pursuit of long-run price stability, but Congress should hold the Fed accountable for achieving that goal—and not require the Fed to respond to supply shocks that would lead to one-time increases or decreases in the price level.

The public's trust and confidence in the future purchasing power of the dollar can be permanently increased by a legal mandate directing the Fed to adopt a monetary rule to achieve long-run price stability. According to Poole:

> The logic, and the evidence, both suggest that the appropriate goal for monetary policy should be price stability, that is, a long-run inflation rate of approximately zero. . . . A central bank's single most important job is preserving the value of the nation's money. Monetary policy has succeeded if the public can reasonably trust that a dollar will buy tomorrow what it will buy today. . . . I am confident that our economy's long-run performance would be enhanced by a monetary policy that aims at, achieves, and maintains a zero rate of inflation.

That institutional change would ensure that the post-Greenspan Fed maintained a credible monetary policy—one that protected the value of money and, hence, safeguarded private property rights.

Recognize the Limits of Monetary Policy

The Fed cannot permanently increase the rate of economic growth or permanently lower the rate of unemployment by increasing money growth, nor can it permanently lower real interest rates. But it can throw the economy off track by policy errors—that is, by creating either too much or too little money to maintain stable expectations about the long-run value of the currency. The most grievous error of discretionary monetary policy, as Milton Friedman and Anna Schwartz have shown in *A Monetary History of the United States*, was the Fed's failure to prevent the money supply from shrinking by one-third between 1929 and 1933, which turned a sharp but otherwise ordinary recession into the Great Depression.

Economics, like medicine, is not an exact science. The guiding principle of economic policy should be the great physician Galen's (A.D. 160) admonition to "first do no harm." Instead of pursuing in vain an activist monetary policy designed to fine-tune the economy and achieve all good things—full employment, economic growth, and price stability—Fed policy ought to be aimed at what it can actually achieve.

Three questions Congress must contemplate in its oversight of monetary policy are (1) What can the Fed do? (2) What can't it do? (3) What should it do?

What the Fed Can Do

The Fed can

- control the monetary base through open market operations, reserve requirements, and the discount rate;
- provide liquidity quickly to shore up public confidence in banks during a financial crisis;
- influence the level and growth rate of nominal variables, in particular monetary aggregates, nominal income, and the price level;
- control inflation and prevent monetary instability in the long run; and
- influence expectations about future inflation and nominal interest rates.

What the Fed Cannot Do

The Fed cannot

- target real variables so as to permanently reduce the rate of unemployment or increase economic growth;
- determine real interest rates;
- peg the nominal exchange rate and at the same time pursue an independent monetary policy aimed at stabilizing the price level, without imposing capital controls;

- fine-tune the economy; or
- make accurate macroeconomic forecasts.

What the Fed Should Do

The Fed should

- keep the growth of nominal GDP on a stable, noninflationary path so that expected inflation is close to zero by controlling the monetary base;
- let market forces determine exchange rates so that the dollar and other key currencies are free to find their equilibrium value in the foreign exchange market; and
- avoid predicating monetary policy on stock market performance.

By recognizing the limits of monetary policy, Congress will also recognize the importance of enacting a law that establishes a clear framework for such policy. Mandating long-run price stability as the Fed's sole objective is a goal the public can understand and a target the Fed can achieve and be held accountable for.

Hold the Fed Accountable

If a law making price stability the sole aim of monetary policy is to be effective, the Fed must be held responsible for failure to meet that target. That means the law must clearly state the price-stability target while letting the Fed choose how best to achieve it.

The New Zealand inflation-targeting law is instructive. The Reserve Bank Act of 1989 states that the sole objective of monetary policy is price stability. A target range is set for inflation, as measured by the consumer price index, which the governor of the Reserve Bank must achieve within a specified time horizon, with exceptions made for supply shocks. The governor is required to sign a contract, the Policy Targets Agreement, with the finance minister, in which the governor agrees to a target range for inflation set by the finance minister, the period for achieving it, and the penalty of dismissal for failing to meet the target. That arrangement has served New Zealand well in terms of achieving a low rate of inflation while letting its currency float on the foreign exchange market. Unlike countries with pegged exchange rates and no monetary rule, New Zealand sailed through the Asian financial crisis quite smoothly.

Congress should draw on the experience of New Zealand to create a credible monetary law that holds the chairman of the Fed accountable for achieving long-run price stability.

Abolish the Exchange Stabilization Fund

If the Fed is to focus solely on maintaining the purchasing power of the dollar, then it cannot also use monetary policy to peg the foreign exchange, or external, value of the dollar. The dollar must be free to float without exchange market intervention. Halting such intervention requires that Congress abolish the Exchange Stabilization Fund, which was created in 1934 by the Gold Reserve Act. The ESF has been used by the Treasury to try to "stabilize" the external value of the dollar, but without success. It has also been used to make dollar loans to support the currencies of less-developed countries. It is time to get rid of this relic of the New Deal and let markets, not the state, determine the relative price of the dollar.

Welcome the Evolution of Alternatives to Government Fiat Money

While Congress should hold the Fed responsible for maintaining the value of money, in terms of its domestic purchasing power, Congress should also welcome the emergence of alternatives to government fiat money, such as digital cash. New monetary institutions should be allowed to evolve as new technology and information become available.

The growth of electronic commerce will increase the demand for new methods of payment, methods that economize on paper currency. As consumers' trust in electronic cash grows, the demand for the Fed's base money may decrease. That may actually make it easier for a monetary rule to be implemented because the Fed need not worry about complications arising from changes in the ratio of currency to deposits, according to University of Georgia economist George Selgin. Indeed, Milton Friedman's simple rule of zero growth of the monetary base may work quite well in the information age, and it may be a step toward private competing currencies, as advocated by F. A. Hayek. Consumers would have greater monetary freedom and money with the best record of stable purchasing power as a result.

A concrete measure to promote greater monetary choice would be for Congress to repeal the 1 percent tax on bank-issued notes that is still on the books (U.S. C., title 12, section 541), as suggested by Kurt Schuler, an economist with the U.S. Treasury.

Conclusion

Monetary disturbances have been either a major cause of or a key accentuating factor in business fluctuations. Reducing uncertainty about the future path of nominal GDP and the price level would help remove erratic money as a disrupting influence in economic life. As Friedman has pointed out, one of the most important things monetary policy can do is "prevent money itself from being a major source of economic disturbance."

It is time for Congress to accept its constitutional responsibility by making the Fed more transparent and holding it accountable for long-run price stability. In testimony before the Joint Economic Committee of the U.S. Congress in March 1995, economist David Meiselman summed up the case for limiting Fed discretion and mandating a stable price-level rule:

> It is . . . dangerous folly to expect or depend on the Fed to achieve what is beyond its power to attain. The best possible monetary policy cannot create jobs or production. It can only prevent the instability, the uncertainty, and the loss of employment and income resulting from poor monetary policy. In my judgment, the best possible monetary policy aims to achieve a stable and predictable price level.

Congress should now heed that advice and create an institutional framework that recognizes the limits of monetary policy and sets a firm basis for a credible long-run commitment to stable money in the post-Greenspan era. Monetary policy should not depend on any one individual. It should depend on rules that limit discretion, mandate price stability, and hold the Fed chairman accountable for failing to achieve money of stable value. Financial markets will then show less anxiety upon the departure of the "wise one."

The Greenspan record can be extended by moving from discretion to a clear rule for price stability, thereby converting trust in a particular individual into confidence in a rule that will long outlast any single Fed chairman. Ending stop-go monetary policy will generate social benefits by reducing the uncertainty due to erratic money, making it easier to plan long-term investment projects, and increasing the efficiency of resource allocation. Economic growth will be more robust as a result.

The major thrust of this chapter has been to call on Congress to make the Fed accountable for maintaining the long-run value of the currency. But Congress should not limit its vision to a monetary system dominated by a government-run central bank, even if that institution is limited by a monetary rule. Rather, Congress should welcome the vision of a future in which the free market plays an important role in supplying money of stable value, in competition with the Fed. The choice of monetary institutions should ultimately be a free choice, made by the market, not dictated by law.

Suggested Readings

Dorn, James A. "Alternatives to Government Fiat Money." *Cato Journal* 9, no. 2 (Fall 1989): 277–94.

Dorn, James A., ed. *The Future of Money in the Information Age.* Washington: Cato Institute, 1997.

Dorn, James A., and Anna J. Schwartz, eds. *The Search for Stable Money.* Chicago: University of Chicago Press, 1987.

Friedman, Milton. "The Role of Monetary Policy." *American Economic Review* 58 (1968): 1–17.

Gwartney, James, Kurt Schuler, and Robert Stein. "Achieving Monetary Stability at Home and Abroad." *Cato Journal* 21, no. 2 (Fall 2001): 183–203.

Keleher, Robert E. "A Response to Criticisms of Price Stability." Study for the Joint Economic Committee of the U.S. Congress, September 1997. www.house.gov/jec.

McCallum, Bennett T. "Choice of Target for Monetary Policy." *Economic Affairs* (Autumn 1995): 35–41.

———. "Misconceptions Regarding Rules vs. Discretion for Monetary Policy." *Cato Journal* 23, no. 3 (Winter 2004): 365–72.

Meiselman, David I. "Accountability and Responsibility in the Conduct of Monetary Policy: Mandating a Stable Price Level Rule." Testimony before the Joint Economic Committee of the U.S. Congress on the Humphrey-Hawkins Act. 104th Cong., 1st sess., March 16, 1995.

Niskanen, William A. "On the Death of the Phillips Curve." *Cato Journal* 22, no. 2 (Fall 2002); 193–98.

———. "On the Fed's Demand Bubble." *Cato Journal* 23, no. 1 (Spring–Summer 2003): 135–38.

———. "A Test of the Demand Rule." *Cato Journal* 21, no. 2 (Fall 2001): 205–9.

Poole, William. "Is inflation Too Low?" *Cato Journal* 18, no. 3 (Winter 1999): 453–64.

———. "Monetary Policy Rules?" Federal Reserve Bank of St. Louis *Review* 81 (March–April 1999): 3–12.

Reynolds, Alan. "The Fed's Whimsical Monetary Tinkering." *Outlook: Ideas for the Future from Hudson Institute* 1, no. 4 (April 1997): 1–16.

———. "The Fiscal Monetary Policy Mix." *Cato Journal* 21, no. 2 (Fall 2001): 263–75.

Schuler, Kurt. "Note Issue by Banks: A Step toward Free Banking in the United States?" *Cato Journal* 20, no. 3 (Winter 2001): 453–65.

Schwartz, Anna J. "Time to Terminate the ESF and the IMF." Cato Institute Foreign Policy Briefing no. 48, August 26, 1998.

Walsh, Carl E. "Accountability in Practice: Recent Monetary Policy in New Zealand." FRBSF Economic Letter no. 96-25, September 9, 1996.

—Prepared by James A. Dorn

43. *Major Policy Lessons from the Corporate Scandals*

Congress should

- clarify that the criminal penalties in the Sarbanes-Oxley Act (SOA) require proof of malign intent and personal responsibility for some illegal act;
- address the potential problem of the delisting of foreign and small firms from the American stock exchanges, maybe by exempting such firms from the regulatory requirements;
- *eliminate* the expensive and wholly unnecessary Public Company Accounting Oversight Board, preferably before it establishes new precedents and creates some special interest;
- consider the wholesale *repeal* of the SOA on the basis that it is unnecessary, harmful, and inadequate to address the major problems in the U.S. corporate economy;
- *eliminate* the current roles of the Financial Accounting Standards Board (FASB), the Securities and Exchange Commission (SEC), and Congress in setting accounting standards, allowing each stock exchange to set the accounting standards for corporations listed on that exchange;
- delay implementation of the FASB ruling that would require the expensing of stock options until the issue of the authority to set accounting standards is resolved;
- encourage the development of a parallel system of the primary *nonfinancial* indicators of the earnings potential of a firm;
- allow each stock exchange to set the disclosure rules for corporations listed on that exchange, to select and monitor the independent public auditors of those corporations, and to establish a market for the voting rights in the shares of those corporations;

(continued next page)

427

> *(continued)*
>
> - consider broadening the certification provisions of the SOA to include the accountants, bankers, and lawyers who abet the misrepresentation of a corporation's financial condition;
> - consider a rule that a lawyer must report a possibly illegal act by a corporate client to a senior partner in his firm and to the board of the corporation;
> - eliminate the authority of the SEC to designate credit-rating agencies as nationally recognized statistical rating organizations (NSROs);
> - reduce and eventually eliminate the reliance of regulators on credit ratings;
> - reduce the standard-setting role of the SEC but increase its effectiveness by modernizing its reporting and review process;
> - repeal the $1 million limit on the salary and bonus that may be deducted as a current expense, and repeal the SOA ban on loans to corporate officers;
> - *replace* the corporate income tax with a broad-based tax on the net cash flow of all nonfinancial businesses; and
> - *repeal* the Williams Act of 1968 and other restrictions on the market for corporate control.

The Flawed Governmental Response to the Corporate Scandals

A $7 *trillion* decline in the value of American equities, a wave of corporate accounting scandals, and the bankruptcy of Enron, WorldCom, and several other large corporations led Congress, the Securities and Exchange Commission (SEC), and a gaggle of state attorneys general to implement the most comprehensive new regulation of corporate behavior since the 1930s. Unfortunately, most of the new regulations authorized by the hurriedly assembled Sarbanes-Oxley Act (SOA) are unnecessary, harmful, or inadequate to address the major problems of the corporate sector.

Unnecessary

Because the stock exchanges had already implemented most of the SOA changes in the rules of corporate governance in their new listing standards, the SEC had full authority to approve and enforce accounting standards, the requirement that CEOs certify the financial statements of their firms, and the rules for corporate disclosure; and the Department of Justice had ample authority to prosecute executives for securities fraud. The expensive new Public Company Accounting Oversight Board (PCAOB) is especially unnecessary. Its role is to regulate the few remaining independent public auditors, but it has no regulatory authority beyond that already granted to the SEC. Moreover, the audit firms still have a potential conflict of interest, because they are selected by and paid by the public corporations that they audit. The PCAOB may also be unconstitutional, because it is a private monopoly that has been granted both regulatory and taxing authority.

Harmful

The SOA is harmful because it substantially increases the risks of serving as a corporate officer or director, the premiums for directors' and officers' liability insurance, and the incentives, primarily for foreign and small firms, not to list their stock on an American exchange. The ban on loans to corporate officers eliminates one of the more efficient instruments of executive compensation. And the SOA may also reduce the incentive for corporate executives and directors to seek legal advice.

Inadequate

The SOA failed to identify and correct the major problems of accounting, auditing, taxation, and corporate governance that have invited corporate malfeasance and increased the probability of bankruptcy.

Unfortunately, the Sarbanes-Oxley Act, the new SEC regulations, and the extortion suits by the state attorneys general are better examples of the incentive for public officials to be seen doing something about a perceived problem than of a patient and informed reflection about the origins of the problem.

The Major Policy Lessons from the Corporate Scandals

The major policy lessons that were illustrated by the collapse of Enron and other corporate scandals are the following:

Don't Count Too Much on Financial Accounting

Financial accounting is backward looking, unusually complex, subject to subjective interpretation, vulnerable to several controversial accounting doctrines, and an invitation to manipulation. More important perhaps, many changes in nonfinancial conditions, which are never recorded on the balance sheet, may affect the value of a firm for better or for worse. For these reasons, corporate financial accounts do not provide accurate or sufficient information to corporate managers, investors, or regulators. This leads us to recommend that the SEC allow each stock exchange to set the accounting standards for all firms listed on that exchange and to promote the development of industry-specific nonfinancial accounts to complement the financial accounts.

Don't Count Too Much on Auditing

The most important lesson of the Enron collapse is that *every* link in the audit chain—including the audit committee and the board, the independent public auditor, the bankers and lawyers that aided and abetted the misrepresentation of Enron's financial condition, the credit-rating agencies, and the Securities and Exchange Commission—failed to deter, detect, and correct the conditions that led to that collapse. Although not a part of the formal audit chain, most of the market specialists in Enron stock and the business press were also late in recognizing Enron's financial weakness. Moreover, this is a characteristic pattern in many other bankruptcies.

This leads us to recommend that most of the audit functions be assigned to the stock exchanges, the only institution with the potential to capture the third-party benefits of a good audit. Each stock exchange would set the disclosure rules for the corporations listed on that exchange and select, monitor, and compensate the independent public auditor of each firm.

I also recommend new rules for the accountants, bankers, and lawyers that contribute to the misrepresentation of a corporation's financial condition, a reduced role for the credit-rating agencies, and a more focused role for the SEC.

Our Tax System Is a Major Part of the Problem

Our tax system encourages too much debt and overly risky investments, the characteristic conditions that lead to bankruptcy. American corporations use too much debt because interest payments are a deductible expense but returns to equity are not. Until the implementation of the 2003 tax law, retained earnings and investment within the corporation were too high because the individual tax rate on long-term capital gains was much lower than on dividends. The effects of those characteristics are magnified by the fact that the combined federal and state U.S. tax rate on corporate income is now among the highest of the industrial nations, second only to that in Japan. The limit of $1 million for salary and bonus as a deductible expense, combined with the increase in the top marginal tax rates on earnings and the reduction of the long-term capital gains rate, strongly increased the incentive to compensate corporate officers by stock options, a form of compensation that encourages risk taking. Our tax system, much like the Generally Accepted Accounting Principles (GAAP) and for much the same reasons, is extraordinarily complex, inviting attention to the many types of legal tax shelters used by Enron. Those characteristics of the current tax system lead me to recommend that the $1 million limit on the deductibility of salary and bonus be repealed and that the corporate income tax be replaced by a broad-based tax on the net cash flow of all nonfinancial corporations.

The U.S. Rules of Corporate Governance Do Not Now Adequately Protect the Interests of General Shareholders

Over the past four decades, beginning with the federal Williams Act of 1968, the combination of federal and state legislation and court rulings and rules approved by corporate boards has led to an accumulation of takeover defenses, even though firm performance is negatively related to the number of such defenses. This has increased the power of incumbent managements relative to their boards and general shareholders, increased the number of unprofitable acquisitions by large corporations, increased executive compensation, and almost destroyed the market for corporate control. The primary policy lesson that we can draw from this experience is that the federal government should withdraw from *any* role in establishing the rules of corporate governance and disclosure, returning this role to the state governments and stock exchanges. The policy actions that would be most helpful in restoring an effective market for corporate control would be for Congress to repeal the Williams Act and for the SEC to allow a market for the voting rights of shares that are separable from the ownership rights.

Conclusion

The corporate scandals illustrated by the Enron collapse were a serious problem, undermining trust in the accounts and the behavior of all corporations and the political support for free-market policies. At the same time, it is important to recognize that the more serious corporate malfeasance was apparently limited to a few dozen of the 12,000 U.S. public corporations and that the general performance of the stock market and the U.S. economy has been better than that of most other industrial nations, both in the last several years and in the last two decades. So it is important not to overreact by such measures as the Sarbanes-Oxley Act.

This chapter, in contrast, advocates addressing the problems illustrated by the Enron collapse by *reducing* and *focusing* the role of government.

Suggested Readings

Culp, Christopher L., and William A. Niskanen, eds. *Corporate Aftershock: The Public Policy Lessons from the Collapse of Enron and Other Major Corporations.* Hoboken, NJ: John Wiley & Sons, 2003.

Litan, Robert E., with George Benston, Michael Bromwich, and Alfred Wagenhofer. *Following the Money: The Enron Failure and the State of Corporate Governance.* Washington: AEI-Brookings Joint Center for Regulatory Studies, 2003.

Niskanen, William A., ed. *After Enron: The Major Lessons for Public Policy.* Lanham, MD: Rowman & Littlefield, 2005.

—Prepared by William A. Niskanen

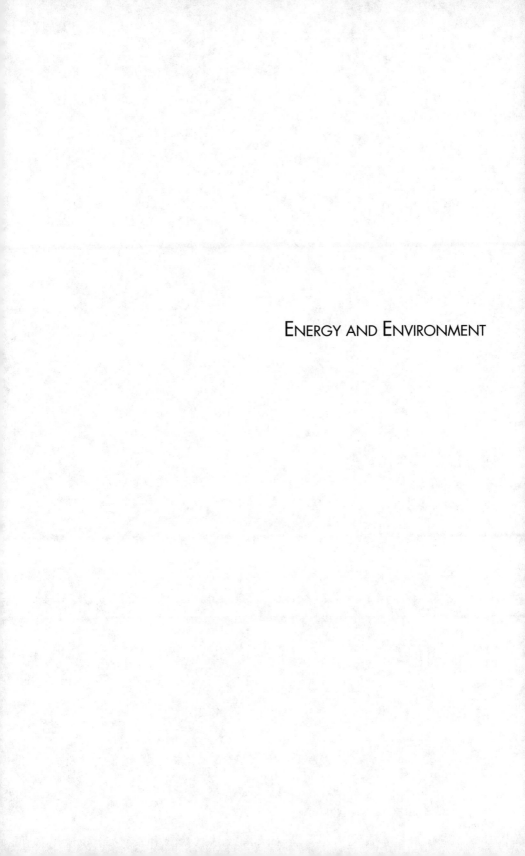

ENERGY AND ENVIRONMENT

44. Electricity Policy

Congress should

- repeal the Federal Power Act of 1935 and abolish the Federal Energy Regulatory Commission (FERC);
- repeal the 1935 Public Utility Holding Company Act (PUHCA) and the 1978 Public Utility Regulatory Policy Act (PURPA);
- privatize federal power marketing authorities, the Tennessee Valley Authority, and all federal power generation facilities;
- eliminate all tax preferences applicable to municipal power companies and electricity cooperatives; and
- declare that any state or municipal regulation of the generation, transmission, distribution, or retail sale of electricity interferes with interstate trade and is a violation of the U.S. Constitution's Commerce Clause.

The debate over electricity regulation is primarily a debate over the regulatory restructuring efforts of the 1990s. At the federal level, the discussion is about (1) the extent to which the federal government should mandate restructuring on states that have yet to give up the old regulatory regime and (2) whether the federal government should impose institutional and regulatory order on an industry still largely under the purview of state governments. At the state level, the debate is moving in the opposite direction; it is about whether and to what extent the entire restructuring experiment ought to be reversed.

Accordingly, a review of the merits of restructuring (sometimes erroneously called "deregulation") is necessary. While most advocates of free markets and competition have embraced electric utility restructuring and favor further steps in that direction, we are skeptical about the merits of those reforms. They are not steps toward a more deregulated market, just a differently regulated market, and they almost certainly introduce more economic complications than they remedy.

435

Electric Utility Restructuring 101

Electric utility restructuring was a political answer to the problem of high-cost electricity in the Northeast and California. By the early 1990s, firms were threatening to leave those states where power costs were far above the national average. The high-cost states attempted to bring low-cost electricity to the firms by ending the monopoly that local utilities had on local customers. In theory, distant (lower-cost) generators as well as new local entrants would compete against the local power companies. Consequently, rates (it was hoped) would fall.

Economists generally put little faith in the hope that competition per se would significantly reduce rates for reasons that we will explain below. Nonetheless, most supported restructuring on two entirely different grounds. First, they believed that restructuring would promote pricing regimes that reflected minute-by-minute changes in supply and demand. "Real-time pricing," as it is known in the trade, could lead (according to one estimate) to a 25 percent increase in power production and a similar percentage decrease in price were it implemented throughout the country. Second, economists believed that restructuring would discourage high-cost generating capacity, a phenomenon that was a major reason why rates were so high in some states in the first place.

Nearly a decade later, it appears that restructuring has indeed improved the performance of the generation sector. Fixed power plant operating costs, for example, have declined in those states that undertook regulatory reforms. Moreover, widespread bankruptcies triggered by low wholesale power prices have reminded investors that returns are no longer guaranteed.

Restructuring, however, has had little observable effect on retail electricity prices. Electricity is still relatively expensive in the high-cost states that undertook restructuring in the 1990s. Whatever price declines have occurred are as much the result of the glut of generation capacity added during the 1990s because of irrational investor exuberance as the result of any permanent effect of regulatory restructuring. Meanwhile, real-time pricing (the development that economists thought would offer the largest efficiency gains from restructuring) has not been implemented on a large scale anywhere.

Why Can't Competition Cut Prices?

Politicians in the high-cost states supported restructuring in the hope that electricity from states like Kentucky (4.3 cents per kilowatthour in

2002) would end up being sold in states like New York (11.3 cents per kWh in 2002). Politicians in the low-cost states, however, have resisted efforts to create the sort of integrated national market for electricity that would allow such a thing to happen. Given how electricity prices are set under most state regulatory systems, the resistance is rational.

Because Kentucky's low prices reflect the cost of electricity *on average* rather than the cost of electricity at the margin, it's unlikely that Kentucky's utilities could produce enough low-cost electricity to serve both its domestic customers and its potential new customers in New York. Expanded output in Kentucky would probably have costs greater than 4.3 cents per kWh because the main source of low-cost electricity in Kentucky is lightly regulated old coal-fired power plants the output of which is strictly controlled under the federal Clean Air Act. Accordingly, politicians in Kentucky resist allowing their utilities to sell to customers in the high-cost states, given the understandable fear that doing so would result in increased electricity costs for domestic consumers. There is, after all, only so much low-cost power to go around, given the regulatory peculiarities of the Clean Air Act, and selling that power to the highest bidder would remove some or much of it from the reach of in-state consumers.

Many economists were skeptical about the prospects for competition reducing retail prices in electricity markets because of the generalizability of the Kentucky story—expanded output would have similar costs everywhere. In a deregulated market, the price of electricity is set by the highest-cost source of supply necessary to meet demand. In all markets and in all regions, that source happens to be natural gas–fired electricity, and the most important factor in gas-fired electricity costs is the cost of natural gas itself, which varies across locations only because of transmission costs.

Has Restructuring Made Crises More Likely?

Although regulatory restructuring was widely embraced in high-cost states during most of the 1990s, resistance is now widespread because most Americans associate electricity restructuring with the California electricity crisis of 2000–2001. That association in the public mind is not entirely unfair.

To be sure, the California electricity crisis was caused by an unusual confluence of events that had nothing to do with restructuring. A severe drought reduced Pacific Northwest hydropower at the same time that demand was increasing because of a hot summer and then a cold winter.

437

Throw in tightening air emissions regulations on gas-fired power generators in the LA Basin and the crisis was on.

Although no regulatory system could have averted the wholesale electricity price increases that followed, the restructuring plan then in place in California exacerbated the crisis. First, the convoluted state-managed wholesale power market left lots of room for generators to game the system and receive prices above what one might expect. Second, retail price controls that were adopted in the course of restructuring removed incentives for generators to price reasonably. Moreover, retail price controls ensured the bankruptcy of the public utility companies because they were prohibited from passing on the prices they paid for wholesale power to retail customers. The declining financial health of California electric utility companies forced wholesale suppliers to mark up the price of their electricity even further because of the increasing risk of nonpayment.

How much did restructuring contribute to the crisis? MIT electricity economist Paul Joskow thinks that about half of the wholesale price increases experienced during the shock can be attributed to poor market design. Other electricity economists, such as Harvard's William Hogan, think that the true figure is much smaller. Still, there is general agreement among economists that restructuring on balance made matters worse.

An important consequence of the California electricity crisis has been the quiet reemergence in many states that have restructured of regulations that require utility companies to maintain adequate reserve generating capacity and socialize the cost among all ratepayers during all hours of electricity use rather than just peak power users. This restores one of the main defects of the old regulated regime (the use of average rather than marginal costs as a basis for prices and the ''need'' to meet excessive peak demand that necessarily results) and undermines an essential rationale for restructuring.

Restructuring and the Public Commons

Before restructuring, the costs of maintaining the power grid and moving power along it were largely internal to companies engaged in generation, transmission, and distribution and paid for by ratepayers in a cost-plus system. Under restructuring and the accompanying separation of generation from the other two components, however, the power grid is the locus of endless battles about investment and cost allocation to which there is no intellectually compelling, nonarbitrary answer. Such battles are a recipe for continuing political intervention and turmoil.

The most important characteristic of electricity systems is the "commons" nature of the alternating current (AC) grid. That is, the physical reality of the grid does not coincide with private property rights or the 50 state regulatory schemes that govern the grid. Power added by any generator on an AC transmission system follows all paths, favoring those with least resistance rather than the shortest distance between generator and customer. Thus bilateral contracts between any willing seller and buyer of electricity involve legal fiction. That is, the power that the buyer is consuming almost certainly does not come from the designated "seller." Moreover, putting power onto the grid and taking it off affects all other parties on the system in ways that are not captured by prices— the textbook definition of "externality." The proper way to manage those externalities is the subject of great dispute and has no obvious answer. Likewise, transmission *additions* confer benefits across all generators and consumers on the grid and thus have public good characteristics. The development of property rights and prices that internalize those characteristics is very difficult.

Prior to restructuring, the commons problem was addressed by allowing one company to service a set block of consumers with generation, transmission, and distribution services. Trade between such companies was never very large and was governed by barter arrangements rather than markets. Where trade was extensive, voluntary arrangements such as the Pennsylvania–New Jersey–Maryland transmission pool arose to manage the flows across separately owned transmission systems through contract. Thus, historically, the "commons" characteristics of the grid did not create large externality issues. Most costs and benefits were borne by the same entity.

The Energy Policy Act of 1992 and orders 888 and 889 from the Federal Energy Regulatory Commission (FERC) changed all that. The law and regulations facilitated (and in some cases, actually ordered) the development of widespread trading on the grid. The mismatch between the physical reality of the grid and its current governance structure has become a matter of serious concern. Unless remedied, it will lead to deterioration of the transmission system, increasingly unstable supplies, and excessively costly power.

Solving the Public Goods Problem

What governance system can best address transmission externalities? The most commonly discussed possibility is aggressive regulation by FERC through mandatory utility participation in regional transmission organizations (RTOs). The RTOs would be responsible for long-term management of the electricity grid. FERC also favors a standard market design for the industry in order to eliminate the discrepancy between the commons nature of the transmission system and the current fragmented system that governs it.

Many of the standard market design rules would be adopted by utilities that wanted to *voluntarily* engage in interstate trade. The problem with that caveat is that many utilities don't really want to engage in interstate trade or allow it to occur over their wires. That's because they own the grid over which trade would take place, and they don't want to be responsible for investment in transmission from which others benefit without payment.

Another problem with FERC's proposals is that they leave state-level regulation intact. Much of that regulation, unfortunately, works to impede electricity trading and ignores the regional spillover effects of transmission investment. The federal solution also takes responsibility for the grid away from its multiple owners and gives it instead to nonprofit corporations, introducing incentives for poor management by separating ownership from control.

While it's certainly true that the FERC could improve matters along the grid by assuming the regulatory powers currently exercised by 47 separate state governments (Texas is the exception because the transmission system there is entirely independent of systems elsewhere), if the existing balkanized system impedes gains to trade. But there may be few gains to trade to be had. Because natural gas is the marginal source of electricity everywhere, efficiency gains from long-distance trade exist only if the transmission costs of gas-fired electricity (from low-cost rural locations) are less than the higher fixed costs (land and labor) of locating generation near urban consumers. Unfortunately, there is little evidence of that. The other potential source of efficiency gains is real-time pricing. But mandatory open access and restructuring have not involved the use of real-time pricing, and states could implement real-time pricing without deregulation and without FERC intervention if they were so inclined.

Back to the Future?

Vertical integration (under which the same company owns both generation and transmission) may be the most efficient form of industrial organization for the electricity industry. Forcing the industry to disaggregate the business of making electricity from the business of moving electricity in order to create competition in the generating sector requires a great deal of regulatory oversight to govern the interaction of independent generators and the public commons that is the current transmission system. Even if some efficiency gains result from the imposition of competition in the generating sector, the revival of installed capacity requirements re-creates the costs of excess capacity that led to the call for generation competition in the first place.

If the static efficiency gains from mandatory open access are smaller than advertised and the costs created by the regulatory apparatus necessary to achieve them are large, what should we do? Traditional vertically integrated utilities are often rather low-cost providers of electricity, but they restrict trade and tend to form state-based cartels. If such firms were totally deregulated (including transmission and distribution), they probably wouldn't change their behavior very much because entry and rivalry are difficult as long as they control the "highways" over which the electricity trade takes place. The only competition they would face would be from large customers who would generate their own power from natural gas cogeneration, but that threat has been considerably weakened by the doubling of natural gas prices in the early part of this decade.

The lack of competition that would occur naturally as the result of simple deregulation led many well-meaning people to propose and implement mandatory open access to "force" competition to occur. But that has required the substitution of legal orders for vertical integration to manage transmission externalities and led to games about transmission investment in which the players all argue that someone else should pay for extra capacity.

Two other scenarios are possible. One is a return to the old model: regulatory oversight of electric power companies (oversight that would include utility prices and investment decisions) combined with management of the transmission commons through vertical integration. The second is complete deregulation. Ironically, the substantive differences between those two radically different approaches are less significant than one might think.

In an unregulated world, the relationship between electric firms and consumers would almost certainly be governed by long-term contracts. That's because the high cost and immobility of electricity generation and transmission assets, and the lack of alternative uses for those assets, would allow producers and consumers to hold each other up—the classic condition under which long-term contracts make the most sense for both parties. Accordingly, the probable relationship between firms and consumers in a deregulated electricity market might very well resemble the regulatory architecture of the old regime—utilities would receive a guaranteed rate of return and consumers some degree of price protection.

But what if residential consumers find it difficult or impossible to negotiate as a group with the electric utility company? Scholars who have examined pricing behavior by power companies under the old regime have discovered that, even when supervised by public regulators, utilities charged profit-maximizing prices for electricity. In short, there's good reason to believe that under normal circumstances rates would be no higher without regulatory supervision than they are with regulatory supervision.

Accordingly, legislators should completely deregulate the electricity sector and not worry about the market power of incumbent utilities. Although complete deregulation may not hold out the promise for static efficiency gains greater than those that might be achieved through a return to the old regime, it does hold out the promise of dynamic efficiency. Market actors do not have the freedom to experiment easily with different business arrangements and contractual relationships under regulation.

If complete deregulation is politically unachievable, legislators should end the experiment in regulatory restructuring and return to the old regime. Fortunately, the economic problems posed by rate regulation are fewer today than they were 30 or 40 years ago because incentive-based regulation has replaced traditional rate-of-return regulation. Under incentive-based regulation, owners have an incentive to reduce costs rather than to pad them and, more to the point, to avoid capital-intensive generating facilities.

Conclusion

Electricity restructuring was originally embraced by many economists because it was believed that reforms would reduce the incentive to build excess generating capacity, eliminate the incentive to build capital-intensive generating facilities, and lead to an introduction of real-time pricing. Only the second of those expectations has been realized.

In addition, restructuring has created problems previously unknown in the electricity sector. Those problems generally arose because electricity restructuring

- focused on generation competition and ignored the pricing and incentive issues involved in managing the transmission system and its public commons characteristics,

- grafted a relatively free wholesale market onto a still heavily regulated retail market, and
- established artificial market institutions that invited manipulation and abuse.

The end result has proven far from satisfactory.

There is little reason to think that the restructuring experiment will produce improved results in the future. The problems with the current regime are systematic. Regulations requiring set amounts of reserve generating capacity essentially return us to the old status quo without saying so.

Suggested Readings

Awerbuch, Shimon, Leonard Hyman, and Andrew Vesey. *Unlocking the Benefits of Restructuring: A Blueprint for Transmission.* Vienna, VA: Public Utilities Reports Incorporated, 1999.

Borenstein, Severin, and James Bushnell. "Electricity Restructuring: Deregulation or Reregulation?" *Regulation* 23, no. 2 (2000): 46–52.

Brennan, Tim. "Questioning the Conventional Wisdom." *Regulation* 24, no. 3 (2001): 63–69.

Chao, Hung-po, and Hillard Huntington, eds. *Designing Competitive Electricity Markets.* Boston, MA: Kluwer Academic, 1998.

Hale, Douglas R., Thomas J. Overbye, and Thomas Leckey. "Competition Requires Transmission Capacity." *Regulation* 23, no. 2 (2000): 40–45.

Lenard, Thomas M. "FERC's New Regulatory Agenda." *Regulation* 25, no. 3 (2002): 36–41.

Michaels, Robert J., "Can Non-profit Transmission Be Independent?" *Regulation* 23, no. 3 (2000): 61–66.

Posner, Richard. *Natural Monopoly and Its Regulation.* Washington: Cato Institute, 1999.

Rassenti, Stephen, Vernon Smith, and Bart Wilson. "Turning Off the Lights." *Regulation* 24, no. 3 (2001): 70–76.

Taylor, Jerry, and Peter Van Doren. "California's Electricity Crisis: What's Going On, Who's to Blame, and What to Do." Cato Institute Policy Analysis no. 406, July 3, 2001.

Van Doren, Peter M. "The Deregulation of Electricity: A Primer." Cato Institute Policy Analysis no. 320, October 6, 1998.

Van Doren, Peter M., and Jerry Taylor. "Rethinking Electricity Restructuring." Cato Institute Policy Analysis no. 530, November 30, 2004.

—Prepared by Peter Van Doren and Jerry Taylor

45. Energy Policy

Congress should

- resist adoption of any additional government interventions in energy markets and, in particular, any packaged interventions under the rubric of "national energy policy";
- eliminate all ethanol subsidies and tax preferences;
- eliminate the U.S. Department of Energy and abolish all of the domestic energy programs under its control;
- transfer the National Nuclear Security Administration, which is responsible for managing the DOE's nuclear-industrial complex, to the Department of Defense;
- sell the oil in the Strategic Petroleum Reserve and eliminate the program;
- spin off the Federal Energy Regulatory Commission, the Energy Information Administration, and the Office of Civilian Radioactive Waste Management as independent agencies within the executive branch; and
- repeal the Price-Anderson Act.

With the exception of electricity markets (see Chapter 44), energy markets are relatively free and only lightly regulated. For instance, the U.S. Energy Information Administration (the analytical arm of the U.S. Department of Energy) reports that federal energy subsidies are relatively inconsequential from an economic standpoint—$6.2 billion annually, or about 1 percent of total energy expenditures in the United States in 1999 (the last year for which reliable data are available). Oil, gas, and coal markets are freer from government intervention than most. And while most fossil fuel production takes place on federal lands, the federal government has proven to be a relatively disengaged landlord, allowing the industry tremendous operational discretion and refraining from imposing particularly excessive rents for access.

That's not to say that there isn't room for policy improvement. Subsidies for energy technologies are unwarranted, and regulatory intervention probably does more to distort energy prices than do the sorts of direct subsidies measured by the Energy Information Administration. Likewise, while oil and gas markets are allowed to operate relatively unhindered by government, the amount of oil and gas traded within those markets is to some degree constrained by questionable federal land management policies (see Chapter 47). But for the most part, legislators interested in promoting free energy markets will spend more of their time fending off bad policy ideas than eliminating the same from the federal code.

Interventions in energy markets are usually packaged with complementary interventions under the rubric of "national energy strategy." Proponents of national energy strategies contend that federal regulators can make better decisions than market agents concerning what fuels to use, how best to use energy, and which technologies are worth researching and developing. While liberals and conservatives in Washington may differ about exactly how the energy market ought to be managed by federal regulators, faith in government planning and distrust of the free market are characteristic of both camps.

Energy Independence

The most popular justification for intervention in energy markets is the alleged necessity of securing energy independence. Market actors, if left to their own devices, will choose to use the cheapest source of energy available, and foreign oil is more often than not less expensive than domestic oil. Consequently, the American economy is rendered vulnerable to embargoes, supply disruptions, and extreme price volatility. The Washington consensus is that the less Middle Eastern oil we import, the less vulnerable we are to such events.

That policy consensus, however, overlooks the fact that energy independence wouldn't make much difference unless we were to abandon oil use altogether or, alternatively, ban all petroleum imports and exports. That's because it costs little to transport oil or refined petroleum commodities around the world, meaning that a supply disruption anywhere in the world will increase the price for all remaining oil traded anywhere in the global market. That's why Great Britain—which had in fact achieved energy independence in the late 1970s due to its exploitation of petroleum fields beneath the North Sea—experienced the same oil price explosion as a consequence of the Iranian Revolution in 1979 as did Japan, which was entirely dependent on imports.

The global nature of the oil market also explains why fears about some future oil embargo are groundless. Once oil is in a tanker or refinery, there is no controlling its destination. During the 1973 embargo on the United States and the Netherlands, for instance, oil that was exported to Europe was simply resold to the United States or ended up displacing non-OPEC oil that was diverted to the U.S. market. Consequently, there was no net reduction in oil imports. Saudi oil minister Sheik Yamani conceded afterwards that the 1973 embargo "did not imply that we could reduce imports to the United States . . . the world is really just one market. So the embargo was more symbolic than anything else."

In sum, reducing or even eliminating oil imports would *not* reduce our vulnerability to OPEC production decisions, lessen the impact of supply disruptions around the world, reduce oil price volatility, or neutralize the risks surrounding some future embargo. Only complete withdrawal from the world oil market would accomplish those ends. Complete withdrawal, however, is not seriously entertained by many politicians or economists for a very good reason—it is a policy of preemptively embargoing ourselves out of fear that our enemies might some day be willing and able to do so.

Promoting Domestic Production

Most elected officials support efforts to increase domestic production of petroleum and natural gas as one way to reduce imports and address upward pressure on energy prices. There are two ways of accomplishing that—increasing industry access to reserves currently off-limits on federal land and providing subsidies to domestic oil and gas producers.

Unfortunately, domestic production is limited by hard geological reality. To whit, there is simply not enough low-cost oil and gas in the United States to meet anything close to current needs. For instance, as of the first quarter of 2004, the United States consumed 20.3 million barrels of oil a day but produced only 5.6 million barrels a day from domestic sources. Because domestic fields have been exploited heavily for decades, reserves are declining and the deficit between domestic production and overall consumption has been growing over time. Even if all public lands currently off-limits to the industry were opened up for exploration and development (particularly the Arctic National Wildlife Refuge, the Rocky Mountain West, and coastal areas off California and the Gulf Coast), an additional

2.0–3.5 million barrels of oil a day might be recoverable in the mid term assuming relatively high oil market prices.

In the natural gas sector, reserves are likewise declining and imports in the form of liquefied natural gas are now the best hope for keeping natural gas prices from embarking on a long-term upward spiral. Under current policy, America is moving from self-sufficiency in natural gas to a condition in which a quarter of it's supply will have to come from overseas to meet expected demand. Opening up public lands currently off-limits to the industry would narrow that deficit but probably not close it completely.

Given such constraints, politicians in both parties have been inclined to subsidize domestic production in order to tease more supply from sources that otherwise would prove uneconomic even given current high market prices. While that might be good politics, it's lousy economics. Subsidizing the production of uneconomic commodities would be a net drain on the economy even if those subsidies were capable of increasing supply.

Subsidizing Renewable Energy

Proponents of renewable energy subsidies have offered multiple justifications for government intervention to promote those technologies. The most popular argument at the moment is that government must promote alternatives to fossil fuels if we're ever to reduce our dependence on oil imports and our vulnerability to events in the Middle East.

There is a germ of truth here. As noted above, there is simply not enough domestic oil available to meet current demand, so if we're serious about promoting energy independence, we must find alternative energy sources to meet current needs. The fundamental problem, however, is that only 2 percent of America's oil consumption goes to electricity generation—most oil is used as transportation fuel and feedstock for various chemicals, plastics, and lubricants. Renewable energy, however, is primarily dedicated to electricity production. Accordingly, even if the market for renewables were to grow substantially, it would not reduce oil consumption, or oil imports, very much if at all. The two fuels compete in entirely different markets. The exception is ethanol and various other biofuels, which are discussed below.

Another argument for government promotion of renewables is that they are environmentally cleaner energy sources than are fossil fuels and nuclear power. If the environmental costs of conventional fuels were incorporated in their market price, the argument goes, renewables would be economically competitive with nonrenewables. Accordingly, subsidies for renewable energy simply correct a market failure and thus enhance overall economic efficiency.

It's unclear, however, whether there are significant environmental costs associated with the consumption of nonrenewable energy that are not incorporated in market prices. If the Environmental Protection Agency is correct about the human health effects of exposure to various pollutants, for instance, Harvard University regulatory analyst W. Kip Viscusi calculates that coal is somewhat undertaxed, natural gas is somewhat overtaxed, and petroleum and gasoline are taxed correctly.

The difficulty, however, is that EPA may not be correct about such things given the vast uncertainty associated with the health effects of exposure to various pollutants. Figure 45.1 illustrates the problem. It is a survey of the published range of external cost estimates associated with the consumption of various fuels for electricity generation. The wide disparity between published estimates in peer-reviewed journals suggests that, whatever the merits of this exercise, it is impossible to conclude scientifically what the correct tax should be. The literature also suggests that renewable energy may not be anywhere near as environmentally benign as proponents believe.

Another argument frequently marshaled for government subsidy of renewable energy is that fossil fuels are unfairly advantaged by their own set of subsidies and that offsetting subsidies would level the economic playing field. Yet with the exception of nuclear power, subsidies to conventional fuels are rather minuscule and are dwarfed by the subsidies already on the books for renewable energy.

Figure 45.2 breaks those subsidies down by fuel and considers them in relation to the size of the industry. Regardless, the best remedy for the market distortions engendered by conventional energy subsidies is to eliminate those subsidies, not to impose a new round of the same.

Finally, proponents of renewable energy subsidies argue upon occasion that fossil fuels are finite and dwindling and that the government would be doing us all a favor by promoting the transition to more sustainable fuel sources. While there is little reason to believe that fossil fuels are growing scarcer in any real economic sense (as measured by finding costs, the sales price of reserves in the ground, inflation-adjusted prices, or known reserves), the argument is irrelevant from an economic standpoint. When fossil fuels begin to become scarcer, their price will rise accordingly,

Figure 45.1
Range of External Cost Estimates

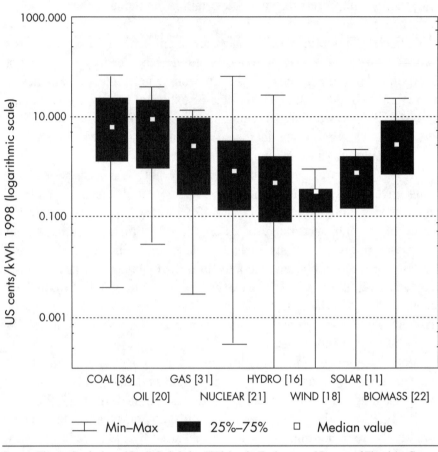

SOURCE: Thomas Sundqvist and Patrik Soderholm, "Valuing the Environmental Impacts of Electricity Generation: A Critical Survey," *Journal of Energy Literature* 8, no. 2, December 2002, p. 19.

providing all the signals and incentives necessary for market actors to switch to alternatives without government guidance or help.

Ethanol Subsidies

There are ethanol producers in the United States only because of federal subsidies; without exemptions from federal fuel taxes and various production tax credits, the industry would completely disappear. The defenses offered by proponents of those subsidies are quite weak.

First, proponents argue that ethanol is environmentally preferable to gasoline. Yet, as Figure 45.2 indicates, that might not be the case. Ethanol's

Figure 45.2
Magnitude of Energy Subsidies, 1999

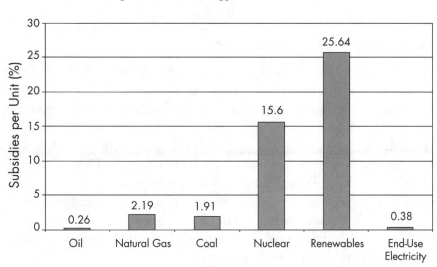

SOURCE: Energy Information Administration, "Federal Financial Interventions and Subsidies in Energy Markets 1999: Energy Transformation and End Use," SR/OIAF/2000–02, Table ES1, p. xiv.

major environmental advantage is that its combustion produces less carbon monoxide than does combustion of conventional gasoline. Yet carbon monoxide is a trivial environmental problem; no city in the United States currently in violation of federal standards. Ethanol combustion, however, emits more ozone precursors than does combustion of conventional gasoline, and 110 million people live in counties where the concentration of low-level ozone (smog) violates federal standards upon occasion. Accordingly, almost every major environmental organization in the country opposes ethanol subsidies.

Second, proponents argue that ethanol reduces America's dependence on foreign oil. Yet oil dependence has increased even as ethanol subsidies have done the same. The reason is that ethanol requires nearly as much or even more oil to produce than is saved at the point of combustion in a vehicle's engine. Accordingly, ethanol is a way of processing oil into fuel; it is not a substitute for oil.

Finally, ethanol proponents echo proponents of renewable energy by arguing that subsidies merely offset countervailing petroleum subsidies. Yet, as shown in Figure 45.2, those subsidies are trivial and scarcely affect market prices.

In sum, ethanol subsidies cannot be defended from an economic or an environmental perspective. Their political appeal is the only rationale for federal support.

Encouraging Energy Conservation

Some energy analysts argue that consumers invest too little in energy conservation measures such as insulation, fluorescent lights, and hybrid cars. Even if that's true, empirical analysis suggests that the record of government-directed conservation is rather poor. Between 1989 and 1999, for example, electric utility companies—primarily at the behest of state public utility commissions—spent $23.1 billion in the United States to subsidize ratepayer energy conservation investments. Yet a recent study found that those expenditures reduced electricity sales by only 0.3 to 0.4 percent and did so at an average cost of 14–22 cents per kilowatt hour—roughly 2–3 times more expensive on average than the energy the conservation effort was attempting to conserve.

Similarly, a recent study found that federal energy efficiency standards for appliances will provide net negative benefits of between $46.4 billion and $56.2 billion through 2050 and that those costs will be borne disproportionately by low- and middle-income households.

Federal automobile fuel efficiency standards are likewise rather inefficient measures to encourage conservation. The Congressional Budget Office estimates that increasing the Corporate Average Fuel Efficiency (CAFE) standards to achieve a 10 percent reduction in gasoline consumption would cost producers and consumers about $3.6 billion a year more than the value of the fuel saved, or about $228 per new vehicle sold. CAFE standards also reduce the marginal cost of driving a mile and thus, ironically, increase vehicle-miles traveled (economists have calculated that for every 10 percent increase in fuel efficiency, people increase the number of miles they drive by 2 percent). In fact, any efficiency standard that reduces the marginal cost of consuming energy will have an analogous effect, known to economists as the "rebound effect."

One of the consequences of the rebound effect in relation to CAFE standards is an increase in congestion. Another is a net increase in air pollution. According to one recent study, a 50 percent increase in fuel efficiency standards would reduce gasoline consumption by about 21 percent but would increase net emissions of volatile organic compounds by 1.9 percent, nitrogen oxides by 3.4 percent, and carbon monoxide by 4.6 percent.

Prices provide all the incentives necessary for consumers to use energy efficiency. Government attempts to force conservation where it has been otherwise resisted by consumers are counterproductive, costly, and injurious to consumer welfare.

Subsidizing Energy R&D

Because investors cannot easily capture all the economic benefits associated with a particular technological advance, proponents of government-supported research and development programs argue that government intervention is necessary to ensure that such investments are sufficient to ensure long-term economic growth.

Unfortunately, the government's record of intelligently targeting support across the universe of potential energy investments is rather poor. The fundamental problem is that decisions about public R&D investments are made by politicians, which means that programs are judged by political, not economic, criteria. Accordingly, while there may be a "market failure" to be found in the R&D sector, there is at least an equally serious problem of "government failure" in the prescribed remedy.

Economist William Niskanen reminds us, however, that "the case for government support of civilian R&D is that the return to the economy is greater than the return to the firm, not that government has better information on what R&D has the highest return." Niskanen accordingly suggests that targeted federal R&D efforts be eliminated and replaced with a robust R&D tax credit and matching grants to universities to supplement funds raised from private sources.

Abolish the Department of Energy

The arguments marshaled above provide not only the rationale for resisting the call for "national energy strategies" but also the rationale for eliminating about half the programs undertaken by the U.S. Department of Energy. Most of the remaining programs within the DOE's portfolio concern the nation's nuclear-industrial complex, particularly the nuclear stockpile; various nuclear wastes attendant thereto; some nuclear nonproliferation programs; and the complex of national defense laboratories. Those programs, which are consolidated under the National Nuclear Security Administration within the Department of Energy, should be transferred to the Department of Defense. The Federal Energy Regulatory Commission, the Energy Information Administration, and the Office of Civilian

Radioactive Waste Management (which is responsible for regulating the longer-term disposal of high-level nuclear waste) should be spun off as independent agencies within the executive branch.

Oil in the U.S. Strategic Petroleum Reserve should be sold in the marketplace and the program shut down. The original purpose of the SPR was to ensure that, in case of some future embargo, the United States would have enough oil on hand to weather the economic storm for at least several months. But as we have seen, embargoes are phantasmic events not worth worrying about. Supply disruptions are more likely, but it's unclear when if ever an administration would release oil within the SPR to address supply disruptions. More important, companies can insure against supply disruptions with futures contracts, so the SPR does not do anything for the economy that market actors couldn't do for themselves if they were so inclined. The cost of maintaining the SPR—and the related uncertainty created in the market by the existence of such reserves under government control—necessitate elimination of the program.

Finally, Congress should repeal the Price-Anderson Act, which protects the nuclear power industry against liability for damages above a certain threshold. If nuclear power is as safe as proponents maintain, then nuclear power companies should be able to find liability insurance in the private market. If they cannot, then it tells us that those with the most incentive to get the risk calculations right are not as sanguine as are our elected leaders about the safety of nuclear power plants. Either way, it's a significant subsidy that cannot be defended on economic grounds.

Suggested Readings

Adelman, M. A. *The Genie Out of the Bottle: World Oil Since 1970.* Cambridge, MA: MIT Press, 1994.

———. "The Real Oil Problem." *Regulation* 27, no. 1 (Spring 2004): 16–21.

Heyes, Anthony. "Determining the Price of Price-Anderson." *Regulation* 25, no 4 (Winter 2002–03): 26–30.

Kleit, Andrew. "CAFE Changes, By the Numbers." *Regulation* 25, no. 3 (Fall 2002): 32–35.

Loughran, David, and Jonathan Kulick. "Demand Side Management and Energy Efficiency in the United States." *Energy Journal* 25, no.1 (2004): 19–43.

Robinson, Colin. "Energy Economists and Economic Liberalism." *Energy Journal* 21, no. 2 (2000): 1–22.

Smil, Vaclav. *Energy at the Crossroads: Global Perspectives and Uncertainty.* Cambridge, MA: MIT Press, 2003.

Stelzer, Irwin. "The Department of Energy: An Agency That Cannot Be Reinvented." American Enterprise Institute Studies in Policy Reform, 1996.

Sundqvist, Thomas, and Patrik Soderholm. "Valuing the Environmental Impacts of Electricity Generation: A Critical Survey." *Journal of Energy Literature* 8, no. 2 (December 2002): 3–41.

Sutherland, Ronald. "Big Oil at the Public Trough? An Examination of Petroleum Subsidies." Cato Institute Policy Analysis no. 390, February 1, 2001.

———. "The High Costs of Federal Energy Efficiency Standards for Residential Appliances." Cato Institute Policy Analysis no. 504, December 23, 2003.

Sutherland, Ronald, and Jerry Taylor. "Time to Overhaul Federal Energy R&D." Cato Institute Policy Analysis no. 424, February 7, 2002.

Taylor, Jerry, and Peter Van Doren. "Evaluating the Case for Renewable Energy: Is Government Support Warranted?" Cato Institute Policy Analysis no. 422, January 10, 2002.

Tilton, John. *On Borrowed Time? Assessing the Threat of Mineral Depletion.* Washington: Resources for the Future, 2003.

Van Doren, Peter. *Politics, Markets, and Congressional Policy Choices.* Ann Arbor: University of Michigan Press, 1991.

—Prepared by Jerry Taylor

46. Pollution Policy

Congress should

- Establish a mechanism by which states can apply for regulatory waivers from the Environmental Protection Agency in order to allow states some flexibility in establishing environmental priorities and to facilitate experiments in innovative regulatory approaches;
- replace the Federal Insecticide, Fungicide, and Rodenticide Act and the Toxic Substances Control Act with a consumer products labeling program under the auspices of the Food and Drug Administration;
- repeal the Comprehensive Environmental Response, Compensation, and Liability Act and privatize the cleanup of Superfund sites;
- replace the Resource Conservation and Recovery Act with minimal standards for discharge into groundwater aquifers;
- eliminate federal subsidies and programs that exacerbate environmental damage; and
- replace the Endangered Species Act and section 404 of the Clean Water Act with a federal biological trust fund.

The Theory of Environmental Regulation

Air sheds, watersheds, groundwater, scenic lands, and ecologically important but sensitive ecosystems are widely considered "public goods." That is, in an unregulated marketplace, people who pay to "consume" environmental goods and services (say, those who purchase a conservation easement for an ecologically important wetland) are unable to keep those who don't pay from enjoying the benefits of that purchase. Accordingly,

457

without government regulation, there would be widespread "free riding" and less investment in environmental goods than would be economically and socially desirable.

Moreover, people who might wish to protect their property against polluters via private action will often find that the transaction costs associated with doing so are prohibitive. For instance, if one owned a small lake and discovered that the fertilizer runoff from hundreds if not thousands of homes and agricultural operations was contaminating water quality, the costs associated with tracking down the responsible parties would almost certainly be larger than the costs associated with the pollution itself.

Accordingly, those "market failures" would necessitate government intervention. While there are numerous ways that the government could intervene in environmental marketplaces to address market failure, the method employed by the federal government is public ownership of air, water, and subsurface resources as well as of some sensitive ecosystems. Congress exercises its power over those resources by delegating to executive agencies the authority to determine how resources can and can't be used—that is, by establishing pollution and public land use regulations—usually, but not always, on the basis of assessments of human health risk. The Environmental Protection Agency (EPA) is further empowered to determine the exact manner in which regulated entities are to go about meeting pollution standards—usually, but not always, dictating the installation of particular control devices or technologies.

Accurate, timely, and accessible information about environmental exposures is also considered by some to be a public good. Absent such laws as the Toxic Substances Control Act and the Federal Insecticide, Fungicide, and Rodenticide Act, individuals, some people think, would be unable to effectively police their exposures to dangerous chemicals. A variation of this argument contends that it is so costly and time-consuming for people to gain access to the environmental health information necessary for intelligent decisionmaking that government must act in the individual's stead and make those decisions for society as a whole.

Debates about the regulation of pollution generally begin with an acceptance of the above claims. The political arguments today are over the details:

- Do concentrations of chemical x in the environment truly pose a health risk to the public? If so, we regulate. If not, we don't.
- Should environmental regulations have to pass a cost/benefit test?

- Should government tell firms exactly how to go about meeting federal environmental standards, or should government simply dictate the permissible concentration of pollutants in a given air shed or water-shed and allow firms some degree of flexibility in complying with those standards?
- How stringently should regulations be enforced, and who should do the enforcing—the EPA, state governments, environmental organizations through third-party lawsuits, or some combination of the three?

The Real Environmental Debate

Although environmental debates sound like they're arguments about science and public health (with a smattering of economics tossed in), they're really debates about preferences and *whose* preferences should be imposed on society. Although participants argue that "sound science" ought to determine whose preferences determine the standards (and that *their* science is better than their opponents'), science cannot referee the debate.

Consider the dispute about the regulation of potentially unhealthy pollutants, the central mission of the EPA. The agency examines toxicological and epidemiological data to ascertain the exposure level at which suspect substances impose measurable human health risks. Even assuming that such analyses are capable of providing the requisite information (a matter, incidentally, that is hotly debated within the scientific and public health community), who is to say whether one risk tolerance is preferable to another?

The amount of resources one is willing to spend on risk avoidance is ultimately subjective. Everyone's risk tolerance is different. Scientists can help inform our decisions, but they cannot point us to the "correct" decision.

Should experts—acting on behalf of regulatory agencies—decide what sort of environmental quality people should or should not have a right to consume? In no other area of the economy do scientists have the power to rule in such a manner. After all, people are allowed to consume all kinds of things—power crystals, magnets, age-defying vitamins, and organic food—that scientists, doctors, and public health officials think are silly or even potentially counterproductive.

Many people, perhaps even a majority of voting Americans, want to secure cleaner air and cleaner water regardless of whether those improvements significantly reduce human health risks. Under the present political regime, however, no such improvements can occur without some alleged scientific justification. That is why people who wish to improve environmental quality are forced to embrace whatever science they can—no matter how dubious—to get what they want. They should not, however, have to engage in such scientific gymnastics to secure desired goods or services.

The Case for Preference Neutrality

A government that is fully respectful of the right of individuals to live their lives as they wish (as long as they respect the rights of others to do likewise) would be neutral regarding the subjective preferences of its citizens. People who are more risk tolerant than others should have a right to exercise their preferences, and those who are less risk tolerant than others should have that same right. This reasonable premise has some striking policy implications because the present order is most definitely not neutral regarding environmental preferences.

Preference neutrality works well when it comes to the consumption of private goods, such as those regulated by the Federal Insecticide, Fungicide, and Rodenticide Act (FIFRA) and the Toxic Substances Control Act (TSCA). It does not work well, however, when it comes to the consumption of public environmental goods, which pose a far more difficult problem. Within the same city, for instance, one person cannot exercise his preference for cleaner air without infringing upon another's preference for, say, more entry-level jobs in the manufacturing sector. After all, nothing is free, and people vary (legitimately) in their willingness to trade off environmental goods and services for other goods and services.

A policy founded on preference neutrality requires that we do as little violence to minority preferences as possible. *When it comes to public goods like air and watersheds, some majority will, of necessity, be imposing its preferences on some minority.* The only way to provide safeguards for minority preferences is to require some sort of supermajority consensus before decisions about public goods are made.

Reform the Clean Air and Clean Water Acts

As noted earlier, within limits, there are no right or wrong air or water quality standards. Political leaders need not constantly war over those issues. Accepting public preferences for cleaner air and water—even without sufficient scientific justification—still leaves a great amount of room for productive reform.

The Problem with Command-and-Control Regulation

There is little reason for government to prescribe exactly how firms are to go about complying with pollution standards. Command-and-control regulations, which require regulators to determine exactly which technologies and what manufacturing methods are to be adopted for pollution control in every single facility in the nation, place on public officials informational requirements that are difficult to meet in the real world. This task is complicated by the fact that every air shed and watershed has different carrying capacities for different pollutants.

Command-and-control regulations may often prove more efficient than alternative regulatory arrangements when dealing with a large number of difficult-to-identify pollution sources (for instance, air emissions from automobile tailpipes and water runoff from the application of fertilizers and pesticides). Yet their utility is reduced when targeting identifiable and immobile pollution sources such as manufacturing and electric power facilities. After all, individual plant managers have better incentives to discover the most efficient ways to control pollution at their facilities than do EPA technicians and consultants. That is the case, not only because those managers have more direct knowledge of their facilities and the technology of production, but because competition forces cost minimization, and even the most dedicated EPA official isn't going to lie awake nights searching for new solutions to pollution control problems.

Most regulatory analysts are in agreement that flexible regulatory approaches—such as performance-based regulation (wherein regulators dictate overall emissions levels from a facility but allow facility managers to decide how best to meet those standards), emissions trading, and pollution taxes—are often more efficient and less costly means of meeting environmental standards than are command-and-control alternatives. Unfortunately, those sorts of flexible regulatory strategies are underutilized in the United States for a host of political reasons. That should concern not only economists but environmentalists as well. The less costly it is to "buy" improvements in environmental quality, the greater the public appetite will likely be for additional initiatives to improve environmental quality.

Provide for State Regulatory Waivers

Despite the well-known problems associated with command-and-control environmental regulation, it's unlikely that Congress will find the political capital necessary to reform thousands of pages of counterproductive rules and regulations found in more than a dozen sprawling environmental statutes, given the entrenched special interests that benefit politically and economically from their existence. Accordingly, Congress should take a page from the welfare reform experience and allow states to appeal for waivers from EPA in order to facilitate experiments in regulatory policy.

Case Western law professor Jonathan Adler proposes that Congress adopt a mechanism similar to Section 160 of the 1996 Telecommunications Act to facilitate this reform. Section 160 allows telecommunication companies to submit a request for a regulatory waiver from the Federal Communications Commission. The FCC "shall forebear from applying any regulation or any provision" of the act to a company or class of service providers if the FCC determines upon review of the petition that

- "enforcement of such regulation or provision is not necessary" to ensure that rates "are just and reasonable and are not unreasonably discriminatory,"
- "enforcement of such regulation or provision is not necessary for the protection of consumers, or
- "forbearance from applying such provision or regulation is consistent with the public interest."

The FCC has one year to respond or the petition is deemed granted, and any decision to grant or deny forbearance is subject to judicial review under the Administrative Procedure Act.

Adapting a mechanism akin to Section 160 of the 1996 Telecommunications Act to the environmental arena would mean allowing states to apply for forbearance from any standard or requirement administered by EPA. The state would be expected to submit supporting material detailing the basis for the request and explain why the waiver would serve the public interest. EPA would then provide public notice, seek comment from interested parties, and make a call one way or the other within one year pending judicial review under the aegis of the Administrative Procedure Act.

Some states may wish to experiment with market-oriented emissions trading programs or pollution taxes in lieu of the existing federally imposed command-and-control regimen. Others may well act to tighten existing standards. A few states might even propose reallocation of regulatory efforts in order to concentrate on some relatively more important environmental issues instead of others. A policy of preference neutrality suggests tolerance regarding any such proposals.

Allowing "50 regulatory flowers to bloom" admittedly entails some degree of risk. Although some state experiments will likely bear economic and environmental fruit, others will probably fail to meet expectations. Such risks will certainly engender political opposition to the entire enterprise, but politicians should remember that useful innovations are virtually impossible without the risk of failure. In fact, the risks of failure underscore the value of decentralized policy experiments since localized policy failures would have far less damaging consequences than federal policy failures. Moreover, failed experiments provide useful information, cautioning reformers in other states about problems to avoid. Successful state experiments, on the other hand, could become models for reform elsewhere.

Repeal FIFRA and TSCA

A policy of preference neutrality would be most easily applicable to consumer preferences that do not directly affect the rights of others to exercise alternative preferences (so-called private goods). TSCA (which governs the use of various chemicals and the abatement of asbestos, indoor radon concentrations, and lead-based paint) and FIFRA (which regulates the use of agricultural chemicals) impose politically derived risk preferences (and their related costs) on individuals without respect for those who are more risk tolerant than the political majority. Accordingly, both statutes should be abolished.

Of course, some people argue that the cost of obtaining good risk information is too great. That's not altogether obvious (a plethora of private, third-party reporting organizations, such as Underwriters Laboratories, Consumer's Union, Green Seal, various kosher and halal food certification groups, the Better Business Bureau, and the Good Housekeeping Institute, are well-known and on the job today), and there are remedies available beyond the uniform imposition of politically derived risk tolerances. Mandatory labeling standards—perhaps accompanied by Food and Drug Administration advisories—would address the concern about this alleged market imperfection and do minimal violence to the marketplace and the rights of individual consumers.

Repeal CERCLA

The Comprehensive Environmental Response, Compensation, and Liability Act (CERCLA), commonly known as "Superfund," addresses the potential risks posed by the past disposal of hazardous wastes. Most scientists and public health officials agree that the risks posed by sites not yet cleaned up under CERCLA are virtually nonexistent. Although those sites might pose a hazard if they were converted to different uses—say, if a school with a dirt playground were built on top of an old Superfund site—such concerns are easily addressed by not converting such sites to problematic uses.

In reality, CERCLA is an extremely expensive land reclamation project, dedicated to turning contaminated land, which at present poses little danger of harm to nearby residents, into land as pure and clean as the driven snow. Congress should acknowledge that some sites are simply not worth reclaiming; containment and isolation should be permitted as an alternative.

Accordingly, CERCLA should be abolished. Superfund sites and potential Superfund sites that have yet to be addressed should be privatized in a reverse Dutch auction in which government offers to *pay* potential bidders for assuming ownership of and responsibility for the land. The amount offered escalates until some private party is willing to accept the deal. Owners would then assume full liability for any future damage that might occur. Such a regime would set up the proper incentives for the private remediation or isolation of potentially dangerous environmental contaminants.

Repeal RCRA

The Resource Conservation and Recovery Act (RCRA) regulates the commercial use and disposal of potentially toxic chemicals primarily as a means of protecting groundwater aquifers from contamination. Yet RCRA is not necessary to remedy any traditional environmental market failure.

Groundwater aquifers are not a public good. Ownership is easily created through unitization, the same means employed by owners of oil wells to allocate property rights across geographically disperse fields. Owners of aquifers are quite capable of restricting consumption to people who pay for water and policing the integrity of their aquifers through the tort system.

But even if groundwater resources remain in government hands, there's little reason for such incredibly prescriptive and excessively costly regulations as the kind imposed by RCRA, a statute that stipulates detailed cradle-to-grave management standards for thousands of substances. Better to repeal RCRA and replace it with a minimal discharge standard. That is, prohibit significant discharges of pollutants (as defined by government) into groundwater and impose heavy fines and penalties—perhaps even shutdown orders—on firms discovered to be in violation of the standard.

A requirement that potential dischargers maintain special liability insurance further ensures that firms have strong incentives to minimize the chance of contamination (insurance companies would be reluctant to issue coverage to those whose practices put the insurance company at risk). Public groundwater monitoring costs would be borne by industry, preferably through a special tax levied on the purchase of liability coverage.

End Subsidies for Resource Exploitation

The foremost engine of environmental destruction in America today is not the private sector but federal and state government. A great deal of environmental harm could be alleviated by eliminating the subsidized use of natural resources.

Five "Brownest" Programs in the Budget

- Agricultural subsidies are responsible for excessive pesticide, fungicide, and herbicide use with corresponding increases in non-point-source pollution.
- Sugar import quotas, tariffs, and price-support loans sustain a domestic sugar industry that might not otherwise exist; the destruction of the Everglades is the ecological result.
- Electricity subsidies via the power marketing administrations and the Tennessee Valley Authority artificially boost demand for energy and thereby are responsible for millions of tons of low-level radioactive waste and the disappearance of wild rivers in the West.
- Irrigation subsidies and socialized water services, which generally underwrite half of the cost of consumption, have done incalculable damage to western habitat while artificially promoting uneconomic agriculture with all the attendant environmental consequences. They also lead to tremendous overuse of water resources and worsen periodic shortages.
- Federal construction grant projects—such as the river maintenance, flood control, and agricultural reclamation undertakings of the Army Corps of Engineers—allow uneconomic projects to go forward and cause an array of serious environmental problems.

Repeal the Endangered Species Act

As Chapter 22 argues, compensating property owners for takings meant to secure public goods such as biological diversity is a simple matter of fairness and constitutional justice. But protecting property rights is also a necessary prerequisite for ecological protection. Property owners who expect to experience economic losses if their property is identified as ecologically important have little incentive to exhibit good ecological stewardship.

The ESA, which prevents private property owners from making certain uses of their land in order to secure the "public good" of biological diversity, should thus be repealed since it provides no compensation to landowners for public takings. Instead, a federal biological trust should be established that would be funded out of general revenues at whatever level Congress found appropriate. The trust fund would be used to purchase conservation easements (in a voluntary and noncoercive fashion) from private landowners in order to protect the habitat of endangered species.

The virtue of such a reform is that landowners would have incentives rather than disincentives to protect species habitat. Moreover, the cost of biological preservation would become more transparent, which allows better-informed decisionmaking about the use of resources. Finally, such a reform would decriminalize the "ranching" of endangered species for commercial purposes. The ESA prohibits such practices out of a misguided belief that any commercial use of an endangered species inevitably contributes to its decline. Yet the experience of the African elephant and other threatened species belies that concern and strongly suggests that, if private parties are allowed to own and trade animals as commodities, their economic value goes up, not down. That in turn provides better incentives for species protection.

Similarly, section 404 of the Clean Water Act—the provision that ostensibly empowers the EPA to regulate wetlands—should be repealed. Like the ESA, it takes private property out of otherwise inoffensive uses for a public purpose and provides disincentives for wetland conservation. Protection of wetlands habitat should be left to the federal biological trust fund.

The "Greenest" Political Agenda Is Economic Growth

There are a number of reasons why economic growth is perhaps the most important of all environmental policies. First, it takes a healthy, growing economy to afford the pollution control technologies necessitated by environmental protection. A poorer nation, for example, could scarcely have afforded the nearly $200 billion this nation has spent on sewage treatment plants over the past 30 years.

Second, growing consumer demand for environmental goods (parks; recreational facilities; land for hunting, fishing, and hiking; and urban air and water quality) is largely responsible for the improving quantity and quality of both public and private ecological resources. Virtually all analysts agree that, for the vast majority of consumers, environmental amenities are "luxury goods" that are in greatest demand in the wealthiest societies. Economic growth is thus indirectly responsible for improving environmental quality in that it creates the conditions necessary for increased demand for (and the corresponding increase in supply of) environmental quality.

Third, advances in technology, production methods, and manufacturing practices—both a cause and a consequence of economic growth—have historically resulted in less, not more, pollution. Even advances in nonenvironmental technologies and industries have indirectly resulted in more efficient resource consumption and less pollution.

Conclusion

Science can inform individual preferences but cannot resolve environmental conflicts. Environmental goods and services, to the greatest extent possible, should be treated like other goods and services in the marketplace. People should be free to secure their preferences about the consumption of environmental goods such as clean air or clean water regardless of whether some scientists think such preferences are legitimate or not. Likewise, people should be free, to the greatest extent possible, to make decisions consistent with their own risk tolerances regardless of scientific or even public opinion.

Policies that override individual preferences in favor of political preferences are incapable of pleasing a majority of people or resolving subjective disputes. No matter what environmental risk thresholds are set, only those at the political mean will be pleased. The best we can do when it comes to the governance of public goods is to establish mechanisms that allow people the right to secure their preferences to the greatest extent possible.

Given the different circumstances of both communities and environmental media, it makes sense to allow those most directly affected by the pollution issue in question to decide for themselves how best to deal with it. Not only will the tradeoffs associated with differing approaches be

467

more fully appreciated, but, given the fact that people prefer to live amidst those more like them than not, local decisionmaking will almost certainly prove less injurious to minority preferences than decisionmaking at some other level of government.

Suggested Readings

Adler, Jonathan. "Let Fifty Flowers Bloom: Transforming the States into Laboratories of Environmental Policy." Roundtable Paper Series, American Enterprise Institute Federalism Project, September 20, 2001.

Anderson, Terry, and Peter Hill, eds. *Environmental Federalism*. Lanham, MD: Rowman & Littlefield, 1997.

DeLong, James. "Privatizing Superfund: How to Clean Up Hazardous Waste." Cato Institute Policy Analysis no. 247, December 18, 1995.

Keohane, Nathaniel, Richard Revesz, and Robert Stavins. "The Choice of Regulatory Instruments in Environmental Policy." *Harvard Environmental Law Review* 22, no. 2 (1998): 313–67.

Leal, Donald, and Roger Meiners, eds. *Government vs. Environment*. Lanham, MD: Rowman & Littlefield, 2002.

Revesz, Richard, and Robert Stavins. "Environmental Law and Policy." Resources for the Future, Discussion Paper 04-30, June 2004.

Sterner, Thomas. *Policy Instruments for Environmental and Natural Resource Management*. Washington: Resources for the Future, 2002.

Stroup, Richard. *Eco-nomics: What Everyone Should Know about Economics and the Environment*. Washington: Cato Institute, 2003.

Sunstein, Cass. *Risk and Reason*. New York: Cambridge University Press, 2002.

VanDoren, Peter. *Cancer, Chemicals, and Choices: Risk Reduction through Markets*. Washington: Cato Institute, 1999.

Yandle, Bruce, Madhusudan Bhattarai, and Maya Vijaaraghavan. "Environmental Kuznets Curves: A Review of Findings, Methods, and Policy Implications." Political Economy Research Center, Research Study 02-1 Update, April 2004.

Yilmaz, Yesim. "Private Regulation: A Real Alternative for Regulatory Reform." Cato Institute Policy Analysis no. 303, April 20, 1998

—Prepared by Jerry Taylor

47. Public Lands Policy

Congress should

- privatize the lands held by the U.S. Department of the Interior and the U.S. Department of Agriculture; or, failing that,
- allow any business entity or interest group to compete for leases to harvest resources from federal lands;
- grant holders of federal leases and permits the right to trade those leases or permits freely in secondary markets;
- reform the national park system by giving individual park administrators greater autonomy but requiring their operations to be self-supporting; and
- eliminate water and rangeland subsidies for agricultural users.

The federal government owns 29 percent of the landmass of the United States—including 82 percent of Nevada, 68 percent of Alaska, 64 percent of Utah, 63 percent of Idaho, 61 percent of California, 49 percent of Wyoming, and 48 percent of Oregon. Recreationists, environmentalists, and resource extraction industries compete fiercely for rights to make use of that land. During the 108th Congress, for instance, competing interest groups engaged in high-profile clashes over snowmobile access to Yellowstone National Park, drilling in the Arctic National Wildlife Refuge, timber road construction in the national forests, water rights in the Klamath River Basin, the future of major hydroelectric dams in the Pacific Northwest, and access to untapped natural gas reserves off the Florida Gulf Coast.

Both liberals and conservatives appear to be comfortable with allowing government officials to resolve disputes between competing claimants for access rights. The disagreement resides in *how* the resource pie is being divided and *who* is doing the dividing. Conservative Republicans typically argue that timber, mineral, and energy resources on federal lands are more valuable than the ecosystems treasured by environmentalists and that more resource extraction is called for. Moreover, they contend that state and local governments should have more of a say than federal officials in Washington about how the resources on federal lands are allocated. Liberal Democrats typically argue the opposite and complain that our national heritage is being destroyed by shortsighted greed.

The Genesis of Conflict

Disagreements are intense because the stakes are often quite high. Resource extraction industries and the politicians who represent the workers in those industries point out that federal lands are a major source of the nation's softwood timber, coal, and hard metals and that much of the nation's grazing lands are federal lands. Federal lands are also the home of large reserves of petroleum and natural gas, some of which are currently being exploited but much of which is not, given the political resistance to drilling in some particularly popular ecosystems. Recreationists counter that millions of Americans each year visit federal lands to enjoy recreational pursuits such as hiking, camping, and sightseeing—all of which to one degree or another conflict with the goal of wilderness preservation and resource extraction. Environmentalists, for their part, argue that the federal lands encompass the most biologically important ecosystems in North America and the most important national treasures in the nation. On much of that land, environmentalists argue, both industrialists and recreationists must by necessity take a backseat to conservation in the interests of both present and future generations.

Although parties to those debates marshal ecological, biological, and economic arguments to justify their claims to the federal estate, the evidence forwarded is remarkably flimsy and unpersuasive.

For instance, how do we know whether any particular parcel of federal land is more valuable if left wild than if developed in some way? Although methods such as contingent valuation surveys exist to measure the "existence value" of land, they yield highly dubious information for the simple reason that what people *say* they're willing to pay in surveys rarely comports with their actual behavior in the marketplace.

Likewise, there's no objectively correct way to measure the economic benefits provided by most ecological services (such as water filtration, soil conservation, and carbon sequestration) because so many of the resources affected are—at the moment—outside the marketplace. If a resource is outside the market, we can't reliably "price" it, and if we can't find a price for a resource, we can't calculate the value of saving the resource.

470

None of this is to say that ecological assets have no value—only that we can't reliably calculate it outside the marketplace and, accordingly, cannot consider those values when conducting an implicit or explicit cost/ benefit examination of various alternative uses of a given resource. In short, there is no way to intelligently adjudicate an argument between those who say that the oil beneath the ANWR is more valuable than the ecosystem above it and those who argue that the wildlife in ANWR is more valuable than the oil.

The upshot is that the debate over federal lands—while often garbed in the cloth of ecological science and economics—is in reality a debate about subjective preferences about how resources ought to be allocated. There is no real way to test whether those subjective preferences represent the "best" use of resources because we lack the information to consider the value of alternatives.

Political Allocations Reconsidered

Leaving the decision about how to allocate scarce resources among competing users to the government is unwise. First, since politicians or their agents make the decisions on how resources are to be allocated, decisions will be based on political criteria. Economically efficient or ecologically sensible decisions will occur only by chance. Moreover, counterproductive subsidies almost always emerge when government is allocating resources, given the fact that the benefits bestowed by those subsidies are highly concentrated while their costs are widely disbursed. Politicians in both parties find significant political profit in bestowing such subsidies on favored constituencies.

Second, because governmental offices change hands frequently, allocations are always subject to reconsideration and reversal. Continuing uncertainty regarding resource rights reduces incentives for conservation. Given that disputes are never permanently settled and that potential gains from subsidies are great, vast sums are poured into lobbying efforts that are pure deadweight losses to the economy.

Third, mutually satisfactory solutions to resource disputes are difficult to achieve because competing interest groups cannot financially bargain with one another. In private markets, economic actors can pay groups of people to surrender their rights to resources or legal claims and, because the transactions are voluntary, conflict is typically resolved with minimal ill will. In political markets, such transactions are impossible and disputes are "all-or-nothing" affairs. Political compromises designed to indemnify losers are not necessarily voluntarily accepted by the losers and can be undone by future political action.

Fourth and finally, the managerial record of public land officials is as abysmal as the managerial record of socialist plant managers in the old Soviet bloc. Environmental organizations publish mountains of reports documenting the sorry state of our national parks, the poor condition of our publicly owned forests, and the overuse of western water and rangeland. The cost of managing commercially attractive resources on federal land greatly exceeds the revenues brought in to the federal treasury. It would appear that ecological socialism is subject to the same problems that bedevil socialism in other economic contexts.

Why Public Lands?

Given the endemic problems of public land ownership, why does it continue to find support?

Economists have defended it because ecologically important and visually compelling lands are generally considered to be "public goods." That is, in an unregulated marketplace, those who pay to "consume" those acres are unable to keep those who *don't* pay from enjoying the benefits of that purchase. For instance, in a laissez-faire world, many if not most Americans would be willing to pay some money to ensure that the Grand Canyon remains unexploited for commercial purposes. Yet only a subset of those Americans might actually contribute to such a cause because they know that others will do so even if they don't. Economists worry that, without government intervention, the incentive to free ride on the activism of others will lead to less investment in conservation than would be economically or socially desirable.

Although there are numerous ways that the government could intervene in environmental markets to address the problem (for instance, some sort of subsidy or tax deduction for conservation investments), the common method is public ownership. Few people, however, seriously consider whether this particular remedy is worse than the malady being addressed.

Regardless, while "national treasures" are indeed a part of the federal estate, the majority of the acres held by the federal government are not lands that have a particularly significant "existence value." Most of the land held by the U.S. Bureau of Land Management, for instance, ended up there by historical accident—nobody filed any claims for it when the federal government was homesteading land in the West during the 19th century. Similarly, the lands held by the U.S. Forest Service were deposited there during the Progressive Era on the assumption that scientific management of timberlands by government experts was economically superior to market-based management of timberlands by private owners.

In short, only a small fraction of the federal estate can be defended on the grounds of market failure. Much land held by the BLM is no longer unwanted. Likewise, given the evidence over the past several decades, few economists would argue today that timber harvests are more efficiently managed by government agents than by private companies. Unfortunately, Americans have grown so accustomed to public ownership of vast stretches of western lands that intellectual justifications of the federal estate are seldom if ever necessary.

The Privatization Option

Privatization is the best way to improve the economic and environmental services provided by federal lands and to ensure that they are being harnessed for the most popular and necessary uses. Although it's not clear whether the ''free-rider'' problem is serious enough to significantly distort the market for certain federal lands, if the problem must be confronted, it is best addressed by some form of public subsidy for conservation activities. Possibilities include federal matching funds for individual contributions to preservationist organizations or tax credits for conservation expenditures.

The most neutral way to divest public lands is to begin by recognizing the implicit claims that different interest groups have on the federal estate. Lands presently devoted to the national parks, wilderness preserves, and wildlife refuges would be simply given to nonprofit conservation groups representing users. Lands presently devoted to resource industries—such as the public grazing lands and forest lands presently devoted to timber operations—would likewise be given to present permit holders and users. Lands, however, that are under mixed use or no use at all would be auctioned off over a set number of years.

To address the concern that corporations and the rich would have an unfair advantage in the subsequent auction, every American would be issued an equal share of land scrip that would be redeemable only in a public land auction. After all, if the public lands truly ''belong to all of us''—as we're constantly told by environmentalists—why not explicitly acknowledge this state of affairs and allow people to decide for themselves what to do with ''their share'' of the federal estate? Individuals would be free to buy, sell, or donate their scrip as they pleased, but only this government-issued scrip would be accepted as currency in the federal land auctions.

The virtue of this privatization scheme is that it minimizes conflict by accepting current political arrangements regarding public resource use while allowing those arrangements to change via voluntary postauction exchange. Equity concerns are addressed, and the financial benefits of privatization would be captured directly by the American people.

Environmental lobbyists may well object to divestiture no matter how it is executed, arguing that, if left to the market, America's ecological crown jewels would end up as Disney-style theme parks, exclusive housing developments, or massive extraction platforms for oil, coal, gas, and timber companies. Yet if the American people are as "Green" as environmentalists say, it's hard to imagine that they would use their scrip to facilitate that sort of development. Likewise, it's hard to believe that environmentalists themselves would surrender the rights they would inherit to govern the national parks, wilderness areas, and wildlife refuges as they see fit without satisfactory compensation.

In truth, there's plenty of reason to think that environmentalists will more often than not find themselves on the winning side of most auctions. When resource extraction industries have competed with conservationists in the private marketplace, they have discovered that the conservationists can usually marshal more dollars for attractive lands than the industries themselves can. Similarly, when the U.S. Forest Service has allowed conservationists to compete against timber companies for use rights, conservationists have won those auctions more often than not. Lobbyists for western agricultural interests labor mightily to prevent laws that would allow their clients to trade federal water or grazing rights to environmentalists out of fear that, were such transactions allowed, conservationists would buy out much of the industry. In fact, "sagebrush rebels" in the West have historically been vigorously opposed to the privatization of public land for exactly those reasons.

It is indeed ironic that *both* resource users and organized conservationists fear that, were federal resources put up for grabs in the marketplace, the *other* side would emerge with more resources than at present. But both can't be right. At root, perhaps, is a reluctance on the part of all parties to pay for access to resources they currently receive from the public for free or at subsidized rates. Granting resource users the right to lands currently dedicated to their use prior to the launch of an auction would probably address this concern.

474

A Second-Best Alternative

No matter how intellectually attractive divestiture of public lands may be, politicians have been reluctant over the years to consider it. If privatization proves politically impossible, a second-best alternative would be to allow competing resource users to freely buy and sell access rights to federal land. Farmers and ranchers with permits for federal water would be allowed to sell those permits to anyone they wished—including environmentalists who might wish to retire the permits in order to restore riparian ecosystems. Similarly, ranchers should be allowed to sell grazing permits to nonranchers, and timber companies should be allowed to sell harvest rights on federal land to nontimber interests.

Anyone interested should likewise be afforded the opportunity to compete in the sale of federal leases for oil, gas, coal, mineral, or timber rights. The idea that federal land managers know a priori that a given tract of land is best used for this or that purpose is dubious for all the reasons addressed earlier. Federal laws that prohibit such secondary transactions violate the interests of all parties, who by definition will gain when voluntary exchanges that would be desirable to both parties are finally allowed by law.

This second-best reform has been embraced by many environmental organizations (most prominently, perhaps, by the Natural Resources Defense Council and Environmental Defense) and is a good first step toward allowing market forces to have a greater say in how federal lands are used.

Eliminate Pubic Subsidies

As noted earlier, public ownership of resources encourages counterproductive subsidies for politically influential groups of resource users. Most criticism of such subsidies targets the unfairness of using federal tax dollars to fatten the income of some at the expense of others; less attention is paid to the fact that subsidizing public resource users has detrimental economic and environmental impacts as well. Unfairness, of course, is in the eye of the beholder. Economic efficiency, however, is not.

Disagreement exists about the extent of the subsidies bestowed upon various user groups. The federal government, for instance, loses money on timber sales from public lands, suggesting to many that the timber industry is paying less than its fair share for access to the national forests. Others counter that leases are disbursed via auctions so by definition fair market values for the land are discovered (at least, concerning the value of those lands to the timber industry). The disparity between lease payments and federal revenue is due primarily to gold-plated and inefficient Forest Service management practices.

Similarly, many observers argue that mining companies pay extremely low rates for access to federal land and that the law governing such transactions—the 1872 Mining Act—denies taxpayers a fair return from mining activity. Yet careful analysis suggests that the fees established by the act may not be that far from what would arise in an auction process.

The best way to dissipate both subsidies (to the extent to that they exist) would be to allow a larger universe of interested parties to bid for timber contracts and to reform the Mining Act to establish similar auction mechanisms. If that's not possible, allowing secondary exchanges between timber and mineral companies and other potentially interested groups would at least allow a remedy for the economic and ecological problems associated with the subsidies. The wealth effects, however, would remain unaddressed.

Subsidies for recreationists and agricultural interests are even more damaging than those for other user groups. Entrance fees at the national parks, for instance, cover only a fraction of the costs associated with park upkeep and maintenance. Despite more than two decades of complaint, legislators continue to refuse to appropriate enough funds to keep the parks in good order—probably because politicians gain political credit when they create and expand parklands but little if any credit when they appropriate money for maintenance. Accordingly, park conditions continue to deteriorate and park ecology is harmed by excessive public intrusion into sensitive areas.

Requiring park visitors to pay the full cost of park management is a necessary but insufficient remedy. Park managers have an incentive to maximize the number of visitors because that strengthens their bid for larger budgets and furthers their career within the park service (managers of popular parks have a career advantage over managers of less popular parks). Accordingly, individual parks should be separated completely from the federal treasury and forced to become self-sufficient. That reform will only work, however, if park managers are given more autonomy to run the parks as they best see fit. Boards of trustees for each park would ensure that public accountability was not completely lost.

Agricultural subsidies are likewise rife for public land users. Myriad rangeland maintenance programs provide valuable services at little or no cost to those who graze cattle on public land. Most important, access to federal water at artificially low rates ensures not only counterproductive land uses in arid regions but also that water scarcity will continue to haunt the West. Indeed, federal water subsidies to farmers may well be the most environmentally destructive program in the federal budget. Forcing agricultural users of the federal estate to pay for rangeland maintenance programs through special fees and requiring agricultural users to pay market rates for water access are obvious remedies.

Suggested Readings

Anderson, Terry, and Pamela Snyder. *Water Markets: Priming the Policy Pump.* Washington: Cato Institute, 1997.

Anderson, Terry, Vernon Smith, and Emily Simmons. "How and Why to Privatize Federal Lands." Cato Institute Policy Analysis no. 363, November 9, 1999.

Baden, John, and Donald Snow, eds. *The Next West: Public Lands, Community, and Economy in the American West.* Washington: Island Press, 1997.

Fretwell, Holly. "Public Lands Report III: Federal Estate: Is Bigger Better?" Political Economy Research Center, December 2000.

Gordon, Richard, and Peter Van Doren, "Two Cheers for the 1872 Mining Law." Cato Institute Policy Analysis no. 300, April 9, 1998.

Hess, Karl Jr. *Visions upon the Land: Man and Nature on the Western Range.* Washington: Island Press: 1992.

Leal, Donald, and Holly Fretwell. "Back to the Future to Save Our Parks." Policy Series PS-10, Political Economy Research Center, June 1997.

Nelson, Robert. "How to Reform Grazing Policy: Creating Forage Rights on Federal Rangelands." *Fordham Environmental Law Journal* 8, no. 3 (1997).

Nelson, Robert. *Public Lands and Private Rights: The Failure of Scientific Management.* Lanham, MD: Rowman & Littlefield, 1995.

Sedjo, Roger, ed., *A Vision for the U.S. Forest Service: Goals for Its Next Century.* Washington: Resources for the Future, 2000.

—Prepared by Jerry Taylor

48. Global Warming and Climate Change

Congress should vote down any legislation restricting emissions of carbon dioxide, the principal human "greenhouse" emission related to global warming.

In October 2003, the Senate voted down a bill (S. 139), sponsored by John McCain (R-AZ) and Joseph Lieberman (D-CT), whose purpose was to limit emissions of carbon dioxide, because of its role in alteration of the earth's surface temperature. Scholars accurately labeled this legislation "Kyoto Lite," because of its strong resemblance to the Kyoto Protocol to the United Nations Framework Convention on Climate Change.

The Kyoto Protocol would have required the United States to reduce its emissions of carbon dioxide to 7 percent below 1990 levels for the period 2008–2012. Because of increases in emissions since 1990, this works out to roughly a 30 percent cut, a dramatic lowering that cannot be accomplished without major infrastructural changes. S. 139 delays the implementation time eight years, to 2016.

The Kyoto Protocol has never been ratified by the required two-thirds majority in the Senate. But S. 139, requiring only a simple majority, was defeated by a relatively narrow margin, 55–43. Sen. McCain has vowed to reintroduce this legislation at regular intervals, citing his perseverance with the McCain-Feingold campaign finance bill as the model for his activity.

The 109th Congress is likely to be confronted by increasing pressure to pass such legislation. It should be resisted.

Background

Global warming—meaning an alteration of the planetary temperature by human activity—was largely brought to public attention in the hot, dry summer of 1988. National Aeronautics and Space Administration research scientist James Hansen testified in a joint House-Senate hearing that there was a "cause and effect relationship" between "the current climate and human alteration of the atmosphere."

Since that landmark testimony, there have been remarkable developments in climate science, many of which have yet to exert their proper influence on climate policy. Many of those changes have taken place since the publication of the widely cited Third Assessment Report of the United Nations' Intergovernmental Panel on Climate Change (IPCC) in 2001.

This chapter first provides an overview of the state of climate science. It will become clear that much more is known about global warming than is generally perceived, and that the most consistent interpretation of that knowledge is that expensive regulation of carbon dioxide is simply not warranted by science. The remainder of the chapter is concerned with aspects of global warming that engage political discussion. Those include whether or not humans are warming the surface temperature, what the related changes in weather are, what the amount of future warming is likely to be, and whether it is of sufficient magnitude to justify the enormous expenses required to prevent it.

The strongest evidence for human "greenhouse" warming is based on recent observations of a disproportionate increase in temperature in cold, dry air, especially in the winter. For over a century, climate theory has predicted that a change in the greenhouse effect—caused by the addition of atmospheric carbon dioxide—would be expressed in this fashion. As shown in Figure 48.1, warming in the last quarter of the 20th century indeed tended to be amplified in the winter, and in dry regions, such as interior Asia and North America.

Warming May Be Overestimated by Surface Thermometers

While the overall pattern of recent warming indeed resembles what one would expect from an increase in atmospheric carbon dioxide, the magnitude of that warming may be overestimated. The temperature trends shown in Figure 48.1 are from the United Nations Intergovernmental Panel on Climate Change (2001 and updates). They have been the subject of much debate concerning the amount of "artificial" warming that they might contain. Cities, for example, tend to grow around the location of their weather stations, which initially tended to be at centers of commerce. Warming because of urban sprawl has little to do with global warming caused by industrial emissions of greenhouse gases.

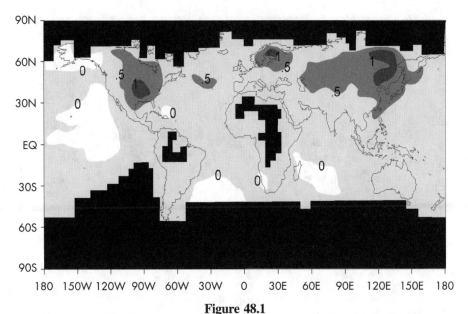

Figure 48.1

Cold season temperature trends (°C/decade) from 1977 to 2000 in the surface
temperature record (black regions indicate a lack of available data).

Kalnay and Cai (2003) compared temperatures calculated from weather-
balloon measurements of the atmosphere to a ground-based thermometer
record that is quite similar to the IPCC's and found a pervasive warm
bias in U.S. temperatures. Figure 48.2 applies that bias to the 100-year-
long U.S. history. The bias is so large that it removes any statistically
significant warming from the record. Kalnay and Cai attributed the effect
to large-scale changes in land use, including urbanization and land-cover
alterations, such as changing from forests to farms.

Michaels et al. (2004) and McKitrick and Michaels (2004) examined
the geographic distribution of the IPCC's temperature trends and found
that these more local "economic" effects were more related to warming
than were changes in the greenhouse effect, with the exception of the
aforementioned dry regions in the cold season, where the human "signal"
still remains.

There are other records of temperature—one from satellites, another
from weather balloons—that tell a different story than the IPCC surface
record. Neither annual satellite nor balloon temperature trends differ significantly from zero since the satellite record started in 1979. These records
reflect temperatures in what is called the lower atmosphere, or roughly
between 5,000 and 30,000 feet.

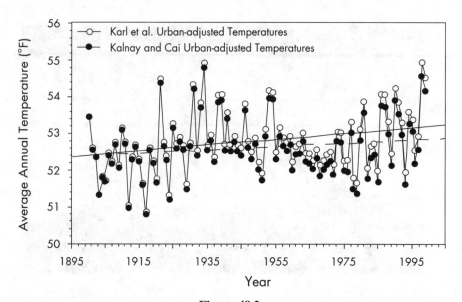

Figure 48.2
The U.S. annual temperature history (open circles) with warm urban bias removed
(filled circles).

Four years ago, a distinguished panel of the National Academy of
Sciences (NAS, 2000) concluded there is a real disparity between the
reported surface warming and the temperature trends measured in the
atmosphere above. Since then, many investigators have tried to explain
the cause of the disparity while others have denied its existence. Recently,
Douglass and others (2004) examined a third record, from seven feet
above the ground, derived from balloon data released by the National
Oceanic and Atmospheric Administration.

When all of those records—the weather balloon data from the lower
atmosphere, from seven feet, from the satellites, and surface thermometers
from the IPCC—are compared, the one that differs most from all of the
others is the IPCC record. While this is not dispositive proof, it lends
credence to the hypothesis that the IPCC record is contaminated with a
significant amount of "artificial" warming, even as the pronounced warming of the Northern Hemisphere land areas in the winter is a "greenhouse"
signal of human-induced change.

Related Climate Changes and Their Effects

As noted above, with an enhanced greenhouse effect, *warming is much
greater in the winter than in the summer.* Since World War II, observed

warming is twice as great in winter as it is in summer. In the winter, three-quarters of the total warming is in the frigid air masses of Siberia and North America. Figure 48.3, from the National Oceanic and Atmospheric Administration (Tinker, 1999), shows how dramatic this effect is in the lower 48 states. The largest warming in the last three decades occurs in winter (January through March), when severity and presence of the cold high-pressure systems that form in northwestern North America largely determine the winter departure from normal. Late summer and early fall temperatures actually show a slight decline.

Temperature Variability Is Decreasing, Not Increasing

Logically, a world in which the winters warm much more than the summers is one in which temperature variability declines. That's because day-to-day temperature changes are greatest in the winter, so making the atmosphere less "winter-like" (which is the main "greenhouse" signal) implies less variability.

No Increase in Overall U.S. Floods or Droughts

Despite popular perception, there is no statistically significant increase in flooding rains or drought on a nationwide basis (Figure 48.4).

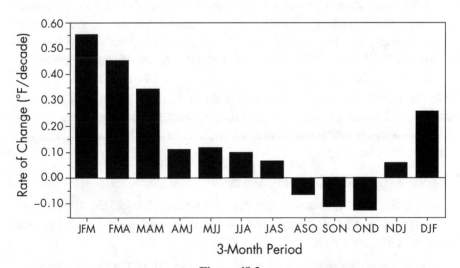

Figure 48.3
Seasonal changes since 1966 in the U.S. record, according to the U.S. National Oceanic and Atmospheric Administration.

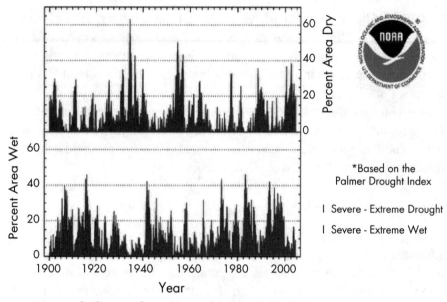

National Climatic data Center / NESDIS / NOAA

Figure 48.4
Historical record of the percentage of the United States that is experiencing either
extreme dry conditions (top) or extreme wet conditions (bottom),
January 1900–July 2004.

Hurricane Frequency and Severity

Hurricanes, known generically as tropical cyclones, are the most destructive storms on earth. Figure 48.5 shows that there is no overall trend in their frequency in the Atlantic and Caribbean basin, the source for U.S. storms. While recent years have seen quite a lot of storms, they are no different than the regime that was dominant in the 1940s, 1950s, and 1960s. Similar results obtain on a worldwide basis. Perhaps more interesting, as shown by Landsea et al. (1996), is that maximum winds in these storms, as measured by hurricane-hunter aircraft, have declined significantly in the last 50 years.

Heat-Related Mortality Is in Decline in American Cities

In its Second Assessment Report on climate change, the IPCC made a statement that is often repeated in discussions of global warming and heat-related mortality.

[Based upon data from several North American cities], the annual number of heat-related deaths would approximately double by 2020 and would increase several fold by 2050.

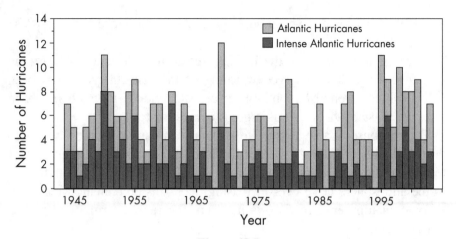

Figure 48.5
Number of hurricanes (and intense hurricanes) in the Atlantic Ocean basin,
1944–2003.

In other words, the IPCC assumed that, as cities warm, people would slowly accept increasing mortality and die in higher numbers as a proportion of the population. In fact, cities have, in general, been slowly warming, without the influence of "global" warming, as their infrastructure, especially masonry and pavement, serves to retain heat more than the vegetated countryside.

So, in reality, we have been conducting a long test of the hypothesis that people do not adapt to changing conditions. I tested this with my colleague Robert Davis and others (2002, 2003). We found that, in almost all North American cities, population-adjusted heat-related mortality is declining significantly because the "threshold" temperature at which people begin to die is rising. In other words, people are adapting and increasingly prospering in slowly warming cities, contrary to the way the United Nations believes they would behave.

Together, the behavior of climate and its impact in these important areas—means, seasonality, droughts, floods, hurricanes, and mortality—indicate that the warming that has occurred cannot glibly be claimed to be harmful; in fact, the evidence indicates the opposite.

Future Warming

One of the most overlooked facts in the vociferous discussions of global warming it that we know, to a very small range of error, how much the planet will warm in the foreseeable future, and that number is reassuringly small. It also provides yet another example of the inaccuracy of IPCC climate science.

Over the next 50 years, the IPCC gives a probable range of warming of 0.9 to 4.5°F; the observed warming of the last 100 years has been 1.4°F. Unless around $10 billion in climate science research has been virtually wasted, this range is a gross overestimate.

The response of temperature to a change in carbon dioxide begins to drop off with time. So, in order to simply maintain a constant rate of temperature rise, computer simulations of climate must add carbon dioxide to the atmosphere at an ever-increasing rate. This combination results in a constant temperature rise, rather than the feared ''runaway greenhouse effect.''

Figure 48.6 shows projected warming from a large family of different climate models called the CMIP-1 study (Meehl et al., 2000). Note that

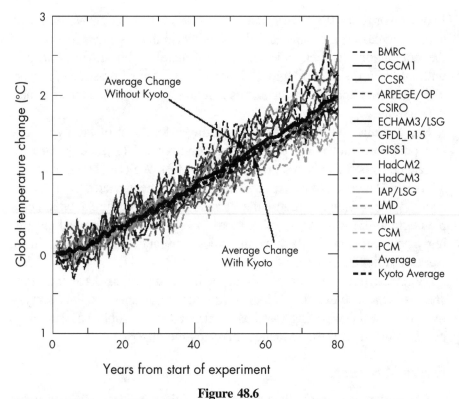

Figure 48.6
Output from several representative climate models. Once warming starts, it takes place at a constant rate. The model average is highlighted, as is the effect of full compliance with the Kyoto Protocol.

the central tendency indeed is to produce a constant rate of warming once human-induced warming begins.

Which of these models is likely to be correct? Global surface temperature has risen as a straight line, too, in the last three decades. Figure 48.7 shows the observed trend superimposed on the model projections of Figure 48.6.

How Much Warming Would Kyoto Prevent?

Soon after negotiating the Kyoto Protocol in December 1997, the Clinton administration asked federal scientists how much warming would be prevented. The answer, which was ultimately published in the journal *Geophysical Research Letters* (Wigley, 1998), is 0.07°C/50 years, which is far beneath the natural level of interannual global temperature variability. In other words, it will be impossible to find the effects of the protocol on global temperature. Nonetheless, because of restrictions on emissions trading that were imposed by several European nations in November 2000,

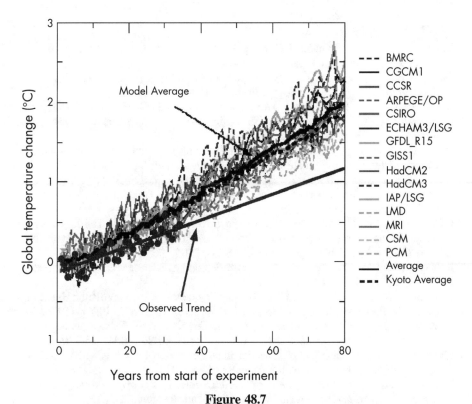

Figure 48.7
The linear temperature trend extrapolated from observed temperatures during the past three decades is lower than the projections of most climate models.

the cost to the United States of the protocol would be approximately 2 percent of GDP per year. As shown by Nordhaus (2001), this forces the economic burden of Kyoto to fall almost exclusively on the United States.

In short, Kyoto would do nothing about global warming but would cost America dearly.

Conclusion

In conclusion, several lines of evidence all point to the likelihood that warming in the next century is likely to be modest, and all evidence demonstrates that Kyoto will have no measurable effect on that warming. But the Kyoto Protocol is enormously expensive, reducing the amount of capital that can be invested in evolving and increasingly efficient technologies.

It is an inescapable conclusion that the Kyoto Protocol, or other similar instruments (such as S. 139), is precisely the wrong thing to do about global climate change.

Suggested Readings

Davis, R. E., et al. "Changing Heatwave Mortality in U.S. Cities," *Proc. 14th Appl. Clim. Con.,* Seattle, 2004, paper no. 18.4.

Davis, R. E., et al. "Decadal Changes in Summer Mortality in the U.S. Cities." *International Journal of Biometeorology* 47 (2003): 166–75.

Davis, R. E., et al. "Heat Wave Mortality in Large U.S. Cities." *Proc. 16th Conf. Biometeorol. Aerobiol.* and *17th ISB Cong. Biometeor.,* Vancouver, 2004, paper no. 6A.3.

Davis, R. E., et al. "Seasonality of Climate-Human Mortality Relationships in U.S. Cities and Impacts of Climate Change." *Climate Research* 26 (2004): 61–76.

IPCC. *Climate Change 1995: The Science of Climate Change.* Working Group I. In Second Assessment Report of the Intergovernmental Panel on Climate Change, edited by J. T. Houghton et al. Cambridge: Cambridge University Press, 1995.

IPCC. *Climate Change 2001: The Scientific Basis.* Working Group I. In Third Assessment Report of the Intergovernmental Panel on Climate Change, edited by J. T. Houghton et al. Cambridge: Cambridge University Press, 2001.

Kalnay, E., and M. Cai. "Impact of Urbanization and Land Use Change on Climate." *Nature* 423 (2003): 528–31.

Landsea, C. W., et al. "Downward Trends in the Frequency of Intense Atlantic Hurricanes during the Past Five Decades." *Geophysical Research Letters* 23 (1996): 1697–1700.

McKitrick, R., and P. J. Michaels. "A Test of Corrections for Extraneous Signals in Gridded Surface Temperature Data." *Climate Research* 26 (2004): 159–73.

Meehl, G. A., et al. "The Coupled Model Intercomparison Project (CMIP)." *Bulletin of the American Meteorological Society* 81 (2000): 313–18.

Michaels, Patrick J. *Meltdown: The Predictable Distortion of Global Warming by Scientists, Politicians, and the Media.* Washington: Cato Institute, 2004.

Michaels, P. J., R. McKitrick, and P. C. Knappenberger. "Economic Signals in Global Temperature Histories." *Proc. 14th Appl. Clim. Conf.,* Seattle, 2004, paper no. J1.1.

Moore, Thomas Gale. *Climate of Fear: Why We Shouldn't Worry about Global Warming*. Washington: Cato Institute, 1998.

National Academy of Sciences. *Reconciling Observations of Global Temperature Change*. Washington: National Academy Press, 2000.

Nordhaus, W. D. "Global Warming Economics." *Science* 294 (2001): 1283–84.

Tinker, R. *U.S. Temperature and Precipitation Trends*. Climate Prediction Center, National Atmospheric and Oceanic Administration, 1999. www.cpc.noaa.gov/trndtext.htm.

Wigley, T. M. L. "The Kyoto Protocol: CO2, CH4 and Climate Implications." *Geophysical Research Letters* 25 (1998): 2285–88.

—Prepared by Patrick J. Michaels

FOREIGN AND DEFENSE POLICY

49. Dismantling Al Qaeda

Policymakers should

- remember that the joint resolution approved by the Senate and the House of Representatives authorized the president "to use all necessary and appropriate force against those nations, organizations, or persons he determines planned, authorized, committed, or aided the terrorist attacks that occurred on September 11, 2001," not to wage an amorphous war on terrorism or evil or to unnecessarily conflate the terrorist threat with rogue regimes that seek weapons of mass destruction;
- focus the war on terrorism only on the Al Qaeda terrorist network and not expand it to other groups or countries that have not attacked, or do not represent a direct terrorist threat to, the United States;
- finish the job of aggressively hunting down Al Qaeda's leadership that fled to Pakistan from Afghanistan;
- recognize that much of the war on terrorism will not involve large-scale military action but will emphasize diplomatic, intelligence, and law enforcement cooperation with other countries;
- work with foreign governments to apprehend Al Qaeda operatives in other countries;
- approve the use of U.S. Special Forces for specific operations against Al Qaeda operatives when foreign governments are unable or unwilling to take action themselves; and
- make domestic counterterrorism to find Al Qaeda operatives in the United States the top priority for the Federal Bureau of Investigation.

A Different Kind of War

Because we use the shorthand phrase "war on terrorism" to describe the U.S. response to the September 11, 2001, terrorist attacks, it is easy to believe that this war—like all previous wars—can be won simply by killing the enemy, wearing them down until they are broken and capitulate. Given that suicide terrorists are, by definition, undeterrable, it seems that we have no choice but to kill them before they kill us.

We call it a "war on terrorism," but a more correct description would be a "war against the terrorists who attacked the United States on September 11, 2001." It might even be called the "un-war" because it is unlike any previous war we've fought. Our enemy does not wear uniforms or command military forces. It does not operate in or emanate from a specific geographic region. So U.S. forces with overwhelming military superiority and advanced technology will not be the appropriate instruments to wage this war. Precision-guided smart bombs and cruise missiles are not smart enough to know who the enemy is and where it is. More important, Carl Von Clausewitz's seminal work *On War* (first published in 1832) is not a suitable manual for this war because he wrote about war between nation-states. The war on terrorism is not against another nation-state and thus not "an act of force to compel our enemy to do our will." Indeed, the war on terrorism is not "merely the continuation of policy by other means."

This is a different kind of war that requires a different paradigm. We must shed conventional Western thinking conditioned by the European wars of the 18th and 19th centuries, two World Wars, Korea, Vietnam, the Gulf War, and Iraq. Rather than Clausewitz, the 2,300-year-old words of Chinese philosopher Sun Tzu from *The Art of War* are applicable. "War" for Sun Tzu meant "conflict" as it occurs throughout all aspects of life. And the "art" of war is conquering without aggression: "Subduing the other's military without battle is the most skillful." The lesson for the war on terrorism is not that aggression is unnecessary or should be avoided. In war, aggression is inevitable. But the weapons and skills for the un-war will be different. Special Forces rather than armor or infantry divisions will be the norm. Unmanned aerial vehicles patrolling expanses of desert or inaccessible mountain regions will often replace fighter pilots and foot soldiers. Arabic and Islam will be part of the syllabus for un-warriors.

Focus on Al Qaeda

Fighting the war on terrorism requires a delicate balance. Working with countries around the world, we must dismantle the Al Qaeda terrorist network—operative by operative, cell by cell. At the same time, we must not engage in actions or follow policies that create sympathy and recruits for Al Qaeda; that is, we must avoid needlessly giving Muslims reasons to hate America. The core question was raised by Secretary of Defense Donald Rumsfeld in his now-famous October 2003 leaked memo: "Are we capturing, killing, or deterring and dissuading more terrorists every day than the madrassas and radical clerics are recruiting, training, and deploying against us?" With more than a billion Muslims in the world, a strategy that focuses only on the former without addressing the latter is a losing strategy.

Although the United States must do everything it reasonably can to defend against future terrorist attacks, the war on terrorism requires aggressively seeking out and destroying the terrorists who would do us harm. Dismantling and degrading the Al Qaeda terrorist network is the one part of U.S. strategy that involves killing or capturing the enemy. But we must first understand who the enemy is and what this so-called war is really all about. Not all Muslims are Al Qaeda. Not all terrorists are Al Qaeda terrorists. Not all Islamic fundamentalists are radical Islamists. In other words, we should not extend the terrorist threat beyond those who directly threaten the United States.

We must be able to understand and make those distinctions in order to differentiate people who pose a genuine threat, those who pose little or no threat, and those who might be helpful. For example, as part of the war on terrorism, the U.S. military is assisting the Philippine government against the Abu Sayef guerrillas. To be sure, some of the Abu Sayef may have graduated from Al Qaeda's Afghanistan training camps, and there are some known contacts between Abu Sayef and Al Qaeda members. But the reality is that the Abu Sayef is a separatist group of financially motivated kidnappers, not radical Islamists who threaten the United States.

Iran is ruled by a fundamentalist Islamic regime that calls the United States the "Great Satan," aspires to possess nuclear weapons, and supports anti-Israeli Palestinian terrorist groups such as Hezbollah and Hamas. But that does not necessarily make Iran an ally of Al Qaeda and a target in the war on terrorism.

A War Not Fought by the Military

Part of the problem of using the phrase "war on terrorism" is that it implies the use of military force as a primary instrument of waging the war. But traditional military operations—such as Operation Enduring Freedom in Afghanistan against the Taliban and Al Qaeda—will be the exception rather than the rule. Al Qaeda is not an army that wears uniforms and operates in a specific geographic region. Rather, it is a loosely connected and decentralized network with cells and operatives in 60 countries around the world. So President Bush was right: "We'll have to hunt them down one at a time."

President Bush was also right to be skeptical about treating terrorism "as a crime, a problem to be solved mainly with law enforcement and indictments." Nonetheless the arduous task of dismantling and degrading the network will largely be accomplished through unprecedented international intelligence and law enforcement cooperation. Military involvement in the war on terrorism will be primarily that of Special Forces in discrete operations against specific targets.

So where will the war against Al Qaeda be fought?

First and foremost, the United States must get serious about mopping up the remnants of Al Qaeda that fled Afghanistan to Pakistan—if for no other reason than because Osama bin Laden and other key senior Al Qaeda leaders are believed to be there. That means that the United States must take an active role in any operations. Successes against Al Qaeda in Pakistan—the capture of Khalid Sheikh Mohammed, the mastermind of the September 11 attacks; Abu Zubaydah, the operational coordinator for Al Qaeda responsible for recruiting and training; and Ahmed Khalfan Ghailani, wanted in connection with the 1998 U.S. embassy bombings in Kenya and Tanzania and whose laptop computer provided information about possible attacks in the United States that resulted in raising the color-coded terrorist threat level to orange in August 2004—have been the result of cooperative efforts of the Pakistanis and the United States. But when left to their own devices, the Pakistanis have largely come up empty-handed. For example, Pakistani claims of having Ayman al-Zawahiri (bin Laden's right-hand man) cornered and killing Al Qaeda's spy chief Abdullah Ahmed Abdullah (one of the FBI's most wanted terrorists for his involvement in the 1998 bombings of the U.S. embassies in Tanzania and Kenya) in March 2004 were both false.

Pakistan is not the only front. With the world's largest Muslim population, Indonesia is a logical place for Al Qaeda both to blend in and to recruit new followers. The October 2002 nightclub bombing in Bali and the August 2003 Jakarta Marriott bombing are both linked to Al Qaeda via the terrorist group Jemaah Islamiyah. Eleven of the 19 hijackers who attacked the World Trade Center and Pentagon were Saudi nationals, and the May 2003 car bombings in Riyadh have been attributed to Al Qaeda. Suicide bombings in Casablanca may be linked to Al Qaeda. Sudan, Somalia, and Yemen are weak states where Al Qaeda has previously operated and could once again hide and reconstitute.

But Al Qaeda's presence is not limited to Muslim countries or to the Middle East and Africa. The March 2004 Madrid train bombings are attributed to Islamic militants sympathetic to Al Qaeda. Subsequently, French authorities arrested 13 people connected to the Moroccan Islamic Combatant Group accused of the Madrid attacks. An Al Qaeda cell in Hamburg, Germany, was allegedly involved in planning the 9/11 attacks. British authorities have arrested Al Qaeda suspects on a number of different occasions. All of those incidents point to Al Qaeda operating in Europe under cover of peaceful and law-abiding Muslim populations (the Muslim populations in France, Germany, and the United Kingdom total more than 10 million people).

Finally, we must prudently assume that Al Qaeda is operating in the United States (with an estimated Muslim population of 5–7 million people). Even America's friendly neighbor to the north, Canada, with a relatively small Muslim population (estimated at about 600,000) is a place where Al Qaeda might hide and from which it might gain access to the United States. So it is not simply a matter of "striking the terrorists in Iraq, defeating them there so we will not have to face them in our country," as President Bush asserted. Every reasonable and prudent effort must be made to bolster homeland security, including making domestic counterterrorism the top priority for the FBI.

Understanding the Enemy

Just as important as knowing where to hunt down Al Qaeda is understanding it. We tend to think of Al Qaeda as an entity or structure, as a centralized organization wholly dependent on its leadership for its existence and operation. Thus the general misconception that all the nodes of the network are directly connected to the leadership and that if the leadership is destroyed, then the organization can be collapsed.

Certainly, Al Qaeda has a leadership hierarchy. At the top is Osama bin Laden. His most trusted lieutenant is Ayman al-Zawahiri, an Egyptian doctor who is the architect of Al Qaeda's ideology and who has been indicted in the United States for his role in the U.S. embassy bombings in Africa in 1998. But Al Qaeda is not a completely centralized top-down hierarchical organization, so simply taking out the leadership will not be enough to destroy it or even degrade it so that it is less effective and able to attack the United States. Such an approach may work for regime change in rogue states ruled by dictators, but it would be a mistake to assume that it will yield the same results against Al Qaeda. In fact, we already know that as elements of Al Qaeda's leadership have either been captured or killed, new leaders have emerged.

According to one U.S. intelligence official, "The strength of the group is they don't need centralized command and control." There is no single target (either an individual or a part of the organization) within Al Qaeda; according to a senior U.S. official: "Now, instead of a large, fixed target we have little moving targets all over the world, all armed and all dangerous. It is a much more difficult war to fight this way."

Thus, it is useful to visualize and conceptualize Al Qaeda's structure as the honeycombs of a beehive—with the cells interconnected by multiple paths and able to be reconstructed if they are damaged or destroyed. That being the case, the task of dismantling the network will not be easy or quick—we should expect that it will take many years. Furthermore, we may not be able to completely destroy the network; the best we can hope for may be degrading Al Qaeda's capabilities so they do not represent a direct catastrophic threat to the United States. For example, if enough of the network is physically destroyed, Al Qaeda may not have the capacity to mount an attack against the U.S. homeland. In a similar vein, Al Qaeda may remain a conventional terrorist threat to America, but if the organization is deprived of weapons of mass destruction—in particular a nuclear weapon—then it does not pose a catastrophic threat.

We must also understand that Al Qaeda is more than just a terrorist organization; it is also an idea. Al Qaeda is representative of a radical brand of Islam, but what is underappreciated by most Americans— although largely understood by most foreign analysts—is that Al Qaeda's real war is not primarily against America but within the Muslim world. It is a struggle for the soul of Islam. Since the war is within the Muslim world (not the Muslim world vs. America), it may not be possible to win the war on terrorism in the traditional sense of winning and losing. But the United States could lose the war if by its policies and actions it creates the perception that the war on terrorism is being waged against all Muslims and polarizes the more than one billion Muslims in the world to view America as the enemy.

And it is important to understand that Al Qaeda's ideology has taken on a life of its own. What is unknown is the extent to which Al Qaeda's radicalism has taken hold throughout the Muslim world, but certainly the U.S. preoccupation with Iraq for more than three years after the September 11 attacks has given time and space for the cancer to spread, as well as a rallying cry for recruiting more Muslims to Al Qaeda's radical cause. According to Omar Bakri Mohammed, the London-based leader of the radical Islamic group al-Muhajiroun: "Al Qaeda is no longer a group. It's become a phenomenon of the Muslim world resisting the global crusade of the U.S. against Islam." We know that Al Qaeda has become a franchise of sorts, bringing other radical Islamic groups, such as Jemaah Islamiyah in Indonesia, into its fold. But it also now appears that a "reverse franchise" effect may be taking place. That is, other groups may conduct terrorist attacks citing sympathy with Al Qaeda but without any direct connection or contact with Al Qaeda (e.g., planning, training, financing). The November 2003 car bombings in Turkey (the Abu Hafs al Masri Brigades and Great Eastern Islamic Raider's Front both claimed responsibility) and the March 2004 train bombings in Spain (the Abu Hafs al Masri Brigades claimed responsibility, but Moroccan Islamic Combatant Group has been the primary target of the Spanish investigation) are signs of that phenomenon.

Allies and Friendly Countries

Because the war on terrorism requires unprecedented cooperation between U.S. intelligence and law enforcement agencies and those in other countries, the United States needs to improve relations with foreign intelligence agencies in order to be able to share information about suspected Al Qaeda operatives. (Such cooperation should be limited to intelligence and law enforcement; the U.S. military should not become involved in fighting other nations' wars for them.) Foreign law enforcement and internal security agencies will have primary responsibility for apprehending suspected Al Qaeda terrorists in their countries. And the hurdles of extradition will have to be overcome so that foreign governments hand over the terrorists who are caught. Again, the United States will need to use its political and diplomatic skill to elicit such cooperation. The threat of military force (let alone its actual use) is not a viable option.

In the final analysis, the United States will not be able to go it alone in the war on terrorism. The United States will need to convince other countries to take actions that are in U.S. interests. Diplomacy and statecraft may ultimately be the most important tools for achieving success against Al Qaeda.

499

Suggested Readings

Anonymous. *Imperial Hubris*. Washington: Brassey's, 2004.

_____. *Through Our Enemies' Eyes*. Washington: Brassey's, 2003.

Bergen, Peter L. *Holy War, Inc.* New York: Free Press, 2001.

Burke, Jason. *Al-Qaeda.* London: I.B. Tauris, 2003.

Carr, Caleb. *The Lessons of Terror.* New York: Random House, 2002.

Gunaratna, Rohan. *Inside Al Qaeda.* New York: Columbia University Press, 2002.

Hoffman, Bruce. *Inside Terrorism.* New York: Columbia University Press, 1998.

Peña, Charles V. "Strategy for the War on Terrorism." Cato Institute *Policy Report* 26, no. 4 (July–August 2004).

Vlahos, Michael. "Terror's Mask: Insurgency within Islam." Johns Hopkins University, Applied Physics Laboratory, May 2002.

_____. "Culture's Mask: War and Change after Iraq." Johns Hopkins University, Applied Physics Laboratory, September 2004.

—Prepared by Charles V. Peña

50. Homeland Security

Policymakers should

- make better screening of visitors at points of entry to the United States the top priority for the Department of Homeland Security and ensure that such screening is tied to terrorist databases;
- focus DHS's efforts on a few areas that will make a significant difference in preventing future terrorist attacks, rather than trying to do everything, and eliminate efforts that are only effective at the margins;
- make it clearer to the public that homeland security efforts cannot make the country absolutely safe against possible terrorist attacks;
- ensure the homeland security efforts are not disproportionately focused on defending against the last attack, for example, another September 11 or the Madrid train bombings, at the expense of other vulnerabilities that need to be remedied;
- not rush to reorganize the intelligence community as a way to fix perceived problems and to satisfy the public's need to feel safer; and
- ensure that civil liberties are not sacrificed for unneeded and ineffective homeland security measures.

A paramount responsibility of the federal government as set forth in the Constitution is to "provide for the common defense." But in the largest open society in the world, providing homeland security is a daunting task. Some of the vulnerabilities include the 2,000-mile-long U.S.-Mexican border, the 3,900-mile-long U.S.-Canadian land border, and 2,300 miles of border over water between the United States and Canada; thousands of bridges, sports stadiums, and shopping malls; and hundreds of skyscrapers and nuclear power plants. Defending against the possibility of terrorist attacks with weapons of mass destruction may be even more challenging.

The Al Qaeda terrorist network poses a unique threat to the United States. Al Qaeda is the one and only terrorist group with demonstrated global reach and willingness to attack the U.S. homeland. Al Qaeda is an agile, nonbureaucratic adversary that has the great advantage of being on the offense—knowing when, where, and how it will attack. Al Qaeda operatives will take advantage of the poor coordination among military, intelligence, law enforcement, and other responsible bureaucracies to exploit gaps in defenses. No other security threat to the United States rivals this one. To fight this nontraditional threat, the U.S. government must think more innovatively and try to be as nimble as the opponent. Indeed, this is the difficult task laid at the doorstep of the Department of Homeland Security.

In taking on this task, it is important to recognize the hard truth: providing absolute and perfect defense against any and all future potential terrorist attacks is impossible. The nature of terrorism is to morph and adapt, to flow around obstacles, and to find the path of least resistance. The problem of trying to defend against terrorism is best illustrated in a statement by the Irish Republican Army after a failed attempt to kill British prime minister Margaret Thatcher in 1984: ''Remember, we only have to be lucky once. You will have to be lucky always.'' That is no less true for the U.S. government defending against Al Qaeda. Homeland security starts with knowing that a perfect defense against terrorism is not possible.

The problem of homeland security is so vast that the DHS will be tempted to do everything. The nature of bureaucracy is to grow and to do more. This is exactly what the department needs to avoid at all costs. To be effective, the department must do everything it can to be as nimble, responsive, and adaptive as our terrorist enemy.

Therefore, instead of trying to do the impossible or attempting to do everything and doing nothing well, homeland security must focus on those threats that pose the most catastrophic consequences and for which there are cost-effective defenses. First and foremost, that means not focusing on the last attack and disproportionately directing homeland security efforts against preventing the same thing from happening again. The March 2004 Madrid train bombings are proof enough that we should not be obsessed with hijacked airplanes. And even with airplanes, hijackings are not the only terrorist threat—passengers with explosives in carry-on baggage are a demonstrated threat to commercial airliners and the effect of such a terrorist attack could be even more chilling for the airline industry and the economy than were the attacks of September 11, 2001.

Preventing Terrorist Entry into the United States

The first priority for homeland security must be to prevent terrorists from entering the country. This is the single most important thing DHS can do to reduce the likelihood of another terrorist attack. It is important to remember that none of the 19 hijackers sneaked into the country the way hundreds of thousands of illegal immigrants come across the U.S.-Mexican border every year. Instead, they entered the United States via known points of legal entry, as millions of visitors to the United States do each year. Therefore, we need to put systems and procedures in place so that known or suspected terrorists can be stopped at the border by the appropriate authorities. The most crucial aspect is ensuring that information from the appropriate agencies (e.g., CIA, FBI, Interpol) about known or suspected terrorists is made directly available in real time to those people responsible for checking passports, visas, and other immigration information.

In theory, US-VISIT (Visa and Immigrant Status Indicator Technology) is supposed to screen for potential terrorists before they enter the country. In practice, however, it seems misdirected. When it was unveiled in January 2004, DHS secretary Tom Ridge claimed, "While processing more than 20,000 travelers . . . US-VISIT has matched 21 hits on the FBI Criminal Watch List, including potential entrants with previous convictions for statutory rape, dangerous drugs, aggravated felonies, and several cases of visa fraud." Instead of flagging garden variety criminals, what's really needed is a "Google search" at the borders where a person's name and passport number can be cross-referenced with U.S. and foreign terrorist databases. And biometric data screening—such as facial recognition technology to compare people to photographs in those databases—might also be a useful technology to employ if tied to relevant databases.

Preventing WMD Entry into the United States

The prospect of terrorists using weapons of mass destruction—chemical, biological, or radiological/nuclear—is something that must be taken seriously. For the terrorists, there are opportunity costs associated with acquiring WMD, and the strategy of DHS should be to take all reasonable, prudent, and cost-effective measures to make those costs as high as possible.

More than 15,000 containers enter the United States via ship and twice that many via truck on a daily basis. DHS undersecretary for border and transportation security Asa Hutchinson has stated that his goal is to inspect 100 percent of the "at risk" shipments into the United States. That is probably the most realistic and cost-effective approach to increasing the opportunity costs to terrorists' ability to smuggle WMD into the country. "At risk" could be defined as containers shipped from or transiting through countries where terrorists are known to operate, where ownership of the vessel is suspect, where the entire manifest cannot be adequately accounted for, or where there might be suspicious activity with regard to the crew. Clearly, in order to streamline the process and not impede the flow of commerce, there should be maximum use of technology to detect and prevent illegal or otherwise unauthorized radiological, chemical, or biological materials from entering the country.

But our homeland security efforts must not be dominated completely by WMD. Terrorists can also use low-tech means. For example, concerns have been raised about the vulnerability of commercial aircraft to shoulder-fired anti-aircraft missiles (i.e., MANPADS or man-portable air defense systems). Given that such aircraft do not currently have defensive counter-measures against such missiles and that it would be virtually impossible to secure the requisite areas around airports (a several-mile radius) to prevent their use, prudence dictates that these types of weapons should also be on the watch list.

Ships, trains, and trucks carrying hazardous materials could be potential bombs (just as hijacked airplanes are potential missiles). The foiled Jordanian terrorist attack in April 2004 demonstrated how trucks laden with chemicals and explosives could be potent homemade chemical bombs. Of course, not every ship, train, or truck is a threat, and the need for security must be balanced by the need to ensure the free flow of goods, which is vital to the health of the U.S. economy. For example, in 2003, 37,000 trucks crossed the border between the United States and Canada and the two-way trade in goods and services between the two countries was more than $441 billion.

Protecting Critical Facilities

There are literally thousands of potential targets for possible terrorist attack. Even with an unlimited budget, it would be impossible to protect all of them because there are too many targets to protect and myriad ways in which they can be attacked. But the government would be remiss to ignore protecting a subset of critical targets—such as nuclear facilities and chemical facilities—whose destruction could have catastrophic consequences. The key to providing such protection is understanding the nature of the catastrophic event that we are trying to prevent, how that event could be precipitated by terrorists, and what barriers can be erected to reduce the threat or minimize the damage. As with homeland security writ large, it will probably not be possible to defend against every potential attack. But reasonable and prudent measures need to be taken to make it as difficult as possible for attacks with catastrophic consequences.

For example, nuclear power plants would be lucrative targets, but it is not simply a matter of providing increased security. The first concern is to safeguard nuclear material so that it can't be stolen for building a radiological weapon. Second, the plant itself must be protected to prevent terrorists from creating a disaster along the lines of Chernobyl. Similarly, security for chemical and biological facilities must be designed to prevent terrorists from creating an accident such as the 1984 Union Carbide chemical pesticide plant accident in Bhopal, India, which killed more than 3,000 people.

Aviation Security

There has been a tremendous emphasis on airline and airport security since September 11. That is only natural. But two truths need to be recognized. First, security did not fail on September 11. The hijackers simply took advantage of a loophole in security, demonstrating that the terrorist mindset is to find the path of least resistance. Second, although we must guard against it, the likelihood of terrorists hijacking jetliners to be used as weapons of mass destruction is probably relatively low given all the new security measures and procedures.

Future terrorist tactics may not be to use jetliners as missiles, but simply to blow them up and kill as many people as possible. Since January 1, 2003, the Transportation Security Agency has screened 100 percent of checked baggage at all 429 commercial airports across the United States to check for explosive devices. But it's not just passengers and their checked baggage that are of concern. As demonstrated by the two Russian airliners blown up in August 2004, carry-on bags with explosives are a real threat. Air cargo (on both passenger and cargo-only aircraft) is currently not inspected 100 percent of the time. Greater emphasis needs to be placed on security for airport operations, especially for those people with access to aircraft (e.g., ground crews, baggage handlers, etc.). Airport perimeter security is also an issue that needs to be addressed.

Emergency Preparedness and Response

The post-9/11 reality that we have to be willing to accept is that, given enough time and opportunities, a determined terrorist group will likely eventually succeed in attacking the United States. Hopefully, it will not be another attack that results in the kind of mass casualties experienced on September 11. But despite all efforts to prevent further terrorist attacks, it is vitally important that the Department of Homeland Security is prepared to respond to such attacks.

Education

First and foremost, the public needs to be educated about how to be prepared for and respond to terrorist attacks, especially the potential use of chemical, biological, or nuclear/radiological weapons. Solid, science-based information needs to be made available about the effects of such weapons and what can be done to mitigate their effects. Resource directories must be published. People need to know where to go and whom to contact in the event of an emergency. And it is just as important that people know what not to do.

In short, if there are effective means of providing protection against certain types of possible terrorist attacks (e.g., potassium iodide used to protect the thyroid gland from the effects of exposure to the radioactive iodine from a dirty bomb), the Department of Homeland Security needs to let people know exactly what those are, how they work, how to use them, and where they can be obtained.

Prevention

It may be possible to take preventive measures against the effects of terrorist attacks, particularly against the prospect of biological pathogens. We have already seen and experienced the use of anthrax by some unknown person or group. We understand that the deadly smallpox virus—if introduced intentionally into a highly mobile population—could have widespread catastrophic effects. Rather than waiting and responding after the fact, it would be more prudent to take preventive measures beforehand.

The president's smallpox vaccination policy is a good example of such action. The best defense against smallpox is a vaccinated population—even just a partially vaccinated population. Unfortunately, that policy is being met with some resistance. There appears to be a reluctance on the part of the first-response force—the very people the rest of the population will depend on in the event of an attack—to be vaccinated. If we cannot even vaccinate our first responders, how can the population reasonably expect that the first responders will be able to vaccinate everyone else? And if the first responders are not getting vaccinated, what does that mean for a plan to allow people to make their own decision about receiving the vaccination?

Emergency Response

As was shown on September 11, emergency response to a terrorist attack (just as with a natural disaster) is at the local level. Therefore, instead of being spent in Washington, a large chunk of the money authorized and appropriated for homeland security by the Congress should be given to state and local governments to allow communities to assess their needs and how best to meet them. Some of that money would likely be spent on improving first responder capabilities, while some would be spent on improving communications and information-sharing capabilities (but not necessarily providing radios that first responders need for their day-to-day duties and responsibilities). But we must, above all, understand that emergency response cannot be accomplished with a federally mandated, top-down approach. The federal government should consider itself a coordinator that can provide guidance and information (and funding, when and where necessary) for emergency response. But the federal government cannot become the micromanager of emergency response, setting mandated guidelines and requirements for local communities with a cookie cutter approach. What is appropriate for a large and densely populated metropolitan area may be overkill (and financially unattainable) for a rural community.

Intelligence

The 9/11 Commission recommended sweeping changes to the U.S. intelligence community in response to failures related to the September 11 attacks. Although the commission was careful not to claim that the attacks could have been prevented, the public's perception seems to be that fixing problems related to intelligence—primarily communication and information sharing—will prevent another September 11. The public's desire to feel safe from another terrorist attack and the impulse to look to the federal government to provide that safety is certainly understandable, but that does not mean that the 9/11 Commission's recommendations are sacred and should be implemented without question.

Resolving the problem of communication and information sharing among the 15 different federal agencies with intelligence functions requires a careful assessment of the costs, benefits, and risks associated with reorganization vs. reform. It is not a question of either-or, but of achieving the right balance. Are there duplicative functions that can be eliminated or consolidated? Do U.S. intelligence-gathering and analysis requirements require 15 different agencies? The important thing is to cut before pasting rather than just pasting together a new government bureaucracy (as was done in creating the Department of Homeland Security). Does reorganization in and of itself break down the barriers to effective communication and information sharing? Or is making the cultural shift from a "need to know" to "need to share" paradigm more of a management and leadership issue?

Admittedly, having 15 different agencies that are not part of an integrated management structure is unwieldy and inefficient. But there are downside risks that must be considered before rushing to consolidate the intelligence community. It is important to remember that intelligence analysis is not an exact science. Competing points of view and the ability to dissent are an important and healthy part of the intelligence process. Consolidating the intelligence function (whether under the aegis of a cabinet-level secretary as recommended by the 9/11 Commission or the Bush administration's approach of a director who reports to the president) might actually decrease the freedom for intelligence analysts to disagree. The result could be more of the groupthink that seemed to plague the CIA's assessment of Iraq's WMD, instead of just a single agency affecting the broader intelligence community. So there are good reasons to keep intelligence separated rather than under the umbrella of a single person and unitary management control.

Before trying to reorganize the intelligence community, it would be useful to assess how well the Department of Homeland Security has been in getting what were the 23 disparate federal agencies that comprise the department to communicate and share information. The bottom line is that a headlong rush to fix what is perceived as broken in the intelligence community may not solve the real problems, may create other problems, and may give the public a false sense of security that it is safe from another September 11.

Civil Liberties

Finally, all homeland security actions must take into account civil liberties implications. We must heed Benjamin Franklin's admonition that "they that can give up essential liberty to obtain a little temporary safety deserve neither liberty nor safety." Before the government infringes on civil liberties, it must pass a litmus test: the government must demonstrate that any proposed new powers are essential, that they would be effective, and that there is no less invasive way to accomplish the same security goal.

Ultimately, we must remember that although terrorists may take advantage of our liberties to exploit vulnerabilities in our society, our liberties are not the problem in trying to defend against terrorism. In the final analysis, homeland security means securing the Constitution and Bill of Rights, not just the country itself.

Suggested Readings

de Rugy, Veronique, and Charles V. Peña. "Responding to the Threat of Smallpox Bioterrorism: An Ounce of Prevention Is Best Approach." Cato Institute Policy Analysis no. 434, April 18, 2002.

Flynn, Stephen. *America the Vulnerable.* New York: HarperCollins, 2004.

Harris, James W. "Building Leverage in the Long War: Ensuring Intelligence Community Creativity in the Fight against Terrorism." Cato Institute Policy Analysis no. 439, May 16, 2002.

Lynch, Timothy. "Breaking the Vicious Cycle: Preserving Our Liberties While Fighting Terrorism." Cato Institute Policy Analysis no. 443, June 26, 2002.

Taylor, Eric R. "Are We Prepared for Terrorism Using Weapons of Mass Destruction? Government's Half Measures." Cato Institute Policy Analysis no. 387, November 27, 2000.

_____. "The New Homeland Security Apparatus: Impeding the Fight against Agile Terrorists." Cato Institute Foreign Policy Briefing no. 70, June 26, 2002.

—Prepared by Charles V. Peña

51. The Defense Budget

Policymakers should

- reduce the budget for national defense from the current sum of more than $400 billion to about $200 billion in increments over five years;
- make it clear that the reduced budget must be accompanied by a more restrained national military posture that requires enough forces to fight a major war anywhere in the world;
- restructure U.S. forces to reflect the American geostrategic advantage of virtual invulnerability to invasion by deeply cutting ground forces (Army and Marines) while retaining a larger percentage of the Navy and Air Force;
- authorize a force structure of 5 active-duty Army divisions (down from 10 now), 1 active Marine division (reduced from 3 now), 14 Air Force fighter wings (down from 20 now), 200 Navy ships (down from 316), and 6 carrier battle groups with 6 Navy air wings (reduced from 12 and 11, respectively);
- require that the armed services compensate for reduced active forces by relying more on the National Guard and the Reserves in any major conflict;
- terminate force structure or weapons systems that are unneeded and use the savings to give taxpayers a break and to beef up neglected mission areas; and
- terminate all peacekeeping and overseas presence missions so that the armed services can concentrate on training to fight wars and to deploy from the U.S. homeland in an expeditionary mode should that become necessary.

The Context for Defense Policy

Paradoxically, the massive amount the United States spends on national defense each year, and the profligate military interventions conducted overseas with the forces generated by such spending, may actually make the United States less, rather than more, secure.

A nation's defense policy (including the defense budget) should reflect its security situation—that is, the geopolitical realities of its environment. U.S. defense policy fails to take such realities into account.

Advocates of higher military budgets regret that U.S. spending on national defense has declined to about 3.5 percent of the nation's gross domestic product, its lowest point since 1940. As a result, they argue that U.S. security is being severely compromised. Although defense spending as a percentage of GDP is a good indicator of what proportion of the national wealth is being appropriated for defense, it is not an indicator of what amount should be spent on a nation's defense. Such spending should be based on the nation's geostrategic situation and the threats to its vital interests (which have declined dramatically since the end of the Cold War). Besides, no nation ever fought another nation with a percentage of its GDP. Nations fight other nations with military forces that are purchased with finite quantities of resources.

When the U.S. annual budget for national defense is compared with that of other nations, the true magnitude of U.S. defense spending becomes clear. The United States alone accounts for more than one-third of the world's military spending. U.S. defense spending roughly equals the combined spending of the next 18 nations and is more than triple the combined defense budgets of the remaining 142 countries in the world. The United States outspends both Russia and China seven to one. More important, the United States spends 54 times the combined amount spent by potential rogue state threats—Iran, Syria, Libya, Cuba, and North Korea.

The United States could probably spend less, not more, than other major nations and remain secure. The United States is blessed with one of the most secure geostrategic environments the world has ever seen. It is virtually invulnerable to a conventional military invasion. The United States has two great oceans separating it from other major powers and weak and friendly neighbors on its borders, and no major power exists in the Western Hemisphere to pose a challenge. Most important, any nation foolish enough to attack the United States would risk devastation of its homeland by the world's most formidable nuclear arsenal. In short, a large portion of the more than $400 billion spent annually on defense (almost $1,400 per American) has nothing to do with U.S. security and lots to do with the expensive, self-appointed role of "world leader."

Of course, the attacks on September 11 brought home the vulnerability of the United States to strikes by terrorists using unconventional means.

The huge U.S. military is much larger than needed to conduct the small brushfire wars required to fight terrorism (much of the war on terrorism will be conducted by U.S. intelligence and law enforcement agencies, not the military)—the only real major threat to U.S. security in the post–Cold War world. In fact, the large military and the temptation to use it to intervene all over the world actually reduce the security of the U.S. homeland. Therefore, adopting a policy of military restraint and cutting the defense budget would actually enhance security at home.

New Criterion for Determining the Size of U.S. Forces Is Needed

The virtual invulnerability of the United States allows it to define its vital interests narrowly and intervene militarily only when they are threatened. There has always been—and will always be—instability in the world (although, since the Cold War ended, most indicators have shown that it is declining). In the vast majority of cases, however, instability will not threaten vital American interests. If the United States pursued a policy of military restraint, it could reduce its budget for national defense by half—from $400 billion to about $200 billion per year—and still be, by far, the most capable military power in the world.

Adopting a policy of military restraint would allow the United States to size its forces to fight one major theater war instead of two concurrently, as envisioned by the Pentagon. Even that reduction in forces would provide some hedge against uncertainty. Acting as a "balancer of last resort," the United States would assist other nations in shoring up a deteriorating balance of power only in such critical regions as Europe and East Asia (the areas of the world with large concentrations of economic and technological power). Like-minded nations in the affected region would provide most of the ground forces and some air forces; the United States would also provide air power—its comparative advantage. U.S. air power could quickly be dispatched to help friendly nations halt the offensive of a serious aggressor state. Some U.S. ground forces eventually might be needed to help retake lost territory, but that is a remote possibility that should not be considered a high-priority mission.

Optimal U.S. Force Structure

The Department of Defense's 1993 Bottom-Up Review (BUR) allocated a block of forces to conduct one major regional conflict. The block consisted of 4–5 Army divisions, 4–5 Marine brigades (between 1 and 2 divisions), 10 Air Force wings, 100 heavy bombers, and 4–5 aircraft carrier battle groups. Prudent military planning might require that this "one war" force structure be augmented to add even more cushion for unforeseen circumstances. Thus, an optimal force structure can be created that still saves money. That force structure would consist of 5 active Army divisions (down from 10 now), 1 active Marine division (reduced from 3 now), 14 Air Force air wings (down from 20 now), 187 heavy bombers (down only slightly from 208 now), 200 ships (down from 317), 6 aircraft carrier battle groups and 6 Navy air wings (reduced from 12 and 11, respectively), and 25 nuclear-powered attack submarines (down from the current force of 55 vessels). See Table 51.1

In this alternative force structure, ground forces—the Army and the Marine Corps—have been reduced more than the Air Force and Navy. Such a shift of emphasis makes sense for a nation that faces no threat from an invading ground force. There are long distances between the United States and any potential adversary. With a small standing army, more reliance would need to be placed on the National Guard and the Reserves. In the case of the rare, large-scale war in a foreign theater that requires substantial ground forces to win back lost territory, plenty of time will be available to mobilize the forces of the National Guard and the Reserves.

Table 51.1
Proposed Cuts in U.S. Military Forces

Force Component	Planned Force	Optimal Force Structure	Percentage Reduction
Active Army divisions	10	5	50
Active Marine divisions	3	1	67
Air Force tactical fighter wings	20	14	30
Air Force heavy bombers	208	187	0
Total Navy ships	317	200	37
Navy aircraft carrier battle groups	12	6	50
Navy carrier air wings	11	6	45
Nuclear-powered attack submarines	55	25	55

SOURCE: Planned force structure from William Cohen, *Annual Report to the President and Congress* (Washington: U.S. Department of Defense, 2001).

A much smaller Marine Corps will also rely more heavily on the Reserves. Although the BUR stated the need for more than one division to fight a major conflict, one existing Reserve division can supplement the active division to meet that requirement. Only one Marine division needs to be active; there has been no large-scale amphibious assault since Inchon during the Korean War. In the post–World War II period, the Marines have most often been used in small-scale interventions in the Third World. Such interventions should be undertaken only rarely.

The Air Force would be cut the least of any service. Air power proved devastatingly effective during the wars in the Persian Gulf and Kosovo, and the United States has traditionally had a comparative advantage in air power. Air Force tactical aircraft should be favored over Navy tactical aircraft because land-based aircraft have a greater range and bomb-carrying capacity (that is, have greater efficiency) than aircraft that operate from carriers.

In any major war, friendly nations can provide land bases from which U.S. aircraft can operate. If such bases become more vulnerable to enemy missile attacks, the United States will need to buy theater missile defenses to protect the bases, purchase short-take-off aircraft that can be dispersed to unfinished airfields, or use long-range heavy bombers that can operate from distant bases in the region. Such measures would be better than relying more on expensive aircraft carriers and naval aircraft. For this reason, the U.S. heavy bomber fleet—which has great range and large bomb-carrying capacity—should be reduced only slightly.

Nonetheless, some aircraft carriers and naval aircraft are needed. Like the Marines, in the post–World War II period Navy carriers have been used primarily to provide forward presence in overseas theaters and for small-scale interventions in the Third World (so-called crisis response). If the United States observed a policy of military restraint, the need for such missions would be rare. Instead, carrier battle groups would sail from the United States and be used to control the seas, to protect American trade if it were threatened, and to provide air power in the rare instance when land bases were not available.

The elimination of the overseas military presence and crisis response missions would allow a substantial reduction in the number of carrier battle groups. Six carrier battle groups would suffice to control the seas and protect trade. The United States—with six carriers—would still have bone-crushing dominance over any other fleet in the world. Although the BUR suggested that four or five carriers would be needed to fight a regional conflict, there has always been a dispute about whether that number included the carrier at the dock undergoing extensive overhaul. To be conservative, another carrier was added, bringing the total to six.

After the Cold War, the Navy's increased emphasis on providing air support for Marine amphibious assaults made Marine air wings redundant; such air wings should be eliminated.

The demise of the Soviet nuclear attack submarine fleet would allow the United States to cut its attack submarine force by more than half, from 55 to 25.

Cut Unneeded Weapons Systems

Many weapons the Pentagon is currently procuring were originally designed during the Cold War (for example, the Marine Corps' V-22 tiltrotor aircraft). Some weapons now in development entered that process during the Cold War and were to be used against a threat that is now gone or never came to fruition (for example, the Army's Comanche helicopter and the Air Force's F-22 fighter). In addition, the tradition-bound military services are buying successors to Cold War systems (for example, the Navy's Virginia-class submarine and F-18E/F aircraft). Some weapons are too costly (for example, the F-22). Finally, both the executive branch and Congress build unneeded weapons to dole out pork to inefficient defense industries and favored congressional districts. Thus, inertia, tradition, and pork undermine the rational development and procurement of weapon systems. Congress should terminate or reduce procurement of the following "white elephant" weapons.

F-22 Raptor and F/A-18E/F Tactical Fighters

The current generation of American aircraft (the Air Force's F-15 and F-16 and the Navy's F-14 and F-18C/D) will enjoy crushing air superiority over all other air forces for the foreseeable future. According to Eliot Cohen, director of the Strategic Studies Program at Johns Hopkins University and an acknowledged expert on air power, "There's not anybody who's going to be comparable to us for as long as you can see."

But the U.S. military services are currently developing or purchasing three new fighter aircraft (the Air Force's F-22, the Navy's F/A-18E/F, and the multiservice Joint Strike Fighter) at a cost of about $340 billion. The three new fighter aircraft alone will consume a quarter of the Pentagon's annual budget for procuring new weapons and "crowd out" the purchase of weapons that should have a higher priority—for example, a modestly priced replacement for aging U.S. bombers. Thus, two of the three aircraft—the F-22 and F/A-18E/F—should be terminated or purchased only in drastically reduced numbers.

The Air Force designed the stealthy F-22 aircraft primarily to fight futuristic Soviet fighters that were never built. The F-22 would replace the best air superiority fighter in the world today—the F-15C. The United States could maintain its current dominance of the skies well into the future using upgraded F-15Cs, superbly trained pilots, new munitions, and Airborne Warning and Control System aircraft (the best aircraft in the world for management of air battle and a potent force multiplier). No current or future threat to U.S. air superiority exists that would justify spending nearly $63 billion for 341 F-22 aircraft. As a result, the aircraft will probably be used mainly for air-to-ground attack, which it is not optimally designed to do. (Besides, the United States already has the F-117 and B-2 planes to perform stealthy ground attack missions.) At nearly $200 million for each aircraft, the F-22 is the most expensive, least needed fighter ever built.

Although the F/A-18E/F is an entirely different aircraft than the F/A-18C/D, it is not much of an improvement for about double the price ($86 million for each E/F model). For example, although the E/F has a longer range and greater payload than the C/D, it still has a shorter range and smaller payload than the retired A-6 attack aircraft at a time when the aircraft carrier is being pushed farther out to sea by enemy mines, cruise missiles, and diesel submarines. Because the air-to-air threat environment is so low, the C/D model will most likely suffice for future air defense of the fleet until the stealthy Navy version of the Joint Strike Fighter comes on line. If a ground attack aircraft with longer range and greater payload is needed before the stealthy Navy Joint Strike Fighter is ready, a special naval version of F-117 Nighthawk might provide an interim capability.

Virginia-Class Submarines

With the demise of the Soviet Union and the Russian submarine fleet rusting in port, the existing U.S. force of Seawolf and 688 Los Angeles–class vessels is unquestionably the best in the world and will remain so for the foreseeable future. No other navy in the world even comes close to U.S. undersea power. But the Navy has already begun constructing 30 new Virginia-class submarines (at an average cost of $2.2 billion per ship) and decommissioning older 688 boats before their useful life is over. The Virginia-class submarines will, in most respects, be less capable than the Seawolf-class—in size, speed, diving depth, and weapons capacity.

According to the U.S. General Accounting Office, the Navy could retain its goal of 55 submarines in the force by merely refueling the nuclear reactors of the older 688 boats. Moreover, the Navy justified hiking its force goal from 50 to 55 submarines on the basis of increased requirements for intelligence collection. During the Cold War the main target of intelligence gathering by U.S. submarines was the Soviet fleet. Because most of that fleet does not get out of port much anymore, the Pentagon has added more countries to the list of reconnaissance targets. Yet justifying the 55-boat goal on the basis of collecting intelligence is questionable. With the end of the Cold War, conventional threats to the U.S. Navy and the United States declined and so should have requirements for gathering intelligence on such threats; instead they have doubled since 1989. Although, in certain instances, the submarine can provide unique collection capabilities, the United States has many other more versatile assets for spying—for example, manned and unmanned aircraft and satellites—that can perform missions less expensively than $2 billion submarines and are not limited to collection in littoral areas. The United States should reduce its submarine goal and terminate the Virginia-class line.

The V-22 Tiltrotor Aircraft

The V-22—which takes off (and lands) like a helicopter, then tilts its rotors and flies as a fixed-wing aircraft—transports Marines and their light equipment from amphibious ships to shore. The aircraft can go faster and farther than a CH-53 heavy-lift helicopter but cannot carry the heavy equipment the CH-53 can.

The V-22 program has been troubled by crashes and is 10 years behind schedule and $15 billion over budget. In the 1980s and 1990s, senior officials from the Reagan, Bush, and Clinton administrations, including Secretary of Defense Dick Cheney, recommended that the aircraft be cancelled. Because of the exorbitant cost of the aircraft, the first Bush administration tried to terminate the program, but Congress reinstated it. The V-22 is truly an albatross.

At more than $100 million per V-22 aircraft, transporting Marines and equipment to shore by air could be done much more cheaply by buying new versions of existing CH-53 rotary aircraft or even smaller helicopters like the Blackhawk CH-60. Besides, against a capable opponent, if faster V-22s transport Marines and their light equipment inland behind enemy lines and if slower CH-53s carry their heavy equipment, the Marines may die before the heavy equipment reaches them.

Some Savings from Cutting Unneeded Weapons Could Fund More Critical Needs

Canceling the F-22 Raptor, the F/A-18E/F Super Hornet, the V-22 Ospry, and the Virginia-class submarine programs could save $12.2 billion in procurement and research, test, and development (RDT&E) costs in the FY05 defense budget and more than $170 billion in future program costs.

Some of the savings generated by cutting unneeded weapons could be used to fund research, development, and procurement in areas that the services usually neglect: Special Forces, long-range bombers, unmanned aerial vehicles, defenses against cruise missiles, technology to detect and neutralize sea mines, and equipment to protect against attacks with biological and chemical weapons (Table 51.2). The war in Afghanistan showed that long-range bombers were devastating when guided to their targets by information from unmanned aerial vehicles and Special Forces on the ground. Much has been invested in defending U.S. forces against ballistic missiles; less effort has been put into defending troops against attacks from cheaper and more effective cruise missiles. More and more terrorists and countries are working on weapons of mass destruction, so more should be invested in defending U.S. forces and civilians at home from biological and chemical weapons. The Navy has neglected capabilities that can detect and neutralize sea mines, which can be devastating to naval operations. Because great advancements can be achieved for small amounts of funding in most of those areas, the remainder of the savings from cuts could be returned to the taxpayer.

Savings achieved through decommissioning some military units and their existing equipment could be supplemented by savings accruing from canceling new weapons systems, currently in development or production, that are either unneeded in principle or relics of the Cold War. Some of those savings could be returned to taxpayers through reductions in the defense budget and some could be reallocated to increase funding for previously neglected, but important, military missions.

Terminate All Peacekeeping and Overseas Presence Missions

Peacekeeping and overseas presence missions (U.S. troops stationed overseas and regular naval deployments in overseas theaters) have nothing

Table 51.2
Weapon Systems to Terminate or Cut and Missions and Weapons That Need Increased Funding

Weapon or Mission	Function	Service
Weapon Systems to Terminate or Cut		
F-22	Air superiority fighter	Air Force
F/A-18E/F	Carrier-based fighter attack aircraft	Navy
Virginia-class submarine	Attack submarine	Navy
V-22	Tiltrotor transport aircraft	Martine Corps
Neglected Missions and Weapons in Need of Increased Funding		
Unmanned aerial vehicles	Reconnaissance, strike, etc.	All
Heavy bomber (R&D)	High-capacity, long-range bomb delivery	Air Force
Special Forces	Intelligence gathering, commando attacks, designation of targets	Army, Navy, Air Force
Cruise missile defenses	Defend U.S. forces against cruise missiles	Army, Marine Corps
Mine countermeasures	Detect and neutralize sea mines	Navy, Marine Corps
Chemical and biological defense	Defend forces and civilian population	All

to do with safeguarding vital U.S. interests. In the more benign security environment of the post–Cold War world, such missions only discourage wealthy U.S. allies from spending the resources needed to provide for their own security. Furthermore, those missions lower morale of U.S. forces and consume resources and time that should be used for training to fight wars and to deploy from the United States in the rare cases in which a foreign conflict threatens U.S. vital interests.

Benefits of Adopting the Alternative Defense Posture

Adopting a foreign policy of military restraint overseas, buying the forces needed to fight one regional war, and reducing the budget for national defense by more than a third would help to keep the United States out of unnecessary foreign wars. Such potential quagmires have little to do with vital American security interests and incur exorbitant costs—in both resources and American lives (both those of U.S. military personnel overseas and those of civilians at home, who will be the victims of terrorist attacks in retaliation for an interventionist American foreign policy). A smaller military would also help safeguard U.S. liberties at home.

Suggested Readings

Carpenter, Ted Galen. *A Search for Enemies: America's Alliances after the Cold War.* Washington: Cato Institute, 1992.

Conetta, Carl, and Charles Knight. "Inventing Threats." *Bulletin of Atomic Scientists,* March–April 1998.

Eland, Ivan. *Putting "Defense" Back in U.S. Defense Policy: Rethinking U.S. Security.* Westport, CT: Praeger, 2001.

_____. "Subtract Unneeded Nuclear Attack Submarines from the Fleet." Cato Institute Foreign Policy Briefing no. 47, April 2, 1998.

_____. "Tilting at Windmills: Post–Cold War Military Threats to U.S. Security." Cato Institute Policy Analysis no. 332, February 8, 1999.

Isenberg, David, and Ivan Eland. "Empty Promises: Why the Bush Administration's Half-Hearted Attempts at Defense Reform Have Failed." Cato Institute Policy Analysis no. 442, June 11, 2002.

Murray, Williamson. "Hard Choices: Fighter Procurement in the Next Century." Cato Institute Policy Analysis no. 334, February 26, 1999.

_____. "The United States Should Begin Work on a New Bomber Program Now." Cato Institute Policy Analysis no. 368, March 16, 2000.

Peña, Charles V. "V-22: Osprey or Albatross?" Cato Institute Foreign Policy Briefing no. 72, January 8, 2003.

Preble, Christopher. "Joint Strike Fighter: Can a Multiservice Fighter Program Succeed?" Cato Institute Policy Analysis no. 460, December 5, 2002.

—Prepared by Ivan Eland and Charles V. Peña

52. Strategic Nuclear Forces and Missile Defense

Policymakers should

- endorse a truly "national" limited land-based missile defense;
- eschew grandiose sea- and space-based missile defenses—which are unnecessary, expensive "international" systems designed to protect wealthy U.S. allies and friends and provide a robust shield for unneeded U.S. interventions overseas;
- not rush development and expanded deployment of land-based missile defense so that the system can be thoroughly tested under realistic conditions before a decision is made to fully deploy it;
- encourage destruction—rather than storage—of warheads as part of the Strategic Defensive Reductions Treaty to reduce operationally deployed forces to 1,700–2,200 warheads by December 2012;
- propose even deeper cuts in offensive strategic nuclear forces—down to a maximum of 1,500 warheads; and
- reduce the triad of U.S. nuclear forces—nuclear-capable bombers, intercontinental ballistic missiles (ICBMs), and sea-launched ballistic missiles (SLBMs)—to a dyad.

Although the Bush administration envisions a global, layered missile defense system (incorporating land-, sea-, and space-based weapons), the reality is that a limited land-based system designed to protect the U.S. homeland against the potential threat of long-range missiles from rogue states is the most mature (though still not thoroughly tested and proven) and closest to fruition. The first deployment of 10 interceptors at Fort Greely, Alaska, is putting the cart before the horse. Rather than be rushed to deployment, a limited missile defense system should be developed at a measured pace because an excessively rapid development program could waste taxpayer dollars on an ineffective system. Missile defense should remain a research and development (R&D) program until it has been thoroughly tested under realistic operational conditions. Only then should a decision be made expanding deployment beyond the current interceptors at Fort Greely.

Any defense expenditures—including those on missile defense—must be commensurate with the threat. More robust missile defenses are not justified by the present limited threat. Also, sinking large amounts of money into more comprehensive missile defenses—when even the limited land-based system might fail because of technical problems or lack of adequate testing—is questionable.

A Limited Missile Defense Is Needed for a Limited Threat

Although it is not certain that North Korea or any other "rogue" state will be capable of launching a missile attack against the United States by 2005, the R&D program for missile defense is being rushed to have a system deployed by that date. Even if the threat from North Korea did materialize by that date, the United States would probably be able to use its offensive nuclear force to deter a missile attack from North Korea, another "rogue" state, or any other state. Thus, missile defense would be a backup system against a missile attack from a pariah state. Rushing development to deploy a system without thorough and realistic operational testing increases the probability that the system will ultimately be delayed, will experience escalating costs, or will simply not work.

More important, rogue states have or will have options for striking the United States other than long-range ballistic missiles. Such countries already possess short- and-medium-range ballistic missiles that could be launched from ships operating in international waters off the U.S. coasts. And a missile defense designed for use against long-range ICBMs will not have the capability to intercept these shorter-range missiles. Moreover, the kinds of missile defense systems designed to counter these threats (commonly referred to as theater missile defense) would be extremely expensive to deploy to protect the entire nation or even the coastlines (the limited areas such systems can protect would require greater numbers of systems) and are not part of the administration's plan for a missile defense system to protect the United States.

"Rogue" nations also may possess or could acquire cruise missiles that could be launched from ships or, possibly, aircraft. Again, a missile defense against long-range ICBMs will not be able to counter these threats, which would require deploying an extensive (and likely expensive) air defense system.

Finally, September 11, 2001, clearly demonstrated that the United States is vulnerable to terrorist attack.

Such threats to the American homeland may be more inexpensive, accurate, reliable, and thus more probable than that posed by ICBMs launched from rogue states. Even the most hostile pariah state is likely to hesitate to launch from its territory an ICBM against the United States. U.S. satellites can detect the origin of such long-range missile launches, and the world's most powerful nuclear force would almost certainly retaliate against the attacking nation. In contrast, the origin of terrorist attacks or missile launches from ships or aircraft may be harder to determine, which makes U.S. retaliation—and therefore deterrence—more difficult. The existence of the other threats does not, of course, refute the argument that long-range ballistic missiles also pose a threat and that the U.S. government should combat the threats that can be defeated. But we must understand that long-range ballistic missiles will be just one of several possible threats.

None of the proposed missile defense systems to protect the United States will have a defensive capability against either short-range ballistic missiles or cruise missiles—delivery systems that rogue states and others already possess. The best reason to have a limited missile defense may be the possibility of accidental—rather than intentional—launches from such states and limited accidental launches from established nuclear powers. Pariah states with newly acquired long-range missiles and nuclear warheads may have poor early warning systems, only rudimentary command and control over such forces, nonexistent nuclear doctrine, and insufficient safeguards against an accidental launch. In addition, in the past, Russia's decrepit early warning systems almost led to accidental launches.

Nevertheless, the primary threat from accidental or intentional launches from rogue states is likely to be relatively modest (a few ICBMs) and unsophisticated (their missiles are unlikely to have multiple warheads or sophisticated decoys), requiring an equally modest response. A thoroughly tested limited ground-based missile defense system of 100 or so interceptors could provide sufficient defensive capability against such threats.

The Limited Threat Does Not Warrant "International" Defenses

Although it is portrayed to the American public as a "national" missile defense, the global, layered system consisting of land-, sea-, and space-based weapons favored by the administration is really an "international" missile defense system that would also defend U.S. allies and "friends," even though they are wealthy enough to build their own missile defenses.

The main objective of observers who support more comprehensive, robust, and layered missile defense systems does not seem to be defense of the U.S. homeland. Instead, their aim seems to be to create a stronger shield behind which the United States can intervene against potential regional adversaries possessing weapons of mass destruction and the long-range missiles to deliver them. According to that reasoning, if such adversaries cannot threaten the United States or its allies with catastrophic retaliation, U.S. policymakers will feel more confident about intervening militarily. But because no missile defense system can guarantee that all incoming warheads will be destroyed, such an increase in U.S. military activism could actually undermine U.S. security in a catastrophic way. Thus, deployment of a missile defense should be confined to a more limited land-based "national" system, which is the most technologically mature system.

Some proponents of missile defense argue that a sea-based system can be deployed more quickly and will be less expensive than the limited land-based system. They contend that the Navy Theater Wide system (a system that is currently being designed to provide midcourse intercept capability against slower, shorter-range theater ballistic missiles) can be upgraded to destroy long-range ICBMs in their boost phase (when under powered flight at the beginning of their trajectories). To intercept faster, longer-range missiles in the boost phase, a new, faster interceptor would need to be developed. That interceptor would probably not be compatible with the vertical launchers of Navy ships. Forward-deployed sea-based missile defense against ICBMs might also experience operational difficulties, including greater vulnerability to attack, and detract from the Navy's other missions, or require expensive new dedicated ships for missile defense.

Some proponents have also advocated a sea-based midcourse system as an alternative to a land-based system. But this would require dedicated Aegis ships deployed near Alaska (where the proposed limited land-based system would be deployed), necessitating an investment in additional ships and crews. And such ships would still be dependent on land-based radars—the Aegis SPY-1B radar system is designed to track shorter-range and slower ballistic and cruise missiles, and an X-band radar for ICBMs is too large to be fitted aboard an Aegis ship. So it is puzzling how such a system would be an improvement over a land-based deployment.

Even if a sea-based missile defense could be developed faster and more inexpensively than the more mature land-based system (a dubious proposition since the sea-based system would depend on sensor, communication, and kill vehicle technology being developed for the land-based system), critical gaps in coverage would necessitate supplementing the sea-based system with expensive space-based weapons. Unlike land-based missile defense against ICBMs, a sea-based system is not a stand-alone system.

Also, many advocates of sea- and space-based weapons want to protect U.S. friends and allies. But the United States should refuse to protect those wealthy nations—which spend too little on their own defense and already benefit from significant U.S. security guarantees—with a missile defense. A layered international missile defense that adds sea- and space-based weapons will escalate the costs of the system dramatically. In addition, an international defense is not warranted by the limited threat and should not be used to defend rich allies who can afford to build their own missile defenses.

A limited land-based system (for example, a hundred or more ground-based interceptors designed to defend against tens of warheads from rogue states) would not enable the United States to undermine nuclear stability by threatening Russia's surviving offensive nuclear forces (even at reduced levels, numbering in the hundreds or thousands of warheads); but more robust defenses might do so. In addition, deploying robust defenses might cause an "action-reaction" cycle with China. As China modernizes and builds up its small nuclear forces (which will probably happen whether or not U.S. defenses are deployed), robust defenses are much more likely to cause a larger Chinese buildup than is a limited system. A limited missile defense would signal to both powers that the United States is not trying to achieve strategic advantage.

Combine Limited Missile Defense with Deeper Cuts in Offensive Strategic Weapons

The most prudent course of action is to pursue development of a limited missile defense system to defend the United States against rogue state threats and accidental launches and negotiate even deeper cuts in strategic offensive forces.

In the much milder nuclear threat environment of a post–Cold War world, if the United States changed its nuclear doctrine from war fighting to deterrence, deep mutual reductions in offensive forces to levels below the 1,700 to 2,200 operationally deployed warheads of the SORT agreement (perhaps a ceiling as low as 1,500 warheads) would still allow the United States to deter Russia and smaller or emerging nuclear powers (Figure 52.1). Also, with much lower numbers of warheads in that more benign environment, it would be more efficient and cost effective to reduce the triad of nuclear forces—nuclear-capable bombers, ICBMs, and SLBMs— to a dyad (possibly ICBMs and bombers or SLBMs and bombers). The reduced threat of nuclear war would require less redundancy among U.S. forces to complicate the attack plans of the adversary.

Perhaps most important, the United States should destroy rather than put in reserve the warheads taken off operational deployment. The primary

Figure 52.1
Proposed Limits on Warheads in Each of the U.S. and Russian Arsenals

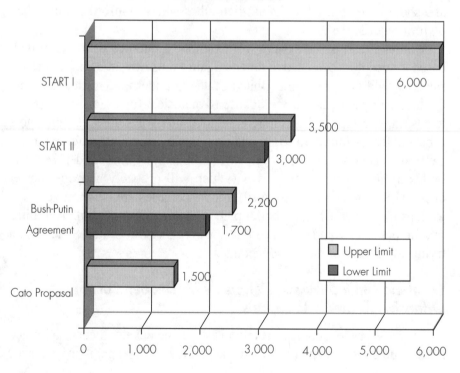

rationale for retaining more weapons in reserve is as a hedge against some unforeseen future threat. The perceived need for a reserve seems to reflect the thinking of many conservatives and military officials that Russia could one day again become a nuclear rival or that China could pose a future nuclear threat. If the United States and Russia have truly entered a new stage in their relationship, then actions should match the rhetoric. Even worse, the "hedging" logic becomes a self-fulfilling prophecy. If the United States retains more weapons, so will Russia. And the Chinese will likely view the entire U.S. strategic arsenal—not just deployed weapons—as a threat and react accordingly. Counting rules that allow the United States to retain more weapons create an incentive for Russia, China, and others to do the same.

Lower numbers of warheads in the inventories of Russia and the United States would probably mean lower numbers of warheads on alert status, and lower numbers of warheads on alert status would substantially reduce the risk of an accidental nuclear launch. The lower inventory levels would also mean that fewer nuclear warheads would be available to be stolen or sold to rogue states or terrorist groups (that possibility is a particular concern for the aging and insecure Russian nuclear stockpile).

Concerns about the safety and security of nuclear warheads put into reserve status further highlight the need to destroy rather than store warheads. If the Russians decide to retain more weapons in storage, there are legitimate concerns about the safety and security of those weapons. By definition, they will be less secure than deployed weapons guarded regularly by military personnel. Their relative lack of security makes them attractive targets for terrorists seeking to acquire weapons of mass destruction. So taking the weapons off operational deployment without destroying them could possibly lessen U.S. security rather than enhance it.

Recommended Readings

Coyle, Phillip. "Rhetoric or Reality? Missile Defense under Bush." *Arms Control Today* 32, no. 4 (May 2002).

Eland, Ivan. "Let's Make National Missile Defense Truly 'National.'" Cato Institute Foreign Policy Briefing no. 58, June 27, 2000.

Graham, Bradley. *Hit to Kill: The New Battle over Shielding America from Missile Attack.* New York: Public Affairs, 2001.

Holum, John. "Assessing the New U.S.-Russian Pact." *Arms Control Today* 32, no. 5 (June 2002).

Jones, Rodney. "Taking National Missile Defense to Sea: A Critique of Sea-Based and Boost-Phase Proposals." Council for a Livable World Education Fund, October 2000.

Krepon, Michael. "Defusing Today's Doomsday Machines." *New Democrat Blueprint* (Winter 2000): 20–24.

Newhouse, John. "The Missile Defense Debate." *Foreign Affairs* 80, no. 4 (July–August 2001).

O'Hanlon, Michael E., James M. Lindsay, and Michael H. Armacost. "Defending America: The Case for Limited National Missile Defense." Brookings Institution, 2001.

Peña, Charles V. "Arms Control and Missile Defense: Not Mutually Exclusive." Cato Institute Policy Analysis no. 376, July 26, 2000.

———. "From the Sea: National Missile Defense Is Neither Cheap Nor Easy." Cato Institute Foreign Policy Briefing no. 60, September 6, 2000.

Peña, Charles V., and Barbara Conry. "National Missile Defense: Examining the Options." Cato Policy Analysis no. 337, March 16, 1999.

Slocombe, Walter B. "Stability Effects of Limited Missile Defenses: The Case for the Affirmative." *The Global Politics and Strategy of Missile Defense*, Pugwash Occasional Papers, 3, no. 1 (March 2002).

Tanks, David. "National Missile Defense: Policy Issues and Technological Capabilities." Institute for Foreign Policy Analysis, April 2000.

—Prepared by Charles V. Peña

53. Transatlantic Relations

Policymakers should

- support the Bush administration's plan to redeploy U.S. forces from Western Europe to the continental United States and implement a plan to withdraw all U.S. forces from Europe during the next five years;
- refuse to appropriate funds to construct new U.S./NATO bases in East Central and Southeastern Europe;
- forge a new, balanced transatlantic relationship based on recognition of the European Union as an independent "pole of power" in the international political system and a geopolitical equal of the United States;
- refrain from interfering in decisionmaking areas—membership and enlargement, for example—that are properly within the EU's province; and
- endorse the EU's efforts to forge an independent foreign and security policy.

Since its inception, NATO—and the transatlantic relationship generally—has always been, in Henry Kissinger's apt phrase, a "troubled partnership." NATO has been strained almost to the breaking point by serious crises, including Suez (1956), French president Charles de Gaulle's challenge to U.S. leadership of the alliance (1958–66), Vietnam, U.S–West European differences over détente with the Soviet Union (during the 1970s), and the deployment of Intermediate Range Nuclear Forces (in the early to mid 1980s). Reflecting the stress those crises have placed on the alliance, predictions of an impending transatlantic divorce—which intensified following the Cold War's end—long have been a staple of the American foreign policy debate.

The history of recurrent transatlantic crisis notwithstanding, U.S.-European relations reached an all-time low during the Bush administration in 2003. In considering American policy toward NATO and Europe, policymakers will face a paradox. On the one hand, events since September 11, 2001, have demonstrated that NATO is militarily irrelevant and its existence contributes little to American security. On the other hand, there is an urgent need to repair America's relations with Europe and to put that relationship on a new footing. This is a daunting challenge, because in a time when transatlantic relations visibly are foundering, it will not be easy to disengage the United States from NATO while simultaneously strengthening U.S.-European relations.

NATO after the Cold War: Tottering toward Irrelevance

The common understanding of most Americans—including policymakers, scholars, and foreign policy commentators—is that the North Atlantic Treaty (1949), which evolved into NATO in 1950–51 following the outbreak of the Korean War, committed the United States to deter a Soviet attack on Western Europe and, if deterrence failed, to help the West Europeans defend the Continent. With the collapse of the Soviet Union in 1989–91, NATO had fulfilled its mission, and it might have been expected to dissolve. That, of course, did not happen. Instead, under the first Bush, the Clinton, and the second Bush administrations, the United States spearheaded efforts to save NATO by vesting in it new, post–Cold War missions.

Specifically, NATO has reinvented itself by declaring that it is no longer just a defensive military alliance but is, rather, a political alliance that reflects its members' shared values. At the same time—especially during the Clinton administration—NATO undertook a process of "double enlargement." One prong of that double enlargement was expansion of the alliance's membership; the former Soviet satellite states of Poland, Hungary, and the Czech Republic were admitted. The other prong was an expansion of NATO's missions to include maintaining regional stability in Europe (and its peripheries), addressing "out-of-area" threats to the alliance's members, and combating terrorism. The Kosovo war was the alliance's first post–Cold War test, specifically assessing its role as an instrument of regional stability. The aftermath of 9/11 triggered NATO's second post–Cold War test.

A Neutered Alliance: The Military Ineffectiveness of Post–Cold War NATO

How has the "new" NATO stacked up with respect to fulfilling its post–Cold War missions? Not very well. Post-9/11 challenges—rooting out the Taliban in Afghanistan and eliminating the threat of alleged weapons of mass destruction (WMD) in Iraq—were precisely the kinds of out-of-area threats with which the "new" NATO is supposed to deal. But NATO, as an *institution*, made no contribution either to the campaign in Afghanistan or to the Iraq War. Although NATO now has made commitments to assist in "nation-building" efforts in Afghanistan, its contribution has been both minimal and of questionable effectiveness. With respect to Iraq, the alliance has made a commitment to assist in training a reconstituted Iraqi security force. But again, NATO has sharply circumscribed its involvement in the reconstruction of postwar Iraq, and its contribution clearly will be no more than marginal. Notwithstanding calls that the ongoing effort to stabilize postwar Iraq should be "internationalized," it is apparent that NATO as an institution is not going to step up to the plate and contribute forces for this purpose.

It is true that after 9/11 the alliance invoked the collective defense provision of Article V for the first time. Certainly, individual members of the alliance have effectively cooperated with the United States on the anti-terror campaign (through intelligence sharing, tracking down terrorist cells operating on their own national territories, and going after the terrorists' sources of financial support). Britain and Canada contributed small contingents to fight against the Taliban and Al Qaeda, and Germany and Turkey have stepped forward to help to stabilize postwar Afghanistan. And the British, of course, have contributed a substantial military contingent to fight alongside U.S. forces in Iraq. All of those contributions, however, have been made on an individual (that is, national) basis, not through the alliance. And a strong case can be made that even if there were no NATO, Washington would have been able to assemble the same limited "coalition of the willing."

Why has the "new" NATO been such a bust? There are three reasons. First, the military capabilities of the European NATO members are limited. Second, the European members of NATO do not share Washington's view of out-of-area threats. Third, Washington has deliberately chosen to bypass the alliance, because it wants to maximize its own strategic freedom of action and it regards the European NATO military capabilities as a drag on American power, rather than as a contributor to it. Simply put, the United States prefers to rely on ad hoc "coalitions of the willing" rather than be constrained by the need to forge consensus among the NATO allies.

Except for Britain and France, NATO-Europe lacks the ability to project military power outside of Europe. And, as became evident during the

Kosovo war, all the European NATO members lag well behind the United States in leading-edge conventional military capabilities such as: precision-guided munitions and advanced command, control, reconnaissance/surveillance capabilities. Even former NATO secretary general Lord Robertson warned that NATO-Europe is a military "pygmy" and must do more to enhance its military capabilities. Although the European NATO members have made some noises about increasing their military spending (and France, notably, is doing so, though not necessarily for "Atlanticist" reasons), it is an open question whether NATO-Europe really is going to allocate the resources to close the transatlantic gap in military capabilities (Table 53.1).

Transatlantic Drift: Differing U.S. and European Perspectives on Out-of-Area Threats

That the Europeans do not view out-of-area threats, including Iraq, in the same way Washington does is clear. But there is nothing new about this. Since the United States failed to back Britain and France in Suez and the French in Algeria in the 1950s, the Europeans have always taken the position that NATO's area of strategic responsibility is confined to the European continent, and consequently the Europeans have been unwilling to have the alliance used in support of the United States outside

Table 53.1
Comparison of Defense Budgets, 2002

	Total Defense Expenditures (millions of U.S. $)	Spending per Capita (in U.S. $)	% of GDP
United States	329,616	1,138	3.3
France	38,005	636	2.5
United Kingdom	35,249	590	2.4
Germany	31,465	383	1.5
Italy	24,210	421	1.9
Turkey	8,727	127	5.1
Spain	8,253	206	1.2
Netherlands	7,330	459	1.6
Greece	6,154	579	4.4
Belgium	3,435	332	1.3
Norway	3,434	759	1.9

SOURCE: International Institute for Strategic Studies, *The Military Balance 2003–2004*.

Europe. That certainly is one reason that France and Germany refused to back the Bush administration in Iraq. A second reason for the divergence between Washington and NATO-Europe is that the Europeans have different interests at stake in the Middle East and Persian Gulf than does the United States, and they believed (and still do) that those interests could be affected adversely by a war with Iraq. Finally, throughout much of NATO-Europe, especially the French and German core, the Bush administration's Iraq policy has been opposed both because many Europeans are uneasy with Washington's "unilateralist" proclivities and because of concerns about the implications of "unipolar" American power in the post–Cold War world.

Atlanticism without NATO: Toward a Balanced U.S.-European Relationship

Analysts of U.S.-European relations long have recognized that the unbalanced nature of that relationship has been a source of serious transatlantic tensions. American policymakers, Congress, and the public believe that the United States contributes far too much to defending common interests and that the Europeans fail to pull their weight. For their part, Europeans feel that an overbearing America uses its power to run roughshod over European interests. Events since 9/11, especially the Iraq war, have sharpened negative feelings on both sides of the Atlantic.

Doubtless, the Bush administration's sledgehammer diplomacy in 2002 and 2003 exacerbated the transatlantic divide. But that divide itself is the product of deeper, structural forces. First, with the end of the Cold War, NATO had no compelling raison d'être. Second, in the absence of the Soviet threat, diverging American and European interests—which never went away, even during the Cold War, but were placed on the back burner—have come to the fore. Third, the European Union has embarked on a process intended to culminate in the EU's emergence as an independent "pole of power" in the international system. This effort gained momentum following the signing of the Maastricht Treaty in 1992 and accelerated during the late 1990s as the European Union sought more formal, legal rights and responsibilities under the EU Constitution. That is, the EU integration process—which now encompasses the realms of foreign and defense policy—is meant to create an EU that can punch its weight in international politics and stand as a geopolitical equal to the United States.

535

American attitudes toward the emergence of a truly independent Europe traditionally have reflected a profound ambivalence. Policymakers should overcome that ambivalence and endorse the EU's efforts to forge an independent foreign and security policy. The price of European independence is bound to be less than the price of Europe's continuing subordination to the United States, which is bound to fan resentment (albeit of a different kind) on both sides of the Atlantic. Second, attempts to maintain American preponderance are bound to trigger a nasty geopolitical backlash against the United States. By gracefully accepting Europe's strategic self-sufficiency—and acknowledging that the EU stands on an equal footing with the United States—U.S. policymakers can go a long way toward repairing the damage caused to the transatlantic relationship by the Iraq war and ultimately put that relationship on a healthier, more sustainable basis.

Atlanticism can exist without an ongoing American military presence in Europe. Here policymakers should revisit the views of President Dwight Eisenhower and his secretary of state, John Foster Dulles, leading Republican internationalists who were instrumental in the creation of the alliance. Unlike their successors of both parties, they welcomed a truly independent Europe instead of fearing it, and they regarded the U.S. role in NATO as temporary. Eisenhower and Dulles eagerly anticipated the day—once the West Europeans recovered from World War II and could again assume full responsibility for their own security—when the American military presence in Europe no longer would be necessary. In historical perspective, the EU's continuing march toward political unity and its quest for military self-sufficiency represent the triumph of the hopes for Europe held by Eisenhower, Dulles, and other leading U.S. policymakers during the late 1940s and 1950s. To be sure, they saw the emergence of a stable, prosperous, and independent Europe as the sine qua non for an exit strategy that would allow the United States to bring its troops back from Europe. But they also viewed the emergence of such a Europe as the foundation for a healthy long-term U.S.-European relationship. A U.S.-European relationship based on mutual independence, equality, and autonomy likely will prove far stronger than NATO, the bonds of which are fast being corroded by the recriminations generated by America's dominance and Europe's subordination.

Working together, the administration and Congress have a historic opportunity to refashion the relationship between the United States and Europe. The time has come for the United States to withdraw from Europe militarily and allow the EU to assume responsibility for defending both the Continent itself and the EU's extracontinental interests. In this respect, while Congress should welcome the Bush administration's plan to reduce substantially U.S. force levels in Europe, especially in Germany, it should insist that the administration go further and commit itself to a five-year plan to withdraw all American forces from Europe. Similarly, Congress should refuse administration requests for funds to build new U.S. bases in the recently admitted NATO members in East Central and Southeast Europe. The time has come to recognize what has become obvious: NATO, as an institution, does not enhance America's strategic power. By the same token, Europe no longer needs to rely on American military guarantees for its security. Europe can take care of itself and should be encouraged to do so.

Recommended Readings

Asmus, Ronald D. *Opening NATO's Door: How the Alliance Remade Itself for a New Era.* New York: Columbia University Press, 2002.

Carpenter, Ted Galen. "The Bush Administration's Security Strategy: Implications for Transatlantic Relations." *Cambridge Review of International Affairs* 16, no. 3 (October 2003): 511–24.

Layne, Christopher. "America as European Hegemon." *National Interest*, no. 72 (Summer 2003): 17–28.

––––––. "Casualties of War: Transatlantic Relations and the Future of NATO in the Wake of the Second Gulf War." Cato Institute Policy Analysis no. 483, August 13, 2003.

Lebl, Leslie. "European Union Defense Policy: An American Perspective." Cato Institute Policy Analysis no. 516, June 24, 2004.

Merry, Wayne. "Therapy's End: Thinking beyond NATO." *National Interest*, no. 74 (Winter 2003–4): 43–50.

Walt, Stephen M. "The Ties That Fray: Why Europe and America Are Drifting Apart." *National Interest*, no. 54 (Winter 1998–99): 3–11.

—Prepared by Christopher Layne

54. Nuclear Proliferation and the Terrorist Threat

Policymakers should

- avoid the assumption that deterrence is inapplicable in the post–Cold War era; the vast U.S. strategic nuclear arsenal still acts as a powerful deterrent against even the most aggressive nation-state actor launching an unprovoked attack against the American homeland;
- recognize that the prospect of stable, democratic countries acquiring nuclear weapons for deterrence and self-defense against regional threats is not necessarily destabilizing and may be preferable to having the United States shield those countries with a nuclear guarantee that puts the American homeland at risk;
- stop threatening preemptive war as a response to nuclear ambitions; such a doctrine actually creates a powerful incentive for adversaries to accelerate their acquisition of nuclear weapons as a deterrent to U.S. efforts to achieve regime change;
- make clear to regimes that acquire nuclear weapons that passing on weapons, material, or technology to terrorists is an intolerable act that will result in immediate U.S. military action against the regime; and
- stop trying to get new nuclear-weapons powers to divest themselves of their weapons and instead work with them to develop more secure command and control over their arsenals and to reject dangerous, destabilizing doctrines such as "launch on warning."

Current thinking about nuclear weapons proliferation tends to be binary in nature. The traditional approach to arms control is to negotiate treaties or agreements and create nonproliferation regimes (including intrusive and unfettered inspections) as a way to curb the spread of materials, technology, and weapons. People who are skeptical of arms control argue that the United States can dissuade countries from acquiring nuclear weapons by developing weapons—including precision low-yield nuclear weapons, or mininukes—that can hold high-value targets (including underground weapons of mass destruction, or WMD, facilities) at risk. Moreover, they argue that the United States must be willing to use military force, unilaterally if necessary, to prevent the acquisition of nuclear weapons if diplomacy fails.

The only way out of that dilemma is to rethink nonproliferation.

A Peculiar Loss of Faith in Deterrence

One increasingly prominent assumption in the foreign policy community is that the United States cannot rely on deterrence the way that it did throughout the Cold War era. That point became evident in the months leading up to the U.S. invasion of Iraq. The Bush administration clearly believed that Saddam Hussein was undeterrable. National Security Advisor Condoleezza Rice expressed that assumption when she rebuked those who asked for definitive evidence that Baghdad had chemical and biological weapons and was attempting to acquire nuclear weapons. Rice warned that we could not wait for a smoking gun in the form of a mushroom cloud.

But the question never should have been whether Iraq had WMD or not, which presumed that if it did it was an undeterrable threat. Rather, the fundamental question should have been: if Iraq has WMD, however undesirable that may be, is it a threat to the United States that cannot be deterred?

The answer is that there was no historical evidence of Iraq or any other rogue state using WMD against enemies capable of inflicting unacceptable retaliatory damage. True enough, Saddam Hussein used chemical weapons against helpless Kurdish villages and Iranian infantry in the 1980s. But during the Gulf War in 1991, when Hussein had vast stocks of chemical weapons, he was deterred from using them against the U.S.-led Coalition and Israel by credible threats of obliteration. More to the point, even if Saddam Hussein had managed to build a few atomic bombs, he would have been no more able to escape the reality of credible U.S. nuclear deterrence than were the Soviet Union and Communist China before him.

Most opponents of the administration seemed to share the Bush foreign policy team's lack of confidence in deterrence with regard to Iraq. The traditional arms control and nonproliferation community could not disagree with the Bush administration's assertion that Iraq's possession of WMD was a threat that required a response because to disagree would have meant admitting that proliferation might be an acceptable outcome. Instead, they were left to disagree about the evidence that Iraq was in violation of UN Security Council resolutions and stress the need to obtain international consensus on the appropriate response.

The assumption that the United States can no longer rely on deterrence dominates Washington's overall strategic thinking. That is a startling departure from a core feature of U.S. security strategy since the end of World War II. U.S. officials have traditionally believed that the vast U.S. strategic arsenal would ultimately deter any would-be aggressor—even a nuclear-capable one.

The Bush administration's National Security Strategy, approved in September 2002, embraced the doctrine of preemptive military action to prevent so-called rogue states from acquiring weapons of mass destruction. The NSS stated that goal succinctly: "We must be prepared to stop rogue states and their terrorist clients *before* they are able to threaten or use weapons of mass destruction against the United States and our allies and friends." On another occasion, the administration emphasized that the United States would not "permit the world's most dangerous regimes" to pose a threat "with the world's most destructive weapons."

That loss of faith in deterrence is puzzling. Shadowy nonstate actors—especially Al Qaeda and its allies—probably are not deterrable, since they can shift locations easily and, therefore, there is no obvious target for retaliation. But nation-states have a return address, and their leaders know that any attack on the United States would be met with an obliterating retaliatory attack by the massive U.S. nuclear arsenal. Also, while individual fanatics may sometimes be willing to commit suicide for a cause, prominent political leaders rarely display that characteristic.

Moreover, over the years, the United States deterred the likes of Joseph Stalin, Nikita Khrushchev, Leonid Brezhnev, and Mao Zedong. None of those leaders seriously contemplated attacking the United States. And the reason for their restraint was quite simple: they knew that such an attack would mean their own annihilation. Why, then, do U.S. officials apparently assume that leaders of radical nation-states are undeterrable? It cannot be that those leaders are more brutal than America's previous adversaries. Khrushchev and Brezhnev were thuggish, and Mao and Stalin were genocidal monsters. A credible case cannot be made that the current crop of tyrants is more erratic and unpredictable than the tyrants the United States deterred in the past. Stalin epitomized paranoia, and Mao was the architect of China's utterly bizarre Cultural Revolution in the late 1960s and early 1970s—at the very time that China was acquiring a nuclear-weapons capability.

U.S. policymakers should regain their faith in deterrence and again make that doctrine the cornerstone of America's security policy. Preemptive action may sometimes be necessary to meet a threat, but only when that threat is clear and imminent. What the Bush administration described as preemptive action was more properly termed ''preventive war''—a willingness to strike first to forestall a vague, largely theoretical security threat. That doctrine not only risks making the United States an aggressor in certain situations; it also has some highly undesirable side effects.

Preemptive War and Perverse Incentives

Washington's goal of nuclear nonproliferation has suffered two serious setbacks in recent years. Both North Korea and Iran appear to be pursuing ambitious nuclear-weapons programs. What U.S. officials do not recognize is that such actions are a logical, perhaps even inevitable, response to the foreign policy the United States has pursued since the end of the Cold War. Consider the extent of U.S. military action since the opening of the Berlin Wall in 1989. Washington has engaged in nine major military operations during that period. Moreover, in his 2002 State of the Union address, President Bush explicitly linked both North Korea and Iran to Iraq (a country with which the United States was clearly headed to war) in an ''axis of evil.'' It is hardly surprising that Pyongyang and Tehran concluded that they were next on Washington's hit list unless they could effectively deter an attack. Yet neither country could hope to match the conventional military capabilities of a superpower. The most reliable deterrent—maybe the only reliable deterrent—is to have nuclear weapons. In other words, U.S. behavior may have inadvertently created a powerful incentive for the proliferation of nuclear weapons—the last thing Washington wanted.

North Korean and Iranian leaders likely noticed that the United States treats nations that possess nuclear weapons quite differently than it treats those that do not possess them. That is not a new phenomenon. Just six years after China began to develop nuclear arms, the United States sought to normalize relations—reversing a policy of isolation that had lasted more than two decades. U.S. leaders show a nuclear-armed Russia a fair amount of respect even though that country has become a second-rate conventional military power and a third-rate economic power. And Washington has treated Pakistan and India with far greater respect since those countries barged into the global nuclear-weapons club in 1998.

Contrast those actions with Washington's conduct toward nonnuclear powers such as Iraq and Yugoslavia. The lesson that North Korea and Iran learned (and other countries may be learning as well) is that possessing a nuclear arsenal is the way to compel the United States to exhibit caution and respect. That is especially true if the country has an adversarial relationship with the United States.

U.S. leaders need to face the reality that America's foreign policy may cause unintended (and sometimes unpleasant) consequences on the nuclear-proliferation front. The people who cheered Washington's military interventions need to ask themselves whether increasing the incentives for nuclear proliferation was a price worth paying—because greater proliferation is the price we are now paying.

Not All Forms of Proliferation Are Equal

The conventional wisdom is that nonproliferation per se creates greater security. Indeed, that was the underlying logic of the Nuclear Nonproliferation Treaty (NPT) adopted by the bulk of the international community in the late 1960s. The NPT is the centerpiece of the existing nonproliferation system. Members of the arms control community have over the decades spent at least as much time and energy agonizing over the possibility that stable, democratic, status quo powers such as Germany, Japan, Sweden, and South Korea might decide to abandon the NPT and develop nuclear deterrents as they have spent over the prospect that unstable or aggressive states might do so.

That unfortunate attitude is evident across the political spectrum. As the North Korean nuclear crisis evolved, some of the most hawkish members of the U.S. foreign policy community became terrified at the prospect that America's democratic allies in East Asia might build their own nuclear deterrents to offset Pyongyang's moves. Neoconservative luminaries Robert Kagan and William Kristol regard such proliferation with horror: "The possibility that Japan, and perhaps even Taiwan, might respond to North Korea's actions by producing their own nuclear weapons, thus spurring an East Asian nuclear arms race . . . is something that should send chills up the spine of any sensible American strategist."

That attitude misconstrues the problem. A threat to the peace may exist if an aggressive and erratic regime gets nukes and then is able to intimidate or blackmail its nonnuclear neighbors. Nuclear arsenals in the hands of stable, democratic, status quo powers do not threaten the peace. Kagan and Kristol—and other Americans who share their hostility toward such countries having nuclear weapons—embrace a moral equivalence between a potential aggressor and its potential victims.

America's current nonproliferation policy is the international equivalent of domestic gun control laws—and exhibits the same faulty logic. Gun control laws have had done little to prevent criminal elements from acquiring weapons. Instead, they disarm honest citizens and make them more vulnerable to armed predators. The nonproliferation system is having a similar perverse effect. Such unsavory states as Iran and North Korea are well along the path to becoming nuclear-weapons powers while their more peaceful neighbors are hamstrung by the NPT from countering those moves.

The focus of Washington's nonproliferation policy should be on substituting discrimination and selectivity for uniformity of treatment. U.S. policymakers must rid themselves of the notion that all forms of proliferation are equally bad. The United States should concentrate on making it difficult for aggressive or unstable regimes to acquire the technology and fissile material needed to develop nuclear weapons. Policymakers must adopt a realistic attitude toward the limitations of even that more tightly focused nonproliferation policy. At best, U.S. actions will only delay, not prevent, such states from joining the nuclear-weapons club.

But delay can provide important benefits. A delay of only a few years may significantly reduce the likelihood that an aggressive power with a new nuclear-weapons capability will have a regional nuclear monopoly and be able to blackmail nonnuclear neighbors. In some cases, the knowledge that the achievement of a regional nuclear monopoly is impossible may discourage a would-be expansionist power from even making the effort. At the very least, it could cause such a power to configure its new arsenal purely for deterrence rather than design it for aggressive purposes.

Although in the general sense it might be true that fewer nuclear weapons in the world (and fewer countries with nuclear weapons) would be a good thing, such logic is not necessarily absolute. Instead of assuming that all proliferation of nuclear weapons is an inherent danger that must be prevented, policymakers should analyze proliferation and assess its consequences on a case-by-case basis rather than use a one-size-fits-all approach.

What If Nonproliferation Efforts Fail?

There are steps that the United States can take to limit some of the harmful effects of proliferation. One worrisome prospect is that new nuclear states may lack the financial resources or the technical expertise to establish reliable command-and-control systems, or to guard their arsenals from theft or accidental or unauthorized launch. (Although the latter two dangers are an acute concern with new nuclear-weapons powers, they are also a problem with Russia's nuclear arsenal.) An equally serious danger is that some of those nuclear powers may fail to develop coherent strategic doctrines that communicate to adversaries the circumstances under which the aggrieved party might use nuclear weapons.

In some cases, Washington can help minimize such problems by disseminating command-and-control technology and assisting in the creation of crisis management hotlines and other confidence-building measures among emerging nuclear-weapons states. That would reduce the danger that a country might adopt a "launch on warning" strategy—launching its weapons on the basis of an indication that the other side has launched an attack without waiting for confirmation that an attack is actually under way. The United States can also encourage potential adversaries to engage in strategic dialogues to delineate the kinds of provocations that might cause them to contemplate using nuclear weapons and outline the doctrines that would govern their use. At the very least, such a dialogue would reduce the chances of a nuclear conflict erupting because of miscalculation or misunderstanding. Finally, Washington can strongly encourage new nuclear powers to configure their arsenals solely for defensive, second-strike roles rather than provocative, first-strike capabilities.

Such measures are not a panacea, but they do limit some of the worst potential effects of nuclear proliferation. There is one other area in which the United States must have a proactive policy—making it clear to new nuclear powers that transferring nuclear technology or weapons to nonstate actors is utterly unacceptable.

Proliferation and Terrorism

The imperatives of the post-9/11 threat environment dictate that the most important U.S. security concern related to nuclear weapons is the potential for transfer of such weapons (or materials and technology) to terrorist groups who are, by definition, undeterrable. Therefore, the single most important criterion to use in assessing the potential dangers of proliferation must be the possibility of nuclear terrorism.

The conventional wisdom is that preventing proliferation of nuclear weapons to countries de facto prevents the transfer of weapons to terrorists. That was the rationale used by the Bush administration to disarm Iraq— including using military force unilaterally. The president argued that Hussein could give his WMD to terrorists who would then attack the United States—the smoking gun in the form of a mushroom cloud. Therefore, the only way to prevent the possibility of WMD terrorism was to rid Iraq of its WMD or its ruler, who was seeking to acquire WMD, including nuclear weapons.

Such an argument was certainly plausible, but the question was whether it was likely. The Bush administration was never able to make a convincing case. The 9/11 Commission has issued a report concluding that there was no evidence of a collaborative relationship between Baghdad and Al Qaeda. Moreover, Saddam Hussein was known to support anti-Israeli Palestinian terrorist groups, including Hamas, for years, but he never gave chemical or biological weapons to those groups to use against Israel, a country he hated as much as he hated the United States.

Regardless of the Bush administration's weak case that Iraq would transfer WMD to terrorists, the logic of its argument creates a conundrum for those who believe that preventing proliferation of nuclear weapons to countries also prevents the transfer of such weapons (or materials or technology) to terrorists. The only way out of the conundrum is a willingness to explore failed nonproliferation efforts as an acceptable (but undesirable) outcome while still developing successful ways to prevent nuclear weapons from falling into the hands of terrorists. There are three specific, worrisome cases.

North Korea

The United States and the major nations of East Asia are engaged in a concerted diplomatic effort to get the Democratic People's Republic of Korea (North Korea) to dismantle its nuclear-weapons program. However, it may not be possible to put that genie back into the bottle. If that proves to be the case, the United States can probably live with a nuclear-armed North Korea, but the danger of proliferation activities by Pyongyang must be addressed.

The United States cannot tolerate North Korea's becoming the global supermarket of nuclear technology. An especially acute danger is that

Pyongyang *may* provide either a nuclear weapon or fissile material to Al Qaeda or other anti-American terrorist organizations. The DPRK's record on missile proliferation does not offer much encouragement that it will be restrained when it comes to commerce in nuclear materials. Perhaps most troubling of all, Pyongyang has shown a willingness to sell anything that will raise revenue for the financially hard-pressed regime. In the spring of 2003, for example, evidence emerged of extensive North Korean involvement in the heroin trade. It is hardly unwarranted speculation that the DPRK might be a willing seller of nuclear weapons or materials to terrorist groups flush with cash.

Washington should communicate to the DPRK that selling nuclear material—much less an assembled nuclear weapon—to terrorist organizations or hostile governments will be regarded as a threat to America's vital security interests. Indeed, U.S. leaders should treat such a transaction as the equivalent of a threatened attack on America by North Korea. Such a threat would warrant military action to remove the North Korean regime. Pyongyang must be told in no uncertain terms that trafficking in nuclear materials is a bright red line that it dare not cross if the regime wishes to survive.

Iran

Clearly, Iran's nuclear-weapons program is a concern because of that country's ties to terrorist groups. According to the State Department, "Iran remained the most active state sponsor of terrorism in 2003." It's no secret that Iran provides funding, safe haven, training, and weapons to anti-Israeli groups, such as Hezbollah and Hamas. But, like Iraq, Iran has not supplied terrorist groups with chemical or biological weapons to use against Israel. So it's not clear what incentive Iran would have to give nuclear weapons to terrorists. Indeed, Israel's nuclear arsenal (believed to be as many as 200 warheads) serves as a powerful deterrent against Iran taking such action.

Iran's terrorist ties were also cited by the 9/11 Commission, which implicated Iran in the 1996 Khobar Towers bombing and cited "strong evidence" that Iran facilitated the transit of several Al Qaeda members before 9/11 (including perhaps eight or more of the hijackers). The commission did not claim, however, that Iran was involved with the attacks. The potential Iran–Al Qaeda connection is a serious one that deserves further investigation. But without clear evidence that the regime in Tehran was involved in 9/11 or is otherwise supporting or harboring Al Qaeda, the

547

United States cannot afford to wage another unnecessary war as it is doing against Iraq.

Just as the United States may have to learn to live with a nuclear-armed North Korea, U.S. policy may have to adjust to Iran's nuclear ambitions. If Iran does eventually acquire nuclear weapons, one thing should be made clear to Tehran: transfer of such weapons, material, or technology to terrorist groups will be justification for regime change. That is a bright line that must be drawn and strictly (and swiftly) enforced, not just with Iran but with any other country that aspires to nuclear status.

Pakistan

Pakistan also demonstrates the limitations of current nonproliferation thinking. Although the Musharraf regime is considered an ally in the war on terrorism and has helped capture some important Al Qaeda operatives, the prospect of that country's nuclear weapons falling into the hands of radical Islamists must be planned for. Pakistan is also a concern because so many nuclear efforts in other countries (e.g., North Korea, Iran, and Libya) were tied to a nuclear bazaar created by Pakistani scientist A. Q. Kahn, who has been hailed as a national hero by Musharraf. Unfortunately, neither the traditional nonproliferation approach nor preemptive war is a real solution to this problem. Preemptive regime change is not a viable option, and it is unrealistic to expect that Pakistan will give up its nuclear weapons. Instead, U.S. efforts should focus on creating better security and command and control over Pakistan's nuclear weapons to prevent them from being used by terrorists. Continuous U.S. pressure must also be exerted on Musharraf's government to make sure that such leakage does not occur.

Conclusion

U.S. policymakers must think beyond traditional nonproliferation policy. That policy may have served us reasonably well in the past, but a rapidly changing global security environment is rendering it obsolete and potentially counterproductive. We can no longer cling to the NPT and all it symbolizes as the answer to all the varied problems of nuclear proliferation. Instead, we need a large policy toolbox with a variety of tools. We can continue to rely on the ability of America's vast nuclear arsenal to deter attacks on the American homeland by nuclear-weapons powers. At the same time, we must recognize the likelihood that the number of nuclear powers in the international system will increase in the next decade and that many of those new members of the global nuclear club will be unsavory regimes. In some cases, we may have to accept that stable, democratic countries may acquire their own deterrents—or even encourage them to do so—to prevent aggressive states from achieving a regional nuclear monopoly.

Washington's own nonproliferation efforts should focus on delaying rogue states in their quest for nuclear weapons, not beating up on peaceful states that want to become nuclear powers. The other key objective of a new U.S. proliferation policy should be to prevent unfriendly nuclear states from transferring their weapons or nuclear know-how to terrorist adversaries of the United States. Those objectives are daunting enough without continuing the vain effort to prevent all forms of proliferation.

Suggested Readings

Atal, Subodh. "Extremist, Nuclear Pakistan: An Emerging Threat?" Cato Institute Policy Analysis no. 472, March 5, 2003.

Bandow, Doug. "All the Players at the Table: A Multilateral Solution to the North Korean Nuclear Crisis." Cato Institute Policy Analysis no. 478, June 26, 2003.

————. "Wrong War, Wrong Place, Wrong Time: Why Military Action Should Not Be Used to Resolve the North Korean Nuclear Crisis." Cato Institute Foreign Policy Briefing no. 76, May 12, 2003.

Carpenter, Ted Galen. "Living with the Unthinkable." *National Interest*, no. 74 (Winter 2003–04): 92–98.

Peña, Charles V. "Mini-Nukes and Preemptive Policy: A Dangerous Combination." Cato Institute Policy Analysis no. 499, November 19, 2003.

Record, Jeffrey. "Nuclear Deterrence, Preventive War, and Counterproliferation." Cato Institute Policy Analysis no. 519, July 8, 2004.

Waltz, Kenneth, and Scott Sagan. *The Spread of Nuclear Weapons: A Debate Renewed.* New York: Columbia University Press, 2002.

—Prepared by Ted Galen Carpenter and Charles V. Peña

55. Strengthening the All-Volunteer Military

Policymakers should

- devote additional resources to recruiting programs and enlistment inducements,
- increase benefits for hard-to-fill occupational specialties,
- change the mix of active and Reserve forces to reflect current military commitments,
- consider creating special Reserve units designed for garrison duty,
- fully withdraw U.S. forces from outdated Cold War deployments in Asia and Europe,
- accelerate turnover of authority in Iraq and the pullout of American troops,
- reduce the frequency and length of overseas tours,
- cut force levels and increasingly devolve defense responsibilities to allied states, and
- drop draft registration and eliminate the Selective Service System.

Three decades ago the United States inaugurated the All-Volunteer Force. The AVF produced the world's finest military, capable of deterring superpower competitors and coercing regional powers with relative ease.

Today, however, the U.S. military is under enormous strain. Although it is the finest fighting force on the planet, it lacks sufficient strength to satisfy the demands of an imperial foreign policy. The ongoing military occupation of Iraq necessitated a massive troop rotation to relieve U.S. forces deployed in that country, but that rotation did nothing to reduce pressure on American service personnel.

The United States has managed so far by turning the Reserves and the National Guard into de facto active duty units. But the Bush administration risks driving down recruitment and retention for both active and Reserve forces. Some members of Congress are promoting a return to conscription. Warns Rep. Charles Rangel (D-NY): "The experts are all saying we're going to have to beef up our presence in Iraq. We've failed to convince our allies to send troops, we've extended deployments so morale is sinking, and the president is saying we can't cut and run. So what's left?"

Unfortunately, no relief for the U.S. military is in the offing. About 10,000 U.S. troops remain in Afghanistan. Despite dramatic initial success, Washington now must cope with increasing attacks on coalition soldiers and foreign aid workers outside the capital. Elections were postponed as the internal security situation deteriorated.

Iraq

Iraq is of greater concern. Defense Secretary Donald Rumsfeld once opined that the number of U.S. troops there could fall to 30,000 by fall 2003. But the garrison currently numbers roughly 160,000, about 140,000 of whom are American. (Another 34,000 perform support duties in Kuwait.) The coalition has made progress in restoring services and rebuilding infrastructure. Yet the administration's goal of creating a liberal, pro-Western democracy remains far distant.

The Iraqi conflict is taking a heavy toll on the U.S. military: not only the thousands of dead and wounded, but the unexpected and unexpectedly lengthy deployments to Iraq. Although administration supporters routinely complained that the media were focusing on bad news, the troops lived the bad news. A poll of 2,000 soldiers in 2003, before the worst of the violence, by *Stars and Stripes*, a newspaper for members of the armed forces funded by the Department of Defense, found that 40 percent believed the Iraq mission was unrelated to their training, one-third believed their mission was not clearly defined, and one-third believed the Iraqi war was of limited value.

After having to face the reality that drawing down the U.S. force in Iraq to 30,000 troops was an overly optimistic plan, the administration hoped to bring down the U.S. garrison to about 110,000 in spring 2004. But that proved to be another example of hysterically high hopes ruined by reality as the insurgency intensified. Even now, many analysts believe that more troops are necessary.

But the Pentagon has had trouble finding sufficient soldiers to man its existing commitments. To maintain training standards and troop morale, the Congressional Budget Office suggests "rotation ratios" of 3.2:1 to 4:1 for active forces and 7.5:1 to 9:1 for Reserves and the Guard. Yet of roughly 480,000 Army active duty and 560,000 Army Reserve and Army National Guard forces, 370,000 are deployed overseas. Even that understates the problem. Only about 300,000 active Army personnel and 470,000 Army Reserve and Guard members are in deployable units.

Reserve and National Guard

The burden falls heaviest on reservists. Nearly 40 percent of the Iraq garrison is made up of members of the Reserve and National Guard. The average annual call-up during the 1990s was about 10,000. Lt. Gen. H. Steven Blum, chief of the National Guard Bureau, admits that the "weekend warrior is dead."

The military can handle such burdens in a temporary emergency. But speaking only of Afghanistan in March 2002, Secretary Rumsfeld observed: "It's helpful to remember that those who developed the concept for peacekeepers in Bosnia assured everyone that those forces would complete their mission by the end of that year and be home by Christmas. We are now heading into our seventh year of U.S. and international involvement in Bosnia."

Thomas Donnelly and Vance Serchuk of the American Enterprise Institute suggest that "the protection of the embryonic Iraqi democracy is a duty that will likely extend for decades." Even President George W. Bush admitted that the United States faced a "massive and long-term undertaking" in Iraq. Democratic challenger John Kerry spoke of trying to reduce the size of America's garrison within six months and withdrawing troops within four years but nevertheless pledged to stay as long as necessary.

Which brings back Rep. Rangel's question, "So what's left?" The administration limited coverage of the return of bodies and of funerals to cut hostile press coverage, but that provided no additional manpower. By fall 2004 allied states were leaving, not coming into, Iraq, and the only serious help came from Great Britain. As Francois Heisbourg, director of the Paris-based Foundation for Strategic Research, bluntly put it, "I don't think anybody is going to jump into an American-run quagmire."

Which means Iraq will remain largely an American show. Yet the active forces don't have much more to contribute. The Pentagon admits that many infantrymen will have to serve back-to-back foreign tours. Even though deployment in countries like Britain and Germany is more pleasant than in Afghanistan and Iraq, few people will join and remain in the Army if they rarely see home.

Adding Marine Corps actives, as DOD did last spring, will help. But the Marines are a relatively small force (175,000) intended to respond to unexpected contingencies. Warns the Congressional Budget Office, "If all Marine regiments were either deployed, recovering after deployments, or preparing for deployments . . . , DoD's ability to quickly deploy substantial combat power in the early phases of an operation would be degraded."

Which leaves the Reserves and National Guard. But those troops are intended to supplement the active force in an emergency. Unfortunately, write Philip Gold and Erin Solaro of the Aretea Institute, Washington is using reservists "not just as reinforcements for the regulars but as substitutes." The Army Reserve has been mobilized more in the last 12 years (10 times) than in the previous 75 years (9 times). Today Guard and Reserve units handle everything from civil affairs to personnel services.

Extended deployments place a greater burden on reservists than on active duty forces because the former, who consciously chose not to join the active force, must leave not only family, friends, and community but jobs as well. The burden has been compounded by discrimination against reservists, who often serve longer deployments than active duty soldiers but are last on the list to receive the best equipment, such as Kevlar vests. Nevertheless, the military has been pressuring reservists to waive the statutory requirement of 12 months home between overseas deployments.

The Specter of the Draft

Where else can bodies be found? When Gen. Eric Shinseki retired as Army chief of staff in June 2003, he warned, "Beware the 12-division strategy for a 10-division Army." Support for adding at least two divisions has been building in Congress, and candidate John Kerry backed that addition.

So far the Defense Department has rebuffed such proposals. Adding forces takes money and time. Concludes the Congressional Budget Office: "Recruiting, training, and equipping two additional divisions would entail up-front costs of as much as $18 billion to $19 billion and would take about five years to accomplish, CBO estimates. In the long run, the cost to operate and sustain these new divisions as a permanent part of the

Army's force structure would be about $6 billion annually (plus between $3 billion and $4 billion per year to employ them in Iraq).''

Moreover, the armed services are having trouble because excessive and unpleasant commitments make it harder for them to attract and keep enough people. Increasing recruiting and retention requirements won't address the underlying problems.

Publicly, many officials and analysts argue that there is no morale problem. Yet the *Stars and Stripes* interview found that one-third of soldiers said their own morale was low and half said their units' morale was low. Half said they would not reup once their tours end and the DOD's "stop-loss" order, which bars retirements, is lifted. Moreover, the *Stars and Stripes* reported that it was hearing "edgier complaints about inequality among the forces and lack of confidence in their leaders"—complaints stronger than the sort of griping common among enlisted personnel.

Also critical is the attitude of service families. Worried Fox News Channel commentator Robert Maginnis, "Either we find a fix to rotate those troops out and to keep the families content . . . or we're going to suffer what I anticipate is a downturn in retention." Army recruiters are finding increasing resistance from parents, especially when they seek to recruit 17-year-olds, who need parental approval to join.

So far, DOD has been making most of its manpower targets. However, in FY03 the Army National Guard and Navy Reserve fell behind their goals; the former ran 87.4 percent and the latter a less worrisome 98.9 percent. Although attrition rates remained low, Defense Under Secretary David Chu admitted, "Certain high-demand (high-use) units and specialties have experienced higher than normal attrition."

But the situation could easily worsen. Secretary Rumsfeld acknowledges that "the effects of stress on the force are unlikely to be felt immediately; they're much more likely to be felt down the road." Similarly, Les Brownlee, acting secretary of the Army, worried that DOD might have to wait "some three to six months after these units return" to judge the impact. The effect might take even longer for retentions, since "stop-loss" remains in effect for some Army active duty soldiers and many Army Reserve soldiers.

A growing economy, by providing more employment alternatives, could discourage new enlistments. And the longer the Afghanistan and Iraq occupations continue, the more likely problems are to arise. Beth Asch of the RAND Corporation explains, "Short deployments actually boost enlistments and reenlistments.'' But ''studies show longer deployments can definitely have a negative impact.'' Lt. Gen. Blum says that a fall in recruits and reenlistees is ''the No. 1 thing in my worry book.''

So all that's left, in Rep. Rangel's view, is renewing the draft. Every recent war has sparked proposals for restarting conscription. Rep. Rangel and retiring Sen. Fritz Hollings (D-SC) introduced legislation to establish a system of conscription-based national service. Indeed, when the Selective Service System, apparently innocently, placed a notice on its website recruiting for local and appeal boards, it sparked a flurry of media stories and administration denials. In October 2004 the Republican House ostentatiously rejected Rangel's bill in an attempt to deflate the rumors.

From a security standpoint, conscription would be foolish. The U.S. military is the finest on earth largely because voluntarism allows the Pentagon to be selective, choosing recruits who are smarter and better educated than their civilian counterparts. Enlistees also are selective; they work to succeed in their chosen career rather than to escape forced service. They serve longer terms and reenlist in higher numbers, increasing the experience and skills of the force.

Since conscription would lower the quality of the U.S. military, advocates of a draft make other arguments. Rangel argues that lower socioeconomic groups ''make up the overwhelming majority of our nation's armed forces, and that, by and large, those of wealth and position are absent from the ranks of ground troops.'' Actually, Rangel is wrong. There are fewer children of elites, but the underclass is entirely absent, barred from volunteering.

Virtually no one who lacks a high school diploma or who doesn't score in the top three of five categories of the Armed Forces Quality Test can join. The U.S. military is overwhelmingly middle class; in fact, the test scores and educational achievements of recruits exceed those of young people generally. African Americans are somewhat overrepresented, but they disproportionately serve in support, not combat, arms. Hispanics are underrepresented.

National Service

Broader national service makes even less sense. It would divert people from military service to civilian tasks, jail young men and women who prefer not to put their lives at the discretion of political officials, and waste people's lives in frivolous, pork-barrel pursuits. How can one compare picking up cigarette butts in a park with patrolling the streets of Baghdad?

Although a volunteer military beats a draft force, Washington risks driving down recruiting and retention, which, over the long term, could wreck the AVF. If forced to choose between a policy of promiscuous military intervention and freedom, an activist administration, whether Republican or Democratic, might turn to a draft. Argues *Washington Times* editorial page editor Tony Blankley, it is critical to increase the size of the military, "whether by draft or by voluntary means."

Ironically, Blankley recognizes the fact that voluntarism impedes an interventionist foreign policy. Which disproves Rep. Rangel's final contention, that "there would be more caution" in going to war if policymakers' children were at risk. The surest barrier to war is not a draft, which allowed the Vietnam War to proceed for years, but the AVF, which empowers average people to say no.

A related argument by *Washington Post* columnist David Broder is that a draft would ensure that more leaders served in the military. But conscription would not increase the incidence of military service, which was low throughout American history until World War II and the Cold War. With new accessions running only about 185,000 a year, the armed services require fewer than 10 percent of male 18-year-olds, and 5 percent of all 18-year-olds, irrespective of how the military is manned.

Ironically, while some legislators advocate renewing conscription, other nations—France, Germany, and Russia, for instance—have moved or are moving to professionalize their forces. In a world where terrorism is a greater threat than a mass attack by the Red Army through Germany's Fulda Gap, the United States has no choice but to build the sort of quality force possible only through voluntarism. Indeed, Congress should eliminate draft registration—the list ages rapidly and a postmobilization sign-up would be available in an emergency—and close down the Selective Service System, an expensive and unnecessary anachronism.

Improve Retention and Recruiting

What to do to strengthen the armed services? The obvious place to start is improved pay and benefits, especially for Guard and Reserve members, who are increasingly being treated like active duty soldiers. For instance, Democratic legislators have proposed extending health insurance for National Guard and Reserve members even when they are not deployed.

Improved treatment of those deployed overseas, particularly in battle zones, also matters. In September 2003 the Pentagon began the first rest and recuperation leave program since Vietnam, allowing soldiers 15 days at home. Congress also approved legislation to pay for the flights from Baltimore (where military flights land) to service members' hometowns.

Resources also need to be put into recruiting. In fact, so far the Pentagon has helped stanch potential personnel losses by increasing signing bonuses, doubling the advertising budget, and developing cyberrecruiting.

Personnel Mix

The armed services could use uniformed personnel more efficiently. Explained Secretary Rumsfeld, "We can get some possibly 300,000 people, military people, who are doing non-military jobs out of those non-military jobs and into military positions." The strategy is sound, though civilian functions in war zones cannot always be easily categorized and civilians do not come cheap.

DOD needs to rethink the mix of duties within services as well as shift some billets between active and Reserve forces. As Acting Army Chief of Staff Gen. John Keane has observed: "We need more infantry. We need more military police. We need more civil affairs [personnel]."

Another creative approach, which runs against military tradition, is to bring in trained personnel laterally. The demand for civil affairs personnel, technology experts, and translators, for instance, varies by conflict.

DOD also should consider establishing a multitiered Reserve force, with some units available for longer-term deployments, others for temporary emergencies, and a number for homeland duties. CBO suggests creating temporary "constabulary" units made up of members of the Individual Ready Reserve and people who recently left active or Reserve or Guard service, which could train for six months, deploy for one year, and then disband. Moreover, the military could offer higher compensation for reservists willing to accept more frequent deployment. In fact, the Navy uses assignment and sea pay, and the Army offers stationing pay, to encourage personnel to accept undesirable jobs and locations. Larger reenlistment bonuses also are employed for some hard-to-fill specialties.

Eliminate Unnecessary Military Commitments

Most important, the United States should drop unnecessary commitments. As part of the Pentagon's review of America's strategic posture, President George W. Bush proposed redeploying 60,000 to 70,000 soldiers from Asia and Europe. That is a good start, but far more could be done.

The first priority should be to expeditiously exit Iraq. Lawrence Korb of the Center for American Progress cites Gen. Maxwell Taylor, who observed that we went to Vietnam to save the country but had to withdraw from Vietnam to save the Army. Plans to turn authority over to Iraqis are welcome and reflect the administration's realization that, as one unnamed official put it, "the Iraqis won't tolerate us staying in power for that long." However, the administration plans an indefinite military occupation.

The administration must recognize—even if it doesn't publicly acknowledge—its mistake in invading and occupying Iraq. This is not the first time that an administration has intervened militarily in potentially disastrous civil wars and irregular conflicts. But, as Korb points out, in the cases of Lebanon and Somalia, "the Presidents admitted their mistakes and withdrew the military before more problems were created for the military and the country." Better to accept the prospect of Iraqi instability with equanimity and focus on preventing the accumulation of weapons of mass destruction and cooperation with terrorists.

The U.S. military won the Cold War, defeated a host of small states with minimal casualties, and could overwhelm any nation. But it cannot do everything. Worries Michael O'Hanlon of the Brookings Institution, "It would be the supreme irony, and a national tragedy, if after winning two wars in two years, the U.S. Army were broken and defeated while trying to keep the peace." Conscription is no answer; fiddling with military compensation and force structure would help but would not address the basic problem. Only abandoning a foreign policy of empire will eliminate pressure to create an imperial military.

Suggested Readings

Anderson, Martin, ed. *Conscription: A Select and Annotated Bibliography.* Stanford, CA: Hoover Institution Press, 1976.

Anderson, Martin, with Barbara Honegger, eds. *The Military Draft: Selected Readings on Conscription.* Stanford, CA: Hoover Institution Press, 1982.

Bandow, Doug, "Draft Registration: The Politics of Institutional Immortality." Cato Institute Policy Analysis no. 214, August 15, 1994.

_____. "Fighting the War against Terrorism: Elite Forces, Yes; Conscripts, No." Cato Institute Policy Analysis no. 430, April 10, 2002.

_____. "Fixing What Ain't Broke: The Renewed Call for Conscription." Cato Institute Policy Analysis no. 351, August 31, 1999.

_____. *Human Resources and Defense Manpower.* Washington: National Defense University, 1989.

_____. "National Service: Utopias Revisited." Cato Institute Policy Analysis no. 190, March 15, 1993.

_____. "The Volunteer Military: Better Than a Draft." Cato Institute Foreign Policy Briefing no. 6, January 8, 1991.

Evers, Williamson, ed. *National Service: Pro & Con.* Stanford, CA: Hoover Institution Press, 1990.

Exiting Iraq: Why the U.S. Must End the Military Occupation and Renew the War against Al Qaeda. Cato Institute Special Task Force Report, 2004.

Military Manpower Task Force, *A Report to the President on the Status and Prospects of the All-Volunteer Force,* rev'd ed. Washington: U.S. Government Printing Office, November 1982.

Morris, Steven, et al. "The Differential Budget Costs of Conscription-Based Alternatives to the All-Volunteer Force." Syllogistics, Inc. (Springfield, VA.), July 23, 1986.

—Prepared by Doug Bandow

56. Toward a Sensible U.S. Policy in the Middle East

Policymakers should

- De-emphasize U.S. alliances in the Middle East, especially with Saudi Arabia and Israel;
- reduce the U.S. role in the Israeli-Palestinian peace process;
- recognize that the Gulf States cannot effectively use the "oil weapon" against the American economy; and
- shape a sensible U.S. policy toward the Middle East that does not inflame anti-American sentiments.

America's approach toward the Middle East has been characterized by considerable continuity since the beginning of the Cold War. Successive U.S. administrations have used largely the same guidelines to define U.S. national security interests in the Middle East, namely: maintaining an American political and military presence in the region, encouraging democracy and respect for human rights, promoting the Israeli-Palestinian peace process, ensuring access to Middle Eastern oil, containing any aspiring hostile hegemonic powers, and limiting the proliferation of weapons of mass destruction.

Washington has tried to achieve that complex set of goals primarily through a network of informal security alliances—with Israel, Saudi Arabia, and Egypt. The United States has also poured vast sums of money into the region to promote economic development. Cooperative relations with corrupt dictatorial regimes, whose policies run contrary to American values in terms of religious freedom, women's rights, and freedom of the press, have been maintained with one goal in mind—advancing America's interests in the region.

Redefining American Security Alliances in the Middle East

For decades Washington has maintained a "special relationship" with both Saudi Arabia and Israel. The relationship with the Saudis was sealed when King Abdul Ibn Saud, the founder of the Saudi Kingdom, shook hands with President Franklin D. Roosevelt aboard a U.S. destroyer 60 years ago. The special relationship with Israel started when President Harry Truman became the first world leader to recognize the new Jewish state in 1948. The cost of maintaining both alliances has steadily increased over the years.

Countries in the Middle East receive a disproportionate share of U.S. aid. Since 1949, according to the Congressional Research Service, Israel has received more foreign aid than any other country, a total of $91 billion. But several other countries in the region, including Egypt, Jordan, and now Iraq, are awarded hundreds of millions of dollars annually from U.S. taxpayers (Table 56.1).

The costs of U.S. policy in the Middle East are not confined to foreign aid, however. Economists have calculated that the deployment of the U.S. military to safeguard oil supplies from Saudi Arabia and the rest of the Persian Gulf—particularly since the first Gulf War—costs the United States between $30 billion and $60 billion a year. That figure does not

Table 56.1
Top 10 Recipients of U.S. Foreign Aid in FY 2004

	Total U.S. Aid (millions of dollars)	Population Mid-2004 (in millions)	Average U.S. Aid per Capita (in U.S. dollars)
Iraq	18,440	25.90	711.97
Israel	2,620	6.80	385.29
Egypt	1,870	73.40	25.48
Afghanistan	1,770	28.50	62.11
Colombia	570	45.30	12.58
Jordan	560	5.60	100.00
Pakistan	390	159.20	2.45
Liberia	210	3.50	60.00
Peru	170	27.50	6.18
Ethiopia	160	72.40	2.21

SOURCES: Curt Tarnoff and Larry Nowels, "Foreign Aid: an Introductory Overview of U.S. Programs and Policy," Congressional Research Service Report for Congress updated April 15, 2004; and Population Reference Bureau, "2004 World Population Data Sheet."

take into consideration the costs of the war against Iraq and the continuing occupation of that country. And no statistic can capture the high costs America is paying in the form of anti-American sentiments among Arabs and Muslims because of Washington's support for Israel and Saudi Arabia.

Resentment of U.S. Policies Leading to Terrorism

America's allies have not helped it to attain its goals in the region. To the contrary, at present, the American position in the region is weaker than it has been in more than 50 years, even though Washington maintains troops throughout the Middle East and, as of this writing, has de facto control over Iraq. The Bush administration has argued that raging anti-Americanism in the Muslim world stems from extremists' hatred of core American and Western values. In reality, it has little to do with cultural incompatibility. Anti-American sentiments are a reaction to America's abrasive policies, including the presence of large military contingents in the Middle East. In the spring of 2002, Zogby International surveyed residents of five Arab nations (Saudi Arabia, Kuwait, Egypt, Jordan, and Lebanon), three non-Arab Islamic countries (Iran, Pakistan, and Indonesia), and two others (France and Venezuela) for comparison purposes. The poll showed that many Muslims are favorably inclined toward America's democracy and freedom, with the numbers especially high in Kuwait (58 percent). Muslim nationals also think highly of U.S.-made products, particularly American technology, science, films, and TV. However, when asked whether they approve of U.S. government policy toward the Palestinians, only a small fraction (9 percent of Pakistanis and just 1 percent of Kuwaitis) said yes. "In essence, they don't hate us; they don't hate what we are about," pollster John Zogby told the *Christian Science Monitor*. Even though the president said that they hate our way of life and our democratic values, "at least in this first poll in the region, we did not find that was the case."

The stationing of U.S. forces in Saudi Arabia after the first Gulf War is known to have stirred such deep hostility that Osama bin Laden made it the initial focal point in his campaign to recruit Muslims from around the globe to attack Americans.

The relationship between Riyadh and Washington has never been easy, but relations have further deteriorated in the aftermath of the events of September 11, 2001. The Saudis have had to deal with Americans' reaction to the fact that 15 of the 19 hijackers in the Al Qaeda attacks of September 11 were Saudi citizens. Meanwhile, Saudi money has been used to spread the puritanical Sunni Wahhabi ideology, the official creed of the Saudi state, through mosques around the world. An opinion poll conducted by *Time* magazine and CNN in September 2003 found that 72 percent of Americans did not trust Saudi Arabia as an ally in the war on terrorism.

Despite that overwhelming popular sentiment, the Bush administration continues to maintain a ''special relationship'' with Riyadh, as demonstrated, among other things, by the decision of the White House to withhold from the public parts of a congressional inquiry into 9/11. Lawmakers who had seen the report implied that the deleted portions listed prominent Saudis under investigation for possible terrorist links. While members of Congress from both parties remain suspicious of the cozy relationship between Washington and Riyadh, there has been no substantial change in the strategic relationship between the two states.

Unfortunately, the move by the Bush administration to end the deployment of U.S. troops in Saudi Arabia in August 2003 was not part of an American strategy to disengage from Saudi Arabia but rather a way to relieve some of the political pressure on the Saudi royal family. Ending a military deployment that dated to the first Gulf War—and that has served as one of Osama bin Laden's chief rallying cries—was a wise decision, but it did not reflect a fundamental change in the U.S.-Saudi relationship.

The House of Saud, which has ruled the Desert Kingdom since the country's founding in 1932, faces an unprecedented threat to its survival. It is caught between criticism from the United States—the kingdom's traditional ally, now feeling betrayed by Saudi Arabia's sponsorship of Wahhabism, a virulently anti-Western strain of Islamism that has become a catalyst for terrorism—and the pressures of a conservative religious establishment on which the regime has long relied for its legitimacy. But those threats to the regime are unlikely to usher in a new age of *Glasnost* in Saudi Arabia. With the survival of the regime at stake, the members of the royal family may well put personal rivalries aside and adopt a policy of attempting to both co-opt and repress dissenters. The collapse of the royal family would most likely give rise to a more radical Islamic regime, one based on an alliance between military and radical religious leaders. Facing a threat of a military coup, the Saudis might preempt such a move by selecting to rule the country a member of the dynasty who would be acceptable to religious leaders.

As long as Washington continues to cling to the assumption that it must maintain its military supremacy in the Persian Gulf, it will not be able to resolve the dilemmas it is currently facing in the Middle East. The alliance with the ruling Arab regimes and the U.S. military presence in the region will continue to foster anti-Americanism and may force the United States into more costly military engagements. Such pressures might prompt a further strengthening of ties with theocracies like Saudi Arabia.

Forced Democratization Not a Panacea

An effort to accelerate "democratization" would likely fail in the near term and could pose a very serious threat to U.S. security in the medium to long term. Observations about the absence of factors supporting genuine, liberal-democratic reform, and of the risks posed to American interests by democratic impulses throughout the Middle East, are affirmed by a classified State Department report released to the media. According to press accounts, the report, prepared by the State Department's Bureau of Intelligence and Research, noted that "Middle East societies are riven by political, economic and social problems that are likely to undermine stability regardless of the nature of any externally influenced or spontaneous, indigenous change." George Downs and Bruce Bueno de Mesquita of New York University observed from their research that no country has "an enviable record of creating democracy" through the use of force. They warned, "There's no guarantee that free, fair, open elections . . . will produce governments that back fundamental American policies."

In short, given the virulent anti-American sentiments in Saudi Arabia and throughout the Middle East, a government that represented the wishes of the Saudi people could well choose to support Al Qaeda or other anti-American terrorist groups that seek our destruction. Accordingly, U.S. policies should not be predicated on the installation of a liberal democratic government in Saudi Arabia or elsewhere in the Middle East. The United States should focus on the policies adopted by the governments in question.

Redefining the American Role in the Israeli-Palestinian Peace Process

In the summer of 2002 the Bush administration endorsed the Roadmap for Peace in the Middle East, a plan that foresees the comprehensive settlement of the Israel-Palestinian conflict by 2005 under the auspices of the so-called Quartet that includes the United States, the European Union, the United Nations, and Russia. The Roadmap is supposed to correct the errors of the failed Oslo process by providing a detailed set of performance criteria that will result in an end to Palestinian violence, Israeli withdrawal from the occupied territories, and creation of an independent Palestinian state.

Although Israel immediately expressed reservations about the plan, it was seen as reasonably successful in its early stage—the Palestinians named Mahmoud Abbas (Abu Mazen) their prime minister, and terrorist attacks against Israeli civilians temporarily ebbed. However, Abbas stepped down in September 2003, and a wave of new attacks effectively put an end to the plan, even as the Bush administration continued to pay it lip service. In August 2004 Israel expanded its settlements in the West Bank, contradicting implicit commitments it had made under the framework of the Roadmap. The Bush administration's refusal to criticize the Israeli settlement plan was widely interpreted as a de facto endorsement of the policy.

Americans who continue to push for a peace settlement according to the Roadmap plan should recognize that the pro-peace factions in both Israeli and Palestinian societies are small and weak; many Palestinians and Israelis are still ready to pay a high price in blood in what they regard as a fight for survival. A settlement can be possible only when the majority of Israelis and Palestinians recognize that their interests would be best served by negotiation and peaceful resolution of the conflict.

Many Israelis and Palestinians are interested in keeping the United States entangled in the conflict. Few seem prepared to solve the conflict regionally. However, the U.S. government does not have to sustain the same level of involvement in the conflict that it maintained during the Cold War. First of all, no Arab regime can present a serious threat to Israel, whose military is unchallenged in the Middle East. Considerable American military aid to Israel might have been justified in the context of the Cold War, but it is unnecessary and even harmful under present conditions. Meanwhile, direct U.S. involvement in the Israeli-Palestinian conflict does not advance American national interests. Washington should reject demands to internationalize the conflict between Israelis and Palestinians, which implicitly assume that the United States should and would be responsible for resolving the dispute and paying the costs involved.

The war, with its national, ethnic, and religious dimensions, is clearly a human tragedy, but—like the conflicts between Hutus and Tutsis in Burundi, persistent civil wars in Burma and Laos, disputes between Indians and Pakistanis over Kashmir, or even continued hostility between Protestants and Catholics in Northern Ireland—it must be solved by the groups involved. The United States can and should express diplomatic support for the peaceful resolution of such conflicts and for the creation of strong civil societies, but we must be aware of the limits of our influence. And policymakers must remain focused on direct threats to the United States, the American people, or American vital interests.

U.S. policymakers should withdraw financial assistance to the Palestinians and phase out aid to Israel. The latter step would create an incentive for Israel to reform its economy, which has become far too dependent upon financial support from the United States. Removing that support would also encourage Israel to integrate itself politically and economically into the region. The United States should encourage diplomatic efforts on the regional level to promote the Middle East peace process. The way to localize and gradually resolve the conflict is not through direct U.S. involvement but through depriving both sides of international support.

Instead of complaining about the failure of the United States to make peace in the Middle East, and warning Americans of the dire consequences of a low diplomatic profile, the Arab states should recognize that it is in their national interests and that of the long-term stability of the region to do something to resolve the Israeli-Palestinian conflict in a regional context. With its geographic proximity to the Middle East, its dependence on Middle Eastern energy resources, and the large number of Arab immigrants living in major European countries, the European Union also has a clear stake in a more peaceful Middle East. U.S. policymakers should encourage the EU to take a more active role in the region.

Middle Eastern Oil and U.S. Interests

Continuing support for American policies in the Middle East, even in the face of the obvious risks and dubious benefits, stems from the erroneous belief that American military involvement in the Middle East protects U.S. access to ''cheap'' oil. Many Americans are willing to pay the cost of the U.S. military presence in the Middle East on the assumption that the oil resources in the Persian Gulf would be shut off if American troops were removed from the region. But the Gulf States have no other significant sources of revenue; they would risk economic suicide if they were to withhold oil from world markets. And once the oil reaches the market, there is no practical way to somehow punish American consumers. In short, the so-called oil weapon is a dud.

A different economic argument holds that the U.S. presence in the Middle East prevents terrorist attacks against oil infrastructure. It is certainly true that disruptions of supply anywhere in the world raise prices everywhere in the world and thus all consuming countries have an interest in preventing terrorist attacks on oil infrastructure. But the producing countries themselves also have a strong incentive to prevent supply disruptions because such disruptions reduce their income. And a permanent U.S. presence in the oil-producing regions seems to create as much insecurity as security, if not more. During the Cold War, the U.S. policy of actively safeguarding a strategic resource may have made sense in terms of maintaining the unity of the noncommunist alliance under American leadership. At present, however, that policy is badly outdated.

Changing Long-Term Strategy in the Middle East

The United States should recognize that its interests would be best served by reconsidering its Cold War–era strategy in the Middle East. Crafting long-term alliances with the "friendly" regimes there and elsewhere in the world, without regard to the long-term cost and while turning a blind eye to the nature of those regimes, was a defensible strategy in the framework of the Cold War. However, in the 21st century Washington finds itself trapped in an intellectual and political quagmire in the Middle East. On the one hand, Washington aims to preserve existing alliances with authoritarian Arab regimes, including those in Saudi Arabia and Egypt, even though maintaining "political friendship" with the House of Saud and Mubarak is completely inconsistent with American ideals, including concern for human rights and the rule of law. On the other hand, Washington's staunch support for Israel, combined with Israel's assertive policies in the Middle East, provokes disapproval within Arab states and ignites anti-American sentiments in the region and throughout the world. Both components of U.S. policy in the Middle East are morally dubious, and neither advances the national security interests of the United States. Indeed, they reinforce the negative image of America in the Middle East, potentially increasing incentives for terrorism.

A responsible policy in the Middle East, consistent with American security interests in the region, should be based on de-emphasizing U.S. alliances, especially those with Saudi Arabia and Israel, to meet the realities of the present day. Also, it should include a change in popular perceptions of U.S. dependence on Middle Eastern oil and of the necessity of U.S. leadership in the negotiations to end the Israeli-Palestinian conflict.

Reshaping U.S. policy in the Middle East would enhance American security and help change the perception that U.S. policies are guided by double standards. Maintaining a frail balance among all of Washington's commitments in the Middle East is becoming ever more costly, dangerous, and unnecessary. To sustain a U.S. military and political presence in the Middle East, ordinary Americans are constantly paying a price in dollars and reduced security both for American service personnel abroad and for American civilians at home. A change in policies is long overdue.

Suggested Readings

Bandow, Doug. "Befriending Saudi Princes: A High Price for a Dubious Alliance." Cato Institute Policy Analysis no. 428, March 20, 2002.

_____. "Settlements Pose Fundamental Threat to Democracy in Israel." Cato Institute Daily Commentary, December 19, 2003.

Fromkin, David. *A Peace to End All Peace: The Fall of the Ottoman Empire and the Creation of the Modern Middle East.* New York: Owl Books, 2001.

Hadar, Leon. "Mending the U.S.-European Rift over the Middle East." Cato Institute Policy Analysis no. 485, August 20, 2003.

_____. *Sandstorm: American Blindness in the Middle East.* New York: Palgrave/ Macmillan, 2005.

Preble, Christopher. "After Victory: Toward a New Military Posture in the Persian Gulf." Cato Institute Policy Analysis no. 477, June 10, 2003.

—Prepared by Leon T. Hadar and Christopher Preble

57. Iraq and the Persian Gulf: Getting Out, Staying Engaged

> **Policymakers should**
>
> - establish a firm timeline for American military withdrawal from Iraq;
> - refocus efforts on the principal task of fighting terrorism: identifying and destroying Al Qaeda and other anti-American terrorist networks;
> - recognize that the United States cannot impose liberal democracy in Iraq by force; political and economic reform must be embraced and nurtured by the Iraqis themselves;
> - follow the withdrawal from Iraq with a military withdrawal from the Persian Gulf; and
> - encourage trade, private investment, and other forms of voluntary exchange (including travel, tourism, and study abroad programs) between Americans and the people of the region.

It is in America's strategic interest to end the military occupation of Iraq at the earliest possible date, because a long-term military presence in the country undermines many of the goals that we are hoping to achieve there. A U.S. military occupation is a lightning rod that enables anti-American terrorists to expand their operations against the American troops in their neighborhood and ultimately to America's shores. Further, the presence of U.S. military garrisons in Iraq weakens the forces of democratic reform by undermining the indigenous government's authority and credibility. Finally, because any attempt to impose democracy by force is likely to fail, our presence in Iraq weakens the United States as a nation, diverting our resources and making the United States less capable of responding to genuine threats to U.S. security elsewhere in the world. Regardless of whether the decision to invade Iraq in 2003 was right or wrong, it cannot

571

be undone now, and policymakers are responsible for crafting a strategy that minimizes the risks to U.S. security, especially the risk of terrorist attacks against the United States.

The Costs and Burdens of Occupation

The primary concern for U.S. policymakers should be defending Americans from known threats. An expeditious end of the military occupation of Iraq serves that end because a withdrawal would free crucial resources for fighting known terrorists and at the same time remove a source of grievance for future terrorists. In the meantime, the presence of U.S. forces in Iraq is costly, in terms of both in lives lost and dollars spent. The U.S. occupation in Iraq has already cost the lives of more than 1,000 American service personnel. Several thousand more have been wounded, many of them grievously. Casualty figures among Iraqi civilians are even higher. Through 2003 and 2004 occupation costs totaled, on average, more than $4 billion per month.

A calculation of the true costs of the military occupation of Iraq must also include the strains on the nation's military. Absent a firm commitment to quickly reduce, and then eliminate, the military presence in Iraq, more and more will be demanded of the men and women in uniform. We're already extending tours of duty involuntarily, a back-door draft for active duty enlistees and for reservists and national guardsmen who have been called to active service. These burdens threaten to undermine the recruitment and retention that are key to the health of the all-volunteer force. Weakening the military diminishes America's ability to deter and defeat challenges to our vital security interests in the Middle East and elsewhere in the world.

As dangerous as the current situation in Iraq is for our troops and for average Iraqis, the risks extend much further. So long as our forces remain in Iraq, they risk becoming caught in the middle of a civil war between Iraq's feuding ethnic and religious factions. Some advocates of "staying the course" have justified a long-term presence on the grounds that our troops will prevent such a conflict from occurring. On the contrary, these forces may succeed in temporarily stifling ethnic tensions, but true reconciliation can only come from Iraqis themselves and will likely take many years, if it occurs at all. Meanwhile, the presence of U.S. forces serves as a lightning rod for domestic dissent and rebellion.

The Occupation of Iraq Is Counterproductive to Addressing the Terror Threat

The American military occupation of Iraq is not merely costly and burdensome for the United States; it is detrimental to fighting the war on terrorism. Bringing an end to the occupation and withdrawing militarily from Iraq will maximize America's ability to refocus its military and intelligence assets on the fight against those terrorists who present the gravest danger to American security—specifically, Al Qaeda and other anti-American terrorist groups with global reach—while minimizing the risks to vital U.S. national security interests.

Most proponents of a long-term military occupation of Iraq seem to disregard the detrimental effect that the occupation is having on the U.S.-led war against terrorism. By staying in Iraq, the United States sends a grim and misleading message to the rest of the world that Washington is using the occupation as a vehicle for asserting its dominance in the Middle East and imposing its will on the region's populace. The killings of Iraqis, including the inadvertent killings of Iraqi civilians, create new jihadis from the ranks of a population that had previously been largely unreceptive to Osama bin Laden's radical message. But even if our forces never fired a shot in anger at Iraqi citizens, the mere presence of our forces in Iraq would be seen as humiliating. Humiliation breeds contempt. And contempt breeds terrorism.

The jihadis will certainly claim that the American withdrawal represents a victory for their side, but it would be the height of irresponsibility for U.S. policymakers to allow that misperception to take hold. An American military withdrawal would not, and must not, signal that the United States has chosen to ignore events in Iraq. Instead, the withdrawal of U.S. forces must be coupled with a clear and unequivocal message to the people and elites of Iraq: do not threaten the United States; do not support anti-American terrorists; do not develop weapons of mass destruction. If you do, we will be back. Anyone who questions U.S. willingness and resolve to use force need only be reminded of the fate of the Taliban.

The end of the U.S. military occupation actually weakens the terrorists over the long term because Al Qaeda and other anti-American terrorist groups have used the U.S. occupation as a vehicle for promulgating their message of hatred and violence. In short, our occupation emboldens the forces of terror. The United States must use withdrawal from Iraq to its own advantage by countering propaganda by the likes of Osama bin Laden and other anti-American extremists who argue that the United States is planning to take control of Middle Eastern oil or to otherwise consolidate its control in the region.

Imposing Democracy by Force Is Doomed to Failure

Some of the most fervent advocates of a long-term presence in Iraq move beyond questions about terrorism and direct threats to the United States and argue that American security depends on the establishment of democracy in Iraq. For many, the creation of an Iraqi democracy is America's primary duty after the fall of Saddam. The general reasons for the support of Iraqi democracy are twofold: first, the humanitarian idea of democracy for democracy's sake and, second, the notion that democratic regimes tend not to threaten U.S. national security interests.

While the rhetoric of democratization and political liberalization is used to justify a continued military occupation of the country, the practice of occupation often entails thwarting the wishes of millions of Iraqis. The deeper problem, however, is that it is unlikely that democracy will take hold in Iraq, and certainly not in short order. Moreover, the very conditions for the formation of liberal democratic institutions are in fact undermined by the presence of foreign troops in Iraq. The handover of political sovereignty in June 2004 left in place approximately 140,000 American soldiers. This massive foreign military presence implies a measure of coercion on the Iraqi polity, playing into legitimate concerns that the United States does not really favor self-rule for the Iraqi people but instead hopes to see the emergence of a compliant government in Iraq, imbued with an aura of democratic legitimacy.

Genuine sovereignty for a new government in Iraq can be achieved only when American military personnel are removed from the country. Anything short of that end will forever leave the impression that the new government does not truly serve the people of Iraq. That is true even if the government of Iraq is afforded the superficial trappings of international legitimacy, such as membership in international organizations, and recognition of new national symbols. Sovereign states must be free and independent, and this independence must include the ability of the Iraqi people to defend themselves from threats and to conduct their own foreign policy.

Assuming that U.S. policymakers sincerely hope to create a self-reliant, stable democracy in Iraq, a model that will then be exportable around the Middle East, a prolonged U.S. occupation is unlikely to do the job. Even if it were possible to export democracy at gunpoint, such a strategy entails a much greater commitment than simply overthrowing unfriendly dictators;

it also requires the formulation, and subsequent stabilization, of democratic institutions. That, in turn, would require a massive commitment of will and resources that would erode America's own political and economic health. A long-term military occupation of Iraq is unsustainable.

U.S. military withdrawal therefore should not be predicated on the establishment of a liberal democratic government in Iraq. Policymakers must make a clear distinction between core U.S. national interests (in other words, those interests worth fighting for) and those goals that, while they may be worthy, are not, and should not be, the central object of U.S. foreign policy. Most Americans welcome the prospects for the emergence of a new government in Iraq, even as they recognize that the process is likely to take many years. Most believe that a liberal democratic government can eventually develop and that trade and economic interaction between Iraqis, Americans, and the rest of the international community can stimulate the process. U.S. policymakers should welcome the participation of private groups and nongovernmental organizations in supporting and, where possible, encouraging institutions of civil society that promote political and economic freedom. Those goals cannot be achieved through the application of military power and are not advanced by the maintenance of a U.S. military presence in Iraq.

The United States cannot ensure that the Iraqis will elect liberal democrats to represent them. Instead of trying to dictate outcomes and create a democracy in America's image, policymakers must allow the Iraqi people to create their own system of governance absent the pressure and humiliation of a foreign occupying army.

The tasks of governing must be left to the Iraqi people. The United States for its part should encourage the widest possible representation for Iraq's religious and ethnic minorities and should not demand that the new government be organized around a strong central authority based in Baghdad. If Iraq's disparate ethnic communities opt for some measure of autonomy, the United States should not stand in the way of a federal solution. However, Iraqis must understand that they will have responsibility for defending themselves from both internal and external threats.

For the United States to remain tied to the fortunes of the government of Iraq places our country, and our citizens, in a no-win situation. For example, in stating its preference for democracy, but in opposing the democratic impulses of the Shiite majority and the Kurds' desire for autonomy, the United States finds itself on a collision course with the wishes of millions of Iraqis. As policymakers juggle various and clashing commitments, Americans—both in Iraq and abroad—could become a target for all unsatisfied Iraqis, Shiite or Sunni, Arab or Kurd. Every month, every year, that the U.S. military remains in Iraq only makes it more difficult and more costly for the United States to extract itself. A decision to remove all U.S. military personnel from Iraq will minimize the enormous costs and risks associated with a military occupation and could eventually set the stage for a stable and sustainable relationship between Iraq and the United States.

Changing American Policies in the Middle East

Many observers believe that the United States must maintain a large military presence in the Middle East to secure its vital national interests in the Persian Gulf. In reality, however, the United States need not retain troops in a region in order to protect our security interests there. This applies both to our physical security—protection from attack by terrorist groups—and our economic security, in this case, ensuring continued access to Middle Eastern oil. The United States has the most capable military in human history; our capacity for projecting our power throughout the entire world is truly unprecedented. In other words, in the highly unlikely event that regional conditions were to threaten vital U.S. security interests, the United States could draw upon the military's capacity for projecting force over great distances to eliminate those threats.

Meanwhile, from a strictly economic standpoint, the United States need not retain troops in the Persian Gulf in order to remain engaged in the region or to secure its access to Middle Eastern oil. The gulf's energy resources are important to the global economy, but goods and services flow on the world market absent explicit "protection" by military forces.

In short, U.S. policy in the Persian Gulf should not be based on the assumption that the region's energy resources will not reach global markets absent the physical presence of the U.S. military. Oil is the principal source of revenue for the Persian Gulf countries; the leaders of those countries could not withhold the precious commodity from the world without committing economic suicide. That is true regardless of the internal composition of the government (i.e., democratic or autocratic) and applies to both pro- and anti-American governments.

The presence of U.S. troops may have temporarily stabilized the Persian Gulf from time to time, but, as the terrorist incidents in Saudi Arabia demonstrated, the troops have also been, and remain, a source of tension and instability. While the withdrawal of U.S. military personnel from

Saudi Arabia in 2003 was both appropriate and welcomed, that action should be the first of several steps leading to a wholesale reduction in the American military's "footprint" in the entire region. The collapse of Saddam Hussein's decrepit regime provides a golden opportunity for a fundamental change in U.S. policy in the Persian Gulf. In addition to the removal of troops from Saudi Arabia and Iraq, U.S. forces should be withdrawn from the other Gulf States, including Qatar and Kuwait.

Focusing on Known Threats As We Reduce Our Risks

Prior to launching the military operation that ultimately resulted in the removal of Saddam Hussein from power, the Bush administration argued that this would set in motion a chain of events that would ultimately democratize the entire region. That may happen, but U.S. policy should not be directed toward that end. Our overriding goal should be the protection of vital U.S. interests and the mitigation or elimination of threats to the United States and its citizens. Given the United States' low standing in the region, skeptics are likely to question U.S. motives, inherently weakening would-be reformers. Rather than take a direct, active role in the creation of new governments in the region, the United States can foster an atmosphere conducive to reform in the Middle East, including the expansion of liberal democratic principles, and free-market economics and entrepreneurship, by adopting a largely hands-off approach.

U.S. policymakers should do so with a clear eye on the lessons of recent history. Many scholars warned of the dangers of a lengthy U.S. presence in the region, long before the events of September 11. There *were* alternatives to a lengthy U.S. presence in the region throughout the 1990s, a presence that most people realized posed grave risks for American military personnel and American interests. There are even more alternatives today. A decision by the Bush administration to substantially reduce the number of U.S. military personnel stationed in the region will be welcomed by the troops and by U.S. taxpayers and could set the stage for a stable and sustainable relationship between Americans and the men and women living there for many years to come.

Suggested Readings

Abramowitz, Morton. "Does Iraq Matter?" *National Interest,* no. 75 (Spring 2004): 39–44.

Basham, Patrick. "Can Iraq Be Democratic?" Cato Institute Policy Analysis no. 505, January 5, 2004.

Eisenstadt, Michael, and Eric Mathewson. *U.S. Policy in Post-Saddam Iraq: Lessons from the British Experience*. Washington: Institute for Near East Policy, 2003.

Eland, Ivan. "Does U.S. Intervention Overseas Breed Terrorism? The Historical Record." Cato Institute Foreign Policy Briefing no. 50, December 17, 1998.

Exiting Iraq: Why the U.S. Must End the Military Occupation and Renew the War against Al Qaeda. Cato Institute Special Task Force Report, 2004.

Lindsey, Brink. "The Trade Front: Combating Terrorism with Open Markets." Cato Institute Trade Policy Analysis no. 24, August 5, 2003.

Record, Jeffrey, and W. Andrew Terrill. "Iraq and Vietnam: Differences, Similarities and Insights." Strategic Studies Institute, May 2004.

—Prepared by Christopher Preble

58. East Asian Defense Commitments

Policymakers should

- withdraw American military forces from South Korea over the next two years and terminate the mutual defense treaty at the end of that period;
- work with other nations in the region to dissuade North Korea (DPRK) from developing a nuclear arsenal, while planning for the possibility that Pyongyang might do so;
- communicate to the DPRK that any proliferation of nuclear technology to hostile actors would be considered an act of war, meriting immediate removal of the Kim Jong Il regime;
- begin a four-year phased pullout of American troops from Japan, beginning with forces on Okinawa;
- replace the bilateral U.S.-Japanese defense treaty with an agreement that allows emergency base and port access and maintains joint military exercises and intelligence cooperation;
- drop proposals for enhanced defense ties with Singapore, eliminate the AUSMIN agreement with Australia, and make clear to the Philippine government and people that the Visiting Forces Agreement and anti-terrorist assistance do not commit the United States to military action on behalf of the Philippines, especially in any territorial disagreement involving the South China Sea;
- promote regional security cooperation through the Association of Southeast Asian Nations (ASEAN) and other appropriate institutions; and
- drop Washington's implicit defense guarantee to Taiwan but sell Taipei any conventional weapons it deems necessary for its defense.

After the end of World War II, the United States established an extensive forward military presence and fought two wars in East Asia as part of its strategy to contain communism. The Cold War ended a decade and a half ago, but America's defense posture has changed little. Washington long was committed to keeping at least 100,000 military personnel in East Asia and the western Pacific, apparently forever. The Pentagon's infamous 1995 assessment of security policy in East Asia (the so-called Nye Report) made the astonishing assertion that "the end of the Cold War has not diminished" the importance of any of America's regional security commitments. Only under pressure created by the unexpectedly difficult occupation of Iraq did the Bush administration propose in mid-2004 to remove 12,500 soldiers from the Korean peninsula.

That modest reduction did not reverse the Bush administration's policy of *increasing* U.S. military ties, such as involving Special Forces in Manila's fight against Abu Sayyaf guerrillas and escalating an implicit defense guarantee to Taiwan against China. Rather than expand America's military presence in East Asia, policymakers should initiate a phased withdrawal of American forces from South Korea and Japan and prepare to center Washington's reduced military presence in the central Pacific rather than East Asia.

Changed Threat Environment

American policy in the Far East has succeeded. For five decades Washington provided a defense shield behind which noncommunist governments throughout East Asia were able to grow economically (despite their recent setbacks) and democratically. Japan is the world's second-ranked economic power; Taiwan's dramatic jump from poverty to prosperity forced the leaders of the communist mainland to undertake fundamental economic reforms. South Korea now outstrips North Korea by virtually every measure of national power. After years of failure, the Philippines seems to be on the path to prosperity, while countries like Thailand have grown dramatically.

Major threats to America's allies and interests have diminished. There is no more Soviet Union; a much weaker Russia has neither the capability nor the will for Asian adventurism.

Elsewhere real, tough-minded communism has dissolved into a cynical excuse for incumbent officeholders to maintain power. More than 15 years after the Tiananmen Square massacre, China is combining support for greater economic liberty with respect for greater individual autonomy. So far Beijing's military renewal has been modest, and China has been assertive rather than aggressive, though its saber rattling at Taiwan remains of concern.

Southeast Asia remains roiled by economic and political instability, but such problems threaten no one outside the immediate region. Only North Korea remains a potential threat, but it is no replacement for the Soviet Union. Pyongyang is bankrupt and starving, essentially friendless, and, despite its willingness to wave the threat of an atomic bomb to gain respect, will only fall further behind the South. Moreover, sporadically warmer relations between the two Koreas after the summit between the South's Kim Dae Jung and the North's Kim Jong Il offer the hope, though obviously not the guarantee, of growing détente between the two states.

Some analysts privately, and a few publicly, say that Japan poses a potential threat to regional peace. However, Tokyo has gained all of the influence and wealth through peace that it had hoped to attain through war and the Greater East Asia Co-Prosperity Sphere in the 1930s.

Moreover, the lesson of World War II remains vivid to most Japanese: in recent years the nation has been convulsed by political debates over such modest actions as providing peacekeeping troops to the UN operation in Cambodia, authorizing military participation in civilian rescues, and sending 550 soldiers for humanitarian duties in Iraq.

Even mainstream politicians committed to a somewhat more assertive posture—which has become increasingly respectable—have routinely sacrificed military spending to budget concerns. The Koizumi government has moved to modestly expand Tokyo's defense responsibilities, but they remain far below both Japan's economic resources and its strategic interests.

Rethinking American Strategy

So far neither the Bush administration nor Congress seems to have noticed the many dramatic changes. Indeed, the Bush administration's proposed $425 billion in military spending for 2005 is more than the next eight countries spend on defense. U.S. taxpayers spent more than $13 trillion (in current dollars) and sacrificed 92,000 lives to win the Cold War. With the dramatic diminution of security threats and the equally dramatic growth of allied capabilities, the American people should no longer be expected to surrender more dollars and risk more lives to police East Asia for as long as friendly states believe it to be convenient. However much it might be in the interest of other nations for Washington to defend them—and what country would not naturally desire that the world's remaining superpower subsidize its defense?—it is not in America's interest to do so.

Unless the administration initiates a full rather than a partial troop drawdown, Congress should take the lead in adjusting U.S. overseas deployments. Legislators should reduce the defense budget as well as overall force levels and foreign deployments; Washington should develop a comprehensive plan for the phased withdrawal of all forces currently stationed in East Asia and the termination of U.S. defense guarantees to allied nations.

The starting point for a new East Asian strategy is disengagement from the Korean peninsula, the international flashpoint that could most easily involve the United States in war. Although North Korea remains unpredictable and potentially dangerous, the South should be able to defend itself. It now possesses twice the population of, around 40 times the gross domestic product of, and a vast technological lead over the North. Especially after having rebounded from the Asian economic crisis, the South is well able to spend whatever is necessary to make up for the withdrawal of 37,000 American troops. The North could then choose to engage in meaningful arms control or lose an inter-Korean arms race.

The potential for a North Korean nuclear bomb is unnerving. Pyongyang's increasingly obvious nuclear-weapons program has significantly raised tensions. That program is a violation of the commitments North Korea made in the 1994 Framework Agreement. Washington should continue working with China, Japan, South Korea, and Russia to encourage continued compliance by North Korea. More generally, the United States should work to reduce tensions on the peninsula. Washington should allow Seoul to take the lead in dealing with the North, supporting rather than undercutting South Korean efforts to draw the DPRK into a more responsible international role. At the same time, Washington should not only lift trade sanctions against the North but also normalize diplomatic relations—modest concessions that would offer the North ongoing benefits in return for adopting a peaceful course.

Although we should remain cautious about any promises by Pyongyang, engagement offers greater prospects of success than does plunging the peninsula into a new cold, or possibly hot, war. There are no good options if Pyongyang ultimately attempts to develop an atomic bomb, and a continued American conventional military presence is certainly not one. U.S. ground forces in the South would become nuclear hostages, enhancing the North's leverage over America. While the United States might be willing to reluctantly tolerate North Korean acquisition of nuclear weapons, Washington should make it very clear that sale of nuclear materials, especially to hostile nonstate actors such as Al Qaeda, would be considered a casus belli, with regime change the result.

Time for a Setting Sun

Washington should follow a similar strategy in Japan, which no longer faces a superpower threat. Whatever dangers to Japan remain or might arise in the future, from, say, an aggressive China or DPRK, could be met by a modest Japanese military buildup. Of course, many of Japan's neighbors have long viewed Washington's presence more as an occupation force to contain Tokyo than as a defense against other threats. But the Japanese do not possess a double dose of original sin; their nation, along with the rest of the world, has changed dramatically over the last half century. The Japanese people have neither the desire nor the incentive to start another conflict, having come to economic prominence in East Asia peacefully.

Moreover, Tokyo is unlikely to accept a permanent foreign watchdog, and tensions will grow as the lack of other missions for the U.S. forces becomes increasingly obvious. Popular anger is already evident in Okinawa, where American military facilities occupy one-fifth of the island's landmass. Washington should develop a four-year program for the withdrawal of all U.S. forces from Japan, starting with those in Okinawa. At the end of that period, Washington and Tokyo should replace their mutual defense treaty with a more limited agreement providing for emergency base and port access, joint military exercises, and intelligence sharing.

The United States need not expand base access elsewhere in the region. Washington should drop proposals to increase defense cooperation with Singapore and tightly circumscribe the scope of its Visiting Forces Agreement with the Philippines, which was promoted by former president Joseph Estrada and other Filipino supporters as a mechanism for drawing the United States into any confrontation between the Philippines and China. The United States needs also to limit any future military training missions, sharply insulating American forces from involvement in domestic conflicts, such as that involving the Abu Sayyaf, essentially a gang of bandits. The United States has suffered no damage attributable to the closing of its bases in the Philippines, which had become expensive anachronisms, in 1992. Instead of upgrading U.S. military ties, Washington should be transferring security responsibilities to its allies and friends.

Even less relevant are the Australia–New Zealand–United States (ANZUS) accord, which went into deep freeze in 1984 after New Zealand blocked port access by nuclear-armed and nuclear-powered American ships, and the annual Australia–United States Ministerial Consultations (AUSMIN). ANZUS, created in the aftermath of World War II, was directed less at containing the Soviet Union, which had no military presence in the South Pacific, than at preventing a new round of Japanese aggression. But since Tokyo had been decisively defeated and completely disarmed, later to be fully integrated into the Western alliance, ANZUS was outmoded the day it was signed.

Which leaves AUSMIN. But Australia faces no meaningful threats to its security. An attack by a serious military power—China, India, Vietnam—is a paranoid fantasy. An Indonesian implosion might flood Australia with refugees, but not hostile troops. Anyway, Australia, blessed with splendid isolation and economic prosperity, can easily provide whatever forces it deems necessary to defend itself.

Washington should simply discard AUSMIN. Australia and America should maintain mutually beneficial military cooperation, such as intelligence sharing and emergency port access. At the same time, Canberra should enhance its own military role in the region—as it now shows some signs of doing.

Regional Security Cooperation

Indeed, the United States should encourage expanded regional security discussions. Either through ASEAN or another organization, smaller countries throughout East Asia should develop a cooperative defense relationship with Australia, New Zealand, South Korea, and especially Japan.

Fear of the latter ignores five decades of dramatic changes. Tokyo could do much to improve regional security. A measured military buildup, focused on defensive weapons and conducted in consultation with Japan's neighbors, would help prevent the creation of a dangerous vacuum following the departure of American forces, which is feared by proponents of continuing U.S. dominance. Washington's position should be that of a distant balancer, leaving its friends to handle their own affairs and most regional contingencies but poised to act if a hegemonic threat arises that allied states cannot contain.

The United States could aid in the creation of a more effective regional security framework by encouraging the peaceful resolution of various boundary and territorial disputes. None presently seems likely to lead to war, but all impede better bilateral and multilateral cooperation. To help dissipate international tensions, Washington should offer its good offices to help mediate the Japanese–South Korean squabble over the Takeshima/ Tokdu islands, the Japanese-Russian quarrel over the "northern territories" (the Kurile islands), and the multifaceted dispute involving China and several other countries that claim the Paracel and Spratly islands. Most important, the United States should make clear that resolution of those (and other similar) controversies is up to the interested parties, not America. Such a "tough love" policy forced Australia to assume the lead role in establishing a UN peacekeeping force in East Timor in the aftermath of that territory's messy divorce from Indonesia.

The end of Cold War rivalry between the United States and the Soviet Union allows Washington to take a more balanced position vis-à-vis the People's Republic of China (PRC). Washington should continue to promote good political relations, expand the military dialogue, and encourage additional economic reform.

However, the United States need not fear bruising the PRC's sensitivities when discussing China's foreign arms sales, human rights abuses, attempted bullying of Taiwan, and interference with America's internal affairs by seeking to block even private visits to the United States by Taiwanese officials. America should speak frankly on those issues, and Congress should resist pressure to limit trade with and investment in China. While nothing is inevitable, extensive economic ties offer what is probably the most powerful tool for weakening central communist control in the PRC.

U.S. leaders also need to carefully calibrate policy toward Taiwan. (See Chapter 61.) The election in 2000 and reelection in 2004 of Chen Shui-bian of the Democratic Progressive Party, which has long championed Taiwanese independence, has further increased tensions across the Taiwan Strait.

The United States does not have sufficient interests at stake to risk war with nuclear-armed China over Taiwan. However, Washington, after making clear that it believes the status of Taiwan, whether reunified with the mainland or independent, is up to the people of Taiwan to decide, should sell the island whatever conventional weapons Taipei desires to purchase for its own defense.

Conclusion

East Asia is likely to grow more important to the United States in coming years. That makes it essential that Washington simultaneously reduce the military burden on the American economy and force its trading competitors to bear the full cost of their own defense. Otherwise, U.S. firms will be less able to take advantage of expanding regional economic opportunities. More important, the United States will be more secure if friendly powers in the region, instead of relying on America, are able and willing to contain nearby conflicts.

Jettisoning antiquated alliances and commitments and reducing a bloated force structure does not mean the United States would no longer be an Asian-Pacific power. After bringing its forces home from South Korea and Japan, America should center a reduced defense presence around Wake Island, Guam, and Hawaii. The United States would remain the globe's strongest military power, with the ability to intervene throughout East Asia if necessary. However, American policy would be dictated by the interests of the American people, not those of the populous and prosperous security dependents that Washington has accumulated throughout the region.

Suggested Readings

Bandow, Doug. "All the Players at the Table: A Multilateral Solution to the North Korean Nuclear Crisis." Cato Institute Policy Analysis no. 478, June 26, 2003.

————. "Bring the Troops Home: Ending the Obsolete Korean Commitment." Cato Institute Policy Analysis no. 474, May 7, 2003.

————. "Instability in the Philippines: A Case Study for U.S. Disengagement." Cato Institute Foreign Policy Briefing no. 64, March 21, 2001.

————. "Needless Entanglements: Washington's Expanding Security Ties in Southeast Asia." Cato Institute Policy Analysis no. 401, May 24, 2001.

————. "Okinawa: Liberating Washington's East Asian Military Colony." Cato Institute Policy Analysis no. 314, September 1, 1998.

————. "Old Wine in New Bottles: The Pentagon's East Asian Security Report." Cato Institute Policy Analysis no. 344, May 18, 1999.

————. Tripwire: Korea and U.S. Foreign Policy in a Changed World. Washington: Cato Institute, 1996.

————. "Wrong War, Wrong Place, Wrong Time: Why Military Action Should Not Be Used to Resolve the North Korean Nuclear Crisis." Cato Institute Foreign Policy Briefing no. 76, May 12, 2003.

Carpenter, Ted Galen. "Managing a Great Power Relationship: The United States, China and East Asian Security." Journal of Strategic Studies 21, no. 1 (March 1998).

————. "Options for Dealing with North Korea." Cato Institute Foreign Policy Briefing no. 73, January 9, 2003.

————. "Washington's Smothering Strategy: American Interests in East Asia." World Policy Journal 14, no. 4 (Winter 1997–98).

Carpenter, Ted Galen, and Doug Bandow. The Korean Conundrum: America's Troubled Relations with North and South Korea. New York: Palgrave/Macmillan, 2004.

Harrison, Selig S. Korean Endgame: A Strategy for Reunification and U.S. Disengagement. Princeton, N.J.: Princeton University Press, 2002.

Johnson, Chalmers, and E. B. Keehn. "The Pentagon's Ossified Strategy." *Foreign Affairs* 74, no. 4 (July–August 1995).

Layne, Christopher. "Less Is More: Minimal Realism in East Asia." *National Journal* 43 (Spring 1996).

Olsen, Edward A. "A Northeast Asian Peace Dividend." *Strategic Review* (Summer 1998).

―――. *U.S. National Defense for the Twenty-First Century: The Grand Exit Strategy.* London: Frank Cass, 2002.

Zich, Arthur. "Okinawa, Seoul: Are the Bases Needed?" *Impact* 12 (March 1997).

—Prepared by Doug Bandow

59. Relations with South and Central Asia

Hard Choices in Pakistan

The 9/11 Commission report stressed that both Islamabad and Washington need to make "hard choices" if they are to make progress in the fight against radical Islamic terrorism. More specifically, the commission

589

recommended that the United States commit itself to a period of sustained aid, including military assistance, to Pakistan, but only on condition that Pakistan's military ruler, Gen. Pervez Musharraf, proves that he stands for "enlightened moderation" by confronting Islamic extremism, curbing nuclear proliferation, and paving the way for the return to democracy.

The commission's recommendations reveal the fundamental conundrum that the United States has faced in its dealings with Pakistan both before and after 9/11. American policymakers have come to recognize that Pakistan's pre-9/11 alliance with the Taliban regime in Afghanistan and its strong ties to radical Islamic terrorist groups helped to create the environment that gave birth to Al Qaeda. But the commission report portrays Pakistan as dramatically different than it was before 9/11. The report implies that the decision by Musharraf to sever his country's links to the Taliban and provide logistical support for the U.S. invasion of Afghanistan marked a dramatic reversal in Pakistan's approach to radical Islamic terrorism. Accordingly, the 9/11 report implies that Pakistan has been evolving into a reliable ally of the United States in the war on terrorism.

That conclusion is flawed. Pakistan is not a dependably effective strategic partner. The decision by Musharraf to abandon the Taliban after 9/11 reflected not a strategic choice but a tactical one. It was based on the clear recognition that anything less than full cooperation with the United States would result in punishing American military retaliation, including the invasion of parts of Pakistan, and possibly the overthrow of the Musharraf government. At a minimum, the refusal by Pakistan to back the American invasion of Afghanistan would have led to the total diplomatic and economic isolation of the regime, which could have played into the hands of rival India in its bid for regional hegemony.

Support for Radical Islamist Causes

The assumption that Pakistan has severed its ties with those who advocate a radical Islamic agenda is based more on the rhetoric emanating from Islamabad than on the policy steps taken there since 9/11. For example, the 9/11 Commission points to "an extraordinary public essay" by Musharraf, in which he called on Muslims to adopt a policy of "enlightened moderation," to shun militancy and extremism, to seek to resolve disputes with "justice," and to help "better the Muslim world."

Contrast that with the reality in Pakistan as described by the members of the commission: "Within Pakistan's borders are 150 million Muslims, scores of al Qaeda terrorists, many Taliban fighters and—perhaps—Usama

Bin Ladin. Pakistan possesses nuclear weapons and has come frighteningly close to war with nuclear-armed India over the disputed territory of Kashmir.'' In addition, when the commission asked American and foreign government officials, ''If you were a terrorist leader today, where would you locate your base?'' Pakistan was at the top of the list.

Policymakers should focus on what attracts terrorists to Pakistan. In many respects, it is a ''failed state'': corruption is widespread, the government is ineffective, and there is immense support among the general public and the elites for radical Islamic causes. Motivated by ideology and cheap tuition, millions of Pakistani families send their children to religious schools, or madrassas, which have become incubators for anti-Western propaganda that contributes to the terrorist problem.

Moreover, radical Islamism is backed not only by leaders of large political parties and by the tribes on the Pakistan-Afghanistan borders. Many reports by Western intelligence and media have found that the Pakistani Army and intelligence services, in particular, are at best ambivalent about confronting Islamic extremists. Meanwhile, Islamic terrorists have found refuge in Pakistan's unpoliced regions, which now provide both a base of operations against U.S. forces in Afghanistan and a safe haven for planning attacks against Americans inside the United States.

Widespread support for extremist Islam in Pakistan may explain why many of the Pakistani government's early efforts to pursue Al Qaeda members hiding along the Pakistan-Afghanistan border failed. That sentiment may also explain why Musharraf's government refused to vigorously pursue former Taliban and Islamic militants gathered in tribal, semiautonomous regions of Pakistan. According to the 9/11 Commission report, during the two years following the 9/11 attacks, ''the Pakistani government tried to walk the fence, helping against al Qaeda while seeking to avoid a larger confrontation with Taliban remnants and other Islamic extremists.'' By most indications, Pakistan either could not or would not pursue Al Qaeda members effectively, even on its own territory.

The disappointing results of Pakistan's early military offensives raise doubts about Musharraf's ability to challenge the power of the local tribal leaders in Waziristan and the semiautonomous regions of northwest Pakistan. Despite the military pressure and the financial rewards offered by the United States, many Pakistanis continue to shelter the militants, including foreigners who operate there. At the same time, two assassination attempts on Musharraf in December 2003 seem to have mobilized the Pakistani president to take action. The capture of several Al Qaeda operatives during the summer of 2004 may indicate a growing willingness on Musharraf's part to pursue Al Qaeda terrorists. Musharraf must understand that this is his fight as well, and U.S. policymakers must understand that Musharraf is in a precarious political position.

Nuclear Proliferation

In addition to Pakistan's uneven record in pursuing Al Qaeda and the Taliban, there were troubling revelations that a leading Pakistani scientist and the father of Pakistan's atomic bomb, Abdul Qadeer Khan, provided nuclear military technology to several countries, including Iran, North Korea, and Libya. Musharraf and other Pakistani officials insisted that the business network led by Khan—which transferred nuclear know-how, including designs, components, and advice to anti-American regimes interested in developing weapons of mass destruction (WMD)—operated without the authorization and knowledge of the government. The officials explained that Khan was a "rogue scientist" motivated by greed and that he was acting alone. But sources in Pakistan dispute that account and suggest that at least some individuals in the government approved of what Khan was doing and saw his proliferation efforts as part of a strategy to help other Islamic countries such as Libya and Iran to develop nuclear military capabilities as a deterrent against the United States and Israel.

The Khan network may also have been a way for the military and intelligence services to gain access to funds for covert operations in Afghanistan, Kashmir, and elsewhere. Musharraf's decision to pardon Khan immediately following the revelations about his activities raises serious questions about Pakistan's commitment to nonproliferation. It also calls into question the security of Pakistan's own nuclear military program and underlines concerns that Pakistan's nuclear secrets could fall into the hands of Al Qaeda and other Islamic terrorists.

The Bush administration accepted Musharraf's pardon of Khan and refrained from challenging the Pakistani leader when he said that he and all senior officials in Pakistan's military and intelligence establishment had been completely unaware of Khan's proliferation activities. Throughout 2003 and 2004, the Bush administration agreed (under pressure from Islamabad) not to dispatch American and British forces to the tribal areas inside Pakistan where senior Al Qaeda and Taliban leaders were believed to be hiding.

Also troubling was the Bush administration's decision to designate Pakistan a "major non-NATO ally," a title that has been granted to Japan,

Israel, South Korea, the Philippines, Thailand, Argentina, Egypt, Kuwait, Bahrain, and Jordan. That new status not only provided Pakistan with added diplomatic prestige; it also afforded Islamabad greater access to American military technology and surplus defense equipment and training. That announcement angered the members of the political establishment in India who regard Pakistan as a sponsor of anti-Indian terrorism.

U.S. officials defend their support for Pakistan by stressing that U.S. policy is driven by the short-term goals of the war on terrorism and also that Musharraf's government may present the only realistic chance to reach an agreement over Kashmir. New Delhi and Islamabad did announce in early 2004—only two years after nearly going to war—that they would restart peace talks. Some American analysts have suggested that, by agreeing publicly to prevent Pakistani territory from being used as a staging ground to support the anti-Indian insurgency in Kashmir, Musharraf has made a "strategic choice" to end the Pakistani-supported proxy war against India in Kashmir.

Musharraf Is Opportunistic; U.S. Policymakers Should Be As Well

Policymakers should consider an alternate interpretation of Pakistan's behavior. Since 9/11, Musharraf has been opportunistic. He responded to political and military pressure from the United States by ending his country's alliance with the Taliban and other radical Islamic groups, taking steps to liberalize his country's political and economic system, and opening the road to an accord with India over Kashmir. But there are no signs that Musharraf and his political and military allies have made a strategic choice to ally themselves with U.S. long-term goals in the war on terrorism by destroying the political and military infrastructure of the radical and violent anti-American Islamic groups in Pakistan. It is highly probable that Musharraf is not strong enough to do so. From that perspective, the partnership with the United States and Musharraf's willingness to negotiate with India over Kashmir are nothing more than short-term moves aimed at winning U.S. assistance and preventing India from emerging as Washington's main ally in the region.

If this alternate interpretation is correct, the current American relationship with Pakistan is, at best, a short-term alliance of necessity. Over the medium and long term, U.S. policymakers should distance themselves from Musharraf's regime, seek out ways to cultivate liberal secular reforms in Pakistan, and engage in more constructive relations with India.

Such a policy shift would reflect present-day reality: Westernized and secular India is a stable democracy and a rising regional power, not a de facto client of the Soviet Union, as it was widely presumed to be during the Cold War. With the Cold War order long since dismantled, the United States has a clear interest in establishing strong ties with India, whose political, economic, and military clout places the country in a position to counterbalance even an increasingly assertive China. As the world's largest democracy and an important bilateral trading partner with the United States, India, not Pakistan, should be the focus of long-term U.S. policy in the region.

U.S. Policy in Central Asia

Given the uncertainties in Pakistan, Afghanistan, and the Middle East, Central Asia will present both historic opportunities and serious challenges for the United States in the 21st century. The presence of oil and natural gas, coupled with the region's geographic location, makes Central Asia strategically important to the United States. Instability in the greater Middle East and the war on terrorism are demanding a new strategic posture.

The United States has indicated that it would like to become more involved in the region, particularly in establishing military basing rights in states such as Uzbekistan and Kyrgyzstan. Though such relationships are strategically important, they present serious problems that policymakers must take into account.

Strategic Value and Dangers of Cooperation

In the wake of U.S. military interventions in Afghanistan and Iraq, support in the Middle East for the United States and its policies has dropped precipitously. During the preparations for invading Iraq, even Turkey refused to allow its territory to be used as a staging ground, and the United States was forced to alter its plans accordingly. As American military planners were forced to look elsewhere for basing rights in the region, access to bases in places like Uzbekistan and Kyrgyzstan became increasingly desirable, particularly in the event of a flare-up in Afghanistan or the potential destabilization of Pakistan.

The Pentagon has cast its new thinking in terms of a Central Asian "lily pad" strategy; that is, the opportunity to "hop" from one base to another in Central Asia rather than maintain large, permanent bases from which U.S. forces could fight directly. Although this proposal has some appeal (reducing the U.S. presence in a given country and maintaining fewer forces on active duty there), it carries serious risks as well.

Even before the regimes in Central Asia started cooperating with the United States, Islamist terrorists had targeted them for destruction. The Islamic Movement of Uzbekistan and several Turkic groups have been branded as terrorists by regional governments. Hizb ut-Tahrir (the Islamic Liberation Party), while generally considered nonviolent, seeks to unite the entire Islamic world under the rule of a new caliphate and is active primarily in Uzbekistan. Sucking those groups into the amalgam of anti-American terror groups that operate worldwide would add fuel to an already hot fire. A U.S. military presence perceived as intrusive and humiliating could serve to push those groups into the arms of Al Qaeda. Although many of the region's leaders are unsavory and unpredictable, their overthrow and the chaos that would ensue in Central Asia would present serious problems for an already overstretched U.S. military.

Entering the Russian and Chinese Spheres of Influence

In addition to the concern of terrorism, the introduction of great power politics into Central Asia could create unnecessary problems for the United States. History, geography, and national interest place the region within both the Russian and the Chinese spheres of influence. A large or long-term American presence in the region would likely rankle both countries, creating needless tension in an already unstable region.

A variety of treaty organizations (such as the Shanghai Cooperation Organization for China and the Collective Security Treaty Organization for Russia) have been used to tie both regional great powers to Central Asia. Thus, there is already competition for strategic space in Central Asia. Expanding the American military presence could aggravate the conflict and alarm both China and Russia.

Russia is already bolstering its military presence in the region; the budding U.S. base in Kyrgyzstan is in close proximity to the expanding Russian base at Kant. Though it is unclear whether Russian president Vladimir Putin himself disapproves of such an American presence in the region, he faces pressure from hardliners who vehemently oppose what they see as an attempt to undermine Russian dominance.

Meanwhile, China's energy needs and its campaign against the Muslim Uighur separatist groups in Xinjiang province have forced the Chinese to look westward. A larger U.S. military presence in the region could draw the United States into the conflict. Taking sides on that issue will anger either China or the Muslim populations of surrounding states, possibly including terrorist groups.

Further, an American presence to China's west, coupled with the existing tensions over the Taiwan issue, could press China into seeing the United States as a genuine threat to its strategic position.

Conclusion: Walk Lightly in Central Asia

Although the potential downsides of involvement in Central Asia present serious dangers, cooperative relationships with governments there can offer important benefits at a manageable cost, if American activities in the region conform to certain characteristics.

First, the American military "footprint" in Central Asia must be small. If the United States were to set up a large-scale, highly visible presence in the region, Osama bin Laden and his adherents would have one more rallying cry. A visible U.S. troop presence and open alliances with corrupt regimes that oppress Muslim populations would likely inflame Muslim resentment and put both U.S. forces and the allies' governments at risk.

Accordingly, the United States should seek to establish agreements that regional bases *could* be used in the event of an emergency that threatened vital U.S. interests. Economic enticements such as trade agreements could be used to encourage Central Asian governments to cooperate. A small-scale American presence may be necessary temporarily to ensure that the bases meet U.S. needs, but there should be no permanent or quasi-permanent garrisons of U.S. troops.

Second, the United States must openly and clearly communicate its objectives in the region to Russia and China and act in accordance with its promises. Although both states would face internal pressure opposing a U.S. presence, neither state's influence would be threatened by a small-scale U.S. plan of basing rights. The United States should not oppose Russian and Chinese military agreements with Central Asian governments and should allow those states to maintain a preponderance of the military capability in the region. The notion that the United States must compete is foolhardy and threatens to upset the already unstable situation.

Third, U.S. policymakers must keep in mind their primary objective—keeping the world's most dangerous weapons out of the hands of the world's most dangerous terrorists. Although the Defense Threat Reduction Agency and the Proliferation Security Initiative are positive steps, Central Asia presents unique challenges for counterproliferation efforts. Radiological and nuclear materials remain in the region, and destabilization would not only create a security and political vacuum—it could also jeopardize U.S. efforts to secure former Soviet nuclear facilities.

In sum, U.S. interests in Central Asia are best served by developing agreements to use bases in the Central Asian states in the event of an emergency. Conversely, U.S. interests could be harmed by a large-scale military presence in the region. By cultivating the regional governments with trade and other mutually beneficial economic agreements, the United States can improve its strategic position in the region. Maintaining a small footprint will prevent the new U.S. strategy from inflaming terrorist groups and their sympathizers. If U.S. intentions are focused on protecting vital U.S. national security interests, a corresponding U.S. policy will not present a significant problem for either Russo-U.S. or Sino-U.S. relations. Accordingly, the United States can enhance its ability to pursue its interests in both Central and South Asia.

Suggested Readings

Atal, Subodh. "Extremist, Nuclear Pakistan: An Emerging Threat?" Cato Institute Policy Analysis no. 472, March 5, 2003.

Bogaturov, Alexei. "International Relations in Central-Eastern Asia: Geopolitical Challenges and Prospects for Political Cooperation." Brookings Institution Working Paper, June 2004.

Ganguly, Sumit. *Conflict Unending: India-Pakistan Tensions since 1947.* New York: Columbia University Press, 2002.

Gobarev, Victor M. "India as a World Power: Changing Washington's Myopic Policy." Cato Institute Policy Analysis no. 381, September 11, 2002.

Gurcharan, Das. *India Unbound.* New York: Knopf, 2001.

Hadar, Leon T. "Pakistan in America's War against Terrorism: Strategic Ally or Unreliable Client?" Cato Institute Policy Analysis no. 436, May 8, 2002.

Kux, Dennis. *The United States and Pakistan, 1947–2000.* Baltimore: Johns Hopkins University Press, 2001.

Maynes, Charles William. "America Discovers Central Asia." *Foreign Affairs* 82, no. 2 (March–April 2003): 120–32.

Merry, E. Wayne. "Governance in Central Asia: National in Form, Soviet in Content." *Cambridge Review of International Affairs* 17, no. 2 (2004): 285–300.

Olcott, Martha Brill. "Taking Stock of Central Asia." *Journal of International Affairs* 56, no. 2 (Spring 2003): 3–17.

Wishnick, Elizabeth. "Strategic Consequences of the Iraq War: U.S. Security Interests in Central Asia Reassessed." Strategic Studies Institute Monograph, May 2004.

—Prepared by Leon T. Hadar

60. The International War on Drugs

Policymakers should

- terminate Plan Colombia and other expensive, counterproductive anti-drug programs in the Andean region of South America;
- not allow anti-drug efforts in Afghanistan to interfere with the far more important effort to destroy the Taliban and Al Qaeda;
- recognize that prohibition creates a huge black-market premium and potential profit from drug trafficking that terrorist groups will exploit;
- remove U.S. trade barriers to the products of developing countries; and
- declare an end to the international war on drugs and assure foreign governments that the United States will no longer pressure them to wage war on their own populations.

Washington's international drug control campaign exhibits every flaw inherent in central planning. The war on drugs—a program whose budget has more than quadrupled over the past 15 years—has failed remarkably in all aspects of its overseas mission. Most telling, illicit drugs continue to flow across U.S. borders, unaffected by the more than $40 billion Washington has spent since 1981 in its supply-side campaign. The purity of cocaine and heroin, moreover, has increased, while the prices of those drugs have fallen dramatically during the same period.

The U.S. government has not only compounded the domestic social problem of drug abuse by treating narcotics use as a criminal offense; it has intruded into the complex social settings of dozens of countries around the globe by pressuring foreign governments to adopt laws and policies of its liking. In the process, the U.S.-led war on drugs has severely exacerbated the political and economic problems of drug-source nations and increased financing for terrorist groups. Counternarcotics strategy thus conflicts with sound foreign policy goals, namely the encouragement of free markets, democracy, and peace. For countless reasons, the international drug war is both undesirable and unwinnable.

Failure on Multiple Fronts

One component of the supply-side campaign has been interdiction of drug traffic coming into the United States. That approach has been ineffective at reducing the availability of cocaine and heroin because authorities seize only 5 to 15 percent of drug imports and because traffickers easily adapt to such disruptions by using new smuggling innovations and routes. In an implicit recognition of the failure of interdiction efforts, Washington has increasingly favored strategies that focus on drug-producing countries. Yet there is little reason to believe that an approach that emphasizes eradication, crop-substitution, and interdiction efforts in drug-source countries will be more successful than interdiction of drugs along transit routes. A reason that supply reduction efforts cannot be expected to affect the use of cocaine, for example, lies in the price structure of the illicit drug industry. Smuggling costs make up only 10 percent of the final value of cocaine in the United States. Those costs, combined with all other production costs outside the United States, account for only 13 percent of cocaine's retail price. Drug traffickers thus have every incentive to continue bringing their product to market; they view eradication and interdiction as a mere cost of doing business. Moreover, even if such efforts were successful at raising the price of coca paste or cocaine in drug-source countries, their effect on the final price of cocaine in the United States would be negligible. As analyst Kevin Jack Riley has observed, "Using source country price increases to create domestic scarcities is similar to attempting to raise glass prices by pushing sand back into the sea."

The efforts of international drug warriors are also routinely frustrated by drug traffickers' dynamic responses to counternarcotics policies. Already expecting interference in their business, traffickers build redundant processing facilities in case current ones are destroyed and stockpile their product inside the United States in case of smuggling interruptions. The massive resources available to the $300 billion global illicit drug industry also enable it to react to counternarcotics strategies with ease. At best, drug war "victories" are ephemeral as the industry accommodates itself to new conditions. That situation has reduced U.S. officials to citing drug seizure figures or expressions of political will by foreign governments as important gains in the U.S.-orchestrated war on drugs.

The evidence from the field is more sobering. According to the State Department's annual International Narcotics Control Strategy Report, the total area planted in coca increased from 176,000 hectares in 1987 to more than 200,000 hectares in 2003. The area planted in opium poppy, mostly in southwest and southeast Asia, increased from 112,585 hectares to more than 140,000 hectares during the same period. Moreover, those figures do not reveal important qualitative information—for example, the destruction of less productive older plants and the cultivation of new, more productive plants.

Indeed, the State Department's estimates of net production of illicit drug crops illustrate the futility of its overseas campaign. From 1987 to 2003, opium production did not surge dramatically. Yet as the State Department once conceded, the quantity of opium available was "more than enough to supply global heroin demand many times over."

A similar situation exists with respect to cocaine. Despite more than $3.3 billion spent on Plan Colombia over the past four years, the supply of cocaine on America's streets remains plentiful. Indeed, John Walters, the White House drug czar, conceded in August 2004 that Plan Colombia had not yet had any significant impact on the amount of cocaine coming out of that country.

Despite increased eradication efforts—the U.S. government pressures source-country governments to eliminate drug crops by spraying pesticides, slashing illegal plants, or burning peasants' fields—farmers still view illegal drug cultivation as advantageous. Less coercive schemes have also been tried. Crop-substitution and alternative development programs, for example, seek to encourage peasants to join the legal market in agriculture or other sectors. U.S. aid finances infrastructure projects, such as roads and bridges, and subsidizes the cultivation of legal agricultural goods, such as coffee and corn.

Here, too, serious obstacles and unintended consequences undermine the best-laid plans of Washington and the governments of drug-source countries. Coca plants, for example, grow in areas and under conditions that are thoroughly inhospitable to legal crops, making a switch to legal alternatives unrealistic. (For example only 5 to 10 percent of the major coca-growing regions in Peru and Bolivia may be suitable for legal crops.)

Farmers can also earn far higher returns from illicit plants than from the alternatives. For that reason, even when they enter crop-substitution programs, peasants often continue to grow drug plants in other areas. Ironically, in such cases, the U.S. government subsidizes the production of illegal drugs.

Indeed, programs that pay peasants not to produce coca and other drug crops can have effects policymakers did not anticipate. As analysts Patrick Clawson and Rensselaer Lee point out: "The voluntary programs are similar to the crop acreage reduction program that the U.S. government uses to raise the income of wheat farmers. It is not clear why Washington thinks that a crop reduction program raises the income of Midwest wheat farmers but lowers the income of Andean coca farmers. In fact, in both cases, the crop reduction program really is a price support program that can raise farmers' income."

The illicit drug trade also benefits from improved infrastructure. One World Bank report on road projects in coca-growing regions in Peru concluded, "While the roads were useful in expanding coca production, they have severely hampered the development of legal activities." It is interesting to note that the major coca-growing regions in Peru and Bolivia—the Upper Huallaga Valley and the Chapare, respectively—were sites of major U.S.-funded development projects in previous decades.

Finally, even if alternative development programs were able to raise the prices of legal crops so that they exceeded or were at least competitive with the price paid for illegal crops, that situation could not last. The cost of growing coca, for example, represents such a small fraction of the final value of cocaine—less than 1 percent—that the illicit drug industry will always be able to pay farmers more than the subsidized alternatives could command.

U.S. Policy Is Not Just Ineffective

Efforts to "get tough" on drug-producing nations have caused an increase in violence and corruption, distorted economies, and undermined fragile democratic governments and the institutions of civil society. As long as drugs remain outside the legal framework of the market and U.S. demand continues, the enormous profit potential that results not only makes eliminating the industry impossible but makes attempts to do so thoroughly destructive.

It is Washington's prohibition strategy—and not the narcotics trade per se—that is responsible for the problems usually associated with drug trafficking. Colombia, the principal target of Washington's international drug control campaign, has over the years seen its judicial, legislative, and executive branches become corrupted by the drug trade. Crackdowns on leading trafficking organizations have produced widespread violence and even dismantled cartels, but they have not affected the country's illicit export performance.

Colombia's efforts to convince the United States that it wishes to cooperate in the fight against narcotics have led Bogotá to undertake coca eradication and other counternarcotic initiatives. Those initiatives have created resentment among peasant populations, who have consequently increased their support of major guerrilla groups and have reinforced the business relationship between drug traffickers and the rebels who protect illicit drug operations. Indeed, Colombia's various guerrilla organizations earn anywhere from $100 million to $500 million a year from drug-related activities.

The U.S.-orchestrated drug war in Colombia and elsewhere has weakened the rule of law and the institutions of civil society and financed terrorism. In Peru, for example, the Maoist Shining Path guerrillas received up to $100 million per year during the 1980s from their marriage of convenience with drug traffickers. That situation prompted Harvard economist Robert Barro to suggest that "the U.S. government could achieve pretty much the same results if it gave the aid money directly to the terrorists."

The crippling of the Shining Path came only after the Peruvian government suspended coca plant eradication programs and concentrated its efforts on anti-terrorist activities and market liberalization. U.S. efforts to get tough on Peru in recent years may compromise those successes. The resumption of coca eradication and other traditional anti-narcotics measures is worrisome in a country that has recently experienced political instability, the return of populist rhetoric, and outbursts of terrorist violence.

Washington's heavy-handed ways have been evident in Bolivia as well. The livelihood of thousands of coca growers in the Chapare region has been wiped out by years of a vigorous, U.S.-backed coca eradication campaign that has not managed to provide the farmers with alternative sources of income. The result has not only been an increase in social unrest; the eradication program has led to the rise of Evo Morales, an anti-American, anti–free market political leader representing the grievances of the dispossessed farmers. In the presidential elections of June 2002, Morales came in a close second. The populist candidate received a further boost from Washington shortly before the elections when the U.S. ambassador warned Bolivians not to vote for Morales, a message that had the opposite effect. The resulting elections gave Morales's party control of the largest bloc in congress—a factor that contributed significantly to market-liberal President Gonzalo Sánchez de Losada's decision to flee Bolivia in the fall of 2003 in the face of anti-government protests.

Mexico provides another urgent warning to leaders of Washington's anti-narcotics crusade. Major Mexican drug cartels gained strength and influence as the U.S.-led interdiction campaign in the Caribbean, which began in the mid-1980s, rerouted narcotics traffic through Mexico. Unfortunately, the result has been a sort of "Colombianization" of Mexico, where drug-related violence has since increased. President Vicente Fox's arrest of hundreds of police officers on drug-related charges is only the latest confirmation that the illicit industry has managed to corrupt government officials at all levels.

Mexico afflicted by drug-related violence has serious implications for the United States. If Mexico eventually experienced the level of social violence and volatility seen in Colombia or Peru, for instance, the United States would be directly affected—a development that would almost certainly provoke Washington's increased involvement in Mexico's complex domestic affairs.

Washington has not only created severe difficulties for drug-producing nations, its drug control efforts have helped disperse the narcotics industry to countries that might otherwise have avoided such penetration. Venezuela, Ecuador, Argentina, and Brazil, for example, have seen an upsurge in drug-related activity. Similarly, international disruptions in the various stages of illicit drug production have encouraged local traffickers to be self-sufficient in all stages of production. For example, the crackdown on Colombia's Cali cartel, which temporarily depressed coca prices in Peru in the 1990s, prompted the Peruvian industry to enter more advanced stages of cocaine production. More dramatic, while supply reduction initiatives have temporarily reduced coca production in Peru and Bolivia, those efforts have resulted in a more than 150 percent increase in coca cultivation in Colombia over the past decade, making it the world's largest producer of the crop.

The Drug War in Afghanistan: A Dangerous Distraction

Latin American societies are not the only ones threatened by the global prohibition model. The war on drugs is interfering with the U.S. effort to destroy Al Qaeda and the Taliban in Afghanistan. That country has been one of the leading sources of opium poppies–and therefore heroin—for many years. Indeed, there has been a steady upward trend in opium production for more than two decades. The only significant interruption to that trend occurred in 2001 following an edict by the Taliban regime banning opium cultivation on pain of death. (Taliban leaders had an ulterior motive for that move. They had previously stockpiled large quantities of opium and wanted to create a temporary scarcity to drive up prices and fill the regime's coffers with additional revenue.) Today, Afghanistan accounts for nearly 75 percent of the world's opium supply.

During the long civil war between the Taliban and the Northern Alliance, both sides were extensively involved in the drug trade. Since U.S. forces and their Northern Alliance allies overthrew the Taliban in late 2001 and drove Al Qaeda operatives into neighboring Pakistan, drug commerce has been even more prominent. The trade now amounts to approximately $2.3 billion, nearly half of the impoverished country's annual gross domestic product. Some 264,000 families are estimated to be involved in growing opium poppies. For many of them, that crop is the difference between modest prosperity and destitution.

Unfortunately, during 2004 the U.S. government increased pressure on the fragile government of President Hamid Karzai to crack down on drug crop cultivation. In August of that year, Secretary of Defense Donald Rumsfeld also ordered American military forces in Afghanistan to make drug eradication a high priority.

Those moves are a big mistake. The Taliban and their Al Qaeda allies have already shown a resurgence in Afghanistan. If zealous American drug warriors alienate tens of thousands of Afghan farmers, the Karzai government's hold on power could become even more precarious than it is now. Washington would then face the unpalatable choice of letting radical Islamists regain power or sending more U.S. troops to suppress the insurgency.

U.S. officials need to keep their priorities straight. Our mortal enemy is Al Qaeda and the Taliban regime that made Afghanistan into a sanctuary for that terrorist organization. The drug war is a dangerous distraction in the campaign to destroy those forces. U.S. officials should look the other way regarding the drug activities of Afghan farmers. Washington should stop putting pressure on the Afghan government to pursue crop eradication programs and should not make U.S. soldiers into anti-drug crusaders. Even those policymakers who oppose ending the war on drugs ought to recognize that, in this case, the war against radical Islamic terrorism must take priority.

Toward a Constructive Approach

Washington's international drug war has failed by every measure. Production of drugs in foreign countries has increased, and the flow of drugs

605

to the United States has continued. The Council on Foreign Relations notes, "For twenty years, these programs have done little more than rearrange the map of drug production and trafficking." In fact, the impact of U.S. narcotics control policies is even worse, severely aggravating political, economic, and social problems in developing countries. Attempts to escalate the drug war, even in a dramatic way, will do little to change those realities.

Similarly, a more multilateral approach to fighting the drug war—through the United Nations or the Organization of American States, for example—will not work. Involving more governments and bureaucracies may marginally deflect political criticism away from the United States, but that approach cannot solve the fundamental problems created by prohibition: corruption, political violence, the destruction of civil society, the distortion of economic activity, and increased financing of terrorism. The multilateral strategy will have especially low credibility if international organizations present wildly unrealistic solutions, such as the UN's 1998 plan to eliminate global drug production in 10 years.

Washington should instead encourage the worldwide shift away from statism toward the creation of markets and civil society by ending its international crusade against drugs and opening its markets to drug-source countries' legal goods. Doing so will hardly affect U.S. drug consumption, but it would at least be a recognition that narcotics abuse is a domestic social problem that foreign policy cannot solve.

Suggested Readings

Bandow, Doug. "Afghanistan: Opium Market to the World." *Chronicles*, July 2004.

Carpenter, Ted Galen. *Bad Neighbor Policy: Washington's Futile War on Drugs in Latin America.* New York: Palgrave/Macmillan, 2003.

———. "Ending the International Drug War." In *How To Legalize Drugs,* edited by Jefferson M. Fish. Northvale, NJ: Jason Aronson, 1998.

———. "How the Drug War in Afghanistan Undermines America's War on Terror." Cato Institute Foreign Policy Briefing no. 84, November 10, 2004.

Clawson, Patrick L., and Rensselaer Lee III. *The Andean Cocaine Industry.* New York: St. Martin's, 1996.

Council on Foreign Relations. *Rethinking International Drug Control: New Directions for U.S. Policy.* New York: Council on Foreign Relations, 1997.

Riley, Kevin Jack. *Snow Job? The War against International Cocaine Trafficking.* New Brunswick, NJ: Transaction, 1996.

Thoumi, Francisco. *Political Economy and Illegal Drugs in Colombia.* Boulder, CO: Lynne Reinner, 1995.

—Prepared by Ted Galen Carpenter and Ian Vásquez

61. Relations with China

Policymakers should

- treat China as a normal great power, not as a "strategic partner" or a probable adversary;
- continue to liberalize U.S.-Chinese relations and hold China to its World Trade Organization commitments;
- avoid imposing economic sanctions against China even for narrowly defined objectives, since such measures will undermine permanent normal trade relations (PNTR);
- support Taiwan's requests to purchase defensive weapons systems but warn Taiwan that the United States will not defend the island with U.S. forces; and
- recognize that advancing economic freedom in China has had positive effects on civil society and personal freedom for the Chinese people.

Constructive Partner or Emerging Threat?

U.S.-Chinese relations have become increasingly unpredictable. During the late 1990s both governments spoke of a "strategic partnership" and sought ways to enhance already substantial economic and political ties. The bombing of the Chinese embassy in Belgrade, the release of the Cox report alleging systematic nuclear espionage by the People's Republic of China, and the forced landing of a U.S. spy plane on Hainan Island produced a new round of tensions. For a time, the Bush administration described the PRC as a strategic competitor, and the United States increased arms sales to Taiwan. In the last two years tensions have again receded, marked by China's membership in the World Trade Organization and by cooperation between Beijing and Washington in the war against terrorism.

But, as the periodic reports by the U.S.-China Economic and Security Review Commission (also known as the U.S.-China Commission) and the Pentagon illustrate, there is a deep concern that China will be an increasing threat to U.S. global economic and military power. The Pentagon's recent report on China's military modernization efforts highlights the point that some members of the policy community worry about China's future capabilities and intentions.

It would be a major mistake to backslide from a policy of engagement into one of containment and to treat China as an adversary rather than as a normal great power. Managing relations with China and avoiding the extremes of confrontation or wishful thinking will be one of the key challenges facing U.S. policymakers in the next decade.

China's economy has grown precisely because Beijing has allowed greater economic freedom. Between 1980 and 2002 China's economic freedom rating increased from 3.8 to 5.7 (with 10 being the highest score), according to the *Economic Freedom of the Word 2004 Annual Report*. The rise would be even more impressive, however, if one focused on the coastal provinces, such as Fujian, Guangdong, and Zhejiang, which are highly market oriented. Moreover, the current index score of 5.7 does not recognize the liberalization that has occurred in China since 2002, including the recent amendment to the constitution that gives greater protection to private property rights.

Trade liberalization has linked China to the international price system, dramatically increased per capita incomes, and provided the Chinese people with new opportunities. In contrast to 1978, when the central government had tight control over foreign trading rights, today virtually all firms are free to import and export.

The growth of China's foreign trade has been breathtaking. In 1978 the total value of Chinese imports and exports amounted to only $20.6 billion. By the end of 2003 their value had increased to $851.2 billion (Figure 61.1)—nearly 62 percent of GDP—making China one of the most open economies in the world.

Protectionists in the United States who point to large and growing trade deficits with China and to increased U.S. investment in China should not be allowed to block trade liberalization by injudicious use of national security and human rights arguments. Further liberalization of U.S.-Chinese trade is a win-win strategy and can play an important role in promoting peace, prosperity, and improved human rights. Containment would do the opposite (just ask the North Koreans).

Figure 61.1
China's Opening to the Outside World

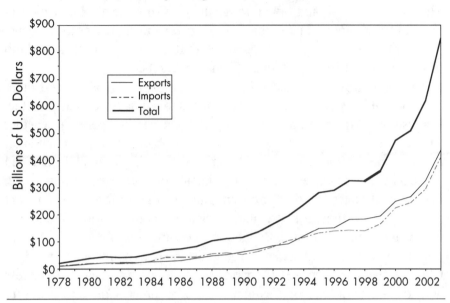

SOURCE: PRC General Administration of Customs, *China's Customs Statistics*.

The U.S.-China Commission's 2002 report, "The National Security Implications of the Economic Relationship between the United States and China," offered more than 40 recommendations, many of which implicitly assume that China is a threat to U.S. economic and military power. The 2004 report, however, dropped many of the more onerous recommendations, such as the creation of a "federally mandated corporate reporting system" designed to force U.S. firms doing business in China to provide extensive data on all their business activities, even those that have no significant impact on national security. Nevertheless, the latest report continues to perceive the large U.S. trade deficit with China—a record $124 billion in 2003—as a threat to the U.S. economy, especially to the manufacturing sector, and hence to national security.

The main premise of the 2004 report, like the earlier report, is that economic liberalization has not led to political change or to greater openness and that China's rapid growth poses a danger to U.S. security. To counter that threat, the commission favors restricting access to U.S. capital markets, invoking WTO safeguards to limit imports of selected manufactured goods such as textiles, and pressuring China to revalue its currency.

609

China should be given ample time to meet its obligations to the WTO and to the United States under the 1999 bilateral market access agreement. The United States should work through the WTO dispute resolution mechanism and target specific cases that are *significant* rather than try to prosecute *every* infraction of the trade agreement. It is in the interests of both Washington and Beijing to open China's markets.

The United States should follow the lead of New Zealand and other countries and extend market economy status to China as soon as possible. The use of production costs in surrogate countries to determine whether China sold at below ''cost'' is highly questionable. Indeed, the nonmarket economy methodology used in antidumping cases is grossly defective and prevents China from realizing its legitimate comparative cost advantage. (The United States and the European Union recognize Russia as a market economy, even though that country began economic reform much later than China and has a lower economic freedom rating.)

Policymakers should not let protectionist interests dominate future U.S.-Chinese relations. The USCC reports send the wrong signal to Congress and to China. Instead of seeing China as a threat, Congress needs to cooperate with China in ways that are mutually beneficial. It is in China's interest to deepen and extend economic reform by opening its capital markets and allowing full convertibility of the yuan. The threat of U.S. sanctions if China fails to do so will only antagonize China and harm U.S.-Chinese relations.

Continued trade liberalization and engagement on a number of fronts, including a more liberal visa policy that permits Chinese students to study in the United States, especially law, economics, and the humanities, will have positive long-term benefits. Visa procedures should be reexamined. So long as individuals pose no threat to our national security, they should be encouraged to learn about our free society firsthand. Free trade can help normalize China and transform it into a modern economy and a civil society under the rule of law. Backsliding into protectionism cannot.

Both the USCC and the Pentagon reports imply that as China grows wealthier its military spending will increase to the detriment of the United States and our Asian allies. That danger cannot be overlooked, but the probability is small compared with the likelihood that, as the nonstate sector in China grows, the Chinese Communist Party will lose power and political reform will ensue.

China is a normal, albeit sometimes difficult, rising great power. China's behavior can sometimes pose challenges, but the country is not a dangerous threat to U.S. security. China's military spending is a tiny fraction of U.S. defense spending. It will take decades before China can even come close to current U.S. spending levels. (China officially spends $25 billion on defense, but the actual figure is $50–70 billion. In contrast, U.S. defense spending for fiscal year 2005 is more than $417 billion.) China's weapons systems are no match for those of the United States—although China is making a serious effort to modernize its armed forces.

The Taiwan Question

The most serious potential flashpoint in relations between the United States and China involves the status of Taiwan. China is primarily concerned with its domestic stability and with Taiwan's ultimate return to the motherland. The United States should insist that China use peaceful means to settle the Taiwan question. Despite Beijing's objections, the United States should remain willing to sell Taiwan the weapons it needs for its own defense. However, policymakers should reject proposals to extend diplomatic recognition to an independent Taiwan or to significantly increase official contacts between the U.S. and Taiwanese governments. Such measures would only provoke the PRC and strengthen hardliners in Beijing. Under no circumstances should the United States intervene with its armed forces to defend Taiwan from the PRC. Such a war would be enormously dangerous and would, at the very least, poison U.S.-Chinese relations for decades.

The best available means of bringing about a peaceful resolution to the Taiwan issue is to further liberalize trade relations between the mainland and Taiwan. During the past 10 years, Taiwan has committed more than $80 billion to Chinese projects and now ranks as the fifth-largest foreign investor in China. Taiwanese investors have a strong incentive to maintain peace to increase their own prosperity. Likewise, they have an incentive to have direct trade, transport, and postal links with the mainland. The sooner those links are established, the better the chance for a cooperative solution to the Taiwan question. U.S. policymakers should recognize that reality.

As a free society, Taiwan obviously has no incentive to become part of the PRC at this time. But if liberal economic policies on both sides of the strait continue, then China may undergo the quiet revolution that has occurred on the island. In that case, a peaceful solution to the Taiwan question could be realized. U.S. policymakers should foster that process.

Taiwan's accession to the WTO, following in China's footsteps, is a positive development that offers hope for the future.

Forging a Constructive Relationship

The dark side of the Chinese communist state is disturbing and must not be ignored. But that unsavory record should not be allowed to hide the progress that the Chinese people have made since economic reforms began in 1978. Increased trade has promoted the growth of markets relative to state planning, given millions of people new opportunities, and substantially raised living standards, especially in the coastal cities where economic liberalization has advanced the most. The primary goal of U.S. foreign policy should be to further the liberalization trend in China by maintaining a cooperative, constructive relationship. The most direct means of achieving that goal is closer trade ties.

China has benefited most not from Western aid but from trade. As Ma Yu, a senior research fellow of the Chinese Academy of International Trade and Economic Cooperation, recently wrote in the *China Daily's Business Weekly*, "The root cause of China's high-speed economic growth . . . is the policy of reform and opening-up." Policymakers should not take any actions that would stall that process.

The challenge for the United States is to exploit opportunities for further gains from trade and move closer to a constructive partnership with the PRC—but at the same time protect vital U.S. interests. Unfortunately, U.S. policy is drifting toward confrontation, as witnessed, in particular, by the USCC and Pentagon reports. That strategy risks creating a self-fulfilling prophecy that China will become an enemy. Indeed, a growing chorus in Congress and the U.S. foreign policy community argues that the PRC is a belligerent dictatorship and an implacable future enemy of the United States.

Painting China as an economic and military adversary is dangerous and misguided. Free trade is mutually beneficial—both China and other countries gain from trade liberalization. There is no doubt that, as the Chinese economy grows, so will the Chinese military budget. But that is not unusual for a large nation-state, and thus far China's military spending and its military modernization effort have been relatively modest.

It is true that no one can be certain how the PRC will behave on security issues in the future. Unlike Nazi Germany or the Soviet Union, however, the PRC is not a messianic, expansionist power; it is a normal rising (or reawakening) great power. At times, that can be difficult for other countries to deal with, but such a country does not pose a malignant security threat.

Proceed with Caution

The best course is to treat China as a normal (albeit sometimes repressive and prickly) great power but avoid the extremes of viewing the PRC as either enemy or strategic partner. The United States would also be wise to encourage other major countries in Asia to think more seriously about how they intend to deal with a rising China. A collection of diffident, militarily weak neighbors, wholly dependent on the United States for protection, is not likely to cause Beijing to behave cautiously.

Beijing's behavior toward regional neighbors has been a curious mixture of conciliation and abrasiveness. Examples of conciliation include efforts to dampen the border disputes with such important land neighbors as India, Vietnam, Russia, and Kazakhstan and a campaign to build close political and economic ties with South Korea. The PRC has also been helpful in trying to discourage the North Korean regime from pursuing nuclear weapons and ballistic missile programs and has facilitated multilateral negotiations on the North Korean nuclear crisis. At the same time, China's relations with Japan, the Philippines, and some other oceanic neighbors are less friendly, and Beijing still pushes its territorial claims in the South China Sea.

Taiwan remains an especially dangerous flashpoint. Any move toward formal independence by Taipei would surely provoke military action by Beijing. Yet China's economic future depends strongly on Taiwan's prosperity, so military action is likely seen as a last resort. The reelection of Taiwanese president Chen Shui-bian has agitated Beijing, and there is growing evidence that the PRC's patience on the reunification issue is beginning to wear thin. That is a matter of concern, but the top priority of the United States should be to stay out of a PRC-Taiwan armed conflict if one should erupt. Beyond that, the United States should take no position on the question of reunification.

China's Changing Tide

Economic liberalization has put cracks in the edifice of the Chinese state. Individuals have more personal space than they did before the growth of the nonstate sector, and a nascent civil society is developing outside of political society. Politics does not dominate everyday life as it did during the Cultural Revolution. As Wang Dan, one of the leaders of the 1989 democracy movement, wrote in the *Asian Wall Street Journal* (May 31, 2004): "Since the early 1990s, shoots of civil society have begun to sprout within China. As more Chinese enter the private sector, the state is no longer able to control every aspect of daily life in the way it used to."

Whether China will go all the way to a true free-market system remains highly uncertain. Private property and capitalism are a threat to the survival of the Chinese Communist Party. To help China make the transition to a more open society, the United States needs a clear, realistic, and prudent foreign policy toward the PRC. Instead of painting China as a serious threat one day and as a de facto strategic ally the next, the United States needs to formulate a balanced view consistent with our own principles— a view that recognizes our long-term interest in engaging China and at the same time protects our national security. The PRC's claims to the South China Sea Islands and its relations with Japan and Taiwan must be viewed from that perspective.

It is also important to consider the future of economic, political, and social reform in China and how that future may be shaped by the liberal influence of Hong Kong and Taiwan. Will freedom spill over from those more open societies to the mainland, or will Chinese communism slowly corrupt the rule of law and weaken the free market in Hong Kong and seek to absorb and subordinate Taiwan?

Ultimately, the creation of real as opposed to pseudo markets in China will require the full recognition of private property rights. The 1999 amendment to Article 11 of the PRC Constitution, which places the nonstate sector and private enterprise on a par with state-owned enterprises, is a step in that direction, as is the March 2004 amendment to Article 13 that makes "the lawful private property of citizens inviolable." Moreover, for the first time, the PRC Constitution (Art. 33) explicitly mentions human rights: "The state respects and protects human rights."

But, like all rights in the constitution, they lack any credible enforcement mechanism. There is no independent judiciary or high-level constitutional commission to safeguard either persons or property. And although the National People's Congress Standing Committee has now established a low-level working group to investigate some breaches of the constitution, this body will be unable to have any real impact as long as the CCP maintains its monopoly on power.

Without further constitutional and political reform that places rights to life, liberty, and property above the party, and allows for both economic and political freedom, there can be no certainty of ownership.

Constitutional Provisions to Protect Property Rights

- "The state protects the lawful rights and interests of the private sector" (Art. 11, sec. 2).
- "The lawful private property of citizens is inviolable" (Art. 13).
- "The state respects and protects human rights" (Art. 33, sec. 3).

Every step in the direction of greater economic freedom will provide further opportunities for the Chinese people to enlarge their private space and shrink the relative size of the state. Pressures will then build for greater social and political freedom.

Liu Junning, an independent scholar in Beijing, gave the best concise answer to the question of whether China will be a constructive partner or an emerging threat. In his view, the answer will "depend, to a very great extent, on the fate of liberalism in China: a liberal China will be a constructive partner; a nationalistic and authoritarian China will be an emerging threat." America must prepare for both possibilities, but its policies should avoid needless snubs and provocations that would undermine the prospect for the emergence of a democratic, peaceful China.

Recommended Readings

Carpenter, Ted Galen. "Going Too Far: Bush's Pledge to Defend Taiwan." Cato Institute Foreign Policy Briefing no. 66, May 30, 2001.

———. "Let Taiwan Defend Itself." Cato Institute Policy Analysis no. 313, August 24, 1998.

———. "Managing a Great Power Relationship: The United States, China and East Asian Security." *Journal of Strategic Studies* 21, no. 1 (March 1998).

———. "President Bush's Muddled Policy on Taiwan." Cato Institute Foreign Policy Briefing no. 82, March 15, 2004.

———. "Roiling Asia: U.S. Coziness with China Upsets the Neighbors." *Foreign Affairs* 77, no. 6 (November–December 1998).

Carpenter, Ted Galen, and James A. Dorn, eds. *China's Future: Constructive Partner or Emerging Threat?* Washington: Cato Institute, 2000.

Dorn, James A. "China's Future: Market Socialism or Market Taoism?" *Cato Journal* 18, no. 1 (Spring–Summer 1998): 131–46.

———. "China's Future Depends upon Protecting Rights." *Asian Wall Street Journal*, July 19, 2004.

———. "Trade and Human Rights: The Case of China." *Cato Journal* 16 (Spring–Summer 1996).

Dorn, James A., ed. *China in the New Millennium: Market Reforms and Social Development*. Washington: Cato Institute, 1998.

Eland, Ivan. "Is Chinese Military Modernization a Threat to the United States?" Cato Institute Policy Analysis no. 465, January 23, 2003.

Gries, Peter Hays. *China's New Nationalism: Pride, Politics and Diplomacy.* Berkeley: University of California Press, 2004.

Kristof, Nicholas D., and Sheryl Wudunn. *China Wakes: The Struggle for the Soul of a Rising Power.* New York: Times Books, 1994.

Lampton, David M., ed. *The Making of Chinese Foreign and Security Policy in the Era of Reform, 1978–2000.* Stanford, CA.: Stanford University Press, 2001.

Lardy, Nicholas R. *Integrating China into the Global Economy.* Washington: Brookings Institution Press, 2002.

Lindsey, Brink, and Daniel J. Ikenson. *Antidumping Exposed: The Devilish Details of Unfair Trade Law.* Washington: Cato Institute, 2003.

Vogel, Ezra F., ed. *Living with China: U.S.-China Relations in the Twenty-first Century.* New York: Norton, 1997.

—Prepared by Ted Galen Carpenter and James A. Dorn

62. Relations with Russia

Policymakers should

- monitor closely the growing strategic ties between Russia and other major Eurasian powers,
- insist on a strong legislative role in U.S.-Russian diplomacy to set a good example for the fragile Russian democracy,
- not base U.S.-Russian relations exclusively on personal ties with Russian president Vladimir Putin,
- ensure that the United States does not make security promises to the nations of Eastern Europe or Central Asia that it might not be able to fulfill, and
- emphasize America's common interests with Russia in fighting terrorism and preventing the proliferation of weapons of mass destruction.

The "honeymoon" of the immediate post–Cold War period is over. It was undermined by U.S. policies originally undertaken to contain and ultimately destroy Soviet power. Ironically, the United States now finds itself allied with Russia to defeat the very same forces Washington helped to unleash during the Cold War —specifically, radical Islamists. But this post–Cold War alliance is built on shaky foundations, without popular enthusiasm or significant institutional underpinning.

The collapse of Soviet power meant that the centrality of Russia to the United States would be diminished. Indeed, it would hardly be an exaggeration to say that Russia went from being a rival to a supplicant. Russians looked to America as a model for their aspirations, and they welcomed the prospect of American assistance in their transformation to capitalism and democracy. But their hopes were disappointed, and their attitude has changed as a result. "The attitude to the U.S. has dramatically worsened," Yuri Levada, one of Russia's leading pollsters, reported in

April 2003. Nevertheless, he was careful to add that this applied to our country and its policies, not to the American people, implying that the deterioration is not irreversible.

The turnabout in Russian opinion has been accompanied by a transformation in Russia's position in the world. When Vladimir Putin ascended to the presidency, he took over a country still recovering from a wrenching economic crisis and whose international position was just a shadow of its former one. Putin has done a remarkable job of stabilizing the economy (aided by a significant increase in oil prices). A banking crisis in the summer of 2004 was an uncomfortable echo of the past, however, indicating that underlying problems remain. Internationally, Putin has successfully used Russia's geographic position, its permanent seat on the United Nations Security Council, and its still-extensive defense industry to make Russia the indispensable Eurasian nation—one that other leaders, including President Bush, feel they must cultivate.

Domestically, Putin has consolidated power relentlessly, particularly since the horrific acts of terrorism in Beslan, and elsewhere in Russia, in August and September 2004. He has, quite simply, crushed all his opponents. To be sure, as a result of the democratic transformation of Russia, he may still be the focus of public criticism, especially in some of the media—but that is not the same thing as effective political opposition. He is, for all intents and purposes, Russia's new tsar, albeit an elected one.

President Bush has tried to forge a strong personal relationship with Putin. Although there have been disappointments—not surprisingly, since state interests typically override personal ties—the effort cannot be faulted. The presence of Mikhail Gorbachev at Ronald Reagan's funeral and his gracious tribute to both the late president and his widow testify to the importance that personal relations can play in resolving even the most intractable disputes.

Such efforts based on personal friendships must be put on a realistic footing, however. The *Washington Post* reported that President Bush was impressed that Putin treasures a cross given him by his mother. It is understandable that President Bush, deeply religious himself, felt a bond to someone who shares a religious conviction, even if it is of another faith. Yet we must be mindful of the overture President Reagan made to the Iranian leadership on religious premises, which ended dismally.

Russia's Identity

As is the case for many European countries, Russia's identity as a state is tied to a religion. Since the beginning of the 17th century, Russian tsars had been baptized exclusively in the Orthodox faith. Following the Bolshevik takeover in 1917, Russia became officially atheist, but religion remained a strong force among the people. Following the collapse of Soviet power, the Orthodox Church was allowed to practice openly once again. The reconstruction in the 1990s of the Church of Christ the Savior in Moscow, which had been destroyed by Stalin, is a testament to Russia's change of direction.

In recent years, especially, there have been growing ties between the church and the state. When Putin met with Russian oligarchs in the Kremlin in 2004, television cameras focused on an icon of an Orthodox saint behind him—an image that replaced the portrait of Lenin from Soviet times. According to the *Moscow Times,* "The central focus that the icon has acquired in the Kremlin's official imagery also points to the essence of the Kremlin's new ideology in which Russian Orthodoxy, as the antithesis of Soviet internationalism, is becoming key."

Samuel Huntington identified the boundary between Orthodox and Protestant/Catholic Europe as one of the areas where different civilizations might clash. The expansion of NATO and the European Union will define the boundaries of Europe, and therefore will have an effect on the formation of Russian identity (and also that of countries adjacent to Russia). Significantly the EU dividing line closely follows Huntington's civilizational divide, but if it were to follow that divide completely, it would split Ukraine in two. The breakup of Yugoslavia along sectarian lines is an ominous reminder of where such divisions can lead if they are not addressed properly.

The Orthodox Church suffered terribly under Soviet rule—it is estimated that 200,000 people lost their lives because of their religious convictions. The ability of believers to practice their religion without fear of persecution is one of the great benefits of the collapse of communism. It would be doubly tragic, therefore, if the fall of the Berlin Wall and the end of the communist-capitalist divide were to be followed by the reemergence of an age-old religious divide. Unfortunately, there are indications of a struggle for influence in the region surrounding Russia—what the Russians call the "near abroad"—that has overtones of long-simmering historical tensions.

Russia and Its Neighbors

When the Cold War ended, Russia effectively abandoned the idea of global competition with the United States. It withdrew from many of its foreign bases, which had become too expensive to maintain. In recent years, however, it has intensified an effort to reintegrate the Commonwealth of Independent States (the 12 non-Baltic states that formerly were part of the Soviet Union). Putin himself underlined the importance of this effort in a speech to his Security Council in July 2004:

> I believe that we have approached a decisive moment in the development of the Commonwealth. Basically, there is only one choice: either we essentially strengthen the CIS, and create a working, globally influential regional structure, or this geopolitical area will inevitably erode and, as a result, will lose any attractiveness for its member states. The latter scenario may not take place. Russia's role in increasing the influence and authority of the CIS is today extremely important.

For the United States there would appear to be two primary areas of concern. One—already noted—is Ukraine (and to a lesser degree, Belarus). There has been the appearance, at least, of a tug of war between Russia and the United States over Ukraine. For example, when Ukrainian president Leonid Kuchma said in July 2004 that Ukraine would attempt to ''deepen relations'' with the EU and NATO, there was immediate speculation that he had abandoned efforts to seek membership in those organizations. Although that interpretation was immediately disputed by Ukrainian officials, the controversy those few words generated is an indication of the sensitive nature of this relationship.

The other area of concern for the United States is Central Asia. Ever since the breakup of the Soviet Union, there has been competition for influence in this region, in particular for its energy resources. The United States, for example, pushed for the construction of a pipeline from Baku, Azerbaijan, to Ceyhan, Turkey, which would bypass both Russia and Iran. The Russians, unsurprisingly, have pushed back and now seem to be enjoying some success. According to a report in the Indian paper, the *Hindu*, ''Russian experts are convinced that Kazakhstan's long-term commitment to use Russian, Chinese and Iranian routes for its oil exports will make the U.S.-pushed BTC pipeline a money-losing project.''

Competition over Central Asian energy resources has been complicated by the war on terrorism. Some observers were impressed with Putin's cooperation with the Bush administration following the September 11 attacks, but there was no reason for him to oppose U.S. efforts since both countries are fighting the same enemy. Russia is wary, however, of any American effort to create a permanent presence, especially if it is designed to counter Russian influence. Some observers have speculated that Russia is teaming up with China to build a security belt in Central Asia and the Caspian to counterbalance the U.S. presence in the region.

The deepening integration of the Shanghai Cooperation Organization is a particularly noteworthy manifestation of this development. "After the September 11 terror attacks, the United States started to deploy military forces in Central Asia; it gained a geopolitical advantage by overthrowing the Taliban regime in Afghanistan and dealing a big blow to such religious extremist groups as the Islamic Movement of Uzbekistan," *China Daily* explained in January 2004, implying that the establishment of a secretariat for the SCO at that time was designed in part to counter that geopolitical advantage. According to the *Hindu,* "Analysts in Russia said the Shanghai grouping was emerging as a counterweight to growing American presence in Central Asia."

The United States must be careful not to overplay its hand with Putin and Russia. So long as the United States requires access to Afghanistan, and so long as access through Iran is out of the question, the goodwill of Russia will be required. A quick look at the map will suffice to explain. Afghanistan is landlocked; in addition to Iran on its western border, its neighbors are Pakistan, Tajikistan, Turkmenistan, and Uzbekistan. The three latter countries are all former members of the Soviet Union, and access to Afghanistan through the territory of any of them would be difficult to sustain without (at least tacit) Russian consent. (China has a small border with Afghanistan, but it is too remote and mountainous to provide access in any meaningful sense.)

This situation provides Russia with exceptional leverage—which would be enormously enhanced if the political situation in Pakistan were to change for the worse. To be sure, since Russia and the United States are on the same side in the war against terrorism, there is no reason for Russia to obstruct U.S. efforts in Afghanistan. But if Moscow were to become convinced that Washington was using its presence in Central Asia to consolidate a position in the region, it would have ways of making its displeasure known.

The United States, unfortunately, does not have good options here. The war against terrorism is also a war for democracy, but the reality of geography means that to prosecute the war in Afghanistan, the United

States must occasionally cooperate with undemocratic regimes. To the extent that cooperation with any one of them (e.g., Iran) is politically unacceptable, cooperation with the others becomes even more important. So long as success in Afghanistan remains a priority for the United States, cooperation with Russia is essential, and it would be unwise for Washington to give Moscow any reason to believe that the United States has a hegemonic agenda for the region.

The Democratic Transformation

When the Cold War ended, there was widespread expectation that Russia was on its way to democracy. Indeed, some Russians publicly acknowledged that they had been wrong to protest Western criticism of the human rights situation under Soviet rule. "One of the most profound ideological and practical divergences between us and the Western-type democracies was our different view of the relations between the state and the *individual*," a commentator wrote in *Izvestia* on the occasion of President Reagan's departure from the presidency in January 1989. "In recent years, while gradually breaking down the Stalinist and Brezhnevian stereotypes, we have been gaining an understanding of the sovereignty of the human individual and have thereby found a common language with the West on a question that we used to regard as an infringement on our internal affairs—human rights."

Language praising the "sovereignty of the individual" has been absent from Russian political discourse for some time now, and Moscow once again bristles at criticism of its human rights situation. In July 2004 Russia and eight other former Soviet states condemned interference by the Organization for Security and Cooperation in Europe, which "does not respect such fundamental principles . . . as non-interference in internal affairs and respect of national sovereignty" and focuses "exclusively on monitoring human rights and democratic institutions."

That is dispiriting language, and it is not the only disappointment in Russia's democratic evolution. Although Russia's economy has recovered well from its dire situation in 1998, that recovery is highly dependent on energy prices, since energy accounts for approximately a quarter of Russian GDP. Such lack of diversification has political as well as economic implications, since accountable (democratic) government thrives only when political leaders must go to the people for money to fund the operations of government. A lack of diversification leads to unhealthy collusion or confrontation between the powerful economic magnates and the government, which in Russia has manifested itself in the relationship between the oligarchs and the president. The arrest and trial of Mikhail Khodorkovsy, the head of the giant energy firm Yukos, was yet another chapter in this saga.

To be sure, setbacks were to be expected in Russia's transformation to a full-fledged, stable democracy. For example, it is impossible to diversify an economy in just a few years. Such an evolution requires time and investment—notably, in the training of people in skills valued in an international economy. Yet some observers worry that the trends might be more ominous. "The resurgence of [Vladimir] Zhirinovsky's [political] party and the blending of confiscatory socialist and ethnic nationalist slogans under the tranquilizing label of 'motherland' raise anew the possibility of a Nazi-type movement developing within a façade of democratic institutions," warns James Billington, the librarian of Congress and a leading authority on Russia. "More likely would be the unintended evolution into some original Russian variant of a corporatist state ruled by a dictator, adorned with Slavophile rhetoric, and representing, in effect, fascism with a friendly face."

Conclusion

We can certainly hope that Billington's concern is unjustified, but we must take it seriously. The question, however, is what the United States can do. Unfortunately, our options are limited. Ironically, given our position as the "sole superpower," Russia has leverage over us because of our difficult position in Afghanistan. Although Russia has an interest in assisting us—after all, it will also suffer if we fail—its interest in our success is not greater than ours. Putin has demonstrated a mastery of diplomacy, quietly forging ties with other countries while America's energy drains into conflicts that show no signs of ending. The first requirement for U.S. policy, therefore, is to abandon the rhetoric about American hegemony and recognize the degree to which international power relationships have shifted in the last few years.

Recognizing the limits on our ability to influence events in Russia in the short term, we need to concentrate our efforts on the long term. And here, historically, we find that our best leverage has come from the power of our example. "Ever since its political emergence the United States has been a model for Russia," Max M. Laserson, an official in the 1917 provisional government, wrote in 1950. Indeed, the 1825 Decembrist uprising was inspired in part by the American example. Testifying before the Committee of Inquiry, which investigated the revolt, one of its leaders, P. I. Pestel, acknowledged that ''all newspapers and political writings have so much extolled the growing prosperity of the North American United States, which they attributed to their state [i.e., federal] organization, that this seemed to me to be a clear proof of the superiority of the republican government.''

Something similar happened when the Cold War ended and Russians embraced their former adversary. They now feel that we did not return their embrace but instead have sought to consolidate a position of victory. In addition, they feel that we are no longer a good model, which helps explain why they are increasingly returning to their traditions and history to reassert their identity.

If we are to be an inspiring model, we must examine our own policy. The alienation of Russians from the United States is not unique; it tracks attitudes toward the United States elsewhere in the world. If we emphasize our power and the importance our power gives us, the lesson the rest of the world will learn is that of the need for power. We should not be surprised, therefore, if Russia and other like-minded countries increase their military power and create ''strategic partnerships'' while questioning our efforts to promote democracy.

The situation in which we find ourselves now is very sad, especially compared with the hopes that existed 15 years ago. It recalls a previous moment that also proved fleeting: in June 1917 the minister for foreign affairs in the Russian provisional government addressed a delegation sent to Russia by President Woodrow Wilson.

> These two great peoples, the free people of Russia and the free people of America, the great people of the United States, the oldest, strongest, and purest democracy, hand in hand, will show the way that human happiness will take in the future.

That is an inspiring vision that, regrettably, was not realized because of Lenin's triumph a few months later. With the end of the Cold War, we were given another opportunity to achieve it. Let us hope it is not too late.

Suggested Readings

Billington, James H. *Russia in Search of Itself*. Washington: Woodrow Wilson Center Press, 2004.

Lieven, Anatol. *Ukraine and Russia*. Washington: U.S. Institute of Peace, 1999.

Lieven, Dominic. *Empire: The Russian Empire and Its Rivals*. New Haven, CT: Yale University Press, 2000.

Powell, Colin. "Partnership, Under Construction." *Izvestia,* January 24, 2004. http://www.state.gov/secretary/rm/28495.htm.

Putin, Vladimir. "Speech at a Russian Security Council Session," July 19, 2004. http://www.kremlin.ru/eng/speeches/2004/07/19/2023_74668.shtml.

"Statement by CIS Member Countries on the State of Affairs in the OSCE," July 8, 2004. http://www.kremlin.ru/eng/text/docs/2004/07/74223.shtml.

—Prepared by Stanley Kober

63. Relations with Cuba

> **Congress should**
> - repeal the Cuban Liberty and Democratic Solidarity (Libertad, or Helms-Burton) Act of 1996,
> - repeal the Cuban Democracy (Torricelli) Act of 1992,
> - restore the policy of granting Cuban refugees political asylum in the United States,
> - eliminate or privatize Radio and TV Marti,
> - end all trade sanctions on Cuba and allow U.S. citizens and companies to visit and establish businesses in Cuba as they see fit, and
> - move toward the normalization of diplomatic relations with Cuba.

In 1970, 17 of 26 countries in Latin America and the Caribbean had authoritarian regimes. Today, only Cuba has a dictatorial regime. To be sure, the transition to market-oriented democracies, which protect individual liberty and property rights under the rule of law, is far from complete in any of the region's countries and has suffered setbacks in some of them. Economic sanctions have not been responsible for the general shift toward liberalization, however. They have, in fact, failed to bring about democratic regimes anywhere in the hemisphere, and Cuba has been no exception. Indeed, Cuba is the one country in the hemisphere against which the U.S. government has persistently and actively used a full economic embargo as its main policy tool in an attempt to compel a democratic transformation.

The failure of sanctions against Cuba should come as no surprise since sanctions are notorious for their unintended consequences—harming those they are meant to help. In Cuba, Fidel Castro is the last person to feel the pain caused by the U.S. measures. If sanctions in the early 1990s failed to dislodge the military regime in Haiti, the poorest and most vulnerable country in the region, it is difficult to believe that they could be successful in Cuba.

A Cold War Relic

Sanctions against Cuba were first authorized under the Foreign Assistance Act of 1961, passed by the 87th Congress. In 1962 President John F. Kennedy issued an executive order implementing the trade embargo as a response to Castro's expropriation of American assets and his decision to offer the Soviet Union a permanent military base and an intelligence post just 90 miles off the coast of Florida at the height of the Cold War. Castro's decision confirmed Cuba as the Soviet Union's main ally in the Western Hemisphere.

For three decades, Cuba was a threat to U.S. national security. Not only did Cuba export Marxist-Leninist revolutions to Third World countries (most notably, Angola, and Nicaragua), but, more important, it served as a base for Soviet intelligence operations and allowed Soviet naval vessels port access rights. However, with the collapse of the Soviet Union and the subsequent end of Soviet subsidies to Cuba in the early 1990s, that threat virtually ceased to exist. (There is always the possibility that Castro will do something reckless.) Indeed, a 1998 report by the Defense Intelligence Agency concluded: "At present, Cuba does not pose a significant military threat to the United States or to other countries in the region. Cuba has little motivation to engage in military activity beyond defense of its territory and political activity." With the demise of the security threat posed by Cuba, all valid justifications for the embargo also disappeared.

Trade sanctions against Cuba, however, were not lifted. The embargo was instead tightened in 1992 with the passage of the Cuban Democracy (Torricelli) Act, a bill that former president George Bush signed into law. The justification for it was not national security interests but the Castro regime's form of government and human rights abuses. That change of focus was reflected in the language of the act, the first finding of which was Castro's "consistent disregard for internationally accepted standards of human rights and for democratic values."

In 1996 Congress passed the Cuban Liberty and Democratic Solidarity (Libertad) Act, a bill that President Clinton had threatened to veto but instead signed into law in the aftermath of the downing of two U.S. civilian planes by Cuban fighter jets in international airspace.

The Unintended Consequences of a Flawed Policy

The Libertad Act, better known as the Helms-Burton Act for its sponsors Sen. Jesse Helms (R-NC) and Rep. Dan Burton (R-IN), is an ill-conceived law. It grants U.S. citizens whose property was expropriated by Castro the right to sue in U.S. courts foreign companies and citizens "trafficking" in that property (Title III). That right—not granted to U.S. citizens who may have lost property in other countries—is problematic because it essentially extends U.S. jurisdiction to the results of events that occurred on foreign territory.

By imposing sanctions on foreign companies profiting from property confiscated by the Castro regime, the Helms-Burton Act seeks to discourage investment in Cuba. But fears that foreign investment there, which is much lower than official figures claim, will save the communist system from its inherent flaws are unfounded; significant capital flows to Cuba will not occur unless and until market reforms are introduced. While Helms-Burton may have slowed investment in Cuba, U.S. allies (in particular, Canada, Mexico, and members of the European Union) have not welcomed that attempt to influence their foreign policy by threat of U.S. sanctions. Consequently, they have repeatedly threatened to impose retaliatory sanctions and to take the United States to the World Trade Organization.

In May 1998 the Clinton administration and the European Union reached a tentative agreement that would exclude citizens of EU countries from Titles III and IV (denying entry visas to the executives of companies "trafficking" in confiscated property) of the Helms-Burton Act in exchange for guarantees from the EU not to subsidize investments in expropriated properties. President Bush has continued the policy of repeatedly waiving Title III of the act. But because only the Congress can repeal Titles III and IV, the possibility that the EU will impose retaliatory sanctions or take the United States to the WTO remains. That confrontation has risked poisoning U.S. relations with otherwise friendly countries that are far more important than Cuba to the economic well-being and security of the United States. It also serves to divert attention, both inside and outside Cuba, from the island's internal crisis.

Moreover, any increase in Washington's hostility would benefit only the hard-liners within the Cuban government. Indeed, the embargo continues to be the best—and now the only—excuse that Castro has for his failed policies. As a Hoover Institution report on Cuba stated, Castro knows that "the embargo to some degree keeps him from becoming just another in a centuries-long string of failed Latin American dictators. . . . Nothing would come so close to 'killing' him while he is still alive as lifting the embargo.''

Although the Soviet Union provided Cuba with more than $100 billion in subsidies and credits during their three-decade relationship, Cuban officials, who have estimated the cumulative cost of the embargo at more than $40 billion, incessantly condemn U.S. policies for causing the meager existence of the Cuban people. Elizardo Sánchez Santa Cruz, a leading dissident in Cuba, has aptly summed up that strategy: ''[Castro] wants to continue exaggerating the image of the external enemy which has been vital for the Cuban Government during decades, an external enemy which can be blamed for the failure of the totalitarian model implanted here.'' The more supporters of the embargo stress the importance of sanctions in bringing Castro down, the more credible becomes Castro's claim that the United States is responsible for Cuba's misery.

Unfortunately, the Bush administration played into Castro's hands when it formed the Commission for Assistance for a Free Cuba. The administration adopted the commission's recommendation to tighten the embargo by restricting travel and remittances to the island even further. The commission also endorsed the administration's policy of providing aid to Cuban opposition groups, thus lending a semblance of credibility to Castro's claims that dissident groups are agents of Washington.

As long as Castro can point to the United States as an external enemy, he will be successful in barring dissent, justifying control over the economy and the flow of information, and stirring up nationalist and anti-U.S. sentiments in Cuba.

Cuba Must Determine Its Own Destiny

Perhaps the biggest shortcoming of U.S. policy toward Cuba is its false assumption that democratic capitalism can somehow be forcibly exported from Washington to Havana. That assumption is explicitly stated in the Helms-Burton Act, the first purpose of which is ''to assist the Cuban people in regaining their freedom and prosperity, as well as in joining the community of democratic countries that are flourishing in the Western Hemisphere.''

But the shift toward democratic capitalism that began in the Western Hemisphere two decades ago has little to do with Washington's efforts to export democracy. Rather, it has to do with Latin America's realization that previous policies and regimes had failed to provide self-sustaining growth and increasing prosperity. The region's ability to benefit from a market system will depend in large part on its success in sustaining market reforms, which, again, will depend entirely on Latin American countries, not on the United States.

Since the end of the Cold War, Cuba has no longer posed a credible threat to the United States. Whether Cuba has a totalitarian or a democratic regime, though important, is not a vital U.S. national security concern. The transformation of Cuban society, as difficult as that may be, should be left to the Cuban people, not to the U.S. government. As William F. Buckley Jr. has stated: "If the Cuban people overthrow Mr. Castro, that is the end for which devoutly we pray. But if they do not, he is their problem."

Furthermore, there is little historical evidence, in Cuba or elsewhere, that tightening the screws on Cuba will produce an anti-Castro rebellion. Cato scholar James Dorn has observed that "the threat of using trade restrictions to advance human rights is fraught with danger . . . [because] it undermines the market dynamic that in the end is the best instrument for creating wealth and preserving freedom."

Even though Cuba—unlike other communist countries, such as China or Vietnam, with which the United States actively trades—has not undertaken meaningful market reforms, an open U.S. trade policy is likely to be more subversive of its system than is an embargo. Proponents of the Cuban embargo vastly underestimate the extent to which increased foreign trade and investment can undermine Cuban communism even if that business is conducted with state entities.

Cuban officialdom appears to be well aware of that danger. For example, Cuba's opening of its tourism industry to foreign investment has been accompanied by measures that restrict ordinary Cubans from visiting foreign hotels and tourist facilities. As a result, Cubans have come to resent their government for what is known as "tourism apartheid." In recent years, Cuban officials have also issued increasing warnings against corruption, indicating the regime's fear that unofficial business dealings, especially with foreigners, may weaken allegiance to the government and even create vested interests that favor more extensive market openings. As the Hoover Institution study concluded: "In time, increasing amounts [of expanded tourism, trade, and investment] would go beyond the state, and although economics will not single-handedly liberate Cuba, it may contribute some to that end. This is so, in part, because the repressive Cubans within the state apparatus are subject to influences that can tilt their allegiances in positive ways."

Further undercutting the regime's authority is the widespread dollar economy that has emerged as a consequence of foreign presence and remittances from abroad, estimated at $800 million annually, which the Helms-Burton Act had banned until the spring of 1998. Today about 50 percent of the Cuban population has access to dollars. The dollarization in the early 1990s of the Cuban economy—a phenomenon legalized by the Cuban regime as a result of its inability to control it—significantly reduced the regime's ability to dictate the country's monetary policy. That development in part prompted the regime to impose restrictive exchange controls in 2003 and to try to "de-dollarize" the economy by penalizing use of dollars beginning in 2004.

Replacing the all-encompassing state with one that allows greater space for voluntary interaction requires strengthening elements of civil society, that is, groups not dependent on the state. That development is more likely to come about in an environment of increased interaction with outside groups than in an environment of increased isolation and state control.

At present, there are signs that civil society is slowly emerging in Cuba, despite Castro's attempts to suppress it. For example, the Catholic Church, the main recipient of humanitarian aid from international nongovernmental organizations, has experienced a resurgence since the Archbishop of Havana was made a cardinal. The Varela project, a Cuban democratization initiative, attracted 25,000 signatures, prompting Castro to crack down on peaceful dissidents, sentencing 75 of them to up to 20 years in prison.

Finally, there are the small-business owners who are able to earn a living in the small but growing nonstate sector. The 150,000 *cuentapropistas*, or "workers on their own account," are approximately 4 percent of the total workforce; half of them are working with government-approved licenses and the other half in the informal sector. According to Philip Peters, vice president of the Lexington Institute, those workers "are dramatically improving their standard of living and supplying goods and services while learning the habits of independent actors in competitive markets." For instance, private farmers bring 85 percent of the produce sold in markets although they cultivate only 15 percent of the arable land. And, because most independent workers are in the service industries (mostly restaurant and food service), they would greatly benefit from the presence of Americans visiting for business or pleasure.

Cuban exiles should also be allowed to participate in the transformation of Cuban society. However, their participation need not require active involvement of the U.S. government. Thus, Radio and TV Marti, government entities that broadcast to Cuba, should be privatized or closed down. If the exile community believes that those stations are a useful resource in their struggle against the Castro regime, they have the means—there are no legal impediments—to finance such an operation.

A New Cuba Policy Based on American Principles

Washington's policies toward Cuba should be consistent with traditional American principles. First, the United States should restore the practice of granting political asylum to Cuban refugees. The 1994 and 1995 immigration accords between the Clinton administration and the Cuban government have turned the United States into Castro's de jure partner in oppressing those Cubans who risk their lives to escape repression. The "wet feet, dry feet" policy, which grants political asylum to Cuban refugees who make it to the U.S. shore on their own and forces the U.S. Coast Guard to return to Cuba those refugees that it picks up at sea, should be eliminated. Instead, the U.S. government should grant political asylum to all Cubans who escape the island.

There is no reason to believe that Cuban refugees would not continue to help the U.S. economy as they always have. The 1980 boatlift, in which 120,000 Cuban refugees reached U.S. shores, proved a boon to the economy of South Florida. In addition, since the Cuban-American community has repeatedly demonstrated its ability and desire to provide for refugees until they can provide for themselves, such a policy need not cost U.S. taxpayers.

Second, the U.S. government should protect its own citizens' inalienable rights and recognize that free trade is itself a human right. As Dorn says: "The supposed dichotomy between the right to trade and human rights is a false one. . . . As moral agents, individuals necessarily claim the rights to liberty and property in order to live fully and to pursue their interests in a responsible manner." In the case of Cuba, U.S. citizens and companies should be allowed to decide for themselves—as they are in the case of dozens of countries around the world whose political and human rights records are less than admirable—whether and how they should trade with it.

Third, U.S. policy toward Cuba should focus on national security interests, not on transforming Cuban society or micromanaging the affairs of a transitional government as current law obliges Washington to do. That means lifting the embargo and establishing with Cuba the types of diplomatic ties that the United States maintains with other states, even dictatorial ones, that do not threaten its national security. Those measures, especially the ending of current sanctions, will ensure a more peaceful and smooth transition in Cuba. After all, as former Reagan National Security Council member Roger Fontaine explains, "It is not in our interest to acquire another economic basket case in the Caribbean."

The Tide Is Turning

Since the pope's visit to Cuba in early 1998 and the Elián González incident—in which the shipwrecked six-year-old lost his mother at sea and was rescued by Florida fishermen during Thanksgiving weekend of 1999—U.S. businesspeople, policymakers, and the U.S. population at large have shown a growing interest in Cuba. For instance, in early 1998 the U.S. Chamber of Commerce joined religious and humanitarian groups to create a coalition to support the end of restrictions on the sale of food and medicine to Cuba. In the fall of 1998, 24 senators, led by Sen. John Warner (R-VA), and several foreign policy experts, including former secretaries of state Henry Kissinger, Lawrence Eagleburger, and George Shultz, unsuccessfully asked President Clinton to appoint a bipartisan congressional commission to reevaluate U.S. policy toward Cuba. Thousands of U.S. business leaders have visited the country in the past several years.

In the closing days of its second session, the 106th Congress passed a measure as part of its agricultural funding bill that allows cash sales of food and medicine to Cuba but prohibits private-sector financing from the United States. It is doubtful that the measure will create a significant or lasting market for U.S. farmers, as proponents of the bill desire, because Cuba is both broke and uncreditworthy.

The 106th Congress also turned the travel ban to Cuba, which had been implemented by executive order, into law. Turning that ban into law makes it more difficult to revoke the restrictions that deny the majority of Americans their right to travel freely. Already, about 200,000 Americans per year travel to Cuba, including 80,000 who do so without the explicit authorization of the U.S. government. If the travel restrictions were to be lifted completely, the number of American citizens traveling to Cuba would certainly increase, as would their contacts with Cuban citizens who work outside the state sector.

Indeed, in the past four years, the House of Representatives voted to overturn the ban on traveling to Cuba. During that time, an increasing number of politicians, including governors and U.S. senators, visited the island. In May 2002 former president Jimmy Carter traveled to Havana and called for an end to the trade and travel embargo. Underlining the liberalizing potential of U.S. travel to Cuba, Carter used his visit to draw Cuba's national attention to the Varela project, which had thus far received no play in the official media. Signs of increasing political dissatisfaction with the embargo show that the tide of opinion is clearly changing.

Conclusion

Sen. Robert G. Torricelli (D-NJ) offered the following justification for U.S. policy after Helms-Burton was passed by Congress: "Different policies might have worked, might have been taken. But the die has been cast. Years ago we decided on this strategy and we are in the end game now. It is too late to change strategy." But even many people who may agree with Torricelli's position recognize, as Cuban exile Carlos Alberto Montaner does, that "the embargo, at this stage of the game, is probably a strategic error, political clumsiness from Washington which provides Castro with an alibi." In fact, it is not too late to change strategy and the "end game" may yet take years to complete. U.S. clumsiness, unfortunately, increases the likelihood of a violent Cuban transition into which the United States would unnecessarily be drawn.

A better policy would recognize that, while Castro may be a clever political manipulator, his economic forecasting and planning have been dismal. Supporters of the embargo casually assume that Castro wants an end to the embargo because he believes that step would solve his economic problems. More likely, Castro fears the lifting of the U.S. sanctions. It is difficult to believe, for example, that he did not calculate a strong U.S. response when he ordered the attack on two U.S. planes in early 1996. It is time for Washington to stop playing into Castro's hands and instead pull the rug out from under him by ending the embargo.

Suggested Readings

Clarke, Jonathan G., and William Ratliff. "Report from Havana: Time for a Reality Check on U.S. Policy toward Cuba." Cato Institute Policy Analysis no. 418, October 31, 2001.

Council on Foreign Relations. "U.S.-Cuban Relations in the 21st Century." Report of an Independent Task Force Sponsored by the Council on Foreign Relations. New York: Council on Foreign Relations, 1999.

Defense Intelligence Agency. "The Cuban Threat to U.S. National Security." Washington: Defense Intelligence Agency, 1998.

Falcoff, Mark. *Cuba the Morning After: Normalization and Its Discontents*. Washington: AEI Press, 2004.

Flake, Jeff. "Will U.S. Trade with Cuba Promote Freedom or Subsidize Tyranny?" Remarks at Cato Policy Forum, July 25, 2002. www.cato.org–events–020725pf.html.

Glassman, James K. "No Sanctions, No Castro." *Washington Post,* January 20, 1998.

Human Rights Watch. "Cuba's Repressive Machinery: Human Rights Forty Years after the Revolution." New York: Human Rights Watch, 1999.

Montaner, Carlos A. "Cuba Today: The Slow Demise of Castroism." In *Essays in English Language*. Madrid: Fundación para el Análisis y los Estudios Sociales, 1996.

Peters, Philip. "A Policy toward Cuba That Serves U.S. Interests." Cato Institute Policy Analysis no. 384, November 2, 2000.

Ratliff, William, and Roger Fontaine. "A Strategic Flip-Flop on the Caribbean: Lift the Embargo on Cuba." Hoover Institution *Essays in Public Policy,* no. 100 (2000).

U.S. Department of State. "Zenith and Eclipse: A Comparative Look at Socio-economic Conditions in Pre-Castro and Present Day Cuba." January 12, 1998. http://usembassy.state.gov/havana/wwwh0013.html.

Vásquez, Ian. "Washington's Dubious Crusade for Hemispheric Democracy." Cato Institute Policy Analysis no. 201, January 12, 1994.

—Prepared by L. Jacobo Rodríguez and Ian Vásquez

INTERNATIONAL ECONOMIC POLICY

64. Trade

Congress should

- recognize that the relative openness of American markets is an important source of our economic vitality and that remaining trade barriers are a drag on growth and prosperity;
- move the focus of U.S. trade policy away from "reciprocity" and "level playing fields" toward commitment here and abroad to free-trade principles;
- take unilateral action to repeal remaining protectionist policies;
- reform U.S. antidumping law to limit abuses and conform with U.S. obligations within the World Trade Organization;
- enact implementing legislation for market-opening trade agreements;
- maintain support for the WTO as a body for negotiating market-opening agreements and settling disputes;
- avoid using trade deficits and concerns about employment levels as excuses for imposing trade restrictions; and
- employ trade expansion, not trade sanctions, as a tool of U.S. foreign policy.

Free Trade Means Free Markets

Its opponents like to portray free trade as an ivory-tower theory, but in fact the case for knocking down trade barriers rests on common sense. It is now widely recognized that free markets are indispensable to our prosperity: when people are free to buy, sell, and invest with each other as they choose, they are able to achieve far more than when governments attempt to control economic decisions. Given that fact, isn't it obvious that free markets work even better when we widen the circle of people with whom we can buy, sell, and invest? Free trade is nothing more than the extension of free markets across political boundaries. The benefits of free trade are the benefits of *larger* free markets: by multiplying our potential business partners, we multiply the opportunities for wealth creation.

From this perspective, it becomes clear that Americans gain from open U.S. markets even when other countries' markets are relatively closed. The fact that people in other countries are not as free as they should be is no reason to restrict the freedom of Americans. When goods, services, and capital can flow over U.S. borders without interference, Americans are able to take full advantage of the opportunities of the international marketplace. They can buy the best and cheapest goods and services the world has to offer; they can sell to the most promising markets; they can choose among the best investment opportunities; and they can tap into the worldwide pool of capital. Study after study confirms that nations that are more open to the global economy grow faster and achieve higher incomes than those that are relatively closed.

Unfortunately, supporters of open markets seldom put their case in those straightforward terms. Instead, trade liberalization in this country is identified almost exclusively with international negotiations in which the removal of U.S. trade barriers is seen as a "concession" contingent upon the removal of barriers abroad. Such negotiations convey the impression that exports are the primary benefit that accrues from international trade and that open markets at home are the price we pay for greater export opportunities. That impression is misleading—and ultimately harmful to prospects for continued liberalization.

The idea that exports are good and imports are harmful is the essence of the mercantilist fallacy that lies at the root of most protectionist thinking. That fallacy turns truth on its head: imports are in fact the primary benefit of trade. Imports give us goods that are cheaper or better than those we can produce ourselves; exports, which represent production that Americans do not get to consume, are actually the price we pay for the imports we enjoy. To the extent that free traders perpetuate the mercantilist fallacy by endorsing the dogmas of "reciprocity" and "level playing fields," they are helping to foster a political culture that is hostile to open markets.

Opinion polls show that many Americans believe that U.S. openness to the rest of the world is destroying jobs and eroding living standards. That such "globalphobia" could be so widespread demonstrates that free traders are doing something wrong. To combat the current intellectual confusion, supporters of trade liberalization should return to their free-market roots. They need to meet mercantilist misconceptions head-on and to make the case that free trade is its own reward.

Alternatives to Reciprocity

Because free trade is first and foremost in our own national interest, the United States should not deny itself the benefits of open markets just because other countries hold on to self-damaging policies. Free traders should expand beyond their traditionally exclusive reliance on negotiated liberalization and launch a campaign for the unilateral reduction or outright elimination of U.S. trade barriers—including the antidumping law, still-high tariffs on many products, import restrictions linked to agricultural price support programs, the Jones Act ban on foreign shipping between U.S. ports, the similar denial of cabotage rights to foreign airlines, and foreign ownership limits for air transport and broadcasting.

Top 12 Most Costly U.S. Trade Barriers

Quota, tariff, and licensing barriers to imported

- Textiles and apparel
- Domestic maritime transport (Jones Act)
- Sugar
- Footwear and leather products
- Tobacco and tobacco products
- Canned tuna
- Beef
- Watches, clocks, watch cases and parts
- Ball and roller bearings
- Ceramic wall and floor tile
- Dairy products
- Table and kitchenware

SOURCE: U.S. International Trade Commission.

Advocating unilateral reform would enable free traders to frame the trade debate in terms that give them the natural advantage. Instead of always defending free trade, they could attack its alternative: protectionism in actual practice. The beneficiaries of protection would be forced to explain why they deserve their special privileges and why the welfare of other American businesses, workers, and consumers should be sacrificed on their account. The U.S. sugar protection program, for example, forces domestic consumers to pay triple the world price for sugar and costs American sugar-using industries and consumers an estimated $1.9 billion a year. Meanwhile, removal of quotas and tariffs on imported textiles and apparel would result in a welfare gain to the U.S. economy of $11.8 billion, according to the U.S. International Trade Commission.

Free traders need to reclaim their populist roots. Free trade benefits American families by injecting greater competition into the marketplace, leading to lower prices, wider choice, and better quality. Protectionism is especially tough on the poor: America's highest remaining trade barriers are aimed at products—such as shoes, clothing, and food—that are disproportionately consumed by poor people at home and produced by poor people abroad. A study by the Progressive Policy Institute found that a single mother of two earning about $20,000 a year pays a much higher effective tariff rate on the goods her family consumes than is paid by a single executive earning six figures.

Unilateral U.S. reforms would do more to encourage liberalization abroad than any trade negotiations ever could. The most sweeping and dramatic moves toward freer trade in recent years—in countries as diverse as Australia, New Zealand, Chile, Mexico, China, and India—have occurred not at the bargaining table but unilaterally. The leaders of those countries finally realized that isolation from the world economy was a recipe for economic stagnation, and therefore they sought to emulate the relatively open-market policies of more prosperous countries. History shows, therefore, that the most effective form of international economic leadership is leadership by example.

Negotiating for Free Trade

Still, pursuing unilateral reform would not mean an end to trade negotiations. International agreements can facilitate the liberalization process by recruiting export interests to support free trade at home; also, such agreements provide a useful institutional constraint against protectionist backsliding. But a new U.S. negotiating posture is needed, one that replaces demands for reciprocity with commitment to free-trade principles.

Instead of seeking to "win" at the negotiating table by "getting" more than it "gives," the United States could define its key liberalization objectives—for example, global tariff reductions, reforms of antidumping laws, rules on treatment of foreign investment, rules against protectionist misuse of health and safety standards, and so on—and offer to elevate its own unilaterally adopted free-trade policies into binding international commitments, provided that some "critical mass" of other countries agreed to exceed a defined minimum threshold of liberalization.

The United States does not need protectionist policies as "bargaining chips" to exert significant leverage. For example, other countries signed on to the 1997 multilateral agreements on telecommunications and financial services even though the only major U.S. "concession" was to lock in current levels of openness. Also, U.S. involvement in international agreements is desirable apart from any consideration of "concessions," since U.S. participation lends legitimacy to an agreement, thereby increasing other countries' confidence in the integrity of each others' commitments.

The same free-trade agenda should animate bilateral or regional trade negotiations. Subsequent free-trade agreements can open markets at home and abroad to more import competition, encourage cross-border integration of industries, and reward economic and political reform in other countries. Although less economically important than a comprehensive WTO agreement, regional and bilateral deals can mark important steps toward the goal of global free trade.

To maximize the benefits of regional and bilateral free-trade agreements, the United States should seek agreements with countries that can provide significant import competition in our domestic market and export opportunities abroad, or countries that are reform leaders in regions of the world where models of successful reform are most needed. U.S. negotiators should avoid the political temptation to exclude or phase in liberalization of the very products or sectors that most desperately need import competition.

Congress should use its constitutional authority over trade policy to facilitate genuine market openings, not to erect roadblocks. Many members of Congress have strongly urged the inclusion of "enforceable" labor and environmental standards in any new trade agreements. The whole purpose of trade negotiations, however, is to reduce governmental interference in cross-border flows of goods and services; international regulatory mandates on labor and environmental matters would threaten to increase government interference in those flows and thus subvert the basic mission of negotiations. Meanwhile, labor and environmental standards are implacably opposed by developing countries, and a U.S. negotiating position that insisted upon such standards could end up dooming negotiations to fail.

The U.S. trade remedy laws—the antidumping, countervailing duty, and Section 201 "safeguard" laws—and their counterparts in other countries are badly in need of reform. In particular, the antidumping law, which purports to focus on "unfair trade," frequently penalizes healthy foreign competition for business practices routinely engaged in by American companies. While the U.S. antidumping law victimizes American import-using industries and consumers, foreign copycat laws now target U.S. exporters with depressing frequency. Indeed, the United States became one of the leading victims of worldwide antidumping actions during the second half of the 1990s.

The prospects for reform here and abroad, however, are dimmed by vehement congressional opposition to any trade negotiations that might "weaken" U.S. trade laws. That opposition threatens, not just to block improvements in trade laws, but to prevent market-opening agreements more generally. Many of our trade partners are demanding changes to antidumping rules as a condition of any new agreements. If congressional pressure forces the administration into adopting an obstructionist position on antidumping, the United States could ultimately pay a grievously heavy price in lost opportunities to open markets around the world.

The World Trade Organization

The World Trade Organization is at present the primary institutional support for an open world trading order. In addition to serving as a forum for ongoing trade negotiations, the WTO and its dispute settlement procedures uphold a limited but real rule of law in international commerce. The WTO strongly advances the U.S. national interest in free markets here and abroad and therefore deserves strong U.S. support.

Congress should support the ongoing Doha Development Round of WTO negotiations. If successfully concluded, those talks could open vast new markets for American exports, raise global welfare by hundreds of billions of dollars, and help protect American consumers from trade-distorting barriers here at home.

Complaints that the WTO impinges on U.S. sovereignty are groundless. The WTO cannot overturn U.S. laws; at most, it can declare that U.S. laws are inconsistent with international agreements we have already signed and ratified. The WTO wields no power of enforcement. The WTO itself has no authority or power to levy fines, impose sanctions, change tariff rates, or modify domestic laws in any way to bring about compliance. If a member government refuses to comply with rules it previously agreed to follow, all the WTO can do is approve a request by the complaining member to impose sanctions—a "power" that member governments have always been able to wield against each other. By establishing procedures for the use of sanctions, the WTO's dispute settlement understanding actually makes their use less likely. So whether we honor our obligations as a member of the WTO is ultimately up to us.

But honor them we should. The principles of market access and nondiscrimination incorporated in WTO agreements are ones that ought to be reflected in U.S. policy. When U.S. laws violate those principles, they ought to be changed. It is a mistake to complain simply because the United States "loses" a case in the WTO; when the dispute settlement process leads the U.S. government to reform protectionist policies, that is a victory, not a defeat, for the American people. Furthermore, by heeding "adverse" WTO decisions, the United States sets an example for the rest of the world. We stand to gain when other countries follow the WTO's free-trade rules. Consequently, we have a large stake in the legitimacy and credibility of the dispute settlement process, which cannot be sustained if we selectively disregard WTO rulings.

Congress should show its support for the WTO process by passing legislation to implement all outstanding adverse WTO rulings as soon as possible. In particular, Congress should move quickly to comply with a large and growing number of outstanding rulings against various aspects of U.S. trade laws. To the extent that legislation is needed to implement those rulings, Congress should move immediately to make the necessary changes to U.S. law.

Trade and the U.S. Economy

Imports benefit the U.S. economy by injecting more competition into domestic markets, delivering lower prices, better quality, and more choice to American families. Imports benefit American producers as well by lowering the cost of raw materials, intermediate parts, and capital equipment, making U.S. companies more competitive in global markets.

Anxieties about job losses and trade are misplaced. Trade is not about more or fewer jobs but about better jobs. Like technology itself, trade changes the mix of jobs by allowing American workers to shift into sectors where we have greater advantages as a nation. Of course, not everyone benefits from expanding trade. Trade does bring new competitive pressure to bear on certain domestic industries. It can cause those industries to shrink and lay off workers. The adjustment can be painful, but those workers who lose their jobs because of trade are not alone.

The number of jobs lost each year because of import competition is quite small in an economy that, as of 2004, employed 138 million workers. Within that labor force, "job churn" is a fact of life in a healthy, dynamic economy. According to the Bureau of Labor Statistics, jobs lost to imports and offshoring represent only 2 percent of annual job losses in the United States. New technology, domestic competition, and changing consumer demand displace far more workers than trade. To impose new trade barriers to supposedly "save" jobs would be as foolish as banning new technologies or restraining domestic competition.

America's trade deficit is not an economic problem. It is the benign consequence of a persistent surplus of foreign capital flowing into the United States. That additional capital has helped to make U.S. workers more productive, raising living standards above what they would be without it and building the foundation for future growth.

The underlying cause of the U.S. trade deficit is the fact that domestic savings in the United States are insufficient to fund all the available domestic investment opportunities. Any savings gap is filled by a net inflow of foreign investment. Those foreign funds allow Americans to buy more than we sell in the international market for goods and services, resulting in a trade deficit. As long as the pool of domestic savings available for investment is smaller than the actual level of investment, the United States will run a trade deficit.

The only real sense in which the trade deficit is a threat to the U.S. economy is its potential effect on public policy. Persistent worries about the trade deficit could prompt policymakers to implement a "cure" for the trade deficit, such as higher tariff barriers, that itself could impose serious damage on the economy. Members of Congress should reject the idea of "balanced trade" as a policy goal. The best policy response would be to ignore the U.S. trade deficit and concentrate on maintaining a strong and open domestic economy that welcomes trade and foreign investment.

Export Barriers, Trade Sanctions, and U.S. Foreign Policy

Although we complain about other countries' barriers to our exports, the fact is that many barriers are homegrown. In particular, America's export control policies remain detached from the realities of the global marketplace. U.S. companies should be allowed to sell technologies that are being sold freely elsewhere in the world by their foreign competitors and the sale of which fails to present a clear danger to U.S. citizens or world peace. That is not the case today for many products, and much bureaucratic wrangling is needed before others can be exported.

Sales and investments abroad by U.S. companies are also hindered by ill-considered foreign policy trade sanctions against Cuba, Burma, and other countries. The Cuban embargo is discussed in Chapter 63. It should be noted here, though, that trade sanctions rarely accomplish their foreign policy objectives. Instead, they end up hurting the very people they are designed to help—the unfortunate subjects of despotic regimes. Absent compelling national security considerations, trade sanctions are almost always a bad idea.

Trade and investment, on the other hand, can improve the lot of despotism's victims while sowing the seeds of political change. As trade and globalization have spread to more and more countries in the last 30 years, so too have democracy and political and civil freedoms. In particular, the most economically open countries today are more than three times as likely to enjoy full political and civil freedoms as those that are relatively closed. Those that are closed are nine times more likely to completely suppress civil and political freedoms than are those that are open. Nations that have followed a path of trade reform in recent decades by progressively opening themselves to the global economy are significantly more likely to have expanded their citizens' political and civil freedoms.

The powerful connection between economic openness and political and civil freedom provides yet another argument for pursuing an expansion of global trade. In the Middle East, China, Cuba, Central America, and other regions, free trade can buttress U.S. foreign policy by tilling foreign soil for the spread of democracy and human rights.

Suggested Readings

Griswold, Daniel T. "America's Maligned and Misunderstood Trade Deficit." Cato Institute Trade Policy Analysis no. 2, April 24, 1998.

———. "America's Record Trade Deficit: A Symbol of Economic Strength." Cato Institute Trade Policy Analysis no. 13, February 9, 2001.

———. "Trade, Labor, and the Environment: How Blue and Green Sanctions Threaten Higher Standards." Cato Institute Trade Policy Analysis no. 15, August 2, 2001.

———. "Trading Tyranny for Freedom: How Open Markets Till the Soil for Democracy." Cato Institute Trade Policy Analysis no. 26, January 6, 2004.

Groombridge, Mark. "America's Bittersweet Sugar Policy." Cato Institute Trade Policy Briefing Paper no. 13, December 4, 2001.

Irwin, Douglas. *Free Trade under Fire*. Princeton, NJ: Princeton University Press, 2002.

Lash, William H. III, and Daniel T. Griswold. "WTO Report Card II: An Exercise or Surrender of U.S. Sovereignty?" Cato Institute Trade Policy Briefing Paper no. 9, May 4, 2000.

Lindsey, Brink. *Against the Dead Hand: The Uncertain Struggle for Global Capitalism.* New York: John Wiley & Sons, 2002.

———. "Job Losses and Trade: A Reality Check." Cato Institute Trade Briefing Paper no. 19, March 17, 2004.

———. "The Trade Front: Combating Terrorism with Open Markets." Cato Institute Trade Policy Analysis no. 24, August 5, 2003.

Lindsey, Brink, and Daniel J. Ikenson. *Antidumping Exposed: The Devilish Details of Unfair Trade Law.* Washington: Cato Institute, 2003.

Norberg, Johan. *In Defense of Global Capitalism.* Washington: Cato Institute, 2003.

U.S. International Trade Commission. "The Economic Effects of Significant U.S. Import Restraints." June 2004.

All Cato Institute trade studies are available online at www.freetrade.org.

—Prepared by Brink Lindsey and Daniel Griswold

65. Immigration

Congress should

- expand, or at least maintain, current legal immigration quotas;
- focus border-control resources on efforts to keep terrorists out of the country;
- create a temporary worker visa for less-skilled immigrants from Mexico and other countries to work in the United States to meet labor shortages and reduce incentives for illegal immigration;
- allow workers already in the United States illegally to apply for temporary legal status provided they pose no threat to national security;
- repeal the arbitrary cap on H1-B visas for highly skilled workers; and
- reverse the recent decline in the number of refugees accepted by the United States.

America was founded, shaped, and built in large measure by immigrants seeking freedom and opportunity. Since 1820, more than 70 million immigrants have entered the United States legally, and each new wave stirred controversy in its day. In the mid-1800s, Irish immigrants were scorned as lazy drunks too beholden to the pope in Rome. At the turn of the century, a wave of "New Immigrants"—Poles, Italians, Austro-Hungarians, and Russian Jews—was believed to be too different to ever assimilate into American life. Today the same fears arise about immigrants from Latin American and Asia, but current critics of immigration are as wrong as their counterparts were in previous eras.

Immigration is not undermining the American experiment; it is an integral part of it. We are a nation of immigrants. Successive waves of immigrants have kept our country demographically young, enriched our culture, and added to our productive capacity as a nation, enhancing our influence in the world.

Immigration gives America an economic edge in the global economy. Immigrants bring innovative ideas and entrepreneurial spirit to the United States, most notably in Silicon Valley and other high-technology centers. They provide business contacts with other markets, enhancing America's ability to trade and invest profitably abroad. They keep our economy flexible, allowing American producers to keep prices down and meet changing consumer demands. An authoritative 1997 study by the National Research Council concluded that immigration delivers a "significant positive gain" to native Americans of as much as $10 billion each year.

Contrary to popular myth, immigrants do not push Americans out of jobs. Immigrants tend to fill jobs that Americans cannot or will not fill in sufficient numbers to meet demand, mostly at the high and low ends of the skill spectrum. Immigrants are disproportionately represented in such high-skilled fields as medicine, physics, and computer science but also in lower-skilled sectors such as hotels and restaurants, domestic service, construction, and light manufacturing. Immigrants also raise demand for goods as well as the supply. During the long boom of the 1990s, and especially in the second half of the decade, the national unemployment rate fell below 4 percent and real wages rose up and down the income scale during a time of relatively high immigration.

Immigrants are not a drain on government finances. The NRC study also found that the typical immigrant and his or her offspring will pay a net $80,000 more in taxes during their lifetimes than they collect in government services. For immigrants with college degrees, the net fiscal return is $198,000. It is true that low-skilled immigrants and refugees consume more in government services than they pay in taxes, but welfare and immigration reform legislation in 1996 made it much more difficult for new immigrants to collect welfare. As a result, immigrant use of welfare has plunged even more steeply than use among the general population. Immigration actually improves the finances of the two largest federal income-transfer programs, Social Security and Medicare.

Despite the claims of opponents of immigration, today's flow is not out of proportion to historical levels. Legal immigration in the last decade averaged about 900,000 people per year, historically high in absolute numbers, but the rate of 4.3 immigrants per year per 1,000 U.S. residents is less than half the rate during the Great Migration at the turn of the last century. (See Figure 65.1) In 2003, 11.7 percent of U.S. residents were foreign born, an increase from 4.7 percent in 1970 but still well below the 14.7 percent who were foreign born in 1910.

Figure 65.1
American Immigration in Perspective, by Decade, 1820–2003

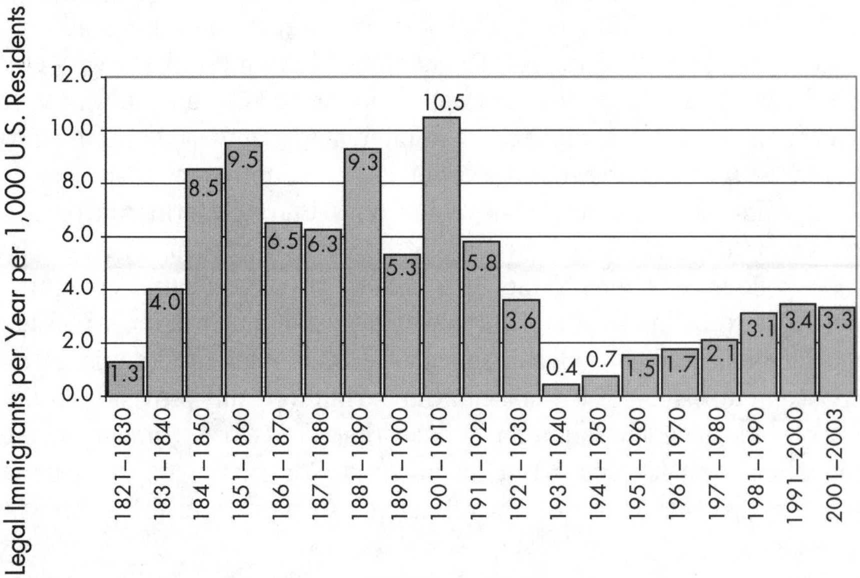

SOURCES: U.S. Census Bureau; and U.S. Office of Immigration Statistics, *2003 Yearbook of Immigration Statistics*.

Immigrants cannot be fairly blamed for causing "overpopulation" or "urban sprawl." America's annual population growth of 1 percent is below the average growth rate of the last century. According to the most recent census, 22 percent of U.S. counties lost population between 1990 and 2000. Immigrants have kept major metropolitan areas vibrant and are revitalizing demographically declining areas of the country.

Border Control and the War on Terrorism

In the wake of the terrorist attacks of September 11, 2001, long-time critics of immigration tried to exploit legitimate concerns about security to argue for drastic cuts in immigration. But "border security" and immigration are two distinct issues. Immigrants are only a small subset of the total number of foreigners who enter the United States every year. Of the 30 million foreigners who typically enter our country every year, fewer than 1 million eventually become immigrants. The vast majority come as tourists, business travelers, and students or are Mexicans and Canadians who cross the border for a few days to shop or visit family and then return home with no intention of settling permanently in the United States.

None of the 19 terrorists who attacked America on September 11, 2001, came as an immigrant. They did not apply to the Immigration and Naturalization Service for permanent status. Like most aliens who enter the United States, they were here on temporary tourist and student visas. We could reduce the number of immigrants to zero and still not stop terrorists from slipping into the country on nonimmigrant visas.

The Enhanced Border Security and Visa Entry Reform Act of 2002 represents the right kind of policy response to terrorism. The new law focuses directly on identifying terrorist suspects abroad and keeping them out of the country. Among its provisions, it requires tamper-resistant, machine-readable entry documents and restricts visas from countries that sponsor terrorism. Notably absent from the bill were any provisions rolling back levels of legal immigration or bolstering efforts to curb undocumented migration from Mexico. Most members of Congress rightly understood that immigrants who come to America to work are not a threat to national security.

The National Commission on Terrorist Attacks upon the United States (the "9/11 Commission") endorsed the major provisions of the 2002 border security law in its final report of August 2004. The commission rejected any calls for reduced levels of legal immigration. "Our borders and immigration system, including law enforcement, ought to send a message of welcome, tolerance, and justice to members of immigrant communities in the United States and in their countries of origin. We should reach out to immigrant communities. Good immigration services are one way of doing so that is valuable in every way—including intelligence," the commission concluded.

America's Legal Immigration System

The United States maintained an essentially unrestricted immigration policy for most of its history. The Chinese Exclusion Act of 1882 and some qualitative restrictions were the only exceptions. But in the 1920s Congress responded to growing xenophobia and fear that new immigrants were racially "inferior" by establishing strict quotas that favored immigrants from northern Europe. In 1965 Congress finally repealed race-based quotas and, in effect, increased the numerical limits. In 1990 Congress raised the numbers and included more visas for people whose immigration is employment based.

Non-Employment-Based Immigration

Current legal immigration is tightly regulated and limited by numerical quotas and per country ceilings that prevent people from a few countries from obtaining all the visas. Legal immigration is limited to refugees, close family members of citizens and legal residents, and individuals with a company to sponsor them. A limited number of "diversity" visas are also distributed to immigrants from "underrepresented" countries. All categories are numerically restricted, except for the "immediate relatives" of U.S. citizens, whose totals have not shown a long-term, upward trend.

Family Reunification

Under U.S. law, an American citizen can sponsor (1) a spouse or minor child, (2) a parent, (3) a married child or a child 21 or older, or (4) a brother or sister. A lawful permanent resident (green card holder) can sponsor only a spouse or child. No "extended family" immigration categories exist for aunts, uncles, or cousins. In 2000, 78 percent of all family-sponsored immigration visas went to spouses and children. The other 22 percent went to the parents and siblings of U.S. citizens.

Refugees

Congress should reject any rigid "cap" on the admission of refugees. Such a cap is designed to slash the number of refugees admitted and would prevent flexible responses to emerging world situations. The annual number of refugees is set each year by consultations between the president and Congress. The number of refugees admitted has been dropping steadily in recent years, from an average of 121,000 per year under the first President Bush, to 82,000 per year under President Clinton, to a 25-year low of only 27,000 in 2002. In fact, the number admitted in FY02 fell well below the 70,000 that the president and Congress had agreed upon in 2001. Although security concerns were cited, refugees are among the most thoroughly screened of visa categories. The U.S. Committee for Refugees estimated that, as of 2004, 11.9 million people had been displaced from their home countries by war, persecution, or natural disaster. To promote a more stable and humane world, Congress should keep the door open to refugees from other nations by raising the number of refugees allowed to the more traditional level of 100,000 or more.

Asylum

Unlike refugees, who are accepted for admission while still outside the United States, people seeking political asylum must first enter the country and then request permission to stay. Contrary to the popular impression, gaining political asylum is not automatic. According to the Homeland Security Department, fewer than one-third of the claims considered from 1996 through 2003 were approved. Administrative reforms corrected the system's key problems (asylum applicants can no longer receive work papers and disappear into the workforce). The number of first-time claims has dropped dramatically, and almost all new cases are completed within 180 days of filing.

The legislative changes contained in the 1996 immigration law were thus unnecessary and have created a new set of problems. There was no need to require individuals to file for asylum within one year of arriving in the United States, as Congress did in the 1996 immigration bill. Many victims of torture and persecution need time for their emotional wounds to heal and view asylum as an inevitable break with their families and followers back home.

Another problem is the "expedited removal" provision of the 1996 law, which allows low-level INS officials to prevent those arriving without valid documents from receiving a full hearing of their asylum claims. It is not difficult to understand why people fleeing torture or other forms of persecution often cannot obtain valid travel documents from their own governments. The "extraordinary circumstances" exception to the one-year time limit and the summary proceedings established to screen those entering without valid documents do not ensure a high enough standard of procedural protection for people with legitimate claims.

It is a human rights as well as an economic imperative that both the one-year time limit and the expedited removal provisions be changed.

Employment-Based Immigration: The H-1B Debate

Foreign-born workers have filled an important role in the American economy. Nowhere is the contribution of immigrants more apparent than in the high-technology and other knowledge-based sectors. Silicon Valley and other high-tech sectors would cease to function if we were to foolishly close our door to skilled and educated immigrants. These immigrants represent human capital that can make our entire economy more productive. Immigrants have founded companies and developed new products that have created employment opportunities for millions of Americans.

The primary means of hiring highly skilled foreign-born workers is the H-1B visa. Though overly bureaucratic, the system works reasonably well. It allows U.S. companies to hire in a timely manner foreign nationals with the right skills for the job. H-1B visas are generally approved within 60 days. They are valid for six years but must be renewed after three years. The company granted the visa must agree to pay the new employee at least the "prevailing wage" for that area and industry. H-1B visa holders are not immigrants or permanent residents, and they cannot progress toward citizenship.

A visa system for highly skilled foreign-born workers existed for decades without a cap, but in 1990 Congress imposed an arbitrary annual quota of 65,000 H-1B visas. As America's information economy gained steam in the second half of the 1990s, the quota proved to be too restrictive. In 2000 Congress raised the annual cap to 195,000 for three years, but under the law, the quota dropped back to the old level of 65,000 in FY04. As the high-tech industry recovers from the 2001 recession, the cap is once again far below demand, which could cripple the ability of America's most dynamic companies to remain ahead of global competition.

Despite the charge of critics, H-1B professionals do not depress wages, create unemployment, or cost taxpayers money. H-1B workers are generally among the best-paid workers in U.S. industry. Among the more than half a million H-1B visas issued from 1991 through September 1999, the Department of Labor found only seven cases of willful underpayment by an employer. The sharp downturn in the high-tech and information technology sectors that began in 2000 has cut the number of H1-B visa requests in half, demonstrating that visa requests are driven by demand, not by firms' desire to replace U.S. workers with lower-paid foreign workers.

Congress should act immediately to raise the cap to a high enough level to meet demand or, preferably, repeal the cap altogether to allow U.S. companies to hire the workers they need when they need them to stay competitive in the global economy. At the very least, Congress should permanently raise the cap to a minimum of 200,000 annually, with automatic annual increases of 10 percent thereafter. Department of Labor certifications should not place uneconomic regulatory burdens on U.S. firms that are already under market pressure to offer competitive wages and benefits to their workers.

Legal Immigration Reform: What Congress Should Do

Congress has followed a policy of "immigrants yes, welfare no" by overwhelmingly rejecting cuts in legal immigration while at the same time passing a welfare bill that makes immigrants ineligible for public assistance. Immigrant welfare use, often overstated, is now a dead issue in the immigration policy debate. Since illegal immigration is the main concern, and legal immigration is not a problem, it is not clear why Congress needs to make more than modest reforms to the current legal immigration system.

Congress should continue to keep the issues of legal and illegal immigration separate. For legal immigrants, Congress should at least maintain current family categories and quotas. Ideally, Congress should raise the current numbers by, among other things, setting aside separate visas for the one-third of spouses and children of lawful permanent residents in the immigration backlog who are physically separated from their sponsors. It should do so without tearing apart the current family immigration system, as the U.S. Commission on Immigration Reform recommended.

Illegal Immigration: What Congress Should Do

To better defend ourselves against terrorism and promote economic growth, America's border-control system requires a reorientation of mission. For the last two decades, U.S. immigration policy has been obsessed with nabbing mostly Mexican-born workers whose only "crime" is their desire to work, save, and build a better life for their families. Those workers pose no threat to national security.

The federal government's two-decade war against Mexican migration has failed by any objective measure. Employer sanctions and border blockades have not stopped the inflow of Mexican workers drawn by persistent demand for their labor. Coercive efforts to keep willing workers out have spawned an underground culture of fraud and smuggling, caused hundreds of unnecessary deaths in the desert, and diverted attention and resources away from real matters of border security. Those efforts have disrupted the traditional circular flow of Mexican migration, perversely increasing the stock of illegal Mexican workers and family members in the United States.

Important sectors of the U.S. economy have turned to low-skilled immigrant workers, documented and undocumented, to fill persistent job vacancies. Hotels and motels, restaurants, construction, light manufacturing, health care, retailing, and other services are major employers of low-skilled immigrant labor. The demand for less-skilled labor will continue to grow in the years ahead. According to the Department of Labor, 13 of the 20 occupation categories with the largest growth in absolute numbers in the next decade will require only "short-term on-the-job training" of one month or less—occupations in which low-skilled immigrants from Mexico and other countries can be expected to help meet the rising demand for workers. Across the U.S. economy, the Labor Department estimates that the total number of jobs in those low-skilled categories will increase by 4.6 million from 2002 to 2012.

Meanwhile, the supply of American workers suitable for such work continues to fall because of an aging workforce and rising education levels. The median age of American workers continues to increase as the large cohort of Baby Boomers begins to near retirement age. Younger and older workers alike are now more educated as the share of adult native men without a high school diploma has plunged, from more than 50 percent in 1960 to less than 10 percent today. Yet U.S. immigration law provides no legal channels through which low-skilled foreign-born workers can enter the United States to fill the growing gap between demand and supply on the lower rungs of the labor ladder.

Repeal Employer Sanctions

Congress should begin by repealing employer sanctions. Passed in 1986 and widely viewed as a failure, employer sanctions have made it a crime to "knowingly" hire an illegal immigrant. It should be the job of the federal government, not private business owners, to keep out of the country people who are not supposed to be here. The U.S. General Accounting Office found that employer sanctions have created a nationwide pattern of discrimination. The nation's largest labor organization, the AFL-CIO, has joined major business organizations such as the U.S. Chamber of Commerce in formally opposing employer sanctions as a tool of enforcement.

Congress must oppose any related expansion of INS "pilot projects" to a full-fledged national computerized employment ID system. It should also prohibit any requirement that government-issued documents, such as birth certificates and Social Security cards, become de facto national ID cards, as was the intention of the 1996 immigration bill. If such a law were enacted, one of our most basic rights, the right to earn a living, would be at the mercy of an unreliable government computer system. Computer verification would also compromise the right to privacy and invite abuse by government officials.

Reinstate Section 245(i)

Section 245(i) of U.S. immigration law is a humane provision that allows people who are residing in the United States and who are legally qualified to stay here to pay a fee to remain in the country while they apply for permanent residency. These are people who are typically married to American citizens or other legal residents, who are working, and who have become productive members of their communities. Although they are in technical violation of U.S. law, they pose no threat to our national security. They can be checked and processed by U.S. authorities more thoroughly here than at our overworked consulates abroad, all without disrupting their work and family life.

Legalize and Regularize Mexican Immigration

The best long-term solution to illegal immigration from Mexico is sustained growth south of the border to create sufficient opportunities and security at home for Mexican workers. Meanwhile, the United States and Mexico should take steps toward an immigration system that recognizes the reality and the benefits of Mexican migration to the United States.

One key element of a more sensible border policy would be a temporary visa system under which workers from Mexico and other countries would be allowed to work in the United States for a fixed time before returning home. Visa holders would be allowed to work in any job in which there was demand for their labor, including those occupations in which illegal immigrants commonly find work today. Such a program would allow Americans to enjoy the many benefits of employing foreign-born workers in sectors where demand for labor is especially high.

Another crucial element of real immigration reform would be a process that would allow undocumented workers already in the country to become legal. An estimated 10 million people were living in the United States without documents as of 2004. Millions of them hold responsible jobs in important sectors of the U.S. economy. Rounding them up and deporting them would impose a high fiscal, economic, and humanitarian cost, yet maintaining the status quo is also unacceptable. The right policy would be to grant temporary legal status to those who are currently working and who pose no national security threat. Such a legalization program need not be an "amnesty." Newly legalized workers could be required to pay a fine and to apply through existing channels before receiving permanent status.

An expanded and orderly visa program would drastically reduce the disorderly and dangerous flow of illegal immigrants across sparsely populated areas of America's 2,000-mile border with Mexico. It would enhance our national security by draining a large section of the underground swamp of smuggling and document fraud that facilitates illegal immigration.

Meanwhile, legalization of those already here would encourage millions of people now living in the shadows to make themselves known to authorities by registering with the government, reducing cover for terrorists who manage to enter the country and overstay their visas. Legalization would allow the government to devote more of its resources to keeping terrorists out of the country. A system that allows peaceful, hardworking immigrants to enter the United States legally would free thousands of government personnel and save resources that would then be available to fight terrorism.

Suggested Readings

Griswold, Daniel T. "Willing Workers: Fixing the Problem of Illegal Mexican Migration to the United States." Cato Institute Trade Policy Analysis no. 19, October 15, 2002.

Jacoby, Tamar, ed. *Reinventing the Melting Pot: The New Immigrants and What It Means to Be American.* New York: Basic Books, 2004.

Massey, Douglas S., Jorge Durand, and Nolan J. Malone. *Beyond Smoke and Mirrors: Mexican Immigration in an Era of Economic Integration.* New York: Russell Sage Foundation, 2002.

Masters, Suzette Brooks, and Ted Ruthizer. "The H-1B Straitjacket: Why Congress Should Repeal the Cap on Foreign-Born Highly Skilled Workers." Cato Institute Trade Briefing Paper no. 7, March 3, 2000.

Micklethwait, John. "The New Americans." *The Economist,* March 11, 2000.

Moore, Stephen. *A Fiscal Portrait of the Newest Americans.* Washington: Cato Institute and National Immigration Forum, 1998.

National Research Council. *The New Americans: Economic, Demographic, and Fiscal Effects of Immigration.* Washington: National Academy Press, 1997.

Pistone, Michele R. "New Asylum Laws: Undermining an American Ideal." Cato Institute Policy Analysis no. 299, March 24, 1998.

Simon, Julian L. *Immigration: The Demographic and Economic Facts.* Washington: Cato Institute and National Immigration Forum, 1995.

—Prepared by Daniel Griswold

66. International Financial Crises and the IMF

Congress should

- reject additional funding requests for the International Monetary Fund;
- close down the Exchange Stabilization Fund at the U.S. Department of the Treasury;
- avoid giving the IMF new missions, including that of overseeing sovereign debt restructuring or becoming a bankruptcy court for countries; and
- withdraw the United States from the IMF.

After the $30 billion bailout of Mexico in 1995, national currency and financial crises in developing countries increased, as did the incidence of IMF-led bailout packages. Since 1997 those packages have totaled more than $280 billion for Latin America, Asia, Russia, and Turkey. Many of those bailouts and the turmoil in international financial markets resulted in the United States contributing $18 billion to massively increase the IMF's resources in 1998. U.S. Treasury officials disingenuously claimed it did not cost U.S. taxpayers a dime, but Cato Institute chairman William Niskanen put the U.S. relationship with the IMF more accurately: "U.S. government membership in the IMF is like being a limited partner in a financial firm that makes high-risk loans, pays dividends at a rate lower than that on Treasury bills, and makes large periodic cash calls for additional funds."

But the monetary costs of supporting the IMF were not the most important reasons to have opposed more funding. The costs to the global economy are high, and the people who are most directly affected by IMF interventions—the world's poor—are those who can least afford it. If the goal is to help developing countries progress economically and to promote a liberal global economy, then, at the very least, rich countries should seek to reduce the IMF's resources and activities.

Free-market economists have long been critical of the IMF. International financial crises may have brought much attention to the fund in recent years, but the lending agency's record over the last 60 years has been dismal, as numerous books and studies have documented. The IMF does not appear to have helped countries either to achieve self-sustaining growth or to implement market reforms.

Despite its poor performance, the IMF has proven to be a remarkably resilient institution. When the system of fixed exchange rates ended in the early 1970s, so did the agency's original mission of maintaining exchange-rate stability by lending to countries experiencing balance-of-payments problems. Instead of closing down, however, the fund has created new missions for itself with each new crisis, each time expanding its economic influence or resources, or both. On average, the IMF has requested and received an increase in resources every five years.

Although the IMF in theory makes short-term loans in exchange for policy changes in recipient countries, it has not helped countries move to the free market. Instead, the fund has created loan addicts. More than 70 nations have depended on IMF aid for 20 or more years; at least 24 countries have received IMF credit for 30 or more years. Once a country receives IMF credit, it is likely to depend on IMF aid for most, if not all, of the following years. That is not evidence of either the success of the fund's so-called conditionality or the temporary nature of the fund's short-term loans.

The fund has thus moved away from its original mission of providing short-term balance-of-payment assistance and has instead fostered dependence on aid. Because of that, a congressional commission on international financial institutions, known as the Meltzer Commission, has advised that the fund should stop providing long-term loans, a recommendation endorsed by former U.S. treasury secretary Lawrence Summers. There has also been more of a consensus about the detrimental effects of bailouts, including strong statements to that effect by former treasury secretary Paul O'Neill. However, neither the IMF nor the U.S. Treasury has discontinued that IMF function. Using the IMF to bail out a country experiencing a currency or debt crisis is a bad idea for three reasons.

Moral Hazard

The first reason is that it creates moral hazard. That is, the more the IMF bails out countries, the more we can expect countries to slip into crises in the future because governments and investors will engage in risky behavior in the expectation that, if anything goes wrong, the IMF will come to their rescue.

Moral hazard at the international level is not new. During each election cycle from 1976 to 1994, for example, Mexico experienced a currency crisis caused by irresponsible monetary and fiscal policy. Each episode was accompanied by U.S. Treasury and IMF bailouts, each time in increasing amounts. And although IMF and U.S. officials claimed that the 1995 Mexican bailout was a success, its legacy was the Asian crisis of 1997— at least in its severity. Indeed, the bailout of Mexico was a signal to the world that, if anything went wrong in emerging economies, the IMF would come to investors' rescue. Moral hazard helps explain the near doubling of capital flows to East Asia in 1995 alone.

Governments in Asia were not discouraged from maintaining flawed policies as long as lenders kept the capital flowing. Lenders, for their part, behaved imprudently with the knowledge that government money would be used in case of financial troubles. That knowledge by no means meant that investors did not care if a crisis erupted, but it led to the mispricing of risk and a change in the investment calculations of lenders. Thailand, Indonesia, and South Korea, after all, shared some common factors that should have led to more investor caution but did not. Those factors included borrowing in foreign currencies and lending in domestic currency under pegged exchange rates, extensively borrowing in the short term while lending in the long term, lack of supervision of borrowers' balance sheets by foreign lenders, government-directed credit, and shaky financial systems. The financial crisis in Asia was created in Asia, but the aggravating effect of moral hazard was extensive. As Michael Prowse of the *Financial Times* commented after the Mexican bailout: "Rubin and Co. wanted to make global capitalism safe for the mutual fund investor. They actually made it far riskier."

The facts that governments would never choose to lead their countries into crises and that national leaders have been replaced after such crises are often cited as evidence that moral hazard is not a problem. In fact, "moral hazard is not all-or-nothing but operates at the margin," explains economist Lawrence H. White. "Any IMF policy that allows finance ministers to delay the day of reckoning reduces their caution, especially so where political instability makes their planning horizons short."

Moral hazard also exists at the national level, where governments explicitly or implicitly guarantee that they will rescue domestic banks, thus encouraging risky bank behavior. The proliferation of government-subsidized risk since 1982 has led to at least 90 severe banking crises in the developing world, and the bailout costs in 20 of those cases have ranged between 10 and 25 percent of gross domestic product. In a world of increasingly liberal capital flows, IMF bailouts only encourage governments to maintain flawed arrangements and foreign lenders to keep lending to those governments. Thus, even in countries whose monetary and fiscal policies appear conservative, crises can break out as malinvestment and the need to pay for bailouts become evident. The claim that markets react irrationally in countries whose macroeconomic fundamentals are sound ignores the liabilities governments face under those conditions—a factor markets take into account.

Still, advocates of the IMF argue that it must lend to prevent a "contagion effect" in other countries. The fund has thus provided bailouts to countries after economic crises have occurred (e.g., Mexico and Thailand) and before potential crises (e.g., Argentina, Brazil, and Russia). Neither timing has successfully prevented future financial turmoil. Countries that have succumbed to financial crises have done so because of poor domestic policies; countries that do not maintain poor policies have not suffered from so-called contagion. The real contagion effect is not what IMF proponents typically have in mind, but rather that of future crises encouraged by the bailouts themselves.

An Expensive, Unjust Solution

IMF bailouts are expensive, bureaucratic, and fundamentally unjust solutions to economic crises. In the first place, the financial aid cuts investors' losses rather than allowing them to bear the full responsibility for their decisions. Just as profits should not be socialized when times are good, neither should losses be socialized during difficult times. "The $57 billion committed to Korea," Columbia economist Jeffrey Sachs observed, "didn't help anybody but the banks." Unfortunately, ordinary Asian citizens who had nothing to do with creating the crisis are being forced to pay the added debt burden imposed by IMF loans.

IMF bailouts pose another burden on ordinary citizens because the bailouts don't work very well. The fund's money goes to the governments that have created the crises to begin with and that have shown themselves to be unwilling or reluctant to introduce necessary reforms. Giving money to such governments does not tend to promote market reforms; it tends to delay them because it takes the pressure off governments to change their policies. Suspension of loans will tend to concentrate the minds of policymakers in the various troubled countries. To the extent that the IMF steps in and provides money, reform will be less forthcoming. Indeed, despite recovery in some Asian countries in the years immediately following the crisis, fundamental structural reform has been slow or lacking. Thus, the citizens of recipient nations suffer the added burden of IMF intervention. Not only do they have to pay a greater debt, they also have to suffer prolonged economic agony that is produced by the fund's bailouts.

But what about the fund's "strong conditionality"? Don't the strict conditions of IMF lending ensure that important policy changes will be made? Again, the record of long-term dependence of countries shows that conditionality has not worked well in the past. The Meltzer Commission, for example, surveyed the research on conditionality, including that of the IMF and the World Bank, and found "no evidence of systematic, predictable effects from most of the conditions." In addition to the fund's poor record, there is another good reason why IMF conditions have little credibility. As we have seen with Russia over the past several years, a country— especially a highly visible one—that does not stick to IMF conditions risks having its loans suspended. When loans are cut off, recipient governments tend to become more serious about reform. Note that the IMF encourages misbehaving governments to introduce reforms by cutting loans off; it is the *cutoff* of credit that induces policy change.

Unfortunately, when policy changes are forthcoming, the IMF resumes lending. Indeed, the IMF has a bureaucratic incentive to lend. It simply cannot afford to watch countries reform on their own because that would risk making the IMF appear irrelevant. The resumption of financial aid starts the process over again and prolongs the period of reform. The fund's pressure to lend money in order to keep borrowers current on previous loans and to be able to ask for more money is well documented. The IMF's bureaucratic incentive to lend is also well known to both recipient governments and the IMF itself, which makes the fund's conditionality that much less credible. It is telling that the conditions of the IMF's $11.2 billion loan to Russia, approved in July 1998 (weeks before the collapse of the ruble), were virtually identical to those of previous loan packages totaling more than $20 billion in 1992, 1993, 1994, 1995, and 1996.

Similarly, a 2004 IMF report on its perfomance in Argentina leading up to the collapse of that country's currency in 2002 concluded: "The IMF on its part erred in the precrisis period by supporting the country's weak policies too long, even after it had become evident in the late 1990s

665

that the political ability to deliver the necessary fiscal discipline and structural reforms was lacking. . . . Even though the annual deficit targets were missed every year from 1994, financing arrangements with Argentina were maintained by repeatedly granting waivers.''

Undermining Better Solutions

Third, IMF bailouts undermine superior, less-expensive market solutions. In the absence of an IMF, creditors and debtors would do what creditors and debtors always do in cases of illiquidity or insolvency: renegotiate debt or enter into bankruptcy procedures. In a world without the IMF, both parties would have an incentive to do so because the alternative, to do nothing, would mean a complete loss. Direct negotiations between private parties and bankruptcy procedures are essential if capitalism is to work. As James Glassman has stated, capitalism without bankruptcy is like Christianity without Hell. IMF bailouts, unfortunately, undermine one of the most important underpinnings of a free economy by overriding the market mechanism. As the Meltzer Commission noted: ''The IMF creates disincentives for debt resolution when it lends to insolvent sovereign borrowers. This is contrary to an early hope that IMF lending to insolvent countries would facilitate debt renegotiation. The opposite often seems to transpire; the provision of an apparently unlimited external supply of funds forestalls creditors and debtors from offering concessions.'' There is simply no reason why international creditors and borrowers should be treated any differently than are lenders and debtors in the domestic market.

Governments would also react differently if no IMF interventions were forthcoming. There would be little alternative to widespread and rapid reforms if policymakers were not shielded from economic reality. Lawrence Lindsey, former chief economic adviser to President Bush, who opposed bailouts, noted, for example, ''All of the 'conditions' supposedly negotiated by the IMF will be forced on South Korea by the market.'' Of course, there is always the possibility that a government would be reluctant to change its ways under any circumstances; but that is a possibility that is larger, and indeed has become a reality, under IMF programs. ''Perhaps, the IMF's assistance cushions the decline in income and living standards,'' reflected the Meltzer Commission. But it found that ''neither the IMF, nor others, has produced much evidence that its policies and actions have this beneficial effect.''

The IMF as Bankruptcy Court for Countries?

Recognizing the dysfunctional relationship between international creditors and debtors, and in an effort to "minimize moral hazard," in the words of former IMF managing director Horst Kohler, the IMF proposed a new way of dealing with sovereign debt and default. The fund's proposed Sovereign Debt Restructuring Mechanism, which would turn the IMF into a sort of bankruptcy court for countries, was subsequently abandoned by the IMF, largely because there was no demand for it from either creditors or debtors. The idea is nevertheless worth reviewing as it is possible that it will be revived in the future.

The international bankruptcy proposal would fundamentally change the mission of the IMF. The spectacular collapse of the highly indebted Argentine economy in 2002, after having received IMF bailout packages of more than $40 billion, indisputably revealed the need for a new approach to debt problems that did not shield lenders and borrowers from economic reality at all costs.

Yet the bankruptcy approach proposed by the fund is fraught with problems. The changes called for require the IMF's charter to be amended, a procedure that would take years to complete if accepted by its members. The fund would play a central role in determining what countries would qualify for default and why, including countries holding IMF debt. IMF financing would still be used during debt negotiations. In practice, that would encourage creditors to prolong the workout process in an effort to extract more IMF financing; debtors could also use the IMF money to game the system and delay needed reforms. The result of putting the fund at the center of debt renegotiations would likely be unpredictability, financial volatility, and higher borrowing costs to emerging markets across the board regardless of whether some countries merit such an outcome or not.

Better approaches involve direct negotiations between creditors and debtors without the IMF's cumbersome, third-party interventions. For example, Undersecretary of the Treasury for International Affairs John Taylor has proposed that creditors begin relying on collective action clauses, which would allow a majority of creditors to negotiate in the name of all creditors in the event of a default, thus eliminating the problem of "holdout" creditors. Carnegie Mellon University economists Adam Lerrick and Allan Meltzer point out that all of the protections offered by a formal bankruptcy court can be incorporated into new debt issues. Lerrick and Meltzer also show how market mechanisms already exist to renegotiate outstanding debt in a short period of time without the aid of the IMF. Such well-established capital market tools as exchange offers and exit consent amendments can be used to voluntarily convert old debt into new debt with majority action clauses and to change the nonpayment terms of the old debt. Those tools, and Argentina's experience with a well-organized creditors' committee formed before the country defaulted, undermine the argument that coordination among creditors would be too difficult to achieve absent an IMF-backed bankruptcy procedure.

The IMF as a Lender of Last Resort and Surveillance Agency?

Many people who recognize the practical problems of IMF bailouts, including moral hazard, questionable policy advice, and the difficulty of enforcing conditions, still believe that the IMF is needed as an international lender of last resort. Yet the IMF does not perform that function now, nor can it. A true lender of last resort provides funds at a penalty rate to solvent banks that are temporarily threatened by panic, thereby containing financial turmoil. By contrast, the IMF provides subsidized funds that bail out insolvent financial institutions, thereby discouraging much-needed bankruptcy proceedings and corporate restructuring. The IMF cannot act quickly or create money as can true lenders of last resort. Countries that experience threats to their financial systems can rely on their own central banks as lenders of last resort. That includes the United States, where the Federal Reserve is charged with such a mission. The Fed's failure to perform that mission in the last century—not the absence of an international lender of last resort—led to the Great Depression. It is highly improbable that the Fed would repeat the same monumental policy mistakes today.

Others have recommended that the IMF strengthen its role as a watchdog agency that provides an "early warning" of potential financial troubles. Yet it is unclear how a warning mechanism would work. As economist Raymond Mikesell asks, "Who would be warned and when? As soon as the financial community receives a warning that a country is facing financial difficulty, a massive capital outflow is likely to occur, in which case crisis prevention would be out of the question."

On the other hand, if the IMF perceives serious financial difficulties in a country and does not disclose that information, then it undermines its credibility as a credit-rating agency for countries. That appears to have been the case in Thailand, where the IMF claimed, postcrisis, that it issued warnings about the economy before the crisis erupted but kept those concerns confidential. The fund's credibility is further undercut by inherent conflicts of interest: in many cases, it would be evaluating countries in which it has its own money at stake; in all cases, it would be evaluating countries that, as member-owners of the IMF, have contributed to the fund's pool of resources. Only by ceasing to lend could the agency increase its integrity. At that point, however, its evaluations would merely replicate a service already available.

The Exchange Stabilization Fund

The executive branch has also used a little-known account, the Exchange Stabilization Fund, at the Treasury Department to circumvent Congress in providing foreign aid. Originally set up in 1934 to stabilize the value of the dollar, the ESF has since been used to prop up foreign currencies and economies. Most recently, it has been used as a bailout fund for countries in crisis. In 1995 the ESF made a $12 billion loan, its largest, to Mexico; it has since made available billions of dollars more to South Korea, Thailand, Indonesia, and other countries.

The ESF should be closed down because its bailout function suffers from the same defects that afflict the IMF: it creates moral hazard, delays reforms, and precludes superior market solutions to financial crises. Moreover, the ESF is an undemocratic institution since it is exempt from legislative oversight and its transactions, under the sole discretion of the executive branch, are secretive. Economist Anna Schwartz finds that the ESF failed even in its original mission, having "always been wasteful and ineffective at controlling the relative price of the U.S. dollar."

Conclusion

Crises in Latin America, Asia, and elsewhere have occurred because of flawed domestic policies. Bailouts by the IMF or the U.S. Treasury only encourage further crises and aggravate current ones. At a time when the world is moving toward the market, the bureaucratic response to government-induced financial turmoil makes matters worse. The market is far more effective in enforcing conditions, promoting reform, and minimizing the risk of a crisis spreading in the near term or far into the future. It is also more effective at dealing with sovereign debt and default. The United States and other major donors should reject further funding for the IMF or schemes in which the IMF has a high degree of influence in creditor-debtor negotiations, as is currently the case with Argentina. That would send a signal to the world that the fund's resources are not, in fact,

669

unlimited and that lenders and borrowers should be held accountable for their actions. Beyond that, the United States should help the world's poor by withdrawing from the IMF.

Suggested Readings

Calomiris, Charles W. "The IMF's Imprudent Role as Lender of Last Resort." *Cato Journal* 17, no. 3 (Winter 1998).

DeRosa, David. *In Defense of Free Capital Markets: The Case against the New International Financial Architecture*. Princeton, NJ: Bloomberg, 2001.

Hoskins, W. Lee, and James W. Coons. "Mexico: Policy Failure, Moral Hazard, and Market Solutions." Cato Institute Policy Analysis no. 243, October 10, 1995.

"International Financial Crises: What Role for Government?" Special issue, *Cato Journal* 23, no. 1 (Spring–Summer 2003).

International Financial Institution Advisory Commission (Meltzer Commission). "Report to the U.S. Congress and the U.S. Department of the Treasury." March 8, 2000. www.house.gov/jec/imf/meltzer.htm.

Lerrick, Adam, and Allan H. Meltzer. "Sovereign Default: The Private Sector Can Resolve Bankruptcy without a Formal Court." Carnegie Mellon Gailliot Center for Public Policy, *Quarterly International Economics Report*, April 2002.

Meltzer, Allan H. "Asian Problems and the IMF." *Cato Journal* 17, no. 3 (Winter 1998).

Schwartz, Anna J. "The IMF's Dubious Proposal for a Universal Bankruptcy Law for Sovereign Debtors." Cato Institute Foreign Policy Briefing no. 75, March 5, 2003.

———. "Time to Terminate the ESF and the IMF." Cato Institute Foreign Policy Briefing no. 48, August 26, 1998.

Shultz, George, William Simon, and Walter Wriston. "Who Needs the IMF?" *Wall Street Journal*, February 3, 1998.

Vásquez, Ian. "The Asian Crisis: Why the IMF Should Not Intervene." *Vital Speeches*, April 15, 1998.

———. "The Brady Plan and Market-Based Solutions to Debt Crises." *Cato Journal* 16, no. 2 (Fall 1996).

———. "Repairing the Lender-Borrower Relationship in International Finance." Cato Institute Foreign Policy Briefing no. 54, September 27, 1999.

———. "A Retrospective on the Mexican Bailout." *Cato Journal* 21, no. 3 (Winter 2002).

Vásquez, Ian, ed. *Global Fortune: The Stumble and Rise of World Capitalism*. Washington: Cato Institute, 2000.

—Prepared by Ian Vásquez

67. U.S. Policy toward Latin America

Policymakers should

- unilaterally open the U.S. market to goods from Latin America,
- support the Central American Free Trade Agreement,
- support the Free Trade Area of the Americas, and
- facilitate dollarization for any country that wishes to adopt the dollar as its national currency.

In limited but important ways, Washington can positively influence economic policy in Latin America. At a time when much of the region is experiencing economic and political instability, the rise of neopopulism, and a general backlash against free-market reforms that were partially implemented in the 1990s, the United States should exercise its influence by opening its market to the region's goods and by encouraging market reforms.

During most of the time since the passage of the North American Free Trade Agreement with Mexico and Canada in 1993, however, the United States showed no such leadership. Instead, Washington promised to create a hemispheric free-trade zone, known as the Free Trade Area of the Americas, but made little effort to promote the idea.

The result was unfortunate and a window of opportunity was lost. Latin American countries that were eager to enter into an FTAA gradually became disillusioned with years of U.S. inaction, and some have now turned decidedly against the idea of free trade. Worse, as economist Sebastian Edwards points out, Washington's promise of promoting the FTAA had the perverse effect of actually halting unilateral trade barrier reductions in Latin America as those countries waited to negotiate reductions as a group with the United States, an expectation that went unfulfilled. Moreover, since the Mexican peso crisis of 1994–95, Washington has supported massive International Monetary Fund bailouts that have encouraged irresponsible behavior by investors and policymakers and have surely increased the severity of economic crises in the region.

President Bush has emphasized the FTAA and bilateral trade agreements as policy priorities. His administration's support for increased steel tariffs and farm subsidies damaged Washington's credibility in a region already wary of U.S. intentions. But the Bush administration regained the initiative, having ushered the U.S.-Chile Free Trade Agreement into law and having negotiated free-trade agreements with Central America and the Dominican Republic. To understand the importance of free trade in Latin America, we must first understand where the region has been.

Latin America since the 1990s

The early 1990s saw the introduction of far-reaching market reforms in many, but not all, Latin American countries, especially in the areas of monetary policy, trade and investment liberalization, and privatization of state-owned enterprises. Countries in the region ended hyperinflation, reduced their tariffs unilaterally, and eventually sold more than $150 billion of state assets. The initial results were high growth and the widespread popularity of the reforms in the countries that did the most to reform. Mexican president Carlos Salinas was the most popular outgoing president in Mexican history in 1994, and Presidents Alberto Fujimori of Peru and Carlos Menem of Argentina were reelected by wide margins in the mid-1990s.

By the end of the decade and the beginning of the next one, however, a number of countries had experienced years of recession, political instability, and economic crises. Even countries that had introduced only timid reforms had that experience. The IMF bailed out Mexico, Argentina, Brazil, and Uruguay, some more than once. Most spectacular was the collapse of the Argentine economy in early 2002. That country's default and devaluation sent it into a deep depression, calling into question market reforms in the minds of many Argentineans. Latin America's disappointing per capita growth of 1.2 percent in the 1990s was still better than that of the "lost decade" of the 1980s (-0.2 percent), but it certainly did not live up to expectations and was too often accompanied by economic turmoil. It is within that context of disillusionment that politicians using populist or demagogic rhetoric have emerged in Argentina, Bolivia, Venezuela, Peru, and elsewhere, vilifying the free market as the source of their countries' troubles.

But to blame the market is hopelessly wrongheaded. It is important to remember that the regionwide shift to the market occurred because of the failure of past policies, not because governments were committed to free-market principles. For example, the left-leaning ruling party in Mexico; the Peronist party in Argentina; and Fujimori's upstart party, which campaigned against radical market reforms in Peru, introduced liberalization. By the mid-1990s, with the success of the early reforms, governments lost interest in liberalization. The unfinished reform agenda was extensive and brought diminishing returns in the form of slower growth and negative economic indicators. Argentina, for example, suffered from chronically high unemployment throughout the 1990s because it never reformed its rigid labor laws. Latin America had only begun to embrace economic freedom.

Indeed, a whole range of institutions and policies has been left untouched. The pervasiveness of a vast informal economy in most Latin American countries attests to that fact. The region's citizens have long responded to the high costs of the formal legal and regulatory system by simply operating outside it. They have found the formal system of rules to be prohibitively expensive. The private property rights of the poor in urban and rural areas, for example, are typically not recognized or protected by the state since property titling is complicated or impossible. Yet private property lies at the heart of a market system, and the absence of property titles severely restrains the creation of wealth. Bureaucratic red tape also pushes people into the informal sector. Opening a small business in Latin America legally can cost thousands of dollars in licensing fees and take months or years for approval—a procedure that costs less and takes days in rich countries. The rule of law, another institution essential to the functioning of a market economy, is severely defective or nonexistent in the region. Latin America has been given low scores on both the rule of law and business regulation in *Economic Freedom of the World*.

Other sectors, including health care, education, and public security have seen virtually no reform although they have continued to deteriorate, often despite increases in spending. That situation has led Argentinean economist Ricardo López Murphy to complain that Argentineans pay Swedish-level tax rates for public services of African quality.

Thus, Latin America in the 1990s moved partially down the path of economic freedom, but it still has a long way to travel if it is to sustain growth and avoid financial turmoil. Indeed, the continued adherence to old policy practices in large part explains the region's economic crises of the past decade. The crash of the Mexican peso, for example, resulted from a government-managed exchange rate and expansionary monetary and fiscal policies during an election year, policies thoroughly inconsistent with market economics. Likewise, Argentina's default resulted from a 90 percent increase in both public spending and debt from 1991 to 2000, far outstripping the 50 percent growth in gross domestic product of that period.

Chile Teaches the Real Lessons from Latin America

Despite such disappointments, the most important lessons coming out of Latin America are encouraging. As Jackson Diehl of the *Washington Post* notes, "The latest debt crisis is serving to underline not just the failures of those countries that embraced liberal economics in the 1990s but the breakthrough success of the two nations that did it right: Chile and Mexico." Those two countries and some Central American nations are increasingly setting themselves apart from the rest of Latin America in terms of economic and political performance.

The sharpest contrast is provided by Chile, the country that has applied and maintained the most far-reaching and coherent set of market-liberal policies for the longest time. The resulting high growth has enabled the country to more than double its per capita income in the last 15 years and to achieve impressive advances in a range of human development indicators. According to the Santiago-based Institute for Liberty and Development, for example, Chilean growth of about 7 percent from 1987 to 1998 reduced the poverty rate from 45 to 22 percent during that period.

Mexico has likewise maintained economic stability and a growth rate higher than the regional average since the peso crisis of 1994–95. Like Chile, it has accomplished much within the context of democratic transfers of power. Mexican growth has raised per capita income above precrisis levels and has done so relatively rapidly. The key to Mexico's performance has been NAFTA. Free trade with the United States enabled Mexico to begin recovering from its crisis within a year. It took Mexico six years to recover from its economic crisis of 1982, at a time when its economy was fairly closed. (Although a free-trade agreement does not guarantee that a country will not backslide on market-oriented policies, it will tend to discourage policymakers from doing so and discipline them when they commit policy mistakes.)

The divergence in performance between the free-trade countries of Chile and Mexico and the more protectionist countries in most of the rest of the region will become even clearer in the coming years, especially if neopopulism holds sway in the latter countries. The United States can buttress that demonstration effect by signing on to a free-trade agreement with Central America and the Dominican Republic. As does the free-trade agreement with Chile, CAFTA would not only benefit the United States and its trade treaty partners; it would also send a signal to the rest of the region that the United States is willing to reward countries that implement free-market policies. Washington should follow suit with other Latin American countries that have liberalized their economies and are eager to sign a trade treaty with the United States. Indeed, Congress should also support efforts to promote a Free Trade Area of the Americas, although that initiative looks increasingly difficult to realize, given the region's political outlook.

Independent of free-trade negotiations, the United States should immediately reduce its barriers to Latin America's exports, especially textiles and agricultural products. At a time when U.S. credibility on trade is recovering from a low point, such a move would restore some goodwill toward Washington and might help persuade reluctant countries to reduce some of their own trade barriers. At the very least, the United States could then not be blamed for hypocrisy, and the welfare of both the United States and Latin America would improve. Such a unilateral policy of reducing trade barriers, moreover, would not be in conflict with the goal of negotiating free-trade agreements. As Cato Institute scholar Brink Lindsey points out, the United States has regularly signed trade agreements affecting sectors of the U.S. economy that enjoy virtually no protectionism. For countries that are interested in free trade with the United States, such agreements offer the advantage of "locking in" free trade both at home and abroad. Indeed, the certainty provided by free-trade treaties is one of their greatest benefits and explains why they tend to result in increases of both trade and investment.

Dollarization

The United States should support another positive trend in the hemisphere: dollarization. In an effort to eliminate currency risk, including sudden and large devaluations and other manifestations of irresponsible monetary policy, Ecuador and El Salvador have joined Panama as countries that use the U.S. dollar as their national currency. Because most of the region's central banks have a poor record of maintaining the value of their currencies, Latin Americans already use the dollar widely, and it has become the currency of choice in many countries. Other countries may wish to replace their currencies with the dollar as well.

The United States should neither discourage nor encourage those moves but should facilitate official dollarization where it occurs. That may mean sharing the dollar's seigniorage—or the profit that derives from printing currency—with countries that decide to dollarize. In that way, the United States would neither gain nor lose money as a result of another country's decision to dollarize, but the dollarizing country might more easily dollarize if it could still earn seigniorage from the currency it uses. Dollarization alone cannot solve a country's economic problems, but for countries with poor monetary policies, dollarization would end currency risk, reduce interest rates, and help stimulate investment and growth.

Time for a U.S. Policy toward Latin America

The United States can play a strategic role in promoting economic freedom, stability, and growth in Latin America—something it has hardly done in the past decade. That means reversing a policy characterized by bailouts, protectionist measures, and mixed messages to the region. It also means that Washington must end its destructive war on drugs in the region, which works at cross-purposes with important U.S. policy priorities (see Chapter 60 on the international war on drugs). In drug-source countries such as Colombia, the drug war is fueling corruption and violence, financing terrorism, undermining the rule of law, and otherwise debilitating the institutions of civil society. The impact of the U.S.-led war on drugs south of the border has been imperceptible in the United States, but its consequences in Latin America are completely at odds with Washington's stated goal of encouraging free markets.

The rhetoric of free trade must be followed by policy actions consistent with such language. Congress should support a unilateral reduction of trade barriers to the region's goods and continue to negotiate free-trade agreements with countries eager to do so. The United States would thus highlight the success of market reformers in the region by rewarding them without penalizing others. The diverging performances of the countries that embrace economic freedom and the rest can have a powerful effect on the policy direction that Latin American countries subsequently take.

Suggested Readings

Carpenter, Ted Galen. *Bad Neighbor Policy: Washington's Futile War on Drugs in Latin America.* New York: Palgrave/Macmillan, 2003.

Falcoff, Mark. "Colombia: A Questionable Choice of Objectives." AEI Latin American Outlook, March 2002.

Griswold, Daniel, and Daniel Ikenson. "The Case for CAFTA: Consolidating Central America's Freedom Revolution." Cato Institute Trade Briefing Paper no. 21, September 21, 2004.

Hanke, Steve. "The Dominican Republic: Resolving the Banking Crisis and Restoring Growth." Cato Institute Foreign Policy Briefing no. 83, July 20, 2004.

Mendoza, Plinio Apuleyo, Carlos Alberto Montaner, and Alvaro Vargas Llosa. *Guide to the Perfect Latin American Idiot.* New York: Madison Books, 2001.

Montaner, Carlos Alberto. *Las Raíces Torcidas de América Latina.* Barcelona: Plaza & Janes, 2001.

Schuler, Kurt. "Fixing Argentina." Cato Institute Policy Analysis no. 445, July 16, 2002.

Vargas Llosa, Alvaro. *Liberty for Latin America.* New York: Farrar, Strauss & Giroux, 2005.

Vargas Llosa, Mario. Foreword to *The Other Path,* by Hernando de Soto. New York: Harper and Row, 1989.

Vásquez, Ian. "A Retrospective on the Mexican Bailout." *Cato Journal* 21, no. 3 (Winter 2002).

Véliz, Claudio. *The New World of the Gothic Fox: Culture and Economy in English and Spanish America.* Berkeley: University of California Press, 1994.

—Prepared by Ian Vásquez

68. Foreign Aid and Economic Development

Congress should

- abolish the U.S. Agency for International Development and end government-to-government aid programs;
- withdraw from the World Bank and the five regional multilateral development banks;
- not use foreign aid to encourage or reward market reforms in the developing world;
- eliminate programs, such as enterprise funds, that provide loans to the private sector in developing countries and oppose schemes that guarantee private-sector investments abroad;
- privatize or abolish the Export-Import Bank, the Overseas Private Investment Corporation, the U.S. Trade and Development Agency, and other sources of international corporate welfare;
- forgive the debts of heavily indebted countries on the condition that they not receive any further foreign aid; and
- end government support of microenterprise lending and nongovernmental organizations.

In 2002 President Bush called for increasing U.S. bilateral development assistance by about 50 percent by fiscal year 2006, gradually raising the aid above the prevailing level of roughly $10 billion. The Millennium Challenge Account, managed by a new government agency, the Millennium Challenge Corporation, was created in 2004 to direct the additional funds to poor countries that have sound policy environments. Likewise, the World Bank is advocating a doubling of the current $60 billion official development assistance worldwide.

Those calls for significant increases in foreign aid are based on the argument that aid agencies have learned from the failure of past foreign aid programs and that overseas assistance can now be generally effective in promoting growth. But what we know about aid and development provides little reason for such enthusiasm:

- There is no correlation between aid and growth.
- Aid that goes into a poor policy environment doesn't work and contributes to debt.
- Aid conditioned on market reforms has been a failure.
- Countries that have adopted market-oriented policies have done so because of factors unrelated to aid.
- There is a strong relationship between economic freedom and growth.

A widespread consensus has formed about the above points, even among development experts. As developing countries began introducing market reforms in the late 1980s and early 1990s, the most successful reformers also experienced noticeably better economic performance. As would be expected, the improvement among the successful reformers also improved the apparent performance of foreign aid in those countries—thus the new emphasis on giving aid to countries that have already adopted good policies. The new approach to aid is dubious for many reasons, not the least of which is the fact that countries with sound policies will already be rewarded with economic growth and do not need foreign aid. In any event, much, if not most, foreign assistance will continue to follow traditional practice.

The Dismal Record of Foreign Aid

By the 1990s the failure of conventional government-to-government aid schemes had been widely recognized and brought the entire foreign assistance process under scrutiny. For example, a Clinton administration task force conceded that, "despite decades of foreign assistance, most of Africa and parts of Latin America, Asia and the Middle East are economically worse off today than they were 20 years ago." As early as 1989 a bipartisan task force of the House Foreign Affairs Committee concluded that U.S. aid programs "no longer either advance U.S. interests abroad or promote economic development."

Multilateral aid has also played a prominent role in the post–World War II period. The World Bank, to which the United States is the major contributor, was created in 1944 to provide aid mostly for infrastructure projects in countries that could not attract private capital on their own. The World Bank has since expanded its lending functions, as have the five regional development banks that have subsequently been created on the World Bank's model: the Inter-American Development Bank, the Asian Development Bank, the African Development Bank, the European Bank for Reconstruction and Development, and the Middle East Development Bank.

Despite record levels of lending, however, the multilateral development banks have not achieved more success at promoting economic growth than has U.S. AID. Numerous self-evaluations of World Bank performance over the years, for example, have uncovered high failure rates of bank-financed projects. In 2000 the bipartisan Meltzer Commission of the U.S. Congress found a 55 to 60 percent failure rate of World Bank projects based on the bank's own evaluations. A 1998 World Bank report concluded that aid agencies "saw themselves as being primarily in the business of dishing out money, so it is not surprising that much [aid] went into poorly managed economies—with little result." The report also said that foreign aid had often been "an unmitigated failure." "No one who has seen the evidence on aid effectiveness," commented Oxford University economist Paul Collier in 1997, "can honestly say that aid is currently achieving its objective."

Although a small group of countries in the developing world (some of which received aid at some point) has achieved self-sustaining economic growth, most recipients of aid have not. Rather, as a 1989 U.S. AID report suggested, aid has tended to create dependence on the part of borrower countries.

There are several reasons why massive transfers from the developed to the developing world have not led to a corresponding transfer of prosperity. Aid has traditionally been lent to governments, has supported central planning, and has been based on a fundamentally flawed vision of development.

By lending to governments, U.S. AID and the multilateral development agencies supported by Washington have helped expand the state sector at the expense of the private sector in poor countries. U.S. aid to India from 1961 to 1989, for example, amounted to well over $2 billion, almost all of which went to the Indian state. Ghanaian-born economist George Ayittey complained that, as late as 1989, 90 percent of U.S. aid to sub-Saharan Africa went directly to governments.

Foreign aid has thus financed governments, both authoritarian and democratic, whose policies have been the principal cause of their countries' impoverishment. Trade protectionism, byzantine licensing schemes, inflationary monetary policy, price and wage controls, nationalization of industries, exchange-rate controls, state-run agricultural marketing boards, and restrictions on foreign and domestic investment, for example, have all been supported explicitly or implicitly by U.S. foreign aid programs.

Not only has lack of economic freedom kept literally billions of people in poverty; development planning has thoroughly politicized the economies of developing countries. Centralization of economic decisionmaking in the hands of political authorities has meant that a substantial amount of poor countries' otherwise useful resources has been diverted to unproductive activities such as rent seeking by private interests or politically motivated spending by the state.

Research by economist Peter Boone of the London School of Economics confirms the dismal record of foreign aid to the developing world. After reviewing aid flows to more than 95 countries, Boone found that "virtually all aid goes to consumption" and that "aid does not increase investment and growth, nor benefit the poor as measured by improvements in human development indicators, but it does increase the size of government."

It has become abundantly clear that as long as the conditions for economic growth do not exist in developing countries, no amount of foreign aid will be able to produce economic growth. Moreover, economic growth in poor countries does not depend on official transfers from outside sources. Indeed, were that not so, no country on earth could ever have escaped from initial poverty. The long-held premise of foreign assistance—that poor countries were poor because they lacked capital—not only ignored thousands of years of economic development history; it also was contradicted by contemporary events in the developing world, which saw the accumulation of massive debt, not development.

Promoting Market Reforms

Even aid intended to advance market liberalization can produce undesirable results. Such aid takes the pressure off recipient governments and allows them to postpone, rather than promote, necessary but politically difficult reforms. Ernest Preeg, former chief economist at U.S. AID, for instance, noted that problem in the Philippines after the collapse of the Marcos dictatorship: "As large amounts of aid flowed to the Aquino government from the United States and other donors, the urgency for reform dissipated. Economic aid became a cushion for postponing difficult internal decisions on reform. A central policy focus of the Aquino government became that of obtaining more and more aid rather than prompt implementation of the reform program."

A similar outcome is evident in the Middle East, which receives about one-fifth to one-quarter of U.S. economic aid, most of which is received by the governments of Egypt and Israel and, more recently, Iraq. It should not be surprising, then, that the region is notable for its low levels of economic freedom and almost complete lack of economic reform. In 1996 the Institute for Advanced Strategic and Political Studies, an Israeli think tank, complained: "Almost one-seventh of the GDP comes to Israel as charity. This has proven to be economically disastrous. It prevents reform, causes inflation, fosters waste, ruins our competitiveness and efficiency, and increases the future tax burden on our children who will have to repay the part of the aid that comes as loans." In 1998 the institute again complained that foreign aid "is the single greatest obstacle to economic freedom in Israel."

Far more effective at promoting market reforms is the suspension or elimination of aid. Although U.S. AID lists South Korea and Taiwan as success stories of U.S. economic assistance, those countries began to take off economically only after massive U.S. aid was cut off. As even the World Bank has conceded, "Reform is more likely to be preceded by a decline in aid than an increase in aid." When India faced Western sanctions in 1998 in response to nuclear tests there, the *International Herald Tribune* reported that "India approved at least 50 foreign-investment projects to compensate for the loss of aid from Japan and the United States" and that it would take additional measures to attract capital. In the end, the countries that have done the most to reform economically have made changes despite foreign aid, not because of it.

Still, much aid is delivered on the condition that recipient countries implement market-oriented economic policies. Such conditionality is the basis for the World Bank's structural adjustment lending, which it began in the early 1980s after it realized that pouring money into unsound economies would not lead to self-sustaining growth. But aid conditioned on reform has not been effective at inducing reform. One 1997 World Bank study noted that there "is no systematic effect of aid on policy." A 2002 World Bank study admitted that "too often, governments receiving aid were not truly committed to reforms" and that "the Bank has often been overly optimistic about the prospects for reform, thereby contributing to misallocation of aid." Oxford's Paul Collier explains: "Some governments have chosen to reform, others to regress, but these choices appear to have been largely independent of the aid relationship. The micro-evidence of this result has been accumulating for some years. It has been suppressed by an unholy alliance of the donors and their critics. Obviously, the donors did not wish to admit that their conditionality was a charade.''

Lending agencies have an institutional bias toward continued lending even if market reforms are not adequately introduced. Yale University economist Gustav Ranis explains that within some lending agencies, ''ultimately the need to lend will overcome the need to ensure that those [loan] conditions are indeed met.'' In the worst cases, of course, lending agencies do suspend loans in an effort to encourage reforms. When those reforms begin or are promised, however, the agencies predictably respond by resuming the loans—a process Ranis has referred to as a ''time-consuming and expensive ritual dance.''

In sum, aiding reforming nations, however superficially appealing, does not produce rapid and widespread liberalization. Just as Congress should reject funding regimes that are uninterested in reform, it should reject schemes that call for funding countries on the basis of their records of reform. This includes the Bush administration's Millennium Challenge Corporation. The most obvious problem with that program is that it is based on a conceptual flaw: countries that are implementing the right policies for growth, and therefore do not need foreign aid, will be receiving aid. The practical problems are also formidable. The Millennium Challenge Corporation and other programs of its kind will require that government officials and aid agencies—all of which have a poor record in determining when and where to disburse foreign aid—make complex judgment calls about what countries deserve the aid and when. Moreover, it is difficult to believe that bureaucratic self-interest, micromanagement by Congress, and other political or geostrategic considerations will not continue to play a role in the disbursement of this kind of foreign aid. It is important to remember that the new aid funds administered by the Millennium Challenge Corporation do not actually reform U.S. aid; rather, they are *in addition to* the much larger traditional aid programs that will continue to be run by U.S. AID—in many cases in the very same countries.

Helping the Private Sector

Enterprise funds are another initiative intended to help market economies. Under this approach, U.S. AID and the Overseas Private Investment Corporation have established and financed venture funds throughout the developing world. Their purpose is to promote economic progress and ''jump-start'' the market by investing in the private sector.

It was always unclear exactly how such government-supported funds find profitable private ventures in which the private sector is unwilling to invest. Numerous evaluations have now found that most enterprise funds are losing money, and many have simply displaced private investment that otherwise would have taken place. Moreover, there is no evidence that the funds have generated additional private investment, had a positive impact on development, or helped create a better investment environment in poor countries.

Similar efforts to underwrite private entrepreneurs are evident at the World Bank (through its expanding program to guarantee private-sector investment) and at U.S. agencies such as the Export-Import Bank, OPIC, and the Trade and Development Agency, which provide comparable services.

U.S. officials justify those programs on the grounds that they help promote development and benefit the U.S. economy. Yet the provision of loan guarantees and subsidized insurance to the private sector relieves the governments of underdeveloped countries from creating an investment environment that would attract foreign capital on its own. To attract much-needed investment, countries should establish secure property rights and clear economic policies, rather than rely on Washington-backed schemes that allow avoidance of those reforms.

Moreover, while some corporations clearly benefit from the array of foreign assistance schemes, the U.S. economy and American taxpayers do not. Subsidized loans and insurance programs merely amount to corporate welfare. Macroeconomic policies and conditions, not corporate welfare programs, affect factors such as the unemployment rate and the size of the trade deficit. Programs that benefit specific interest groups manage only to rearrange resources within the U.S. economy and do so in a very wasteful manner. Indeed, the United States did not achieve and does not maintain its status as the world's largest exporter because of agencies like the Export-Import Bank, which finances less than 2 percent of U.S. exports.

Even U.S. AID claims that the main beneficiary of its lending is the United States because close to 80 percent of its contracts and grants go to American firms. That argument is also fallacious. "To argue that aid helps the domestic economy," renowned economist Peter Bauer explains, "is like saying that a shop-keeper benefits from having his cash register burgled so long as the burglar spends part of the proceeds in his shop."

685

Debt Relief

Some 42 poor countries today suffer from inordinately high foreign debt levels. Thus, the World Bank and the IMF have devised a $29.3 billion debt-relief initiative for the world's heavily indebted poor countries (HIPCs). To fund the HIPC program, the aid agencies are requesting about half of that money from the United States and other donors. The initiative, of course, is an implicit recognition of the failure of past lending to produce self-sustaining growth, especially since an overwhelming percentage of eligible countries' public foreign debt is owed to bilateral and multilateral lending agencies. Indeed, 97 percent of those countries' long-term debt is public or publicly guaranteed (Table 68.1).

Forgiving poor nations' debt, of course, is a sound idea, on the condition that no other aid is forthcoming. Unfortunately, the multilateral debt initiative promises to keep poor countries on a borrowing treadmill, since they will be eligible for future multilateral loans based on conditionality. There is no reason, however, to believe that conditionality will work any better in the future than it has in the past. Again, as a recent World Bank study emphasized, "A conditioned loan is no guarantee that reforms will be carried out—or last once they are."

Nor is there reason to believe that debt relief will work better now than in the past. As former World Bank economist William Easterly has documented, donor nations have been forgiving poor countries' debts since the late 1970s, and the result has simply been more debt. From 1989 to 1997, 41 highly indebted countries saw some $33 billion of debt forgiveness, yet they still find themselves in an untenable position. Indeed, they have been borrowing ever-larger amounts from aid agencies. Easterly notes, moreover, that private credit to the HIPCs has been virtually replaced by foreign aid and that foreign aid itself has been lent on increasingly easier terms. Thus, when the World Bank and IMF call for debt forgiveness, it is the latest in a series of failed attempts by rich countries to resolve poor countries' debts.

At the same time, it has become increasingly evident that the debt-relief scheme is a financial shell game that allows the multilaterals to repay their previous loans without having to write-down bad debt and thus without negatively affecting their financial status. If official donors wished to forgive debt, they could do so easily. Contributing money to the multilateral debt-relief initiative, however, will do little to promote reform or self-sustaining growth.

Table 68.1
Heavily Indebted Poor Countries: Amount of Debt Attributable to Official Aid and Other Government-Backed Schemes, 2002

	Total Long-Term Debt (billion dollars)	Total Public and Publicly Guaranteed Debt (billion dollars)	Total Public and Publicly Guaranteed Debt as a Percentage of Long-Term Debt
Angola	8.88	8.88	100.00
Benin	1.69	1.69	100.00
Bolivia	4.30	3.38	78.60
Burkina Faso	1.40	1.40	100.00
Burundi	1.09	1.09	100.00
Cameroon	7.42	7.24	97.57
Central African Rep.	0.98	0.98	100.00
Chad	1.15	1.15	100.00
Comoros	0.24	0.24	100.00
Congo Dem. Rep.	7.39	7.39	100.00
Congo, Rep.	3.97	3.97	100.00
Cote D'Ivoire	10.37	9.11	87.85
Ethiopia	6.31	6.31	100.00
The Gambia	0.50	0.50	100.00
Ghana	6.38	6.13	96.08
Guinea	2.97	2.97	100.00
Guinea-Bissau	0.66	0.66	100.00
Guyana	1.22	1.21	99.18
Honduras	4.67	4.21	90.15
Kenya	5.19	5.14	99.04
Lao PDR	2.62	2.62	100.00
Liberia	1.06	1.06	100.00
Madagascar	4.14	4.14	100.00
Malawi	2.69	2.69	100.00
Mali	2.49	2.49	100.00
Mauritania	1.98	1.98	100.00
Mozambique	4.04	2.53	62.62
Myanmar	5.39	5.39	100.00
Nicaragua	5.76	5.58	96.88
Niger	1.66	1.60	96.39
Rwanda	1.30	1.30	100.00
Sao Tome and Principe	0.31	0.31	100.00

(continued)

Table 68.1
(continued)

	Total Long-Term Debt (billion dollars)	Total Public and Publicly Guaranteed Debt (billion dollars)	Total Public and Publicly Guaranteed Debt as a Percentage of Long-Term Debt
Senegal	3.37	3.34	99.11
Sierra Leone	1.26	1.26	100.00
Somalia	1.86	1.86	100.00
Sudan	9.54	9.04	94.76
Tanzania	6.20	6.18	99.68
Togo	1.34	1.34	100.00
Uganda	3.69	3.69	100.00
Vietnam	12.18	12.18	100.00
Yemen, Rep.	4.56	4.56	100.00
Zambia	4.85	4.74	97.73
Total	159.07	153.53	96.52

SOURCE: World Bank, *World Development Indicators Online.* http://publications.worldbank.org/WDI.

Other Initiatives

The inadequacy of government-to-government aid programs has prompted an increased reliance on nongovernmental organizations (NGOs). NGOs, or private voluntary organizations (PVOs), are said to be more effective at delivering aid and accomplishing development objectives because they are less bureaucratic and more in touch with the on-the-ground realities of their clients.

Although channeling official aid monies through PVOs has been referred to as a "privatized" form of foreign assistance, it is often difficult to make a sharp distinction between government agencies and PVOs beyond the fact that the latter are subject to less oversight and are less accountable. Michael Maren, a former employee at Catholic Relief Services and U.S. AID, notes that most PVOs receive most of their funds from government sources.

Given that relationship—PVO dependence on government hardly makes them private or voluntary—Maren and others have described how the charitable goals on which PVOs are founded have been undermined. The nonprofit organization Development GAP, for example, observed that U.S. AID's "overfunding of a number of groups has taxed their management capabilities, changed their institutional style, and made them more bureaucratic and unresponsive to the expressed needs of the poor overseas."

"When aid bureaucracies evaluate the work of NGOs," Maren adds, "they have no incentive to criticize them." For their part, NGOs naturally have an incentive to keep official funds flowing. In the final analysis, government provision of foreign assistance through PVOs instead of traditional channels does not produce dramatically different results.

Microenterprise lending, another increasingly popular program among advocates of aid, is designed to provide small amounts of credit to the world's poorest people. The loans are used by the poor to establish livestock, manufacturing, and trade enterprises, for example.

Many microloan programs, such as the one run by the Grameen Bank in Bangladesh, appear to be highly successful. Grameen has disbursed more than $1.5 billion since the 1970s and achieved a repayment rate of about 98 percent. Microenterprise lending institutions, moreover, are intended to be economically viable, able to achieve financial self-sufficiency within three to seven years. Given those qualities, it is not clear why microlending organizations would require subsidies. Indeed, microenterprise banks typically refer to themselves as profitable enterprises. For those and other reasons, Princeton University's Jonathan Morduch concluded in a 1999 study that "the greatest promise of microfinance is so far unmet, and the boldest claims do not withstand close scrutiny." He added that, according to some estimates, "if subsidies are pulled and costs cannot be reduced, as many as 95 percent of current programs will eventually have to close shop."

Furthermore, microenterprise programs alleviate the conditions of the poor, but they do not address the causes of the lack of credit faced by the poor. In developing countries, for example, about 90 percent of poor people's property is not recognized by the state. Without secure private property rights, most of the world's poor cannot use collateral to obtain a loan. The Institute for Liberty and Democracy, a Peruvian think tank, found that where poor people's property in Peru was registered, new businesses were created, production increased, asset values rose by 200 percent, and credit became available. Of course, the scarcity of credit is also caused by a host of other policy measures, such as financial regulation that makes it prohibitively expensive to provide banking services for the poor.

In sum, microenterprise programs can be beneficial, but successful programs need not receive aid subsidies. The success of microenterprise programs, moreover, will depend on specific conditions, which vary greatly from country to country. For that reason, microenterprise projects should be financed privately by people who have their own money at stake rather than by international aid bureaucracies that appear intent on replicating such projects throughout the developing world.

Conclusion

Numerous studies have found that economic growth is strongly related to the level of economic freedom. Put simply, the greater a country's economic freedom, the greater its level of prosperity over time. Likewise, the greater a country's economic freedom, the faster it will grow (Figure 68.1). Economic freedom, which includes not only policies, such as free trade and stable money, but also institutions, such as the rule of law and the security of private property rights, does not only increase income. It is also strongly related to improvements in other development indicators such as longevity, access to safe drinking water, lower corruption, and dramatically higher incomes for the poorest members of society (Figure 68.2).

Those developing countries, such as Chile and Taiwan, that have most liberalized their economies and achieved high levels of growth have done far more to reduce poverty and improve their citizens' standards of living than have foreign aid programs.

In the end, a country's progress depends almost entirely on its domestic policies and institutions, not on outside factors such as foreign aid. Congress

Figure 68.1
Economic Freedom and Growth of GDP per Capita, 1980–2000

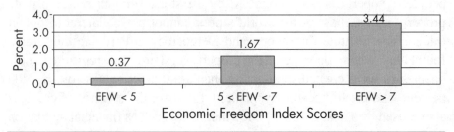

SOURCE: James Gwartney and Robert Lawson, *Economic Freedom of the World: 2004 Annual Report* (Vancouver: Fraser Institute, 2004), p. 30.

Figure 68.2
Economic Freedom and Income of the Poorest 10 Percent

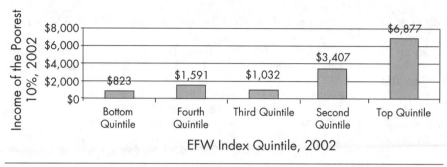

SOURCE: James Gwartney and Robert Lawson, *Economic Freedom of the World: 2004 Annual Report* (Vancouver: Fraser Institute, 2004), p. 23.

should recognize that foreign aid has not caused the worldwide shift toward the market and that appeals for more foreign aid, even when intended to promote the market, will continue to do more harm than good.

Suggested Readings

Anderson, Robert E. *Just Get Out of the Way: How Government Can Help Business in Poor Countries*. Washington: Cato Institute, 2004.

Bandow, Doug, and Ian Vásquez, eds. *Perpetuating Poverty: The World Bank, the IMF, and the Developing World*. Washington: Cato Institute, 1994.

Bauer, P. T. *Dissent on Development*. Cambridge, MA: Harvard University Press, 1972.

Bhalla, Surjit. *Imagine There's No Country: Poverty, Inequality and Growth in the Era of Globalization*. Washington: Institute for International Economics, 2002.

Brumm, Harold J. "Aid, Policies, and Growth: Bauer Was Right." *Cato Journal* 32, no. 2 (Fall 2003).

De Soto, Hernando. *The Mystery of Capital: Why Capitalism Triumphs in the West and Fails Everywhere Else*. New York: Basic Books, 2000.

Dollar, David, and Aart Kraay. "Trade, Growth and Poverty." World Bank research paper, March 2001.

Dorn, James A., Steve H. Hanke, and Alan A. Walters, eds. *The Revolution in Development Economics*. Washington: Cato Institute, 1998.

Easterly, William. *The Elusive Quest for Growth: Economists' Adventures and Misadventures in the Tropics*. Cambridge, MA: MIT Press, 2001.

Gwartney, James, and Robert Lawson. *Economic Freedom of the World: 2004 Annual Report*. Vancouver: Fraser Institute, 2004.

International Financial Institution Advisory Commission (Meltzer Commission). "Report to the U.S. Congress and the Department of the Treasury." March 8, 2000. www.house.gov/jec/imf/meltzer.htm.

Lal, Deepak. *The Poverty of "Development Economics."* London: Institute of Economic Affairs, 1983, 1997.

Lewis, William W. *The Power of Productivity: Wealth, Poverty, and the Threat to Global Stability*. Chicago: University of Chicago Press, 2004.

691

Lindsey, Brink. *Against the Dead Hand: The Uncertain Struggle for Global Capitalism.* New York: John Wiley & Sons, 2002.

Lukas, Aaron, and Ian Vásquez. "Rethinking the Export-Import Bank." Cato Institute Trade Briefing Paper no. 15, March 12, 2002.

Maren, Michael. *The Road to Hell: Foreign Aid and International Charity.* New York: Free Press, 1997.

Vásquez, Ian. "Ending Mass Poverty." *Economic Perspectives,* U.S. Department of State electronic journal, September 2001. http://usinfo.state.gov/journals/ites/0901/ijee/toc.htm.

———. "The New Approach to Foreign Aid: Is the Enthusiasm Warranted?" Cato Institute Foreign Policy Briefing no. 79, September 17, 2003.

Vásquez, Ian, and John Welborn. "Reauthorize or Retire the Overseas Private Investment Corporation." Cato Institute Foreign Policy Briefing no. 78, September 15, 2003.

Walters, Alan. "Do We Need the IMF and the World Bank?" Institute of Economic Affairs Current Controversies no. 10, September 1994.

World Bank. *Assessing Aid: What Works, What Doesn't, And Why.* New York: Oxford University Press, 1998.

———. "Doing Business in 2005: Removing Obstacles to Growth." Washington: World Bank, 2005.

—Prepared by Ian Vásquez

69. U.S. Policy toward Sub-Saharan Africa

Congress should

- expand the Africa Growth and Opportunity Act by granting tariff- and quota-free access to all imports from sub-Saharan Africa,
- forgive sub-Saharan African debt on the condition of ending future official lending to governments in the region,
- oppose International Monetary Fund and World Bank lending to sub-Saharan Africa, and
- impose "smart" sanctions on leaders suspected of corruption and human rights abuses.

Sub-Saharan Africa (herein sometimes referred to simply as "Africa") consists of 48 countries, which spread over nine million square miles and include 688 million people. It is one of the poorest regions in the world. The UN Human Development Index measures quality of life around the world on a scale from 0 (low) to 1 (high). In 2003 sub-Saharan Africa's score was 0.468. The scores for the developing world and the United States were 0.655 and 0.937, respectively. Africa lags behind most of the world in practically all indicators of human well-being, including longevity, infant mortality, HIV, incidence of malaria and tuberculosis, nourishment, school enrollment, economic growth, and income per capita.

The ability of the United States to help Africa is limited, because the solutions to most of Africa's problems must be determined internally. Those problems are extensive. For most of independent Africa's history, arbitrary and authoritarian rule has been the norm. The resulting casualties have included political stability, the rule of law, the protection of individuals and private property, and growth.

Indeed, most African governments have imposed central control over their economies, a development strategy not conducive to economic growth. Inflationary monetary policies; price, wage, and exchange rate controls; marketing boards (which keep the prices of agricultural products artificially low, thus impoverishing Africa's farmers); and state-owned enterprises and monopolies are commonplace.

Microeconomic policy in the region has also been counterproductive. For example, business regulation in Africa remains much too restrictive. It takes only 2 days for an entrepreneur to start a business in Australia but 215 days in the Republic of Congo. No minimum capital is required to start a business in Singapore, but the Ethiopian government imposes a minimum capital requirement that is 17 times higher than average annual per capita income. It takes only 7 days to enforce a contract in Tunisia, but in Ethiopia it takes 895 days.

African governments also restrict foreign and domestic investment, and Africa's tariffs are among the highest in the world. Following the Uruguay Round of trade liberalization, the average applied tariff in sub-Saharan Africa was 28 percent. The comparable figure for fast-growing economies, including Taiwan, Singapore, and Hong Kong, was 9.12 percent. Nontariff barriers in Africa were also higher (39 percent) than nontariff barriers in fast-growing economies (9.4 percent).

On the whole, African economies continue to be largely unfree. According to the *Economic Freedom of the World* report, economic freedom in Africa has stagnated. On a scale from 0 to 10, where 10 represents the highest measured level of freedom, Africa moved from 5.3 in 1970 to 5.6 in 2002. The ranking of the United States, one of the world's freest economies, was 8.2 in 2002.

Botswana is a rare exception. Botswana's economic freedom increased from 5.6 in 1980 to 7.4 in 2002, making it Africa's freest economy. Between 1980 and 2002, Botswana's gross domestic product per capita grew at an average annual rate of 4.58 percent. Over the same period, African GDP per capita contracted at an average annual rate of 0.47 percent. Today Botswana's citizens enjoy one of Africa's highest standards of living. Their 2002 GDP per capita in constant 1995 U.S. dollars was $4,102. Only oil-rich Gabon and market-friendly Mauritius had higher incomes of $4,323 and $4,538, respectively. In 2002 average GDP per capita in sub-Saharan countries was $575.

As long as its economic freedom remains low, Africa's economic performance will continue to disappoint. Similarly, African countries are unlikely to escape poverty as long as their governments remain unaccountable and their actions arbitrary. Unfortunately, there is little the United States can do to positively influence the evolution of Africa's governing institutions and the policies that African countries adopt.

Free Trade

The United States can help by further opening its markets to African exports. Congress has taken a step in the right direction, by adopting the Africa Growth and Opportunity Act in 2000 and later extending it to 2015. As a consequence of AGOA, two-way trade between the United States and AGOA nations increased by 36 percent in 2003 alone. Its value has now reached $33 billion per year. Between 2002 and 2003, AGOA exports to the United States increased by 43 percent to $25.6 billion. More than half of those exports were covered by AGOA and its generalized system of preferences. AGOA apparel imports grew by 50 percent, transportation equipment by 34 percent, and agricultural goods by 13 percent. American exports, especially those of aircraft, vehicles, and computer and telecommunications equipment, to AGOA countries grew by 15 percent.

The benefits of free trade are political and economic. First, free trade can be a potent weapon against terror directed against the United States. Apparel trade with the United States alone has created 250,000 jobs in the AGOA countries. Such increased economic interconnectedness between the world's trouble spots and the United States may help to dissuade potential terrorist sympathizers from harming the United States. National security considerations are clearly relevant to Africa. American lives and assets were targeted in the 1998 embassy bombings in Kenya and Tanzania. Al Qaeda activities have been reported in Somalia and Sudan.

Second, trade increases specialization. Increased specialization leads to increasing productivity. Reductions in the cost of production lead to cheaper goods and services, which, in turn, increase the standard of living for Americans and Africans alike. Unfortunately, Washington limits the economic benefits of AGOA by excluding a variety of products, including those in which Africa has a comparative trade advantage, from tariff- and quota-free treatment. The United States restricts imports of dairy goods, soft drinks, cocoa, coffee, tea, tobacco, nuts, and many types of fabrics. Researchers at the World Bank, the IMF, and the University of Maryland found that AGOA yields only 19 to 26 percent of the benefits that it could if it were comprehensive and unconditional. Concerns that further trade opening would negatively affect the number of American jobs are misplaced, especially since AGOA's share of American imports remains very small. For example, AGOA apparel imports constitute just 2.1 percent of the American market. AGOA should be extended to offer tariff- and quota-free access to all imports from Africa.

Foreign Aid

Between 1961 and 2000, U.S. official development assistance to sub-Saharan Africa increased from $358 million to $1.14 billion in constant 2000 dollars, an inflation-adjusted increase of 218 percent. U.S. aid to Africa as a percentage of the entire U.S. aid budget rose more than fourfold, from 2.5 percent in 1961 to 11.4 percent in 2000. But that aid has had poor results.

British economist Peter Bauer once described foreign aid as "an excellent method for transferring money from poor people in rich countries to rich people in poor countries." That is an especially accurate description of aid to Africa. Aid there has increased the size of government to the detriment of the private sector. It has enabled government officials to embezzle large amounts of money and misspend much on loss-making projects. Citizens have been left with large debt. Africa receives one of the largest amounts of aid per capita. But, as the accompanying figures show, African economic performance has been very poor. Today, most researchers agree that economic growth depends on market-oriented domestic policies.

Countries that follow sound economic policies grow regardless of aid. A comparison of two similarly poor regions, sub-Saharan Africa and South Asia (Afghanistan, Bangladesh, Bhutan, India, Maldives, Nepal, Pakistan, and Sri Lanka), may be instructive. As Figure 69.1 shows, between 1975 and 2000, aid to Africa averaged $24 per capita per year. The comparable figure for South Asia was $5. Over those 25 years, South Asian GDP per capita grew at an average annual rate of 2.94 percent. In contrast, African GDP per capita declined at an average annual rate of 0.59 percent.

As Figure 69.2 shows, South Asian GDP per capita adjusted for purchasing power parity (PPP) grew from $1,010 in constant 1995 international dollars to $2,056. By the same measure, African GDP per capita declined from $1,770 to $1,479.

The percentage of people in Africa living on less than $1 a day increased from 47.4 percent in 1990 to 49 percent in 1999. During the same period, absolute poverty in South Asia declined from 45 percent to 36.6 percent. In 1970 the National Bureau of Economic Research estimated that 1 in

Figure 69.1
Foreign Aid and Economic Growth in Sub-Saharan Africa and South Asia

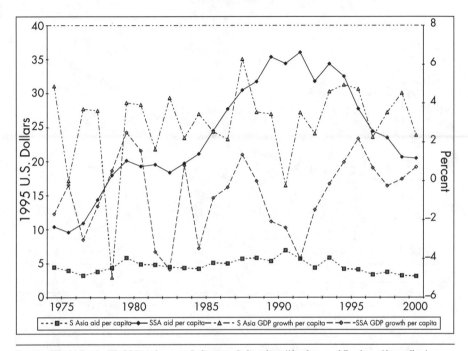

SOURCE: World Bank, *World Development Indicators Online*, http://devdata.worldbank.org/dataonline/.

10 people surviving on less than $1 a day lived in Africa. Today that number is close to 1 in 2.

In addition to giving bilateral aid, Washington also participates in multilateral aid schemes overseen by a variety of international institutions, including the World Bank, the African Development Bank, and the IMF. Those multilateral institutions have also backed African regimes that have engaged in gross macroeconomic mismanagement. And although the World Bank's structural adjustment programs and IMF lending were designed to provide credit in exchange for economic reforms in the region, African compliance with lending conditions has been poor or nonexistent. For example, Daniel arap Moi of Kenya "sold" the same package of reforms to the World Bank and the IMF several times. Similarly, Robert Mugabe broke a number of promises to liberalize the Zimbabwean economy. When policy mistakes resulted in Zimbabwe's economic decline, Mugabe blamed the World Bank and IMF and their main sponsor, the United States.

697

Figure 69.2
Purchasing Power Parity–Adjusted GDP per Capita in Sub-Saharan Africa and South Asia

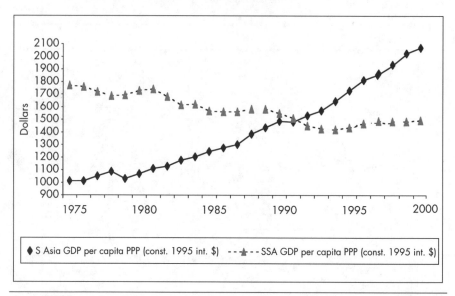

SOURCE: World Bank, *World Development Indicators Online*, http://devdata.worldbank.org/dataonline/.

The World Bank and IMF do not have the ability to enforce compliance with their loan conditions. Yet both agencies keep lending, and Africa's debt continues to accumulate. Of the 42 Heavily Indebted Poor Countries (HIPCs), which the World Bank and IMF deem too poor to pay back debt, 34 are in sub-Saharan Africa. The total long-term debt of HIPCs was approximately $158 billion in 2000. Africa's share of that debt was $122 billion, or 77 percent. Approximately 85 percent of HIPCs' long-term debt was owed to public lenders (i.e., governments and international organizations). That is a dramatic testament to the failure of foreign aid in Africa.

Much of the debt incurred by African governments was caused by misallocation by incompetent government officials or theft. The African people received few or no benefits. The United States could forgive its share (3.7 percent) of the HIPCs' debt, but debt cancellation will work only if the United States and other official creditors refuse to lend to African governments in the future. Indeed, despite receiving $33 billion in debt relief between 1989 and 1997, HIPCs keep borrowing and falling further into debt. To break this vicious cycle, HIPCs should rely only on private lenders. Private lenders should be made aware that Western governments will not bail them out in case of sovereign default. That will make lenders more circumspect when lending money to African countries. Greater scarcity of capital and higher interest rates may encourage African governments to liberalize.

Smart Sanctions

In the past, few international sanctions have met with success. Global agreement on imposition of sanctions is difficult to reach. Moreover, sanctions tend to harm the poor much more than the ruling elite. The United States could help Africa, however, by targeting those leaders in the region who are suspected of corruption and abuses of human rights. "Smart sanctions" are unlikely to bring about change in government, but they do make the lives of the ruling elite more difficult. Measures that should be considered against African dictators and their collaborators include international arrest warrants, freezing of personal assets abroad, prohibitions on travel, and arms embargos.

Suggested Readings

Ayittey, George. *Africa Unchained: The Blueprint for It's Future.* New York: Palgrave/Macmillan, 2005.

Beaulier, Scott A. "Explaining Botswana's Success: The Critical Role of Post-Colonial Policy." *Cato Journal* 23, no. 2 (Fall 2003).

Guest, Robert. *The Shackled Continent: Power, Corruption, and African Lives.* Washington: Smithsonian Books, 2004.

Mattoo, Aadita, Davesh Roy, and Arvind Subramanian. "The Africa Growth and Opportunity Act and Its Rules of Origin: Generosity Undermined?" *World Economy* 26 (June 2003): 829–51.

Ng, Francis, and Alexander Yeats. *Good Governance and Trade Policy: Are They the Keys to Africa's Global Integration and Growth?* Washington: International Monetary Fund, 1999.

————. "Open Economies Work Better! Did Africa's Protectionist Policies Cause Its Marginalization in World Trade?" *World Development* 25, no. 6 (1997): 889–904.

—Prepared by Marian L. Tupy

Contributors

Radley Balko is a policy analyst at the Cato Institute.

Doug Bandow is a senior fellow at the Cato Institute and author of *Tripwire: Korea and U.S. Foreign Policy in a Changed World.*

Patrick Basham is a senior fellow in the Cato Institute's Center for Representative Government.

David Boaz is executive vice president of the Cato Institute and author of *Libertarianism: A Primer.*

Michael F. Cannon is director of health policy studies at the Cato Institute.

Ted Galen Carpenter is vice president for defense and foreign policy studies at the Cato Institute and author of *Peace and Freedom: Foreign Policy for a Constitutional Republic.*

Edward H. Crane is president of the Cato Institute.

James A. Dorn is vice president for academic affairs at the Cato Institute and coeditor of *China's Future: Constructive Partner or Emerging Threat?*

Chris Edwards is director of tax policy studies at the Cato Institute and coeditor of *The Republican Revolution 10 Years Later: Smaller Government or Business As Usual?*

Ivan Eland was formerly director of defense policy studies at the Cato Institute and is author of *Putting "Defense" Back in Defense Policy: Rethinking U.S. Security in the Post–Cold War World.*

Daniel Griswold is director of the Cato Institute's Center for Trade Policy Studies and coeditor of *Economic Casualties: How U.S. Foreign Policy Undermines Trade, Growth, and Liberty.*

Leon T. Hadar is a research fellow in foreign policy studies at the Cato Institute and author of *Sandstorm: American Blindness in the Middle East.*

Jim Harper is director of information policy studies at the Cato Institute.

Gene Healy is senior editor at the Cato Institute and editor of *Go Directly to Jail: The Criminalization of Almost Everything.*

Stanley Kober is a research fellow in foreign policy studies at the Cato Institute.

Christopher Layne is a visiting fellow in foreign policy studies at the Cato Institute.

Robert A. Levy is senior fellow in constitutional studies at the Cato Institute and author of *Shakedown: How Corporations, Government, and Trial Lawyers Abuse the Judicial Process.*

Brink Lindsey is vice president for research at the Cato Institute and author of *Against the Dead Hand: The Uncertain Struggle for Global Capitalism.*

Timothy Lynch is director of the Cato Institute's Project on Criminal Justice and editor of *After Prohibition: An Adult Approach to Drug Policies in the 21st Century.*

Neal McCluskey is a policy analyst at the Cato Institute's Center for Educational Freedom.

701

Patrick J. Michaels is a professor of environmental sciences at the University of Virginia, senior fellow in environmental studies at the Cato Institute, and author of *Meltdown: The Predictable Distortion of Global Warming by Scientists, Politicians, and the Media.*

Mark K. Moller is a senior fellow at the Cato Institute's Center for Constitutional Studies and editor of the *Cato Supreme Court Review.*

Michael New is an assistant professor of political science at the University of Alabama and an adjunct scholar of the Cato Institute.

William A. Niskanen is chairman of the Cato Institute and author of *Policy Analysis and Public Choice.*

Tom G. Palmer is a senior fellow at the Cato Institute.

Charles V. Peña is director of defense policy studies at the Cato Institute.

Roger Pilon is vice president for legal affairs at the Cato Institute where he holds the B. Kenneth Simon Chair in Constitutional Studies and is director of Cato's Center for Constitutional Studies.

Christopher Preble is director of foreign policy studies at the Cato Institute.

Sheldon Richman is editor of *The Freeman.*

L. Jacobo Rodríguez was formerly the assistant director of the Cato Institute's Project on Global Economic Liberty.

Gabriel Roth is a transportation and privatization consultant and author of *Roads in a Market Economy.*

David Salisbury is director of the Center for Educational Freedom at the Cato Institute and coeditor of *Educational Freedom in Urban America.*

John Samples is director of the Center for Representative Government at the Cato Institute and editor of *James Madison and the Future of Limited Government.*

David Schoenbrod, a former senior attorney of the Natural Resources Defense Council and now a professor at New York Law School, is an adjunct scholar of the Cato Institute and author of *Power without Responsibility: How Congress Abuses the People through Delegation.*

Stephen Slivinski is director of budget studies at the Cato Institute.

Michael Tanner is director of health and welfare studies at the Cato Institute, author of *The End of Welfare: Fighting Poverty in the Civil Society*, and coauthor of *A New Deal for Social Security.*

Jerry Taylor is director of natural resource studies at the Cato Institute.

Adam Thierer is director of telecommunications studies at the Cato Institute and coeditor of *Who Rules the Net?*

Marian L. Tupy is assistant director of the Cato Institute's Project on Global Economic Liberty.

Peter Van Doren is editor of *Regulation* magazine and author of *Chemicals, Cancer, and Choices: Risk Reduction through Markets.*

Ian Vásquez is director of the Project on Global Economic Liberty at the Cato Institute and editor of *Global Fortune: The Stumble and Rise of World Capitalism.*

Jenifer Zeigler is a welfare policy analyst at the Cato Institute.